THE

Expositor's Bible Commentary

with The New International Version

MATTHEW

CHAPTERS 13 THROUGH 28

THE Expositor's Bible Commentary

with The New International Version

MATTHEW

CHAPTERS 13 THROUGH 28

D. A. Carson

ZondervanPublishingHouse
Grand Rapids, Michigan

A Division of HarperCollins*Publishers*

General Editor:

FRANK E. GAEBELEIN

Former Headmaster, Stony Brook School

Former Coeditor, *Christianity Today*

Associate Editors:

J. D. DOUGLAS

Editor, *The New International Dictionary of the Christian Church*

RICHARD P. POLCYN

Requests for information should be addressed to:
Zondervan Publishing House
Grand Rapids, Michigan 49530

Library of Congress Cataloging-in-Publication Data

The expositor's Bible commentary : with the New International Version of the Holy Bible / Frank E. Gaebelein, general editor of series.
p. cm.
Includes bibliographical references and index.
Contents: v. 1–2. Matthew / D. A. Carson — Mark / Walter W. Wessel — Luke / Walter L. Liefeld — John / Merrill C. Tenney — Acts / Richard N. Longenecker — Romans / Everett F. Harrison — 1 and 2 Corinthians / W. Harold Mare and Murray J. Harris — Galatians and Ephesians / James Montgomery Boice and A. Skevington Wood
ISBN: 0-310-49971-2 (softcover : v. 2)
1. Bible N.T. — Commentaries. I. Gaebelein, Frank Ely, 1899–1983.
BS2341.2.E96 1995
220.7-dc 00 94-47450
CIP

Printed in the United States of America

98 99 00 /❖DH/ 10 9 8 7 6 5 4 3

CONTENTS

PREFACE

The title of this work defines its purpose. Written primarily by expositors for expositors, it aims to provide preachers, teachers, and students of the Bible with a new and comprehensive commentary on the books of the Old and New Testaments. Its stance is that of a scholarly evangelicalism committed to the divine inspiration, complete trustworthiness, and full authority of the Bible. Its seventy-eight contributors come from the United States, Canada, England, Scotland, Australia, New Zealand, and Switzerland, and from various religious groups, including Anglican, Baptist, Brethren, Free, Independent, Methodist, Nazarene, Presbyterian, and Reformed churches. Most of them teach at colleges, universities, or theological seminaries.

No book has been more closely studied over a longer period of time than the Bible. From the Midrashic commentaries going back to the period of Ezra, through parts of the Dead Sea Scrolls and the Patristic literature, and on to the present, the Scriptures have been expounded. Indeed, there have been times when, as in the Reformation and on occasions since then, exposition has been at the cutting edge of Christian advance. Luther was a powerful exegete, and Calvin is still called "the prince of expositors."

Their successors have been many. And now, when the outburst of new translations and their unparalleled circulation have expanded the readership of the Bible, the need for exposition takes on fresh urgency.

Not that God's Word can ever become captive to its expositors. Among all other books, it stands first in its combination of perspicuity and profundity. Though a child can be made "wise for salvation" by believing its witness to Christ, the greatest mind cannot plumb the depths of its truth (2 Tim. 3:15; Rom. 11:33). As Gregory the Great said, "Holy Scripture is a stream of running water, where alike the elephant may swim, and the lamb walk." So, because of the inexhaustible nature of Scripture, the task of opening up its meaning is still a perennial obligation of biblical scholarship.

How that task is done inevitably reflects the outlook of those engaged in it. Every biblical scholar has presuppositions. To this neither the editors of these volumes nor the contributors to them are exceptions. They share a common commitment to the supernatural Christianity set forth in the inspired Word. Their purpose is not to supplant the many valuable commentaries that have preceded this work and from which both the editors and contributors have learned. It is rather to draw on the resources of contemporary evangelical scholarship in producing a new reference work for understanding the Scriptures.

A commentary that will continue to be useful through the years should handle contemporary trends in biblical studies in such a way as to avoid becoming outdated when critical fashions change. Biblical criticism is not in itself inadmissible, as some have mistakenly thought. When scholars investigate the authorship, date, literary characteristics, and purpose of a biblical document, they are practicing biblical criticism. So also when, in order to ascertain as nearly as possible the original form of the text, they deal with variant readings, scribal errors, emendations, and other phenomena in the manuscripts. To do these things is essential to responsible exegesis and exposition. And always there is the need to distinguish hypothesis from fact, conjecture from truth.

The chief principle of interpretation followed in this commentary is the grammatico-historical one—namely, that the primary aim of the exegete is to make clear the meaning of the text at the time and in the circumstances of its writing. This endeavor to understand what in the first instance the inspired writers actually said must not be confused with an inflexible literalism. Scripture makes lavish use of symbols and figures of speech; great portions of it are poetical. Yet when it speaks in this way, it speaks no less truly than it does in its historical and doctrinal portions. To understand its message requires attention to matters of grammar and syntax, word meanings, idioms, and literary forms—all in relation to the historical and cultural setting of the text.

The contributors to this work necessarily reflect varying convictions. In certain controversial matters the policy is that of clear statement of the contributors' own views followed by fair presentation of other ones. The treatment of eschatology, though it reflects differences of interpretation, is consistent with a general premillennial position. (Not all contributors, however, are premillennial.) But prophecy is more than prediction, and so this commentary gives due recognition to the major lode of godly social concern in the prophetic writings.

THE EXPOSITOR'S BIBLE COMMENTARY is presented as a scholarly work, though not primarily one of technical criticism. In its main portion, the Exposition, and in Volume 1 (General and Special Articles), all Semitic and Greek words are transliterated and the English equivalents given. As for the Notes, here Semitic and Greek characters are used but always with transliterations and English meanings, so that this portion of the commentary will be as accessible as possible to readers unacquainted with the original languages.

It is the conviction of the general editor, shared by his colleagues in the Zondervan editorial department, that in writing about the Bible, lucidity is not incompatible with scholarship. They are therefore endeavoring to make this a clear and understandable work.

The translation used in it is the New International Version (North American Edition). To the International Bible Society thanks are due for permission to use this most recent of the major Bible translations.The editors and publisher have chosen it because of the clarity and beauty of its style and its faithfulness to the original texts.

To the associate editor, Dr. J. D. Douglas, and to the contributing editors—Dr. Walter C. Kaiser, Jr. and Dr. Bruce K. Waltke for the Old Testament, and Dr. James Montgomery Boice and Dr. Merrill C. Tenney for the New Testament—the general editor expresses his gratitude for their unfailing cooperation and their generosity in advising him out of their expert scholarship. And to the many other contributors he is indebted for their invaluable part in this work. Finally, he owes a special debt of gratitude to Dr. Robert K. DeVries, executive vice-president of the Zondervan Publishing House; Rev. Gerard Terpstra, manuscript editor; and Miss Elizabeth Brown, secretary to Dr. DeVries, for their continual assistance and encouragement.

Whatever else it is—the greatest and most beautiful of books, the primary source of law and morality, the fountain of wisdom, and the infallible guide to life—the Bible is above all the inspired witness to Jesus Christ. May this work fulfill its function of expounding the Scriptures with grace and clarity, so that its users may find that both Old and New Testaments do indeed lead to our Lord Jesus Christ, who alone could say, "I have come that they may have life, and have it to the full" (John 10:10).

FRANK E. GAEBELEIN

ABBREVIATIONS

A. General Abbreviations

A	Codex Alexandrinus
Akkad.	Akkadian
א	Codex Sinaiticus
Ap. Lit.	Apocalyptic Literature
Apoc.	Apocrypha
Aq.	Aquila's Greek Translation of the Old Testament
Arab.	Arabic
Aram.	Aramaic
b	Babylonian Gemara
B	Codex Vaticanus
C	Codex Ephraemi Syri
c.	*circa*, about
cf.	*confer*, compare
ch., chs.	chapter, chapters
cod., codd.	codex, codices
contra	in contrast to
D	Codex Bezae
DSS	Dead Sea Scrolls (see E.)
ed., edd.	edited, edition, editor; editions
e.g.	*exempli gratia*, for example
Egyp.	Egyptian
et al.	*et alii*, and others
EV	English Versions of the Bible
fem.	feminine
ff.	following (verses, pages, etc.)
fl.	flourished
ft.	foot, feet
gen.	genitive
Gr.	Greek
Heb.	Hebrew
Hitt.	Hittite
ibid.	*ibidem*, in the same place
id.	*idem*, the same
i.e.	*id est*, that is
impf.	imperfect
infra.	below
in loc.	*in loco*, in the place cited
j	Jerusalem or Palestinian Gemara
Lat.	Latin
LL.	Late Latin
LXX	Septuagint
M	Mishnah
masc.	masculine
mg.	margin
Mid	Midrash
MS(S)	Manuscript(s)
MT	Masoretic text
n.	note
n.d.	no date
Nestle	Nestle (ed.) *Novum Testamentum Graece*
no.	number
NT	New Testament
obs.	obsolete
OL	Old Latin
OS	Old Syriac
OT	Old Testament
p., pp.	page, pages
par.	paragraph
‖	parallel passage(s)
Pers.	Persian
Pesh.	Peshitta
Phoen.	Phoenician
pl.	plural
Pseudep.	Pseudepigrapha
Q	Quelle ("Sayings" source in the Gospels)
qt.	quoted by
q.v.	*quod vide*, which see
R	Rabbah
rev.	revised, reviser, revision
Rom.	Roman
RVm	Revised Version margin
Samar.	Samaritan recension
SCM	Student Christian Movement Press
Sem.	Semitic
sing.	singular
SPCK	Society for the Promotion of Christian Knowledge
Sumer.	Sumerian
s.v.	*sub verbo*, under the word
Syr.	Syriac
Symm.	Symmachus
T	Talmud
Targ.	Targum
Theod.	Theodotion
TR	Textus Receptus
tr.	translation, translator, translated
UBS	The United Bible Societies' Greek Text
Ugar.	Ugaritic
u.s.	*ut supra*, as above
viz.	*videlicet*, namely

vol.	volume	Vul.	Vulgate
v., vv.	verse, verses	WH	Westcott and Hort, *The New Testament in Greek*
vs.	versus		

B. Abbreviations for Modern Translations and Paraphrases

AmT	Smith and Goodspeed, *The Complete Bible, An American Translation*	LB	The Living Bible
ASV	American Standard Version, American Revised Version (1901)	Mof	J. Moffatt, *A New Translation of the Bible*
Beck	Beck, *The New Testament in the Language of Today*	NAB	The New American Bible
BV	Berkeley Version (The Modern Language Bible)	NASB	New American Standard Bible
JB	The Jerusalem Bible	NEB	The New English Bible
JPS	*Jewish Publication Society Version of the Old Testament*	NIV	The New International Version
KJV	King James Version	Ph	J. B. Phillips *The New Testament in Modern English*
Knox	R.G. Knox, *The Holy Bible: A Translation from the Latin Vulgate in the Light of the Hebrew and Greek Original*	RSV	Revised Standard Version
		RV	Revised Version — 1881–1885
		TCNT	Twentieth Century New Testament
		TEV	Today's English Version
		Wey	*Weymouth's New Testament in Modern Speech*
		Wms	C. B. Williams, *The New Testament: A Translation in the Language of the People*

C. Abbreviations for Periodicals and Reference Works

AASOR	*Annual of the American Schools of Oriental Research*	BAG	Bauer, Arndt, and Gingrich: *Greek-English Lexicon of the New Testament*
AB	*Anchor Bible*	BC	Foakes-Jackson and Lake: *The Beginnings of Christianity*
AIs	de Vaux: *Ancient Israel*	BDB	Brown, Driver, and Briggs: *Hebrew-English Lexicon of the Old Testament*
AJA	*American Journal of Archaeology*	BDF	Blass, Debrunner, and Funk: *A Greek Grammar of the New Testament and Other Early Christian Literature*
AJSL	*American Journal of Semitic Languages and Literatures*	BDT	Harrison: *Baker's Dictionary of Theology*
AJT	*American Journal of Theology*	Beng.	Bengel's *Gnomon*
Alf	Alford: *Greek Testament Commentary*	BETS	*Bulletin of the Evangelical Theological Society*
ANEA	*Ancient Near Eastern Archaeology*	BJRL	*Bulletin of the John Rylands Library*
ANET	Pritchard: *Ancient Near Eastern Texts*	BS	*Bibliotheca Sacra*
ANF	Roberts and Donaldson: *The Ante-Nicene Fathers*	BT	*Babylonian Talmud*
ANT	M. R. James: *The Apocryphal New Testament*	BTh	*Biblical Theology*
A-S	Abbot-Smith: *Manual Greek Lexicon of the New Testament*	BW	*Biblical World*
AThR	*Anglican Theological Review*	CAH	*Cambridge Ancient History*
BA	*Biblical Archaeologist*	CanJTh	*Canadian Journal of Theology*
BASOR	*Bulletin of the American Schools of Oriental Research*	CBQ	*Catholic Biblical Quarterly*

CBSC	*Cambridge Bible for Schools and Colleges*
CE	*Catholic Encyclopedia*
CGT	*Cambridge Greek Testament*
CHS	Lange: *Commentary on the Holy Scriptures*
ChT	*Christianity Today*
Crem	Cremer: *Biblico-Theological Lexicon of the New Testament Greek*
DDB	*Davis' Dictionary of the Bible*
Deiss BS	Deissmann: *Bible Studies*
Deiss LAE	Deissmann: *Light From the Ancient East*
DNTT	*Dictionary of New Testament Theology*
EBC	*The Expositor's Bible Commentary*
EBi	*Encyclopaedia Biblica*
EBr	*Encyclopaedia Britannica*
EDB	*Encyclopedic Dictionary of the Bible*
EGT	Nicoll: *Expositor's Greek Testament*
EQ	*Evangelical Quarterly*
ET	*Evangelische Theologie*
ExB	*The Expositor's Bible*
Exp	*The Expositor*
ExpT	*The Expository Times*
FLAP	Finegan: *Light From the Ancient Past*
GR	*Gordon Review*
HBD	*Harper's Bible Dictionary*
HDAC	Hastings: *Dictionary of the Apostolic Church*
HDB	Hastings: *Dictionary of the Bible*
HDBrev.	Hastings: *Dictionary of the Bible*, one-vol. rev. by Grant and Rowley
HDCG	Hastings: *Dictionary of Christ and the Gospels*
HERE	Hastings: *Encyclopedia of Religion and Ethics*
HGEOTP	Heidel: *The Gilgamesh Epic and Old Testament Parallels*
HJP	Schurer: *A History of the Jewish People in the Time of Christ*
HR	Hatch and Redpath: *Concordance to the Septuagint*
HTR	*Harvard Theological Review*
HUCA	*Hebrew Union College Annual*
IB	*The Interpreter's Bible*
ICC	*International Critical Commentary*
IDB	*The Interpreter's Dictionary of the Bible*
IEJ	*Israel Exploration Journal*
Int	*Interpretation*
INT	E. Harrison: *Introduction to the New Testament*
IOT	R. K. Harrison: *Introduction to the Old Testament*
ISBE	*The International Standard Bible Encyclopedia*
ITQ	*Irish Theological Quarterly*
JAAR	*Journal of American Academy of Religion*
JAOS	*Journal of American Oriental Society*
JBL	*Journal of Biblical Literature*
JE	*Jewish Encyclopedia*
JETS	*Journal of Evangelical Theological Society*
JFB	Jamieson, Fausset, and Brown: *Commentary on the Old and New Testament*
JNES	*Journal of Near Eastern Studies*
Jos. Antiq.	Josephus: *The Antiquities of the Jews*
Jos. War	Josephus: *The Jewish War*
JQR	*Jewish Quarterly Review*
JR	*Journal of Religion*
JSJ	*Journal for the Study of Judaism in the Persian, Hellenistic and Roman Periods*
JSOR	*Journal of the Society of Oriental Research*
JSS	*Journal of Semitic Studies*
JT	*Jerusalem Talmud*
JTS	*Journal of Theological Studies*
KAHL	Kenyon: *Archaeology in the Holy Land*
KB	Koehler-Baumgartner: *Lexicon in Veteris Testament Libros*
KD	Keil and Delitzsch: *Commentary on the Old Testament*
LSJ	Liddell, Scott, Jones: *Greek-English Lexicon*
LTJM	Edersheim: *The Life and Times of Jesus the Messiah*

MM	Moulton and Milligan: *The Vocabulary of the Greek Testament*
MNT	Moffatt: *New Testament Commentary*
MST	McClintock and Strong: *Cyclopedia of Biblical, Theological, and Ecclesiastical Literature*
NBC	Davidson, Kevan, and Stibbs: *The New Bible Commentary*, 1st ed.
NBCrev.	Guthrie and Motyer: *The New Bible Commentary*, rev. ed.
NBD	J. D. Douglas: *The New Bible Dictionary*
NCB	*New Century Bible*
NCE	*New Catholic Encyclopedia*
NIC	*New International Commentary*
NIDCC	Douglas: *The New International Dictionary of the Christian Church*
NovTest	*Novum Testamentum*
NSI	Cooke: *Handbook of North Semitic Inscriptions*
NTS	*New Testament Studies*
ODCC	*The Oxford Dictionary of the Christian Church*, rev. ed.
Peake	Black and Rowley: *Peake's Commentary on the Bible*
PEQ	*Palestine Exploration Quarterly*
PNF1	P. Schaff: *The Nicene and Post-Nicene Fathers* (1st series)
PNF2	P. Schaff and H. Wace: *The Nicene and Post-Nicene Fathers* (2nd series)
PTR	*Princeton Theological Review*
RB	*Revue Biblique*
RHG	Robertson's *Grammar of the Greek New Testament in the Light of Historical Research*
RTWB	Richardson: *A Theological Wordbook of the Bible*
SBK	Strack and Billerbeck: *Kommentar zum Neuen Testament aus Talmud und Midrash*
SHERK	*The New Schaff-Herzog Encyclopedia of Religious Knowledge*
SJT	*Scottish Journal of Theology*
SOT	Girdlestone: *Synonyms of Old Testament*
SOTI	Archer: *A Survey of Old Testament Introduction*
ST	*Studia Theologica*
TCERK	Loetscher: *The Twentieth Century Encyclopedia of Religious Knowledge*
TDNT	Kittel: *Theological Dictionary of the New Testament*
TDOT	*Theological Dictionary of the Old Testament*
Theol	*Theology*
ThT	*Theology Today*
TNTC	*Tyndale New Testament Commentaries*
Trench	Trench: *Synonyms of the New Testament*
UBD	*Unger's Bible Dictionary*
UT	Gordon: *Ugaritic Textbook*
VB	Allmen: *Vocabulary of the Bible*
VetTest	*Vetus Testamentum*
Vincent	Vincent: *Word-Pictures in the New Testament*
WBC	*Wycliffe Bible Commentary*
WBE	*Wycliffe Bible Encyclopedia*
WC	*Westminster Commentaries*
WesBC	*Wesleyan Bible Commentaries*
WTJ	*Westminster Theological Journal*
ZAW	*Zeitschrift für die alttestamentliche Wissenschaft*
ZNW	*Zeitschrift für die neutestamentliche Wissenschaft*
ZPBD	*The Zondervan Pictorial Bible Dictionary*
ZPEB	*The Zondervan Pictorial Encyclopedia of the Bible*
ZWT	*Zeitschrift für wissenschaftliche Theologie*

D. Abbreviations for Books of the Bible, the Apocrypha, and the Pseudepigrapha

OLD TESTAMENT

Gen	2 Chron	Dan
Exod	Ezra	Hos
Lev	Neh	Joel
Num	Esth	Amos
Deut	Job	Obad
Josh	Ps(Pss)	Jonah
Judg	Prov	Mic
Ruth	Eccl	Nah
1 Sam	S of Songs	Hab
2 Sam	Isa	Zeph
1 Kings	Jer	Hag
2 Kings	Lam	Zech
1 Chron	Ezek	Mal

NEW TESTAMENT

Matt	1 Tim
Mark	2 Tim
Luke	Titus
John	Philem
Acts	Heb
Rom	James
1 Cor	1 Peter
2 Cor	2 Peter
Gal	1 John
Eph	2 John
Phil	3 John
Col	Jude
1 Thess	Rev
2 Thess	

APOCRYPHA

1 Esd	1 Esdras
2 Esd	2 Esdras
Tobit	Tobit
Jud	Judith
Add Esth	Additions to Esther
Wisd Sol	Wisdom of Solomon
Ecclus	Ecclesiasticus (Wisdom of Jesus the Son of Sirach)
Baruch	Baruch
Ep Jer	Epistle of Jeremy
S Th Ch	Song of the Three Children (or Young Men)
Sus	Susanna
Bel	Bel and the Dragon
Pr Man	Prayer of Manasseh
1 Macc	1 Maccabees
2 Macc	2 Maccabees

PSEUDEPIGRAPHA

As Moses	Assumption of Moses
2 Baruch	Syriac Apocalypse of Baruch
3 Baruch	Greek Apocalypse of Baruch
1 Enoch	Ethiopic Book of Enoch
2 Enoch	Slavonic Book of Enoch
3 Enoch	Hebrew Book of Enoch
4 Ezra	4 Ezra
JA	Joseph and Asenath
Jub	Book of Jubilees
L Aristeas	Letter of Aristeas
Life AE	Life of Adam and Eve
Liv Proph	Lives of the Prophets
MA Isa	Martyrdom and Ascension of Isaiah
3 Macc	3 Maccabees
4 Macc	4 Maccabees
Odes Sol	Odes of Solomon
P Jer	Paralipomena of Jeremiah
Pirke Aboth	Pirke Aboth
Ps 151	Psalm 151
Pss Sol	Psalms of Solomon
Sib Oracles	Sibylline Oracles
Story Ah	Story of Ahikar
T Abram	Testament of Abraham
T Adam	Testament of Adam
T Benjamin	Testament of Benjamin
T Dan	Testament of Dan
T Gad	Testament of Gad
T Job	Testament of Job
T Jos	Testament of Joseph
T Levi	Testament of Levi
T Naph	Testament of Naphtali
T 12 Pat	Testaments of the Twelve Patriarchs
Zad Frag	Zadokite Fragments

E. Abbreviations of Names of Dead Sea Scrolls and Related Texts

CD	Cairo (Genizah text of the) Damascus (Document)
DSS	Dead Sea Scrolls
Hev	Nahal Hever texts
Mas	Masada Texts
Mird	Khirbet mird texts
Mur	Wadi Murabba'at texts
P	Pesher (commentary)
Q	Qumran
1Q,2Q,etc.	Numbered caves of Qumran, yielding written material; followed by abbreviation of biblical or apocryphal book.
QL	Qumran Literature
1QapGen	Genesis Apocryphon of Qumran Cave 1
1QH	*Hodayot* (Thanksgiving Hymns) from Qumran Cave 1
1QIsa[a, b]	First or second copy of Isaiah from Qumran Cave 1
1QpHab	Pesher on Habakkuk from Qumran Cave 1
1QM	*Milhamah* (War Scroll)
1QS	*Serek Hayyahad* (Rule of the Community, Manual of Discipline)
1QSa	Appendix A (Rule of the Congregation) to 1QS
1QSb	Appendix B (Blessings) to 1QS
3Q15	Copper Scroll from Qumran Cave 3
4QFlor	Florilegium (or Eschatological Midrashim) from Qumran Cave 4
4Qmess ar	Aramaic "Messianic" text from Qumran Cave 4
4QPrNab	Prayer of Nabonidus from Qumran Cave 4
4QTest	Testimonia text from Qumran Cave 4
4QTLevi	Testament of Levi from Qumran Cave 4
4QPhyl	Phylacteries from Qumran Cave 4
11QMelch	Melchizedek text from Qumran Cave 11
11QtgJob	Targum of Job from Qumran Cave 11

TRANSLITERATIONS

Hebrew

א = ʾ	ד = ḏ	י = y	ס = s	ר = r
בּ = b	ה = h	כּ = k	ע = ʿ	שׂ = ś
ב = ḇ	ו = w	כ = ḵ	פּ = p	שׁ = š
גּ = g	ז = z	ל = l	פ = p̄	תּ = t
ג = ḡ	ח = ḥ	מ = m	צ = ṣ	ת = ṯ
דּ = d	ט = ṭ	נ = n	ק = q	

◌ָ(ה) = â (h)	◌ָ = ā	◌ַ = a	◌ֲ = ^{a}
◌ֵי = ê	◌ֵ = ē	◌ֶ = e	◌ֱ = ^{e}
◌ִי = î	◌ֹ = ō	◌ִ = i	◌ְ = ^{e} (*if vocal*)
וֹ = ô		◌ָ = o	◌ֳ = ^{o}
וּ = û		◌ֻ = u	

Aramaic

ʾ b g d h w z ḥ ṭ y k l m n s ʿ p ṣ q r ś š t

Arabic

ʾ b t ṯ ǧ ḥ ḫ d ḏ r z s š ṣ ḍ ṭ ẓ ʿ ġ f q k l m n h w y

Ugaritic

ʾ b g d ḏ h w z ḥ ḫ ṭ ẓ y k l m n s ś ʿ ġ p ṣ q r š t ṯ

Greek

α — a	π — p	αι — ai
β — b	ρ — r	αὐ — au
γ — g	σ,ς — s	ει — ei
δ — d	τ — t	εὐ — eu
ε — e	υ — y	ηὐ — ēu
ζ — z	φ — ph	οι — oi
η — ē	χ — ch	οὐ — ou
θ — th	ψ — ps	υι — hui
ι — i	ω — ō	
κ — k		ῥ — rh
λ — l	γγ — ng	‛ — h
μ — m	γκ — nk	
ν — n	γξ — nx	ᾳ — ā
ξ — x	γχ — nch	ῃ — ē
ο — o		ῳ — ō

MATTHEW

D.A. Carson

con't.

B. *Third Discourse: The Parables of the Kingdom* (13:1–53)

1. *The setting*

13:1–3a

[1]That same day Jesus went out of the house and sat by the lake. [2]Such large crowds gathered around him that he got into a boat and sat in it, while all the people stood on the shore. [3]Then he told them many things in parables, saying:

1 Doubtless *en tē hēmera ekeinē* must be rendered "that same day," but NIV introduces an insurmountable problem by translating *palin* in Mark 4:1 "on another occasion." *Palin* does not mean that; indeed, it can often be translated "furthermore" or "thereupon" (BAGD, s.v.). At any rate Matthew links the parabolic discourse in chapter 13 to the preceding controversies (either 12:38–50 or 12:22–37) and ends it with a formulaic conclusion (13:53), which implies that all these parables were given on this occasion. The statement "Jesus went out of the house" implies the same thing by setting a specific scene carried forward by 13:36.

Jesus "sat by the lake," taking the normal position of a teacher (see on 5:1–2). The explanation that Jesus' posture was a symbol drawn from apocalyptic literature representing God sitting in judgment (cf. Rev 7:9–12; Kingsbury, *Parables*, pp. 23f.) is not only overly subtle and needlessly anachronistic but misunderstands the parables. Although in some parables Jesus portrayed himself as the Judge coming at the end of the age (esp. vv.40–43), such a judicial session is future. During his ministry Jesus' chosen role was that of a teacher who taught others about the kingdom so that they might teach others (see on vv.51–52).

2 This is the only one of the five major discourses in Matthew that is addressed, not to the "disciples" (in the broad sense of 5:1–2), but to the crowds. Therefore Matthew includes in it two major digressions (vv.10–23, 36–43) to explain to his disciples the significance of parables and to interpret two of them. While these digressions doubtless took place after the public discourse, Matthew moves them back as parentheses so that the significance of the parables will not be lost to the reader. Some scholars contend that the crowds, unlike the Jewish leaders, are portrayed favorably, since they are the group Matthew wants immediately to reach. But that is farfetched. In Matthew, Jesus has already criticized "this generation" (11:16–24) and can treat the Jewish leaders as typical of it (12:38–39). Here the crowds are not given "the secrets of the kingdom" (v.11).

Matthew changes Mark's "taught" (4:2) to "told" (v.3a)—a change that has encouraged many to suppose that he is turning the parables into "proclamation narratives" (e.g., W. Wilkens, "Die Redaktion des Gleichniskapitels Mark.4 durch Matth.," *Theologische Zeitschrift* 20 [1964]: 305–27). On the other hand, Kingsbury (*Parables*, pp. 28–31) holds that the change from "taught" to "told" owes everything to the structure of Matthew's Gospel. After Matthew 12 Jesus never teaches or preaches to the Jews. So Matthew looks on this chapter as a sort of "apology." To base such large theological implications on the change of a single verb is not convincing, because Matthew often shows considerable independence in verbal expression. What he understands Jesus to be doing in the parables must be based on the exegesis of the whole chapter, and especially on that of Matthew 13:10–17, which purports to answer that very question. Kingsbury's view that Jesus does not teach or preach to the crowd after Matthew 12 is in any case manifestly wrong. Little of such teaching occurs before Matthew 12; most references to it are general (e.g., 4:23; 9:35); and after Matthew 12 we find similar remarks (13:54; 15:10; 21:23; cf. 22:16; 26:55; and implicitly 14:13–36; 15:29–31). These and similar reconstructions attempt to see in the antithesis between the "crowds" and the "disciples" a covert disjunction between the church and the synagogue. J. Dupont ("Point de vue," pp. 221–59) analyzes these efforts in detail and shows that the language is simply not specific enough to draw such far-reaching conclusions. In particular he shows that the disciples-crowds contrast relates to what is just or unjust and with either doing or not doing the will of the Father.

3a Jesus told the crowd "many things in parables." Before we examine them, however, three comments are needed.

1. The history of the interpretation of parables is very complex, and the number of new developments in parable scholarship has accelerated in recent years. This has been set forth concisely by J.G. Little ("Parable Research in the Twentieth Century," ExpT 87 [1975–76]: 356–60; 88 [1976–77]: 40–44, 71–75) and comprehensively by W.S. Kissinger (*The Parables of Jesus: A History of Interpretation and Bibliography* [Metuchen, N.J.: Scarecrow, 1979]).

Commentators tended to interpret the parables more or less by appeal to allegory (with notable exceptions such as Augustine and, to a lesser extent, Calvin) till Adolph Jülicher's huge study (*Die Gleichnisreden Jesu*, 2 vols. [Tübingen: J.C.B. Mohr, 1910]), which contends that Jesus told not allegories but parables—simple stories with a single point. Traces of allegorical interpretation of parables in the Gospels must therefore be assigned to the postapostolic church. Studies by Dodd (*Parables*) and Jeremias (*Parables*) have proceeded along similar lines. Dodd has tried to show that some parables demonstrate the eschatological orientation of Jesus' preaching and the "presentness" of the kingdom, while Jeremias has established "laws" of parable transmission to determine how Jesus' simple stories were progressively changed in the process of oral and written retelling and application. Using these "laws," Jeremias has argued that we can strip off later accretions and discover what the historical Jesus really taught.

Two essays challenge Jeremias's view. Both Matthew Black ("The Parables as Allegory," BJRL 42 [1959–60]: 273–87) and Raymond E. Brown ("Parable and Allegory Reconsidered," NovTest 5 [1962]: 36–45) convincingly demonstrate that the allegory-parable distinction is too facile, that Jesus himself occasionally derived more than one or two points from certain of his parables, and that all "allegorizing" of the parables cannot be automatically assigned to the postapostolic church. Two things follow: (1) what Jeremias calls allegorization does not by itself prove secondary accretion; (2) as McNeile (p. 186) observed long ago, a certain unavoidable ambiguity is built into the parables. For it is not always easy to distinguish illustrative details and details that are merely part of the story structure. While there is room for difference of opinion here, the slight loss in certainty of meaning is more than compensated for by the greater flexibility in understanding the parables.

More recent developments in parable scholarship have moved in different directions. Hans Weder (*Die Gleichnisse Jesu als Metaphern* [Göttingen: Vandenhoeck und Ruprecht, 1978], pp. 69–75) distinguishes parabolic (as opposed to allegorical) elements as those tied to the narrative flow and lacking independent existence both in the narrative and its interpretation. His work largely follows the studies of Eta Linnemann (*Parables of Jesus* [London: SPCK, 1966]), D.O. Via (*The Parables* [Philadelphia: Fortress, 1967]), and J.D. Crossan (*In Parables* [New York: Harper and Row, 1973]), who say that what distinguishes parable from allegory is not that only the former has one central point but that the former alone ties all its elements to one another within the parable's framework. These interconnections are determined not so much by a one-to-one link with the historical or theological situation to which the parable refers but by the demands of the story—viz., the parable itself. Therefore some parabolic elements may have a historical referent; others none. But where such "outside" connections are made, they are subsidiary to the connections "inside" the parable, the point of which is contained within the story's internal movement.

These are important insights. Yet those who have developed them unfortunately tend to think deeply on the literary level but naively on the historical one. Many recent interpreters tend to be far less conservative than Jeremias in what they ascribe to the historical Jesus. And it is astonishing how often, once they have finished their interpretations, they exhort their readers to choose authentic existence, trust the benevolence of the universe, or the like. Whatever else Jesus was, he was no twentieth-century existentialist! Coupling these literary studies with insights from "the new hermeneutic," Mary Ann Tolbert (*Perspectives on the Parables: An Approach to Multiple Interpretations* [Philadelphia: Fortress, 1979]) tries to establish the legitimacy of interpreting the parables in different ways that depend largely on the stance of the interpreter, and argues that the parables' "dynamic indeterminacy" (p. 115) requires such an approach. Questions raised by such studies and the German works on which many of them are based cannot be handled here. For a responsible treatment of the issues involved, see A.C. Thiselton, *The Two Horizons* (Grand Rapids: Eerdmans, 1980).

Suffice it to say that historical doubts are not always tied as intimately to the genuine literary insights of these writers as they seem to think. Jesus, though he did indeed confront people and demand existential choices, did so within a message that was, and can still be, defined and defended propositionally. Moreover the criteria for distinguishing between Jesus' parables and church accretions to them are becoming less and less justifiable. Although there are many *kinds* of parables (see below), Thiselton is right in pointing out how many of them are designed to capture the listener and make him a participant, overturning his world view and leading him to call in question his most basic values (cf. esp. pp. 12–15, 344–47). These convictions undergird the following exposition.

2. Some areas of disagreement might be eliminated if more attention were paid to the word "parable" itself. Behind it stands the Hebrew *māšāl* (twenty-eight of

thirty-three instances in the OT are rendered *parabolē* [parable] in the LXX), a word referring to proverbs, maxims, similes, allegories, fables, comparisons, riddles, taunts, stories embodying some truth (Num 23:7, 18; 1 Sam 10:12; 24:13; Job 27:1; Pss 49:4; 78:2; Prov 1:6; Eccl 12:9; Isa 14:4; Ezek 12:2; 17:2; 24:3; 13; Mic 2:4; Hab 2:6). And the word "parable" in the NT comes close to duplicating this range (cf. esp. DNTT, 2:743–60). Thus a parable can be a proverb (Luke 4:23; something John calls a *paroimia* ["figure of speech," John 10:6; 16:25, 29; cf. Job 27:1 LXX]); a profound or obscure saying (Matt 13:35); a nonverbal symbol or image (Heb 9:9; 11:19); an illustrative comparison, whether without the form of a story (Matt 15:15; 24:32) or with (in the most familiar kind of "parable"—e.g., 13:3–9); an illustrative story not involving comparison of unlikes (e.g., the rich fool, Luke 12:16–21); and more. So it becomes obvious that much learned discussion actually focuses on only one or two kinds of NT "parables." Most, though not all, parables are extended metaphors or similes. Yet even so broad a definition as this eliminates some of the material listed above that NT writers label "parable." Most generalized conclusions about parables require painful exceptions; and on the whole it is best to deal inductively with parables, while at the same time being aware of the questions posed by recent studies and the scholarly analyses of some parable material.

One of the most responsible of these is Boucher's recent work, some of whose conclusions are adopted later (see on vv.10–17). But even Boucher narrows down parable to "a *narrative* having two levels of meaning" (p. 23) and confusingly defines allegory as merely "a device of meaning, and not in itself a literary form or genre" (p. 20), while insisting that allegory must extend a metaphor over a whole story, thus tying it inescapably to a form. By this definition some parables are allegories. Yet it is useful, for instance, to be able to distinguish allegories that are types from those that are not. Progress in understanding parables depends, it seems, in greater scholarly agreement over the semantics of the labels and in greater willingness to recognize the diversity of kinds of parables in the NT. (On this point, cf. G.B. Caird, *The Language and Imagery of the Bible* [London: Duckworth, 1980], pp. 161–67; Robert H. Stein, *The Method and Message of Jesus' Teachings* [Philadelphia: Westminster, 1978], pp. 34–39.)

3. The structure of the third discourse (13:3–52) bears directly on its interpretation. Certain things are obvious. Two of the parables are also found in Mark and Luke: viz., the sower and its interpretation (13:3–9, 18–23; Mark 4:3–9, 13–20; Luke 8:5–15) and the mustard seed (13:31–32; Mark 4:30–32; Luke 13:18–19). One is paralleled in Luke but not Mark (the yeast [13:33; Luke 13:20–21]), and the other four (or five; see below) are found only in Matthew. Mark 4:26–29 adds still another to this discourse; and both Mark 4:33 and Matthew 13:3 suggest there was a great deal more left unreported.

These are the agreed facts, but the structure of the discourse as it stands is more disputed (cf. Dupont, "Point de vue," pp. 231f.; Kingsbury, *Parables*, pp. 12–15). The best analysis has been provided by David Wenham ("Structure," pp. 516–22), who argues, with Lohmeyer and Kingsbury (*Parables*), that v.52 is a parable (note the form "is like [plus dative]" and the opening words of v.53). The discourse may then be broken down into two parts of four parables each (vv.3–33, 44–52). The first four are addressed to the crowds, the last four to the disciples. Wenham's distinctive contribution lies in identifying the emergent chiastic structure. Of the first four parables, the first stands apart from the other three, separated by discussion about the purpose of parables (vv.10–17) and the interpretation of the parable (vv.18–23).

It has a formally different introduction (the other three begin "Jesus told them another parable, 'The kingdom of heaven is like . . .' "). The matching chiastic four in the second half begin with three parables with the same opening ("The kingdom of heaven is like . . ."), separated from the fourth, which has a different beginning, by the explanation in vv.49–50 and the question and answer about the disciples' understanding of parables. The central section separating the two sets of parables (vv.34–43) divides the chiasm and further explains the function of parables while expounding one of them. (See outline, Introduction, section 14.) The implications are important.

1. Matthew reports two rationales for parables, one related to their function for outsiders and one related to their function for disciples.

2. The detailed structure reveals Matthew's skill as an author; and the alleged dislocations (esp. vv.12, 34–35), often taken to support Markan priority, turn out to be, not aporias (i.e., a break that demands explanation), but an integral part of the outline (see below). This does not of course disprove Mark's priority here; but if Matthew is indeed prior or independent for all or part of this chapter (as Wenham argues in "The Synoptic Problem Revisited"), it supports an important point—viz., that it is methodologically doubtful to think that the only access to information Matthew has when following Mark is Mark itself.

3. This structure also calls in question the traditional dispensational interpretation of the parables in this chapter. Typical is Walvoord: "Jesus deliberately adopted the parabolic method of teaching at a particular stage in His ministry for the purpose of withholding further truth about Himself and the kingdom of heaven from the crowds, who had proved themselves to be deaf to His claims and irresponsive to His demands. . . . From now onwards, when addressing the unbelieving multitude, He speaks only in parables which He interprets to His disciples in private."

There is insight here: Walvoord rightly detects the note of judgment bound up with some parables. Walvoord's position, however, is too cut and dried. First, remembering the broad definition of "parables" in the NT, it is doubtful that we are to think that chapter 13 contains Jesus' first use of parables in Matthew (cf. 7:24–27; 9:15–17; 11:16–19). Second, if Walvoord were to respond that such passages are not labeled "parables," the historical problem recurs when any synoptic harmony is attempted (a procedure he would approve). Historically Jesus does not use parables for the first time at this stage in his ministry (cf. Luke 5:36; 6:39). What does seem likely is that rising opposition to Jesus encouraged his greater and greater use of parables (see on vv.10–17, 34–35). But there is little ground for the sudden switch in method Walvoord sees. Third, parables are not restricted to Jesus' ministry to outsiders: he also uses them positively for his disciples (cf. structure, above). Fourth, there has been no extensive teaching to outsiders before this third discourse and there is none after it to test Walvoord's claim that Jesus' use of parables is a new departure here. We have only the fact that Jesus' preaching to outsiders is repeatedly mentioned but no extended samples of it (see on 13:11).

2. *To the crowds* (13:3b–33)

a. *The parable of the soils*

13:3b–9

3b"A farmer went out to sow his seed. 4As he was scattering the seed, some fell along the path, and the birds came and ate it up. 5Some fell on rocky places, where it did not have much soil. It sprang up quickly, because the soil was shallow. [6]But when the sun came up, the plants were scorched, and they withered because they had no root. [7]Other seed fell among thorns, which grew up and choked the plants. [8]Still other seed fell on good soil, where it produced a crop—a hundred, sixty or thirty times what was sown. [9]He who has ears, let him hear."

3b–7 The focus of the parable is not the sower (the article is used in v.3 to designate a class; cf. 12:43) but the soils. The farmer scatters the seed (v.3b), which falls in various places. Paths run through and around the unfenced fields (see on 12:1); and the earth paths are too hard to receive the seed, which is eaten by birds (v.4). "Rocky places" (v.5) are those in which the limestone bedrock lies close to the surface: there is little depth of soil. As the rainy season ends and the sun's heat increases, the shallow soil heats up quickly (v.6). The seeds sprout and promise to be the best of the crop (on the appropriateness of these details to the Palestinian setting, cf. P.B. Payne, "The Order of Sowing and Ploughing in the Parable of the Sower," NTS 25 [1978–79]: 123–29). But the unrelenting summer heat demands that plants send deep roots down for water, and the bedrock prevents this. Like grass on rooftops, the young plants wither before they can grow (Ps 129:6). Other seed falls into hedges of thorns that deprive the plants of sun and nourishment (v.7).

8–9 But some seed falls on good soil and produces crops of various yields (v.8), which, contrary to what many think, are not extremely high, symbolic of the fertility of the Messianic Age, but well within ordinary expectations (cf. Payne, "Authenticity," pp. 181–86). The same seed produces no crop, some crop, or much crop according to the soil's character. The final exhortation (v.9; see on 11:15) warns Jesus' hearers and Matthew's readers that the parable needs careful interpretation.

At this point many commentators, believing vv.18–23 to be unauthentic, attempt to interpret vv.3b–9 without reference to vv.18–23. Their efforts fail to produce interpretations more believable than the one Matthew ascribes to Jesus. Typical is that of Hill (*Matthew*), who says the parable means that just as every (Palestinian) sower does his work in spite of many frustrations, so the kingdom makes its way in spite of many difficulties. It will be established in time, with a sure and glorious harvest, but only after much loss. The parable has little to do with how to hear the word of God. But Hill's interpretation depends on treating the parable serially—i.e., the sower sows seed in all the bad places first. On the face of it, the differences lie in the soils, not in the order of sowing: i.e., the kingdom, while advancing now by the promulgation of the good news about the kingdom (4:23), is meeting many different responses.

b. *Interlude* (13:10–23)

1) *On understanding parables*

13:10–17

[10]The disciples came to him and asked, "Why do you speak to the people in parables?"

[11]He replied, "The knowledge of the secrets of the kingdom of heaven has been given to you, but not to them. [12]Whoever has will be given more, and he will have an abundance. Whoever does not have, even what he has will be taken from him. [13]This is why I speak to them in parables:

"Though seeing, they do not see;
though hearing, they do not hear or understand.

14 In them is fulfilled the prophecy of Isaiah:

" 'You will be ever hearing but never understanding;
you will be ever seeing but never perceiving.
15 For this people's heart has become calloused;
they hardly hear with their ears,
and they have closed their eyes.
Otherwise they might see with their eyes,
hear with their ears,
understand with their hearts
and turn, and I would heal them.' "

16 But blessed are your eyes because they see, and your ears because they hear.
17 For I tell you the truth, many prophets and righteous men longed to see what
you see but did not see it, and to hear what you hear but did not hear it.

Matthew's treatment is not only longer than Mark's (4:10–12) and Luke's (8:9–10; 10:23–24), but it includes more OT Scripture and is structured with great care. The disciples' question (v.10) evokes Jesus' basic answer (vv.11–12), which is then applied in greater detail first to "them" (vv.13–15) and then to the disciples (vv.16–18). The latter two sections are a well-ordered chiasm whose inversion echoes OT form (e.g., Ps 89:28–37) and emphasizes the climax of judgment and mercy (so K.E. Bailey, *Poet and Peasant* [Grand Rapids: Eerdmans, 1976], pp. 61f.):

Therefore I speak to them in parables,
1 because seeing *they see not* and hearing *they hear not,* nor understand.
2 And *it is fulfilled to them* the *prophecy* of Isaiah which says,
3 "Hearing *you shall hear* and shall *not understand,*
4 and seeing you *shall see* and shall *not perceive.*
5 For this people's *heart* is become dull
6 and the *ears* are dull of hearing
7 and their *eyes* they have closed,
7′ lest they should perceive with the *eyes*
6′ and hear with the *ear*
5′ and understand with the *heart,* and should turn again and I should heal them."
4′ But blessed are *your eyes,* for they see,
3′ and your *ears,* for they *hear.*
2′ For truly *I say unto you* that many *prophets* and righteous men
1′ desired to see what *you see,* and *did not see,* and to hear what *you hear,* and *did not hear.*

10 "The disciples" (Mark: "the Twelve and the others around him") approached Jesus, apparently in private (cf. Mark 4:10). If this occurred at the end of the discourse, the plural "parables" would be well accounted for. Kingsbury (*Parables,* pp. 40–41) detects in the verb *proselthontes* ("came to him") a "cultic connotation": the disciples approached Jesus "with the same reverence that would be due to a king or deity." He defends this doubtful view with a prejudicial selection of the evidence that could in some cases be taken that way, while ignoring contrary evidence regarding Matthew's use of the verb (cf. 4:3; 8:19; 9:14; 15:1, 30; 16:1; 17:24; 22:23 et al.).

Recent scholarship rightly sees in this chapter the distinction between the disciples and the crowds, presupposed by the above outline. But there has been a regrettable tendency to think Matthew has absolutized the distinction, idealized the disciples, and played down their lack of understanding (Bornkamm, *Tradition*, pp. 105ff.; Kingsbury, *Parables*, pp. 42ff.; Schmid; Grundmann). This idealization, it is alleged, is very strong in vv.10–17 and emerges in v.10. The disciples ask why Jesus speaks to the crowds in parables, not what the parables mean—and this presupposes they already know. But Mark's question is ambiguous (Mark 4:10); Matthew typically has merely clarified the point. The critics' contention is based on an argument from silence. But if the disciples did understand the parable of the sower, why does Jesus proceed in a few verses to give them an explanation (vv.18–23)? And why do they ask for an explanation to a later parable (v.36)? The focus of Jesus' reply (vv.11–17) is not so much on the disciples' understanding as on the fact that the revelation is given to some and not to others and why. (On this recurring question, cf. Trotter.)

11–12 Jesus' answer cannot legitimately be softened: at least one of the functions of parables is to conceal the truth, or at least *to present it in a veiled way*. This point is strengthened if the *hoti* is not "recitative" (equivalent to the quotation marks in NIV) but fully causal, "because." The disciples ask, "Why do you speak, etc?" and Jesus replies, "Because the secrets of the kingdom have been given to the disciples but not to others." The strength of this translation turns not only on its suitability after "Why?" but also on the fact that *hoti* is nowhere else in the NT "recitative" after the particular formula used: *ho de apokritheis eipen* ("he replied," v.11; cf. D. Wenham, "Structure," p. 519, n. 5) and literature there cited). The pronoun *autois* ("to them") does not refer first to the Jews in Matthew's day but to "the people" mentioned by the disciples in the previous verse.

Ta mysteria tēs basileias ("the secrets of the kingdom") is not explained; its meaning may be deduced by the context and by the use of *mysterion* ("secret") elsewhere. *Mysterion* has no obvious connections with pagan mystery religions but reflects a thoroughly Semitic background (cf. R.E. Brown, *The Semitic Background of the Term "Mystery" in the New Testament* [Philadelphia: Fortress, 1968]). It appears in the OT in Daniel (Aram. *rāz*), which refers to some eschatological secret, some portent of what God has decreed will take place in the future. The Greek term can also reflect the Hebrew *sôḏ* ("secret," "confidential speech"), taken from the heavenly council (cf. Brown, *Mystery*, pp. 2–6; DNTT, 3:502). The same range of meanings is found in the DSS. "Mysteries" are divine plans or decrees, often passed on in veiled language, known only to the elect, and usually relating to eschatological events.

For the "secrets of the kingdom" to be "given" the disciples suggests that to them certain eschatological realities are being revealed. What is revealed is not who Jesus is, the nature of God, or the power of love (all of which have been suggested); rather, the "mystery of the Kingdom is the coming of the Kingdom into history in advance of its apocalyptic manifestation" (Ladd, *Presence*, pp. 218–42, esp. p. 222). That God would bring in his kingdom was no secret. All Jews looked forward to it. "The new truth, now given to men by revelation in the person and mission of Jesus, is that *the Kingdom which is to come finally in apocalyptic power, as foreseen by Daniel, has in fact entered into the world in advance in a hidden form to work secretly within and among men*" (ibid., p. 225, emphasis his).

It is unlikely that the plural "secrets," as opposed to Mark's "secret," refers to everything Jesus has taught (so Kingsbury, *Parables*, pp. 44f.). The strongest reason for the latter view is that some of the parables deal with ethical matters, not eschatology, reflecting, it is argued, the full gamut of Jesus' teaching (e.g., parables of the hidden treasure, of the pearl, of the unforgiving servant). But in reality all such parables, as we shall see, necessarily presuppose some form of realized eschatology to make their ethical demands meaningful. The plural "secrets" is best accounted for as a typical Matthean preference for the plural (cf. Matt 4:3–Luke 4:3; Matt 8:26–Mark 4:39; Matt 26:15–Mark 14:11) and a regular changing of "crowd" to "crowds" (at Matt 12:46; 13:2; 14:22; 15:36; 21:46; 23:1; 27:20) or as a reflection of a non-Markan source (there are several Matt–Luke "minor agreements" against Mark here; for details cf. D. Wenham, "Synoptic Problem") or perhaps as a reference to the multiple elements bound up with the basic eschatological truth that the age to come has already dawned.

The antithesis of v.12 is proverbial and repeated elsewhere (25:29; cf. Mark 4:25; Luke 8:18). It warns against taking spiritual blessings for granted and serves to increase gratitude and a sense of privilege among those who continue to enjoy them. What is lost in the second part of the antithesis is not the law but one's standing as the expected subject of the kingdom (cf. 8:11–12).

13 Jesus now explicitly applies his answer (vv.11–12) to those who are not disciples. Discussion of this verse turns on Matthew's change of *hina* plus subjunctive in Mark 4:12 ("in order that, etc.")—which implies that the parables' blinding outsiders is a function of divine election—to *hoti* ("because"), which means that Jesus speaks in parables because the people are spiritually insensitive. Though they "see," they do not *really* "see." There are four possible approaches to the above data.

1. Some argue that Matthew's change of *hina* to *hoti* is motivated by his editorial desire to blame the Jews or to establish a moral basis for their being rejected (e.g., Kingsbury, *Parables*, pp. 48–49; Dupont, "Point de vue," pp. 233f.). But this badly oversimplifies the matter because of the strong note on election in the best rendering of v.11 (above).

2. Others suggest a sort of additive harmonization: "because" (*hoti*, Matt) the willful rejectors refused to see and hear, Jesus spoke to them in parables "in order that" (*hina*, Mark–Luke) they might not (truly) see and hear (Hendriksen). This may be theologically sound, but it is doubtful whether simple addition best explains what Matthew has done.

3. Many attempt to soften the *hina* in Mark to lose its telic force ("in order that") and take on a consecutive force ("with the result that"; cf. NIV's ambiguous "so that"). Mark and Matthew would then be very close in thought in this verse. Certainly *hina* can have consecutive force in Hellenistic Greek, a distinct departure from the classical; but Mark has *hina . . . mēpote* (lit., "in order that . . . lest"; NIV, "otherwise"), and it is very difficult to give such an expression anything else than full telic force. Moule (*Idiom Book*, p. 143) recognizes the strength of this argument; but because he judges the notion of parables told to prevent any who are not predestined for salvation from hearing "too incongruous with any part of the N.T. period to be plausible," he is forced to appeal to Semitic idiom or even the much later linguistic development of causal *hina*. But attempts to ground Mark's *hina* in a Semitic mistranslation (cf. esp. T.W. Manson, *The Teachings of Jesus*, 2d ed. [Cambridge: University Press, 1935], pp. 76ff.) have proved futile (cf. Gundry, *Use of OT*, pp. 34–35, n. 1; Boucher, pp. 43–44; J. Gnilka, *Die Verstockung Israels* [Mün-

chen: Kösel-Verlag, 1961]). And appeals to rabbinic parables and their function have turned out to support the telic view, since rabbis did indeed use parables to mask truth: the rabbinic parable "is not a universalistic form" (D. Daube, "Public Pronouncement and Private Explanation in the Gospels," ExpT 57 [1945–46]: 177).

4. Though the last two approaches are not convincing, the first can become plausible if presented with greater awareness of the relationship v.12 enjoys with v.11 and v.13. Verse 11 most likely embraces a strictly predestinarian viewpoint, more strongly than Mark 4:11 and doctrinally, though not verbally, like Mark 4:12. The reply to the disciples' question (Matt 13:10) is thus given in terms of election in v.11, which is further explained in v.12. Verse 13 recapitulates the reason for speaking in parables but now frames the reason, not in terms of election, but in terms of spiritual dullness. Matthew has already given Jesus' answer in terms of divine election (v.11); now he gives the human reason. While this brings him into formal conflict with Mark 4:12, he has already sounded the predestinarian note of Mark 4:12. Here Matthew includes much more material than Mark; and in the ordered structure (see parallelisms, above) that results from the inclusion of such new material, verbal parallels are lost in favor of conceptual ones.

Three broader reflections help resolve the problem.

1. Biblical writers in both the OT and the NT have, on the whole, fewer problems about the tension between God's sovereignty and man's responsibility than do many moderns. This is not because they fail to distinguish purpose and consequence, as many affirm (e.g., Moule, *Idiom Book*, p. 142), but because they do not see divine sovereignty and human responsibility as antitheses. In short they are compatibilists and therefore juxtapose the two themes with little self-conscious awareness of any problem (cf. Gen 50:19–20; Judg 14:4; Isa 10:5–7; Hag 1:12–14; John 11:49–52; cf. Carson, *Divine Sovereignty*).

2. Thus, even though he records Jesus' answer in terms of election, Mark does not thereby mean to absolve the outsiders of all responsibility. How could he, in the light of the interpretation of the parable of the sower he records (4:13–20), his record of John's demand for repentance (1:4), and much more? Matthew has taken up these themes in greater detail because he wishes simultaneously to affirm that what is taking place in the ministry of Jesus is, on the one hand, the decreed will of God and the result of biblical prophecy and, on the other hand, a terrible rebellion, gross spiritual dullness, and chronic unbelief. This places the responsibility for the divine rejection of those who fail to become disciples on their own shoulders while guaranteeing that none of what is taking place stands outside God's control and plan. The same sort of pairing has already been expressed in 11:25–30.

3. This sheds much light on the parables. It is naive to say Jesus spoke them so that everyone might more easily grasp the truth, and it is simplistic to say that the sole function of parables to outsiders was to condemn them. If Jesus simply wished to hide the truth from the outsiders, he need never have spoken to them. His concern for mission (9:35–38; 10:1–10; 28:16–20) excludes that idea. So he must preach without casting his pearls before pigs (7:6). He does so in parables: i.e., in such a way as to harden and reject those who are hard of heart and to enlighten—often with further explanation—his disciples. His disciples, it must be remembered, are not just the Twelve but those who were following him (see on 5:1–12) and who, it is hoped, go on to do the will of the Father (12:50) and do not end up blaspheming the Spirit (12:30–32) or being ensnared by evil more thoroughly than before (12:43–45). Thus the parables spoken to the crowds do not simply convey information, nor

mask it, but challenge the hearers. They do not convey esoteric content only the initiated can fathom but present the claims of the inaugurated kingdom and the prospects of its apocalyptic culmination in such a way that its implications are spelled out for those in the audience with eyes to see (overstated but rightly defended by Boucher, pp. 83–84).

The parables of the soils not only says that the kingdom advances slowly and with varied responses to the proclamation of that kingdom but implicitly challenges hearers to ask themselves what kinds of soil they are. Those whose hearts are hardened and who lose what little they have do not participate in the messianic kingdom they have been looking for, and for them the parable is a sentence of doom. Those who have ears to hear, to whom more is given, perceive and experience the dawning of the Messianic Age; and for them the parable conveys the mysteries of the kingdom. In the varied responses given to the challenge of the parables, God's act of judgment and his self-disclosure in Jesus are both seen to be taking place in exactly the same way that various "soils" respond to the "seed," which is the message about the kingdom. (See further on 15:10–13.)

14–15 Stendahl and others advance several reasons for taking this quotation as a late gloss on the Gospel, including an anomalous introductory formula, and insist that the quotation is tautologous after v.13. But parallels to this introductory formula are common in the LXX and other Greek-Jewish literature with which Matthew is familiar, and vv.14–15 are not strictly tautologous since they go on to stress the theme of fulfillment. Moreover, if Matthew follows Mark (4:12) in v.13, it is unlikely that he abridged his source by omitting the entire last clause of Mark 4:12 ("otherwise they might turn and be forgiven"). The one area where Matthew almost invariably gives more material than the other synoptists is in OT quotations and allusions. "We must rather assume that verse 13 leads up to the formal quotation in verses 14, 15" (Gundry, *Use of OT*, pp. 116–18). These two verses thus become the rough equivalent of Mark 4:12–13.

The text form is LXX (as also in Acts 28:26–27), which follows the MT of Isaiah 6:9–10 pretty closely, except that the LXX is a description of the people, whereas MT makes this a command to the prophet ("Be ever hearing, but never understanding. . . . Make the heart of this people calloused"). But this is not as significant a change as some have thought; for judging by the prophet's later messages, the words in Isaiah 6:9–10 are steeped in bitter irony. After all, Isaiah was not given this charge because the result was desirable but because it inevitably came on people who were calloused. So also in Jesus' day! The Messiah who comes to reveal the Father (11:25–27) succeeds only in dulling what little spiritual sense many of the people have, for they do not want to turn and be healed. Indeed, the context of Isaiah 6:9–10 reveals that their dullness will continue "until the cities lie ruined . . . and the fields ruined and ravaged . . . and the land is utterly forsaken. And though a tenth remains in the land, it will again be laid waste" (Isa 6:11–13). The reference is to the Exile; but the events surrounding the Exile are seen as a paradigm, the classic case of rejection of God and resulting judgment, repeated in Jesus' generation on a new level and so fulfilling the words of the prophecy. It is unclear whether any claim that Isaiah 6:9–10 has predictive force is implied (if so, see on 2:15). What is certain is the racial connection (cf. also Acts 28:26–27; cf. John 12:38–40): the failure of most Jews to discern spiritual realities was no new thing. Moreover, if the context of Isaiah 6:9–10 goes with the quotation, a strong hint of judgment accompanies the description.

The first two lines of the quotation are in the second person plural: the people are directly addressed. But v.15 gives us God's description of the people in the third person. This makes it at least possible to interpret the "otherwise" clauses (*mēpote*, "lest"), not as the people's purpose (they have closed their eyes lest they see and turn and be healed), but as God's judgment (they have closed their eyes as the result of divine judicial action, otherwise they might see and turn, etc.). The thought then becomes similar to 2 Thessalonians 2:11. Again, of course, neither Jesus nor Matthew would see anything incongruous in God's judicial hardening (see on v.13).

16–17 (For "blessed," see on 5:3; and cf. Luke 10:23–24.) The disciples were blessed by God and privileged above the crowd because they saw and heard (v.16) what "many prophets and righteous men" (v.17; see on 10:40–42) longed to see but did not. The reference is to OT prophets and others who were just before God—people who looked forward to the coming of the kingdom. Here one cannot help but include Simeon (Luke 2:25–35) and Anna (Luke 2:36–38). Implicitly there is in Jesus' saying a rich christological and eschatological claim: no mere prophet could say as much as he did.

Those who think Matthew idealizes the disciples (see on v.10) observe that the parallel in Luke 10:23–24 contrasts Jesus' generation with earlier generations but argue that Matthew contrasts the disciples ("your" is emphatic) with the hard people of that same generation (Bornkamm, *Tradition*, p. 107). In fact Matthew does something of both. Verse 16, in connection with the preceding verses, contrasts the disciples with the calloused crowd; but v.17 contrasts them with prophets and righteous men of past generations. So the crowd in Jesus' day stands in the line of the willfully blind in the OT (vv.14–15), and Jesus' disciples stand in the line of the prophets (as in 5:11–12). The fulfillment motif is operating, showing that the division taking place in Jesus' time with the coming of the kingdom stands in succession to the divisions already spelled out in the Scriptures. The disciples are not idealized; they will later have to ask for an explanation (v.36). But by contrast with the crowds, they really did follow Jesus and gradually grasped the critical turning point in redemption history Jesus was even then introducing.

Notes

14 The addition of a cognate participle or a cognate dative to a verb in order to strengthen the verb is a customary way for the LXX to render the Hebrew infinitive absolute (cf. BDF, par. 422; Zerwick, par. 369). Both are found here in this LXX quotation: ἀκοῇ ἀκούσετε (*akoē akousete*, lit., "in hearing you will hear"), βλέποντες βλέψετε (*blepontes blepsete*, lit., "seeing you will see"). In English these are confusing tautologies, and their meaning is rightly rendered by NIV: "You will be ever hearing," or "you will be hearing acutely," etc.

2) *Interpretation of the parable of the soils*

13:18–23

18"Listen then to what the parable of the sower means: 19When anyone hears
the message about the kingdom and does not understand it, the evil one comes
and snatches away what was sown in his heart. This is the seed sown along the
path. 20The one who received the seed that fell on rocky places is the man who
hears the word and at once receives it with joy. 21But since he has no root, he
lasts only a short time. When trouble or persecution comes because of the word,
he quickly falls away. 22The one who received the seed that fell among the thorns
is the man who hears the word, but the worries of this life and the deceitfulness
of wealth choke it, making it unfruitful. 23But the one who received the seed that
fell on good soil is the man who hears the word and understands it. He produces
a crop, yielding a hundred, sixty or thirty times what was sown."

Jeremias (*Parables*, p. 62) thinks the interpretation provided in all three Gospels (cf. Mark 4:14–20; Luke 8:11–15) is a later church creation, but we have already questioned the cogency of some of his criteria. Payne ("Authenticity") has taken up the points in question and offered comprehensive rejoinders, some of which will be noted below. Here it is enough to say that (contra Jeremias, *Parables*, p. 79) not every point in the parable is interpreted allegorically: no explanation is given of the sower, the path, the rocky ground, or the diverse yield. What "allegorical" points are scored emerge naturally from the story (even the identification of the birds: see on v.19), once the main point of the extended metaphor is established.

The general point is that the "message about the kingdom" (v.19) receives a varied reception among various people, and that during this time of difficulty and frustration there is an implied delay while the seed produces in some soils its various yields. The interpretation therefore demands that each person look to himself as to how he "hears" the message. Broadus cites Chrysostom: "Mark this, I pray thee, that the way of destruction is not one only, but there are differing ones, and wide apart from one another. Let us not soothe ourselves upon our not perishing in all these ways, but let it be our grief in whichever way we are perishing."

18 The *hymeis* ("you") is probably emphatic: in light of the great privilege extended to you, which prophets and righteous men wanted to enjoy and the calloused spurn, *you* listen.

19 Matthew omits "The farmer sows the word" (Mark 4:14) and plunges right into the significance of the various soils. This does not mean that he is concerned with the ecclesiastical implications at the expense of the christological ones (so Kingsbury, *Parables*, p. 72) since Mark himself does not identify the sower as Jesus. If he here depends on Mark, Matthew simplifies to get to the point. But D. Wenham ("Interpretation") has provided a plausible source reconstruction that would invalidate redaction-critical conclusions in this pericope that depend on Markan priority. Possibly Matthew and Mark share a common source.

Neither "word" (Mark) nor "word of the kingdom" (Matt; NIV, "message about the kingdom") indicates later ecclesiastical tradition (cf. Payne, "Authenticity," pp. 178–79; contra Jeremias, *Parables*, pp. 77f.; Hill, *Matthew*). On the change from "word" to "word of the kingdom," compare Matthew's "gospel of the kingdom" (4:23; 9:35; 24:14). More difficult is the mixed metaphor: the seed appears to be "the message about the kingdom," but in the last sentence of the verse it is *ho para tēn hodon spareis* (lit., "he who was sown along the path"; NIV has smoothed out the difficulty by treating the masculine participle as if it were neuter).

A similar problem occurs in Mark's parallel. Several ways for resolving the problem have been suggested. Box and McNeile are among those who take the text literally but think there is a purposeful link between the seed and human character, which grows from the seed. But surely the point of this part of the parable is that the seed is taken away before it has time to grow. Others have suggested some sort of ellipsis: "This is [the situation of] the seed sown along the path," understanding "This" to refer to the situation, not the seed or the person, which would also explain vv.20–23, though the masculine *houtos* ("this"), instead of the neuter, is somewhat surprising. Alexander and Hendriksen therefore opt for a fairly complex ellipsis: "He is the one that [in his reaction to the message resembles the reaction of the ground to the seed that] was sown along the path"—which is possible but rather finely drawn.

D. Wenham ("Interpretation") offers a complex but plausible source-critical solution; Payne ("Authenticity," pp. 172–77) proposes an underlying Aramaic too literally translated and observes that the Greek can be understood to mean, not "this is he who was sown along the path," but "this is the man who received the seed along the edge of the path" (JB; cf. NASB), understanding the passive participle *ho spareis* to mean, not "the one [seed] sown," but "the one [*soil*] sown." C.F.D. Moule ("Mark 4:1–20 Yet Once More," in Ellis and Wilcox, p. 112) has shown that the ambiguity is no indication that the interpretation is secondary; the same thing occurs in Colossians 1:6, 10, where the metaphor of growing and bearing fruit is applied first to the seed sown and then to the ground in which it is sown.

Two further features of this verse require explanation.

1. The words "in his heart" make the heart the place of decision, the center of personality (see on 5:8). Kingsbury (*Parables*, p. 55) is wrong to conclude from this that the person in view actually becomes a Christian and church member and then rejects the message. He argues that the words "when anyone hears the message about the kingdom" is "tantamount to saying that he becomes a Christian." The conclusion is untenable if one considers the next words: "and does not understand it" (cf. the same verbs in vv.13–14). The hunt for anachronisms can distort scholarly judgment.

2. The evil one (cf. 6:13; 12:45; 13:38–39), called "Satan" in Mark 4:15 and "the devil" in Luke 8:12, has been symbolized by the birds (a point Via (*Parables*, p. 8) uses to argue that this interpretation goes beyond the range of the natural and understandable symbolism inherent in the parable and must therefore be judged guilty of falling into allegorizing). In fact, close study of birds as symbols in the OT and especially in the literature of later Judaism shows that birds regularly symbolize evil and even demons or Satan (cf. b. *Sanhedrin* 107a; cf. Rev 18:2).

Jesus' interpretation is clear. Some people hear the message about the kingdom; but like hardened paths, they do not let the truth penetrate, and before they really understand it the devil has snatched it away.

20–21 The language of these verses is often taken to reflect the apostolic age, not Jesus (cf. Jeremias, *Parables*). But "root" (v.21) is appropriate to the extended agricultural metaphor, and "persecution" is amply treated by Jesus elsewhere in nonparabolic settings (e.g., 5:10–12, 43–44; 10:16–25; 24:9; see further Payne, "Authenticity," pp. 177–80). Jesus' interpretation is coherent. The person who receives "the word" (same Gr. word as "message" in v.19) in a thoughtless way may show immediate signs of life and promise to be the best of the crop: he receives the truth "with joy" (v.20). But without real root, there is no fruit; and external pressures, trouble, and persecution (cf. 24:9, 21, 29), like sun beating on a rootless plant, soon reveal the shallowness of this soil. "At once" (*euthys*) he receives the word with joy, and as "quickly" (*euthys*) "falls away" (for *skandalizetai,* see on 5:29). Such temporary disciples are always numerous in times of revival and were so in Jesus' ministry (cf. comments on 12:32).

22 This person does not hear the word "with joy" (as in v.20) but simply never permits the message about the kingdom to control him: life has too many other commitments that slowly choke the struggling plant, which never matures and bears fruit. The competing "thorns" are summed up under two headings—the worries of this life (lit., this "age," as opposed to the age to come; see on 6:25–34) and "the deceitfulness of wealth." The latter category, *hē apatē tou ploutou,* may possibly be rendered "the delight in wealth," since in late Greek *apatē,* which earlier meant "deceitfulness," came to mean "pleasure" or "delight," usually involving sin (e.g., 2 Peter 2:13; cf. BAGD, s.v.). The idea is clear: worries about worldly things or devotion to wealth (cf. 1 Tim 6:9) snuff out spiritual life. If "deceit" is understood, there is an added warning that these "thorns" are so subtle that one may not be aware of the choking that is going on. The warning is timeless. Moreover it is as unconvincing to deduce from this verse that Matthew's church was wealthy (contra Kilpatrick, *Origins,* pp. 124ff.; Kingsbury, *Parables,* p. 61) as to deduce from 6:28–32 that his church was poverty-stricken. What must be avoided is unfruitfulness, for only fruitfulness, not its opposite, indicates spiritual life (cf. John 15:1–8). This person finds "all the seeming good effect is gone, leaving the soul a very thicket of thorns" (Broadus).

23 By contrast with the negative results of the preceding verses, we now come to the person who hears the word and understands it (thus reverting to the categories of Isa 6:9–10 used in vv.13–15, 19). The use of *synienai* ("to understand") in vv.19, 23, a verb not found in the Markan parallels, has led some to say that "understanding" is a fundamental characteristic of discipleship in Matthew, and that his disciples have again become idealized (see on v.10): they are made to "understand" more than the disciples really did at this point in their pilgrimage (cf. Bornkamm, *Tradition,* p. 107; Schniewind; Kingsbury, *Parables,* pp. 61f.). But this may be premature. Certainly *synienai* with its nine occurrences is an important part of Matthew's vocabulary. But Mark uses *synienai* six times, in a book about two-thirds the length of Matthew.

David Wenham has shown that granted Matthew's syntax in v.19, he could not very well have omitted *synienai* ("to understand") there ("Interpretation," pp. 308f., n. 5). Its use in v.23 picks up the Isaiah quotation given more briefly in Mark. Moreover v.23 does not apply the verb directly to the disciples but interprets the parable aphoristically; and in so doing it is merely in line with Mark's "hear the word, *accept it*" (4:20). In this chapter the disciples are distinguished from the crowd; but their understanding is only relatively better (v.36), and they are not idealized. Misunderstanding of this point springs from too ready a willingness to read the later church into every phrase of the parable and from a failure to recognize the absolute categories that any competent preacher, including Jesus, uses (see on 6:5–8).

The interpretation, like the parable itself, ends positively. And we must not fail to notice that the soil that produces only a small crop is nevertheless called "good" (cf. 25:22–23).

Notes

23 The particle δή (*dē*, used for various kinds of emphasis) is normally employed in the NT in sentences of command or exhortation. This is the sole NT exception (though there are good classical parallels): "he is just the man who, etc." (cf. BDF, par. 451[4]). The anomaly has prompted a variant reading in the Western textual tradition.

c. *The parable of the weeds*

13:24–30

24Jesus told them another parable: "The kingdom of heaven is like a man who sowed good seed in his field. 25But while everyone was sleeping, his enemy came and sowed weeds among the wheat, and went away. 26When the wheat sprouted and formed heads, then the weeds also appeared.

27"The owner's servants came to him and said, 'Sir, didn't you sow good seed in your field? Where then did the weeds come from?'

28" 'An enemy did this,' he replied.

"The servants asked him, 'Do you want us to go and pull them up?'

29" 'No,' he answered, 'because while you are pulling the weeds, you may root up the wheat with them. 30Let both grow together until the harvest. At that time I will tell the harvesters: First collect the weeds and tie them in bundles to be burned; then gather the wheat and bring it into my barn.' "

This parable occurs only in Matthew. For the reasons why its interpretation (vv.36–43) is separated from it, see above on 13:3a regarding the structure of the chapter. A few (e.g., Manson, *Sayings*, p. 143) have argued that this parable is not authentic but a creation of Matthew, constructed out of the parable of the seed growing quietly (Mark 4:26–29). But the similar language on which this theory is based owes more to the common agricultural setting than to borrowing. Though many affirm the authenticity of the parable but deny the authenticity of the interpretation (Dodd, *Parables*, pp. 183–84; Jeremias, *Parables*, pp. 81ff.; Kingsbury, *Parables*, pp. 65–66), the criteria for such distinctions are faulty (see on v.3a); and specific arguments can be advanced to defend their joint integrity in this case (see on vv.36–43). David R. Catchpole ("John the Baptist, Jesus and the Parable of the Tares," SJT 31 [1978]: 557–70) unwittingly supports the view that the parable and its interpretation stand or fall together when, in the course of defending his reconstruction of a much shorter parable (vv.24b, 26b, 30b) that Matthew allegedly expanded, he expresses dissatisfaction with this parable because it includes elements that invite the "allegorizing" interpretations of vv.36–43.

The parable of the sower shows that though the kingdom will now make its way amid hard hearts, competing pressures, and even failure, it will produce an abundant crop. But one might ask whether Messiah's people should immediately separate the crop from the weeds; and this next parable answers the question negatively: there will be a delay in separation until the harvest.

24 Jesus *paretheken* ("told") the people another parable (lit., "he set another before them"). This verb is used in the NT only here and in v.31 in the sense of teaching, though that meaning is attested elsewhere. "Them" must be the crowd, not the disciples (cf. vv.34, 36).

The kingdom of heaven is not "like a man" but "like the situation of a man who . . .": the "is like" formula reflects an Aramaic idiom meaning "It is the case with X as with Y" (cf. Jeremias, *Parables*, pp. 100f.; Zerwick, par. 65). But the peculiar tense used here (cf. Notes) also implies that the kingdom *has become* like the situation of a man who, etc. The thought is intriguing; for whereas Judaism was accustomed to delays in waiting for the coming of Messiah (cf. R.J. Bauckham, "The Delay of the Parousia," *Tyndale Bulletin* 31 [1980]: 3–36) what Jesus argues is both that the kingdom has come (see 4:17; 12:28) and that the Parousia is still delayed (i.e., the kingdom has become like . . . —a parable dealing with the *delay* of the kingdom's arrival).

25–26 "Sleeping" (v.25) does not imply that the servants were neglectful but that the enemy was stealthy and malicious. What he sowed was *zizania* ("weeds"—almost certainly bearded darnel (*lolium temulentum*) which is botanically close to wheat and difficult to distinguish from it when the plants are young. The roots of the two plants entangle themselves around each other; but when the heads of grain appear on the wheat, there is no doubt which plant is which (v.26). This weed the enemy sowed "among the wheat"; the Greek suggests thorough distribution. The growing plants gradually become identifiable, and the servants tell their master about the weeds.

27 For *oikodespotes* ("owner"), see on 10:25; 13:52. The servants are not identified; their function in the parable is to elicit information from the owner. In v.27 *kyrios* ("sir") has no special significance; but later Christian readers doubtless saw in it further evidence that the owner is the "Lord" Jesus. The interrogative pronoun *pothen* ("where") can refer to a person as well as to a location (cf. use in 13:54, 56; 21:25) as Jesus' answer (v.28) presupposes.

28–30 The owner blames (v.28) an enemy (lit., "a man [who is] an enemy": the construction occurs again in v.52). But the owner forbids his servants from attempting to separate weed from wheat till the harvest (v.29). Then, as the workers reap the field, only the wheat will be gathered; the weeds, apparently so plentiful they must first be gathered up and burned (v.30—though nothing is made of this point in vv.40–42), contaminate the wheat no longer. "Harvest" is a common metaphor for the final judgment (see on 9:37–38). In this light the "good seed" (v.24) cannot be the "word" or "message" of vv.19–23 but people who must face final judgment.

An astonishing number of scholars treat this parable as if there were behind it a Matthean church riddled with problem people, perhaps even apostates. So Jesus' answer in Matthew becomes, in effect, advice not to try to have a pure church, because the Lord will make the right distinctions at the end (most recently, G. Barth, "Auseinandersetzungen um die Kirchenzucht im Umkreis des Matthäusevangelium," ZNW 69 [1978]: 158–77). But this is a major error in category. Nowhere in Matthew does "kingdom" (or "reign"—see on 3:2) become "church" (see on 16:18; and esp. 13:37–39). The parable does not address the church situation at all but explains how the kingdom can be present in the world while not yet wiping out all opposition. That must await the harvest. The parable deals with eschatological expectation, not ecclesiological deterioration.

Notes

24 The normal way for synoptic parables of the sort "the kingdom is like" to express "is like" consists of ὁμοία ἐστίν (*homoia estin,* "is like") plus dative. In Matthew, however, this pattern sometimes changes to aorist passive ὁμοιώθη (*homoiōthē,* "has become like," here and in 18:23; 22:2) or to future passive ὁμοιωθήσεται (*homoiōthēsetai,* "will become like," 7:24, 26; 25:1). The future passive usages of the verb focus on the kingdom at its consummation and the aorist passive on the kingdom as it has already been inaugurated (cf. Strecker, *Weg,* pp. 214f.; Kingsbury, *Parables,* p. 67; and esp. Carson, "Word-Group"). If so, Pamment's view (see on 5:3; 11:12), that "kingdom of heaven" is always future, referring to the consummated kingdom, receives a fatal blow.

29 Only here in the NT does the adverb ἅμα (*hama,* "at the same time"; NIV, "when") function as an improper preposition "with," "along with" (plus dative; cf. Moule, *Idiom Book,* p. 81; BDF, par. 194[3]).

d. *The parable of the mustard seed*

13:31–32

> [31]He told them another parable: "The kingdom of heaven is like a mustard seed, which a man took and planted in his field. [32]Though it is the smallest of all your seeds, yet when it grows, it is the largest of garden plants and becomes a tree, so that the birds of the air come and perch in its branches."

31–32 Close comparison with Mark 4:30–32 and Luke 13:18 suggests that Matthew may have slightly modified the Q form of this parable under Mark's influence. Yet it is easy to exaggerate the differences. (See discussion and chart at 19:1–2.) Many have held that in Mark the contrast in size is of greatest importance, in Luke the process of growth, and that Matthew has conflated the two ideas. Such distinctions are too finely drawn: if size were for Mark the most important factor, one wonders why Mark's Jesus would choose a plant that reaches a height of only ten to twelve feet.

There is a better interpretation. In all three Gospels the parable begins with a mustard seed (for the introductory formula and the verb *parethēken* ["he told"], see on v.24). This seed is designated "the smallest of all your seeds," but it becomes "the largest of garden plants" (*meizon tōn lachanōn,* v.32; cf. Notes). In rabbinical thought the mustard seed was proverbial for smallness (cf. M *Niddah* 5:2; cf. SBK, 1:669). It becomes a tree, large in comparison with the tiny seed, large enough for birds to perch in its branches (Matt; Luke) or in its shade (Mark). The image recalls OT passages that picture a great kingdom as a large tree with birds flocking to its branches (Judg 9:15; Ezek 17:22–24; 31:3–14; Dan 4:7–23).

But if the greatness of the kingdom is in view, why a mustard plant? The contrast in size between seed and plant does not itself establish the greatness of the kingdom; and, contrary to Kingsbury (*Parables*, p. 81) and Huffmann (p. 21), it is doubtful whether Jesus' point is that the kingdom grows supernaturally. Instead, the point is the organic unity of small beginning and mature end (cf. Dahl, *Jesus in Memory*, pp. 155–56). No pious Jew doubted that the kingdom would come and that it would be vast and glorious. What Jesus is teaching goes beyond that: he is saying that there is a basic connection between the small beginnings taking place under his ministry and the kingdom in its future glory. Though the initial appearance of the kingdom may seem inconsequential, the tiny seed leads to the mature plant.

We can now see why Jesus chose the mustard seed. For him it was not essential to stress the greatness of the future kingdom; few would dispute that. It was more important for him to find a metaphor emphasizing the kingdom's tiny beginning. Jacques Dupont ("Le couple parabolique du sénevé et du levain: Mt 13, 31–33; Lc 13, 18–21," in Strecker, *Jesus Christus*, pp. 331–45) has suggested another reason for this metaphor. He convincingly shows that the parables of the mustard seed and of the yeast, linked in Matthew and Luke but only the first occurring in Mark, actually belonged together from the beginning. He argues that Mark has structural reasons for dropping the parable of the yeast, and so his silence is scarcely determinative. But one of the links he finds between the two parables is the incongruity of both metaphors. He quotes authors who find the mustard plant an incongruous or even bizarre symbol for the kingdom, while everyone knows that yeast normally symbolizes evil (see further on v.33). But that, Dupont says (pp. 344–45), is just the point. In both parables the strange choice of images evokes surprise, encourages the reader to penetrate the parable's meaning, and accords with other parables designed to jar the unthinking (e.g., the coming of the kingdom is like the coming of a thief in the night [24:43]).

Notes

---

31 The construction ὃν λαβὼν ἄνθρωπος ἔσπειρεν (*hon labōn anthrōpos espeiren*, lit., "which having taken a man sowed") represents a Semitic auxiliary construction and occurs only here in the NT and at 13:33, 44; Luke 12:37; 13:19, 21.

32 The word μεῖζον (*meizon*, "the largest") is neuter and is therefore in agreement with τὸ σίναπι (*to sinapi*, "mustard," "mustard plant") rather than ὁ κόκκος (*ho kokkos*, "seed"). There is no smooth way of translating the anomaly.

---

e. *The parable of the yeast*

13:33

33He told them still another parable: "The kingdom of heaven is like yeast that a woman took and mixed into a large amount of flour until it worked all through the dough."

33 The general thrust of this parable is the same as that of the mustard seed. The kingdom produces ultimate consequences out of all proportion to its insignificant beginnings. Efforts by most dispensationalists (e.g., Walvoord) to interpret the yeast as a symbol for evil are not very convincing in this setting because they require the introduction of anachronistic ideas like "the professing church." Moreover, though yeast is *normally* associated with evil in the OT, this is *not always* so (cf. Lev 7:13; 23:15–18). Metaphors may have diverse uses: the lion at different times symbolizes both Satan and Jesus. In any case the anomalous metaphor is here best explained along the lines suggested by Dupont (on vv.31–32).

If there is a distinction between this parable and the last one, it is that the mustard seed suggests extensive growth and the yeast intensive transformation. The yeast doesn't grow, it permeates; and its inevitable effect, despite the small quantity used, recalls Jesus' words in 5:13. In both parables it is clear that at present the kingdom of heaven operates, not apocalyptically, but quietly and from small beginnings.

There seems little merit in trying to identify the woman, any more than the man in v.31. Some have thought that *enekrypsen* ("hid," RSV) resonates with "hidden" (*kekrymmai*) in vv.35, 44: "The Kingdom was inaugurated without display or pomp; its silent, secret character must have surprised those who were zealously impatient for its expected manifestation in power and glory" (Hill, *Matthew*). These comments, while relevant to the parable as a whole, read too much into the verb itself. It simply means "put something into something," even in nonbiblical Greek (cf. BAGD, p. 216); NIV's "mixed" is therefore not bad. Usage of *enekrypsen* in later verses of this chapter (vv.35, 44) is best interpreted in other ways.

Notes

---

33 The phrase εἰς ἀλεύρου σάτα τρία (*eis aleurou sata tria*, "into three satas of flour") is anomalous (an anarthrous noun that depends on a preposition is normally placed before a case governed by it) but not unprecedented (cf. BDF, par. 474[4]).

Far more difficult is the expression σάτα τρία (*sata tria*, "three satas"). NIV has "a large amount of flour," which is true enough; but it is not an unreasonable amount of flour, adopted for parabolic purpose, since the same amount was mixed by Sarah in Genesis 18:6. It probably represents the largest amount of flour a woman might make up into bread at one time. But how much is it? The NIV margin specifies "about ½ bushel or 22 liters." In fact, the standard reference works (including ISBE; EBC, 1:609–10 et al.) adopt an unrecognized and conflicting pair of computations leading to mutually exclusive results. If one follows OT ratios and equivalences, τὸ σάτον (*to saton*) = Aram. סָאתָא (*sā'tā'*) = Heb. סְאָה (*se'āh*) = 1/3 of an ephah or bath. Therefore three satas, as here, equal 1 ephah, known to be 1/10 of a homer.

Now an ephah (or bath) is normally reckoned at about 22 liters. Measurements were imprecise in the ancient world, ranging substantially in place and time (cf. Jeremias, *Jerusalem*, p. 32). That this estimate is approximately correct has been confirmed by an archaeological find that has measured what is almost certainly a "bath" jar and found it to have the capacity of about 21 liters (David Ussishkin, "Excavations at Tel Lachish—1973–1977," *Tel Aviv* 5 [1978]: 87, n. 9. I am indebted to Hugh G.M. Williamson for this reference.). This agrees with the NIV margin. But Josephus (Antiq. IX, 85 [iv. 5]) and other Jewish sources (cf. SBK, 1:669–70) establish that one *saton* = 1½ *modii*, where 1 *modius* = 16 sextarii = approx. 8.75 liters (confirmed by Jos. Antiq. VIII, 57 [ii. 9], which says a bath contains 72 sextarii); and in that case 3 *sata* (as in Matt 13:33) = 1.5 ×

3 × 8.75 = approx. 39.4 liters—a long way from the 22 suggested by the alternative computation. Both approaches are unwittingly juxtaposed in the standard reference works (cf. Douglas, *Illustrated Dictionary*, 3:1637–39; IDB, 4:833–35), though the writer in the former mentions in passing that "the bath is variously calculated between 20.92 and 46.6 litres." The matter has not been finally resolved. D.J. Wiseman, in a private communication (2 December 1980), suggests that the solution may be analogous to the "greater" and "lesser" (half) weights measures (cf. the approximately double "royal bath").

---

3. *Pause* (13:34–43)

a. *Parables as fulfillment of prophecy*

13:34–35

[34]Jesus spoke all these things to the crowd in parables; he did not say anything to them without using a parable. [35]So was fulfilled what was spoken through the prophet:

"I will open my mouth in parables,
I will utter things hidden since the creation of
the world."

Mark 4:33–34 concludes Mark's report of Jesus' parables on this occasion. But Matthew has already departed from Mark at 13:16–17 and 13:24–30 and by omitting Mark 4:21–29. Now he continues on his own. To believe that he has simply modified Mark in this section is difficult because of the great differences between the two accounts. Speculating about Matthew's dependence on an earlier form of Mark (Schniewind) seems too uncontrolled. It is better to assume that Matthew had independent information (Lohmeyer).

34 The Greek's chiasm puts the emphasis on parables: Jesus did not speak to the crowds without using them. The first verb is aorist (*elalēsen*, "spoke"), referring to the situation at hand; the second is imperfect (*elalei*, "used to say"), implying that this was Jesus' constant custom. But *chōris parabolēs* ("without a parable") does not mean that he told nothing but parables to the crowd but that he said nothing to them without using parables. In short parables were an essential part of his spoken ministry.

35 The quotation is from Psalm 78 (LXX 77):2, a psalm of Asaph. In addition to two difficult textual variants (cf. Notes), the text form is notoriously difficult to resolve. The first line follows the LXX exactly; hence it uses the plural *en parabolais* ("in parables") to translate the Hebrew *b*ᵉ*māšāl* ("in a parable" or "in a wise saying"; for the meaning of these words, see on 13:3a). But the singular is probably generic; so LXX has caught the main point. The second line means roughly the same thing as both LXX and MT but is quite independent. The verb *ereuxomai* (lit., "I belch forth," "I utter") is an etymological rendering of the MT and may have been chosen above the LXX's *phthenxomai* ("I will utter") simply because it is stronger (Goulder, *Midrash*, p. 371) and may indicate the richness of the revelation: "I will pour forth things hidden" (as in Ps 19:2 [LXX 18:3]). Matthew's *kekrymmena* ("things hidden") is likewise closer to the Hebrew *ḥîḏôṯ* ("enigmas," "dark sayings") than LXX's *problēmata* ("tasks," "problems").

But in what sense can Jesus' ministry in parables be said to be a fulfillment of Asaph's psalm? The problem does not arise just because the quotation is from a psalm: in 22:43–44 another psalm is quoted as prophecy. Matthew 11:11–13 has already established that the entire OT is in some sense prophetic (see on 2:15, 17–18; 5:17–20) and 2 Chronicles 29:30 attests that Asaph is a "seer." The problem arises rather in the way Psalm 78:2 is applied to Jesus. Contemporary NT scholars almost universally agree that Matthew has taken Psalm 78:2 badly out of context. Psalm 78 repeats Israel's well-known history, none of which is "mysterious" or "hidden." But Matthew presents Jesus as uttering hidden things. He speaks to the people in parables, in a hidden way, whereas his disciples are enlightened and understand all things. Thus, though Mark 4:33 presents Jesus using the parables to communicate as much truth to the crowds as they could understand, Matthew sees parables as a means of hiding the truth from the outsiders (so, more or less, Lindars, *Apologetic*, pp. 156–57; Kingsbury, *Parables*, pp. 88–90; Rothfuchs, pp. 78–80; Hill, *Matthew;* and others).

Despite its popularity, this approach misunderstands both Psalm 78 and Matthew 13. It is true that Psalm 78 recounts the known history of Israel; but there is no escaping the fact that Psalm 78:2 nevertheless finds the psalmist declaring that he will open his mouth "in parables, wise sayings," and pour forth *ḥîḏôṯ* ("enigmas," "dark sayings"). The point is that though the history of the Jews, which Asaph relates, is well known, the psalmist selects the historical events he treats and brings them together in such a way as to bring out things that have been riddles and enigmas "from of old." The pattern of history is not self-evident; but the psalmist will show what it is really all about. He enlarges on God's might at the time of the Exodus and at other major turning points, a might exercised on behalf of his people. With these events the psalmist juxtaposes the people's persistent rebellion, the result being a vivid portrayal of God's justice and mercy and the people's obtuseness, need, and privilege.

The psalmist teaches all this by opening his mouth "in parables" (i.e., by comparing various things) and in so doing utters "things hidden from of old" (NIV)—"things we have heard and known, things our fathers have told us" (v.3), yet enigmatic and hidden. They are "deep and hidden teachings, which the events of the past embrace" (Louis Jacquet, *Les Psaumes*, 3 vols. [Bruxelles: Duculot, 1975–81], 2:522). Thus the psalmist makes his deep points, as does Stephen in Acts 7, by comparing events in redemptive history.

We turn to Matthew 13:35 and discover a similar pattern. If Jesus pours forth things hidden from the beginning, does this mean that those things remain hidden, i.e., that Jesus pours forth teaching in so hidden a form that outsiders cannot understand them? That is what the popular interpretation of the passage requires; but its death knell is the final phrase: "from the beginning." Whatever that phrase means—NIV has "since the creation of the world" (cf. Notes)—it modifies *kekrymmena* ("things hidden"), the unavoidable implication being that those hidden things are no longer hidden since Jesus has revealed them. Otherwise Jesus is saying no more than this: "I will reveal things that have always been hidden so that they will remain hidden"—an unnatural way to take the sentence.

Apparently, then, as applied to Jesus the second line of the quotation pictures him as revealing things formerly hidden. This does not necessarily mean that he is teaching entirely new things any more than the psalmist was teaching such things. In both cases the patterns of redemptive history may be so stressed that when rightly interpreted they point toward new revelation—viz., they are fulfilled (see on 2:15; 5:17–20). This admirably suits v.52: the "teacher of the law . . . instructed about the kingdom of heaven is like the owner of a house who brings out of his storeroom new treasures as well as old." But Jesus teaches these hitherto hidden things "in parables," i.e., by comparing various things. The parables of this chapter are not exactly like the comparisons and wise sayings offered in Psalm 78. Yet the term "parable" can embrace both kinds of utterance. So we must be careful not to impose on the text too narrow an understanding of what a parable is.

It follows that vv.34–35 are much closer in thought to Mark 4:33–34 than is commonly believed. Jesus does teach the crowds, in parables, revealing new things. How much they understand is a different matter. Yet we have already seen that even Matthew 13:11–13 must not be taken to mean that in Matthew the parables for nondisciples are designed only to conceal. Actually they have a dual role; and here Matthew, rightly understanding the psalmist and reverting to the Hebrew from the LXX so as not to miss his desired nuance, insists that Jesus reveals new truth to the crowds.

But what are these "hidden things" Jesus is now uttering? In Psalm 78 they are "the righteous acts of God in redemption" (Lindars, *Apologetic*, p. 157). Likewise that is what Jesus is now revealing—the righteous acts of God in redemption taking place in his teaching, miracles, death, and resurrection. Matthew insists that the OT Scriptures prophesied these things. They are not novel. If in one sense they have not been known before, it is because they have not all been brought together in the same pattern before. Jesus' kingdom parables to the crowds declare new things, secrets (v.11), hidden things (v.35). Yet they are secret and new chiefly because they depend on an approach to Scripture not unlike Asaph's—bringing together various pieces of previous revelation into new perspectives. Thus Messiah is Son of David but also Suffering Servant. Jesus is the royal King and Son of David foreseen in Scripture (21:4–11) but also the stricken Shepherd equally foreseen in Scripture (26:31). Who clearly foresaw that both streams would merge in one person?

Taken as a whole, Jesus' parables preserve the expectation of the apocalyptic coming of Messiah. They also introduce a new pattern of an inaugurated kingdom that anticipates the Parousia. Moreover this pattern rests on Jesus' self-understanding as the Messiah who unites in himself streams of revelation from the old covenant that had not been so clearly united before.

The connection between Matthew 13:35 and Psalm 78:2 is thus very close. But what does Matthew mean when he says that Jesus' ministry of parables "fulfilled" the word spoken through the prophet? Elsewhere when psalms are treated as prophecies, there is normally a Davidic typology, but not so here. A number of things probably led Matthew to this psalm. The phrase "in parables" may have drawn his attention to Psalm 78 but in itself that does not account for the notion of "fulfillment." But a second connection presents itself: it is possible that, as Psalm 78 recounts Israel's history, so Jesus is presented as the one who is the supreme embodiment of Israel and her history, the one who fulfills all the patterns of the OT regarding Israel. We have noticed this theme before in Matthew, though it is stronger in the fourth Gospel.

But there may be a third and more subtle factor. Matthew understands that "prophecy" does not necessarily predict the future; it may reveal hidden things (cf. 26:68 with parallels in Mark and Luke). This sense of "prophecy" and its predictive sense "converge" in a passage like 11:13, where, as we have seen, the entire OT Scripture, both Law and Prophets "prophesy"—i.e., they comprehend certain patterns, types, predictions, declarations, which cumulatively look forward to him who "fulfills" them. Now in Psalm 78 Asaph claims to be explaining such earlier patterns in redemptive history; but in so doing, from a NT perspective he is also himself becoming a constituent element of the recorded redemptive history the NT explains. As such Psalm 78 becomes part of the "Law and Prophets" that prophesy. If part of this sacred record interprets and brings new truth out of an earlier part, it establishes a pattern that looks to one who will interpret and bring new truth out of the whole. Jesus, Matthew claims, fulfills that role and is exercising it in his own parabolic teaching.

Notes

35 There are two important and extremely difficult variants in this verse.

1. Most MSS read διὰ τοῦ προφήτου (*dia tou prophētou,* "through the prophet"). A few witnesses in Jerome's day read διὰ 'Ασὰφ τοῦ προφήτου (*dia Asaph tou prophētou,* "through Asaph the prophet"); but none have come down to us, and "Asaph" is certainly an interpolation. But an impressive group of witnesses (א* H f 1 f 13 33 eth ms et al.) read διὰ 'Ησαΐου τοῦ προφήτου (*dia Esaiou tou prophētou,* "through Isaiah the prophet"); and precisely because the quotation does not come from Isaiah, the reading could lay claim to being the *lectio difficilior* that scribes would want to correct. On the other hand, transcriptional evidence favors the probability of adding a prophet's name where none is mentioned (e.g., 1:22; 2:5; 21:4; Acts 7:48). This factor is even more compelling in Matthew than elsewhere since the first evangelist tends not to name the prophet except when quoting Isaiah or Jeremiah, a habit that makes it less likely that he would falsely ascribe to Isaiah, a book with which he was intimately familiar, something extraneous to Isaiah. Scribal misascription is therefore more likely than misascription by Matthew.

2. A majority of the witnesses support the reading ἀπὸ καταβολῆς κόσμου (*apo katabolēs kosmou,* "from the foundation of the world"); but a second reading, ἀπὸ καταβολῆς (*apo katabolēs,* "from the foundation"), is attested by a small but diversified number of Alexandrian, Western, and Eastern text types (א b B f 1 it e,k syr c,s eth et al.). Although the preponderance of external evidence supports inclusion of *kosmou,* yet the phrase "the foundation of the world" is so stereotyped in the NT (25:34; Luke 11:50; John 17:24; Eph 1:4; Heb 4:3; 9:26; 1 Peter 1:20; Rev 13:8; 17:8) that there is far greater transcriptional probability that the word was added rather than omitted.

There is another reason for thinking the shorter text is original. While we have already seen that in the second line of the quotation Matthew stops following the LXX and apparently offers his own rendering of the MT, I did not discuss this closing phrase of the second line. The Hebrew here reads מִנִּי-קֶדֶם (*minnî-qedem,* "from of old"), which the LXX renders ἀπ' ἀρχῆς (*ap' archēs,* "from the beginning"). Now MT's "from of old" can mean "from the beginning" or "from eternity" (cf. parallelism in Prov 8:23; cf. also Deut 33:27; Ps 55:19). Yet the expression itself is indefinite and in the context of Psalm 78 may only refer to the beginning of the nation, since God's dealings with Israel constitute the focus of discussion. If so, then LXX's "from the beginning" might sound too absolute; and this could account for Matthew's "from the foundation [i.e., of the nation]." Certainly καταβολή (*katabolē,* "foundation") does not have to be taken to refer to the foundation of the world: cf. ἡ καταβολὴ τῆς ἀποστάσεως (*hē katabolē tēs apostaseōs*, "the beginning of the insurrection") in Jos. War II, 260 (xiii. 4) (other examples in BAGD, s.v.). The shorter expression in Matthew might then easily have been lengthened by later scribes. If this reasoning is right, then "since the creation of the world" (NIV) is wrong; and the probability that Matthew is treating his OT text thoughtfully and with profound theological understanding is all the more increased. For fuller discussion of the technical questions of translation and related bibliography, see Gundry (*Use of OT*, pp. 118f.) and Rothfuchs (pp. 78–80).

---

b. *Interpretation of the parable of the weeds*

13:36–43

36Then he left the crowd and went into the house. His disciples came to him and said, "Explain to us the parable of the weeds in the field."
37He answered, "The one who sowed the good seed is the Son of Man. 38The field is the world, and the good seed stands for the sons of the kingdom. The weeds are the sons of the evil one, 39and the enemy who sows them is the devil. The harvest is the end of the age, and the harvesters are angels.
40"As the weeds are pulled up and burned in the fire, so it will be at the end of the age. 41The Son of Man will send out his angels, and they will weed out of his kingdom everything that causes sin and all who do evil. 42They will throw them into the fiery furnace, where there will be weeping and gnashing of teeth. 43Then the righteous will shine like the sun in the kingdom of their Father. He who has ears, let him hear.

For comments on the authenticity of this interpretation, see on 13:3a, 24. The reasons for separating the parable from its interpretation relate to Matthew's plan for this chapter (see on vv.3a, 10–17) and on the need for a setting for this explanation to disciples only (cf. Bonnard).

Those who see more of Matthew's church than of Jesus in the Gospel commonly identify the kingdom in vv.41, 43 with Matthew's church. There is, they argue, a double level of meaning. At one level the passage tells the church not to excommunicate its members because there will be a mixture of "wheat" and "weeds" in the church till the end of the age. For Hill (*Matthew*) this leads to an anomaly: 18:8–9, which he applies to church government, suggests excommunication. But it is doubtful whether Matthew ever confuses kingdom and church: these are two quite distinct categories (see further on vv.37–39).

Hendriksen recognizes the distinction in principle but then ignores it, arguing (1) if tares are "sown *among* the wheat, not alongside of it or on some other field," then it is "natural to think of the intermingling of true and false members within the church"; (2) that the parables shed light on "mysteries" (13:11), and there is no "mystery" in both kinds of people living on the same earth, but it is "far more of a mystery . . . that *within the church visible* God allows both the true and the merely nominal Christians to dwell side by side"; and (3) that the gathering "out of his kingdom" (v.41) assumes the weeds were inside, "in this case inside the church visible" (emphasis his).

We make this reply.

1. Jesus explicitly says the "field is the world" (v.38), not the church; so how could there be "some other field"? The intermingling is adequately explained if it takes place on the field of the world. See further on v.38.

2. The "mysteries" of 13:11 are bound up, not with the intermingling of good and evil per se, in church or world, but in a preliminary or inaugurated form of the kingdom that is not yet the apocalyptic and totally transforming kingdom belonging to the end of the age.

3. The gathering "out of his kingdom" (v.41) is perfectly clear on a synoptic understanding of "kingdom" (see on 3:2; 5:3; 13:41). But to say that "in this case" the expression refers to the church visible is to assume the very thing that must be proved (see esp. Bonnard).

36 The Greek *apheis tous ochlous* could mean either that Jesus sent the crowds away (KJV) or that he left them (NIV). The house referred to is the one Jesus left in order to preach to the crowds (13:1) and was located, presumably, in Capernaum. In Matthew's narrative the house provides the setting both for Jesus' private explanations (vv.37–43; cf. vv.10–23) and for the parables aimed at his disciples (vv.44–52).

Whether the verb "explain" is *diasaphēson* (used elsewhere in the NT only in 18:31) or *phrason* (used elsewhere in the NT only in 15:15) is uncertain but of little consequence. More important is the fact that the disciples need explanations (cf. also 15:15–16). They are not distinguished from the crowds by their instant and intuitive understanding but by their persistence in seeking explanations. Jesus' disciples come to him and ask, and therefore a full explanation is given them (see on vv.10–13).

37–39 On "Son of Man," see on 8:20. The title recurs at v.41: Jesus is the one who both sows the good seed (v.37) and directs the harvest. One of the most significant details in Jesus' parables is the way key images that in the OT apply exclusively to God, or occasionally to God's Messiah, now stand for Jesus himself. These images include sower, director of the harvest, rock, shepherd, bridegroom, father, giver of forgiveness, vineyard owner, lord, and king (cf. Philip B. Payne, "Jesus' Implicit Claim to Deity in His Parables," *Trinity Journal* [1981]: 3–23).

"The field is the world" (v.38). This brief statement presupposes a mission beyond Israel (cf. 10:16–18; 28:18–20) and confirms that the narrower command of 10:5–6 is related exclusively to the mission of the Twelve during the period of Jesus' earthly ministry. Of greater importance in the history of the church has been the view that this actually means that the field is the church. The view was largely assumed by the early church fathers, and the tendency to interpret the parable that way was reinforced by the Constantinian settlement. Augustine made the interpretation official: struggling against the Donatists, who were overzealous in their excommunication practices, he went so far as to say that a mixture of good and evil in the church is a necessary "sign" of the church (cf. esp. his *Breviculus Collationis cum Donatistis* and his *Ad Donatistas post Collationem*). Most Reformers followed the same line: Calvin went so far as to say that the "world" here represents the church by synecdoche.

Ironically some modern redaction criticism has returned to this interpretation because it sees more of Matthew's church than of Jesus in this Gospel. Nevertheless this interpretation is without exegetical foundation. The kingdom is a category flexible enough to be used simultaneously for the saving reign of God (so that "sons of the kingdom" can refer to those who are truly God's people, v.38) and for his reign more broadly considered (so that the kingdom in this sense might well embrace wheat and tares; see on 3:2; 5:3; 28:18); but it is not demonstrable that "church" ever has such semantic flexibility, or that "church" is ever confused with "kingdom" (cf. Ladd, *NT Theology*, pp. 105ff.; Guthrie, *NT Theology*, pp. 702–6).

In this parable and its interpretation, unlike the parable of the sower, the good seed stands for the sons of the kingdom—a healthy reminder that images can symbolize different things in different contexts (see on v.33). But "sons of the kingdom" has also changed its meaning from its use in 8:12. There it refers to those who by birth into the Jewish race have a covenant right to look forward to the messianic kingdom but who, by and large, are forfeiting that right. Here it refers to those who truly are the objects of messianic favor and participants in the messianic kingdom. For their sake the "weeds" are now preserved, and at the "harvest" for their sake the "weeds" will be destroyed. These weeds are "the sons of the evil one." (On "sons of," see on 5:9; and with the entire expression compare John 8:44; 1 John 5:19). The devil himself is the enemy (v.39); the harvest is the end of the age (see on 9:37; cf. Jer 51:33; Hos 6:11; Joel 3:13; 4 Ezra 4:28–29; 2 Bar 70:2); and the harvesters are angels (24:30–31; 25:31; cf. 18:10; Luke 15:7; Heb 1:14; 1 Peter 1:12; also cf. 1 Enoch 63:1).

What must also be pointed out is how many features in the parable are not given nonsymbolic equivalents. These include the conversation between the man and his servants, the servants' sleep, and the fact that the wheat was sown before the tares. This selective use of elements in the story is not atypical of parables (see on v.3a), and the other elements should not be allegorized.

40–42 The identification of the actors is over, and the description of the action begins. As the weeds are "pulled up" (v.40; same verb as "collect" in v.30b) and burned, so it is at the end. The kingdom we have known as the kingdom of heaven or the kingdom of God is also seen as the kingdom of the Son of Man, Jesus' kingdom (cf. 20:21; 25:31; cf. Dan 2:35; Rev 11:15). This is not the church (contra Bornkamm, *Tradition*, p. 44: see above), for Jesus' reign after the Resurrection extends to the farthest reaches of the universe (28:18). In that sense "everything that causes sin and all who do evil" may be weeded out of his kingdom (v.41). For the meaning of *panta ta skandala* ("everything that causes sin"), see on 5:29; with "all who do evil" (lit., "those who do lawlessness") compare 7:23.

The entire expression "everything that causes sin and all who do evil" appears to be a periphrastic rendering of the Hebrew of Zephaniah 1:3 (*hammak̲šēlôṯ ʾeṯ-hārᵉšāʿîm*) (lit., "the stumbling blocks with the wicked"), a phrase so difficult in its context that emendations have been suggested and the best MSS of LXX omit it. The first of the two Hebrew words occurs elsewhere only at Isaiah 3:6, where it means "ruins." Hence NIV translates the phrase in Zephaniah 1:3 as "The wicked will have only heaps of rubble." If this is correct, Matthew is either not referring to Zephaniah 1:3 or else is freely adapting it. But the Hebrew word may well mean "stumbling-blocks," "offenses." For what it is worth, etymology supports it; and the Targum understands it that way. Thus in Zephaniah 1:3 the word may refer to idols, or, better yet, in a figurative manner to people seen as "things that cause offense." If so, Matthew's rendering is appropriate.

The "sons of the evil one" (v.38) may be metaphorically considered as "everything that causes sin," or, without any metaphor, "all who do evil." They, like the weeds, are thrown into the fiery furnace (v.42; see on 3:11; 5:22; cf. Jer 29:22; Dan 3:6; Rev 20:15), where there will be weeping and gnashing of teeth (see on 8:12; cf. 4 Ezra 7:36)—viz., eschatological doom. Nothing is made of the word "first" in v.30, and here the order is reversed. What is clear is that Jesus ascribes to himself the role of eschatological Judge that Yahweh assigns himself in the OT, including Zephaniah 1:3 (cf. France, *Jesus*, pp. 156f.; Payne, "Jesus' Claim").

43 In contrast to the evil-doers, "the righteous will shine like the sun in the kingdom of their Father." The allusion is to Daniel 12:3 LXX, somewhat shortened by omitting *hoi synientes* (= Heb. *hammaśkîlîm*, "those who are wise" or "those who understand"), further evidence that Matthew has not idealized the disciples as those who have understanding (see on 13:10–13, 19, 23, 36). Hill (*Matthew*) remarks that early in the tradition there may have been a word-play on *maśkîlîm* (Aram. *maśkîlîn*) ("wise" or "understanding") in v.43 and *makšēlot* (Aram. *makšelān*) ("stumbling blocks" or "things that cause offense") in v.41. These righteous people (see on 5:20, 45; 9:13; 10:41; 13:17; 25:37, 46), once the light of the world (5:13–16), now radiate perfections and experience bliss in the consummation of their hopes.

The "kingdom of their Father" must not, as is commonly done, be set over against the kingdom of the Son of Man (v.41) on the supposed ground that the former alone is eternal, or that the Son of Man hands over the elect to him (1 Cor 15:24). The Son's postascension reign is a mediated reign. All God's kingly authority is given Jesus (28:18) and mediated through him; and for all that time the kingdom can be called the kingdom of God or the kingdom of the Son of Man or, more generally, the kingdom of heaven. But even when that mediation ceases, halted by the destruction of the last enemy (1 Cor 15:24–26), in Matthew's terminology it is still appropriate to call Jesus Messiah the King (20:31; 25:34; cf. 26:64), for the kingdom remains no less his.

Notes

39 In the final two identifications of the list in vv.37–39, the subjective complement precedes the copula verb and becomes anarthrous, in conformity with the rules developed by E.C. Colwell and extended by Lane C. McGaughy (*Toward a Descriptive Analysis of EINAI* [Missoula, Mont.: SBL, 1972]). The absence of articles in *συντέλεια αἰῶνος* (*synteleia aiōnos*, "the end of the age") is therefore no evidence for a construction built on analogy to the Hebrew construct state (contra Hill), not least because the construction is very common in the NT (706 occurrences) and widely distributed.

4. *To the disciples* (13:44–52)

a. *The parable of the hidden treasure*

13:44

44"The kingdom of heaven is like treasure hidden in a field. When a man found it, he hid it again, and then in his joy went and sold all he had and bought that field.

For the way these parables relate to the structure of the chapter, see on vv.10–17. The parables of the hidden treasure and the pearl are a pair; and pairing is not uncommon in Matthew (e.g., 5:14b–16; 6:26–30; 7:6; 9:16–17; 10:24–25; 12:25; 13:31–33; 24:43–51), an excellent way of reinforcing a point. Like the paired parables with which these two are chiastically coordinated (mustard seed and yeast, vv.31–33), these two make the same general point but have significant individual emphases.

Unlike the parables earlier in the chapter, these two do not deal so much with the hidden, inaugurated form of the kingdom and the concomitant delay of the Parousia as with the superlative worth of the kingdom of heaven. Yet even here the previous eschatological structure underlies them; for in traditional Jewish apocalyptic, one could scarcely liken the kingdom to a man finding a treasure or buying a pearl: the kingdom was to come apocalyptically at the end of the age by an act of God alone. In contrast to this, some kind of realized or inaugurated eschatology is here presupposed.

44 On the "is like" language, see on v.24. The kingdom is not simply like a treasure, but its situation is like the situation of a treasure hidden in a field. The Greek articles are generic (cf. Turner, *Syntax*, p. 179). Finding the treasure appears to be by chance. In a land as frequently ravaged as Palestine, many people doubtless buried their treasures; but, as Huffman (p. 213) points out, actually to find a treasure would happen once in a thousand lifetimes. Thus the extravagance of the parable dramatizes the supreme importance of the kingdom.

Derrett (*Law*, pp. 1–16) has pointed out that under rabbinic law if a workman came on a treasure in a field and lifted it out, it would belong to his master, the field's owner; but here the man is careful not to lift the treasure out till he has bought the field. So the parable deals with neither the legality nor the morality of the situation (as with the parable of the thief in the night) but with the value of the treasure, which is worth every sacrifice. When the man buys the field at such sacrifice, he possesses far more than the price paid (cf. 10:39). The kingdom of heaven is worth infinitely more than the cost of discipleship, and those who know where the treasure lies joyfully abandon everything else to secure it.

Two alternative interpretations must be dismissed.

1. The first, represented by Walvoord, understands the treasure to represent Israel and Jesus as the man who sold everything to purchase her. He rejects the above view by making the parable mean that "a believer in Christ has nothing to offer and the treasure is not for sale" and proposes his own interpretation by noting that in Exodus 19:5 Israel is called God's treasure. But any view, including Walvoord's, can be made to look foolish by pressing a parable into a detailed allegory: for instance one could rebut his view by showing that it entails Israel's being worth far more than the price paid. But would Walvoord be comfortable with this implicit depreciation of Christ's sacrifice? He must come to grips with the nature of parables (see on 13:3a). And "treasure" has a vast range of associations in the OT and NT; on what basis does he select Exodus 19:5? Above all, his interpretation does not adequately handle the opening clause.

2. J.D. Crossan (*Finding Is the First Act* [Philadelphia: Fortress, 1979], esp. pp. 93ff.) argues that "sold all he had" must be taken so absolutely that "all" includes the parable itself. One must give up the parable itself and, in abandoning all, abandon even abandonment. The parable is therefore a paradox, like the sign that reads "Do not read this sign." Crossan's interpretation is unacceptable for exegetical, literary, historical, and theological reasons: exegetical, in that this parable does not speak of "abandoning" or "giving up" things but of "selling," and one cannot imagine giving the parable away by selling it; literary, in that Crossan, like Walvoord, fastens on one word and rides it so hard that the nature of parables is overlooked; historical, in

that ascription of such existentialist results to Jesus or to Matthew is so anachronistic as to make a historian wince; theological, in that his interpretation of "paradox" is defective and is used in undifferentiated ways. Crossan oscillates between paradox construed as a merely formal contradiction and paradox construed as antinomy or even incoherence.

b. *The parable of the expensive pearl*

13:45–46

45"Again, the kingdom of heaven is like a merchant looking for fine pearls.
46When he found one of great value, he went away and sold everything he had
and bought it.

45–46 The word *palin* ("again") ties this parable fairly closely to the preceding one (cf. 5:33). Walvoord recognizes that this parable is roughly equivalent to the last. But here, he says, the pearl represents not Israel but the church. The church, like the pearl, is formed organically; and "there is a sense in which the church was formed out of the wounds of Christ." This does not take us much beyond patristic allegorizing. The real connection with the last parable is the supreme worth of the kingdom. But here we deal with a merchant whose business it is to seek pearls, and who chances on one of supreme value. Derrett (*Law*, p. 15) sees a rabbinic parallel: "One wins eternal life after a struggle of years, another finds it in one hour" (b *Abodah Zarah* 17a): contrast the conversions of Saul and the Ethiopian eunuch.

Unlike the man in the last parable, the merchant, though he sells everything he has to purchase the pearl, apparently pays a full price. Although he is an expert in pearls, this single find so far surpasses any other pearl the merchant has ever seen that he considers it a fair exchange for everything else he owns. Thus Jesus is not interested in religious efforts or in affirming that one can "buy" the kingdom; on the contrary, he is saying that the person whose whole life has been bound up with "pearls"—the entire religious heritage of the Jews?—will, on comprehending the true value of the kingdom as Jesus presents it, gladly exchange all else to follow him.

Notes

45–46 There is no obvious explanation for the change from present tense (v.44) to aorist (vv. 45–46, but the latter are not gnomic but narrative (Moule, *Idiom Book*, p. 13). The perfect πέπρακεν (*pepraken*, "sold") with obvious aorist force is probably not an early instance of the later use of the perfect in narrative but a tense chosen because there is no aorist active form for this verb. For discussion, cf. Zerwick, par. 289; Moulton, *Prolegomena*, pp. 142–46; Turner, *Syntax*, p. 70; RHG, p. 897; BDF, pars. 343–44.

c. *The parable of the net*

13:47–48

47"Once again, the kingdom of heaven is like a net that was let down into the
lake and caught all kinds of fish. 48When it was full, the fishermen pulled it up on

the shore. Then they sat down and collected the good fish in baskets, but threw the bad away.

47–48 This parable, like the last two, is peculiar to Matthew. In the chiastic structure of the chapter (see on v.3b), it is parallel to the parable of the weeds and has a somewhat similar meaning. But whereas the parable of the weeds focuses on the long period of the reign of God during which tares coexist with wheat and the enemy has large powers, the parable of the net simply describes the situation that exists when the Last Judgment takes place: the kingdom embraces "good" fish and "bad" fish, and only the final sweep of the net sorts them out. That is why the introductory formula uses the present tense (cf. further on v.24; Carson, "Word-Group"). The chief concern of the parable is neither the consummated kingdom (which in Matthew would call forth a future tense—"the kingdom of heaven will become like") nor the inaugurated kingdom ("the kingdom of heaven has become like") but the situation that exists at the End. And, once again, kingdom and church must not be equated.

A *sagēnē* (lit., "drag net," used only here in the NT) was drawn along between two boats or tied on shore at one end and put out by a boat at the other end, which was then drawn to land by ropes. "All kinds of fish" (v.47) might hint at the multiracial character of the subjects of the kingdom, but more probably this refers to "good" and "bad" fish (v.48). In the parable itself, "good" and "bad" fish have no moral overtones but refer simply to fish ceremonially suitable and large enough for eating and those for some reason unacceptable, respectively. The word *sapron* ("bad") can mean "decayed," but here it simply means "worthless."

d. *Interlude* (13:49–51)

1) *Interpretation of the parable of the net*

13:49–50

49This is how it will be at the end of the age. The angels will come and separate the wicked from the righteous 50and throw them into the fiery furnace, where there will be weeping and gnashing of teeth."

49–50 Many separate the parable (vv.47–48), supposedly about the disciples on mission as "fishers of men," and the interpretation (vv.49–50), which transforms the parable into a last judgment scene. Hill (*Matthew*) insists that this is "not a suitable ending, for the furnace is hardly the place for bad fish." But that is to confuse symbol with what is symbolized; the furnace is not for the fish but for the wicked. To be consistent, Hill (and many others; e.g., Jeremias, *Parables*, p. 85; Strecker, *Weg*, pp. 160f.) would also have to object that the tares, when burned (v.42), do not weep and gnash their teeth (Kingsbury, *Parables*, pp. 165f., n. 143). The parable itself cannot easily be made to refer to the missionary activity of the church; for it describes a separation *when the net is full*, not a continuous separation. Nor may one attach some deep significance to the distinction between catching all the fish (v.47) and separating them (v.48)—as if the original parable referred to both the church's witness in catching men and the final separation (so Kingsbury, *Parables*, p. 120)—any more than it is legitimate in interpreting the tares to divide the harvesting from the final separation of weeds and wheat. Both the parable and its interpretation point to the Last Judgment. On the angels and the image of the fiery furnace, see on vv.41–42.

But this does not mean that the parable and its interpretation are about the Last Judgment in the same way 25:1–13 (the ten virgins) and 25:31–46 (the sheep and the goats) are, the one warning of the need for readiness and the other establishing a basis for judgment. The focus here is on the state of the kingdom when the Judgment occurs. Though it includes both the righteous and the wicked, a thorough sorting out will certainly take place.

2) *On understanding parables*

13:51

> [51]"Have you understood all these things?" Jesus asked.
> "Yes," they replied.

51 Both "Jesus says to them" and "Lord" (KJV) are late additions to the text; it is difficult to explain why they were dropped if part of the original text.

Jesus' question picks up the disciples' request for an explanation (v.36) but goes beyond it, since the question is introduced, not after v.43, but after three additional parables. The words "all these things" have been taken to refer to what Jesus means by his parables (Filson, Plummer, Schweizer, Schmid) or to the unexplained parables (Robinson) or to the "secrets of the kingdom" in v.11 (Grundmann, Bonnard, Hill, Fenton). In fact, all these are so tightly linked that it is hard to imagine how one could understand one of these areas and not the other two.

This is the only place in this chapter where the disciples themselves are explicitly said to understand, and they say it by themselves. It is as wrong to say that Matthew has portrayed them as understanding everything as it is to say that they understood nothing. The truth lies between the extremes. The disciples certainly understood more than the crowds; on the other hand, they are shortly to be rebuked for their dullness (15:16). Like another positive response in this Gospel (see on 20:22–23), this one cannot be simply dismissed as presumptuous enthusiasm (as if they think they know everything when in fact they know nothing) nor taken at face value (as if their understanding were in fact mature). In any event the disciples' *claim* is not as important as the last parable to which it leads (for the structure of this section, see on v.3a).

e. *The parable of the teacher of the law*

13:52

> [52]He said to them, "Therefore every teacher of the law who has been instructed about the kingdom of heaven is like the owner of a house who brings out of his storeroom new treasures as well as old."

52 Interpretations of this difficult verse are legion. It has been variously held that it refers to scribes who become disciples of the kingdom (Jeremias, *Parables*, p. 216) or join the Christian community (Hummel, pp. 17ff.); that Matthew here refers to the way he himself functions within the community (C.F.D. Moule, "St. Matthew's

Gospel," *Studia Evangelica* 2 [1964]: 98f.); that the verse demonstrates the existence of Christian "scribes" or "teachers of the law" in Matthew's church, men who exercise much the same role as scribes in Judaism (Kilpatrick, *Origins*, p. 111; Strecker, *Weg*, pp. 37–38; Grundmann), or even that disciples within Christianity are more important than scribes within Judaism (Manson, *Sayings*, pp. 198f.); that each disciple who is able to qualify may present himself as a "teacher of the law" (Lagrange); that any scribe who understands what has been taught about the kingdom is like the lord of a house "who handles everything in a carefree manner, who does not save anything and even uses what is old" (van Tilborg, p. 132; R. Walker, pp. 27–29).

The verse's parabolic structure must be noted and a number of exegetical details explored before its meaning can be grasped or the significance of the introductory "therefore" rightly perceived. The "is like" formula (see on v.24) means "it is with a teacher of the law who has been instructed about the kingdom as it is with the owner of a house." The problem is to discern the point of the comparison. The *oikodespotēs* ("owner of a house") is a frequent figure in Jesus' parables and can stand for God (21:33), Jesus (10:25), or disciples (24:43). Very often he is a figure who dispenses wealth in some way (20:1–16; 21:33–43). So here he brings out of his "storeroom" (same word as "treasure" in 2:11; 6:19–21; 12:35[*bis*]; 13:44, 19:21) new things and old things. Why would an owner of a house do this? Presumably it is not simply to ogle his wealth but for some useful purpose. The point is that his treasure *includes* both the new and the old, and that he can use both.

The point of comparison becomes clearer when we remember that a *grammateus* ("scribe") in Jesus' day was not simply a theological interpreter of the Scriptures capable of rendering Halakic decisions (rules for conduct) but a teacher (hence NIV's "teacher of the law"; see on 2:4; 8:19). From this he derived much of his prestige and power (HJP, 2:332–34; Trotter); indeed, he was seen as having esoteric knowledge that could only be passed on to committed initiates (cf. Jeremias, *Jerusalem*, pp. 237–40). But Jesus adds a qualifying factor: the scribe with whom he is concerned (*mathēteutheis tē basileia tōn ouranōn*) ("has been instructed about the kingdom of heaven"). Whether the verbal form is construed as deponent ("has become a disciple") or strictly passive ("has been made a disciple"), it is not at all clear that the dative expression means "*about* the kingdom of heaven"; and in the one NT passage with similar construction (27:57), Joseph of Arimathea had become a disciple *of* Jesus, not *about* Jesus. By analogy the scribes in this verse have become disciples *of the kingdom of heaven.*

If the preceding exegetical observations are correct, the points of comparison in the parable are two. The emphasis in the first part of the verse rests, not on the supposition that the scribe has been instructed *about* the kingdom and therefore understands, but that he has become a disciple *of* the kingdom and therefore his allegiance has been transformed. It is with such a person as with "the owner of a house"—a discipled scribe brings out of his storeroom new things and old.

The *thēsauros* ("storeroom") so regularly stands for a man's "heart," its wealth and cherished values (see above; esp. on 12:35) that we must understand the discipled scribe to be bringing things out of his heart—out of his understanding, personality, and very being. What he brings out are *kaina kai palaia*, not "new things as well as old" (NIV), which suggests the new things have been added to the old, but "new things and old things"—a subtle touch that reminds the alert reader that in Matthew the gospel of the kingdom, though new, takes precedence over the old revelation and is its fulfillment (cf. 5:17–20). The new is not added to the old; there is but one revelation, and its focus is the "new" that has fulfilled and thereby renewed the old, which has thereby become new (Bonnard). Thus the OT promises of Messiah and kingdom, as well as OT law and piety, have found their fulfillment in Jesus' person, teaching, and kingdom; and the scribe who has become a disciple of the kingdom now brings out of himself deep understanding of these things and their transformed perspective affecting all life.

But the order is of great importance. The parable shows that a discipled scribe has this understanding, *not* that understanding generates discipleship. This conforms perfectly to the chapter's structure: the disciples are not defined as having understanding but are described as having been given revelation and understanding (vv.11–12). When the disciples ask for an explanation, they are given it (vv.36–43) and thus claim some measure of understanding (v.51). "Therefore" (v.52) a *discipled* scribe is like, etc. Discipleship to Jesus, recognition of the revelation he is and brings, and submission to the reign he inaugurates and promises are necessary prerequisites to understanding and bringing out from oneself the rich treasures of the kingdom (see further on 25:31–46).

But there is a second point of comparison in the parable. The last one could have been made by stressing discipleship but omitting any reference to scribes. Scribes were "teachers of the Scriptures." If they are likened to the owner of a house who brings treasures out of his storeroom, the further implication is unavoidable—they are not bringing forth things new and old for purely private or personal reasons *but in their capacity as teachers*. Jesus' disciples claim they have understood what he has been teaching. "Therefore," he responds, discipled teachers of the Scriptures, if they have understood, must themselves bring out of their storeroom the treasures now theirs so as to teach others (cf. Trotter).

This interpretation admirably fits in with three other Matthean themes.

1. The disciples have a major responsibility in evangelizing and making disciples, both during Jesus' ministry (ch. 10) and after his departure (28:18–20).

2. In the latter instance they are told to "disciple" the nations and teach them all Jesus has commanded them: i.e., the focus of their mission is Jesus and the revelation—the new "fulfillment" revelation—he has brought.

3. This interpretation, which places some teaching responsibility on the disciples, also fits the purpose of the parables described in the comments on vv.12–17, 34–35. Indeed, part of the reason for private instruction may again be linked to the place of Jesus' earthly ministry in redemptive history; for what he tells his disciples in secret they are to proclaim from the rooftops (10:27). Jesus explains the parables to his disciples in private; they are to bring out of their treasure rooms "new things and old."

If this interpretation of v.52 is correct, then though "disciples" in this chapter most probably refers to the Twelve, they epitomize the church to come. In that event "disciples" does not refer to a special group of "teachers of the law" within Matthew's community (see further on 23:34) but to those who by Matthew's day were called Christians. Just as they have been aligned with prophets and righteous men from past ages (e.g., 5:11–12; 10:41), so are they aligned with "teachers of the law." In fact, only Jesus' "disciples" are able to bring forth new things and old: the Jewish teachers of the law could bring forth only the old.

5. *Transitional conclusion: movement toward further opposition*

13:53

53When Jesus had finished these parables, he moved on from there.

53 On the Greek preliminary formula, see on 7:28–29. The common view that v.53 properly introduces the following pericope fits neither that beginning nor the structure of Matthew. Gooding's claim (p. 229) that v.24 is syntactically tied to v.53 is incorrect: compare the same openings at 8:14; 9:23, where new pericopes are introduced. This verse, as Hill (*Matthew*) points out, "suggests that Jesus spoke all the preceding parables at once"—though he thinks this "is unlikely" (cf. further on 5:1–12; 13:3a). What is clear is that Jesus' movement from Capernaum to "his home town" (vv.53–54) turns out to be a further fulfillment of vv.14–15: these people will be ever hearing but never understanding.

Notes

53 The verb *μετῆρεν* (*metēren,* "he moved on"), found in the NT only here and at 19:1 (again in a formulaic discourse ending), is normally transitive and probably owes its present intransitive force to Semitic influence (Moisés Silva, "New Lexical Semitisms?" ZNW 69 [1978]: 256).

V. The Glory and the Shadow: Progressive Polarization (13:54–19:2)

A. *Narrative* (13:54–17:27)

The danger of outlines is oversimplification. Even genuine insight in outline form may eliminate or minimize various themes that occur in sections where the discovered "structure" does not allow for them. Matthew, as we have seen, can use structure most effectively; and several complex structures have been found in, or imposed on, these chapters (cf. J. Murphy-O'Conner, "The Structure of Matthew XIV–XVII," RB 82 [1975]: 360–84; Gooding, pp. 248ff.). No detailed and comprehensive outline of these chapters is quite convincing; so it seems best to deal with them pericope by pericope.

The principal themes of these chapters are clear. There is a progressive polarization along several axes. As Jesus extends his ministry, the opposition sharpens (15:1–9; 16:1–14). When he reveals himself to his disciples, they perceive some truth clearly and entirely reject other truth (16:13–22; 17:1–13). As Jesus is increasingly opposed by Jewish leaders, so his own disciples become increasingly important (18:1–10). Over it all is the contrast between Christ's glory, goodness, and grace, and the blind misunderstanding of the disciples (15:15–16, 33; 16:22; 17:4, 19; 18:21) and Jewish leaders (15:2, 8; 16:6, 12; 17:24) alike. And rising less ambiguously now is the shadow of the Cross (16:21–22; 17:22–23).

In the narrative section (13:54–17:27), Matthew follows Mark 6–9 fairly closely until Mark 9:33. Of course Matthew leaves out all the material between Mark's parables and the rejection at Nazareth (viz., Mark 4:35–5:43) because he has presented it earlier (chs. 8–9).

1. *Rejected at Nazareth*

13:54–58

54Coming to his hometown, he began teaching the people in their synagogue, and they were amazed. "Where did this man get this wisdom and these miraculous powers?" they asked. 55"Isn't this the carpenter's son? Isn't his mother's name Mary, and aren't his brothers James, Joseph, Simon and Judas? 56Aren't all his sisters with us? Where then did this man get all these things?" 57And they took offense at him.

But Jesus said to them, "Only in his hometown and in his own house is a prophet without honor."

58And he did not do many miracles there because of their lack of faith.

Placing this pericope immediately after the discourse on parables extends the hostility and rejection of the scribes and Pharisees even to Jesus' hometown (cf. Mark 6:1–6). It is almost universally assumed that this is the same rejection recorded in Luke 4:16–31, which ties the event to OT prophecy. Though not unlikely, this is not certain. Unlike Luke, Mark and Matthew mention no hostility so great as to lead people to kill Jesus. If there were two incidents, the one recorded by the first two evangelists may reflect an abating of instinctive rage as the village's most famous son has grown in reputation in the area.

54 On the formal connection between this verse and the preceding one, see on v.53. Jesus' *patris* ("home town") is here understood to be Nazareth, explicitly named only by Luke (4:16; cf. Matt 2:23; 4:13). That Jesus taught extensively in the synagogues is certain (cf. 4:23; 12:9); but he did not limit himself to this environment. (On "their" synagogue, see on 4:23; 7:29; 9:35; 10:17; 11:1; 12:9–10.) The imperfect *edidasken* (lit., "he was teaching") could suggest that Jesus taught here on more than one occasion (Filson, Schweizer) but is more probably inceptive (cf. NIV's "began teaching").

The interrogative *pothen* ("Where"; repeated in v.56) is not so much concerned with location as with source of authority (cf. also v.27; Bonnard). Do Jesus' wisdom and powers—his teaching and miracles, both evidences of his authority—reflect God's authority or something else (cf. 12:24)?

55–57a Obviously some of the questioners' motivation springs less from a serious desire to know whence Jesus derives his authority than from personal pique that a hometown boy has outstripped them. The questions (vv.55–56) do not call for answers but merely reveal that there has already been a denial of who Jesus is. Mark 6:3 has "the carpenter," not Matthew's "the carpenter's son" (v.55); but in a day when most lads followed their father's trade, both are correct. *Tektōn* can mean "carpenter"—one who works with wood—or perhaps even "builder," in a time and place when most homes were made of mud brick. Justin Martyr (*Dialogue* 88.8, c. A.D. 150) says Jesus was a maker of plows and yokes. The definite article ("*the* carpenter's son") suggests there was only one in town. On the question of Jesus' brothers and sisters, see on 12:46–50. The four names listed (cf. Notes) are typically Jewish.

In one sense, of course, the questions of the people are understandable, if not justifiable. Here was a young artisan from a rough town, with no special breeding or education. Whence, then, his wisdom and miracles? (Incidentally, their questions render impossible the fanciful miracles ascribed to Jesus' childhood by the apocryphal gospels.) But by their questions the people merely condemn themselves: they cannot doubt the fact of his wisdom and miracles (v.56) yet reject his claims (v.57). "They took offense at him" (*eskandalizonto en autō*), i.e., found in him obstacles to faith (see on 5:29; 11:6), even though the biggest obstacles were in their own hearts. It is sad that every time in the NT somebody is "scandalized" by someone, that someone is Jesus (cf. Bonnard, citing G. Stählen, TDNT, 7:349; cf. Matt 11:6; 26:31, 33; Mark 6:3; Luke 7:23).

57b–58 The proverb in v.57b recurs at Mark 6:4; Luke 4:24; John 4:44 (cf. Hennecke, 1:109). Most often a person is better received at home than anywhere else; but if he enjoys an elevated position, the reverse is true.

Many say that v.58 softens Mark's "He could not do any miracles there, except lay his hands on a few sick people and heal them. And he was amazed at their lack of faith" (Mark 6:5–6). But two factors must be borne in mind: (1) Mark mentions some miracles, and Matthew, typically condensing, may be referring to these rather than commenting on Jesus' ability to do miracles; and (2) it is doubtful whether Mark's "could not" is ontological or absolute, for Mark records other miracles in which the beneficiaries exhibit no faith (feeding the five thousand, stilling the storm, healing the Gadarene demoniac). The "could not" is related to Jesus' mission: just as Jesus could not turn stones to bread without violating his mission (4:1–4), so he could not do miracles indiscriminately without turning his mission into a sideshow. The "lack of faith" (*apistia*, used only here in Matthew) of the people was doubtless a source of profound grief and frustration for Jesus (cf. *apistos*, "unbelieving," in 17:17), rather than something that stripped him of power.

Notes

---

55 Many MSS read Ἰωσῆς (*Iōsēs*, "Joses," KJV), instead of Ἰωσήφ (*Iōsēph*, "Joseph," NIV), doubtless following the Galilean pronunciation יוֹסֵי (*yôsê*) of the correct Hebrew יוֹסֵף (*yôsēp̄*).

56 The phrase πρὸς ἡμᾶς (*pros hēmas*, "with us") with the sense of position instead of motion (i.e., having the force of παρ' ἡμῖν [*par' hēmin*, "with us"]) represents a Hellenistic Greek far more fluid than its Attic forbear (cf. Moule, *Idiom Book*, p. 52).

---

2. *Herod and Jesus* (14:1–12)

a. *Herod's understanding of Jesus*

14:1–2

[1]At that time Herod the tetrarch heard the reports about Jesus, [2]and he said to his attendants, "This is John the Baptist; he has risen from the dead! That is why miraculous powers are at work in him."

1–2 Of the two parallels (Mark 6:14–16; Luke 9:7–9), only Mark (6:17–29) goes on to give the story of John's death; and Matthew follows this account (vv.3–12). On the chronological problem raised by a comparison of vv.1–2 and v.13, see on v.13.

The phrase "At that time" is very loose (see on 11:25; 12:1) and should not be tied to the previous pericope. Mark sets the scene after the mission of the Twelve; and certainly the multiplication of Jesus' influence through his disciples would upset Herod, one of whose motives in imprisoning the Baptist had been to thwart any threat to political stability (cf. Jos. Antiq. XVIII, 116–19[v.2]).

Herod Antipas, son of Herod the Great (see on 2:1), was tetrarch (v.1; see on 2:22), not king—though doubtless "king" was used popularly (Mark 6:14). His tetrarchy included Galilee (4:12) and Perea (19:1). Because John the Baptist's ministry had been exercised in Perea (John 1:28), he had come under Herod's power. Herod had been ruling more than thirty years, and at this time he lived primarily at Tiberias on the southwest shore of Galilee. Thus Jesus' ministry was taking place largely within Herod's jurisdiction.

How the reports of Jesus' ministry reached Herod is unknown; it may have been through Cuza (Luke 8:3). So extensive a ministry could not have been kept from Herod for long. His conclusion, that this was John the Baptist risen from the dead (v.2), is of great interest. It reflects an eclectic set of beliefs, one of them the Pharisaic understanding of resurrection. During his ministry John had performed no miracles (John 10:41); therefore Herod ascribes the miracles in Jesus' ministry, not to John, but to John "risen from the dead." Herod's guilty conscience apparently combined with a superstitious view of miracles to generate this theory.

b. *Background: Herod's execution of John the Baptist*

14:3–12

[3]Now Herod had arrested John and bound him and put him in prison because of Herodias, his brother Philip's wife, [4]for John had been saying to him: "It is not lawful for you to have her." [5]Herod wanted to kill John, but he was afraid of the people, because they considered him a prophet.

[6]On Herod's birthday the daughter of Herodias danced for them and pleased Herod so much [7]that he promised with an oath to give her whatever she asked. [8]Prompted by her mother, she said, "Give me here on a platter the head of John the Baptist." [9]The king was distressed, but because of his oaths and his dinner guests, he ordered that her request be granted [10]and had John beheaded in the prison. [11]His head was brought in on a platter and given to the girl, who carried it to her mother. [12]John's disciples came and took his body and buried it. Then they went and told Jesus.

3–5 Both Mark (6:16–29; cf. Luke 3:19–20) and Matthew insert this story as an excursus, a bit of explanatory background (see further on v.13). Typically Matthew is more condensed than Mark, yet does add one detail (see on v.12); but in this case it is doubtful whether Matthew is a condensation of Mark. More likely Matthew follows independent information (cf. Hoehner, *Herod Antipas*, pp. 114–17). Many scholars have insisted the Gospel reports of John's death and the report of Josephus (Ant. XVIII, 116–19[v.2]) cannot be reconciled, especially because Josephus assigns a political motive to the execution of the Baptist and the synoptists a moral and religious one. Hoehner (*Herod Antipas*, pp. 124–49) has exhaustively treated these problems and points out that the two motives are not as far apart as some have thought.

Herod's first wife was the daughter of Aretas (cf. 2 Cor 11:32), Arabian king of the Nabateans, whose land adjoined Perea on the south. To divorce her in favor of Herodias was politically explosive. Indeed, some years later border fighting broke out, and Antipas was defeated, but saved by Roman intervention. John's rebuke would be like a spark on tinder; and his powerful preaching about the nearness of the messianic kingdom fueled the expectations of the populace, not least for the reestablishment of the law by which John was rebuking Herod. Religious fanaticism with messianic overtones is more politically dangerous than mere political extremism. This Herod well knew. Josephus and the Gospel writers blend together.

Herodias was married to Herod Philip (not Philip the tetrarch, Luke 3:1), son of Herod the Great and Mariamne II (for this identification, cf. Hoehner, *Herod Antipas*, pp. 131–36), and therefore half-brother to Herod Antipas. John probably did not denounce Antipas for divorcing his former wife, an action probably judged allowable (cf. b *Ketuboth* 57b; Jeremias, *Jerusalem*, p. 371, n. 60), but for incestuously marrying his half-brother's wife (Lev 18:16; 20:21); and John probably kept on repeating his rebuke (imperfect *elegen* means "he used to say [repeatedly]"; so McNeile). John's courage in denouncing Herod distinguishes him from the Essenes (with whom many scholars associate him), for they tended to refuse to meddle in political life, no matter how evil it became (Bonnard). Herodias was not only Antipas's sister-in-law but also his niece, the daughter of his half-brother Aristobulus; but for most Jews there was no bar to marrying a niece (cf. Hoehner, *Herod Antipas*, pp. 137–39, n. 4, for the literature).

Some think Matthew's statement that "Herod wanted to kill John, but he was afraid of the people" (v.5) conflicts with Mark's picture of a Herod who wants to spare John but is pushed into killing him by Herodias (cf. esp. Mark 6:19–21). The total situation is psychologically convincing. Like Ahab, Antipas was wicked but weak; and Herodias, like Jezebel, wicked and ruthless. Herod's grief (not mere distress) in v.9 shows his ambivalence. Moreover if he was "afraid of the people" because they held John to be a prophet (cf. 21:26, 46), then Matthew confirms Josephus's view that Herod's actions were largely motivated by politics.

6–8 "On Herod's birthday"—or, better, "At Herod's birthday feast" (cf. Notes)—Herodias's daughter by her former marriage, Salome, a girl between twelve and fourteen yeas of age (Hoehner, *Herod Antipas*, pp. 151–56), danced before the king and his lords (v.6). The dance may have been very sensual, but the text does not say so. The outrageous morals of the Herodians suggest it, as does the low status of dancing girls. At any rate, Salome pleased Herod Antipas enough for him to put on the airs of a lavish and powerful emperor; petty ruler though he was, he imitated the grandiloquence of ancient Persian monarchs (Esth 5:3, 6; 7:2)—the story also has certain parallels with a later oath made by the Roman emperor Gaius to Herod Agrippa (cf. Hoehner, *Herod Antipas*, pp. 165–67)—and with drunken dignity made a fool of himself. Salome, still young enough to ask her mother's advice, became the means for accomplishing Herodias's darkest desire—the death of the man whose offense had been telling the truth.

9–11 Though grieving because of his oath (the Greek is plural but refers to the single oath Herod had made: see on 2:20; Turner, *Insights*, p. 27, n.; BDF, par.

142) and his loss of face before his guests if he were to renege on his vow (cf. Notes), Herod gave the order (v.9). "Like most weak men, Herod feared to be thought weak" (Plumptre). His oath should neither have been made nor kept. Decapitation (v.10) though sanctioned by Greeks and Romans was contrary to Jewish law, which also forbade execution without trial.

The Gospel writers have been charged with fabrication on the ground that the prompt execution of John would have quenched the merriment. But hardened men are unlikely to let a little gore spoil their merriment. While Alexander Jannaeus feasted with his concubines in a public place, he ordered eight hundred rebels to die by crucifixion, their wives and children being slaughtered before the eyes of the victims (Jos. Antiq. XIII, 380[XIV. 2]). When Cicero's head was brought to Fulvia, the wife of Antony, she spat on it and pierced its tongue with a pin in spite against the man who had opposed Antony. Jerome says Herodias did the same thing to the head of John. We do not know where Jerome got his information, and it may not be historical; but it would not have been out of character for a cruel and ruthless woman intent on aping the imperial court. So John died, the last of the OT prophets (11:9, 13) who through persecution became models for Jesus' disciples (5:11–12). (For the significance of *korasion* ("girl," v.11), see Hoehner (*Herod Antipas*, pp. 154–56).)

12 Though both Mark and Matthew tell of the burial of John the Baptist's body by his disciples, only Matthew mentions the report to Jesus. This report does not become the reason why Jesus withdraws (see on v.13) but serves other purposes: (1) it draws John and Jesus together against the opposition; (2) it suggests, though it does not prove, a positive response to Jesus by John and his disciples following 11:2–6; and (3) it supports the view that Matthew often finishes his longer narrative pericopes by returning to the opening theme (see on 12:45; 15:20)—Herod hears reports of Jesus (14:1); Jesus hears reports of Herod (v.12). The frequency of this device gains importance in interpreting Matthew's later chapters.

Notes

6 The Greek γενεσίοις δὲ γενομένοις (*genesiois de genomenois*, "at the birthday feast") is so difficult that it has generated a nest of variant readings. It appears to be a dative absolute, which, though apparently common in Plutarch, has no other certain example in the NT (cf. further Moule, *Idiom Book*, pp. 44f.).

9 There are two principal readings: (1) λυπηθεὶς ὁ βασιλεὺς διά (*lypētheis ho basileus dia*) attested by B D Θ f[1] f[13] 700 it[a,b,d] et al.; (2) ἐλυπήθη ὁ βασιλεύς; διὰ δέ (*elypēthē ho basileus; dia de*) attested by ℵ C K (L omit *de*) L[c] W X Byz et al. The first, adopted here, is supported by witnesses of Alexandrian, Western, and Caesarean text types but has an ambiguity: does the *dia* phrase qualify *lypētheis* ("grieving")—i.e., "the king, grieving because of his oath and his dinner guests, ordered, etc."—or ἐκέλευσεν (*ekeleusen*, "he ordered")—i.e., "the king was grieved; but because of his oath and his dinner guests, he ordered, etc."? The second reading, most likely secondary, removes the ambiguity (usually evidence of being secondary) and requires the second interpretation. The difference is one of emphasis only; but the harder reading may be taken to support the more nuanced interpretation of Herod's motives given above.

3. *The feeding of the five thousand*

14:13–21

[13]When Jesus heard what had happened, he withdrew by boat privately to a solitary place. Hearing of this, the crowds followed him on foot from the towns. [14]When Jesus landed and saw a large crowd, he had compassion on them and healed their sick.

[15]As evening approached, the disciples came to him and said, "This is a remote place, and it's already getting late. Send the crowds away, so they can go to the villages and buy themselves some food."

[16]Jesus replied, "They do not need to go away. You give them something to eat."

[17]"We have here only five loaves of bread and two fish," they answered.

[18]"Bring them here to me," he said. [19]And he directed the people to sit down on the grass. Taking the five loaves and the two fish and looking up to heaven, he gave thanks and broke the loaves. Then he gave them to the disciples, and the disciples gave them to the people. [20]They all ate and were satisfied, and the disciples picked up twelve basketfuls of broken pieces that were left over. [21]The number of those who ate was about five thousand men, besides women and children.

The feeding of the five thousand is found in all four Gospels (cf. Mark 6:30–44; Luke 9:10–17; John 6:1–14; cf. further on Matt 15:32–39 = Mark 8:1–10). Comprehensive interpretations are too numerous to list. There is probably an implicit anticipation of the messianic banquet (see on 8:11); but the text focuses more on Jesus' compassion (v.14), on the responsibility of the disciples to minister to the crowds (v.16), and on this miracle of creation. Suggestions that what "really happened" was that the people started sharing their lunches have much more in common with late nineteenth-century liberalism than with the text. Those who see Eucharistic significance in the event (Benoit, Gundry) make it meaningless at the time it occurred; the most that can be said is that after the institution of the Lord's Supper and after the Passion and Resurrection, some Christians may have seen parallels to the Eucharist. John 6, often taken to support this, is not as convincing as is commonly thought (cf. Carson, "Historical Tradition," pp. 125–26).

Possible OT allusions to Exodus 16 or 2 Kings 4:42–44 cannot be more than allusions, for the differences between this story and those are more significant than the similarities. Hence, as Davies notes (*Setting*, pp. 48f.), that Matthew here develops a "new Moses" theme based on a manna typology (Exod 16) is unlikely since (1) none of the synoptists stresses the desert setting; (2) in the OT the manna was not to be kept, but here the fragments are to be kept; (3) Jesus ministers to a crowd from which he has tried to escape, and Exodus has no parallel to this. It is far more likely that this pericope shows that Jesus himself cannot be reduced to one of the readymade categories of the day—prophet, rabbi, teacher of the law (cf. van der Loos, esp. pp. 634–37).

13–14 If "what had happened" (v.13) refers to John's death, then the chronology is either contradictory (so Bultmann, *Synoptic Tradition*, pp. 351f.) or a return to a much earlier time, since the beginning of the chapter presupposes the Baptist's death (v.2). But vv.3–12 must be seen as an excursus: the section opens with *gar* ("for"), commonly used to introduce excursuses, and the *de* ("and") in v.13 is resumptive (cf. L. Cope, "The Death of John the Baptist in the Gospel of Matthew, or, The Case of the Confusing Conjunction," CBQ 38 [1976]: 515–19). Therefore v.13 picks up from vv.1–2: when Jesus heard, viz. Herod's response to his preaching and miracles, he decided to withdraw. He had done so previously to escape the animus of the Pharisees (12:15); he now does so to avoid Antipas. But as elsewhere (e.g., Mark 7:24–25), it was often not possible for Jesus to escape the crowds even when it was possible for him to leave a place.

Luke (9:10) specifies that the "solitary place" was in the region belonging to Bethsaida—i.e., Bethsaida Julius (see on 11:21) on the northeast shore of Galilee. The crowds ran "on foot" around the top of the lake, presumably crossing the upper Jordan at a ford two miles north of where the river enters Galilee. They "followed" Jesus, seeing where he was going and setting out after him; but arriving first, they were already there when he landed with his tired disciples (v.14). Lohmeyer (*Matthäus*) finds profound symbolism—Jesus "withdraws" from the presence of God in prayer, like a high priest leaving the Holy of Holies, and presents himself to the people. But this is as uncontrolled a piece of allegorizing as any church father ever thought of. (On Jesus' neverfailing compassion, see 9:36.)

15–17 "Evening" (*opsios*) is a flexible word, referring to any period from mid-afternoon to just after sunset. The later period is in view in v.23; here (v.15) the earlier one.

On the face of it, the conversation between Jesus and his disciples is straightforward, though very condensed compared with the other Gospels. The "villages" to which the disciples wished to send the crowds were small, unwalled hamlets. Bread and fish were staples in Galilee, especially for the poor. John 6:9, 13 specifies *barley* loaves—the cheaper, coarser bread. The numbers "five" and "two" (v.17) are simply accurate details: efforts to explain them (e.g., as referring to the Pentateuch and two tables of the law) are as fanciful as Christian frescoes making them Eucharistic symbols, which would turn fish into wine!

But in recent years the influence of Held (Bornkamm, *Tradition*, pp. 181–83) has convinced many that Matthew's changes of Mark (assuming absolute dependence in this pericope) demonstrate two other themes operating: (1) the disciples take part in the miracle, and so discipleship is prominent; (2) the omission of Mark 6:37b shows that though in Mark the disciples do not understand Jesus' words—"You [emphatic] give them something to eat" (v.16; i.e., they do not understand that they themselves should perform a miracle)—in Matthew they do understand but lack the requisite faith. This will not do.

1. Held is establishing a great deal on the basis of an omission in a book characterized by condensations and omissions, and he does not even raise the question whether Mark 6:37b was omitted for nontheological reasons.
2. Similarly, would a first-century reader of Matthew perusing this Gospel without critically comparing it with Mark at every turn suspect that Matthew was any easier on the disciples than Mark was at this point?
3. Neither "understanding" nor "faith" is explicitly raised in this pericope.
4. Jesus' words "you give them something to eat" are not easy to understand; but whatever they mean, it is possible that the disciples do not understand them, even in Matthew. If (and this is doubtful, though Held seems to assume it) Jesus means that they should perform such a miracle, then their response (v.17) betrays their complete misunderstanding; for miracles of creation cannot be thought to require something first. If on the other hand Jesus is simply making them responsible to

find out what is needed, buy food, or pray—if they remembered the miracle of the wine in Cana (John 2:1–11), they should have asked Jesus to meet the need, not send the people away—then their answer not only reveals limited vision but an approach to the problem betraying a lack of both understanding and faith.

5. The disciples' role in the miracle is limited to the organization and distribution needed for a crowd of thousands. This can scarcely mean that the disciples contribute to the miracle. Indeed, the story could more easily be taken as contrasting Jesus with his disciples in this miracle rather than elevating them to major roles.

18–21 Jesus alone multiplies the loaves and fishes. He gives the orders, gives thanks, and breaks the loaves (vv.18–19). The actions—looking up to heaven, thanking God, and breaking the loaves—are normal for any head of a Jewish household (cf. Moore, *Judaism*, 2:216f.; SBK, 1:685f.; M *Berakoth* 6–8) and have no special Eucharistic significance. A common form of prayer before eating was "Blessed art thou, O Lord our God, King of the Universe, who bringest forth bread from the earth."

Matthew omits many details—the green grass, the groups of fifty and one hundred—but points out that all ate and were satisfied (v.20), perhaps an anticipation of the messianic banquet, and at least evidence that there was lots to eat! The twelve baskets (*kophinos*, a stiff wicker basket) of leftovers and the size of the crowd (which might have been fifteen or twenty thousand total, if there were five thousand "men," v.21) also support the latter point. But the "twelve basketfuls" may be significant: that there were twelve tribes and twelve apostles—emphasized in 19:28—cannot be coincidence. Yet the precise significance is uncertain. The best suggestion may be that Messiah's supply is so lavish that even the scraps of his provision are enough to supply the needs of Israel, represented by the Twelve.

4. *The walk on the water*

14:22–33

22Immediately Jesus made the disciples get into the boat and go on ahead of him to the other side, while he dismissed the crowd. 23After he had dismissed them, he went up on a mountainside by himself to pray. When evening came, he was there alone, 24but the boat was already a considerable distance from land, buffeted by the waves because the wind was against it.

25During the fourth watch of the night Jesus went out to them, walking on the lake. 26When the disciples saw him walking on the lake, they were terrified. "It's a ghost," they said, and cried out in fear.

27But Jesus immediately said to them: "Take courage! It is I. Don't be afraid."

28"Lord, if it's you," Peter replied, "tell me to come to you on the water."

29"Come," he said.

Then Peter got down out of the boat, walked on the water and came toward Jesus. 30But when he saw the wind, he was afraid and, beginning to sink, cried out, "Lord, save me!"

31Immediately Jesus reached out his hand and caught him. "You of little faith," he said, "why did you doubt?"

32And when they climbed into the boat, the wind died down. 33Then those who were in the boat worshiped him, saying, "Truly you are the Son of God."

Many scholars since Bultmann (*Synoptic Tradition*, p. 216) have surmised that two stories are woven together in Mark's account (6:45–52; cf. John 6:16–21)—an account of walking on the water and a later storm-calming miracle. But Scot

McKnight ("The Role of the Disciples in Matthew and Mark: A Redactional Study" [Master's thesis, Trinity Evangelical Divinity School, 1980], pp. 153–56) has shown the two to be integrally related. Some of the points arising from the differences between Mark and Matthew are briefly treated below. On the theological thrust of the passage, see John P. Heil, *Jesus Walking on the Sea* (Rome: Biblical Institute Press, 1981), who notes the association in the OT between chaos and sea. The stilling of the sea is therefore not only christological in orientation but also eschatological: Jesus is even now stilling the deep.

22 Why Jesus "made" (the verb is very strong and might be translated "compelled") the disciples go on ahead of him may be deduced from these bits of information: (1) he wanted to be alone to pray (v.23); (2) he wanted to escape the crowd with his disciples to get some rest (Mark 6:31–32); and (3) he may have dismissed the disciples forcefully to help tame a messianic uproar (John 6:15).

The omission of "Bethsaida" (Mark 6:45) in Matthew raises a difficult geographical problem. From the perspective of the site where the feeding took place, "to the other side" means the west shore; and that is where the boat ultimately landed, at Gennesaret (Mark 6:53 = Matt 14:34), a small triangular plain on the northwest shore of the lake (Kinnereth in the OT, 1 Kings 15:20). John 6:17 specifies the town of Capernaum. But Mark (6:45) says Jesus sent his disciples "on ahead of him to the other side [in the best MSS] to Bethsaida, while he dismissed the crowd." This was most likely Bethsaida Julius, just up the coast to the north, on the same side of the lake. The apparent discrepancy has prompted some MSS of Mark to omit "to the other side." The explanation that the boat was blown off course and landed on the west side does not explain the reference to Bethsaida, if this be Bethsaida Julius.

The problem is knotty. The simplest solution is that defended by Westcott and also by Morris on John—viz., Jesus sent the disciples off to cross the lake, with the command to wait for him on the eastern shore near Bethsaida Julius, but not beyond a certain time. The delay in waiting for Jesus would then account for the actual walking on the water not occurring till the fourth watch (v.25), i.e., after 3:00 A.M. A bit of syntax may support this view. Matthew's *heōs hou* plus the aorist subjunctive verb should normally be rendered "until" (as in 13:33; 17:9; 18:34; though cf. 26:36)—i.e., the disciples were "to go on ahead" (*proagein*) of him *until*, not *while*, he was free of the crowds, after which he hoped to join them, after some time alone in prayer; and they would then cross "to the other side." Mark (6:45) specifies Bethsaida but has *heōs* plus the indicative [in the best MSS]: the disciples were to go "to Bethsaida while," not "until," he sent the crowds away.

23–24 If this interpretation is correct, then it is the length of Jesus' prayer time that delays his coming and sends the disciples across the lake on their own. On the phrase "into the hills" (v.23), see on 5:1–2. The burden of Jesus' prayer is not revealed; but it is possible that the crowd's attempts to make him king (John 6:15) prompted him to seek his Father's face. If so, it is not a Matthean concern here (as is a similar crisis at 26:39).

NIV's "a considerable distance" (v.24) masks a considerable textual difficulty. The most likely reading is "many *stadia* [one *stadion* was about two hundred yards] from land" (Metzger, *Textual Commentary*, p. 37). In any event the boat was out towards the middle of the lake. If *enantios* is taken literally to mean "against," and not metaphorically to mean "hostile to," then the clause "the wind was against it," on the basis of the movements suggested above, refers to a strong wind from the west—a regular feature during the rainy season (Mark's "green grass" [6:39] confirms the season).

Many eager to find signs of the Matthean church take the boat as a symbol of that church—a community of disciples in stormy times (e.g., Bonnard, Schweizer). But if so, why did Peter want to step "out of the boat"?

25–27 The ancient Hebrew world divided the night from sunset to sunrise into three watches (Judg 7:19; Lam 2:19), but the Romans used four (v.25); and their influence prevailed in the evangelists' chronologies. Jesus' approach to the boat therefore occurred between 3:00 A.M. and 6:00 A.M. Matthew omits the difficult words "He was about to pass by them" (Mark 6:48), on which see Lane (*Mark*, pp. 235–36). The disciples were terrified (v.26), thinking they were seeing a *phantasma* ("apparition"; NIV, "ghost"; used in the NT only here and in Mark 6:49). There is no merit in the supposition that this is a transposed resurrection appearance. Jesus' "Take courage!" (v.27, as in 9:2, 22) and his "Don't be afraid" bracket the central reason for these calming exhortations: "It is I." Although the Greek *egō eimi* can have no more force than that, any Christian after the Resurrection and Ascension would also detect echoes of "I am," the decisive self-disclosure of God (Exod 3:14; Isa 43:10; 51:12). Once again we find Jesus revealing himself in a veiled way that will prove especially rich to Christians after his resurrection (see on 8:20; cf. Carson, "Christological Ambiguities").

28 Verses 28–32 have no parallel in the other Gospels; and two of the verbs ("to sink" and "to doubt") are used elsewhere in this Gospel only in exclusively Matthean sections (18:6 and 28:17 respectively). Perhaps Matthew was the first to commit this part of the story to writing, though the evidence from two verbs each used but once elsewhere is not commanding. This is the first of three scenes in which Peter receives special treatment, all in chapters 14–17 (cf. 16:13–23; 17:24–27). Benoit thinks that already in this story Peter gains primacy over the rest of the Twelve; but "if so, it is a primacy which reveals weakness in faith" (Hill, *Matthew*; similarly Bonnard). See further on v.31.

Peter's protasis ("if it's you") is a real condition, almost "since it's you." The request is bold, but the disciples had been trained for some time and given power to do exactly the sort of miracles Jesus was doing (10:1). What is more natural than for a fisherman who knew and respected the dangers of Galilee to want to follow Jesus in this new demonstration of supernatural power?

29–31 How far Peter got is unclear (cf. Notes), but at Jesus' command (v.29) he walked on the water (the plural "waters" in Greek may be in imitation of Hebrew, which uses "water" only in the plural; cf. Mark 9:22; John 3:23). But his outlook changed: when he saw the wind (synecdoche for the storm), he began to sink (v.30). It was not that he lost faith in himself (so Schniewind), but that his faith in Jesus, strong enough to get him out of the boat and walking on the water, was not strong enough to stand up to the storm. Therefore Jesus calls him a man "of little faith" (v.31; see on 6:30; 8:26; and esp. on 17:20), and his rhetorical question—"Why [cf. Notes] did you doubt?"—helps both Peter and the reader recognize that doubts and fears quickly disappear before a strict inquiry into their cause. Thus Peter in this pericope is both a good example and a bad example (cf. R.E. Brown, K.P. Donfried, and J. Reumann, edd., *Peter in the New Testament* [Minneapolis: Augsburg, 1973]. p. 83). His cry for help is natural, not a liturgical creation—Did not liturgy have to choose some formulas on which to build?—and Jesus' rescuing him is akin to God's salvation in the OT (Pss 18:16; 69:1–3; 144:7).

32–33 The climax of the story is not the stilling of the storm (v.32) but the confession and worship of the disciples: "Truly you are the Son of God" (v.33). This is the first time Jesus has been addressed by the disciples with this full title (cf. 16:16; 26:63; 27:40, 43, 54). But it already lurks behind 3:17 ("my Son"), and the devil has used it of Jesus (4:3, 6). It is most likely abbreviated to "the Son" in Jesus' self-references in 11:25–27. In the earlier passage (cf. also 3:17) we have seen how the title would most likely have been understood by the disciples at the time and how it would have been fleshed out in light of the Resurrection. On the absence of the Greek articles, see on 13:39.

The objection that v.33 so anticipates 16:16 as to make the latter anticlimactic is psychologically unconvincing. Similar reasoning would make the rebuke of Peter (16:21–23) following his grand confession (16:13–20) impossible or preclude defection from Jesus at his passion. The synoptic Gospels show us that the disciples understand only by degrees. Therefore their confessions of Christ must not be interpreted as if they had postresurrection understanding of him. One of the marks of the evangelists' fidelity to the historical development of the disciples' understanding of Christ lies precisely in this—that they show the disciples coming around to the same points again and again, each time at a deeper level of comprehension, but always with a mixture of misapprehension.

Exactly what the disciples meant by "Son of God" is uncertain. It is very doubtful that at this point they understood the title in a genuine ontological sense (though they would later). It is even less likely that they thought of Jesus as a *theios anēr* ("divine man"), allegedly an understood category in Hellenistic Judaism for various miracle workers. Carl Holladay (*Theios Anēr in Hellenistic Judaism: A Critique of the Use of This Category in New Testament Christology* [Missoula, Mont.: SP, 1977]) has shown the category was not well defined, that it had no fixed content in our period, and that it was not that common (contra Cullmann, *Christology*, p. 277; E. Lövestam, "Wunder und Symbolhandlung: Eine Studie über Matthäus 14, 28–31," *Kerygma und Dogma* 9 [1962], esp. p. 135; and many others). Probably they used the title in a messianic way (see on 3:17; 11:25–30), but still with superficial comprehension.

Many feel that vv.32–33 decisively alter Mark 6:51–52 (cf. esp. Bornkamm, *Tradition*, pp. 204ff.). Mark, it is alleged, leaves a final impression of confusion: no mention is made of the disciples' worship; instead they are amazed, they do not understand the previous miracle of the loaves, and their hearts are hardened. But Matthew portrays them worshiping, uttering an important christological confession, with no mention of amazement, hard hearts, or failure to understand. These are indeed undeniable differences; but the two evangelists are not so far apart as one might think.

1. Mark says they are "amazed"; but the verb used is often associated, not with fear, but with joyful worship (Lev 9:24 LXX; similarly the cognate noun, Luke 5:26). When used in Mark, the word usually, but not always, denotes amazement in response to some divine self-disclosure, but without fear. Why should they be afraid? The storm had ceased!

2. The comment in Mark 6:52 that the disciples' hearts were hardened does not refer to their amazement but to an underlying attitude that could allow for amazement after having seen so much of Jesus' work. The same point could be deduced from Matthew, even though it is not spelled out there.

3. Matthew may have omitted the censure in Mark 6:52 because he thought it would be repetitive: he had already shown the fear and lack of faith of the disciples (vv.26–27). (On these points, cf. Meyer, Gaechter, and esp. Trotter.)

This is not to deny differences in emphasis between Matthew and Mark but to deny that the historical reality behind the two accounts is too small to sustain both emphases. Mark focuses on the disciples' "hardness" that continued despite another miracle like a previous one (cf. 8:23–27; Mark 4:35–41) by someone who could multiply loaves. Matthew hints at such unbelief through his narrative—he is capable of much more subtle characterization than Mark—and by the example of Peter (if he is a man of little faith, what about the rest of them?) but focuses explicitly on the disciples' confession of Jesus as God's Son. But even there, in view of later developments in Matthew, a reader might think that the disciples' confessions are much greater than their actual comprehension (see on 16:21–28).

Notes

---

29 The principal textual options are (1) καὶ ἦλθεν (*kai ēlthen*, "he came *or* went [to Jesus]") and (2) ἐλθεῖν (*elthein*, "to come," "to go"). The latter signifies intent, the former accomplishment. (NIV does not translate the word.) The external evidence is neatly divided. Metzger's argument (*Textual Commentary*, p. 37) that "he went" was changed to "to go" because the former seemed to say too much may be right; but one might argue instead that "to go" seems to say too little, since the text claims that Peter actually walked on the water; yet, when Peter began to sink, Jesus needed only reach out his hand to seize him, which implies Peter had walked almost all the way.

31 Εἰς τί (*eis ti;* "Why," NIV), probably equivalent to לָמָּה (*lᵉmâh*, "why"), is extraordinary: the customary form is διὰ τί (*dia ti*, "why"), as in 9:14. Turner (*Syntax*, pp. 266f.) detects a subtle difference: the latter means "because of what" = "why," whereas the former means "in order to what" = "why"; and in this instance the latter nuance in "why" makes good sense. Jesus does not ask "because of what" Peter doubted (any fool could see that!) but for what purpose, to what end: what was the point of his doubt, having come so far?

---

5. *Transitional summary of constant and unavoidable ministry*

14:34–36

> [34]When they had crossed over, they landed at Gennesaret. [35]And when the men of that place recognized Jesus, they sent word to all the surrounding country. People brought all their sick to him [36]and begged him to let the sick just touch the edge of his cloak, and all who touched him were healed.

34–36 Gennesaret (v.34) was the fertile plain on the northwest side of the lake (see on v.22), vividly described by Josephus (War III, 516–21[x.8]). The crowds' instant recognition of Jesus (v.35) showed the extent of his ministry; again, word-of-mouth reports led to crowds (cf. 3:5; 4:24). Like the woman with the hemorrhage (9:20–22), the people were satisfied if only they could touch the edge of his cloak (v.36); and even that degree of faith brought thorough healing (the preposition compounded with the verb in *diesōthēsan* ["were healed"] is perfective).

This little pericope does three things: (1) it again stresses the sweeping extent of Jesus' public ministry (cf. 4:23–25; 8:16; 9:35–36); (2) it also shows that Jesus' ministry extended to all the people, though his close disciples had special access to him and his more intimate instruction; and (3) because the stricter groups, such as the Pharisees and the Essenes, counted it an abomination to rub shoulders in a crowd—one never knew what ceremonial uncleanness one might contract—Jesus' unconcern about such things neatly sets the stage for the confrontation over clean and unclean (15:1–20). As in 8:1–4; 9:20–22, he himself cannot become unclean: instead, he makes clean.

6. *Jesus and the tradition of the elders*

15:1–20

1Then some Pharisees and teachers of the law came to Jesus from Jerusalem
and asked, 2"Why do your disciples break the tradition of the elders? They don't
wash their hands before they eat!"
3Jesus replied, "And why do you break the command of God for the sake of
your tradition? 4For God said, 'Honor your father and mother' and 'Anyone who
curses his father or mother must be put to death.' 5But you say that if a man says
to his father or mother, 'Whatever help you might otherwise have received from
me is a gift devoted to God,' 6he is not to 'honor his father' with it. Thus you nullify
the word of God for the sake of your tradition. 7You hypocrites! Isaiah was right
when he prophesied about you:

> 8" 'These people honor me with their lips,
> but their hearts are far from me.
> 9They worship me in vain;
> their teachings are but rules taught by men.' "

10Jesus called the crowd to him and said, "Listen and understand. 11What goes
into a man's mouth does not make him 'unclean,' but what comes out of his
mouth, that is what makes him 'unclean.' "
12Then the disciples came to him and asked, "Do you know that the Pharisees
were offended when they heard this?"
13He replied, "Every plant that my heavenly Father has not planted will be
pulled up by the roots. 14Leave them; they are blind guides. If a blind man leads
a blind man, both will fall into a pit."
15Peter said, "Explain the parable to us."
16"Are you still so dull?" Jesus asked them. 17"Don't you see that whatever
enters the mouth goes into the stomach and then out of the body? 18But the
things that come out of the mouth come from the heart, and these make a man
'unclean.' 19For out of the heart come evil thoughts, murder, adultery, sexual
immorality, theft, false testimony, slander. 20These are what make a man 'unclean'; but eating with unwashed hands does not make him 'unclean.' "

Controversies become sharper and more theological as Matthew's narrative moves on. This controversy is of great importance in grasping Jesus' understanding of the law. Some have tended to draw radical conclusions as to Matthew's distinctive emphases by comparing this pericope with Mark 7:1–23 (e.g., Bornkamm, *Tradition*, pp. 86–89). The most prominent differences between Matthew and Mark are these: Matthew omits Mark 7:3–4, adds Matthew 15:12–14, omits Mark's interpretation

(7:19) that Jesus made all foods clean, and adds Matthew 15:20b to keep the focus on food eaten with washed or unwashed hands. Thus many argue that whereas in Mark Jesus annuls the law, in Matthew he does not do more than annul one small bit of Halakah (rabbinic interpretation affecting conduct). These issues must be kept in mind in interpreting the text more closely. (See esp. Bank's balanced study, *Jesus*, pp. 132–46.)

1 "Then" (see on 2:7) certain Pharisees (see on 3:7, and Introduction, section 11.f) and teachers of the law (see on 2:3) came to Jesus "from Jerusalem." These did not belong to the many such leaders scattered throughout the land but came from Jerusalem. They would probably therefore be held in special esteem (cf. SBK, 1:-691). But from Matthew's perspective, they were probably a quasi-official deputation (cf. John 1:19) and a source of Jesus' most virulent opposition.

2 As in 9:14, the attack on Jesus comes through the behavior of his disciples, though elsewhere we learn that the disciples reflected his own practices (Luke 11:37–41). Matthew is much more condensed than Mark, for two reasons: (1) unlike Mark, Matthew does not need to explain Jewish customs to his readers; and (2) Mark deals with an array of Pharisaic Halakic regulations (Mark 7:1–3), whereas Matthew stresses the one issue of eating food with unwashed hands. It must be emphasized that this distinction says nothing about the sharpness of the Pharisees' attack on Jesus' response but only about the concentration of issues (see on v.20). (For other differences between Matthew and Mark, cf. Banks, *Jesus*, pp. 132–34.)

The "tradition of the elders," the "tradition of men" (Mark 7:8; Col 2:8), "your tradition" (Matt 15:3, 6; Mark 7:9, 13), and the "traditions of the fathers" (Gal 1:14) refer to the great corpus of oral teaching that commented on the law and interpreted it in detailed rules of conduct, often recording the diverse opinions of competing rabbis. This tradition in Jesus' time was largely oral and orally transmitted; but the Pharisees, though not the Sadducees, viewed it as having authority very nearly equal to the canon. It was later codified under Rabbi Judah the Prince (c. A.D. 135–200) to form the Mishnah (cf. SBK, 1:691–95); TDNT, 6:661f.; Moore, *Judaism*, 1:251–62). One entire tractate, *Yadaim*, deals with "hands" (i.e., *yāḏayim*), specifying such details as how much water must be used for effective ceremonial purification: e.g., "If a man poured water over the one hand with a single rinsing, his hand is clean; but if over both hands with a single rinsing, R. Meir declares them unclean unless he pours over them a quarter-log or more" (M *Yadaim* 2:1).

3–6 Jesus' words, in slightly different order in Mark, are less a response than a counterattack. He made a fundamental distinction between the authority of "the command of God" (as found in Scripture) and the Halakic tradition; and he insisted that the Pharisees and teachers of the law were guilty of breaking the former for the sake of (lit., "on account of") the latter (v.3). The two texts cited are Exodus 20:12 and 21:17 (cf. also Deut 27:16; Prov 1:8; 20:20; 30:17; 1 Tim 5:3), and their point is clear enough. The English verb "curses" (v.4) is too narrow: *kakologeō* means "to insult," "to speak evil of," "to revile" (used in the NT only here and at Mark 7:10; 9:39; Acts 19:9). The one who speaks evil of his parents must surely be put to death (on the construction of the latter clause, cf. Zerwick, par. 60).

"But you" (v.5)—the "you" is emphatic—have evaded through your traditions God's command (v.6), broadly interpreted by Jesus to lay responsibility on children to take responsibility for their parents. Greed could keep a son from discharging this duty by simply declaring the goods or money that might have gone to support his parents *korbān*, a gift devoted to God (cf. Lev 27:9, 16), set aside for the temple treasury (cf. M *Nedarim*, esp. 1, 9, 11; cf. SBK, 1:711–17). Such a vow could be annulled in various ways. It would not mean that one could use the goods or money in question but that he could withhold it from his parents (for legal questions, cf. Derrett, *NT Studies*, 1:112–17). Thus Halakic tradition was nullifying the word of God (the textual variants "law of God" or "command of God" are not critical).

A further observation may be important, though it should not be overstressed. For Jesus and the kingdom, a man must be willing to put aside family loyalties and love Jesus supremely (10:37–39). Yet here Jesus accuses the Pharisees and teachers of the law of breaking God's command when they use similar arguments to support vows devoting certain gifts to God. Apparently neither Jesus nor Matthew sees any inconsistency here, because in their view Jewish Halakah cannot take precedence over the law, whereas Jesus and the kingdom may do so because they "fulfill" it. Other factors are also relevant. The Halakic regulations Jesus opposed permitted a son sometimes to act against his parents, whereas 10:37–39 presupposes family opposition against disciples. Not only is the rule different, but the victim is also different.

7–9 This is the first recorded instance of Jesus' calling the Pharisees and teachers of the law hypocrites (v.7; see on 6:2): Luke 11–12 probably refers to a later time. The charge was that, while they made a show of devotion to God, their religious traditions took precedence over God's will. In referring to Isaiah 29:13, Jesus did not say, Isaiah was right when he said . . . and now I make a secondary application, but, "Isaiah was right when he prophesied about you." Yet Isaiah 29:13 is addressed to men of Isaiah's day. What then did Jesus mean? There are three points of contact: (1) in each case those warned were Jews, (2) from Jerusalem, (3) with a religion characterized by externals that sometimes vitiated principle. Moreover the Jews of Jesus' day thought of themselves as preserving ancient traditions; but Jesus said that what they were actually preserving was the spirit of those whom Isaiah criticized long before. The thought is close to, though different in categories from, 23:29–32.

The quotation essentially follows the shorter form of the Septuagint (for details, cf. Gundry, *Use of OT*, pp. 14–16). The burden of the Scripture Jesus quotes is that the Pharisees and teachers of the law have displaced the true religion of the heart (v.8), of the entire personality and will, with a religion of form. Therefore their worship is vain (v.9) and their teachings their own with nothing of God's authority behind them.

The judgment is so sweeping that it calls in question not only the Jews' Halakah but their entire worship and teaching.

10–11 Jesus' sharpest barb against the Pharisees and teachers of the law had been private. Now he teaches the crowd the same things (v.10). These two verses also answer the Pharisees' question (v.2) directly, not just by countercharge (vv.3–9).

What Jesus now says, the disciples call a "parable" (v.15; so also Mark 7:17; see on 13:3a). In presenting it to the crowd (v.10), Jesus exhorts them to understand; for the parable was not meant to be cryptic, though only few seemed to have grasped it at the time, and the disciples had trouble with it (vv.15–16). This confirms our earlier comments on Jesus' parables (13:10–17, 34–35).

The verb *koinoi* ("makes [him] 'unclean' "), here used (v.11) for the first of thirteen times in the NT, literally means "to render common"; but because participation in what was common was for a practicing Jew to become ceremonially unclean, the customary NT meaning is very similar.

Perhaps Mark 7:15 is a shade more generalized than Matthew's form of the "parable" (v.11), but the differences are slight. "[If] Matthew really wished to exclude the kind of laxity represented by his Markan source, it is hard to see why he kept the potentially dangerous parable around which this whole controversy is constructed" (C.E. Carlston, "The Things That Defile (Mk 7.14) and the Law in Matthew and Mark," NTS 15 [1968–69]: 77). The language is so general it lets in everything Mark allows, even though the final application is to food eaten with unwashed hands (v.20). The form of the argument is from this principle to that application, the former being broader than the latter. Thus, though Matthew omits Mark's parenthetical interpretation—"(In saying this, Jesus declared all foods 'clean')" (Mark 7:19b)—yet retention of the "parable" and its interpretation (vv.17–20) lead precisely to that conclusion.

12–14 These verses are peculiar to Matthew and reflect what took place after Jesus and his disciples had retired from the crowd and entered the house (cf. Mark 7:17). The disciples' question shows that the Pharisees understood enough of Jesus' parable to take offense (v.12). The disciples' request to have the parable explained (v.15) does not reveal them as being more obtuse than the Pharisees but shows that, in common with most Jews at the time, they held the Pharisees in high regard and therefore wanted to be certain of exactly what Jesus had said that had offended them so badly. Therefore vv.12–14 are not out of place. Jesus must disillusion his disciples as to the reliability of the Pharisees and teachers of the law as spiritual guides, as well as explain the parable. This is not to say that these verses turn the entire section (vv.1–20) into a personal attack on the Pharisees rather than on their use of the law (so Kilpatrick, *Origins*, p. 180); for the chief point for which they are blamed relates to their misunderstanding of the law.

Jesus uses two images. The first (v.13) predicts the rooting up of any plant the heavenly Father has not planted. Israel often saw herself as a plant God had planted (Ps 1:3; Isa 60:21; cf. 1QS 8:5; CD 1:7; 1 Enoch 10:16; Pss Sol 14:2), and the prophets turned the image against them (Isa 5:1–7). Thus Jesus is not saying that every false doctrine will be rooted up (so Broadus) but that the Pharisees, the leaders of the Jewish people, are not truly part of God's planting. This shocking idea has already been hinted at in Matthew (3:9; 8:11–12) and will recur.

The second image (v.14) may depend on a title some Jewish leaders apparently took on themselves. They had the law, they reasoned, and therefore were fit to serve as "guides of the blind" (Rom 2:19; cf. Luke 6:39). This Jesus disputes. In his view they were "blind guides of the blind" (NIV mg., so the most likely variant; cf. Metzger, *Textual Commentary*, p. 39); and "both will fall into a pit" (cf. also Luke 6:39). Though the Pharisees and teachers of the law had the scrolls and interpreted them in the synagogues, this does not mean that they really understood them. On the contrary, they were blind and failed to comprehend the Scriptures they claimed to follow. Jesus' denunciation presupposes that anyone who truly understands the "word of God" (v.6) will discern who he is and follow him (cf. John 5:39–40). The Pharisees did not follow Jesus; so they did not understand and follow the Scriptures.

15–16 Peter speaks on behalf of the other disciples (v.15): Jesus' answer shows that the "parable" to which Peter refers is v.11. The disciples' failure to understand shocks Jesus. (1) *Kai* ("also")—are you, too, "still so dull?" Dullness might be understandable in others, but in you disciples? (2) *Akmēn* ("still," used only here in Matthew) may mean either "Are you *still* without understanding?" (NIV; Hill, McNeile) or "Are you still—*but not for long*—without understanding?" (Schlatter). The context strongly favors the former; and therefore the question, far from toning down the disciples' failure to grasp Jesus' teaching (so Schweizer), magnifies its enormity.

17–20 Verse 17 explains that "what goes into a man's mouth" (v.11) is merely food, which passes through the body and is excreted (lit., "is cast into a latrine"). On the sanitary conditions of the time, cf. Edward Neufeld, "Hygiene Conditions in Ancient Israel," *Biblical Archaeologist* 34 (1971): 42–66. Verses 18–20 explain that "what comes out of a man's mouth" (v.11), and what makes him unclean, comes from his heart (see on 12:34–35). Matthew's list of the heart's products (v.19) is shorter than Mark's. After the first, "evil thoughts," the list follows the same order as the sixth and seventh commandments, followed by *porneia* ("sexual immorality"; see on 19:3–12), the order of the eighth and ninth commandments, and finally "slander," which probably includes blasphemy (cf. 12:31). The list itself negates (as Banks [*Jesus*, pp. 143–44] points out) Kilpatrick's suggestion that Matthew has transformed Mark's principle of morals into a precept of law (*Origins*, p. 38).

It would be puerile to ask how every item on the list results directly in defiling speech. The point, as in 12:34–35, is that what a man truly *is* affects what he says and does. Jesus presupposes that the heart is essentially evil (cf. 7:11). But the burden of this pericope is not to be pure on the inside and forget the externals but that what ultimately defiles a man is what he really is. Jesus is not spiritualizing the OT but insisting that true religion must deal with the nature of man and not with mere externals.

Because v.20b does not occur in Mark, many have thought it to be Matthew's way of limiting the application of the controversy to the single question of eating food with unwashed hands. Two things militate against this view: (1) Jesus deals with a broad principle touching *all* foods and applies it to this situation, but the application can be no more valid than the broader principle on which it is based; and (2) Matthew frequently ends his pericopes by referring back to the questions that precipitate them (see on 12:45; 14:12; 16:11–12; 17:13); so v.20b requires no more explanation than that.

The way one interprets this pericope relates to a larger understanding of how Matthew deals with Jesus' attitude to the law and the situation in his own church.

1. It goes beyond the evidence to argue, as does Ernst Käsemann (*Essays on New Testament Themes* [London: SCM, 1964], p. 101), that Jesus now abrogates the distinction between the sacred and the profane; or, as Lohmeyer (*Matthäus*) does, that Jesus now distinguishes "word of God" from "word of man" even within Scripture itself; or, as McNeile and R. Walker (p. 142) do, that Jesus now undermines, as in Mark, *all* Mosaic distinctions between clean and unclean. He deals, principially, with the clean-unclean distinctions as to foods and applies this principle to foods eaten with unwashed hands.

2. On the other hand, it does not go as far as the exegetical evidence to pit

Matthew against Mark so that the former, unlike the latter, is seen as absolutely restricting Jesus' words to the single problem of foods eaten with unwashed hands. Verses 3, 7–9, 11, 14, 17–19 cannot be taken so narrowly.

3. The approach that sees a Jewish-Christian church behind this pericope—whether still related to the synagogue or recently separated from it—is exegetically unsatisfying. Matthew is slightly more cautious than Mark and perhaps a shade less explicit, but that is not solid enough evidence to support Barth's reconstruction of the Matthean church (in Bornkamm, *Tradition*). Though Ebionite groups doubtless flourished, Matthew neither belonged to one, nor anything like one; for no Ebionite could write vv.11, 17–20.

4. Banks (*Jesus*, pp. 140–41) contends that if Jesus explicitly repudicated the food laws contained in Leviticus 11 and Deuteronomy 14 (Dan 1:8–16; cf. Jud 10:5; Tobit 1:10–11), then the hesitations of the primitive church on the issue (Acts 10:14–15; 15:28–29; Rom 14:14; Gal 2:11–13) are inexplicable. But he avoids falling into the trap of thinking that Jesus' original teaching on this matter was no more than Semitic hyperbole, with the meaning that "pollutions from within are more serious than pollutions from without" (Banks, *Jesus*, p. 141; cf. Hos 6:6). Rather, he holds that Jesus' approach neither attacked nor affirmed the law but moved on a different level, expressing "an entirely new understanding of what does and does not constitute defilement" (Banks, *Jesus*, p. 141). Abrogation was latent within the saying, but not more. This is a shade too timid.

The hesitations of the early church regarding the food laws are not inexplicable: a great deal of what Jesus taught became *progressively* clear to the church after the Resurrection and did not immediately gain universal assent. The same is true of Jesus' words on Gentile conversion, on the Great Commission, on the delay of the Parousia. What can be said is that Jesus' teaching in this pericope (and in its Markan parallel) opens up an entirely fresh approach to the question of the law. It does not simply subordinate the ritual to the moral (these are not the categories appealed to); instead it discounts the Pharisees' oral tradition while defending the law (vv.3–6) and yet insists that real "cleanness" is of the heart, so discounting some of the law's formal requirements.

The only way to explain these phenomena is the one Matthew has already developed (see esp. 5:21–48): Jesus insists that the true direction in which the OT law points is precisely what he teaches, what he is, and what he inaugurates. He has fulfilled the law; therefore whatever prescriptive force it continues to have is determined by its relationship to him, not vice versa. It is within this framework that Jesus' teaching in this pericope theologically anticipates Romans 14:14–18; 1 Corinthians 10:31; 1 Timothy 4:4; Titus 1:15, and that historically it took some time for the ramifications of Jesus' teaching to be thoroughly grasped, even by his own disciples. Once again it is a mark of Matthew's fidelity to the historical facts that he does not overstate Jesus' teaching, and a mark of his literary skill that he does not find it necessary to draw Mark's parenthetical conclusion (Mark 7:19b), even though he obviously shares it.

5. It follows that Jesus not only rejected the Pharisees and teachers of the law as authentic interpreters of Scripture (esp. vv.12–14) but assigned that role finally and absolutely to himself (cf. 5:21–48). Historically the conflict between Jesus and the traditional interpreters of Scripture would wax fierce and would ultimately bring him to the Cross; theologically the fundamental distinctions between a Christian and a Jewish reading of Scripture must be traced to Jesus himself.

6. What concerned Jesus was not so much the form of religion as human nature. He wanted to see people transformed and their hearts renewed (cf. 6:1–33; 12:34–35; comments on 25:31–46) because he came to save his people from their sins (1:21).

7. *More healings* (15:21–31)

a. *The Canaanite woman*

15:21–28

[21]Leaving that place, Jesus withdrew to the region of Tyre and Sidon. [22]A Canaanite woman from that vicinity came to him, crying out, "Lord, Son of David, have mercy on me! My daughter is suffering terribly from demon-possession."

[23]Jesus did not answer a word. So his disciples came to him and urged him, "Send her away, for she keeps crying out after us."

[24]He answered, "I was sent only to the lost sheep of Israel."

[25]The woman came and knelt before him. "Lord, help me!" she said.

[26]He replied, "It is not right to take the children's bread and toss it to their dogs."

[27]"Yes, Lord," she said, "but even the dogs eat the crumbs that fall from their masters' table."

[28]Then Jesus answered, "Woman, you have great faith! Your request is granted." And her daughter was healed from that very hour.

It is by no means clear which way—if at all—the literary dependency of this pericope on Mark (cf. 7:24–30) runs. (For the most recent analysis, see E.A. Russell, "The Canaanite Woman and the Gospels," in Livingston, 2:263ff.) Of greater interest is the placing of this pericope in both Gospels. It not only records Jesus' withdrawal from the opposition of the Pharisees and teachers of the law (cf. 14:13) but contrasts their approach to the Messiah with that of this woman. They belong to the covenant people but take offense at the conduct of Jesus' disciples, challenge his authority, and are so defective in understanding the Scriptures that they show themselves not to be plants the heavenly Father has planted. But this woman is a pagan, a descendant of ancient enemies, and with no claim on the God of the covenant. Yet in the end she approaches the Jewish Messiah and with great faith asks only for grace; and her request is granted (cf. 8:5–13).

This essentially christological approach to the pericope is more defensible than the one that sees in these verses guidance for Matthew's Jewish church in its relations to Gentiles: they could not claim immediate access to salvation, but exceptions would be made where there was deep faith (Hill, *Matthew*). This begs too many issues. Would they, or would they not, then have to conform to all Jewish law? How do we know so much of Matthew's church (cf. Introduction, section 2)? What this explains to Matthew's readers (Matthew's "church," though this designation may give the wrong impression of a group hermetically sealed off from other churches) is not what attitude they ought to adopt toward Gentile evangelism, whether opposition or occasional acquiescence, but rather "how we got from there to here"—i.e., how the development of redemptive history changed the position of God's people from late OT concepts to the full Christian concept. This story is a step along the way, focused on the self-disclosure of the Messiah and his attitudes to his own mission, his pivotal role in salvation history. But if Matthew's Jewish-Christian readers want to learn more about what their attitude should be toward Gentile evangelism, they must also read the words of the resurrected and glorified Jesus after the climax of his self-disclosure (28:18–20).

The worst feature of many redaction-critical attempts to reconstruct Matthew's church and its problems is the implicit elimination of the salvation history insisted on by the Gospels themselves, a persistent refusal to believe that the evangelists are interested in writing about Jesus to explain him, and therefore "how we got from there to here," rather than to address their "churches" from the perspective of a theology infinitely flexible and shaped by contemporary problems alone. Once the perspective of redemptive history is granted, we may cheerfully acknowledge that the evangelists include material and write it down in such a way that it will prove of interest and/or use (not necessarily both) to their readers. But the loss of the historical perspective from which the evangelists claim to write leads to an unnecessary and basic distortion of their Gospels.

21 Jesus "withdraws" (as in 2:12, 22; 4:12; 12:15; 14:13) to the region of Tyre and Sidon, cities on the Mediterranean coast lying about thirty and fifty miles respectively from Galilee. Kilpatrick (*Origins*, pp. 130ff.) notes Matthew's interest in them (cf. 11:21–24) and suggests that Matthew and his church were there—a possibility, but without much supporting evidence. "The vicinity of Tyre" (Mark 7:24) leads us to ask whether Jesus actually entered the region of Tyre and Sidon or went only to the border—which would mean the woman came out to meet him. But v.21 and Mark 7:31 make it clear that Jesus left Galilee and entered pagan territory. According to Mark 3:8 and Luke 6:17, some crowds had come from Tyre and Sidon to be helped by him; but there he would hardly be known.

22 The introductory *idou* (lit., "behold," untranslated in NIV) probably points to the extraordinary nature of the story. Mark (7:26) calls the woman "a Greek [i.e., a non-Jewess], born in Syrian Phoenicia." Matthew's use of the old term "Canaanite" shows that he cannot forget her ancestry: now a descendant of Israel's ancient enemies comes to the Jewish Messiah for blessing. *Exelthousa* (lit., "coming out") does not mean that she came out of that pagan region to meet Jesus (see on v.21) but either that her ancestry was there or that she had left her home (Lohmeyer, Bonnard). Her calling Jesus "Son of David" shows some recognition of Jesus as the Messiah who would heal the people (see discussion at 9:27; 12:23); "Lord" is ambiguous (see on 8:2). For other instances of demon possession in this Gospel, see on 4:24; 8:16, 28, 33; 9:32; 12:22.

23–24 That these verses are peculiar to Matthew is not surprising. Matthew's Jewish readers would be intensely interested in Jesus' doing a miracle to aid a Gentile, on Gentile territory. Mark's Gentile readers would, however, have needed much explanation had this saying been included in his Gospel. Jesus had healed Gentiles before (4:24–25; 8:5–13), but always in Jewish territory.

Jesus' silence does not quiet the woman; so his disciples beg him to stop her persistent cries (v.23). If they mean "Send her away without helping her," either they suppose she is annoying him or they themselves are being annoyed. But their words could also be taken to mean "Send her away with her request granted" (so Meyer, Benoit). Indeed only this interpretation makes sense, because v.24 gives a reason for Jesus' not helping her rather than for not sending her away.

Bultmann (*Synoptic Tradition*, p. 155), Arens (pp. 315–19) and others judge

Jesus' answer (v.24) to be inauthentic, largely on the grounds that "I was sent" sounds Johannine and thus for them is late and inauthentic. Regardless of this similarity the particularism of the thought supports its authenticity, since the church, even before Paul, engaged in Gentile evangelism and could therefore hardly be thought to have created the saying (cf. Jeremias, *Promise*, pp. 26–28; Bonnard; Hill). The thought echoes 10:6, where the same language is used (lit., "the lost sheep of the house of Israel"). But even chapter 10 recognizes that one day the mission of the disciples will take them to Gentiles (10:18). But that time was not yet. Meanwhile Jesus, doing the Father's will (cf. 11:27), recognized that his own mission was to Israel; and he delighted to do the will of him who sent him.

Either "the lost sheep of the house of Israel" means "the lost sheep *among* the house of Israel"—i.e., some in the house of Israel are not lost—or "the lost sheep *who are* the house of Israel"—i.e., all Israel, regarded as lost sheep. The latter is correct, for in the identical expression at 10:6 the contrast is, not between these lost sheep and others in Israel who are not lost, but between these lost sheep and Gentiles or Samaritans. Flender (pp. 23ff.) errs in the opposite direction, holding that Jesus sees himself gathering *all* Israel, not just a remnant. But Jesus is not so naive (cf. 7:13–14; 10:17–22, 34–37), for there is a categorical distinction between a target people and a converted people.

It appears, then, that Jesus wanted his disciples and the Canaanite woman to recognize "that His activities were circumscribed not only by the inevitable limitations of His manhood, but by the specific part that He had been called to play during His brief earthly life" (Tasker). True, he was "Son of David," as the woman said; but that did not give her the right to enjoy the benefits covenanted to the Jews. The kingdom must first be offered to them. The thought is like John 4:22: "Salvation is from the Jews." The Samaritan woman, like this Canaanite woman, had to recognize this—even if a time was coming when true worship would transcend such categories (John 4:23–26).

25 The woman knelt (see on 2:2; 8:2) before Jesus (probably the imperfect is used to make the action more vivid) and cried, as only the mother of an afflicted child could, "Lord, help me!"

26 Still Jesus made certain that she grasped the historic distinction between Jew and Gentile. Jesus' short aphorism supposes that the "children" are the people of Israel and the "dogs" are Gentiles. The "crumbs" (v.27) do not designate the quantity of blessing bestowed; and still less does the table refer to the Eucharist (rightly Bonnard). The question is one of precedence: the children get fed *first*.

27 The woman's answer is masterly. "Yes, Lord," she agrees, "for even [not 'but even,' NIV; cf. Notes] the dogs eat the crumbs that fall from their masters' table." Those two words "for even" reveal immense wisdom and faith. She does not phrase her answer as a counterstroke but as a profound acquiescence with the further implications of "dogs." She does not argue that her needs make her an exception, or that she has a right to Israel's covenanted mercies, or that the mysterious ways of divine election and justice are unfair. She abandons mention of Jesus as "Son of David" and simply asks for help; "and she is confident that even if she is not entitled to sit down as a guest at Messiah's table, Gentile 'dog' that she is, yet at least she may be allowed to receive a crumb of the uncovenanted mercies of God" (Tasker; cf.

Schlatter). There may be no significance to the use of the diminutive "dogs" (*kynaria*) in vv.26–27, because in Hellenistic Greek the diminutive force is often entirely lacking; but if there is such force here, it does not make the dogs more acceptable—i.e., "pet dogs" or "house dogs" as opposed to "wild dogs"—but more dependent: i.e., little, helpless dogs eat little scraps of food (*psichiōn*—equally diminutive in form). As does Paul in Romans 9–11, the woman preserves Israel's historical privilege over against all radical idealization or spiritualization of Christ's work, yet perceives that grace is freely given to the Gentiles.

28 The faith that simply seeks mercy is honored. Again Jesus speaks, this time with emotion (cf. Notes); and the woman's daughter is healed "from that very hour" (cf. 8:13; 9:22). The Clementine homilies (end of the second century) call the woman Justa and her daughter Berenice, but the names may have been invented.

Notes

---

27 The words καὶ γάρ (*kai gar;* "but even") are used approximately thirty-nine times in the NT. In no other place does NIV render them adversatively ("but even"); and there is no justification for doing so here. The natural translation is "for even." The Markan parallel (Mark 7:28) exhibits far more variants; but the correct reading almost certainly omits both γάρ (*gar,* "for") and ἀλλά (*alla,* "but") in favor of a simple "Lord, even the dogs," whose precise nuance is a shade more ambiguous.

28 The ejaculation ὦ (*ō,* "O [woman]," omitted in D) has emotional force (cf. BDF, par. 146 [1*b*], which contrasts with use of the vocative "woman" without the word in Luke 22:57; John 2:4; 4:21 et al.), as seems usual in the Hellenistic Greek of the NT, with the exception of Acts, which prefers the classical usage (cf. Zerwick, par. 35).

---

b. *The many*

15:29–31

29Jesus left there and went along the Sea of Galilee. Then he went up on a
mountainside and sat down. 30Great crowds came to him, bringing the lame, the
blind, the crippled, the mute and many others, and laid them at his feet; and he
healed them. 31The people were amazed when they saw the mute speaking, the
crippled made well, the lame walking and the blind seeing. And they praised the
God of Israel.

Mark 7:31–37 here tells of the healing of a deaf mute; Matthew provides a summary of more extensive healings (cf. T.J. Ryan, "Matthew 15:29–31: An Overlooked Summary," *Horizons* 5 [1978]: 31–42; for other summaries, cf. 4:23–25; 9:35–38; 12:15–21; 14:14–36). Ryan points out the echoes of Isaiah 29:18–19; 35:5–6. Of greater consequence is the geographical location. Contrary to Bonnard, these healings and the subsequent feeding of the four thousand take place in Gentile territory—viz., in the Decapolis (see below). Jesus had already displayed the power of the kingdom here (8:28–34). His reluctance to respond to the request of the Canaanite woman (vv.21–28) must therefore turn not just on her being a Gentile, or on this being Gentile territory (cf. 8:28–34), but more on her appealing to him as Son of

David and on his being conscious of his primary aims during his earthly ministry. Because of her faith, making appeal to his mercy, the woman receives the "crumbs." Then lest anyone think the crumbs betray a restricted blessing for Gentiles, Matthew immediately tells us of the feeding of four thousand Gentiles. If Jesus' aphorism about the children and the dogs merely reveals *priority* in feeding, then it is hard to resist the conclusion that in the feeding of the four thousand Jesus is showing that blessing for the Gentiles is beginning to dawn.

29–31 "Jesus left there" (v.29) refers to the region of Tyre and Sidon (v.21). But to which (not "along" which, as in NIV; cf. Moule, *Idiom Book*, pp. 50f.) side of the Sea of Galilee did he go? If to the west, he was in Jewish Galilee; if to the east, in predominantly Gentile Decapolis (on which see on 4:25). Mark 7:31 has Jesus traveling north from the vicinity of Tyre to Sidon, and then south and east to the Decapolis on the southeastern side of the lake, still outside Herod's jurisdiction (cf. Matt 14:13). This places him not far from where he had healed the demoniacs and may account for the growing crowds.

But all this depends on reading Mark into Matthew. Could it be that Matthew simply does not care about where Jesus was at this point? No; the evidence suggests rather that he assumes it: (1) the clause "they praised the God of Israel" (v.31) could be naturally said only by Gentiles; (2) the remoteness of the place (v.33) suggests the eastern side of the lake; and (3) the number of "basketfuls of broken pieces" (v.37) left over avoids the symbolic "twelve" (cf. 14:20). More incidental bits of information point in the same direction (see below).

Jesus did many miracles over the course of several days (cf. vv.30–32). The order of the ailments varies in the MSS, possibly owing in part to homoeoteleuton (cf. further Metzger, *Textual Commentary*, p. 40). (For "into the hills" [v.29], see on 5:1–2.)

8. *The feeding of the four thousand*

15:32–39

32Jesus called his disciples to him and said, "I have compassion for these people; they have already been with me three days and have nothing to eat. I do not want to send them away hungry, or they may collapse on the way."

33His disciples answered, "Where could we get enough bread in this remote place to feed such a crowd?"

34"How many loaves do you have?" Jesus asked.

"Seven," they replied, "and a few small fish."

35He told the crowd to sit down on the ground. 36Then he took the seven loaves and the fish, and when he had given thanks, he broke them and gave them to the disciples, and they in turn to the people. 37They all ate and were satisfied. Afterward the disciples picked up seven basketfuls of broken pieces that were left over. 38The number of those who ate was four thousand, besides women and children. 39After Jesus had sent the crowd away, he got into the boat and went to the vicinity of Magadan.

Many scholars hold that this miracle, reported here and in Mark 8:1–10, is a doublet of the feeding of the five thousand, though there is little agreement about why Matthew should include a doublet here. A few have thought the requirements of a liturgical calendar led him to do this—a theory lacking in substantial evidence. More common is the view that Mark put in the doublet to affirm that Gentiles as well as Jews will enjoy the messianic banquet. "The repetition of the story therefore serves theology, not history" (Hill, *Matthew*).

This is not very satisfactory; for if even one of Mark's or Matthew's readers knew there was only one miraculous feeding, *and that of Jews*, the point about the Gentiles would be lost and the credibility of the two evangelists impugned. The events were within the lifetime of many of Matthew's readers: we are dealing with a few decades, not centuries. Thus the validity of the theological point depends here on the credibility of the historical record. Moreover both Mark 8:17–19 and Matthew 16:9–11 report that Jesus referred to the two feedings as separate occasions. Even if one rejects the authenticity of what Jesus said, it argues that the evangelists themselves believed in two miraculous feedings.

Close comparison of the two miracles shows similarities only where there could scarcely be anything else: (1) they both take place in the country; (2) bread and fish appear in both, but this was the common food of the area; (3) Jesus gives thanks and breaks the bread, as one would expect him to (see on 14:19); (4) both portray the disciples distributing the food, a necessity because of the many thousands; and (5) both end in a boat trip, but so do many other stories located near Galilee, especially when Jesus desires to escape the crowds.

On the other hand, the differences between the two miracles are impressive (cf. esp. Maier): (1) the different numbers, five thousand and four thousand; (2) the different locales, northeast shore and southeast shore of Galilee (clearest in Mark); (3) no mention of grass in the second story, implying a different season of the year; (4) a different supply of food at the beginning; (5) a different number of basketfuls of leftovers and even different words for "basket"; and (6) the longer stay of the people in the second miracle (15:32).

It might be wise to remember that two feeding miracles by Moses (Exod 16; Num 11) and Elisha are reported (2 Kings 4:1–7, 38–44). The only impressive reason for taking this account as a doublet is the disciples' response in v.33, and this is best accounted for in other ways (below).

32–33 On Jesus' compassion, see on 9:36. It appears that Jesus' preaching and miracles so captivated the people (cf. their exuberant praise, v.31) that they refused to leave him till he hesitated to dismiss them, fearing that many of them would collapse for hunger on their way home (v.32). Some had come a long distance (Mark 8:3). The response of the disciples is not surprising and not sufficient to prove this pericope a doublet of the feeding of the five thousand, for:

1. The disciples may have understood the feeding of the five thousand Jews as anticipating the messianic banquet. But, though they might have been prepared for Jesus to perform miracles of healing and exorcism on Gentiles as expressions of his mercy and compassion, they might still have been a long way from admitting that Gentiles could share in any anticipation of the messianic banquet.

2. According to John 6:26, after the feeding of the five thousand, Jesus rebuked the crowds for just wanting food; and the disciples may therefore have thought better of bringing the subject up again.

3. More important, we must never lose sight of a human being's vast capacity for unbelief. After this healing, whether a doublet of the feeding of the five thousand or not, Jesus' disciples completely misinterpreted one of his enigmatic sayings because even then they did not understand that those with Jesus could never starve (16:5–12)

34–39 Here in v.36 the verb *eucharisteō* ("I give thanks") is used, not *eulogeō* (lit., "I bless"), as in 14:19, though there is no substantial difference in meaning. The *spyridas* ("baskets") were woven of rushes and used for fish or other food (cf. *kophinous* ["baskets"] in 14:20). A.E.J. Rawlinson (*The Gospel According to St. Mark*, 5th ed. [London: Methuen, 1942], p. 87) cites Juvenal to the effect that, at least in Rome, Jews commonly used *kophinous* to carry kosher food. If so, the use of *spyridas* in this setting may imply that the locale and its people were non-Jewish.

If the number of baskets of leftovers in 14:20 is symbolic, it is hard to see why the seven baskets here (v.37) are not symbolic (see on vv.29–31). The number seven may be significant because it is not twelve and therefore not allusive to the twelve apostles or twelve tribes. This seems more sensible than seeing an allusion to the seven deacons (Acts 6:1–6; so Lohmeyer)—an anachronistic view that ignores that: (1) the seven in Acts 6 are not explicitly called deacons; (2) the church was then entirely Jewish; and (3) the twelve apostles exercised general oversight. It is barely possible that the seven baskets represent the fullness of the people of God now being touched by Jesus' power, as the twelve baskets bore an allusion to Israel; but what is surprising on this view is that the audience here was not apparently comprised of both Jew and Gentile but only the latter.

As before, *hoi esthiontes* ("those who ate," v.38; on the tense, cf. Zerwick, par. 291) are all satisfied, and the men only are numbered. The whole crowd may have exceeded ten thousand.

The site of Magadan (v.39; cf. Notes) is unknown. Both Mark and Matthew now speak of a conflict with the Pharisees and Sadducees (16:1–4). If this occurred when Jesus and the disciples landed, it must have been on Jewish territory, probably on the western shores of Galilee.

Notes

39 Mark 8:10 has τὰ μέρη Δαλμανουθά (*ta merē Dalmanoutha*, "the region of Dalmanoutha"); but we do not know where that is. The uncertainty of the site of Μαγαδάν (*Magadan*) has prompted several textual variants, including Μαγδαλάν (*Magdalan*) and Μαγδαλά (*Magdala*), which may have been influenced by a Semitic word for "tower" (Heb. מִגְדָּל [*migdāl*]; Aram. מִגְדְּלָא [*migdelā'*]).

9. *Another demand for a sign*

16:1–4

[1]The Pharisees and Sadducees came to Jesus and tested him by asking him to show them a sign from heaven.

[2]He replied, "When evening comes, you say, 'It will be fair weather, for the sky is red,' [3]and in the morning, 'Today it will be stormy, for the sky is red and overcast.' You know how to interpret the appearance of the sky, but you cannot interpret the signs of the times. [4]A wicked and adulterous generation looks for a miraculous sign, but none will be given it except the sign of Jonah." Jesus then left them and went away.

Doubtless there were many requests for signs (see on 12:38–40), as there continued to be after Jesus' resurrection and ascension (1 Cor 1:22–24). Moreover itinerant preachers develop standard responses to standard questions. But this pericope (cf. Mark 8:11–13) has a crucial place in the narrative. Jesus has barely returned to Jewish territory when the opposition of Jewish leaders again surfaces, prompting him to leave the area once more, cross the lake, and head far north to Caesarea Philippi (v.13), where in God's providence and in the heart of Gentile territory, Peter makes the great confession that Jesus is the Messiah (v.16).

1 The single article in *hoi Pharisaioi kai Saddoukaioi* ("the Pharisees and Sadducees") implies that they acted together. Because the two groups were so frequently at odds theologically and politically, many think such united action improbable. Moreover critical orthodoxy dates this Gospel at about A.D. 85, a time when the Sadducees, closely connected with Jerusalem and the temple, destroyed in A.D. 70, no longer existed as a coherent force. Therefore many feel that since only Pharisaism was dominant in Judaism at that time, this reference to the Sadducees implies no more than that Matthew vaguely remembered all official Judaism being opposed to Jesus.

A better approach is possible.

1. It is precarious to identify, without remainder, the Pharisees of Jesus' day and the rabbis of A.D. 85 (cf. Introduction, section 11.f) and the Sadducees did not continue as a group with genuine influence after A.D. 70. Matthew's use of these terms might therefore be taken as evidence for historical accuracy in the pre–A.D. 70 setting and not as an anachronism.

2. The Introduction has already questioned critical orthodoxy regarding the date and setting of Matthew's Gospel. A date in the ninth decade should not be lightly assumed. Overcoming that barrier, references to the Sadducees in the synoptic Gospels can be taken to support the evangelists' accuracy. Would not failure to mention the Sadducees have raised questions about how close the evangelists were to what they were writing about? Why then should mention of them not argue for the evangelists' fidelity? If the Sadducees do not appear more often than they do, it is because they were a small group, and closely tied to Jerusalem—a long way from Galilee where Jesus exercised so much of his ministry. Indeed the controversy between Jesus and the Sadducees, recorded in 22:23–34; Mark 12:18; Luke 20:27, occurs in the south, where, too, there is much more frequent mention of "priests" and "chief priests," exactly as one would expect from an accurate historian.

3. The other references to the Sadducees in the Gospels are all in Matthew (3:7; 16:1, 6, 11, 12), exactly as might be expected of a writer who often relies on the understanding of his Jewish readers.

4. Pharisees and Sadducees may here be lumped together because they represent the Sanhedrin, which included both groups (cf. Acts 23:6), or because a common opponent transforms enemies into friends (cf. Luke 23:12; cf. Ps 2:2). Also Matthew elsewhere distinguishes between the two groups (22:33–34; see Introduction, section 11.f).

These men came to Jesus to "test" him (see on 4:1, 7; cf. 19:3; 22:18, 35), asking for "a sign from heaven" (see on 12:38).

2–3 Jesus' words in vv.2–3 are omitted by a small but important group of witnesses. Jerome reports that most MSS known to him omit the words; and many scholars consider them an assimilation to Luke 12:54–56. But if that were so, one wonders why the wording is not closer. (Lagrange, Metzger (*Textual Commentary*, p. 41), and others have postulated that the words are original but were dropped from some MSS by scribes living in climates such as Egypt, where a red sky in the morning (v.3) does not presage rain. The evidence is rather finely balanced, and it is probably best to include the words. If so, Jesus' point is clear enough: the Pharisees and Sadducees can read the "signs" that predict weather, but they remain oblivious to the "signs of the times" already happening. Here these "signs of the times" neither point to the future, nor (contra Hoekema, p. 133) to what God has done in the past. Instead, they testify to Jesus and the kingdom now dawning (cf. 11:4–6; 12:28). The proof that they cannot discern the "signs" is that they ask for a sign (v.1)! For those with eyes to see, the "signs of the times," if not the kind of "sign" the Pharisees and Sadducees demanded, were already abundant.

4 But if a definitive sign is demanded, none but the sign of Jonah will be given (see on 12:39). Mark 8:12 is no exception. In one sense both evangelists are right, for the Jews would not have recognized Jonah as the kind of sign they were after (so there was no exception, Mark) even though that was the only definitive sign Jesus would allow (so there was an exception, Matthew). For exposition, see on 12:38–42.

Mark also says that Jesus sighed: the controversies were wearying. Jesus leaves his opponents and withdraws by boat to the other side of the lake (v.5) and points north (v.13). But his withdrawal is emotional and judicial as well as geographical.

10. *The yeast of the Pharisees and Sadducees*

16:5–12

> [5]When they went across the lake, the disciples forgot to take bread. [6]"Be careful," Jesus said to them. "Be on your guard against the yeast of the Pharisees and Sadducees."
>
> [7]They discussed this among themselves and said, "It is because we didn't bring any bread."
>
> [8]Aware of their discussion, Jesus asked, "You of little faith, why are you talking among yourselves about having no bread? [9]Do you still not understand? Don't you remember the five loaves for the five thousand, and how many basketfuls you gathered? [10]Or the seven loaves for the four thousand, and how many basketfuls you gathered? [11]How is it you don't understand that I was not talking to you about bread? But be on your guard against the yeast of the Pharisees and Sadducees." [12]Then they understood that he was not telling them to guard against the yeast used in bread, but against the teaching of the Pharisees and Sadducees.

This is Jesus' last and most important withdrawal from Galilee before his final trip south (19:1), and it continues to 17:20. Close comparison of these verses with Mark 8:13–21 shows significant differences. In particular, (1) Matthew omits Mark 8:17b–18; (2) Matthew 16:9–11a shortens and rearranges Mark 8:19–21; (3) Matthew adds 16:11b–12; and (4) Matthew refers to the yeast of the Pharisees and Sadducees, but Mark to the yeast of the Pharisees and of Herod.

What do we make of these differences? Some writers (Barth, in Bornkamm [*Tradition*, pp. 114–16]; Strecker [*Weg*, p. 193]; Zumstein [p. 203]) argue that Matthew minimizes the disciples' lack of understanding, so pronounced in Mark, and separates understanding from faith (see on 13:10–15). Though the differences must not be minimized, the question is, What prompts them?

The single-strand theological motivation advanced by many is reductionistic, when on the face of it numerous factors must be weighed.

1. Commentators on Mark complain that Mark 8:13–21 lacks cohesion or is verbose. In part Matthew, as usual, is simply tightening things up and condensing his source.

2. Matthew 16:9 is still very negative: the disciples do not understand (a verb no weaker than the one used in Mark 8:17–18).

3. When they finally do understand (v.12), it is as a result of Jesus' explanation—as in the case of the parables (13:36–43; 15:15–16). The disciples are *beginning* to understand (Trotter), exactly as we might expect from their position in salvation history.

4. Far from driving a wedge between faith and understanding, the charge in vv.8–9a links them. Yet faith in Christ is made the prerequisite to understanding Jesus' remark (cf. comments on 13:34–35). This makes explicit what is merely implicit in Mark.

5. Matthew's distinctive emphases, as compared with Mark, are two: first, he takes the story to the point where the disciples do achieve some understanding, whereas Mark leaves the outcome hanging. This rounded-off conclusion is typical of Matthew (see on 15:20). Second, in Matthew Jesus specifies that the "yeast" metaphor refers to the "teaching" of the Pharisees and Sadducees, whereas in Mark it extends to Herod but is not explained. From the context of Mark we may deduce that yeast refers to "the disposition to believe only if signs which compel faith are produced" (Lane, ***Mark***, p. 281), evidenced by the Pharisees in the preceding pericope and by Herod a short while before (Matt 14:1–2; Mark 6:14). Matthew may not be very different. Jesus is surely not telling his disciples to beware of *all* the teaching of the Pharisees and Sadducees. These two groups did not always agree; and Jesus can stand with the Sadducees against the Pharisees on the authority of Halakah (rules of conduct derived from interpretations of Scripture, preserved in oral tradition) and with the Pharisees against the Sadducees on the Resurrection (22:23–33). The "teaching of the Pharisees and Sadducees" to which Jesus refers (vv.5–12), therefore, is an attitude of unbelief toward divine revelation that could not perceive Jesus to be the Messiah (vv.1–4) but that tried to control and tame the Messiah they claimed to await. The disciples are to avoid that. That is why the next pericope (vv.13–20) is so important: Peter makes the confession that Jesus is the Messiah, not on the basis of manipulative signs, but by revelation from the Father.

5–7 The setting may be the boat in which Jesus and his disciples cross the lake (v.5; Notes). The conversation reveals the contrasting attitudes of Jesus and his disciples: he is still thinking about the malignity of the Pharisees and Sadducees (vv.1–4), and the disciples are thinking about food (15:29–38), which they forgot to bring. Mark 8:14 says they were down to one loaf. (For "Pharisees and Sadducees" governed by one article, see on v.1.)

"Yeast" (v.6) was a common symbol for evil (see on 13:33) and could therefore be applied to different kinds of wickedness (e.g., Luke 12:1; cf. Exod 34:25; Lev 2:11; 1 Cor 5:6–8), but always with the idea that a little of it could have a far-reaching and insidious effect. The disciples do not understand what Jesus is saying but find his words enigmatic and discuss them (v.7).

8–12 Because they were men of little faith (v.8; cf. 6:30; 8:26; 14:31), they came to an unimaginative conclusion (v.7; cf. Notes). Jesus could not have been talking about bread because he had already shown his power to provide all the bread they needed (vv.9–10; cf. 14:13–21; 15:32–39). He had performed two "food" miracles, and there had been basketfuls of leftovers each time.

Jesus' charge (v.11) against the disciples ran deep. Jesus had already denounced the Pharisees and Sadducees for their particular "teaching" that demanded manipulative signs instead of believing in the bountiful evidence already supplied. And now the disciples are perilously close to the same unbelief in Jesus' person and miracles. The miracles Jesus performs, unlike the signs the Pharisees demand, do not compel faith; but those with faith will perceive their significance. Moreover, it is just possible that Jesus was asking his disciples to recognize symbolic meaning in the numbers of leftover baskets, here reiterated (see on 14:20; 15:37). Jesus is the Messiah who spreads bounty and invites both the twelve tribes of Israel and the Gentiles to his messianic banquet. But whether or not this thought is valid, Jesus' criticism of his disciples was sharp.

Instead of explaining the meaning of his metaphor of the yeast, Jesus repeats it in both Matthew and Mark. This suggests that, great teacher that he is, he is trying to train his disciples to think deeply about the revelation he is giving and is not content to keep on spoonfeeding them. Only Matthew provides the interpretation (v.12); Mark leaves it to the reader to discern (but cf. Matt 15:19–20 and Mark 7:19).

Notes

5 NASB (et al.) handles the tenses awkwardly: "The disciples came to the other side and had forgotten to take bread." Ἔρχομαι (*erchomai*) can mean "I come" as well as "I go," and its aorist participle ἐλθόντες (*elthontes*) can indicate either action antecedent to ("having come," "having gone") or coordinate with ("coming," "going") the main verb. NIV's "When they went . . . , the disciples forgot" is coherent and renders the verbs accurately.

7 The ὅτι (*hoti*) could be (1) recitative: the disciples said, "We didn't bring any bread"; (2) causal: the disciples said, "[It is] because we didn't bring any bread"; or (3) an abbreviated form of τί ἐστιν ὅτι (*ti estin hoti*), introducing a question, "Why did we bring no bread?" In light of v.7a, where the disciples discuss Jesus' enigmatic saying among themselves, the second option is to be preferred.

11. *Peter's confession of Jesus and its aftermath* (16:13–23)

a. *The confession*

16:13–20

13When Jesus came to the region of Caesarea Philippi, he asked his disciples, "Who do people say the Son of Man is?"

14They replied, "Some say John the Baptist; others say Elijah; and still others, Jeremiah or one of the prophets."

15"But what about you?" he asked. "Who do you say I am?"

16Simon Peter answered, "You are the Christ, the Son of the living God."

17Jesus replied, "Blessed are you, Simon son of Jonah, for this was not revealed to you by man, but by my Father in heaven. 18And I tell you that you are
Peter, and on this rock I will build my church, and the gates of Hades will not
overcome it. 19I will give you the keys of the kingdom of heaven; whatever you

bind on earth will be bound in heaven, and whatever you loose on earth will be loosed in heaven." [20]Then he warned his disciples not to tell anyone that he was the Christ.

Broadly speaking Matthew and Mark treat Peter's confession similarly. All three Synoptics (cf. Mark 8:27–30; Luke 9:18–21) immediately follow it by Jesus' prediction of his sufferings, a theme Matthew develops (17:12, 22–23; 20:17–19). (For questions of structure, see on v.21 and Introduction, section 14.)

The connections between this key passage and the rest of Matthew are intricate. Some have already been dealt with (cf. on vv.5–12). Peter recognizes Jesus as the Messiah by revelation, not by signs Peter dictates and thus uses to manipulate the Messiah. That Jesus is the Messiah leads inexorably to his self-disclosure as the suffering Messiah (vv.21–23), a theme anticipated earlier (see on 8:17; 10:24–25; 12:15–21). Moreover the suffering of the Servant is not only redemptive (20:28) but exemplary (16:24–26). Therefore the fourth discourse (18:3–35) is grounded in christology.

Peter's role in this passage has been analyzed hundreds of times and is further discussed below. At the risk of oversimplification, we may classify the positions defended in this century into two classes. The first thinks of Peter as a "typical" disciple who speaks for the other disciples, who in turn represent all believers. Thus everything said about Peter becomes a lesson for all Christians (e.g., R. Walker, p. 118; Strecker, *Weg*, p. 205). The second sees Peter as in some way unique: he becomes a kind of supreme rabbi on whom Jesus builds his church, a rabbi who guarantees and transmits the traditions of Jesus in Matthew's church (cf. esp. Hummel, pp. 59ff.; Paul Hoffmann, "Der Petrus-Primat im Matthäusevangelium" in Gnilka, *Neues Testament*, pp. 94–114; C. Kähler, "Zur Form- und Traditionsgeschichte von Matth.xvi. 17–19," NTS 23 [1977]: 36–58).

In a balanced essay J.D. Kingsbury ("The Figure of Peter in Matthew's Gospel as a Theological Problem," JBL 98 [1979]: 67–83) has shown how both alternatives distort the text. The second will not stand: Matthew's Gospel insists that only Jesus is to be called rabbi (23:8, 10) and that after his resurrection he himself will remain with his disciples to the end of the age (28:20; cf. 18:20). Moreover, if Peter is given power to bind and loose, so also is the church (18:18); and all of Jesus' followers are to be involved in discipling and teaching the nations (28:18–19). Yet the first view is also simplistic. Matthew 16:16–17 is intensely personal, not merely representative. Whatever the precise meaning of these verses, Matthew presents Peter as the "first" disciple to be called (4:18–20; 10:2–4) and now the first one truly to understand that Jesus is the promised Messiah, the Son of God. So these passages honor his "salvation-historical primacy" (Kingsbury's expression), and we must not do less.

For brief comments on problems connected with the authenticity of vv.17–19, see below.

13 Caesarea Philippi was built by Herod Philip the tetrarch (cf. 2:20, 22), who enlarged a small town on a plane 1150 feet above sea level at the base of Mount Hermon, renaming it in honor of Caesar, "Philippi" being added to distinguish it from the coastal city of the same name. It lies twenty-five miles north of Galilee; snow-capped Mount Hermon can be seen on a clear day from as far away as Nazareth, where Jesus grew up. The inhabitants were largely Gentile. Though Jesus exercised some broader ministry here (17:14; cf. Mark 8:34), primarily he gave himself to the Twelve. Matthew omits Mark's casual details (Mark 8:27).

In Mark and Luke, Jesus' question leaves out the "Son of Man": "Who do people say I am?" (For the title, see excursus on 8:20.) This clear self-designation must have been somewhat ambiguous or else Jesus' question would have been fatuous. Which form of the question is original is not certain. But that only Jesus uses the title in the Gospels, and that it can serve as a self-designation with some ambiguous messianic significance, favors the view that Matthew is original, while Mark and Luke preserve the self-designation ("I") but delete the title for fear that their non-Jewish readers, who have learned to see messianic significance in it but not Jesus' self-designation, might think the question odd.

14 Opinion on Jesus' identity was divided. Some thought he was John the Baptist risen from the dead—Herod Antipas's view (14:2). Those who thought he was Elijah saw him as forerunner to a Messiah still to come (see on 3:1–3; 11:9–10; 17:10–13; Mal 4:5–6). Only Matthew mentions Jeremiah, the first of the so-called latter prophets in the Hebrew canon (cf. on 27:9). There may have been late Jewish traditions about Jeremiah's death that supported this identification (cf. 2 Macc 2:1–12; 15:14–15) and it is possible that some onlookers had been struck by the mixture of authority and suffering characteristic of Jesus' ministry and well exemplified by Jeremiah (Bonnard). J. Carmignac ("Pourquoi Jérémie est-il mentionné en Matthieu 16,14?" *Tradition und Glaube,* edd. G. Jeremias et al. [Göttingen: Vandenhoeck und Ruprecht, 1971], pp. 283–98) suggests that Jesus, like Jeremiah, must have seemed to many like a prophet of doom because of his negative prognosis for Israel.

"One of the prophets" testifies to the diversity of eschatological expectations in Jesus' day, some of the people expecting a long series of prophetic forerunners. But no group was openly and thoughtfully confessing Jesus as Messiah. Probably aberrations such as 9:27; 15:22 were considered extravagant devices used by desperate people, not maliciously, but in deep hope that their own needs might be met. What we must recognize is that christological confession was not cut and dried, black or white. It was possible to address Jesus with some messianic title without complete conviction, or while still holding some major misconceptions about the nature of his messiahship, and therefore stopping short of unqualified allegiance or outright confession. If Peter had some misconception (vv.21–23), how much more misconception would there be in disciples outside the Twelve? Thus confessions like those in 9:27; 15:22 may not be so surprising.

15–16 The "you" is emphatic and plural (v.15). Therefore, at least in part, Peter serves as spokesman for the Twelve (as he often does: cf. 15:15–16; 19:25–28; 26:40; Mark 11:20–22; Luke 12:41; John 6:67–70; cf. Acts 2:37–38; 5:29). Peter's confession (v.16) is direct: "You are the Christ" (Mark); "The Christ of God" (Luke); "You are the Christ, the Son of the living God" (Matthew). (For comments regarding Messiah = Christ, see on 1:1.)

Majority opinion assigns "the Son of the living God" to Matthean redaction, a sort of explanatory gloss. Yet this may be premature. Ben F. Meyer (pp. 189–91) has given good reason for accepting Matthew's form as authentic: (1) it better explains the genesis of the other forms, not only in Mark and Luke, but also "the Holy One of God" in John 6:69, than does Mark's "You are the Christ"; (2) "Son of God" may well have had purely messianic significance in Peter's mind (see on 3:17; 11:27; 14:33) even though it came to indicate divinity (Bonnard; cf. excursus on "Son of Man" at 8:20) and (3) other details in this pericope support Matthew's priority (see on vv.17–19). Guthrie (*NT Theology*, pp. 305f.) reminds us that since the other synoptists record the application of "Son of God" to Jesus in other contexts, it is not intrinsically unlikely here.

17–19 Many scholars doubt the authenticity of these verses because they are missing in Mark and Luke. We may note that in addition to positions that simply deny that these words are authentic (e.g., Bultmann, *NT Theology*, 1:45; J. Kahmann, "Die Verheissung an Petrus," in Didier, pp. 261–80), there are more sophisticated options. O. Cullmann (*Peter: Disciple-Apostle-Martyr* [London: SCM, 1953], pp. 158–70) holds that the *saying* is authentic, but not the *setting*, which originally lay during the passion period, in some such place as Luke 22:31–38. R.E. Brown et al. (*Peter*, pp. 85ff.) argue that the origin of this saying lies in some tradition on the Resurrection. And recently Max Wilcox ("Peter and the Rock: A Fresh Look at Matthew xvi.17–19," NTS 22 [1976]: 73–88) has held that these verses spring from some ecclesiastical linking of Jesus as the Son with the "rejected stone" and related testimonia (Ps 118:22–23; Isa 8:14; 28:16), and that the possibility of linking "stone" with Peter's name prompted the transfer of this category from Jesus to Peter. Critical orthodoxy largely concurs that "church" is an anachronism; that the omission of the word "this" in the Greek text of v.17 suggests that the words did not originally stand here (Cullmann); and that words such as "blessed," "my Father," and "in heaven" are characteristically Matthean and are therefore probably inauthentic.

But B.F. Meyer (pp. 185–97) has recently mounted a detailed defense of the authenticity of vv.17–19. Some of his points, plus one or two others, are included below.

1. "Blessed" is not exclusively Matthean; and "my Father in heaven" no more vitiates the authenticity of this saying than it does of the opening line of the Lord's prayer (6:9). This is so of any view of the relation between 6:9–13 and Luke 11:2–4, since a redactional formulation says nothing about authenticity unless we are thinking in terms only of *ipsissima verba*, not *ipsissima vox*.

2. The omission of "this" from the Greek in v.17 does not prove the saying was moved from some other place. Greek transitive verbs often omit the direct object where it is obvious. The verb in question, *apokalyptō* ("I reveal"), is used transitively seven other times in the NT. Three of these require for clarity inclusion of the direct object. Of the remaining four (11:27; Luke 10:22; 1 Cor 2:10; Phil 3:15), where the meaning is so clear that no direct object must be included, only one of the four has it (viz., Phil 3:15). Matthew 16:17 fits the majority usage.

3. The use of "church" is not anachronistic: see on v.18.

4. B.F. Meyer (pp. 189f.) advances good reasons for doubting Mark's priority in this pericope but rightly points out that even if Matthew depends on Mark, this says nothing at all about the historical value of Matthew's redaction (pp. 71f.; cf. Introduction, sections 1–3).

5. The verb "reveal" has its closest links, not with any resurrection text, but with 11:25, where, as in 16:17, "the Father's revealing is correlative to the insight of faith, and the correlation 'revelation/faith' is placed in the present of the ministry" (B.F. Meyer, p. 192). Similar things can be said for the next closest parallel, viz., 11:27.

Though the history of the interpretation of these verses is even more tortuous than the recent history of critical opinion about them, part of it has been well chronicled by Joseph A. Burgess (*A History of the Exegesis of Matthew 16:17–19 from 1781 to 1965* [Ann Arbor: Edwards Brothers, 1976]).

17 For "Blessed," see on 5:3. Jesus is the "Son of the living God" (v.16); Peter is the "son of Jonah" (cf. Notes). Yet Jesus' Father has revealed to Peter the truth he has just confessed. Indeed, no one knows the Son except the Father (11:27; cf. John 6:44), who has now graciously revealed his identity to Peter. Such knowledge could not have originated in "flesh and blood"—a common Jewish expression referring to man as a mortal being (cf. 1 Cor 15:50; Gal 1:16; Eph 6:12; Heb 2:14; cf. Ecclus 14:18; 17:31.) We must neither minimize nor exaggerate this revelation of the Father to Peter. Similar confessions by others do not necessarily evoke similar theological conclusions (e.g., 21:9; 27:54); so Peter's confession assumes a God-given insight deeper than these.

On the other hand we need not suppose that the idea that Jesus was Messiah was here entering the apostles' minds for the first time. If so, Jesus' closest disciples were remarkably obtuse (e.g., see on 5:17–48; 7:21–23; 11:2–6). John's witness is surely sound: the disciples began following Jesus in the hope that he was the Messiah (John 1:41, 45, 49). But their understanding of the nature of Jesus' messiahship was hindered by their own expectations (see on 16:21–23); and they did not come into a full "Christian" understanding till after Easter. This verse marks a crucial stage along that growth in understanding and faith. Partial as it was (16:21–23), Peter's firm grasp of the fact that Jesus is the Messiah set him apart from the uncertainty and confusion of the crowd and could only be the result of the Father's disclosure. Indeed, the depth of Peter's conviction was the very thing that simultaneously made talk of Jesus' suffering and death difficult to integrate and prevented more serious defection when the one confessed as Messiah went to his death on a Roman cross.

18 *And I tell you . . . :* Weiss sees a contrast between Jesus and his Father, as if Jesus were saying, "Just as the *Father* revealed something to you and thereby honored you, so now *I* do the same." But the formula is common enough in places without such a contrast, and this may be an unwarranted refinement. The words simply point to what is coming.

that you are Peter . . . : The underlying Aramaic *kêpā'* ("Cephas" in John 1:42; 1 Cor 15:5; Gal 1:18 et al.) was an accepted name in Jesus' day (see on 4:18). Though B.F. Meyer (pp. 186–87) insists that Jesus gave the name Cephas to Simon at this point, Jesus merely made a pun on the name (4:18; 10:2; Mark 3:16; John 1:42). Yet Meyer is right to draw attention to the "rock" motifs on which the name Cephas is based (pp. 185–86, 194–95), motifs related to the netherworld and the temple (and so connoting images of "gates of Hades" and "church": see below.) The Greek *Kēphas* (Eng. "Cephas") transliterates the Aramaic, and *Petros* ("Peter") is the closest Greek translation. P. Lampe's argument ("Das Spiel mit dem Petrusnamen—Matt.xvi.18," NTS 25 [1979]: 227–45) that both *kêpā'* and *petros* originally referred to a small "stone," but not a "rock" (on which something could be built), until Christians extended the term to explain the riddle of Simon's name is baseless. True, the Greek *petros* commonly means "stone" in pre-Christian literature; but the Aramaic *kêpā'*, which underlies the Greek, means "(massive) rock" (cf. H. Clavier,

"Πέτρος καὶ πέτρα," *Neutestamentliche Studien*, ed. W. Eltester [Berlin: Alfred Töpelmann, 1957], pp. 101–3).

and on this rock . . . "Rock" now becomes *petra* (feminine); and on the basis of the distinction between *petros* (above) and *petra* (here), many have attempted to avoid identifying Peter as the rock on which Jesus builds his church. Peter is a mere "stone," it is alleged; but Jesus himself is the "rock," as Peter himself attests (1 Peter 2:5–8) (so, among others, Lenski, Gander, Walvoord). Others adopt some other distinction: e.g., "upon this rock of revealed truth—the truth you have just confessed—I will build my church" (Allen). Yet if it were not for Protestant reactions against extremes of Roman Catholic interpretation, it is doubtful whether many would have taken "rock" to be anything or anyone other than Peter.

1. Although it is true that *petros* and *petra* can mean "stone" and "rock" respectively in earlier Greek, the distinction is largely confined to poetry. Moreover the underlying Aramaic is in this case unquestionable; and most probably *kêpā'* was used in both clauses ("you are *kêpā'* and on this *kêpā'*"), since the word was used both for a name and for a "rock." The Peshitta (written in Syriac, a language cognate with Aramaic) makes no distinction between the words in the two clauses. The Greek makes the distinction between *petros* and *petra* simply because it is trying to preserve the pun, and in Greek the feminine *petra* could not very well serve as a masculine name.

2. Paronomasia of various kinds is very common in the Bible and should not be belittled (cf. Barry J. Beitzel, "Exodus 3:14 and the Divine Name: A Case of Biblical Paronomasia," *Trinity Journal* [1980]: 5–20; BDF, par. 488).

3. Had Matthew wanted to say no more than that Peter was a stone in contrast with Jesus the Rock, the more common word would have been *lithos* ("stone" of almost any size). Then there would have been no pun—and that is just the point!

4. The objection that Peter considers Jesus the rock is insubstantial because metaphors are commonly used variously, till they become stereotyped, and sometimes even then. Here Jesus builds his church; in 1 Corinthians 3:10, Paul is "an expert builder." In 1 Corinthians 3:11, Jesus is the church's foundation; in Ephesians 2:19–20, the apostles and prophets are the foundation (cf. also Rev 21:14), and Jesus is the "cornerstone." Here Peter has the keys; in Revelation 1:18; 3:7, Jesus has the keys. In John 9:5, Jesus is "the light of the world"; in Matthew 5:14, his disciples are. None of these pairs threatens Jesus' uniqueness. They simply show how metaphors must be interpreted primarily with reference to their immediate contexts.

5. In this passage Jesus is the builder of the church and it would be a strange mixture of metaphors that also sees him within the same clauses as its foundation.

None of this requires that conservative Roman Catholic views be endorsed (for examples of such views, cf. Lagrange, Sabourin). The text says nothing about Peter's successors, infallibility, or exclusive authority. These late interpretations entail insuperable exegetical and historical problems—e.g., after Peter's death, his "successor" would have authority over a surviving apostle, John. What the NT does show is that Peter is the first to make this formal confession and that his prominence continues in the earliest years of the church (Acts 1–12). But he, along with John, can be sent by other apostles (Acts 8:14); and he is held accountable for his actions by the Jerusalem church (Acts 11:1–18) and rebuked by Paul (Gal 2:11–14). He is, in short, *primus inter pares* ("first among equals"); and on the foundation of such men (Eph 2:20), Jesus built his church. That is precisely why Jesus, toward the close of his earthly ministry, spent so much time with them. The honor was not earned but stemmed from divine revelation (v.17) and Jesus' building work (v.18).

I will build my church . . . : Ekklēsia ("church") occurs only here and at 18:17 in the Gospels. Etymologically it springs from the verb *ekkaleō* ("call out from") and refers to those who are "called out"; but usage is far more important than etymology in determining meaning. In the NT *ekklēsia* can refer to assemblies of people in a nonreligious setting (Acts 19:39); and once it refers to God's OT people, the "church" in the desert at the giving of the law (Acts 7:38; cf. Heb 2:12). But in Acts and in the Epistles it usually refers to Christian congregations or to all God's people redeemed by Christ. Therefore R. Bultmann ("Die Frage nach der Echtheit von Mt 16, 17–19," *Theologische Blätter* 20 [1941]: col. 265–79) argues that the use of *ekklēsia* in Matthew 16:18; 18:17 cannot be authentic. It refers to a practicing group of Christians, a separate community, or a Christian synagogue in contrast to the Jewish synagogues, and is presided over by Peter.

K.L. Schmidt (TDNT, 3:525) suggests that the Aramaic term behind *ekklēsia* in Matthew is a late term, *kᵉništā'*, which could mean either "the people [of God]" or "a [separate] synagogue." In fact the strongest linguistic evidence runs in another direction. Whenever *ekklēsia* in the LXX is translating Hebrew, the Hebrew word is *qāhāl* ("assembly," "meeting," "gathering"), with reference to various kinds of "assemblies" (cf. E. Jenni and C. Westermann, eds., *Theologisches Handwörterbuch zum Alten Testament*, 2 vols., 3d ed. [München: Chr. Kaiser Verlag, 1978–79], 2:610–19), but increasingly used to refer to God's people, the assembly of Yahweh.

The Hebrew *qāhāl* has a broad semantic range and is not always rendered *ekklēsia;* sometimes in the LXX it is translated "synagogue" or "crowd." "Synagogue" customarily translates an entirely different Hebrew word (*'ēḏâh*, "corporate congregation"), which the LXX never translates *ekklēsia* (on these words, see DNTT, 1:291ff.). Thus *ekklēsia* ("church") is entirely appropriate in Matthew 16:18; 18:17, where there is no emphasis on institution, organization, form of worship, or separate synagogue. Even the idea of "building" a people springs from the OT (Ruth 4:11; 2 Sam 7:13–14; 1 Chron 17:12–13; Pss 28:5; 118:22; Jer 1:10; 24:6; 31:4; 33:7; Amos 9:11). "Jesus' announcement of his purpose to build his *ekklēsia* suggests . . . that the fellowship established by Jesus stands in direct continuity with the Old Testament Israel" (Ladd, *NT Theology*, p. 110), construed as the faithful remnant with the eyes of faith to come to terms with the new revelation. Acknowledged as Messiah, Jesus responds that he will build his *ekklēsia*, his people, his church—which is classic messianism. "It is hard to know what kind of thinking, other than confessional presupposition, justifies the tendency of some commentators to dismiss this verse as not authentic. A Messiah without a Messianic Community would have been unthinkable to any Jew" (Albright and Mann).

Implicitly, then, the verse also embraces a claim to messiahship. The "people of Yahweh" become the people of Messiah (cf. also 13:41). If the Qumran community thinks of itself as the "people of the covenant," Jesus speaks of his followers as *his* people—*his* church—who come in time to see themselves as people of the new covenant established by Messiah's blood (26:28).

Jesus' "church" is not the same as his "kingdom" (contra Hill, *Matthew*): the two words belong to different concepts, the one to "people" and the other to "rule" or "reign" (see on 13:28–30, 36–43). But neither must they be opposed to each other, as if both cannot occupy the same place in time (contra Walvoord). The messianic reign is calling out the messianic people. The kingdom has been inaugurated; the people are being gathered. So far as the kingdom has been inaugurated in advance of its consummation, so far also is Jesus' church an outpost in history of the final eschatological community. "The implication is inescapable that, in the establishment of the church, there was to be a manifestation of the kingdom or rule of God" (Stonehouse, *Witness of Matthew*, p. 235). When the kingdom is consummated, then Messiah's "assembly" shall also attain the richest blessings Messiah's reign can give. Nothing, therefore, can eliminate Messiah's church or prevent it from reaching that consummation.

The gates of Hades will not overcome it (On Hades, see DNTT, 2:206–8; SBK, 4:1016–29; comments on 5:22; 11:23.) The "gates of Hades" have been taken to represent the strength of Satan and his cohorts (since "gates" can refer to "fortifications," Gen 22:17; Ps 127:5): the church, because Jesus is building it, cannot be defeated by the hosts of darkness. Other scholars focus, not on "gates," but on "Hades" and, turning to Revelation 1:18, think this means that death will not prevent Messiah's people from rising at the last day. But "gates of Hades" or very similar expressions are found in canonical literature (Job 17:16; 38:17; Pss 9:13; 107:18; Isa 38:10) noncanonical Jewish literature (Wisd Sol 16:13; 3 Macc 5:51; Pss Sol 16:2) and pagan literature (Homer *Iliad* 9. 312; *Odyssey* 11.277; Aeschylus *Agam*. 1291; Euripedes *Hecuba* 1) and seem to refer to death and dying. Hence RSV: "The powers of death shall not prevail against it." Because the church is the assembly of people Jesus Messiah is building, it cannot die. This claim is ridiculous if Jesus is nothing but an overconfident popular preacher in an unimportant vassal state of first-century Rome. It is the basis of all hope for those who see Jesus as the Messiah who builds his people.

19 *I will give you the keys of the kingdom of heaven:* As in v.18, the promise goes beyond the days of Jesus' earthly ministry. What Jesus' disciples thought this meant at the time is uncertain. Perhaps they hoped that when Jesus established his earthly reign and defeated the Romans, they would hold major posts under his reign (cf. Bonnard). In the postresurrection period, the nature of this inaugurated kingdom became progressively clearer.

Here, as in 7:21, the "kingdom" (see on 3:2; 5:3) is to be entered. The metaphor therefore changes: from being the rock-foundation of the church, Peter now becomes the one who wields the keys of the kingdom (as Alexander points out, the metaphor would be equally mixed if Jesus–rock–foundation "gives" the keys). The person with the keys has power to exclude or permit entrance (cf. Rev 9:1–6; 20:1–3) There may be an allusion here to the chief stewards of monarchs (Isa 22:15, 22). But we cannot go on without understanding the binding and loosing (v.19b) to which the keys are related.

whatever you bind . . . loosed in heaven . . . : Five separate and difficult questions must be considered to understand the force of this verse, and some answers must be tentative.

1. How are the future periphrastic perfects to be translated? In 1938, J.R. Mantey ("The Mistranslation of the Perfect Tense in John 20:23, Matthew 16:19, and Matthew 18:18," JBL 58 [1939]: 243–49) argued that the perfects in all three instances must have their normal force. The finite perfect in John 20:23 must be rendered "If you forgive anyone his sins, they have already been forgiven"; and when the perfect participle is given its full force in the Matthean passages, the periphrastic future perfect in 16:19 becomes "whatever you bind on earth *shall have been* bound in heaven, and whatever you loose on earth *shall have been loosed* in

heaven" (similarly for 18:18). Thus, as Mantey insisted, there is no evidence for "sacerdotalism or priestly absolution" in the NT.

In the same issue of JBL, H.J. Cadbury ("The Meaning of John 20:23, Matthew 16:19, and Matthew 18:18," pp. 251–54) noted that the six perfects or future perfects in the three passages all occur in the apodosis of a general condition. The question, then, is "whether a perfect in the apodosis indicates an action or condition prior to the time of the apodosis" (p. 251) and, citing 1 John 2:5; James 2:10; Romans 13:8; 14:23, along with certain grammarians (BDF, par. 344; Moulton, *Prolegemona*, p. 271; RHG, pp. 897–98, 908) he denied that this must be so. Although he thought the future an acceptable translation here, he suggested that in Matthew the perfects have the force "shall be once for all" (cf. Allen's "Whatsoever thou bindest *shall remain bound*, etc.").

The matter was picked up by W.T. Dayton ("The Greek Perfect Tense in Relation to John 20:23, Matthew 16:19, and Matthew 18:18" [Th.D. dissertation, Northern Baptist Theological Seminary, 1945]) and once more by J.R. Mantey ("Evidence that the Perfect Tense in John 20:23 and Matthew 16:19 is Mistranslated," JETS 16 [1973]: 129–38). Both works are marred by the tendency to cite quotations from grammarians in their favor without a fair handling of counterarguments. Of more use are Dayton's short lists of periphrastic future perfects in Strabo, Lucian, and some papyri; for all these retain perfect force, even when used in the apodosis of a general condition. This is valuable comparative material, since periphrastic future perfects in the NT are very rare; and there are no finite future perfects at all.

While the question is partly grammatical, it must be noted that, regardless of whether v.19 is translated as an English future perfect or as an English future, there are difficulties in interpretation. If the tense is translated as a future ("shall be bound"), the passage can be taken to justify some form of extreme sacerdotalism without unambiguous defense elsewhere in the NT. But if it is translated as a future perfect ("shall have been bound"), it can be taken to support the notion that the disciple must therefore enjoy infallible communication from God in every question of "binding and loosing," a communication that is the role of the so-called charismatic gifts. Paul Elbert ("The Perfect Tense in Matthew 16:19 and Three Charismata," JETS 17 [1974]: 149–55) introduces them here with no sensitivity to broader questions of context, awareness of anachronism, or consciousness that the gifts do not provide infallible guidance (cf. 1 Cor 14:29). But in neither case do these conclusions *necessarily* follow. More moderate interpretations of both grammatical options are possible. But the extremes must be noted, especially because some give the impression that if the Greek is rendered as an English future perfect, we have eliminated sacerdotalism. The truth is that sacerdotalism will neither stand nor fall by these texts alone, though it may be helped or hindered by them. Meanwhile a future perfect rendering is itself not without theological problems.

Recent commentators and grammarians are divided on this question. Hendriksen, who finds Mantey's way of taking the perfects "artificial," opts for "shall be and shall definitely remain bound/loosed," a variation of Allen; and Hendriksen can scarcely be called a sacerdotalist. Many grammarians treat the perfect participle in this construction as little more than an adjective, with little perfect sense remaining (K.L. McKay, "On the Perfect and Other Aspects in New Testament Greek," unpublished, graciously sent me by the author; Moule, *Idiom Book*, p. 18; cf. esp. Luke 12:52, where it is very difficult to find any perfect force at all ["there will be . . . divided": the parallel future passive in the next verse makes this clear]). But Turner (*Insights*, pp. 80–82; id., *Syntax*, p. 82) challenges these views. In disagreeing with

Allen and Hendriksen, he points out that the future force is restricted to the auxiliary verb *estai* ("will be") and is not found in the participle, which must retain its perfect sense, thereby agreeing with Mantey. Turner further argues that this is even clearer in John 20:23, where the finite perfect, not the periphrastic future perfect, is used. Similarly Albright and Mann say, "The church on earth carries out heaven's decisions, not heaven ratifying the church's decisions," which is something of a caricature of the options.

What Turner (*Syntax*, pp. 82–83) and Zerwick (pars. 288f.) point out, however, is that where finite perfects have some force other than the normal perfect in the NT, they tend to be in well-known stereotyped forms: *oida* ("I know," not "I have known"); *pepoitha* ("I am persuaded"); *hestēka* ("I stand"). Similar is the periphrastic future perfect in Hebrews 2:13: although *esomai pepoithōs* means "I will put my trust" (NIV), not "I will have put my trust," this participle commonly takes on perfect form with present meaning. Likewise, when the perfect has an aorist force (Zerwick, pars. 288–89; as at 13:46), there are normally good reasons for it, as when the verb is defective and has no aorist form (cf. further discussion in BDF, pars. 340ff.).

This leads us to the following conclusion: Where questions dealing strictly with Greek syntax are asked, it seems impossible to reach a firm decision, because there are too many clear instances where perfects, whether finite or participial, have something other than perfect force. But where paradigmatic questions are asked—Why was this word or syntax used instead of something else?—we can make some progress. In John 20:23 the Greek perfects must be taken as retaining their normal force as perfects, because both verbs have acceptable present and future tenses used elsewhere: neither verb exhibits a preferential pattern for the perfect. The perfect participles in the periphrastic constructions of Matthew 16:19; 18:18 are based on the two verbs *lyō* ("I loose") and *deō* ("I bind"). Evidence regarding the latter is ambiguous; it often occurs as a perfect participle in the NT, sometimes as an aorist participle, never as a present participle; so one might hold that its perfect-participle form has purely adjectival or present force in some instances—a debatable point. But the former is unambiguous. *Lyō* has a full range of forms, and it is difficult to see why Matthew did not use either the future or the present participle in a periphrastic future if that was all he meant. This result spills over onto *deō* ("I bind"), since the two verbs are so tightly linked in these verses. But though they must therefore be rendered "shall have been bound/loosed," what that means here awaits the rest of the argument.

2. Does the "whatever" (*ho*) refer to things or people? Formally *ho* is neuter, and "things" might be expected. Moreover the rabbis spoke of "binding" and "loosing" in terms of laying down Halakah (rules of conduct): Shammai is strict and "binds" many things on the people, while Hillel allows greater laxity and "looses" them. It might be argued, then, that in Acts 15:10 Peter looses what certain Judaizers want to bind. Yet despite this, it is better to take the binding and loosing in Matthew 16:19 to refer to persons, not rules. The neuter *hosa* ("whatever") occurs in 18:18, where the context demands that persons are meant. Indeed, Greek often uses the neuter of people for classes or categories rather than for individuals. The context of v.19 supports this; for the keys in the preceding clause speak of permission for entering the kingdom or being excluded from it, not rules of conduct under heaven's rule. Acts 15:10 is scarcely an example of the opposite viewpoint, for there Peter does not proceed by legislative fiat. The church in Acts 15 seeks spiritually

minded consensus, not imposed Halakoth; and James is more prominent than Peter.

3. But exactly what is meant by this "binding and loosing" of persons, and is it absolute? And how is it related to the power of the keys? Substantial help comes from comparing Jesus' denunciation of the teachers of the law in Luke 11:52. There they are told that they "have taken away the key to knowledge" and have not only failed to enter [the kingdom] themselves but have "hindered those who were entering." Clearly, then, by their approach to the Scriptures, Jesus says, they are making it impossible for those who fall under the malign influences of their teaching to accept the new revelation in Jesus and enter the kingdom. They take away "the key to knowledge."

In contrast, Peter, on confessing Jesus as Messiah, is told he has received this confession by the Father's revelation and will be given the keys of the kingdom: i.e., by proclaiming "the good news of the kingdom" (4:23), which, by revelation he is increasingly understanding, he will open the kingdom to many and shut it against many. Fulfillments of this in Acts are not found in passages like 15:10 but in those like 2:14–39; 3:11–26, so that by this means the Lord added to the church those who were being saved (2:45), or, otherwise put, Jesus was building his church (Matt 16:18). But the same gospel proclamation alienates and excludes men; so we also find Peter shutting up the kingdom from men (Acts 4:11–12; 8:20–23). The periphrastic future perfects are then perfectly natural: Peter accomplishes this binding and loosing by proclaiming a gospel that has already been given and by making personal application on that basis (Simon Magus). Whatever he binds or looses will have been bound or loosed, so long as he adheres to that divinely disclosed gospel. He has no direct pipeline to heaven, still less do his decisions force heaven to comply; but he may be authoritative in binding and loosing because heaven has acted first (cf. Acts 18:9–10). Those he ushers in or excludes have already been bound or loosed by God according to the gospel already revealed and which Peter, by confessing Jesus as the Messiah, has most clearly grasped.

4. Does this promise apply to Peter only, to the apostolic band, or to the church at large? The interpretation given so far broadly fits a major theme of Matthew's Gospel: the disciples were called to be fishers of men (4:19), to be salt (5:13) and light (5:14–16), to preach the good news of the kingdom (10:6–42), and, after the Resurrection, to disciple the nations and teach them all that Jesus commanded (28:18–20). Within this framework Matthew 16:18–19 fits very well. Unlike the messianic kingdom expected by so many Jews, which would come climactically without any agreement or action taken by men, Jesus announces something different. In full Christian perspective the kingdom will be consummated in sudden, apocalyptic fashion at the Parousia, when God's actions are final and quite independent of human means. But now the keys of the kingdom are confided to men. They must proclaim the Good News, forbid entrance, urge conversion. They constitute a small minority in a big world; their mission will be to function as the eschatological *ekklēsia*, the people of God Jesus is building within this world. Inevitably the assignment involves them in using the keys to bind and loose. These verses are therefore the result of the partially realized—and one day to be consummated—eschatology implicit in the NT.

Understanding the text thus largely answers the question as to how far the promise applies; for the focus is no longer on the individual and what he does or does not represent but on his place in salvation-history. In one sense Peter stands with the other disciples as fishers of men, as recipients of the Great Commission (notice in v.20 that Jesus warns *all* his disciples, not just Peter, to tell no one). In that sense the disciples stand as paradigms for all believers during this period of redemptive history. But this does not exclude a special role for Peter or the apostles (see on v.18). Peter was the foundation, the first stone laid: he enjoys this "salvation historical primacy," and on him others are laid. This results in certain special roles in the earliest years of the Christian church. But notions of hierarchy or sacerdotalism are simply irrelevant to the text.

Confirmation that this is the way 16:19 is to be taken comes at 18:18. If the church, Messiah's eschatological people already gathered now, has to exercise the ministry of the keys, if it must bind and loose, then clearly one aspect of that will be the discipline of those who profess to constitute it. Thus the two passages are tightly joined: 18:18 is a special application of 16:19. Again, if we may judge from Paul's ministry, this discipline is a special function of apostles, but also of elders and even of the whole church (1 Cor 5:1–13; 2 Cor 13:10; Titus 2:15; 3:10–11)—an inescapable part of following Jesus during this age of the inaugurated kingdom and of the proleptic gathering of Messiah's people. The church of Jesus the Christ is more than an audience. It is a group with confessional standards, one of which (viz., "Jesus is the Christ") here precipitates Jesus' remarks regarding the keys. The continuity of the church depends as much on discipline as on truth. Indeed, faithful promulgation of the latter both entails and presupposes the former.

It appears, then, that the text is not interested in whether Peter's (or the church's) decisions are infallible. Its concern is with the role Jesus' disciples must play within this new phase of redemptive history. To press the "whatever" absolutely not only misunderstands the context but fails to reckon with Jesus' tendency to use absolutist language even when he cannot possibly mean to be taken that way (see on 5:33–37).

5. How is the contrast between "heaven" and "earth" to be understood? Our exegesis determines the answer. Some have understood the contrast temporally: what is bound or loosed now on earth will be bound or loosed then in heaven. But if our remarks on the periphrastic future perfect are correct, then such an interpretation is impossible. Rather, "heaven" (= "God," as in "kingdom of heaven") has revealed the gospel in the person of Jesus the Messiah, and heaven's rule has thereby broken in. Thus Jesus' disciples, in accordance with his gospel of the kingdom, take up the ministry of the keys and bind and loose on earth what has with the coming of the kingdom been bound and loosed in heaven. The thought is akin to, though more comprehensive than, Acts 18:9–10.

20 Jesus' warning his disciples not to tell anyone that he was the Christ does not stem from personal reluctance to accept the title, nor from merely qualified acceptance subject to teaching that he was a suffering Messiah (vv.21–26), still less because all the commands to keep silence are church constructions designed to create a "messianic secret" to explain why Jesus failed openly to present himself to the people as Messiah. The categories are wrong. "Contrary to common misappropriation of the messianic secret, it was not Jesus' purpose to conceal his messianic identity. It was his purpose to set before Israel symbol-charged acts and words implying a persistent question: Who do you say that I am?" (B.F. Meyer, p. 305, n. 59; see also pp. 250; 309–10, nn. 119–20). Jesus steadily refuses to make an explicit messianic claim, refusing to bow to demands for a definitive sign (12:38–39; 16:4) and insisting that the "step into messianic faith would be taken only under the combined impact of his densely symbolic career and of a divine illumination disclosing its sense" (ibid., p. 250; cf. 11:4, 25–26; 16:17).

The disciples are now charged with the same reticence. Having come to faith, they must not go beyond the Master himself in the means and limitations of his self-disclosure. The aim must not be to hide Jesus' identity from Israel or to keep it an esoteric secret but to guarantee (1) that the decisive factors in the conversion of men are not nationalistic fervor and impenitent messianic expectation but faith, obedience, and submission to Jesus; and (2) that the events leading to the Cross are not to be short-circuited by premature disclosure. After the Resurrection there could be unqualified proclamation (cf. 10:27), but not yet. The disciples were beginning to comprehend the first of these two aims; but the second, as the next pericope shows, completely eluded them (cf. comments on 13:10–17, 34–35, 51–52).

Notes

14 On the anomalous mixing of ἄλλοι (*alloi*, "others") and ἕτεροι (*heteroi*, "others"), see BDF, par. 306(2).

17 Βαριωνᾶ (*Bariōna*) is a Greek transliteration of בַּר יוֹנָה (*bar yônāh*), where *bar* means "son of" (cf. English John*son*, Robin*son* et al.). In John 1:42 Peter is called "son of John" (in Gr.; there is no transliteration from the Aram.). Probably Peter was called בר יוֹחָנָן (*bar yôḥānᵉn*, "son of Johanan"), and "Jonah" is a shortened form of "Johanan" whereas Ἰωάννης (*Iōannēs*, "John") is the closest Greek translation of the name.

18 Often cited as a parallel to Peter as a rock is Isaiah 51:1–2. But the analogy is not close: the point of the Isaiah passage is that Israel should remember her poor beginnings and be conscious of Yahweh's goodness toward her. Still less relevant, though formally closer, is the Jewish Midrash on Isaiah 51:1–2, where God before creating the world looks ahead till he finds Abraham and says, "Behold, I have found a rock on which I can build and found the world"; but there the point concerns Abraham's merits and worth, quite clearly not paralleled by Peter in Matthew 16. For rabbinic references and some of the impact of the exegesis on the Targums, see N.A. van Uchelen, "The Targumic Versions of Deuteronomy 33:15: Some remarks on the origin of a traditional exegesis," JSS 31 (1980): 199–209.

b. *The first passion prediction*

16:21–23

21From that time on Jesus began to explain to his disciples that he must go to Jerusalem and suffer many things at the hands of the elders, chief priests and teachers of the law, and that he must be killed and on the third day be raised to life.

22Peter took him aside and began to rebuke him. "Never, Lord!" he said. "This shall never happen to you!"

23Jesus turned and said to Peter, "Get behind me, Satan! You are a stumbling block to me; you do not have in mind the things of God, but the things of men."

21 Kingsbury (Matthew, pp. 7ff.), following Lohmeyer (*Matthäus*) and Stonehouse (*Witness of Matthew*, pp. 129–31), argues strongly that *apo tote* ("From that time"), both here and at 4:17, marks a major turning point in Matthew. Turning point there is, but it is not at all clear that the structure of the entire Gospel is dominated by these twin foci. The same expression is found in 26:16, which marks a turning point in Judas Iscariot's pilgrimage but scarcely a major turning point in the book. On the contrary, the very nature of the expression links what follows with what precedes (cf. Introduction, section 14).

For the meaning of "began," see on 11:7, 20, and compare 16:22. At the very least the verb implies that Jesus gave this explanation again and again. This is not the first time he alludes to his death (cf. 9:15; 10:38; 12:40; cf. also John 2:19; 3:14), but it is the first time he discusses it openly with his disciples. The time for symbols and veiled language was largely over now that they had recognized him as Messiah. That is probably the significance of the change from Mark's *didaskō* ("I teach") to Matthew's *deiknyō* ("I point out," "I show"—not, as in NIV, "I explain"). Jesus had taught the Passion earlier but in symbolic language. Now he shows these things to his disciples clearly. Matthew's verb (*deiknyō*) is equivalent to Mark's clause: "He spoke plainly about this" (8:32).

The prediction is remarkably detailed. Jesus must go to Jerusalem (cf. Luke 13: 33); but the "must" of Jesus' suffering lies, not in unqualified determinism, nor in heroic determination (though some of both is present), but in willing submission to his Father's will. At Jerusalem, the killer of prophets (23:37), he will suffer many things (more details specified in 20:19) at the hands of the elders, chief priests, and teachers of the law—the three groups that largely constituted the Sanhedrin (see on 3:7; 26:59; one governing article, as in 16:1, 6; Pharisees would overlap with the first and third groups). There he would be killed and rise again the third day (see on 12:40).

The parallel in Mark 8:31 uses "Son of Man" language (see on 8:20; 16:13). The authenticity of this and other passion predictions has been widely discussed. Bultmann (*Synoptic Tradition*, p. 151) flatly denies it. Jeremias and Zimmerli (pp. 57ff.) approach the question by examining whether there are any Jewish antecedents to the notion of a suffering Messiah. Hill (*Matthew*) thinks Jesus foresaw confrontation in Jerusalem, typical of the prophets, and the possibility of suffering and death, but doubts that he could have spoken so explicitly. C.F.D. Moule ("From Defendant to Judge—and Deliverer: An Inquiry into the Use and Limitations of the Theme of Vindication in the New Testament," NTS 3 [1952–53]: 40–53) argues that the "Son of Man" (Mark 8:31), related to the "saints of the Most High" in Daniel 7, is vindicated after trial and suffering; so if Jesus takes this title and role to himself, he might well perceive the need to suffer before being exalted (cf. 26:64).

Lindars (*Apologetic*, pp. 60ff.) turns to Hosea 6:2 and suggests that historically Jesus spoke of resurrection, of being "raised to life," in a metaphor, as referring to the restoration of God's people. If so, what is surprising, especially in a book as studded with OT quotations as Matthew, is that Hosea is not mentioned nor his words clearly referred to, even allusively. On the face of it, our texts speak of Jesus' resurrection after being killed, not of Jesus' death followed by the restoration of God's people. Others have suggested that Jesus is thinking of Isaiah 53.

These approaches seek to make some part of Jesus' passion predictions historically credible through some historical antecedent on which Jesus allegedly based his predictions. While this is not wrong, it is too restrictive for dealing with one who claims exclusive and intimate knowledge of the Father (11:27). Is it reasonable to think that Jesus could have predicted the details of his passion only if he read about them somewhere? This is not to question the applicability of some of the OT allusions to him; it is rather to question the historical reductionism of some Gospel research.

How much of Jesus' sayings about his death did the disciples understand before the event? The Gospel evidence points in two complementary directions. On the one hand the disciples understand perfectly well: otherwise, for instance, Peter could not possibly have rebuked Jesus (v.22). On the other hand they cannot believe that Messiah will really be killed because their conceptions of the Messiah do not allow for a Suffering Servant. Therefore Peter dares to rebuke Jesus, and the disciples begin to think Jesus' predictions of his sufferings must be in some way nonliteral (Mark 9:10; Luke 9:45; see on Matt 17:4).

22 Peter's rebuke reveals how little he understands the kind of messiahship Jesus has in mind. "Began" (cf. v.21) suggests that Peter gets only so far before Jesus cuts him off (v.23). Peter uses very strong language. "Never, Lord!" (cf. Notes) is a vehement Septuagintalism. "This shall never happen to you!" renders *ou mē* ("never") plus a future indicative, instead of the expected aorist subjunctive. The future indicative after *ou mē*, which makes a strong expression even stronger, is comparatively rare in the NT (only here and in 15:6; 26:35; Mark 13:31; 14:31; Luke 21:33; John 4:14; 6:35; 10:5; Heb 10:17; Rev 9:6; 18:14), and most of these occurrences have textual variants. Peter's strong will and warm heart linked to his ignorance produce a shocking bit of arrogance. He confesses that Jesus is the Messiah and then speaks in a way implying that he knows more of God's will than the Messiah himself.

23 That "Jesus turned" means "Jesus turned away from Peter" or "turned his back on Peter" (B.F. Meyer) is doubtful: the connection with what follows is too awkward. If Jesus told Peter to get out of his way, even metaphorically, it must have been that Jesus was confronting him face to face, not turning away from him. It is better to assume that Jesus turned toward Peter to speak to him, the detail implying an indelible historical reminiscence. The sharp rebuke is made up of three parts.

1. *Hypage opisō mou, Satana* (lit., "Go behind me, Satan") could, by itself, be a call to discipleship (cf. the same adverb in Mark 1:17, 20; 8:34) and therefore be a sharp reminder for Peter to remember that as a disciple he must follow, not lead. But this ill suits the vocative "Satan." The verb *hypagō* is therefore best taken in the way it is used in Matthew 4:10 ("Away from me, Satan"). It is not simply that Peter should get out of Jesus' sight (so NIV) but, as a stumbling block, out of Jesus' way.

2. A few moments earlier Jesus had called Peter a rock. Now he calls him a different kind of "rock," a *skandalon* ("a stumbling block"; see on 5:29). This is one of several striking parallels between vv.13–20 and vv.21–23 (cf. A. Vögtle, "Messiasbekenntnis und Petrusverheissung: Zur Komposition Mt 16,13–23 Par.," *Biblische Zeitschrift* 1 [1957]: 269). As Satan offered Jesus kingship without suffering (4:8–9), so Peter does the same, adopting current expectations of victorious messianic conquest (Pss Sol 17; cf. HJP, 2:517–25, and bibliography, pp. 488–92). Jesus recognizes the same diabolical source behind the same temptation. For him to acquiesce would be to rebel against the will of his Father. The notion of a suffering Messiah, misunderstood by Peter so that he became a stumbling block to Jesus, itself becomes, after the Resurrection, a stumbling block to other Jews (1 Cor 1:23).

3. Peter was not thinking (the verb *phroneō* ["have in mind," NIV], common in Paul, is used elsewhere in the NT only here, in Mark 8:33, and in Acts 28:22) God's

thoughts (viz., that Jesus must go to Jerusalem and die, v.21), but men's thoughts (viz., that he must *not* go). In vv.13–17 Peter, unlike other men, did think God's thoughts because divine revelation was given him. Here, however, he has switched sides, aligning himself not only with men but with Satan.

Many scholars have thought the contrast between Peter in vv.13–20 and vv.21–23 so remarkable that they have worked out elaborate explanations of it. The most common view is that Peter is a stumbling block during Jesus' earthly ministry but becomes a foundation stone after the Resurrection (Brown et al., *Peter*, p. 94). There is an element of truth in this because Jesus' promise to Peter (vv. 17–19) does look to the future. But it looks to the future on the basis of the revelation Peter has *already* grasped (vv.16–17). This means that historically Peter did and did not understand. Along with the other disciples, he understood much more than the crowds; yet even so he did not reach full understanding till after the Resurrection. The juxtaposition of vv.13–20 and vv.21–23 clearly shows the (at best) qualified understanding of Jesus' disciples at this point in salvation history (Trotter).

Notes

21 The variants are very difficult. Most witnesses support ὁ Ἰησοῦς (*ho Iēsous*, "Jesus"); א* B* cop^sa mss, bo^ offer Ἰησοῦς Χριστός (*Iēsous Christos*, "Jesus Christ"). The latter has early and important but very limited attestation. Its strength is that it admirably fits the context, after Jesus has just been confessed as being the Christ. By the same token a copyist might well think the same. The title in the second reading is very rare, which makes it the *lectio difficilior* ("the harder reading"). Internal evidence is therefore ambivalent. On external grounds alone the first reading is to be preferred. A few witnesses omit both, probably due to accidental deletion, something easily done in uncial scripts where the names were regularly abbreviated to $\overline{\text{IC}}$ and $\overline{\text{XC}}$ respectively.

22 Ἵλεώς σοι, κύριε (*Hileōs soi, kyrie*, "Never, Lord") has been understood two ways.

1. The word *hileōs*, used in the NT only here and in Heb 8:12, is taken to mean "propitious," "merciful," "gracious"; and the entire expression is an abbreviation of something longer, either ἵλεως εἴη σοι ὁ θεός (*hileōs eiē soi ho theos*, "May God be merciful to you") or ἵλεως ἔσται σοι ὁ θεός (*hileōs estai soi ho theos*, "God will be merciful to you"). Coupled with what Peter next says, the rebuke is still there but in rather soft language: "This won't happen to you, Lord, for God will be merciful to you" or "may God be merciful to you" (cf. Moulton, *Prolegomena*, p. 240; TDNT, 3:300–301).

2. It is far more likely that *hileōs* is merely a homonymic rendering of the Hebrew חָלִילָה (*ḥālîlāh*, "far be it from"). This is a common Septuagintalism and has the force in confrontational situations of a very strong "Never!" or "Be it far from you!" or "God forbid!" For references and discussion, see Turner, *Syntax*, p. 309; P. Katz, *Theologische Literaturzeitung* 82 (1957): 113f.; H.St.J. Thackeray, *A Grammar of the Old Testament in Greek According to the Septuagint* (Cambridge: University Press, 1909), 1:38; BDF, par. 128(5).

12. *The way of discipleship*

16:24–28

[24]Then Jesus said to his disciples, "If anyone would come after me, he must deny himself and take up his cross and follow me. [25]For whoever wants to save his life will lose it, but whoever loses his life for me will find it. [26]What good will it

be for a man if he gains the whole world, yet forfeits his soul? Or what can a man give in exchange for his soul? [27]For the Son of Man is going to come in his Father's glory with his angels, and then he will reward each person according to what he has done. [28]I tell you the truth, some who are standing here will not taste death before they see the Son of Man coming in his kingdom."

Matthew omits mention of the crowds (cf. Mark 8:34) and omits Mark 8:38 because he has provided a parallel thought elsewhere (10:33). In v.27 Matthew adds some words from Psalm 62:12. This pericope does two things: (1) after the passion prediction in vv.21–23, it demands the disciples' willingness to deny themselves absolutely, a kind of death to self; (2) yet it assures us that the consummated kingdom will at last come. (For the pericope's structure, see on v.28.)

24 Though addressed to Jesus' "disciples" (see on 5:1–2), the thought is expressed in widest terms—"if anyone." As in 10:33, Jesus speaks of "disowning" or "renouncing" oneself. The Jews renounced the Messiah (Acts 3:14); his followers renounce themselves (cf. Rom 14:7–9; 15:2–3). They "take up their cross" (cf. 10:38): any Jew in Palestine would know that the man condemned to crucifixion was often forced to carry part of his own cross (see on 27:32)—a burden and a sign of death. Though Jesus does not explicitly mention the mode of his death till a few days before it takes place (20:19), the impact of this saying must have multiplied after Golgotha. Death to self is not so much a prerequisite of discipleship to Jesus as a continuing characteristic of it (see on 4:19; cf. John 12:23–26). (On the differences between discipleship to Jesus and discipleship to first-century rabbis, see Bornkamm, *Jesus*, pp. 144f.)

25–26 The logic is relentless: *gar* ("for") begins vv.25, 26, 27. For the sense of v.25, see on 10:39. The orientation is eschatological: saving one's *psychē* ("life," NIV; see on 10:28) *now* will result in losing it *at the end*, and losing it *now* will result in finding it *at the end*. Verse 26 (compare 2 Bar 51:15) furthers the argument by asking twin rhetorical questions, showing the folly of possessing all created abundance and wealth at the expense of one's *psychē*. NIV here changes its rendering "life" (v.25) to "soul" (v.26). This is not necessarily wrong. The abrupt change from the physical to the spiritual is amply attested elsewhere (cf. 8:22; John 4:10; 6:27), but the change in English is perhaps too sharp (cf. Luke 9:25: "his very self"). The focus is still eschatological, and the loss is the eternal loss of one's soul = life = self (on the afterlife, see on 22:23–33). Terminology aside, the bargain is a bad one.

27 Not only Jesus' example (v.24; cf. 10:24–25), but the judgment he will exercise is an incentive to take up one's cross and follow him. The Son of Man (see on 8:20; 16:13) will come "in his Father's glory"—the same glory God his Father enjoys (cf. 26:64; John 17:1–5), another implicit claim to the status of deity—along with his angels, who both enhance his glory and serve as his agents for the eschatological ingathering (13:41; 24:31; 25:31–32; Luke 9:26). They are *his* angels: he stands so far above them that he owns them and uses them. At that time he will reward each person *kata tēn praxin auton* ("according to what he has done"). The language is that of Psalm 62:12, where Yahweh rewards his people; and the Yahweh–Jesus exchange is not uncommon. The use of *praxis* ("conduct," "deeds") is Matthew's rendering of the Hebrew collective singular by a corresponding singular in Greek (Gundry, *Use of OT*, p. 138). For the concept of rewards, see on 5:12.

28 Many of the possible interpretations and difficult issues bound up with this verse have been treated at 10:23 and need not be repeated. Martin Künzi (*Das Naherwartungslogion Markus 9, 1 par: Geschichte seiner Auslegung* [Tübingen: J.C.B. Mohr, 1977]) has an excellent history of interpretation.

The parallel in Mark 9:1 has a somewhat different "before" clause: "before they see the kingdom of God come with power." But this and Matthew's "before they see the Son of Man coming in his kingdom" may mean much the same thing, when it is remembered that "kingdom" is a dynamic concept (see on 3:2), and that "the coming of the Son of Man" also has a wide range of possible meanings (see on 10:23). The principal explanations of this verse may be briefly listed.

1. C.H. Dodd (*Parables*, pp. 53–54) interprets Mark's form of the saying as meaning "there are some who stand here who will never taste death until they have seen that the kingdom of God has come with power." In other words, the kingdom *had come* when Jesus was speaking (perfect participle *elēlythuian*) and the disciples "see"—i.e., perceive—that this is so. But, as many have shown, this is an unnatural way of taking the verb "to see"; and it introduces an insurmountable problem in Matthew, where the participle is *erchomenon* ("the kingdom of God *coming*").

2. Many have held that this verse refers to the Transfiguration, the very next pericope in both Matthew and Mark. The problem is twofold. First, "some who are standing here will not taste death before they see" is an extraordinary way to refer to Peter, James, and John, who witness the Transfiguration a mere six days later (17:1). Second, as magnificent as the Transfiguration was, it is not entirely clear how the Son of Man comes in his kingdom (Matt) or the kingdom comes in power (Mark) through this event.

3. Others take this to refer to the Resurrection or to Pentecost. This view has been strenuously defended, but again it faces the difficulty that even these events are not far enough off to warrant the phrasing "some standing here who will not taste death."

4. Still others (Plummer, Gaechter) think the saying refers to the Fall of Jerusalem (a view this commentary defends for 10:23). The chief problem is that the context does not encourage this interpretation here, as it does in 10:23: there is no mention of the cities of Israel, of persecution in synagogue settings, etc. Indeed, the preceding verse (16:27) appears to refer to the Parousia.

5. Others interpret this verse as referring to the Parousia but draw divergent conclusions. Some think the saying shows that Jesus expected history to end within a few years but was clearly wrong; others that "some who are standing here" refers, not to those then standing there, but to the final generation, prophetically foreseen. If Matthew believed that the former was what Jesus meant, we would expect a Gospel full of the Thessalonian heresy, loaded with expectation of the Second Coming because few of the first generation would still be alive. Instead, the disciples' mission is to continue to the end of the age (28:20). The second alternative means that the words were calculated to be misunderstood by "those who [were] standing here."

6. Recently Bruce Chilton has offered a novel interpretation (*God in Strength*, pp. 251–74; id., "An Evangelical and Critical Approach to the Sayings of Jesus," *Themelios* 3 [1977–78]: 78–85). He argues that "those not tasting death" is a technical reference to "immortals" like Elijah and Enoch (cf. Gen R 9:6; 4 Ezra 6:26); that what Jesus actually said was that the immortals, like Elijah and Moses in the Trans-

figuration scene that immediately follows, do indeed witness the reality of the kingdom, understood as God's revelation on behalf of his people. If this is correct, then the problem of trying to find a suitable period to explain Jesus' prediction in Matthew 16:28 and Mark 9:1 is resolved: there is no prediction left. But Chilton's argument depends on adopting a doubtful reading in Mark 9:1 (cf. Brower, pp. 30–31) and on reasoning that maintains that both Mark and Matthew so completely misinterpreted Jesus that they make him say something quite different from what he really said. The word "here," despite Chilton's contention that it contrasts those not tasting death with Jesus' hearers, is most naturally understood to refer to them.

Moreover, most of Chilton's sources for nailing down "those not tasting death" ("taste death" itself simply means "die"; cf. Heb 2:9) as a special phrase for "immortals" are either certainly or probably late. Whereas some elements of Jewish tradition did treat Moses, along with Elijah, as a "deathless figure," the OT firmly insists that "Moses the servant of the LORD died" (Deut 34:5). Furthermore, what "those who are standing here" will see is, in Mark, the kingdom "coming with power" or "having come with power"—i.e., they see evidence of the kingdom's powerful operation. This is interpreted by Matthew to be the equivalent of "the Son of Man coming in [or perhaps 'with'; cf. BDF, par. 198(2)] his reign"—i.e., they see evidence of the Son of Man's reigning authority. But Chilton's interpretation allows for none of this. In his view the "deathless figures" merely perceive the reality of God's reign; and thus Chilton confuses the kingdom with evidence for the coming of the kingdom.

Jesus refers to those who "will not taste death," but Chilton treats them as if they are generically "those not tasting death." He does this by rightly pointing out that the words do not necessarily mean that those "standing" there will necessarily taste death *after* they have seen the kingdom coming in power. The words *ou mē . . . heōs an* ("not . . . until") reflect a Semitic construction, used in Genesis 28:15, where God says to Jacob, "I will not leave you until I have done what I have promised you," which does not mean God will leave him afterwards. From this Chilton deduces that "will not taste death until ['before,' NIV]" refers to "immortals," or "deathless figures," because the "until" does not necessarily mark the end of something. But this, though correct, misses two crucial points.

First, whether "those standing" must one day die or not, with this expression the part of the sentence *before* the "until" clause always expresses something new or the ending or changing of something. The main clause always demands sequence and change. For example, in the Genesis passage just quoted, "until" may not mean that God will then leave Jacob; but the main clause does mean that God will keep every word of his promises and remain with Jacob, *at least* "until" all the promises have been fulfilled. Likewise in Mark 9:1 and Matthew 16:28, the "until" clause ("before," NIV) does not necessarily mean those "standing" must die; but the verse as a whole does mean they will at some future time witness the powerful operation of the reign of God (Mark), the coming of the Son of Man with his reign (Matthew), and that *at least* until then they will not die. Thus even Chilton's reconstruction does not eliminate the difficulty of determining what time period within salvation is in view. He has sidestepped the problem but not resolved it.

Second, the *ou mē . . . heōs an* ("not . . . until") construction *can* mean that at the "until" the action or state of the first clause will cease (as in 23:39). There are numerous NT occurrences of this construction (5:18, 26; 10:23; 16:28; 23:39; 24:34;

Mark 9:1; 14:25; Luke 9:27; 12:59; 13:35; 21:32); and in addition there are important variations with the same meaning, none more so than Luke 2:26, where it had been revealed to Simeon that he would not see death *until* (*prin an* or *prin ē an* or *heōs an*) he saw the Lord's Christ, after which, apparently, he died. Many of these references give evidence of the termination of the action of the first clause when the time of the "until" clause has passed. Along with comments on the natural force of "here," these data suggest that the best way to take "some who are standing *here* will not taste death *until* they see the Son of Man coming with his reign" therefore depends solely on the meaning of "the Son of Man coming with his reign." If this is a reference to the Parousia, then the "some who are standing here" will not die even then; but in that case Jesus' chronology would be very wrong. If it is a reference to the demonstrable evidences of powerful kingship, then "some who are standing here" will die at some point after seeing those evidences. Moreover it must be said that Chilton's redaction-critical methods, though done with rigor, are so procrustean in distinguishing between the "traditional" and the "redactional" that they can only produce suspect results.

7. It seems best to take 16:28 as having a more general reference—viz., not referring simply to the Resurrection, to Pentecost, or the like, but to the manifestation of Christ's kingly reign exhibited after the Resurrection in a host of ways, not the least of them being the rapid multiplication of disciples and the mission to the Gentiles. Some of those standing there would live to see Jesus' Gospel proclaimed throughout the Roman Empire and a rich "harvest" (cf. 9:37–38) of converts reaped for Jesus Messiah. This best suits the flexibility of the "kingdom" concept in the synoptic Gospels (see on 3:2; 10:23; 12:28) and the present context. Thus 16:28 does not refer to the same thing as 10:23. But the distinction is made, not on the basis that consistency is "the hobgoblin of little minds," but on the basis of context.

This pericope contains an important chiasm:

v.24: challenge to take up the cross and follow Christ in the immediate future
  v.25: incentive—reward and punishment at the Parousia
    v.26: central weighing of values
  v.27: incentive—reward and punishment at the Parousia
v.28: promise of witnessing the kingdom power of Jesus in the immediate future

The setting is quite different from that in 10:23. But if the evidence of the kingdom is seen in the church, this does not mean that the church and the kingdom are to be identified. Rather, at this point in salvation history it is the power of the kingdom working through Jesus' disciples that calls the church into being (see further on 13:36–43). Moreover, as Brower (pp. 32ff.) points out, the larger context also offers important insights. Though the Transfiguration is not the fulfillment of v.28, it is related to it in an important way. Sections that stress suffering and the Cross (16:21–28; 17:9–13) envelop the Transfiguration and bracket this clearest manifestation of divine glory by suffering. The way to glory is the way of the Cross; and the reign of the Son of Man, which "some standing here" will see before they "taste death," will be inaugurated by the Cross.

13. *The Transfiguration* (17:1–13)

a. *Jesus transfigured*

17:1–8

1After six days Jesus took with him Peter, James and John the brother of
James, and led them up a high mountain by themselves. 2There he was transfigured before them. His face shone like the sun, and his clothes became as white
as the light. 3Just then there appeared before them Moses and Elijah, talking with
Jesus.
4Peter said to Jesus, "Lord, it is good for us to be here. If you wish, I will put up
three shelters—one for you, one for Moses and one for Elijah."
5While he was still speaking, a bright cloud enveloped them, and a voice from
the cloud said, "This is my Son, whom I love; with him I am well pleased. Listen
to him!"
6When the disciples heard this, they fell facedown to the ground, terrified. 7But
Jesus came and touched them. "Get up," he said. "Don't be afraid." 8When they
looked up, they saw no one except Jesus.

This passage raises difficult literary, historical, and theological questions. The *literary* questions arise largely from the several important "minor agreements" of Matthew and Luke (9:28–36) against Mark (9:2–8), raising doubts about the adequacy of the two-source hypothesis (cf. Introduction, section 3). These have recently been scrutinized by F. Neirynck ("Minor Agreements of Matthew-Luke in the Transfiguration Story," in Hoffmann et al., pp. 253–66) and judged to be of greater relevance to the tendencies of Matthew and Luke than to source-critical relationships.

The *historical* questions arise because there have been numerous attempts to explain the origin of this story in some setting other than what the evangelists present. Schweitzer (pp. 380ff.) holds that when Jesus' dreams were shattered following the mission of the Twelve (he thought that mission would usher in the kingdom), he experienced an ecstatic, perhaps glossalalic, vision later reinterpreted by his disciples. This historical reconstruction depends on Schweitzer's broader theories, now long discredited (see on 10:23). More influential is Bultmann's view that this story is a misplaced resurrection narrative (*Synoptic Tradition*, p. 259). But this has been decisively rebutted by Robert H. Stein ("Is the Transfiguration [Mark 9:2–8] a Misplaced Resurrection-Account?" JBL 95 [1976]: 79–96), who shows that in language and form the theory of Bultmann and many others will not work.

More recently B.D. Chilton ("The Transfiguration: Dominical Assurance and Apostolic Vision," NTS 27 [1980]: 115–24) has followed up his interpretation of v.28 (details above) by positing that the genesis of the transfiguration narrative is his reconstruction of Jesus' saying behind v.28—viz., Jesus swears by "deathless witnesses" that the "kingdom," the revelation of "God in strength," continues in forceful operation. These "deathless witnesses" were understood by the disciples to be Moses and Elijah, a step not dominical but consistent with it. Then Peter, James, and John, who saw themselves as Aaron, Nadab, and Abihu with reference to the new Moses (i.e., Jesus), emphasized the continuity of Jesus' disclosure with the prophetic revelation of old in this "visio-literary fashion." Chilton's first and essential step we have seriously questioned (see on v.28), and the rest is little more than mere assertion without further supporting evidence. Even if his understanding of v.28 were correct, it is difficult to see on what evidential grounds he holds that 17:1–8 is meant by the evangelist to be nonhistorical.

The *theological* questions arise because the story has so many nuances—allusions to Moses, his experience of glory and his role in redemptive history, Elijah and his role as eschatological forerunner, Jesus' baptism (the Voice from heaven saying much the same thing, cf. 3:17), the Parousia, perhaps the shekinah glory, and others. The narrative is clearly a major turning point in Jesus' self-disclosure, and some attempt must be made to weave these themes together without merely allegorizing the passage. The best recent exposition is that of Liefeld. Also, G.H. Boobyer (*St. Mark and the Transfiguration Story* [Edinburgh: T. & T. Clark, 1942], pp. 1–47) provides a useful survey of theological options.

1 Precise time indicators like "after six days" are rare in the Synoptics apart from in the passion narrative. Luke's "about eight days after Jesus said this" (9:28) is based on a Greek way of speaking and means "about a week later." Numerous suggestions have been made as to why "six days" should be mentioned. Bonnard, following H. Baltensweiler (*Die Verklärung Jesu* [Zürich: Zwingli, 1959]), sees an allusion to the six days separating the Day of Atonement from the Feast of Tabernacles. In this view the first explicit mention of Jesus' passion (16:21–23) occurs on the former day and the Transfiguration, with its "shelters" (v.4) or "tabernacles," on the latter. But it seems highly unlikely that Jesus and his disciples would travel from Caesarea Philippi to this mountain during the feast. Nor is there any direct evidence of its being that time of year. Others see a reference to Exodus 24:16 ("For six days the cloud covered the mountain, and on the seventh day the LORD called to Moses from within the cloud"). Such views are probably too subtle—especially for Luke! The "six days" may simply indicate the time it took to travel from one place (16:13) to another (17:1) and thus establish the fact, noted by all three synoptists, that the Transfiguration took place within a few days of the prediction that Jesus must go to Jerusalem and be killed. The two passages must therefore be read together.

Mount Tabor, the traditional "high mountain," lies south of Galilee; but it is not at all "high" (about 1,900 feet), and going to it would have been a roundabout way of traveling from Caesarea Philippi to Capernaum (vv.22, 24; Mark 9:30, 33). Moreover, according to Josephus it had a walled fortress at its summit (War II, 573 [xx.6]; IV, 54–55 [i.8]). Mount Hermon, rising above Caesarea Philippi, is the most popular alternative (9,232 feet); but it is so high and cold at its summit—if indeed they went to the top—it seems a strange place to pass the night (Luke specifies they descended the next day). Immediately after their descent Jesus and the inner three faced crowds that included "teachers of the law" (Mark 9:14). This is almost inconceivable at Mount Hermon in Gentile territory. Liefeld (p. 167, n. 27) has plausibly suggested Mount Miron (3,926 feet), the highest mountain within Israel and on the way from Caesarea Philippi to Capernaum. The "mountain" calls to mind Moses and Elijah, both of whom received revelation on a mountain (Exod 19; 24; 1 Kings 19), though here part of the purpose was to ensure privacy ("by themselves," Matt 17:1; "all alone," Mark 9:2).

Those Jesus "took with him" (the verb, contrary to some recent expositions, has no obvious connection with master-disciple relations; cf. its use in 2:13; 4:5; 12:45) were Peter, James, and John, the inner circle of the Twelve (see on 10:2; 20:20; 26:37; cf. Mark 5:37) and the continued friendship of Peter and John, Acts 8:14; Gal 2:9 [with a different James]).

2 Moses' face shone because it reflected something of God's glory (Exod 34:29–30). But as for Jesus, he himself was transfigured. The verb *metamorphoō* ("transfigure," "transform," "change in form") suggests a change of inmost nature that may be outwardly visible (as here; cf. Exod 34:29; 2 Bar 51:3, 5) or quite invisible (Rom 12:2; 2 Cor 3:18). That Jesus was transfigured "before them" implies that it was largely for their sakes: whatever confirmation the experience may have given Jesus, for the disciples it was revelatory. As they would come to realize, they were being privileged to glimpse something of his preincarnate glory (John 1:14; 17:5; Phil 2:6–7) and anticipate his coming exaltation (2 Peter 1:16–18; Rev 1:16). Their confession of Jesus as Messiah and his insistence that he would be a suffering Messiah (16:13–21; 17:9) were confirmed. Therefore they had reason to hope that they would yet see the Son of Man coming in his kingdom (16:28). The contrast between what Jesus had just predicted would be his fate (16:21) and this glorious sight would one day prompt Jesus' disciples to marvel at the self-humiliation that brought him to the cross and to glimpse a little of the height to which he had been raised by his vindicating resurrection and ascension.

3 The word *idou* should not be pressed to mean "Just then" (NIV): it is used twice more in v.5 where it stresses the marvel of the experience (see on 1:20). Unlike Mark, Matthew puts Moses before Elijah, giving him slightly greater status; and only Matthew mentions the brightness of the cloud (v.5), reminiscent of the shekinah glory (cf. Davies, *Setting*, pp. 50–56). Both Moses and Elijah had eschatological roles: Moses was the model for the eschatological Prophet (Deut 18:18) and Elijah for the forerunner (Mal 4:5–6; Matt 3:1–3; 11:7–10; 17:9–13). Both had strange ends; both were men of God in times of transition, the first to introduce the covenant and the second to work for renewed adherence to it. Both experienced a vision of God's glory, one at Sinai (Exod 31:18) and the other at Horeb (1 Kings 19:8). Now, however, the glory is Jesus' glory, for it is he who is transfigured and who radiates the glory of Deity. Both suffered rejection of various kinds (for Moses, cf. Stephen's summary, Acts 7:35, 37; and for Elijah, cf. 1 Kings 19:1–9; Matt 17:12). Together they may well summarize the Law and the Prophets. This is the more plausible when we recall that these two figures very rarely appear together in Judaism or in the NT (possibly Rev 11:3; cf. Zech 4:14; J. Jeremias, TDNT, 4:863–64). All these associations gain importance as the narrative moves on and Jesus is perceived to be superior to Moses and Elijah and, indeed, to supersede them (vv.5, 8).

The verb *ōphthē* ("appeared"), sometimes used in connection with Jesus' resurrection, does not in itself suggest a resurrection setting, since Moses and Elijah are the ones who "appear," not Jesus.

4 Peter "answered" Jesus (NIV, "said"): the peculiar verb form (*apokritheis*) may mean that his suggestion was called forth by the circumstances, but more likely it has no force of "response" (see on 11:25). Peter, speaking for the three ("it is good for *us* to be here"), sensing something of the greatness of what he, James, and John are seeing, suggests building three *skēnas* ("tabernacles"; NIV, "shelters"). While the word looks back to the tabernacle in the wilderness, forerunner of the temple, the idea of building "tabernacles" also reflects the Feast of Tabernacles, when Jews built shelters for themselves and lived in them for seven days (cf. Lev 23:42–43). The feast had eschatological overtones. So Peter may have been saying that in gratitude for witnessing Jesus' transfiguration and recognizing the imminent dawn of the Messianic Age, he would build three "tabernacles"—one for Jesus, one for Moses, and one for Elijah.

The rebuke that follows does not offer criticism of Peter's eschatology, nor even of its timing, but is administered solely because what Peter blurted out compromised Jesus' uniqueness. *Jesus* was transfigured; they must bear witness concerning *him* (v.5). Mark says Peter spoke out of fear; Luke that he made his suggestion as Moses and Elijah were about to leave. Mark and Luke point out the foolishness of Peter's remark. Matthew simplifies and so highlights the christological error of Peter.

Mark (9:5) has "Rabbi," Luke (9:33) "Master," and Matthew "Lord." Mark is probably original; Luke translates "Rabbi" by "Master" for his non-Jewish readers; and Matthew probably uses "Lord" in its general sense (see on 7:21), connoting no more respect than "rabbi." But why Matthew's different form of address? Perhaps it is to stress what Peter is doing. Earlier Peter confessed Jesus as Christ and yet rebuked him because Peter did not understand the full meaning of "Christ." Here he again treats Jesus with respect ("Lord") but suggests something that compromises his identity. Matthew's readers know very well that "Christ" means more than messianic political conqueror and that "Lord" would in time include unqualified supremacy. But Peter does not yet know these things.

5 The "cloud" is associated, in both the OT and intertestamental Judaism, with eschatology (Ps 97:2; Isa 4:5; Ezek 30:3; Dan 7:13; Zeph 1:15; cf. 2 Baruch 53:1–12; 4 Ezra 13:3; 2 Macc 2:8; b *Sanhedrin* 98a; cf. Luke 21:27; 1 Thess 4:17) and with the Exodus (Exod 13:21–22; 16:10; 19:16; 24:15–18; 40:34–38). Of the synoptists only Matthew says that the cloud was "bright," a detail that recalls the shekinah glory. The latter eschatological associations (Luke 21:27; 1 Thess 4:17) show Jesus in his role as the one who succeeds Moses the eschatological prophet; the former associations (Ps 97:2 et al.) assure us that Jesus is the messianic King whose kingdom is dawning. But as Liefeld (p. 170) points out, common to both sets of passages and to others as well is the more fundamental idea of the presence of God.

It is uncertain whether *epeskiasen* means "enveloped" (NIV) or "overshadowed" (cf. Exod 40:35). What the Voice from the cloud says is largely a repetition of 3:17, an apparent mingling of Psalm 2:7 and Isaiah 42:1, stressing that Jesus is both Son and Suffering Servant. This is the high point of the narrative (cf. S. Pedersen, "Die Proklamation Jesu als des eschatologischen Offenbarungsträgers," NovTest 17 [1975]: 241–64) (Mark omits the allusion to Isa 42:1; but both Matthew and Luke, not to mention 2 Peter 1:17, attest the connection in different ways: cf. Gundry, *Use of OT*, pp. 36–37.) But if Matthew 3:17 identifies Jesus, this verse in its context goes further and places him above Moses and Elijah.

The additional words "Listen to him"—an allusion to Deuteronomy 18:15—confirm Jesus is the Prophet like Moses (Deut 18:15–18; cf. Acts 3:22–23; 7:37). This does not mean Jesus is another prophet of Moses' stature but the eschatological Prophet patterned on Moses as a type; for, as Liefeld has suggested (p. 173), Moses' primary role here is typological, whereas Elijah's, not explained till vv.9–13, is eschatological. As Moses' antitype, Jesus so far outstrips him that when Moses is put next to him, men must "listen" to Jesus, as Moses himself said. The climax of biblical revelation is Jesus, the Son and Servant God loves and with whom God is well pleased. Even Moses and Elijah (the Law and the Prophets) assume supporting roles where he is concerned. This confirms our interpretation of 5:17–48; 11:11–15.

6–8 The effect of the Transfiguration on the disciples reminds us of Daniel (Dan 10:7–9; cf. also Deut 5:25–26; Heb 12:19). The visible glory of Deity brings terror, but Jesus calms his disciples' fears (cf. 14:26–27; cf. Dan 8:18; 10:18). Mark relates fear to Peter's foolish words; Matthew, to the disciples' response to the Voice from the cloud. Both are psychologically convincing; both make different points in the narrative. In Mark fear helps explain Peter's folly. In Matthew it magnifies the greatness of the Transfiguration. Matthew alone tells us that at the divine splendor the disciples "fell facedown to the ground" (v.6), a prelude to their seeing no one "except Jesus" (v.8). These words are pregnant with meaning. Compared with God's revelation through him, all other revelations pale. Supporting, pointing, prophetic roles such revelation may enjoy; but that Jesus is God's Son (and here Matthew's readers must have remembered chs. 1–2) is primary. Therefore all must "listen to him!" (v.7).

The Transfiguration was largely for the disciples (Jesus brought the inner three to it; he was transfigured before "them"; the Voice spoke to "them": cf. Allison A. Trites, "The Transfiguration of Jesus: The Gospel in Microcosm," EQ 51 [1979]: 77f.). This does not mean that they understood it fully; but it was a crucial step in the symbol-charged self-disclosure of Jesus that would be much better understood (2 Peter 1:16–19) following the Resurrection. For the present, it indelibly confirmed the disciples' conviction that Jesus was the Messiah.

Notes

4 BDF, par. 372(2c), suggests that "If you wish," found only in Matthew, is Hellenistic for "please" (cf. French *s'il vous plaît*).

5 There have been many attempts to relate the words of the Voice from heaven to the story of the near sacrifice of Isaac in Genesis 22, as that story is developed in late Judaism into vicarious atonement motifs. But P.R. Davies and B.D. Chilton ("The Aqedah: A Revised Tradition History," CBQ 40 [1978]: 514–46) have clearly shown that such Jewish traditions did not develop until after A.D. 70.

b. *The place of Elijah*

17:9–13

[9]As they were coming down the mountain, Jesus instructed them, "Don't tell anyone what you have seen, until the Son of Man has been raised from the dead."

[10]The disciples asked him, "Why then do the teachers of the law say that Elijah must come first?"

[11]Jesus replied, "To be sure, Elijah comes and will restore all things. [12]But I tell you, Elijah has already come, and they did not recognize him, but have done to him everything they wished. In the same way the Son of Man is going to suffer at their hands." [13]Then the disciples understood that he was talking to them about John the Baptist.

Luke has no parallel, but see Mark 9:9–13. Matthew omits Mark 9:10; and his handling of Mark 9:12–13 in 17:11–13 is so independent, though complementary, that some scholars think Matthew here draws on an independent source (e.g., Schlatter, Lohmeyer).

9 In Matthew this is Jesus' fifth and last command for the disciples to be silent (see on 8:4). This time Jesus permits his disciples to tell everything after the Son of Man (see excursus on 8:20) "has been raised from the dead." Jesus could scarcely have attached this permission to earlier warnings to keep silent (16:20), since he had not yet spoken clearly about his sufferings and death. Nevertheless the same salvation-historical change—first silence, then proclamation—occurs as early as 10:27.

The command must have been in some ways disappointing and its lifting a delight. Why did Jesus impose it? Probably for two principal and complementary reasons:

1. The story would only stir up superficial political messianism, already a menace. If Jesus' closest disciples found it hard to understand a suffering and dying Messiah, how would the crowds fare—till after the Resurrection?

2. The strongest evidence for Jesus' messiahship would be his resurrection, by which he "was declared with power to be the Son of God" (Rom 1:4). Premature self-disclosure in a direct fashion, without the supreme "sign of Jonah," the Resurrection (see on 12:40), would not only foster false expectations but would also quickly disillusion those who held them. Thus with his prospective converts in mind, Jesus knew it was better for their sakes to wait till after the Resurrection before allowing Peter, James, and John to tell what they had seen.

This does not mean that Jesus' full glory could be known only through the Resurrection. On the contrary, it means that though his true glory antedated the Resurrection and was revealed to three intimates before the Passion, it could be made known to others only after the Resurrection.

10 Why did the disciples ask this question, connecting it (in Matthew) with *oun* (normally a logical connective, "therefore," "then")? There are two false solutions:

1. If Jesus was the Messiah, how were the disciples to answer the objection of the scribes that Elijah must *precede* Messiah's coming (Mal 4:5–6; see on 11:7–15; M *Eduyoth* 8:7; M *Baba Metzia* 3:5; SBK, 4:764–98)? In this view the *oun* follows the fact of Jesus' messiahship and the disciples' acceptance of Jesus' reiteration of his death and resurrection: *because* the disciples understand who Jesus is, they ask why, therefore, the scribes insist Elijah precedes Messiah, since apparently Elijah has not yet appeared. This interpretation is intrinsically unlikely, as Mark's account shows: the disciples are there pictured "discussing what 'rising from the dead' meant" (Mark 9:10), thereby showing they did *not* truly understand what Jesus was talking about; and as a result of this discussion, they ask the question in Mark 9:11 and Matthew 17:10. Commentators on Mark assume this is a second relevant question but do not show how it ties in with the disciples' discussion. Trench (*Studies,* p. 222) goes so far as to say that the disciples do not venture to raise the first subject and so move on to this one; Lagrange says Matthew omits Mark 9:10 because that text leads nowhere. Yet a tight connection can be established.

2. A few scholars have suggested that the disciples' question was prompted by an assumption that Elijah's appearance during the Transfiguration was itself the fulfillment of Malachi 4:5; and then the question becomes, Why did Messiah (Jesus) appear before Elijah did, when the scribes say the order should be reversed (B.F. Meyer; Robertson, 1:141)? But this interpretation suffers from the weakness of the

former view (viz., that the disciples properly understand Jesus' teaching of 17:9 and par.), while resting on the dubious assumption that the disciples would interpret this brief vision of Elijah as the fulfillment of a prophecy that promised that Elijah would "turn the hearts of the fathers to their children, and the hearts of the children to their fathers" (Mal 4:6).

The real connection is deeper. Elijah was expected to restore all things—to bring about a state of justice and true worship. If that were so, how could it be that Messiah would be killed in such a restored environment—killed, Jesus had told them only a week before, by elders, chief priests, and teachers of the law (16:21)? This interpretation makes sense both of Matthew's *oun* ("therefore") and of Mark 9:10. If Jesus as Messiah (whose messiahship the disciples do not now doubt) must *suffer*, then how could it be said that Elijah must first come *to restore all things?* Their confusion is not merely chronological, though that may be involved; it is their inability to find a framework in which they can believe that the Messiah could die.

11–12 Jesus' answer confirms this interpretation. He approves the teaching of the scribes but insists that another fact must be taken into account. NIV's "To be sure, . . . But" structure accurately reflects this duality (Gr. *men, . . . de*). On the one hand, Elijah comes "first" (*prōton*, in some MSS) and "will restore all things" (v.11; the combination of present and future tenses is less consistent than Mark 9:12 but reflects the OT prophecy; see Zerwick, par. 281). John's mission was a success (3:5–6; 14:5); but, on the other hand, "restore all things" must not be taken absolutely. The Baptist stood in succession of the OT prophets who were persecuted and even killed. The unrecognized fact is that although the scribes' *interpretation* is right—Elijah must precede the Messiah—their grasp of recent *history* is wrong, for Elijah has already come (v.12; cf. 11:14; Luke 1:17); but the people in general and the scribes and leaders in particular did not recognize him and did to him "everything they wished"—a vague expression hinting at John's rejection by most Jewish leaders (cf. 21:24–27) and his death, for which the Jewish leaders were not directly responsible.

Jesus' point is general: the Baptist (Elijah) did fulfill his mission, but he was killed doing it. "In the same way the Son of Man is going to suffer [cf. BDF, par. 315] at their hands" (v.12b). If the Baptist's restoration of "all things" did not prevent his own death, why should Messiah be any better received?

13 Matthew's conclusion, not found in Mark, has provoked much speculation. G. Barth (Bornkamm, *Tradition*, p. 106) takes it as further evidence for his idea that in Matthew "understanding" is essential to discipleship. Others think it a turning point in Matthew's narrative—the disciples now arrive at true understanding (Klostermann; Trilling, p. 92). Still others hold that this introduces a split between what the disciples understand and the teachers of the law don't (McNeile; Schweizer; Frankmölle, p. 151; Meier, *Vision*, p. 123). Though this has some validity, there are two other factors: (1) Matthew again rounds off a pericope by returning to the question first raised (see on 15:20); and (2) what the disciples understand is that John the Baptist is Elijah. It is not at all clear, however, that they have understood much more about the death and resurrection of the Son of Man, and it becomes very obvious during the passion narrative that they have not understood (cf. esp. 26:50–56). In short, this pericope marks another small step in the understanding of Jesus' disciples.

Notes

9 Because Matthew has τὸ ὅραμα (*to horama,* lit., "the vision"; NIV, "what you have seen") for Mark's ἃ εἶδον (*ha eidon,* "what they had seen," NIV), many suggest that Matthew is seeking to explain the Transfiguration in acceptable terms to his readers. But *horama* does not necessarily mean "vision" as a result of a dream or a trance; it can simply refer to what is seen (BAGD, s.v.). Therefore too much should not be made of the difference between the two expressions.

14. *The healing of an epileptic boy*

17:14–20[21]

14When they came to the crowd, a man aproached Jesus and knelt before him.
15"Lord, have mercy on my son," he said. "He has seizures and is suffering greatly. He often falls into the fire or into the water. 16I brought him to your disciples, but they could not heal him."

17"O unbelieving and perverse generation," Jesus replied, "how long shall I stay with you? How long shall I put up with you? Bring the boy here to me."
18Jesus rebuked the demon, and it came out of the boy, and he was healed from that moment.

19Then the disciples came to Jesus in private and asked, "Why couldn't we drive it out?"

20He replied, "Because you have so little faith. I tell you the truth, if you have faith as small as a mustard seed, you can say to this mountain, 'Move from here to there' and it will move. Nothing will be impossible for you."

All three synoptists (cf. Mark 9:14–29; Luke 9:37–43) put this miracle right after the descent from the Mount of Transfiguration. Matthew's account is much shorter than Mark's, which has led some to think Matthew used independent information here. It introduces v.20 (the thrust of which occurs again at 21:21) and thus makes faith pivotal in the narrative. The contrast between the glory of the Transfiguration and Jesus' disciples' tawdry unbelief (see v.17) is part of the mounting tension that magnifies Jesus' uniqueness as he moves closer to his passion and resurrection.

14–16 Matthew's account, with its sudden introduction of the crowd (v.14), clearly presupposes some fuller narrative (cf. Mark). The word for "knelt" (*gonypeteō,* used in the NT only here and at 27:29; Mark 1:40; 10:17) has no overtones of worship but suggests humility and entreaty. For "Lord" (v.15; Mark has "Teacher"), see on 8:2; 17:4. *Selēniazetai* ("is an epileptic") occurs only twice in the NT (see on 4:24). Mark 9:18–20 describes the boy's symptoms more vividly. "Epilepsy" in this instance is associated with demon possession (see on 8:28). The "disciples" who are unable to heal him are presumably the nine left behind when Jesus took Peter, James, and John with him when he was transfigured.

The disciples' failures are a recurring theme throughout this section (14:16–21, 26–27, 28–31; 15:16, 23, 33; 16:5, 22; 17:4, 10–11). This failure in their healing ministry at first seems strange, since Jesus had clearly given them power to heal and exorcise demons (10:1, 8). Yet it is part of the pattern of the disciples' advance and failure. In other situations they had shown lack of faith (14:26–27, 31; 15:5, 8)—a reminder that their power to do kingdom miracles was not their own but, unlike magic, was entirely derivative and related to their own walk of faith.

17–18 Jesus' response is reminiscent of Deuteronomy 32:5, 20. *Apistos* (v.17) can mean either "untrustworthy" or "unbelieving." The latter is dominant here (cf. v.20); yet it does not mean "this generation" has no faith whatsoever but that unbelief is characteristic of "this generation." The perfect passive participle *diestrammenē* ("perverse") probably has adjectival force, rather than denoting a state consequent on some previous action (see on 16:19). Juxtaposing "perverse" and "unbelieving" implies that the failure to believe stems from moral failure to recognize the truth, not from want of evidence, but from willful neglect or distortion of the evidence. *Diastrephō* ("to pervert") is used seven times in the NT (cf. Luke 9:41; 23:2; Acts 13:8, 10; 20:30; Phil 2:15). In the last of these, Paul applies to the entire world the same words Jesus uses here.

But what does "generation" (*genea*) cover? Assuredly it extends Jesus' excoriation beyond the disciples (cf. also 11:16; 12:39–42; 16:4; 23:36; 24:34). But it goes past the evidence to hold with R. Walker (pp. 35ff.) that the word here means "race," and therefore that the Jews are henceforth excluded from salvation, or to say with Frankmölle (pp. 21ff.) that Israel alone is being addressed. That the disciples' unbelief is central to Jesus' exasperation is made clear by Matthew's omitting Mark 9:23–24; if his description extends beyond them to the entire contemporary generation, it must principally extend also to all guilty of the same unbelief, regardless of their race.

The rhetorical questions—"How long shall I stay with you? How long shall I put up with you?"—express not only personal disappointment but also Jesus' consciousness of his heavenly origin and destiny. His disciples' perverse unbelief is actually painful to him. He must endure ("put up with," NIV) it, though this theme is stronger in Mark than in Matthew (cf. Mark 8:12 and Matt 16:4; Mark 3:5 and Matt 12:13). As for the miracle, Matthew describes it succinctly, leaving no doubt of Jesus' power to heal and exorcise demons (v.18). The boy is healed "from that moment" (lit., "from that hour"; cf. 9:22; 15:28).

19–20 [21] The disciples, presumably the nine who had tried and failed (v.16), ask Jesus, in private (cf. also Mark 9:28), why "we" (emphatic) could not drive out the demon (v.19). The reason, Jesus says, is because of their *oligopistia* ("little faith," v.20; cf. Notes). Despite the etymology of the word, it probably does not refer so much to the littleness of their faith as to its poverty (Bonnard). Little faith, like a little mustard seed, can be effectual; poor faith, like that of the disciples' here, is ineffectual. The noun occurs only here in Matthew, but the cognate adjective occurs at 6:30; 8:26; 14:31; 16:8, and always refers to disciples. Removal of mountains was proverbial for overcoming great difficulties (cf. Isa 40:4; 49:11; 54:10; Matt 21:21–22; Mark 11:23; Luke 17:6; 1 Cor 13:2). Nothing would be impossible for them—a promise that, like its analogue in Philippians 4:13, is limited by context, not by unbelief. Here it refers to the accomplishment of the works of the kingdom for which they had been given authority.

Jesus' answer in Matthew is not the same as the one in Mark 9:29 ("This kind can come out only by prayer"); but if the comment on *oligopistia* ("poverty of faith") is correct, then at least the two answers are complementary, each shedding light on the other. At a superficial level the disciples did have faith: they expected to be able to exorcise the demon. They had long been successful in this work, and now they are surprised by their failure. But their faith is poor and shoddy. They are treating the authority given them (10:1, 8) like a gift of magic, a bestowed power that works *ex opere operato*. In Mark, Jesus tells them that this case requires prayer—not a form or an approved rite, but an entire life bathed in prayer and its concomitant faith. In Matthew, Jesus tells his disciples that what they need is not giant faith (tiny faith will do) but true faith—faith that, out of a deep, personal trust, expects God to work.

Notes

---

14 The genitive absolute here, in v.26, and in Acts 17:14 is defective—a participle without a substantive (cf. Zerwick, par. 50; Moule, *Idiom Book*, p. 203). This evokes the introduction of a pronoun in many later MSS, or a change in the participle to the nominative singular in a few of them.

17 In exclamations expressing very strong emotion, ὦ (ō, "O") is not restricted to the vocative but may color an entire sentence, which is often, as here, a question (cf. BDF, par. 146[2]).

18 For the confusion between the prepositions ἀπό (*apo,* "from," "away from") and ἐκ (*ek,* "from," "out from") in Hellenistic Greek, see on 3:16.

20 'Ολιγοπιστίαν (*oligopistian,* "little faith," or, better, "poor faith") is read by ℵ B H f[1] f[13] 33 700 892 et al., and ἀπιστίαν (*apistian,* "faithless," as in v.17) by the rest. But the first reading has strong witnesses; it is a NT *hapax legomenon* (single occurrence); its cognate is distinctively, if not exclusively, Matthean (6:30; 8:26; 14:31; 16:8); and the change to the second reading may well have been prompted by v.17, where the text is firm.

21 "But this kind does not go out except by prayer and fasting" is omitted by a powerful combination of witnesses. It is obviously an assimilation to the synoptic parallel in Mark 9:29. There is no obvious reason why, if original, it should have been omitted; and textual harmonization is quite demonstrably a secondary process.

---

15. *The second major passion prediction*

17:22–23

[22]When they came together in Galilee, he said to them, "The Son of Man is going to be betrayed into the hands of men. [23]They will kill him, and on the third day he will be raised to life." And the disciples were filled with grief.

This is the second major passion prediction (see on 16:21–24), though there are earlier allusions to Jesus' death (9:15; 10:38; 12:40) and one intervening specific reference (17:12b). Jesus not only foresees the inevitability of his death but, precisely because he knows this to be the Father's will (26:39), recognizes it as an essential part of the divine plan. But that death issues in the Resurrection.

22 Thompson (pp. 13ff.) finds here the beginning of a new literary unit, ending at 18:35, based partly on the references to Galilee here and at 19:1. But the departure from Galilee (19:1) not only ends this brief stay but also this entire period of Jesus' northern ministry (4:23–25). From 19:1 on, Jesus moves toward Jerusalem and

Judea. "When they came together" (the best reading) does not necessarily suggest new activities but the general time when Jesus and the inner circle of disciples joined the other nine in Galilee (see on vv.1, 14–20). No sooner are they all together after the Transfiguration than Jesus again takes up the theme he introduced to them earlier (16:21–23). The verb *paradidosthai* ("to be betrayed") is doubly ambiguous. First, it can have either a weak meaning ("to hand over") or a strong meaning ("to betray"), depending on context; second, the passive ("to be handed over") is perhaps a studied ambiguity leaving it unclear whether God or Judas Iscariot is the one who hands Jesus over or betrays him respectively.

23 Mark and Luke say the disciples do not understand. Matthew, adept at fine characterization, establishes the same point by noting the disciples' grief. They are beginning to absorb the announcement of Jesus' death, but of his resurrection they have no comprehension.

16. *The temple tax*

17:24–27

[24]After Jesus and his disciples arrived in Capernaum, the collectors of the two-drachma tax came to Peter and asked, "Doesn't your teacher pay the temple tax?"

[25]"Yes, he does," he replied.

When Peter came into the house, Jesus was the first to speak. "What do you think, Simon?" he asked. "From whom do the kings of the earth collect duty and taxes—from their own sons or from others?"

[26]"From others," Peter answered.

"Then the sons are exempt," Jesus said to him. [27]"But so that we may not offend them, go to the lake and throw out your line. Take the first fish you catch; open its mouth and you will find a four-drachma coin. Take it and give it to them for my tax and yours."

This incident is peculiar to Matthew (cf. Mark 9:33 for geographical detail). Its significance in Matthew depends heavily on its interpretation at several critical points.

24 Although the point is disputed (see on v.25), the *didrachma* (lit., "two drachmas") was probably not a civil tax in support of Rome (cf. on 22:15–22) but a Jewish "tax" levied on every male Jew between the ages of twenty and fifty in support of the temple and its services. The *didrachma,* worth one-half a *statēr* or shekel, was seldom minted at this time; and probably two people joined to pay a *tetradrachma* ("a four-drachma coin," v.27) or shekel. Originally half a shekel was levied on each Jew at every census (Exod 30:11–16), the money going to support the tabernacle; after the Exile one-third of a shekel was gathered annually. In Jesus' day the amount was two drachmas (half a shekel) annually. This is well attested in both Josephus (Antiq. III, 193–96 [viii.2]; XVIII, 312 [ix.1]) and Mishnah (*Shekalim*). The imposition of this "tax" lacked the sanction of Roman law, but it was understood that the Jews would pay it.

25–26 Peter's defense of Jesus (v.25) is misguided. Once they are alone in the house (perhaps Peter's; cf. 4:13; 8:14), Jesus takes the initiative—whether he overheard

Peter's response or knew it supernaturally is unclear—and asks Peter a provocative question. The vast literature on this pericope stems largely from Jesus' question being cast in *civil* terms: "kings of the earth," "duty," "taxes." The majority view today (e.g., Kilpatrick, *Origins*, pp. 41f.; Walker, pp. 101–3; Bonnard; Hill, *Matthew*) holds that the original question was recast in the period after A.D. 70 (when Matthew is alleged to have been writing) to address questions faced by Christians about taxes paid to Rome. The effect of the pericope, then, is like that of 22:15–22, though Jesus' reported answer here is anachronistic. Jesus is made to say that the Son of God, and therefore Christians, *need* not pay taxes to Rome because of their allegiance to God but *should* do so in order not to cause offense. This will not do, for in Jesus' reply the "king" who collects the tax is Jesus' "Father." Therefore this cannot refer to Rome.

Others (Thompson, pp. 50–68) suggest that this is the tax paid the post-Jamnia patriarchate and that the question Matthew is facing is whether Christians at his time of writing should bow to Jewish religious authority. This means not only that Jesus' question and Peter's answer are anachronistic but that the redaction here is inept. Would Jews at the end of the first century think of the Jamnia rabbis as kings or of Jesus Messiah as their son? The suggestion that the tax is the one imposed by Vespasian in support of the temple of *Jupiter Capitolinus* after the Fall of Jerusalem (Jos. War VII, 218 [vi.6]—so H.W. Montefiore [cf. Hill, *Matthew*] and others) is incredible. No Christian willingly advocated direct subsidy of pagan idolatry in order not to offend Rome, and on this reading Jesus' question becomes even more obscure.

Because of such difficulties, Richard J. Cassidy ("Matthew 17:24–27—A Word on Civil Taxes," CBQ 41 [1979]: 571–80) argues that the entire pericope deals, not with the temple tax, but with civil taxes. The terminology of v.25 supports him; but again it is less than clear how sonship to an imperial "king" fits Jesus.

It is better to allow the most likely interpretations of both v.24 and v.25 to stand —temple tax and civil tax respectively—but to recognize that, whereas v.24 establishes the topic of the entire pericope, v.25 is parabolic. This is suggested by the generalized "kings of the earth"—scarcely an adequate way to refer to Caesar. The point is that, just as royal sons are exempt from the taxes imposed by their fathers, so too Jesus is exempt from the "tax" imposed by his Father. In other words Jesus acknowledges the temple tax to be an obligation to God; but since he is uniquely God's Son, therefore he is exempt (v.26). The focus of the pericope is thus supremely christological and, unlike 22:15–22, says nothing about responsibilities to Caesar.

27 Exempt though he is, Jesus will pay the tax so as not to offend (for the verb, see on 5:29). Thus he sets an example later followed by Paul (1 Cor 8:13; 9:12, 22). The plural "we" and the four-drachma coin to pay for Jesus and Peter at first sight makes the above interpretation seem difficult. In what sense are we to suppose that Peter's reason for paying the tax is akin to Jesus'? Part of the explanation may lie in the freedom Jesus extends to his disciples: e.g., he alone is Lord of the Sabbath, and this has implications for his disciples (see on 12:1–8). More important, Jesus here implicitly frees his followers from the temple tax on the grounds that they, too, will belong to the category of "sons," though derivatively.

Both the christological implication and the relevance to Peter and the disciples are made clear in the course of the narrative. Jesus has just been declared God's unique Son (v.5); yet his glory is veiled as he moves toward betrayal and death, thus establishing a pattern of humility for his followers (18:1–5). At the same time Jesus' death and resurrection have again been introduced (vv.22–23), a foretaste of the lengthy passion and resurrection narratives about to begin and the means by which the Son of Man, in giving his life "a ransom for many" (20:28), completes the redemptive act inaugurating the gathering of his "church" (16:18; 28:18–20). At that point the redemptive-historical significance of the temple will end. Its claims for the two-drachma tax may continue till its destruction forty years later; the sons of God (cf. 5:9) are exempt. But that time is not yet. Like so many of Jesus' actions at this turning point, the full significance of what Jesus was saying could not be grasped even by Peter till after the Resurrection.

The miracle itself has no close canonical parallel. This is the only place in the NT where a fish is caught with a hook (nets were normally used). Extravagant symbolism for "fish" and "lake" (e.g., Neil J. McEleney, "Mt 17:24–27—Who Paid the Temple Tax?" CBQ 38 [1976]: 189–92) is fanciful. This miraculous way of paying the tax is something only Jesus could do; it therefore suggests that though Jesus as the unique Son is free from the law's demands, he not only submits to them but makes provision, as only he can, for the demands on his disciples (cf. Gal 4:4–5)—and this right after a passion prediction (17:22–23)! Perhaps, too, we are reminded again of Jesus' humility: he who so controls nature and its powers that he stills storms and multiplies food now reminds Peter of that power by this miracle, while nevertheless remaining so humble that he would not needlessly cause offense (cf. 11:28–30; 12:20). The lesson in humility is for Peter and the other disciples. We have no evidence that the tax collectors witnessed it. (The nonhealing miracles in Matthew are almost always for the sake of the disciples: see Gerhardsson, *Mighty Acts*). But humility is about to be explained to the disciples in some detail (18:1–35).

Notes

---

26 As in v.14, the genitive absolute is defective and has led to many variants (cf. Metzger, *Textual Commentary*, p. 46).

27 Although some (e.g., Zerwick, par. 93) suggest ἀντί (*anti*, "instead of," "in substitution for") here has the force of ὑπέρ (*hyper*, "on behalf of"), it is perhaps better to think of Exod 30:11–16 as the background, remembering that this tax was perceived as a ransom payment *instead* of the person (cf. Turner, *Insights*, p. 173).

B. *Fourth Discourse: Life Under Kingdom Authority* (18:1–19:2)

1. *Setting*

18:1–2

[1]At that time the disciples came to Jesus and asked, "Who is the greatest in the kingdom of heaven?"

[2]He called a little child and had him stand among them.

This fourth discourse, like the previous three, is bracketed by remarks suggesting that it was delivered on the one occasion specified (see on 5:1; 7:28–29). The chapter parallels Mark 9:33–50 to some extent but omits Mark 9:38–41 (cf. Matt 10:42). The differences between Mark and Matthew are so great that some scholars assume separate sources (Lohmeyer) or wisely advocate cautious agnosticism (Thompson, pp. 147–51).

Many writers compare Matthew 18 with 1QS, the "Manual of Discipline" at Qumran, and interpret it as regulation for the life of the Christian community. But two major reservations forbid too easy a comparison.

1. There is very little in Matthew 18 that has the flavor of regulation and much that deals with principles. The contrasts with 1QS are far more noticeable than the similarities. Even vv.15–17, the closest approximation to "regulation," is far less concerned with mechanical details than with the importance and means of reconciliation. And the whole chapter shows up the carnality of the opening question (v.1) and establishes a radical set of values for greatness in the kingdom.

2. The Qumran covenanters had little doubt about their identity or place in God's eschatological scheme. But here we are dealing with disciples at a critical turning-point in salvation history, men of seriously defective understanding who remain such till after the Cross.

1–2 Mark (9:33–38) says that the disciples were disputing along the way, and when challenged they fell silent. Luke (9:46–48) says Jesus discerned their thoughts. It is not difficult or unnatural to suppose that Jesus detected their rivalry (Luke), challenged them, and thereby silenced them (Mark), and that they then blurted out their question (Matthew). Alternatively Matthew uses this brief question to summarize what was truly on their minds.

"At that time" (lit., "hour," v.1) may only mean "in that general phase of the ministry" (cf. 10:19; 26:45), but it alerts the reader to the transition from what precedes. "At that time," when Jesus has again spoken of his suffering and death, the disciples' grief (17:23) proves short lived; and they busy themselves with arguing about who is greatest in the kingdom. Jesus has already said that there will be distinctions in the kingdom (5:19; cf. also 1QS 3:19–25; 6:9–13) and recently three of them have been specially favored (17:1–3), while Peter has been repeatedly singled out (14:28–29; 15:15; 16:16–18, 22–23; 17:4, 24–27)—though sometimes for rebuke! Perhaps these things set off the dispute, which continues in the ambition of James, John, and their mother to the period right before the Cross (20:20–23) and which embraces the jealousy of the other ten (20:24). Substantial misunderstanding of Jesus by his disciples is presupposed throughout Jesus' entire earthly ministry.

The "disciples" are probably the Twelve but may include others (cf. Thompson, pp. 83–84; see on 5:1–2). The child (v.2) may have been Peter's, if the house is his (17:25; Mark 9:33).

2. *Humility and greatness*

18:3–4

[3]And he said: "I tell you the truth, unless you change and become like little children, you will never enter the kingdom of heaven. [4]Therefore, whoever humbles himself like this child is the greatest in the kingdom of heaven.

3–4 With the solemn introductory formula "I tell you the truth" (v.3; see on 5:18), Jesus warns his disciples that they must "change and become like little children"; for unless they do, they will "never enter the kingdom of heaven." Clearly, the consummated kingdom is in view. The child is held up as an ideal, not of innocence, purity, or faith, but of humility and unconcern for social status. Jesus advocates humility of mind (v.4), not childishness of thought (cf. 10:16). With such humility comes childlike trust (cf. TDNT, 8:16–17). The disciples must "change" (lit., "turn," probably not to be taken as a Semitic auxiliary to "become," i.e., "become again a little child"; cf. J. Dupont, "Matthieu 18, 3," in Ellis, and Wilcox, pp. 50–60) from their present conduct and attitudes and adopt this new norm or be excluded from the kingdom. Conversely, the person who truly humbles himself (cf. Notes) like this child is "the greatest in the kingdom of heaven": the expression completes a link with v.1, and the present tense may suggest that the disciple's greatness, doubtless made obvious in the consummated kingdom in the future, has already begun here as far as kingdom norms are concerned.

The thought is not far removed from 5:3 and vitiates any thought that the kingdom can be gained by personal merit or violent force (see on 11:12). It is to "little children" that the Lord of heaven and earth reveals his truth (11:25).

Notes

4 The verb ταπεινώσει (*tapeinōsei*, lit., "will humble") is one of the few instances in which the distinction between a future indicative and an aorist subjunctive plus ἄν (*an*, untranslatable particle used to suggest some kind of contingency) is obliterated (cf. BDF, par. 380[2]).

3. *The heinousness of causing believers to sin*

18:5–9

[5]"And whoever welcomes a little child like this in my name welcomes me. [6]But if anyone causes one of these little ones who believe in me to sin, it would be better for him to have a large millstone hung around his neck and to be drowned in the depths of the sea. [7]Woe to the world because of the things that cause people to sin! Such things must come, but woe to the man through whom they come! [8]If your hand or your foot causes you to sin, cut it off and throw it away. It is better for you to enter life maimed or crippled than to have two hands or two feet and be thrown into eternal fire. [9]And if your eye causes you to sin, gouge it out and throw it away. It is better for you to enter life with one eye than to have two eyes and be thrown into the fire of hell.

Although some read v.5 with vv.3–4, it is better to link it with vv.6–9, because (1) v.4 already rounds off 18:1–4 with a summary, and (2) vv.5–6 taken together constitute a neat promise-warning proverb (cf. esp. Thompson, pp. 101–7). This pericope is held tightly together by its repeated *skandalon* ("stumbling block") language (see on 5:29), what Paul calls a *proskomma* ("obstacle," "cause of stumbling"; cf. Rom 14:13; 1 Cor 8:9). Rabbinic literature contains denunciations of the evil of causing others to sin (cf. Bonnard), but never with reference to "little ones."

5–6 This promise-warning couplet (like 12:32 in structure) advances the thought by turning attention from the self-humiliation of the true disciple (vv.3–4) to the way others receive such "little ones." The opening clauses of v.5 and v.6 are roughly parallel. The one who welcomes "a little child like this *in my name*" is not welcoming literal children but "children" defined in the previous verses—those who humble themselves to become like children, i.e., Jesus' true disciples. They are not welcomed because they are great, wise, or mighty, but because they come in Jesus' name (v.5)—i.e., they belong to him. "In my name" (v.5), the parallel clause "who believe in me" (v.6), and the necessity of becoming childlike even to enter the kingdom (v.3) all confirm the view that those referred to in vv.5–6 are simply Jesus' disciples—Christians (to use a later term), not literal children or some smaller group of especially humble disciples (see Warfield, 1:234–52; Trotter). These "little ones" (cf. 25:40, 45) can stumble, even the greatest of them (14:28–31; 26:30–35); but whoever causes them to stumble (NIV, "to sin") stands in grave peril.

It is no objection to this identification of "little ones" with believers that Jesus is here addressing his disciples and not the world that is most in need of the warning, for (1) the "whoever" takes in everybody; (2) despite the fact that Jesus is speaking to disciples (v.1), he utters a woe on the world in v.7; (3) this suggests that the passage aims at encouraging the disciples who are going to have to face the world's opprobrium (as also 10:40–42); and (4) the warnings against the world, though not at this moment directed to the world, will in due course become part of the disciples' arsenal in their preaching.

The person who welcomes one of these "little ones," these disciples of Jesus, simply because they are his, welcomes Jesus himself (cf. 10:42). Presupposed is the world's animosity. Mere hospitality is not in view but hospitality given because of the "little ones'" link with Jesus; and it is probably presupposed that hospitality motivated in this way would be shown only if the benefactor were already well disposed toward Jesus, or at least moving in that direction. The antithetic alternative, causing the "little ones" to stumble, does not mean that the "little ones" are led into apostasy. Rather, they are not welcomed but are rejected, ignored. This causes them to stumble in their discipleship. It may lead to serious sin; but, as in 10:40–42 and 25:31–46, the really grave aspect of the rejection is that it signifies rejection of Jesus.

Implicitly, the offense is gravely magnified when with particular perversity some wicked people self-consciously try to entice Christ's "little ones" into sin; but the evil is broader than that. Because it signals a rejection of Jesus as well as damaging his people, drowning at sea before the evil was committed is much preferable to eschatological judgment, the eternal fire of hell (vv.8–9) that awaits the perpetrators. Drowning was a not uncommon punishment in Greek and Roman society. Though rare in Jewish circles, it was done at least once in Galilee (Jos. Antiq. XIV, 450[xv.10]). Most millstones were hand tools for domestic use (see on 24:41); here it is the heavy stone pulled around by a donkey. The picture is more graphic than in Mark, the horror of the judgment sharpened.

7 The Greek text proclaims a "woe" (here, clearly, a proclamation of judgment, not of "sympathetic sorrow" [McNeile], since Matthew heightens the judgment language; see further on 23:13–32) on the "world," understood not merely as the neutral "setting for the struggle between belief and unbelief" (Thompson, pp. 109–10), but the source of all stumbling. Jesus pronounces this woe *apo tōn skandalōn*, which, contrary to NIV, should not be rendered "because of the things that cause *people* to sin," as if the discussion had progressed from Jesus' "little ones" to "people" in general, but "because of stumbling blocks," i.e., because of the things that cause the stumbling already referred to in v.6. Such things must come; but this inevitably does not mitigate the responsibility of those through whom they come (cf. Isa 10:5–12; Acts 4:27–28; see on Matt 13:13). The necessity does not spring from divine compulsion but, like all things, falls nonetheless within the sphere of his sovereignty so that he may use those very things to accomplish his plan and perfect his people (cf. 24:10–13; 1 Cor 11:19). Thus on the one hand the disciples are not to think such opposition strange, for Jesus himself has declared it must occur; on the other hand they are assured that justice will be done in the end (cf. 26:24).

8–9 Jesus now abandons denunciation of the world's causing his disciples to stumble and tells his disciples they may prove to be not only victims but aggressors. The adversative *de* is given its full force: "*But,* beyond all this, if *your* hand" (v.8). This does not mean that the church, pictured as a body in anticipation of Paul's language (e.g., 1 Cor 12:12–27) is here exhorted to excommunicate offending members. The word "body" is not used, and the language is akin to that in 5:29–30 (q.v.). Certain attitudes nurtured by Jesus' disciples toward other believers could also be sinful; thus, instead of being enticed to sin by outsiders, they would cause their own stumbling. Perhaps the particular believer-to-believer attitude that most needs rooting out is pride; so vv.8–9 prepare for v.10.

The argument is clear. Jesus' followers must become like children in humility if they are to enter the kingdom (vv.3–4). Those who receive such "little ones" because they belong to him in effect receive Jesus; those who reject them, causing them to stumble, are threatened with condemnation (vv.5–6). Things causing Jesus' people to stumble are inevitable yet damning (v.7). But the disciples themselves must beware: failure to deal radically with similar sin in their own lives betrays their allegiance to the world and threatens them with the eternal fire of hell (vv.8–9; see on 5:22). Jesus' disciples must deal as radically with pride as they were earlier commanded to deal with lust (5:29–30).

Notes

---

7 The γάρ (*gar,* "for") retains its normal causal force but applies to the next clause, here introduced by πλήν (*plēn,* "but"). The content of the *gar* itself is parenthetical so far as the force of *gar* is concerned. The same construction is found elsewhere (cf. 22:14; 24:6; cf. Zerwick, pars. 474–75).

---

4. *The parable of the lost sheep*

18:10–14

[10]"See that you do not look down on one of these little ones. For I tell you that their angels in heaven always see the face of my Father in heaven.

[12]"What do you think? If a man owns a hundred sheep, and one of them wanders away, will he not leave the ninety-nine on the hills and go to look for the

one that wandered off? [13]And if he finds it, I tell you the truth, he is happier about that one sheep than about the ninety-nine that did not wander off. [14]In the same way your Father in heaven is not willing that any of these little ones should be lost.

Verse 10 clearly follows vv.5–9; but because it also forms a neat inclusion with v.14, vv.10–14 must be read together in the light of the preceding pericope. This link raises important questions concerning the relation between this parable and the parable of the lost sheep in Luke 15:3–7, where it is addressed, not to disciples, but to Pharisees and teachers of the law, in defense of Jesus' attitude to sinners. Almost all scholars hold that one parable stands behind both Gospels, and then they debate over which form and setting are most primitive (for discussion, cf. Jeremias, *Parables*, pp. 38ff.; Marshall, *Luke*, pp. 600–601; Hill, *Matthew*), some arguing in favor of the form in Gospel of Thomas 107 (most recently W.L. Petersen, "The Parable of the Lost Sheep in the Gospel of Thomas and the Synoptics," NovTest 23 [1981]: 128–47; but cf. Blomberg, "Tendencies," pp. 29–63, 96–100). All these views presuppose that at least one of the two settings defined by Matthew and Luke is a late creation by the church or by one of the evangelists to apply the parable to some new problem.

But if the original parable was "simple enough and rich enough to be applied to more than one situation" (Hill, *Matthew*), why did not Jesus apply it to more than one situation? What methodological reasons are advanced for distinguishing between multiple usage by Jesus and multiple usage by the church? It is remarkable how different Matthew's and Luke's forms of the parable are when closely compared in the Greek text. Almost every relevant term is not the same as in the parallel, and the few that are the same are well within the bounds of repetition expected in an itinerant ministry (see on 5:1–2). The evidence suggests that these are two similar parables, both taught by Jesus, but with very different aims: see on 19:1–2 for the bearing of the problems of "Luke's central section" on this discussion. Matthew is not concerned with "faithful pastorship in the community" (Hill, *Matthew*) but, following the preceding pericope, with the importance in Messiah's community of harming no member, of sharing the Father's concern that none of "these little ones" be lost.

10[11] Verse 10 continues the note of humility struck at the discourse's beginning (vv.3–4) and the concern for "these little ones" (vv.5–9). There is no conflict between "you" and "these little ones." At this stage of their pilgrimage, even the disciples must change and become like little children (v.3). Jesus is discussing what will be normative when his passion and resurrection fully inaugurate the messianic community. Its members will be poor in spirit (5:3), humble (18:3–4), and none will be admitted to it without these graces. If his disciples become like that, they will belong to the "little children"; if they look down on them, they will share in the woes (vv.8–9). The warning was not irrelevant: at least one disciple left Jesus.

Jesus says that the "little ones"—believers in him—must be treated with respect because "their angels in heaven" always see the face of the heavenly Father. Many believe this supports the idea of a guardian for each "little one." That these angels are "in heaven" is thought to mean that they are of highest rank and that their seeing the Father's face means they always have access to his presence. This is based largely on Jewish sources (cf. SBK, 1:781ff.; 3:48ff., 437ff.; TDNT, 1:82, 86; see esp. Tobit 12:14–15). Yet the idea will not bear close scrutiny.

It is true that angels are sent to minister to those who will inherit salvation (Heb 1:14). But nowhere in Scripture or Jewish tradition of the NT period is there any suggestion that there is one angel for one person. Daniel and Zechariah imply one angel for each nation. Appeal to Acts 12:15 does not help. Why should Peter's supposed guardian angel sound like Peter? And if ministering angels are sent to help believers, what are the angels in Matthew 18:10 doing around the divine throne, instead of guarding those people to whom they are assigned? References in the DSS to angels who share in the community's worship (1QSa 2:9–10) or minister to the Lord (1QH 5:20–22) are even less relevant, for this context does not deal with corporate worship.

The most likely explanation is the one Warfield (1:253–66) defends. The "angels" of the "little ones" are their spirits after death, and they always see the heavenly Father's face. Do not despise these little ones, Jesus says, for their destiny is the unshielded glory of the Father's presence. The present tense (they "always see") raises no difficulty because Jesus is dealing with a class, not individuals. The same interpretation admirably suits Acts 12:15: what the assembled group thinks is standing outside is Peter's "spirit" (angel), which accounts for Rhoda's recognition of his voice.

But can the word "angel" be pressed into this interpretation? Certainly Jesus teaches that God's people in the Resurrection "will be like the angels in heaven" as to marriage (22:30) and immortality (Luke 20:36). Similar language is also used in 2 Baruch 51:5, 12 (cf. also 1 Enoch 51:4): the righteous will become angels in heaven, will be transformed into the splendor of angels, and will even surpass the excellency of angels. The evidence, though not overwhelming, is substantial enough to suppose that "their angels" simply refers to their continued existence in the heavenly Father's presence.

12–13 Here is another reason not to despise these "little ones": the shepherd—the Father (v. 14)—is concerned for each sheep in his flock and seeks the one who strays (v. 12). His concern for the one wandering sheep is so great that he rejoices more over its restoration than over the ninety-nine that do not stray (v. 13). With a God like that, how dare anyone cause even one of these sheep to go astray?

14 Jesus drives the lesson home: the heavenly Father is unwilling for any of "these little ones" (see on vv. 3–6) to be lost. If that is his will, it is shocking that anyone else would seek to lead one of "these little ones" astray. This love for the *individual* sheep is not at the expense of the entire flock but so that the flock as a whole may not lose a single one of its members. On God's preservation of his own, see comments on 12:32; 13:3–9, 18–23.

Notes

---

11 This verse is omitted by the earliest witnesses of the Alexandrian, pre-Caesarean, Egyptian, and Antiochene text types. Inclusion in various forms appears to be an assimilation to Luke 19:10.

12 Some commentators argue that the verb πλανηθῇ (*planēthē*, "wanders away") signifies for Matthew apostasy from the Christian community (cf. 24:4–5, 11, 24). Two of these references (24:4–5) are taken from Mark 13:5–6, but Matthew ignores two other good references (Mark 12:24, 27). *Planēthē* has for Matthew no technical force and in 22:29 cannot possibly refer to such apostasy. It is general and suits the pastoral setting of the parable. Doubtless Jesus' teaching looks forward to the established church, but there is no evidence here to support theories about Matthew's anachronisms.

---

5. *Treatment of a sinning brother*

18:15–20

[15]"If your brother sins against you, go and show him his fault, just between the two of you. If he listens to you, you have won your brother over. [16]But if he will not listen, take one or two others along, so that 'every matter may be established by the testimony of two or three witnesses.' [17]If he refuses to listen to them, tell it to the church; and if he refuses to listen even to the church, treat him as you would a pagan or a tax collector.

[18]"I tell you the truth, whatever you bind on earth will be bound in heaven, and whatever you loose on earth will be loosed in heaven.

[19]"Again, I tell you that if two of you on earth agree about anything you ask for, it will be done for you by my Father in heaven. [20]For where two or three come together in my name, there am I with them."

15 Jesus has just spoken to his disciples to warn them not to cause one of these "little ones" to stumble. Now the thought shifts. What the shift is depends on the variant reading chosen. If the words "against you" are included, Jesus is looking at offenses within the messianic community from the opposite perspective—from the viewpoint of the brother against whom the sin is committed. If "against you" is omitted (cf. Notes), Jesus is telling the community as a whole how to handle the situation when a brother sins; and in the immediate context, the sin is that of despising another brother.

Either way the proper thing is to confront the brother privately and "show him his fault." The verb *elenchō* probably suggests "convict" the brother, not by passing judgment, but by convicting him of his sin. The aim is not to score points over him but to win him over (same verb as in 1 Cor 9:19–22; 1 Peter 3:1) because all discipline, even this private kind, must begin with redemptive purposes (cf. Luke 17:3–4; 2 Thess 3:14–15; James 5:19–20; cf. Ecclus 19:13–17). Jesus assumes that the individual (second person singular) who personally confronts his brother will do so with true humility (vv.3–4; cf. Gal 6:1): if it is hard to accept a rebuke, even a private one, it is harder still to administer one in loving humility. Behind this verse stands Leviticus 19:17: "Do not hate your brother in your heart. Rebuke your neighbor frankly so you will not share in his guilt."

16 If private confrontation does not work, the next step (backed by Deut 19:15) is to take two or three witnesses (though the text form of the quotation is much disputed: cf. Gundry, *Use of OT*, p. 139). Doubtless this Deuteronomic law was designed for what we would call "secular" cases. But the distinction is artificial and should not be pressed for the Israelite nation understood itself to be not a nation like others but a theocratic nation, God's chosen people. In conformity with his customary interpretation of the Scriptures, Jesus perceives the link joining his messianic community with ancient Israel.

It is not at first clear whether the function of the witnesses is to support the one who confronts his erring brother by bringing additional testimony about the sin committed (which would require at least three people to have observed the offense) or to provide witnesses to the confrontation if the case were to go before the whole church. The latter is a bit more likely, because Deuteronomy 19:15 deals with judicial condemnation (a step taken only by the entire assembly), not with attempts to convince a brother of his fault. By the united testimony of two or three witnesses, every matter "may be established" (*stathē*, lit., "may be made to stand"—though the rise of deponents in Hellenistic Greek, including the use of *stathē*, implies that "may stand" is a superior rendering; cf. Zerwick, par. 231; Turner, *Syntax*, p. 57).

17 The same three-step procedure is known elsewhere (1QS 5:25–6:1; cf. CD 9:2–3; cf. Davies, *Setting*, pp. 221ff.). Refusal to submit to the considered judgment of Messiah's people means that they are to treat the offender as "a pagan or a tax collector." It is poor exegesis to turn to 8:1–11; 9:9–13; 15:21–28 and say that such people should be treated compassionately. The argument and the NT parallels (Rom 16:17; 2 Thess 3:14) show that Jesus has excommunication in mind. That his words should be preserved in this form, with the mention of "pagan and tax collector," suggests that the people for whom Matthew is writing are predominantly Jewish Christians. NIV's "treat him as you would" catches the idea; but in the Greek expression, "let him be to you as," the "you" is singular. This suggests that each member of the church is to abide by the corporate judgment and reminds the reader of the individual responsibility each believer has toward the others, already presupposed by the singular "your brother" in v.15.

18 For comments on the grammar and theology of this verse, see on 16:19.

19–20 These two verses should not in this setting be taken as a promise regarding any prayer on which two or three believers agree (v.20). Scripture is rich in prayer promises (21:22; John 14:13–14; 15:7–8, 16), but if this passage deals with prayer at all, it is restricted by the context and by the phrase *peri pantos pragmatos* (NIV, "about anything"), which should here be rendered "about any judicial matter": the word *pragma* often has that sense (cf. 1 Cor 6:1; BAGD, s.v.), a sense nicely fitting the argument in Matthew 18.

Recently, however, J. Duncan M. Derrett ("'Where two or three are convened in my name . . .': a sad misunderstanding," ExpT 91 [1979–80]: 83–86) has argued that vv.19–20 do not deal with prayer at all. The two who agree are the offender and the one against whom the offense has been committed. They come to agreement on earth about any judicial matter they have been pursuing: the verb *aiteisthai* can refer to "pursuing a claim," as well as asking in prayer (cf. F. Preisigke, *Wörterbuch der griechischen Papyrusurkunden, mit Einschluss der griechischen Inschriften, Aufschriften, Ostraka, Mumienschilder, usw. aus Ägypten*, ed. E. Kiessling, 4 vols. [Berlin: 1927–31], s.v.). The promise, then, is that if two individuals in the church come to agreement concerning any claim they are pursuing (presumably on the basis of the church's judgment, v.18), "it will be allowed, ratified (literally it shall succeed, 'come off') on the part of my heavenly Father" (Derrett, "Two or three," p. 84). This is because God's will and purpose stand behind the binding and loosing of v.18 and also because ("for," v.20) the presence of Jesus is assured with the two or three who are (lit.) "brought together"—judges solemnly convened before the church and by the church to render a decision (cf. Notes). It is a truism of the biblical revelation that God's presence stands with the judges of his people (Ps. 82:1).

Here as elsewhere, Jesus takes God's place: Jesus will be with the judges. As he has identified himself with God before (cf. on 2:6; 3:3; 11:4–6, 7–8), so he does again, and thus anticipates the broader promise of 28:20: he will be with his people "to the very end of the age." Jesus thereby implicitly points forward to a time when, as "God with us" (1:23), he will be spiritually present with the "two or three" and with all his followers; and he presupposes that this time will be of considerable duration (see on 24:1–3).

Notes

15 Εἰς σέ (*eis se*, "against you") is omitted by ℵ B f¹ cop^{sa, bo mss} Origen Basil 3/6 Cyril. If the omission was original, the words were added very early, perhaps to make the general case (suggested by the omission) apply more tightly to the sins of the immediate context. But one might equally argue that omission was an early change designed to generalize the passage. Moreover, because η (*ē*), ῃ (*ē*), and ει (*ei*) were all pronounced the same way in NT times, it is very easy to see how ἁμαρτήσῃ [εἰς σέ] (*hamartēsē* [*eis se*], "sins against you") could foster errors in writing down dictation. UBS (3d ed.) and Nestle (26th ed.) include the words with square brackets, indicating considerable doubt.

The aorist indicative, ἐκέρδησας (*ekerdēsas*, "you have won over") after a future condition is to some extent futuristic itself (cf. BDF, par. 333[2]).

19 The word οὗ (*hou*, "which") is one of only three instances in Matthew in which the relative is attracted to the case of its antecedent (cf. 24:50; 25:24; cf. Zerwick, par. 16).

20 Derrett ("Two or three") suggests that the "two or three" [judges] reflect known Jewish legal practice. Each of the disputing parties would nominate his own "judge," a layman known to be impartial; and these two would try to settle the problem. If this effort failed, they would approach a third, unconnected with the disputants, who worked with the others either along the lines of arbitration or adjudication. The parallel is very neat and nicely accounts for Jesus' "two or three." My chief hesitation comes from the fact that Jesus has just told the complainant to "tell it to the church" (v.17), not to judges appointed by the disputants. Here the DSS (referred to above) may offer a closer parallel. Moreover Derrett assumes that the "two" in v.19 and the "two or three" in v.20 are not the same individuals but disputants and judges respectively. But these points are not decisive. We have as parallels not only 1 Cor 5, where the entire church meets on an issue, but also 1 Cor 6:4, where the church becomes involved *through appointed judges*. Verses 19–20 remain difficult; at this point we must be content with a balance of probabilities.

6. *Forgiveness* (18:21–35)

a. *Repeated forgiveness*

18:21–22

21Then Peter came to Jesus and asked, "Lord, how many times shall I forgive my brother when he sins against me? Up to seven times?"

22Jesus answered, "I tell you, not seven times, but seventy-seven times.

21–22 "Then" (v.21) is probably to be taken strictly (see on 3:13). The issue is not the adjudication of the church, still less the absolute granting of forgiveness by the church (only God and Jesus can forgive sins in so absolute a fashion), but personal forgiveness (cf. 6:14–15). In rabbinic discussion the consensus was that a brother might be forgiven a repeated sin three times; on the fourth, there is no forgiveness. Peter, thinking himself big-hearted, volunteers "seven times" in answer to his own question—a larger figure often used, among other things, as a "round number" (cf. Lev 26:21; Deut 28:25; Ps 79:12; Prov 24:16; Luke 17:4).

Jesus' response (v.22) alludes to Genesis 4:24 (cf. Notes): Lamech's revenge is transformed into a principle of forgiveness. In this context Jesus is not saying that seventy-seven times is the upper limit, nor that the forgiveness is so unqualified it vitiates the discipline and procedural steps just taught (vv.15–20). Rather he teaches that forgiveness of fellow members in his community of "little ones" (brothers) cannot possibly be limited by frequency or quantity; for, as the ensuing parable shows (vv.23–35), all of them have been forgiven far more than they will ever forgive.

Notes

---

21 The Greek is literally "How many times will my brother sin against me and I will forgive him?"—an excellent example of parataxis under Semitic influence, especially in interrogative sentences (cf. BDF, par. 471[2]; Zerwick, par. 453, who compares Isa 50:2).

22 The Greek could just barely be taken to mean 70 × 7 (490) instead of 70 + 7 (77); but it follows the LXX of Gen 4:24 exactly, which is a rendering of the Hebrew 77. For discussion and bibliography, cf. Gundry, *Use of OT*, p. 140.

---

b. *The parable of the unmerciful servant*

18:23–35

23"Therefore, the kingdom of heaven is like a king who wanted to settle accounts with his servants. 24As he began the settlement, a man who owed him ten thousand talents was brought to him. 25Since he was not able to pay, the master ordered that he and his wife and his children and all that he had be sold to repay the debt.

26"The servant fell on his knees before him. 'Be patient with me,' he begged, 'and I will pay back everything.' 27The servant's master took pity on him, canceled the debt and let him go.

28"But when that servant went out, he found one of his fellow servants who owed him a hundred denarii. He grabbed him and began to choke him. 'Pay back what you owe me!' he demanded.

29"His fellow servant fell to his knees and begged him, 'Be patient with me, and I will pay you back.'

30"But he refused. Instead, he went off and had the man thrown into prison until he could pay the debt. 31When the other servants saw what had happened, they were greatly distressed and went and told their master everything that had happened.

32"Then the master called the servant in. 'You wicked servant,' he said, 'I canceled all that debt of yours because you begged me to. 33Shouldn't you have had

mercy on your fellow servant just as I had on you?' 34In anger his master turned
him over to the jailers to be tortured, until he should pay back all he owed.
35"This is how my heavenly Father will treat each of you unless you forgive
your brother from your heart."

23 "Therefore," since Jesus requires his followers to forgive, the kingdom of heaven has become like (not "is like"; see on 13:24) a king who . . . : the reference is to the kingdom already being inaugurated. The reign of God establishes certain kinds of personal relationships, portrayed by this parable, whose point is spelled out in v.35. It quite misses the point to identify kingdom and church and argue that just as the king, though merciful, must be severe in judging the unforgiving, so the church must follow a similar pattern (so Hill, *Matthew*). "Kingdom" and "church" are distinct categories (see esp. on 13:37–39) and the immediate context has returned to the question of *repeated, personal* forgiveness (vv.21–22) and the reasons for it. Those in the kingdom serve a great king who has invariably forgiven far more than they can ever forgive one another. Therefore failure to forgive excludes one from the kingdom, whose pattern is to forgive.

The "servants" (*douloi*, lit., "slaves") may include high-ranking civil servants in a huge colonial empire, for the amount of indebtedness is astronomical (v.24). Yet Jesus may simply be using hyperbole to make clear how much the heirs of the kingdom have really been forgiven.

24–27 We glimpse some idea of the size of the indebtedness when we recall that David donated three thousand talents of gold and seven thousand talents of silver for the construction of the temple, and the princes provided five thousand talents of gold and ten thousand talents of silver (1 Chron 29:4, 7). Some recent estimates suggest a dollar value of twelve million; but with inflation and fluctuating precious metal prices, this could be over a billion dollars in today's currency. (For "talent," see on 25:15.)

Such indebtedness could not possibly be covered by selling the family into slavery (v.25): top price for a slave fetched about one talent, and one-tenth that amount or less was more common. The practice of being sold for debt was sanctioned by the OT (Lev 25:39; 2 Kings 4:1), but such slaves had to be freed in the year of Jubilee (every fiftieth year). (For Jewish and Gentile slavery in Jesus' day, cf. EBC, 1:489; SBK, 4:697–716; Jeremias, *Jerusalem*, pp. 312ff., 345ff.)

In this parable selling the slave and his family does not mean the debt is canceled but rather highlights the servant's desperate plight. With neither resources nor hope, he begs for time and promises to pay everything back (v.26)—an impossibility. So the master takes pity on him and cancels the indebtedness (v.27). The word *daneion* ("loan," a *hapax legomenon*) suggests that the king mercifully decides to look on the loss as a bad loan rather than embezzlement; but by v.32 he abandons that terminology and calls it a "debt."

28–31 The servant's attitude is appalling. The amount owed him is not insignificant: though worth but a few dollars in terms of metal currency, a hundred denarii (v.28) represented a hundred days' wages for a foot soldier or common laborer. Yet the amount is utterly trivial compared with what has already been forgiven him. The similarity of his fellow servant's plea (v.29) to his own (v.26) does not move this unforgiving man. He has him thrown into a debtor's prison (v.30). Even an inexpensive slave sold for five hundred denarii, and it was illegal to sell a man for a sum greater than his debt. But the other servants (v.31), deeply distressed by the inequity, tell the master everything (*diesaphēsan* is a strong verb meaning "explained in detail," not merely "told" [NIV]; it occurs in the NT only here and at 13:36).

32–34 When the servant owes ten thousand talents, the king forgives him; but when the servant shows himself unforgiving toward a fellow servant, the king calls him wicked (v.32) and, foregoing selling him, turns him over to the "torturers" (*basanistais,*) not merely "jailers," NIV); the word reminds us of earlier warnings in this chapter (18:6, 8–9). The servant is to be tortured till he pays back all he owes (v.34), which he can never do.

35 Jesus sees no incongruity in the actions of a heavenly Father who forgives so bountifully and punishes so ruthlessly, and neither should we. Indeed, it is precisely because he is a God of such compassion and mercy that he cannot possibly accept as his those devoid of compassion and mercy. This is not to say that the king's compassion can be earned: far from it, the servant is granted freedom only by virtue of the king's forgiveness. As in 6:12, 14–15, those who are forgiven must forgive, lest they show themselves incapable of receiving forgiveness.

Notes

28 Ἀπόδος εἴ τι ὀφείλεις (*apodos ei ti opheileis,* lit., "pay back, if you owe anything") is not an expression of pitiless logic (B.F. Meyer) but the Hellenistic equivalent of ἀπόδος ὅ τι ἂν ὀφείλῃς (*apodos ho ti an opheilēs,* "pay back what you owe," NIV; cf. BDF, par. 376).

30 In negations the aorist is normally used, "because usually the action as a whole is negated" (BDF, par. 327). When the imperfect is used in negations, the durative or iterative force is usually clear—e.g., Mark 14:55; οὐχ ηὕρισκον (*ouch hēuriskon,* "they did not find any [in spite of repeated attempts]"). In this light οὐκ ἤθελεν (*ouk ēthelen,* "he refused") is very telling: he repeatedly refused, maintained a sustained unwillingness (as in 22:3).

32 BDF (par. 328) points out that—especially in verbs to command, order, request, or send—if an action is complete in itself but the accomplishment of a second action toward which the first points is represented as unaccomplished or still outside the scope of the assertion, then the first verb takes the imperfect, not the aorist. Hence the use of aorist παρεκάλεσάς με (*parekalesas me,* "you begged me to"), pointing toward the forgiveness (ἀφῆκά σοι [*aphēka soi,* "I canceled . . . yours"]) means that "the simple request sufficed" (similarly at 26:53).

7. *Transitional conclusion: introduction to the Judean ministry*

19:1–2

[1]When Jesus had finished saying these things, he left Galilee and went into the region of Judea to the other side of the Jordan. [2]Large crowds followed him, and he healed them there.

1–2 For the formula used in this transition and the manner in which it points ahead, see on 7:28–29. Jesus "left" (*metairō;* for the verb, see on 13:53) Galilee and began to make his way toward Jerusalem, traveling by way of Perea, on the east side of the Jordan, thus avoiding Samaria—at least that is the customary explanation (v.1). But it is possible that *peran tou Iordanou* (lit., "across the Jordan") modifies "Judea" on the west bank. This implies that the writer describes the movements from a stance on the *east* bank (so Slingerland; see on 4:15). The parallel in Mark 10:1 is difficult because of the textual uncertainty concerning *kai* ("and [across the Jordan]"): if the *kai* is original, Mark is thinking of *two* areas—Judea *and* Perea ("across the Jordan"). But Matthew's expression "the other side of Jordan" could be taken as an awkward adverbial modifier of "went": Jesus "went across the Jordan [by that route] into the region of Judea."

The large crowds (v.2) and the many healings show that Jesus did in Judea what he had already done in Galilee. But the many summaries of Jesus' ministry in this Gospel (cf. 4:23; 9:35; 14:14; 16:30) along with showing how busy Jesus was, have another function. Because this Gospel contains so many discourses, "the picture of Jesus might easily become that of a *prophet,* attended by certain signs and wonders but with one single main task: to speak." These summaries help maintain balance and declare the full-orbed ministry of the Messiah (Gerhardsson, *Mighty Acts*, p. 36, emphasis his).

Behind these two verses lurks a very complex problem in synoptic harmony. Although Matthew and Mark are roughly parallel from Matthew 14 to the end, here Luke goes his own way. He pictures Jesus going through Samaria (Luke 9:51–56) and then begins a lengthy series of accounts, some having no synoptic parallel and others appearing to be parallel to earlier material in Mark and Matthew, material Matthew has omitted (e.g., cf. Luke 11:14–36 with Matt 12:22–45; Mark 3:19–30; and Luke 12:22–31 with Matt 6:25–34). Not till 18:15 does Luke rejoin Matthew (19:13) and Mark (10:13), thereafter running roughly parallel with them. The long section, Luke 9:51–18:14 (though the precise ending is disputed), formerly called Luke's "travel narrative" but now commonly referred to as his "central section," is a problem for commentators on Luke, not Matthew; but it cannot be ignored by any synoptic commentator, because the way we perceive Luke's "central section" bears directly on the question of how many of the pericopes in Luke 9:51–18:14 are taken as real parallels to similar ones in the other Synoptics.

Because in Luke's "central section" Jesus is regularly portrayed as heading for Jerusalem (Luke 9:51–53; 13:22; 17:11), some have argued that there is a direct route to Jerusalem, with various side trips; but the chronology and topography become so tortuous as to render this unbelievable. Others see the three chief references to Jerusalem as parallels to (1) Jesus' journey to Jerusalem at the Feast of Tabernacles (John 7:2–10), (2) Jesus' journey south at the time of the raising of Lazarus (John 11:17–18), and (3) the journey terminating in the final Passover and the Cross. Therefore the entire "travel narrative" stands under the shadow of the Cross. This is possible, but it raises more questions of Gospel chronology and harmony than can be discussed here; and, in particular, it means that none of the apparent parallels to similar synoptic material can possibly spring from the same historical event. That too is just possible and is defended by many older commentators (e.g., Broadus). But it is unlikely that an evangelist like Luke—whose "orderly account" (1:3) clearly organizes much material in topical, not chronological or geographical, order—abandons this in 9:51–18:14.

Therefore even if (as I am willing to assume) Luke's central section is framed by certain historical journeys to Jerusalem, used theologically to point to the final journey, it is only to be expected that topical material is also incorporated, because many of Luke's transitions between pericopes (when he uses them at all) are chronologically imprecise. What this means for a commentator on Matthew is that each apparent parallel between a pericope in Matthew and one in Luke's "central section" must be assessed on its own merits. In some cases they probably refer to the same event, in others not; and in some instances the evidence may be such that a convincing decision is impossible.

Craig Blomberg ("Tradition-history") has made some of the careful comparisons that are necessary. In the following chart of parables found in Luke's central section, prepared by Blomberg, column *a* lists the total number of words in Luke's account that appear in identical form in the synoptic parallel, *b* lists the number of words common to both texts but in different lexical or grammatical forms, and *c* the number of words in Luke that are clear synonyms for corresponding words in the other text. Column *d* provides the percentage of words in Luke falling into category *a*, and column *e* the percentage falling into *a*, *b*, or *c*.

Lukan parable	*Synoptic parallel*		*No. of words in Luke*	*a*	*b*	*c*	*d*	*e*
12:39–40	Matt	24:43–44	34	29	2	3	85.3	100.0
13:20–21	Matt	13:33	21	15	4	1	71.4	95.2
12:42–46	Matt	24:45–51	102	83	5	4	81.4	90.2
8:5–8	Mark	4:3–9	76	44	11	7	57.9	81.5
7:31–35	Matt	11:16–19	76	45	14	2	59.2	80.3
11:11–13	Matt	7:9–11	48	34	2	2	70.8	79.2
13:18–19	Matt	13:31–32	38	19	5	4	50.0	73.7
20:9a–16a	Mark	12:1–9	120	64	11	6	53.3	67.5
14:5	Matt	12:11	17	2	6	1	11.7	52.9
6:47–49	Matt	7:24–27	83	21	16	3	25.3	48.2
19:12–27	Matt	25:14–30	253	54	23	28	21.3	41.5
15:4–7	Matt	18:12–14	81	15	12	2	18.5	35.8
14:16–24	Matt	22:2–10	159	10	14	4	6.3	17.6
12:35–38	Mark	13:33–37	67	2	4	3	3.0	13.4

The chart reveals three groups of parables: (1) those with considerable verbal similarity, 53.3%–85.3% in column *d*, and 67.5%–100% in column *e*; (2) those with very little verbal similarity, 3.0%–6.3% in column *d*, and 13.4%–17.6% in column *e*; and, bunched between these two extremes, (3) those with a significant but not high verbal similarity, 18.5%–25.3% in column *d*, and 35.8%–52.9% in column *e*. As far as these statistics alone are concerned, one might be tempted to think that parables in group (1) probably have a common source, parables in group (2) are distinct, and parables in group (3) have to be handled one by one. This is largely the way they have worked out in this commentary.

Yet other mitigating factors must be kept in mind. For instance, if a parable is brief and aphoristic, then high verbal similarity is less likely to indicate a common source: the parable may have been repeated many times. Again, contrary to Jeremias (*Parables*, pp. 33ff.), P.B. Payne ("Metaphor as a Model for Interpretation of the Parable of the Sower" [Ph.D. diss., Cambridge University, 1975], pp. 308–11) has shown in detail that in almost all instances the audience claimed by the evangelist for any parable found in two or more synoptic Gospels does not contradict the audience claimed by another synoptic evangelist for what appears to be the same parable. If the Gospel writers are careful to preserve the correct audience in all but two cases, one suspects that, if there is independent reason in those two cases to think the parallels may not be parallels but *independent* parables, that is reasonable evidence to believe the alleged parables were separate stories with similar plot lines and vocabularies from the beginning. One such case is the parable of the lost sheep (see on Matt 18:10–14), which falls at the bottom of the intermediate group on the accompanying chart (cf. further Blomberg, "Tradition-history," ch. 2).

While the work of Blomberg and Payne is largely restricted to the parables in Luke's central section (or in Payne's case to synoptic parables), their methods and general observations are applicable to other materials in that section that are paralleled in Matthew. (See comments on 18:10–14; 22:2–10; 24:43–44; 25:14–30.)

VI. Opposition and Eschatology: The Triumph of Grace (19:3–26:5)

A. *Narrative* (19:3–23:39)

1. *Marriage and divorce*

19:3–12

3Some Pharisees came to him to test him. They asked, "Is it lawful for a man to divorce his wife for any and every reason?"

4"Haven't you read," he replied, "that at the beginning the Creator 'made them male and female,' 5and said, 'For this reason a man will leave his father and mother and be united to his wife, and the two will become one flesh'? 6So they are no longer two, but one. Therefore what God has joined together, let man not separate."

7"Why then," they asked, "did Moses command that a man give his wife a certificate of divorce and send her away?"

8Jesus replied, "Moses permitted you to divorce your wives because your hearts were hard. But it was not this way from the beginning. 9I tell you that anyone who divorces his wife, except for marital unfaithfulness, and marries another woman commits adultery."

10The disciples said to him, "If this is the situation between a husband and wife, it is better not to marry."

11Jesus replied, "Not everyone can accept this word, but only those to whom it has been given. 12For some are eunuchs because they were born that way; others were made that way by men; and others have renounced marriage because of the kingdom of heaven. The one who can accept this should accept it."

On the dangers and difficulties of constructing detailed outlines, see on 13:54–58. Yet certain themes in these chapters (19:3–26:5) are crystalized. The opposition to Jesus becomes more heated and focused: the stances of Jesus and the Jewish leaders become more irreconcilable. Jesus not only reveals more of himself and his mission to his disciples but centers more attention on the End, the ultimate eschatological hope, the consummation of the kingdom. Within these two poles, opposition and eschatology, the grace of God toward those under the kingdom becomes an increasingly dominant theme. Without ever using the word "grace," Matthew returns to this theme repeatedly (e.g., 19:21–22; 20:1–16). But grace does not mean there is no judgment (23:1–39). Rather, it means that despite the gross rejection of Jesus, the chronic unbelief of opponents, crowds, and disciples alike, and the judgment that threatens both within history and at the End, grace triumphs and calls out a messianic people who bow to Jesus' lordship and eagerly await his return.

By and large 19:3–26:5 follows the structure of Mark; but there are substantial additions (20:1–16; 21:28–32; 22:1–14), expansions (esp. 23:1–39; cf. Mark 12:38–44), alterations (esp. 21:10–17), and additional parables after the Olivet Discourse (ch. 25).

For three reasons the first pericope in this section of Matthew has called forth an enormous quantity of comment and exposition: (1) it deals with a perennially burning pastoral issue in society and in the church; (2) it includes some notoriously difficult words and phrases (see esp. v.9); and (3) its relation to the parallel in Mark 10:2–12 is hotly disputed. Only some of these issues can be directly addressed here. (For the cultural background to marriage in the Bible, see Edwin M. Yamauchi, "Cultural Aspects of Marriage in the Ancient World," BS 135 [1978]: 241–52; and for post-Pentateuchal developments on divorce, canonical and other, see Sigal, "Halakah," pp. 130–42.)

3 Pharisees (see on 3:7) are often found in Matthew's Gospel testing or opposing Jesus in some way (12:2, 14, 24, 38; 15:1; 16:1; 19:3; 22:15, 34–35). Their "test," here, is probably delivered in the hope that Jesus would say something to damage his reputation with the people or even seem to contradict Moses. Perhaps, too, they hoped that Jesus would say something that would entangle him in the Herod–Herodias affair so that he might meet the Baptist's fate. Machaerus was not far away (see on 14:3–12).

The question whether it is right for a man to divorce his wife "for any and every reason" (NIV has rightly rendered a difficult phrase: cf. Turner, *Insights*, p. 61) hides an enormous diversity of Jewish opinion. Among the Qumran covenanters, divorce was judged illicit under all circumstances (CD 4:21; and esp. 11QTemple 57:17–19; on which see J.R. Mueller, "The Temple Scroll and the Gospel Divorce Texts," *Revue de Qumran* 38 [1980]: 247ff.).

In mainstream Palestinian Judaism, opinion was divided roughly into two opposing camps: both the school of Hillel and the school of Shammai permitted divorce (of the woman by the man: the reverse was not considered) on the grounds of *ʿerwaṯ dāḇār* ("something indecent," Deut 24:1), but they disagreed on what "indecent" might include. Shammai and his followers interpreted the expression to refer to gross indecency, though not necessarily adultery; Hillel extended the meaning beyond sin to all kinds of real or imagined offenses, including an improperly cooked meal. The Hillelite R. Akiba permitted divorce in the case of a roving eye for prettier women (M *Gittin* 9:10).

On any understanding of what Jesus says in the following verses, he agrees with neither Shammai nor Hillel; for even though the school of Shammai was stricter than Hillel, it permitted remarriage when the divorce was not in accordance with its own Halakah (rules of conduct) (M *Eduyoth* 4:7–10); and if Jesus restricts grounds for divorce to sexual indecency (see on v.9), then he differs fundamentally from Shammai. Jesus cuts his own swath in these verses, as Sigal ("Halakah," pp. 104ff.) rightly points out; and he does so in an age when in many Pharisaic circles "the frequency of divorce was an open scandal" (Hill, *Matthew*). Josephus, for instance, himself a divorcé, was a Pharisee; and in his view divorce was permitted "for any causes whatsoever" (Jos. Antiq. IV, 253[viii.23]).

Thus the setting of the divorce question in this pericope is different from 5:31–32. There divorce is set in a discourse that gives the norms of the kingdom and the sanctity of marriage; here it is set in a theological disputation that raises the question of what divorces are allowed.

4–6 Jesus aligns himself with the prophet Malachi, who quotes Yahweh as saying, "I hate divorce" (2:16), and also refers to creation (2:14–15). Jesus cites first Genesis 1:27 and then Genesis 2:24. The Creator made the race "male and female" (v.4): the implication is that the two sexes should be united in marriage. But lest the implication be missed, the Creator then said that "for this reason" (v.5)—because God made them so—a man will leave father and mother, be united to his wife, and become one flesh (cf. Ecclus 25:26; Eph 5:28–31).

The words "for this reason" in Genesis 2:24 refer to Adam's perception that the woman was "bone of his bone and flesh of his flesh" because she had been made from him and for him—i.e., the man and the woman were in the deepest sense "related." The same thing is implied by Genesis 1:27—i.e., the "one flesh" in every marriage between a man and a woman is a reenactment of and testimony to the very structure of humanity as God created it.

"So" (*hōste* here is "simply an inferential particle" [Moule, *Idiom Book*, p. 144]), Jesus concludes, the husband and wife are no longer two but one, and that by God's doing (v.6). If God has joined them together, according to the structure of his own creation, divorce is not only "unnatural" but rebellion against God. God and man are so far apart on this issue that what God unites, man divides.

Jesus' response cuts through a great deal of casuistry and sets forth a dominant perspective that must not be lost in the exegetical tangles of v.9. Two profound insights must be grasped.

1. Although Jewish leaders tended to analyze adultery in terms, not of infidelity to one's spouse, but of taking someone else's wife (cf. M *Ketuboth* and M *Kiddushin*), Jesus dealt with the sanctity of marriage by focusing on the God-ordained unity of the couple.

2. Jesus essentially appealed to the principle, "The more original, the weightier," an accepted form of argument in Jewish exegesis (cf. Paul in Gal 3:15–18); and it is impossible to go further back than creation for the responsibilities of mankind. If marriage is grounded in *creation*, in the way God has made us, then it cannot be reduced to a merely covenantal relationship that breaks down when the covenantal promises are broken (contra David Atkinson, *To Have and to Hold: The Marriage Covenant and the Discipline of Divorce* [London: Collins, 1979], esp. pp. 114ff.). But the argument in this instance leaves unanswered the question of how the Mosaic law is to be taken; and therefore the stage is set for the Pharisees' next question.

7–8 The Pharisees refer to Deuteronomy 24:1–4, which they interpret to mean something like this: "If a man takes a wife . . . and she does not find favor in his eyes . . . he shall write a bill of divorce . . . and shall send her away from his house" (so also Vul.). But the Hebrew more naturally means something like this: "If a man takes a wife . . . and she does not find favor in his eyes . . . and he writes a bill of divorce . . . and he sends her away from his house . . . and her second husband does the same thing, then her first husband must not marry her again" (presumably because that would be a kind of incest (cf. Zerwick, par. 458; G.J. Wenham, "The

Restoration of Marriage Reconsidered," *Journal of Jewish Studies* 30 [1979]: 36–40). In other words Moses did not *command* divorce but permitted it for *'erwaṯ dāḇār* ("something indecent"); and the text is less concerned with explaining the nature of that indecency (the precise expression is found in only one other place in the OT—Deut 23:14, with reference to human excrement) than with prohibiting remarriage of the twice-divorced woman to her first husband. Divorce and remarriage are therefore presupposed by Moses: i.e., he "permitted" them (v.8).

The general thrust of Mark 10:2–9 is the same as in Matthew 19:3–8. But there (1) the Pharisees ask their test question without "for any and every reason"; (2) Jesus mentions Moses' command; (3) the Pharisees reply in terms of what Moses permitted; and (4) only then does Jesus offer his basic perspective in terms of the creation ordinance. The net effect of the two passages this far is the same. But it is not easy to reconstruct the historical details. Matthew seems more concerned about the thrust of the exchange than about who said what first.

Both Matthew and Mark show that Jesus taught that Moses' concession reflected not the true creation ordinance but the hardness of men's hearts. Divorce is not part of the Creator's perfect design. If Moses permitted it, he did so because sin can be so vile that divorce is to be preferred to continued "indecency." This is not to say that the person who, according to what Moses said, divorced his spouse was actually committing sin in so doing; but that divorce could even be considered testified that there had already been sin in the marriage. Therefore any view of divorce and remarriage (taught in either Testament) that sees the problem only in terms of what may or may not be done has already overlooked a basic fact—divorce is never to be thought of as a God-ordained, morally neutral option but as evidence of sin, of hardness of heart. The fundamental attitude of the Pharisees to the question was wrong.

It should be noted also that Jesus, when speaking of the sin of the people, invariably refers to *their* sin, *your* sin, never *our* sin (cf. 6:14–15).

But what was the "indecency" in Moses' day that allowed for divorce? "Something indecent" could not be equated with adultery, for the normal punishment for that was death, not divorce (Deut 22:22)—though it is not at all clear that the death penalty was in fact regularly imposed for adultery (cf. Henry McKeating, "Sanctions Against Adultery in Ancient Israelite Society," JSOT 11 [1979]: 57–72). Nor could the indecency be suspicion of adultery, for which the prescribed procedure was the bitter-water rite (Num 5:5–31). Yet the indecency must have been shocking: ancient Israel took marriage seriously. The best assumption is that the indecency was any lewd, immoral behavior, sometimes including, but not restricted to, adultery—e.g., lesbianism or sexual misconduct that fell short of intercourse.

9 Four problems contribute to the difficulty of understanding this verse. The first is textual. The "except" clause appears in several forms, doubtless owing to assimilation to 5:32; but there can be no doubt that an except clause is original. Though some MSS add a few more words (e.g., "and the divorcée who marries another commits adultery"), the diversity of the MS additions and the likelihood of assimilation to 5:32, not to mention the weight of external evidence, support the shorter text (cf. Metzger, *Textual Commentary*, pp. 47–48).

The second problem concerns the meaning of *porneia* ("marital unfaithfulness," NIV; "fornication," KJV). H. Baltensweiler (*Die Ehe im Neuen Testament* [Zürich: Zwingli, 1967], p. 93) thinks that it refers to marriage within prohibited degrees

(Lev 18), i.e., to incest. Many others, especially Roman Catholic scholars, have defended that view in some detail (cf. J.A. Fitzmyer, "The Matthean Divorce Texts and Some New Palestinian Evidence," *Theological Studies*, 37 [1976]: 208–11). Appeal is often made to 1 Corinthians 5:1, where "a man has his father's wife" (his stepmother). But it should be noted that even here Paul gives no indication he is dealing with an incestuous marriage but only an incestuous affair. It is very doubtful whether Paul or any other Jew would have regarded an incestuous relationship as marriage: Paul would not have told the couple to get a divorce but to stop what they were doing. And in the next chapter Paul uses the same word (*porneia*) to describe prostitution (1 Cor 6:13, 16).

Others have argued that *porneia* refers to premarital unchastity (Isaksson, pp. 135ff.; Mark Geldard, "Jesus' Teaching on Divorce," *Churchman* 92 [1978]: 134–43): if a man discovers his bride is not a virgin, he may divorce her. This has the advantage (it is argued) of being no *real* exception to Jesus' prohibition of divorce, making it easier to reconcile Matthew and Mark, who omits the "except" clause. Moreover it provides a neat background for the disciples' shock (v.10); for if *porneia* refers to every sexual sin, Jesus is saying no more than what many rabbis taught. The latter objection is best treated at v.10. The former is a possible way of reconciling Matthew and Mark, but there are many other possibilities; and there is no reason to adopt this one if *porneia* is being squeezed into too narrow a semantic range.

Still others hold that *porneia* here means "adultery," no more and no less (e.g., T.V. Fleming, "Christ and Divorce," *Theological Studies* 24 [1963]: 109; Sigal, "Halakah," pp. 116ff.). Certainly the word can include that meaning (Jer 3:8–9; cf. MT and LXX; cf. Ecclus 23:23). Yet in Greek the normal word for adultery is *moicheia*. Matthew has already used *moicheia* and *porneia* in the same context (15:19), suggesting some distinction between the words, even if there is considerable overlap. A. Mahoney ("A New Look at the Divorce Clauses in Mt 5, 32 and 19, 9," CBQ 30 [1968]: 29–38) suggests *porneia* refers to spiritual harlotry, a metaphor often adopted by the OT prophets. Jesus then prohibits divorce except where one spouse is not a Christian. But it is almost impossible to conceive how such a response, couched in such language, could have any relevance (let alone intelligibility) to the disputants here. Moreover Paul knows no dominical word on the subject of mixed marriages (1 Cor 7:12), and the answer he provides (1 Cor 7:12–16) seems somewhat stricter.

The reason these and many other creative suggestions have been advanced lies in the difficulty of the verse as a whole, both in its immediate context and as a parallel to Mark–Luke. But it must be admitted that the word *porneia* itself is very broad. In unambiguous contexts it can on occasion refer to a specific kind of sexual sin. Yet even then this is possible only because the specific sexual sin belongs to the larger category of sexual immorality. *Porneia* covers the entire range of such sins (cf. TDNT, 6:579–95; BAGD, s.v.; Joseph Jensen, "Does *porneia* Mean Fornication? A Critique of Bruce Malina," NovTest 20 [1978]: 161–84) and should not be restricted unless the context requires it.

The third problem is why Matthew alone of the synoptic Gospels includes the except clause; and the fourth is just what that clause means. These may be handled together. Proposed solutions are legion; but there are seven important ones.

1. Some hold that the except clause here and in 5:32 is really no exception at all. The preposition *epi* plus the dative can have the sense of addition: "in addition to"

or even "apart from" (cf. Luke 3:20; Col 3:14; Zerwick, par. 128). In this verse the words should be rendered "not apart from sexual promiscuity" in v.9; and similar reasoning applies to the slightly different construction in 5:31: "whoever repudiates his wife, in addition to the *porneia* [for which he repudiates her], causes her to be defiled by adultery." There is then no exception to Jesus' prohibition of divorce as reported in Mark–Luke. But all this requires almost impossible Greek. When *epi* has this "additive" force, it is nowhere preceded by *mē* ("not"), which most naturally introduces an exception. Dupont (*Mariage et divorce*, pp. 102–6) has clearly shown that a real exception is meant.

2. The majority of recent commentators hold that Matthew has simply taken over Mark's pericope but liberalized it. The absolute prohibition was no longer possible in the Matthean church, and so the except clause was introduced (so David R. Catchpole, "The Synoptic Divorce Material as a Traditio-Historical Problem," BJRL 57 [1974–75]: 92–127; R.H. Stein, " 'Is It Harmful for a Man to Divorce His Wife?' " JETS 22 [1979]: 115–21; H. Reisser, DNTT, 1:500). The particular reason for adding the exception is variously put: (1) Jesus' absolute prohibition was only meant to be a guideline, which the evangelists felt free to adapt—after all, "Jesus was not a legalist" (Stein); (2) Matthew felt it necessary to align Jesus with the school of Shammai in the context of rabbinic debates in his day (Bornkamm, *Tradition*, pp. 25–26); and (3) *porneia* refers to incestuous marriages, not uncommon among Gentiles; so Matthew added the except clause because an increasing number of Gentile converts were entering his predominantly Jewish church, and Jesus' prohibition of divorce must not be thought to apply to their illicit marriages (Mahoney, "New Look"; cf. also Benoit, Bonnard).

But all these views have serious problems.

a. There is serious debate about whether Matthew has actually *added* something to the tradition or whether he is independent of Mark at this point.

b. To stigmatize an absolute prohibition by suggesting it would make Jesus a "legalist" is to beg a number of questions. Could not any absolute prohibition be subjected to the same cavalier labeling? The word "legalist" is a loaded word that can refer either to someone who sets up absolutes or to someone who thinks he is accepted by God on the basis of his obedience. In the first sense Jesus *is* a "legalist" (e.g., 22:37–38); in the second sense he is not. But only the first sense is relevant to this verse.

c. It is not clear why Matthew would feel it necessary to align his Gospel with a particular rabbinic school that, as he knew, already existed in Jesus' day. There is no new situation, in this respect, in A.D. 85.

d. The new situation suggested by Mahoney ("New Look") is not very plausible because it requires an unnatural reading of *porneia*, it assumes that Matthew would see an incestuous "marriage" as a genuine marriage subject to divorce (instead of a sinful affair that must be terminated), and it introduces an unsupported major anachronism.

e. Moreover simple alignment with the school of Shammai is implausible in a book demanding a righteousness surpassing that of the Pharisees (5:20) and in a context where Jesus' teaching on divorce evokes a cynical response from the disciples (19:10).

3. Hill, Sigal, and others argue that *porneia* simply means "adultery" in this context and that Jesus is interpreting the *'erwaṯ dāḇār* ("something indecent") of Deuteronomy 24:1 in this way. This does not necessarily mean that Matthew softens

Mark: as Hill (*Matthew*) points out, in Jewish circles of the first century, Jewish law *required* a man to divorce an adulterous wife (M *Sotah* 5:1); and this may well be assumed by the other Gospels "as an understood and accepted part of any teaching on the subject of divorce" but spelled out only in Matthew. This interpretation probably narrows down the meaning of *porneia* too far; but apart from that, the objections against it can be satisfactorily answered (cf. below on 7).

4. Bruce Vawter, in two articles ("The Divorce Clauses in Mt 5, 32 and 19, 9," CBQ 16 [1954]: 155–67; and "Divorce and the New Testament," CBQ 39 [1977]: 528–48), argues strongly that the except clauses have been misunderstood: they are preteritions, i.e., exceptions to the proposition itself, not simply to the verb. The except clause in 19:9 therefore "means that *porneia* [which he takes to be equivalent to the 'something indecent' of Deut 24:1] is not involved"—i.e., "I say to you, whoever dismisses his wife—the permission in Deut 24:1 notwithstanding—and marries another, commits adultery." Similarly, in 5:32 he understands the crucial phrase to mean "quite apart from the matter of *porneia*." Vawter is followed by Banks (*Jesus*, pp. 156–57). The effect of this interpretation is similar to 1: Matthew allows no more of an exception than Mark, and Jesus specifically abrogates the Mosaic permission. It makes good sense of the disciples' next remarks (v.10)—though Jesus' rejoinder (vv.11–12) seems a bit of a letdown, in a book in which the redactional pattern is *not* to have Jesus agree with his misunderstanding disciples but to reemphasize the point just made (cf. Q. Quesnell, " 'Made Themselves Eunuchs for the Kingdom of Heaven' (Mt 19, 12)," CBQ 30 [1968]: 340ff.). Moreover it is not at all obvious that the except clauses are preteritions: certainly the earliest Greek commentators did not take them that way, as Quesnell (p. 348) points out.

5. What Quesnell himself argues is that Jesus by using the verb *apolyō* (v.9) permits, in the case of the wife's marital infidelity, separation but not divorce (similarly G.J. Wenham, "May Divorced Christians Remarry?" *Churchman* 95 [1981]: 150–61; Dupont, *Mariage et divorce*, pp. 93–157), and therefore no remarriage under any circumstances. Such separation without possibility of remarriage was unheard of in Jewish circles and, of course, would have been much stricter than the school of Shammai; and this prompts the disciples' reaction (v.10). But two considerations stand against this view. First, *apolyō* has already been used in v.3 with the undoubted meaning "to divorce." It is unwarranted to understand the same verb a few verses later in some other way, unless there is some compelling contextual reason for the change. Again, though it is formally true that the except clause is syntactically linked to the divorce clause, not the remarriage clause, this is scarcely decisive. Locating the except clause anywhere else would breed even more ambiguity. For instance, if it is placed before the verb *moichatai* ("commits adultery"), the verse might be paraphrased as follows: "Whoever divorces his wife and marries another, if it is not for fornication that he divorces one and marries another, commits adultery." But this wording suggests that fornication is being advanced as the actual *reason* for marrying another, and not only for the divorce—an interpretation that borders on the ridiculous. Moreover, if the remarriage clause is excluded, the thought becomes nonsensical: "Anyone who divorces his wife, except for *porneia*, commits adultery"—surely untrue unless he remarries. The except clause must therefore be understood to govern the entire protasis. We may paraphrase as follows: "Anyone who divorces his wife and marries another woman commits adultery—though this principle does not hold in the case of *porneia*."

6. John J. Kilgallen ("To What Are the Matthean Exception-Texts [5, 32 and 19, 9] an Exception?" *Biblica* 61 [1980]: 102–5) suggests that the except clauses need only mean that in some cases divorce is not adulterous, rather than that in some cases divorce is not morally wrong. He renders 5:32: "Everyone who divorces his wife (except in the case of *porneia*) makes her adulterous." But in the case of *porneia,* he does not *make* her adulterous; she is *already* adulterous (similarly Westerholm [pp. 118f.] and the literature he cites). This is not convincing; for the Greek does not read "makes her adulterous" or "makes her an adulteress," but "makes her commit adultery" (the passive infinitive does not mean "to become an adulter[ess]" but "to commit adultery"; cf. BAGD, s.v., 2.b). If the woman has already committed *porneia,* doubtless divorce (and the remarriage that would ensue) could scarcely be said to make her an adulteress; but such divorce and remarriage would make her commit adultery. And this approach does not work in v.9, where the result is not that the man makes his wife commit adultery but that he commits adultery.

7. It seems best, then, to permit both *porneia* and the except clause to retain their normal force. Jesus is then saying that divorce and remarriage always involve evil; but as Moses permitted it because of the hardness of men's hearts, so also does he—but now on the sole grounds of *porneia* (sexual sin of any sort). The principal exegetical difficulties surrounding this view may be treated as follows:

a. Formally Jesus is abrogating something of the Mosaic prescription; for whatever the *'erwaṯ dāḇār* ("something indecent") refers to (Deut 24:1), it cannot easily be thought to refer to adultery, for which the prescribed punishment was death. That this was rarely carried out (McKeating, "Sanctions Against Adultery"; cf. Joseph in 1:19–20) is beside the point: as a legal system, irrespective of whether it was enforced, the Deuteronomic permission for divorce and remarriage could scarcely have adultery primarily in view. But *porneia* includes adultery even if not restricted to it. Jesus' judgments on the matter are therefore both lighter (no capital punishment for adultery) and heavier (the sole exception being sexual sin).

b. This exception is not in contradiction with Jesus' strong words in vv.4–8, despite frequent insistence on the contrary. In vv.4–8 Jesus lays out the true direction in which Scripture points (cf. Jesus' treatment of oaths, 5:33–37, where there is also formal abrogation of a Mosaic command). Even here Jesus acknowledges that the Mosaic concession springs not from divine desire but human hardheartedness. Would Jesus say human hearts were any less hard in his own day? Might there not therefore be some exception to the principle he lays out, precisely because *porneia* was not on the Creator's mind in Genesis 1–2? More importantly sexual sin has a peculiar relation to Jesus' treatment of Genesis 1:27; 2:24 (in Matt 19:4–6), because the indissolubility of marriage he defends by appealing to those verses from the creation accounts is predicated on sexual union ("one flesh"). Sexual promiscuity is therefore a de facto exception. It may not necessitate divorce; but permission for divorce and remarriage under such circumstances, far from being inconsistent with Jesus' thought, is in perfect harmony with it.

c. Although it is commonly held that the except clauses are secondary and bring Matthew into a clash with Mark, the issue is not so simple. Not a few scholars hold that, at least on this point, Matthew 19:9 is authentic and that Mark omits the obvious exception (e.g., Schlatter; Isaksson, pp. 75–92; D.L. Dungan, *The Sayings of Jesus in the Churches of Paul* [Philadelphia: Fortress, 1971], pp. 122–25). Catchpole ("Synoptic Material"), on the other hand, argues for Markan priority on the ground that the aporias he finds in Matthew 19:3–12 can all be explained by recognizing that they have been introduced precisely where Matthew has changed Mark. His argument has some weight only if the aporias are real; but the four he mentions are either imagined or explainable in other ways. For instance, Catchpole holds that v.9 does not cohere with vv.4–8, and this problem can be remedied only by the removal of the except clause in v.9—which is precisely the new bit Matthew has added. But we have shown above at b that v.9 *does* cohere with vv.4–8. This does not prove Matthew did not depend on Mark, but it forbids claiming he *did*. And even if Mark's priority prevails in this pericope, Matthew's redactional additions cannot be assumed to be nonhistorical unless we have evidence that Matthew had access to no other information (cf. Introduction, sections 1–3). We conclude, therefore, that there is no decisive evidence for literary dependence either way, and that there is no overwhelming reason why the except clauses, both here and in 5:32, should not be authentic.

Certainly, on the interpretation adopted here, Matthew and Mark–Luke have this in common—they abrogate any permission for divorce in Deuteronomy 24:1 if that permission extends, or is thought to extend, beyond sexual sin. If Mark has priority, the except clause in Matthew seems best explained along the line suggested by Hill above at 3; if the reverse, or if the two Gospels preserve independent accounts of the same incident, Mark may think the exception so obvious (because it concerns sexual infidelity, the heart of the union according to Genesis) as not worth mentioning. Moreover the exception is particularly appropriate to Jesus' day and to Matthew's Jewish readers; for though Jesus had formally dismissed the Mosaic divorce provisions and substituted marital unfaithfulness as the sole basis of a rupture of the "one flesh," this exception collided with the Mosaic sentence of stoning in such cases—a fact of which Jewish audiences were doubtlessly aware. With the death penalty for marital *porneia* effectively abolished, "the termination of the relationship might appropriately be effected by divorce" (James B. Hurley, *Man and Woman in Biblical Perspective* [Leicester: IVP, 1981], p. 104; cf. further John Murray, *Divorce* [Philadelphia: Presbyterian and Reformed, 1953], pp. 51ff.).

d. The final problem is whether this interpretation adequately accounts for the disciples' reaction (v.10). Before turning to this, we may observe that Mark 10:12 makes the same responsibilities and privileges concerning divorce and remarriage extend to the woman as well as the man—probably a pointed rebuke of Herodias (cf. Lane, *Mark*, p. 358). Mark omits the except clause and retains the remark about women, Matthew the reverse. (The related question of the so-called Pauline privilege [1 Cor 7:15] must be left to commentaries on 1 Corinthians.)

10–12 Dupont (*Mariage et divorce*, pp. 161–222) argues that these verses deal, not with celibacy, but with continence after divorce. Believing that no remarriage is legitimate, Dupont argues that the divorced believer must remain continent "for the sake of the kingdom"—i.e., in order to enter it—because remarriage would be adulterous. Somewhat similar is Francis J. Moloney's position ("Matthew 19, 3–12 and Celibacy. A Redactional and Form-Critical Study." *Journal of the Study of the New Testament* 2 (1979): 42–60, esp. 47ff.). But in addition to the difficulties entailed by holding that no remarriage is permitted (see on v.9), "eunuch" is a strange figure for continence after marriage, especially since if the divorced spouse died, the survivor could remarry (Dupont's view).

There is a better way to look at these verses. First, the disciples' reaction (v.10) must not be exaggerated. Unlike v.25, there is no mention of astonishment. Jesus, though not forbidding *all* divorce and remarriage, has come close to the school of Shammai on the grounds for exceptions, while taking a far more conservative stance than Shammai on who may remarry. In the light of the position, tacitly adopted by most Jews, that marriage was a duty, the disciples rather cynically conclude that such strictures surely make marriage unattractive. This virtually makes the appeal of marriage contingent on liberal divorce and remarriage rights—a stance that fails miserably to understand what Jesus has said about the creation ordinance.

Verse 11 can then be understood in one of two ways. Either *ton logon touton* (lit., "this word"—regardless of whether *touton* is original, since *ton* can be a mild demonstrative) refers to Jesus' teaching in vv.4–9 or to the disciples' misguided remark in v.10. NIV's "this teaching" (v.11) favors the former; but this is unlikely, for it makes Jesus contradict himself. After a strong prohibition, it is highly unlikely that Jesus' moral teaching dwindles into a pathetic "But of course, not everyone can accept this."

It helps little to say with Bonnard that those to whom the teaching is given are Christians who must follow Jesus' moral standards but that others cannot accept what he says, for Jesus' appeal has been to the creation ordinance, not to kingdom morality. It is better to take "this word" to refer to the disciples' conclusion in v.10: "it is better not to marry." Jesus responds that not everyone can live by such a verdict, such abstinence from marriage. But some do, namely those to whom it is given—those born eunuchs, those made eunuchs by men (possibly in groups like the Essenes, but more likely a reflection of the rabbinic distinction between two types of eunuch: the impotent and the castrated—the latter very often for some high court position where there were royal women (cf. Acts 8:26–39; SBK, 1:805–7)—and those who have made themselves eunuchs because of the kingdom of God. The latter is not a commendation of self-castration but of renunciation of marriage in light of the disciples' remark, "it is better not to marry."

Jesus, like Paul after him (1 Cor 7:7–9), is prepared to commend celibacy "because of the kingdom" (not "for the sake of attaining it," but "because of its claims and interests": cf. J. Blinzler, "Εἰσὶν εὐνοῦχοι: Zur Auslegung von Mt 19, 12," ZNW 28 [1957]: 254–70). Thus, far from backing down at the disciples' surliness, Jesus freely concedes that for those to whom it is given "it *is* better not to marry"; and "The one who can accept this should accept it." But it is important to recognize that neither Jesus nor the apostles see celibacy as an intrinsically holier state than marriage (cf. 1 Tim 4:1–3; Heb 13:4) nor as a condition for the top levels of ministry (Matt 8:14; 1 Cor 9:5) but as a special calling granted for greater usefulness in the kingdom. Those who impose this discipline on themselves must remember Paul's conclusion: it is better to marry than to burn with passion (1 Cor 7:9).

Two final observations: (1) The authenticity of v. 12 has been admirably defended by T. Matura ("Le célibat dans le Nouveau Testament," *Nouvelle Revue Théologique* 107 [1975]: 481-500); and (2) Jesus' remarks betray a certain self-conscious independence of the OT law, which excluded eunuchs from the assembly of Yahweh (Deut 23:1; cf. Lev 22:24; SBK, 1:806–7; Schweizer). One cannot forget the conversion of the Ethiopian eunuch (Acts 8:26–40) who, though he would have been excluded from the assembly of Yahweh, was joyfully welcomed to the assembly of Messiah.

Notes

5 On the use of *εἰς σάρκα μίαν* (*eis sarka mian*, "one flesh") instead of a predicative nominative, see Moule, *Idiom Book*, pp. 183, 208; Zerwick, par. 32.

10 Οὕτως (*houtōs*, lit., "thus") here takes on a relatively rare adjectival function (NIV, "this"; cf. BDF, par. 434[1]).

Contrary to B.F. Meyer, *αἰτία* (*aitia*) here means not "cause" but "case" or "situation" (NIV; cf. BDF, par. 5[3*b*]).

2. *Blessing little children*

19:13–15

[13]Then little children were brought to Jesus for him to place his hands on them and pray for them. But the disciples rebuked those who brought them.
[14]Jesus said, "Let the little children come to me, and do not hinder them, for the kingdom of heaven belongs to such as these." [15]When he had placed his hands on them, he went on from there.

13 "Then" is ambiguous (see on 2:7). Children in Jesus' day were often brought to rabbis and elders to be blessed, customarily by placing hands on them (cf. Gen 48:14; Num 27:18; Acts 6:6; 13:3; cf. Matt 9:18, 20; Mark 10:16). The disciples "rebuked them" (lit.): both the context and the synoptic parallels show that "them" refers, not to the children, but to "those who brought them" (NIV).

Why did the disciples stoop to this rebuke? Perhaps they were annoyed that Jesus was being delayed on his journey to Jerusalem; perhaps they felt they were being interrupted in their important discussion. Although children in Judaism of the time were deeply cherished, they were thought in some ways to be negligible members of society: their place was to learn, to be respectful, to listen. But two deeper insights suggest themselves: (1) the preceding pericope (vv.3–12) implicitly stresses the sanctity of the family, and vv.13–15 continue by saying something important about children; and (2) in 18:1–9 children serve as models for humility, patterns for Jesus' "little ones"; yet Jesus' disciples, his "little ones," show little humility here.

14–15 Jesus does not want the little children prevented from coming to him (v.14), not because the kingdom of heaven belongs to them, but because the kingdom of heaven belongs to those like them (so also Mark and Luke, stressing childlike faith): Jesus receives them because they are an excellent object lesson in the kind of humility and faith he finds acceptable.

Notes

14 O. Cullmann (*Baptism in the New Testament* [London: SCM, 1950], pp. 71–80) finds in *μὴ κωλύετε* (*mē kōluete*, "do not hinder") an echo of a primitive baptismal formula, because this verb refers to baptism elsewhere (3:14; Acts 8:36; 10:47; 11:17). He does not argue that here Jesus teaches infant baptism but that the church transmitted the story in a way Christians would remember an event in Jesus' ministry "by which they might be led to a solution of the question of infant Baptism" (p. 78). Apart from the propriety of finding a solution to a later problem in a story all agree does not address it, the suggestion that *mē kōluete* was a technical term that connoted baptism is very doubtful. The verb occurs twenty-three times in the NT, and only five of these relate to baptism. The four (outside this passage) allegedly referring to baptism fail to establish a clear baptismal formula: at 3:14 John tries "to deter" Jesus; in Acts 8:36 the Ethiopian eunuch asks what "prevents" him from being baptized; and the remaining two occurrences (Acts 10:47; 11:17) justify the baptism of the Gentile Cornelius on the grounds that the Spirit had fallen on him.

---

3. *Wealth and the kingdom* (19:16–30)

a. *The rich young man*

19:16–22

16Now a man came up to Jesus and asked, "Teacher, what good thing must I do to get eternal life?"
17"Why do you ask me about what is good?" Jesus replied. "There is only One who is good. If you want to enter life, obey the commandments."
18"Which ones?" the man inquired.
Jesus replied, " 'Do not murder, do not commit adultery, do not steal, do not give false testimony, 19honor your father and mother,' and 'love your neighbor as yourself.' "
20"All these I have kept," the young man said. "What do I still lack?"
21Jesus answered, "If you want to be perfect, go, sell your possessions and give to the poor, and you will have treasure in heaven. Then come, follow me."
22When the young man heard this, he went away sad, because he had great wealth.

Some of the differences between Matthew and Mark–Luke (cf. Mark 10:17–31; Luke 18:18–30) are so sharp (cf. vv.16–17) that they have frequently served as tests for redaction criticism. Many, of course, are of little significance. Matthew introduces the central figure as "a man" and later says he was "young" (v.20). Mark (10:17) says nothing about his age but provides more details of the initial meeting: it was "as Jesus started on his way" that a man "ran up" to him and "fell on his knees before him." These and many similar differences have been treated elsewhere (cf. Carson, "Redaction Criticism"). The nub of the problem turns on vv.16–17 and parallels.

16–17 A certain man—identified by all three evangelists as rich, by Matthew (v.20) as young, and by Luke (18:18) as a ruler—asks Jesus what he must do to inherit "eternal life" (v.16). The latter expression refers to a life "approved by God and to which access to the kingdom (present and eschatological) is promised (cf. the rabbinic 'life of the age to come')" (Hill, *Matthew;* cf. 7:14; 25:46; Hill, *Greek Words*, pp. 163–201).

The problem arises when Matthew is compared with Mark and Luke. In the latter, the questioner asks, "Good teacher, what must I do to inherit eternal life?" (Luke 18:18). Jesus replies, "Why do you call me good? No one is good—except

God alone" (v.19). In Matthew, however, the questioner asks, "Teacher, what good thing must I do to inherit eternal life?" (v.16). "Good" no longer modifies "teacher"; and therefore Jesus' response is correspondingly adapted: "Why do you ask me about what is good? There is only One who is good" (v.17). A majority of modern scholars hold that Matthew has transformed the exchange because, at his later time of writing, the church can no longer live with the suggestion that Jesus himself is not sinless.

It is logically possible to achieve harmonization by mere addition ("*Good* teacher, what *good* thing?" followed by Jesus giving both answers); indeed, later copyists of NT MSS sometimes opted for such an approach (hence KJV). But the procedure is notoriously implausible. The evangelists, as we have often witnessed, are far more concerned with Jesus' *ipsissima vox* than his *ipsissima verba* (see note on 3:17); and we do the Scriptures disservice when we fail to consider the implications. Nevertheless the christological explanation ventured by many is equally implausible. A better understanding of the text is gained from the following observations.

1. Stonehouse (*Origins*, pp. 93–112) has convincingly demonstrated that christological concerns do not stand at the heart of *any* of the three synoptic accounts. The argument of G.M. Styler ("Stages in Christology in the Synoptic Gospels," NTS 10 [1963–64]: esp. pp. 404–6), that Matthew reflects a growing interest in ontology, is especially weak. Styler argues that, unlike Mark, Matthew believes Jesus is divine. But Hill (*Matthew*) rightly points out that Matthew still preserves the words "There is only One who is good," a clear reference to God; and the alteration says nothing about Jesus' status in relation to God. Moreover Styler has adopted a historical reconstruction of the development of doctrine that not all find convincing (cf. D.A. Carson, "Unity and Diversity: On the Possibility of Systematic Theology," in Carson and Woodbridge), especially here where Luke, probably writing after Matthew or at least very close to him, senses no embarrassment in Mark's words but records them verbatim—and this despite the fact that Luke elsewhere feels free to drop bits that could be taken as detrimental to Jesus. We must therefore look for nonchristological explanations for Matthew's alteration.

2. The thrust of the passage in both Mark and Matthew must be grasped. Irrespective of what "good" refers to, the man approaches Jesus with a question showing how far he is from the humble faith that, as Jesus has just finished saying, characterizes all who belong to the kingdom (vv.13–15). He wants to earn eternal life; and in the light of v.20, he apparently thinks there are good things he can do, beyond the demands of the law, by which he can assure his salvation. Many Jews believed that a specific act of goodness could win eternal life (SBK, 1: 808ff.); and this young man, assuming this opinion is correct, seeks Jesus' view as to what that act might be. Whatever differences exist between Matthew and Luke, Jesus' response is not designed either to confess personal sin (Mark) nor to call in question his own competence to discuss what is good (Matthew), for such topics are not in view (see esp. B.B. Warfield, "Jesus' Alleged Confession of Sin," PTR 12 [1914]: 127–228). Instead Jesus calls in question his interlocutor's inadequate understanding of goodness. In the absolute sense of goodness required to gain eternal life, only God is good (cf. Ps 106:1; 118:1, 29; 1 Chron 16:34; 2 Chron 5:13; and there is no discussion of whether Jesus shares that goodness). Jesus will not allow anything other than God's will to determine what is good. By approaching Jesus in this way (esp. vv.16, 20), the young man reveals simultaneously that he wants something beyond God's will (v.20) and that he misconstrues the absoluteness of God's goodness.

3. In this light Matthew's phrasing of the initial exchange between Jesus and the young man focuses on the issue central for both Matthew and Mark more clearly than Mark does. To that extent it also ties this pericope more closely to the preceding one than Mark does. This young man stands in stunning contrast to those to whom, according to Jesus, the kingdom belongs. This may help explain Matthew's wording.

4. Within this framework Mark 10:18 no more calls in question Jesus' sinlessness than Matthew 19:17 calls in question Jesus' competence to judge what is good. Apart from the assumption of Mark's priority without either evangelist having access to other traditions, it is difficult to see why, if we charge Matthew with eliminating the possibility that readers might think Jesus could sin, we should not charge Mark with eliminating the possibility that some readers might think Jesus could not pronounce on what was good. Both charges would miss the central point of both Matthew and Mark.

5. "If you want to enter life, obey the commandments" (v.17) does not mean that Matthew, unlike Mark, thinks eternal life is *earned* by keeping the commandments. After all, Mark himself is about to report Jesus' exhortation to keep specific commandments. The entire debate has been bedevilled by a false split between grace and obedience to the will of God. No less staunch a supporter of grace than Paul can insist that without certain purity a man cannot inherit the kingdom (1 Cor 6:9–10). Jesus tells this young man, in similar vein, what good things he must do if he is to gain eternal life, precisely because he perceives his questioner has little understanding of such things. But that is still far from telling him that by doing these things he will *earn* eternal life.

6. But why, then, has either Matthew or Mark edited the exchange? Or, if the two reports are independent, or if Matthew depends on Mark but has eyewitness knowledge of the events, how is it possible that both accounts can be accepted as trustworthy representations of the same incident? Lohmeyer (*Matthäus*) suggests that the variations stem from different translations of an Aramaic report of the incident. Better yet is a reconstruction of the incident that, though not simple additive harmonization, provides a historical basis broad enough to support reports of both Matthew and Mark–Luke and fits well within the normal latitude the evangelists show in their reportage. This reconstruction is worked out in more detail elsewhere (Carson, "Redaction Crticism"). Briefly, it suggests the young ruler's question was "Good teacher, what must I do to inherit eternal life?" and that Jesus' reply was "Why do you ask *me* questions regarding the good? There is only one who is good, namely God."

18–20 Jesus lists the sixth, seventh, eighth, ninth, and fifth commandments of Exodus 20 in that order. He omits "do not defraud" (Mark 10:19, apparently an application of the eighth and ninth) and adds "love your neighbor as yourself" (Lev 19:18; cf. Matt 22:34–40). On the text form, compare Gundry (*Use of OT*, pp. 17–19) and K.J. Thomas ("Liturgical Citations in the Synoptics," NTS 22 [1975–76]: 205–14). The man's impulsive reply is reflected by Paul (Phil 3:6; cf. SBK, 1:814) on a certain understanding of the law; but the man's further words, "What do I still lack?" show his uncertainty and lack of assurance of ever being good enough for salvation, as well as his notion that certain "good works" are over and above the law (cf. SBK, 4:536ff., 559ff.). Wealth he enjoyed (v.22), while suffering barrenness of soul.

21–22 Many have taken these verses to indicate a two-tier ethic: some disciples find eternal life, and others go further and become perfect by adopting a more compassionate stance (e.g., Klostermann; DNTT, 2:63). But G. Barth (Bornkamm, *Tradition* pp. 95ff.) convincingly disproves this exegesis. In particular the young man's question in v.20, "What do I still lack?" clearly refers to gaining eternal life (v.17); and Jesus' answer in v.21 must be understood as answering the question. A two-tier Christianity is implicitly contradicted by 23:8–12; and the same word "perfect" is applied to all of Jesus' disciples in 5:48. Matthew shows no strong tendency toward asceticism. Therefore the basic thrust of v.21 is not "Sell your possessions and give to the poor" but "Come, follow me."

What the word "perfection" suggests here is what it commonly means in the OT: undivided loyalty and full-hearted obedience. This young man could not face that. He was willing to discipline himself to observe all the outward stipulations and even perform supererogatory works; but because of his wealth, he had a divided heart. His money was competing with God; and what Jesus everywhere demands as a condition for eternal life is absolute, radical discipleship. This entails the surrender of *self*. "Keeping the individual commandments is no substitute for the readiness for self-surrender to the absolute claim of God imposed through the call of the gospel. Jesus' summons in this context means that true obedience to the Law is rendered ultimately in discipleship" (Lane, *Mark*, p. 367).

Formally, of course, Jesus' demand goes beyond anything in OT law (cf. Banks, *Jesus*, p. 163): no OT passage stipulates v.21. Equally remarkable is the fact that the focus on *God's will* (vv.17–19) should culminate in following *Jesus*. The explanation of this is that Jesus is prophesied by the OT. The will of God, as revealed in Scripture, looks forward to the coming of Messiah (see on 2:15; 5:17–20; 11:11–13). Absolute allegiance to him, with the humility of a child, is essential to salvation. The condition Jesus now imposes not only reveals the man's attachment to money but shows that all his formal compliance with the law is worthless because none of it entails absolute self-surrender. What the man needs is the triumph of grace; for as the next verses show, for him entering the kingdom of heaven is impossible (v.26). God, with whom all things are possible, must work. The parable in 20:1–16 directly speaks to this issue. But the young man is deaf to it: he leaves because, if a choice must be made between money and Jesus, money wins (cf. 6:24).

Notes

---

20 Here and elsewhere (Allen, p. xxiii), Matthew uses the aorist active verb—this time ἐφύλαξα (*ephylaxa,* "I have kept")—rather than the middle Mark uses—but the distinction is hardly worth mentioning (cf. Moule, *Idiom Book*, p. 24).

---

b. *Grace and reward in the kingdom*

19:23–30

23Then Jesus said to his disciples, "I tell you the truth, it is hard for a rich man to enter the kingdom of heaven. 24Again I tell you, it is easier for a camel to go through the eye of a needle than for a rich man to enter the kingdom of God."

[25]When the disciples heard this, they were greatly astonished and asked, "Who then can be saved?"

[26]Jesus looked at them and said, "With man this is impossible, but with God all things are possible."

[27]Peter answered him, "We have left everything to follow you! What then will there be for us?"

[28]Jesus said to them, "I tell you the truth, at the renewal of all things, when the Son of Man sits on his glorious throne, you who have followed me will also sit on twelve thrones, judging the twelve tribes of Israel. [29]And everyone who has left houses or brothers or sisters or father or mother or children or fields for my sake will receive a hundred times as much and will inherit eternal life. [30]But many who are first will be last, and many who are last will be first.

23–24 Jesus is not saying that all poor people and none of the wealthy enter the kingdom of heaven (v.23; see on 3:2). That would exclude Abraham, Isaac, and Jacob, to say nothing of David, Solomon, and Joseph of Arimathea. The point of Jesus' teaching lies elsewhere. Most Jews expected the rich to inherit eternal life, not because their wealth could buy their way in, but because their wealth testified to the blessing of the Lord on their lives. Jesus' view is a different and more sober one. (On "I tell you the truth," see on 5:18). The proverbial saying of v.24 refers to the absolutely impossible. The camel was the biggest animal in Palestine (a similar proverb in BT [B *Berakoth* 55b] prefers "elephant" to "camel" because elephants were not uncommon in Babylon). Attempts to weaken this hyperbole by taking "needle," not as a sewing needle, but as a small gate through which an unladen camel could just squeeze—and only on his knees—are misguided. This conjecture may come from some of Jerome's allegorizing (cf. Broadus).

25–26 "Saved" (v.25) is equivalent to entering the kingdom of God (v.24) or obtaining eternal life (v.16). The disciples, reflecting the common Jewish view of the rich, are astonished and ask that if rich men, blessed of God, cannot be saved, then who *can* be? Jesus agrees: "With man this [the salvation of anyone] is impossible, but with God all things are possible" (v.26; cf. Gen 18:14; Job 42:2; Luke 1:37).

27–28 Peter, impressed by "impossible" and speaking for his fellow disciples, thinks Jesus' words are unfair to the Twelve (v.27). Peter emphatically replies, "We have left everything to follow you" (cf. 4:20). Even here he and the others are thinking in terms of deserving or earning God's favor. Yet Jesus does not castigate his disciples for being mercenary: they have made sacrifices and deserve an answer. But what he says—that the blessing to come, whether belonging exclusively to the Twelve at the renewal (v.28) or to all believers now (vv.29–30), far surpasses any sacrifice they might make—implies that it is a gentle rebuke.

Verse 28 has no parallel in Mark and only a loose one in Luke 22:28–30. The solemn "I tell you the truth" points to something important. Jesus looks forward to the session of the Son of Man (see on 8:20). He will sit on his "glorious throne" (lit., "throne of glory"; cf. Zerwick, par. 41; Turner, *Syntax*, p. 214; cf. 7:22; 16:27; 25:31, 34) at the *palingenesia* ("renewal" of all things), a word used only twice in the NT, the other occurrence dealing with "rebirth . . . by the Holy Spirit" (Titus 3:5). Here it has to do with the consummation of the kingdom (RSV, "in the new world"). (For its use elsewhere, cf. TDNT, 1:686–89; DNTT, 1:184–85; and cf. 13:32; Acts 3:21; Rom 8:18–23; 2 Peter 3:13; Rev 21:1, 5; 1QS 4:25.)

Contrary to Schweizer (*Matthew*), there is no allusion to the endless Stoic cycles of conflagration and "renewal"; the idea moves strictly within Jewish teleological and apocalyptic expectation. But the remarkable feature of this verse is that the Twelve will "sit on twelve thrones," sharing judgment with the Son of Man. The idea that believers will at the consummation have a part in judging is not uncommon in the NT (Luke 22:30; 1 Cor 6:2). What is less clear is whether (1) the twelve apostles exercise judgment over the twelve tribes of Israel physically and racially conceived, or whether (2) the twelve apostles will exercise some kind of judgment over the entire church, symbolized by "Israel" (cf. Rev 21:12–14), or whether (3) the Twelve represent the entire assembly of Messiah, who will exercise a juridical role over racial Israel. The third supposition has no scriptural parallel; the second is possible but an unnatural way of taking "Israel" in a book that, though applying OT promises to Gentiles and Jews alike—viz., the "church" of Messiah—distinguishes between the two. The most plausible interpretation is the first one. At the consummation the Twelve will judge the nation of Israel, presumably for its general rejection of Jesus Messiah. (On the symbolism, cf. Joseph M. Baumgarten, "The Duodecimal Courts of Qumran, Revelation, and the Sanhedrin," JBL 95 [1976]: 59–78, esp. pp. 70–72; France, *Jesus,* pp. 65f.)

29–30 Jesus now extends his encouragement to all his self-sacrificing disciples (cf. Mark 10:30). The promise is not literal (one cannot have one hundred mothers). God is no man's debtor: if one of Jesus' disciples has, for Jesus' sake, left, say, a father, he will find within the messianic community a hundred who will be as a father to him—in addition to inheriting eternal life (v.29).

The proverbial saying (v.30) is one Jesus repeats on various occasions. Here he immediately illustrates it by a parable (20:1–16), climaxed by the proverb in reverse form (20:16) as a closing bracket. It indicates something of the reversals under the king's reign. Attempts to restrict the application of this parable to one setting are not successful.

1. Some say the rich become poor at the consummation and the poor rich (cf. vv.16–29), as in Luke 16:19–31: the story of Lazarus and the beggar. But such reversals are not absolute: Zacchaeus (Luke 19:1–10) was a rich man to whose house salvation came; and Abraham, to whose "bosom" the beggar went, had great wealth.

2. Many of the Fathers hold that the first-last idea refers to Jews and Gentiles respectively. Doubtless it may, but this theme is not dominant in these chapters.

3. Some think the proverb assumes that the disciples had been arguing about priority on the basis of who was first called, to which Jesus responds that "the last will be first, etc." But this better suits the situation in Matthew 18 than in Matthew 19.

4. It seems preferable, therefore, to take the proverb as a way of setting forth God's grace over against *all* notions that the rich, powerful, great, and prominent will continue so in the kingdom. Those who approach God in childlike trust (vv.13–15) will be received and advanced in the kingdom beyond those who, from the world's perspective, enjoy prominence now.

4. *The parable of the workers*

20:1–16

1"The kingdom of heaven is like a landowner who went out early in the morning to hire men to work in his vineyard. 2He agreed to pay them a denarius for the day and sent them into his vineyard.

[3]"About the third hour he went out and saw others standing in the marketplace doing nothing. [4]He told them, 'You also go and work in my vineyard, and I will pay you whatever is right.' [5]So they went.

"He went out again about the sixth hour and the ninth hour and did the same thing. [6]About the eleventh hour he went out and found still others standing around. He asked them, 'Why have you been standing here all day long doing nothing?'

[7]" 'Because no one has hired us,' they answered.

"He said to them, 'You also go and work in my vineyard.'

[8]"When evening came, the owner of the vineyard said to his foreman, 'Call the workers and pay them their wages, beginning with the last ones hired and going on to the first.'

[9]"The workers who were hired about the eleventh hour came and each received a denarius. [10]So when those came who were hired first, they expected to receive more. But each one of them also received a denarius. [11]When they received it, they began to grumble against the landowner. [12]'These men who were hired last worked only one hour,' they said, 'and you have made them equal to us who have borne the burden of the work and the heat of the day.'

[13]"But he answered one of them, 'Friend, I am not being unfair to you. Didn't you agree to work for a denarius? [14]Take your pay and go. I want to give the man who was hired last the same as I gave you. [15]Don't I have the right to do what I want with my own money? Or are you envious because I am generous?'

[16]"So the last will be first, and the first will be last."

On parables generally, see on 13:3a. From this one, found only in Matthew, we learn how "the last" person can become "first" (19:30)—by free grace (Schlatter; see esp. v.15). The point is not that those who work just an hour do as much as those who work all day (unlike a Jewish parable c. A.D. 325 that tells of a man who on those grounds is paid a month's wages for a few hours' discussion), nor that the willingness of the latecomers matches that of the all-day workers (contra Preisker, TDNT, 4:717 and n. 91), nor that Gentiles are the latecomers in contrast to the Jews (the context knows no such distinctions), nor that all men are equal before God or that all kingdom work is equal. (Still less acceptable is Derrett's lengthy explanation (*NT Studies*, 1:48–75). He rightly holds that the entire parable portrays working conditions in the first century; but the eleventh-hour men, entitled to a certain minimum wage, actually get more. But Derrett's view depends on late sources for minimum wage laws; and he assumes that the grapes were urgently in need of harvesting and that it must have been Friday afternoon—none of which the text implies.)

Huffmann (pp. 209–10) is right. The parable begins with a typical scene and introduces atypical elements to surprise the reader and make a powerful point. "Jesus deliberately and cleverly led the listeners along by degrees until they understood that if God's generosity was to be represented by a man, such a man would be different from any man ever encountered" (p. 209).

1–2 On "the kingdom of heaven is like" formula (v.1), see on 13:24. The normal working day was ten hours or so, not counting breaks. The landowner in the parable finds his first set of men at about 6 A.M. (*hama prōi* means "at dawn"; NIV, "early in the morning": on the construction, see Moule, *Idiom Book*, p. 82) and agrees to pay each worker a denarius (v.2)—the normal wage for a foot soldier or day laborer (Tobit 5:14; Tacitus *Annales*, 1.17; Pliny 33.3).

3–7 There were twelve "hours" from dawn to sundown. The third hour (v.3) would be about 9:00 A.M., the sixth about 12:00 M., and the eleventh about 5:00 P.M. The marketplace would be the central square, where all kinds of business was done and casual labor hired. Why the landowner kept returning to hire more men—lack of foresight, not finding enough workers earlier in the day at the marketplace, the poor work of the first laborers—is not spelled out and therefore cannot be the key to the parable. The third-hour men are promised "whatever is right" (v.4); and, trusting the landowner's integrity, they work on that basis (v.5). The last group (v.6) were standing around ("idle" [KJV] is a late addition) because no one had hired them (v.7).

8–12 Some take "when evening came" (v.8) as an allusion to the judgment, but this is doubtful. It is essential to the story in a time when laborers were customarily paid at the end of each day (cf. Lev 19:13). The foreman is told to pay each man (lit.) "the wage"—the standard day-laborer's wage. Who gets paid first is crucial: it is only because the last hired receive a day's wage (v.9) that those first hired expect to get more than they bargained for (v.10). They "grumble against" (v.11) the owner because he has been generous to others and merely just to them. They have borne "the heat of the day" (v.12, either direct sunlight or hot wind [BAGD, s.v. *kausōn*]), which could drive workers from the field; and, though fairly paid, they feel unfairly treated because others who worked much less received what they did. Nothing in the parable implies that Jews have borne the burden of the law and now Gentile outcasts are made equal to them.

13–15 "Friend" (v.13) suggests that this rebuke is only a mild one. "I am not being unfair to you"—I am not cheating you, defrauding you (cf. M. Black, "Some Greek Words with 'Hebrew' Meanings in the Epistles and Apocalypse," in McKay and Miller, pp. 142ff.). The owner has paid the agreed wage (v.14). Should he want to pay others more, that is his business. Provided he has been just in all his dealings, does he not have the right to do what he wants with his money (v.15)? NIV translates "is your eye evil" (lit. Gk.) by "are you envious," because the "evil eye" was an idiom used to refer to jealousy (cf. Deut 15:9; 1 Sam 18:9; see on Matt 6:22–23).

These rhetorical questions (vv.13b–15) show that God's great gifts, simply because they *are* God's, are distributed, not because they are earned, but because he is gracious (cf. W. Haubeck, "Zum Verständnis der Parabel von den Arbeitern im Weinberg [Mt. 20, 1–15]," in Haubeck and Bachmann, pp. 95–107, esp. pp. 106f.). Jesus is not laying down principles for resolving union-management disputes. On the contrary, "the principle in the world is that he who works the longest receives the most pay. That is just. But in the kingdom of God the principles of merit and ability may be set aside so that grace can prevail" (Kistemaker, pp. 77f.). (See note on 5:12 and G. de Ru's article "The Conception of Reward in the Teaching of Jesus," NovTest 8 [1966]: 202–22.)

16 God's grace makes some who are last first. The point of the parable is not that all in the kingdom will receive the same reward but that kingdom rewards depend on God's sovereign grace (cf. v.23). For the inclusion around the parable, see on 19:30.

Notes

10 The article in τὸ ἀνὰ δηνάριον (*to ana dēnarion*) is anaphoric, i.e., "a denarius to each man *as to the others who preceded*": cf. BDF, par. 266(2).

15 "Or" is omitted by some MSS, with the evidence rather evenly divided (cf. Metzger, *Textual Commentary*, pp. 50f.).

16 Many MSS add to the end of the verse "for many are invited, but few are chosen." The shorter reading is Alexandrian and Western. The longer reading, if original, might have been dropped by homoeoteleuton; but it is equally possible the extra words are an assimilation to 22:14 (so Metzger, *Textual Commentary*, p. 5).

5. *Third major passion prediction*

20:17–19

[17]Now as Jesus was going up to Jerusalem, he took the twelve disciples aside and said to them, [18]"We are going up to Jerusalem, and the Son of Man will be betrayed to the chief priests and the teachers of the law. They will condemn him to death [19]and will turn him over to the Gentiles to be mocked and flogged and crucified. On the third day he will be raised to life!"

See on 16:21–23; 17:9, 22–23; and for the synoptic parallels, see Mark 10:32–34; Luke 18:31–34. Here there is the first mention of the mode of Jesus' death and of the Gentiles' part in it (only the Romans could crucify people). These three verses may look back to the preceding parable by implying the grounds of God's grace—viz., what his Son did on the cross. Also, just as 19:13–15 sets the stage for 19:16–30, so 20:17–19 sets it for 20:20–28. While Jesus faces crucifixion, his disciples, still blind to the nature of his messiahship, squabble over their places in the kingdom.

17 "Going up" does not necessarily mean that Jesus has left Perea, crossed the Jordan, passed through Jericho, and begun the ascent to Jerusalem; for it had become customary to speak of "going up" to Jerusalem regardless of where one was in Palestine, as in England one "goes up" to London from every place except Oxford or Cambridge. We should therefore not be surprised to find Jesus still in Jericho (20:29). Before setting out for Jerusalem, doubtless to attend the festival, Jesus took the Twelve aside from the throngs of pilgrims choking the roads to Jerusalem at such times (see on 21:9). Only the Twelve were even remotely ready to hear this passion prediction.

18–19 Jerusalem was the focal point of Jewish worship. We are going there, Jesus says, because there the Son of Man will be betrayed and crucified. He will be "condemned"—his death will result from legal proceedings (v.18). Mention of the Resurrection is brief (v.19) and apparently not understood (cf. Luke 18:34)—though in Matthew the disciples' misunderstanding is not spelled out as in Luke but exemplified by the succeeding story (vv.20–28), which Luke omits.

6. *Suffering and service*

20:20–28

20Then the mother of Zebedee's sons came to Jesus with her sons and, kneeling down, asked a favor of him.
21"What is it you want?" he asked.
She said, "Grant that one of these two sons of mine may sit at your right and the other at your left in your kingdom."
22"You don't know what you are asking," Jesus said to them. "Can you drink the cup I am going to drink?"
"We can," they answered.
23Jesus said to them, "You will indeed drink from my cup, but to sit at my right or left is not for me to grant. These places belong to those for whom they have been prepared by my Father."
24When the ten heard about this, they were indignant with the two brothers.
25Jesus called them together and said, "You know that the rulers of the Gentiles lord it over them, and their high officials exercise authority over them. 26Not so with you. Instead, whoever wants to become great among you must be your servant, 27and whoever wants to be first must be your slave— 28just as the Son of Man did not come to be served, but to serve, and to give his life as a ransom for many."

Luke parallels Matthew both before and after this pericope but omits it (cf. Mark 10:35–45). He has a somewhat similar account (Luke 22:24–30), but it is probably a different occasion.

Again the question of rank returns (cf. 18:1–5). Despite Jesus' repeated predictions of his passion, two disciples and their mother are still thinking about privilege, status, and power.

S. Légasse ("Approche de l'Épisode préévangélique des Fils de Zébédée [Mark x.35–40 par.]," NTS 20 [1974]: pp. 161–77) represents those who discount the historicity of this narrative largely on the hypothesis that "cup" and "baptism" are theological symbols around which a fictional episode was woven to convey certain theological truths. Bultmann (*Synoptic Tradition*, p. 24) goes farther and says that even the "prospect" of James's and John's death could not have been implied till after their martyrdom. The grounds for such theorizing are slender indeed. Why cannot theologically loaded terms be used in a historical narrative? Bultmann's critique reflects presuppositional antisupernaturalism in its most naive form. Jesus predicts his death (vv.17–19); and, when two of his disciples ask for preferential treatment, it is entirely natural that he should ask them if they are prepared to face similar suffering and death (cf. 5:10–12; 10:37–39). Moreover it is highly unlikely the church would invent a story so damaging to two of its leading apostles.

20 In Mark, John and James approach Jesus themselves; here, it is through *their mother*. Many find this historically improbable because in v.22 Jesus responds to her sons only. But the following points make the obvious synthesis plausible:

1. According to v.20, the mother *and her sons* approach Jesus, the implication being that all three are asking this favor, with the mother as the speaker.

2. This is confirmed by the other apostles' indignation (v.24), showing that James and John as well as their mother were involved.

3. That the mother should be the one to approach Jesus becomes the more plausible if she is Jesus' aunt on his mother's side—not certain, but not unlikely (see on 10:2; 27:56).

4. By adding the mother, Matthew cannot be shielding James and John: they still get the same response as in Mark. Matthew has no obvious theological motive for introducing their mother; he is simply recording a historical detail.

5. That the request should come from James and John, whether through their mother or not, accords with what we know of their aggressiveness (cf. Mark 9:38; Luke 9:54).

The "kneeling down" is not "worship" of Deity but may imply homage to the one increasingly recognized as King Messiah (see on 2:2).

21 The "right hand" and "left hand" suggest proximity to the King's person and so a share in his prestige and power. Such positions increase as the King is esteemed and has absolute power (cf. Pss 16:11; 45:9; 110:1; Matt 27:64; Acts 7:55–56; cf. Jos. Antiq. VI, 235 [xi. 9]). Mark has "in your glory," Matthew "in your kingdom." Mark's phrase clearly points to the Parousia, "when Jesus is enthroned as eschatological judge" (Lane, *Mark*, p. 379). Hill (*Matthew*) proposes that the "kingdom" in Matthew is the kingdom of Christ (13:41–43; 25:31–46), identified as the church; and the change from "glory" to "kingdom" therefore means that the original story is now being applied to competition for leadership in the church. But we have already seen that "kingdom" is never identified with "church" in Matthew (see on 13:37–39), and Christ's kingdom is equivalent to the kingdom of heaven (13:41; 20:21; 25:31). Because the "kingdom" comes in stages, there is no substantial difference between Matthew and Mark: the kingdom here is the reign of Messiah at the consummation. The link with 19:28—a verse that speaks (cf. Gk.) of both "throne" and "glory"—is unmistakable. What the sons of Zebedee want and their mother asks for is that they might share in the authority and preeminence of Jesus Messiah when his kingdom is fully consummated—something they think to be near at hand without the Cross or any interadvent period.

22 The additional words "or be baptized with the baptism I am baptized with" (cf. KJV)—and similarly in v.23—are almost certainly an assimilation to Mark 10:38–39. Jesus' answer is not severe but mingles firmness with probing. It is often ignorance that seeks leadership, power, and glory: the brothers do not know what they are asking. To ask to reign with Jesus is to ask to suffer with him; and not only do they not know what they are asking for (cf. 10:37–39; Rom 8:17; 2 Tim 2:12; Rev 3:21), they have as yet no clear perceptions of *Jesus'* sufferings. To ask for worldly wealth and much honor is often to ask for anxiety, temptation, disappointment, and envy; and in the spiritual arena to ask for great usefulness and reward is often to ask for great suffering (cf. 2 Cor 11:23–33; Col 1:24; Rev 1:9). "We know not what we ask, when we ask for the glory of wearing the crown, and ask not for grace to bear the cross in our way to it" (Henry).

The "cup" (cf. 26:39) characteristically refers, in OT imagery, to judgment or retribution (cf. Ps 75:8; Isa 51:17–18; Jer 25:15–28). If the disciples grasped anything of Jesus' passion predictions, they probably thought the language partly hyperbolic (Jesus did use hyperbole elsewhere [e.g., 19:24]) and referred to the eschatological conflict during which Messiah's side would suffer losses; but these could scarcely be too severe for one who could still storms and raise the dead. Thus by their bold response, James and John betray their misunderstandings of the timing of the dawn of the kingdom in all its glory (cf. Luke 19:11), and equally of the uniqueness and redemptive significance of Jesus' sufferings (cf. v.28) now imminent.

23 Jesus answers them first on their own terms before speaking of his own death as a ransom (v.28). In a sense they can and will drink from his cup of suffering. James would become the first apostolic martyr (Acts 12:2); and John (if it is the same one) would suffer exile (Rev 1:9). But it is not Jesus' role to determine who sits on his right hand and his left. Here, as elsewhere (see on 11:27; 24:36; 28:18; cf. John 14:28), Jesus makes it clear that his authority is a derived authority. These positions have already been assigned by the Father: Jesus cannot assign them at a mother's request.

24–27 The indignation of the ten (v.24) doubtless sprang less from humility than jealousy plus the fear that they might lose out. If these verses scarcely support egalitarianism—choice positions, after all, will be allotted—they demonstrate that interest in egalitarianism may mask a jealousy whose deepest wellsprings are not concern for justice but "enlightened self-interest." The disciples revert to the squabbling of an earlier period (Mark 9:33–37; cf. Matt 18:1). Jesus calls them together and draws a contrast between greatness among *ta ethnē* ("pagans" or "Gentiles," v.25) and greatness among heirs of the kingdom. The "pagans" or "Gentiles" who would spring to mind were Romans: power and authority characterized their empire. NIV's "lord it over" gives a false impression. Jesus is not criticizing abuse of power in political structures—the verb never has that meaning (cf. K.W. Clark, "The Meaning of [κατα] κυριεύειν" in Elliott, pp. 100–105) and should be translated "exercise lordship over," parallel to "exercise authority over" in the next line—but insists that the very structures themselves cannot be transferred to relationships among his followers.

Greatness among Jesus' disciples is based on service. Anyone who wants to be great must become the *diakonos* ("servant," v.26) of all. Here *diakonos* does not mean "deacon" or "minister" (KJV) in the modern church use. One of the ironies of language is that a word like "minister," which in its roots refers to a helper, one who "ministers," has become a badge of honor and power in religion and politics. But lest the full force of his teaching be lost, Jesus repeats it in v.27 with the stronger word *doulos* ("slave"; cf. 1 Cor 9:19; 2 Cor 4:5; 1 Peter 1:22; 5:1–3). In the pagan world humility was regarded, not so much as a virtue, but as a vice. Imagine a slave being given leadership! Jesus' ethics of the leadership and power in his community of disciples are revolutionary.

28 At this point Jesus presents himself—the Son of Man (see on 8:20)—as the supreme example of service to others. The verse is clearly important to our understanding of Jesus' view of his death. Three related questions call for discussion.

1. *Authenticity.* Many reject the authenticity of v.28, or at least of v.28a (and, correspondingly, Mark 10:45), on the grounds that it ill suits the context, since Jesus' atoning death cannot be imitated by his disciples, that nowhere else is he reported as speaking of his death in this way, and that the language reflects the influence of the Hellenistic church. On the contrary, the language has been shown to be Palestinian (Jeremias, *Eucharistic Words*, pp. 179–82); and Jesus speaks of his death in not dissimilar terms when instituting the Lord's Supper (26:26–29) and also in Luke 22:37, assuming that it relates to a different occasion. It is quite common in the NT, both in words ascribed to Jesus and elsewhere, to begin with the disciples' need to die to self and end up with Jesus' unique, atoning death as an ethical example—or, conversely to begin with Jesus' unique death and find it applied as an

example to the disciples (John 12:23–25; Phil 2:5–11; 1 Peter 2:18–25). There are no substantial reasons for denying the authenticity of this saying (cf. esp. S.H.T. Page, "The Authenticity of the Ransom Logion [Mark 10:45b]," in France and Wenham, 1:137–61); and its nuances seem much more in keeping with the way Jesus progressively revealed himself (cf. Carson, "Christological Ambiguities") than with a clear-cut, postresurrection, apostolic confession.

2. *Meaning*. It is natural to take "did not come" as presupposing at least a hint of Jesus' preexistence, though the language does not absolutely require it. He came not to be served, like a king dependent on countless courtiers and attendants, but to serve others. Stonehouse (*Witness of Matthew*, pp. 251ff.; id. *Origins*, p. 187) rightly points out that the verse assumes that the Son of Man had every right to expect to be served but served instead. Implicit is a self-conscious awareness that the Son of Man who, because of his heavenly origin, possessed divine authority was the one who humbled himself even to the point of undergoing an atoning death. (The tripartite breakdown of the Son of Man references (see excursus on 8:20) is to this extent artificial.) The display of divine glory shines most brightly when it is set aside for the sake of redeeming man by a shameful death. This stands at the very heart of Jesus' self-disclosure and of the primitive gospel (1 Cor 1:23: "We preach Christ [Messiah] crucified").

The Son of Man came "to give his life a ransom for many." Deissmann (LAE, pp. 331f.) points out that *lytron* ("ransom") was most commonly used as the purchase price for freeing slaves; and there is good evidence that the notion of "purchase price" is always implied in the NT use of *lytron* (cf. esp. Morris, *Apostolic Preaching*, pp. 11ff.). Others, however, by examining the word in the LXX conclude that, especially when the subject is God, the word means "deliverance" and the cognate verb "to deliver," without reference to a "price paid" (see esp. Hill, *Greek Words*, pp. 58–80). The matter may be difficult to decide in a passage like Titus 2:14. Is wickedness a chain from which Jesus by his death *delivers* us or a slave owner from whom Jesus by his death *ransoms* us? The parallel in 1 Peter 1:18 suggests the latter, even though (as Turner, *Christian Words*, pp. 105–7, insists) there is never any mention in the NT of the one to whom the price is paid; and in Matthew 20:28 this meaning is virtually assured by the use of *anti* ("for"). The normal force of this preposition denotes substitution, equivalence, exchange (cf. esp. M.J. Harris, DNTT, 3:1179f.). "The life of Jesus, surrendered in a sacrificial death, brought about the release of forfeited lives. He acted on behalf of the many by taking their place" (ibid., p. 1180).

"The many" underlines the immeasurable effects of Jesus' solitary death: the one dies, the many find their lives "ransomed, healed, restored, forgiven," a great host no man can number (cf. J. Jeremias, "Das Lösegeld für Viele," *Judaica* 3 [1948]: 263). But it should be remembered that "the many" can refer, in the DSS and the rabbinic literature, to the elect community (cf. Ralph Marcus, "'Mebaqqer' and 'Rabbim' in the Manual of Discipline vi, 11–13," JBL 75 [1956]: 298–302). This suggests Jesus' substitutionary death is payment for and results in the eschatological people of God. This well suits "the many" of Isaiah 52:13–53:12.

3. *Dependence on Isaiah* 53. C.K. Barrett ("The Background of Mark 10.45," *New Testament Essays*, ed. A.J.B. Higgins [Manchester: University Press, 1959], pp. 1–18; id., "Mark 10.45: A Ransom for Many," *New Testament Essays* [London: SPCK, 1972], pp. 20–26), Hooker (*Son of Man*, pp. 140–47), and others have argued that there is no allusion to Isaiah in Mark 10:45 and Matthew 20:28. They argue this

on two grounds: linguistic and conceptual. Linguistically, they point out that the Greek verb *diakonein* ("to serve," v.28) and its cognates are never used in the LXX to render *'ebed* ("servant" of Isaiah's "Servant Songs") and its cognates. But the evidence is slight and the conceptual parallels close—Isaiah's Servant benefits men by his suffering, and so does Jesus. Hooker is certainly incorrect in restricting *diakonein* to *domestic* service (cf. France, "Servant of the Lord," p. 34). Both France and Moo ("Use of OT," pp. 122ff.) have also shown that "to give his life" springs from Isaiah 53:10, 12, and that *lytron* ("ransom") is not as impossible a rendering of *'āšām* ("a guilt offering") as some allege. The Hebrew word *'āšām* includes the notion of substitution, at least of an equivalent. The guilty sinner offers an *'āšām* to remove his own guilt; and in Leviticus 5 *'āšām* refers to compensatory payment. Thus, though *'āšām* has more sacrificial overtones than *lytron*, both include the idea of payment or compensation. Most scholars have also recognized in "the many" a clear reference to Isaiah (cf. esp. Dalman, pp. 171–72). The implication of the cumulative evidence is that Jesus explicitly referred to himself as Isaiah's Suffering Servant (see on 26:17–30) and interpreted his own death in that light—an interpretation in which Matthew has followed his Lord (see on 3:17; 12:15–21).

Notes

---

21 Compare this use of εἰπὲ ἵνα (*eipe hina,* "Grant that") with the use in 4:3. "Command that" is the idea common to both. The mother believes Jesus need only say the word for it to be done.

28 For an interesting and extended gloss on this verse, see Metzger, *Textual Commentary,* p. 53.

---

7. *Healing two blind men*

20:29–34

[29]As Jesus and his disciples were leaving Jericho, a large crowd followed him.
[30]Two blind men were sitting by the roadside, and when they heard that Jesus was going by, they shouted, "Lord, Son of David, have mercy on us!"

[31]The crowd rebuked them and told them to be quiet, but they shouted all the louder, "Lord, Son of David, have mercy on us!"

[32]Jesus stopped and called them. "What do you want me to do for you?" he asked.

[33]"Lord," they answered, "we want our sight."

[34]Jesus had compassion on them and touched their eyes. Immediately they received their sight and followed him.

Mark (10:44–52) and Luke (18:35–43) mention only one blind man, and Mark names him (Bartimaeus, Mark 10:46); but Matthew habitually gives fuller details on numbers of persons (cf. 8:28). This story is not a doublet of 9:27–31, which stresses faith and ends with a command to be silent. It lacks those twin foci but has other purposes. It pictures Jesus still serving and again links his healing ministry with his death (v.28; see on 8:17). Moreover it reminds us that the one going up to Jerusalem to give his life a ransom for many is the Messiah, the Son of David, whose great power, used mercifully (v.30) and compassionately (v.34), is not used to save himself.

29 Matthew and Mark say that Jesus was "leaving," Luke that he was "entering" Jericho. While there are several possible reasons for this, none is certain. Many "explanations" are inadequate: that Jesus healed one blind man on entering the town and two on leaving; that the healings occurred while Jesus was going "in and out"; that Jesus went through Jericho (Luke 19:1) without finding lodging and on his way out healed the blind men, met Zacchaeus, and returned to his place—so that Jesus' "leaving" was really his "entering." Calvin's "conjecture," followed by many, is that Jesus on his way into the city did not respond to the petitions of the blind men (perhaps in order to increase their faith: cf. 15:21–28) but healed them on his way out. Marshall (*Luke*, pp. 692f.) offers a literary explanation—viz., Luke made the change to accommodate the ensuing Zacchaeus story that takes place in Jericho and which Luke wants to place as a climax. One might have thought that Luke's simpler course would have been to drop any mention of Jericho in this healing, since he gains nothing by it and his alteration brings him into conflict with Mark.

Many avoid geographical contradiction by noting that in this period there were *two* Jerichos—an older town on the hill, largely in ruins, and the new Herodian town about one mile away (cf. Jos. War IV, 459 [viii. 3]). In this view Matthew and Mark, under Jewish influence, mention the old town Jesus was leaving; Luke the Hellenist refers to the new one, which Jesus is entering. This may well be the explanation. But there is no certain evidence that the old town was still inhabited at this time, and we do not know the local names of the two sites.

Jericho was not only the home of Jesus' ancestor Rahab (1:5) but was also a day's journey from Jerusalem. The "large crowd" implies more than messianic excitement; it also reflects the multitudes of pilgrims from Galilee and elsewhere heading to Jerusalem for the feast.

30 The rather common suggestion that Matthew increases the number of blind men to two because two was the minimum number of witnesses for attesting Jesus' messiahship is misguided. To *experience* the healings would not prove Jesus was the Messiah. He might simply be a prophet. On the other hand, if the miracle confirmed or promoted belief in Jesus' messiahship, it might do so as easily for *those who witnessed the miracle* as for those who experienced it. The "large crowd" would have provided witnesses aplenty. The "two" therefore has no theological motivation, but shows personal knowledge of the events. There may have been many blind people in the Jericho area; for the region produced large quantities of balsam, believed to be very beneficial for many eye defects (cf. Strabo 16.2.41). These two were sitting by the roadside, doubtless begging (Mark–Luke), and, hearing that Jesus was passing, cried out, "Lord, Son of David, have mercy on us!" (in the most likely text; cf. Metzger, *Textual Commentary*, pp. 53–54). On the title "Son of David" in relation to healing, see on 9:27.

31–34 Matthew's account is simple but stresses that Jesus mercifully healed the men despite the opposition of the crowds (v.31) that, like the disciples (cf. 19:13–15), wanted to bask in his glory but not practice his compassion. After this healing, unlike 9:30, there is no command to be silent. That point in Jesus' ministry has been reached when more public self-disclosure could not change the course of events. The two healed men joined the crowds following Jesus (v.34), pressing on to the Passover they expected and the Cross they did not.

8. *Opening events of Passion Week* (21:1–23:39)

a. *The Triumphal Entry*

21:1–11

1As they approached Jerusalem and came to Bethphage on the Mount of
Olives, Jesus sent two disciples, 2saying to them, "Go to the village ahead of you,
and at once you will find a donkey tied there, with her colt by her. Untie them and
bring them to me. 3If anyone says anything to you, tell him that the Lord needs
them, and he will send them right away."
4This took place to fulfill what was spoken through the prophet:

5"Say to the Daughter of Zion,
'See, your king comes to you,
gentle and riding on a donkey,
on a colt, the foal of a donkey.' "

6The disciples went and did as Jesus had instructed them. 7They brought the
donkey and the colt, placed their cloaks on them, and Jesus sat on them. 8A very
large crowd spread their cloaks on the road, while others cut branches from the
trees and spread them on the road. 9The crowds that went ahead of him and
those that followed shouted,

"Hosanna to the Son of David!"
"Blessed is he who comes in the name of the Lord!"
"Hosanna in the highest!"

10When Jesus entered Jerusalem, the whole city was stirred and asked, "Who
is this?"
11The crowds answered, "This is Jesus, the prophet from Nazareth in Galilee."

T.W. Manson ("The Cleansing of the Temple," BJRL 33 [1951]: 271–82) suggests the feast in question is Tabernacles (autumn), not Dedication (winter) or Passover (spring). Because Jesus died at Passover, Manson spreads Matthew 21–28 (and parallels) over six months, instead of six days. His view rests largely on the observation that figs do not usually appear on the trees around Jerusalem till June and September, which seems to rule out Passover (usually April) as the right period for 21:18–21. But figs are regularly found in Jericho much earlier—and sometimes also in Jerusalem—and Manson's view introduces some difficult problems in the passion chronology.

For the moment we shall assume that this trip to Jerusalem occurred a few days before the Passover on which Jesus was crucified. Matthew does not mention the stay at Bethany (John 12:1–10) where Jesus arrived "six days before Passover," probably Friday evening (at the beginning of the Sabbath) before the Passion Week, and stayed there for Sabbath, entering Jerusalem on Sunday. Apparently Jesus went back and forth to Bethany throughout the week (21:17). (For the most recent detailed chronology of Passion Week, cf. Hoehner, *Chronological Aspects;* for close study of the question of authenticity, cf. Dhyanchand Carr, "Jesus, the king of Zion: A Traditio-Historical Enquiry into the So-called 'Triumphal' Entry of Jesus" [Ph.D. diss., University of London, 1980], pp. 128–218, 350–92.)

1–2 The Roman military road from Jericho to Jerusalem was about seventeen miles long and climbed three thousand feet. It passed through Bethany and nearby Bethphage ("house of figs"), which lay on the southeast slope of the Mount of Olives, then crossed over the mount and the Kidron Valley and entered Jerusalem (v.1). The mount itself stands about three hundred feet higher than the temple hill and about one hundred feet higher than the hill of Zion, affording a spectacular, panoramic view of the city.

Jesus sent two disciples (unnamed, but cf. Luke 22:8) ahead to Bethphage (for the grammar, cf. RHG, pp. 643–44) to fetch the animals (v.2). The distinguishing feature of the synoptic accounts, as opposed to John 12, is that Jesus arranged for the ride. The applause and the crowds were not manipulated; they would have occurred in any case. But the ride on a colt, because it was planned, could only be an acted parable, a deliberate act of symbolic self-disclosure for those with eyes to see or, after the Resurrection, with memories by which to remember and integrate the events of the preceding weeks and years. Secrecy was being lifted.

3 "Lord" (also Mark–Luke) might mean "owner"; but then the disciples' response would be untrue, unless Jesus owned the animals, which is extremely unlikely. The title might refer to Yahweh—the animals are needed in Yahweh's service. But the most natural way to take "Lord" is Jesus' way of referring to himself. This step is not out of keeping with the authority he has already claimed for himself and fits this late period of his ministry, when he revealed himself with increasing clarity. J. Gresham Machen (*The Origin of Paul's Religion* [New York: Macmillan, 1928, 1947], pp. 296–97) notes that even the church's ascription of "Lord" to Jesus in a full christological sense finds its roots in Jesus' self-references.

4–5 It is possible that Matthew presents these verses as having been spoken by Jesus. The perfect *gegonen* should then be translated "This has taken place" (v.4), spoken somewhat proleptically because the order had been given (see discussion on 1:22). The alternative is to take the verses as Matthew's comment. This requires taking the perfect as either having aoristic force or meaning "This stands as something that happened." John's statement that the disciples did not understand all this at the time (12:16) does not necessarily support the alternative, since Jesus said many things they did not understand at the time (cf. John 2:20–22).

A few MSS add "Zechariah" or "Isaiah" to "prophet," doubtless because the quotation comes from both. The introductory words of the quotation are from Isaiah 62:11 and the rest from Zechariah 9:9. The omitted words "righteous and having salvation" (Zech 9:9) may be understood as implicitly included, or omitted because the chief stress is on Jesus' humility (Stendahl, *School*, pp. 118–20).

The text form of the quotation (v.5) is disputed, but at least the latter parts depend directly on the MT (cf. Gundry, *Use of OT*, pp. 120–21; Moo; "Use of OT," pp. 178f.). The last word, *hypozygion*, means a "beast of burden," which in Palestine was usually a donkey. Such an animal was sometimes ridden by rulers in times of peace (Judg 5:10; 1 Kings 1:33; cf. Rev 19:11). Jews certainly understood Zechariah 9:9 to refer to the Messiah, often in terms of the Son of David (SBK, 1:842–44). Therefore for those with eyes to see, Jesus was not only proclaiming his messiahship and his fulfillment of Scripture but showing the kind of peace-loving approach he was now making to the city.

Many scholars find difficulty with the fact that Matthew alone of the four evangelists mentions *two* animals: a donkey and her colt (vv.2, 7); and only he cites the Hebrew text so fully that the unwary might think there *were* two animals. The Hebrew, of course, refers to only one beast: the last line is in parallelism with the next-to-the-last line and merely identifies the "donkey" (line 3) as a colt (a young, male donkey). But it is quite unreasonable to suggest that Matthew, who demonstrably had a good command of Hebrew (cf. Gundry, *Use of OT*, p. 198), added the extra animal to fit a text he radically misunderstood (contra McNeile, Schniewind). Nor is it more reasonable to assume that Matthew knows there actually were two animals and quotes Zechariah because the prophet's words might barely refer to two; for his Jewish readers would not likely be convinced. Still less likely is the appeal to unassimilated sources (cf. R. Bartnicki, "Das Zitat von Zach IX, 9–10 und die Tiere im Bericht von Matthäus über dem Einzug Jesu in Jerusalem (Mt XXI, 1–11)," NovTest 18 [1976]: 161–66).

The most reasonable suggestion is that Mark's "which no one has ever ridden" prompted Matthew to mention both animals (cf. Stendahl, *School*, pp. 118–20; Lindars, *Apologetic*, p. 114; Longenecker, *Biblical Exegesis*, pp. 148–49). Gundry (*Use of OT*, pp. 198–99) holds that Matthew witnessed the scene. Matthew's reference to both animals is his way of highlighting what the other synoptists affirm—the animal Jesus rode on *was* "a colt." If we assume that Matthew understood Hebrew, the full quotation affirms that Jesus rode on the "colt," not its mother. Mark and Luke say the animal was so young that it had never been ridden. In the midst, then, of this excited crowd, an unbroken animal remains calm under the hands of the Messiah who controls nature (8:23–27; 14:22–32). Thus the event points to the peace of the consummated kingdom (cf. Isa 11:1–10). Though Matthew may have something of the same thing in mind, in addition he stresses that Jesus fulfills Scripture even in this detail—that the animal he rode was a colt. Without warrant is the appeal to Midrash, at least in its technical, fourth-century sense (cf. Introduction, section 12.b). Although Jewish midrashic writers occasionally give a separate meaning to each part of Hebrew parallelism (cf. examples in Carr), the continuity of the Midrash lies in the passage being expounded, not in the narrative explanations. But here the continuity lies in the narrative. Still less credible is the allegorizing of many of the Fathers, and even of Lange: the donkey symbolizes Jews accustomed to the yoke of the law and the colt hitherto untamed Gentiles ("The old theocracy runs idly and instinctively by the side of the young Church, which has become the true bearer of the divinity of Christ," CHS).

6–8 The two disciples returned from their errand (v.6) and put their cloaks (their outer garments; see on 5:40) on the beasts—both animals were in the procession (v.7). Jesus sat "on them." Not a few critics take the antecedent of "them" to be the animals and ridicule the statement. But as Plummer remarks, "The Evangelist credits his readers with common sense." The antecedent of "them" may be the cloaks; or the plural may be a "plural of category" (cf. "He sprang from the horses"; cf. Turner, *Insights*, p. 41; see on 2:20). Less convincing is appeal to very weak textual traditions: "he sat on *it*" or "they sat him on *it*" ("thereon," KJV; cf. Broadus; BDF, par. 141).

A "very large crowd" (v.8, the Gr. superlative is merely elative; cf. Moule, *Idiom Book*, p. 98) spread their cloaks on the road, acknowledging Jesus' kingship (cf. 2 Kings 9:13). Still others "cut branches" and "spread them" (the Gr. imperfects make the action vivid) on the road. It has been argued that cutting down tree branches well suits the activities of the Feast of Tabernacles, when the people built "booths" to live in for the week (cf. Lev 23:41–42). But those "branches" were substantial boughs, big enough to support a lean-to; these "branches," thrown before the animals, were not more than twigs. The somewhat parallel entrance of Simon Maccabaeus into Jerusalem (1 Macc 13:51; 2 Macc 10:7) does not depend on the season of the year but on the man.

9 Crowds ahead and behind may be incidental confirmation of two other details. First, John 12:12 speaks of crowds coming out of Jerusalem to meet Jesus. Apparently the Galilean pilgrims accompanying Jesus and the Jerusalem crowd coming out to greet him formed a procession of praise. Second, that the Jerusalem crowds knew he was approaching supports the stopover in Bethany, which allows time for the news to spread. Messianic fervor was high, and perhaps this contributed to Jesus' desire to present himself as Prince of Peace.

The words of praise come primarily from Psalm 118:25–26. "Hosanna" transliterates the Hebrew expression that originally was a cry for help: "Save!" (cf. 2 Sam 14:4; 2 Kings 6:26). In time it became an invocation of blessing and even an acclamation, the latter being the meaning here (cf. Gundry, *Use of OT*, pp. 41–43). "Son of David" is messianic and stresses the kingly role Messiah was to play (cf. Mark, Luke, and John for explicit references to "kingdom" or "king"). "He who comes in the name of the Lord" is cited by Jesus himself a little later (23:39; cf. 3:11; 11:3), but some scholars object that if this phrase had been a messianic acclamation by the people, the authorities would have stepped in. The words, they say, must be a formula of greeting to pilgrims on the way to the temple.

Such an assessment betrays too stark an "either-or" mentality to weigh the evidence plausibly. "Son of David" in the previous line is unavoidably messianic, and the authorities *do* raise objections (v.16). But crowd sentiments are fickle. On the one hand, acclamation can rapidly dissipate; so instant action by the authorities was scarcely necessary. On the other hand, it is foolish to antagonize the crowd at the height of excitement (cf. 26:4–5, 16). "Hosanna in the highest" is probably equivalent to "Glory to God in the highest" (Luke 2:14). The people praise God in the highest heavens for sending the Messiah and, if "Hosanna" retains some of its original force, also cry to him for deliverance.

Two final reflections on this verse are necessary: first, Psalm 118 was not only used at the Feast of Tabernacles (M *Succoth* 4:5) but also at the other two major feasts, Dedication and Passover—at the latter as part of "the great Hallel" (Pss 113–18). The use of Psalm 118 is therefore no support for Manson's suggestion. Second, Walvoord's interpretation stumbles badly: "They recognized that He was in the kingly line, although they do not seem to have entered into the concept that He was coming into Jerusalem as its King." On the contrary, it is hard to think of the crowd's making fine distinctions between "kingly line" and "king." Moreover one growing thrust of this Gospel is, as we have seen, that even where Jesus was perceived, however dimly, as King Messiah, he was not perceived as Suffering Servant. In the expectations of the day, it was fairly easy for the crowd, after hearing Jesus' preaching and seeing his miracles, to ascribe messiahship to him as much in their hope as in conviction. But it was far harder for them to grasp the inevitability of his suffering and death and the expansion of the "people of God" beyond the Jewish race.

10–11 Only Luke (19:41–44) pictures Jesus weeping over the city as he approaches it. Mark 11:11 establishes chronology; Matthew's information stands alone. Jesus probably entered Jerusalem through what some now call Saint Stephen's gate, near the north entrance to the outer court of the temple. As the city was stirred earlier (2:3), so here (v.10): news of Jesus' presence is inevitably disturbing. "Who is this?" does not mean that Jesus was virtually unknown in Jerusalem, and so needed to be identified (Bonnard), but "Who really is this about whom there is so much excitement?" The answer of the crowds accurately reflects the historical setting: many of his contemporaries saw him as a prophet (cf. 16:14; 21:46) "from Nazareth in Galilee"—his hometown and primary field of ministry respectively. The phrase probably also connotes surprise that a prophet should come from so unlikely a place (see on 2:23). In the light of the messianic acclamation (v.9), some may well have seen Jesus as the eschatological Prophet (Deut 18:15–18; cf. John 7:40, 52; Acts 3:22; 7:37), though there is no more than a hint of that here. Yet there is also no evidence that Matthew deprecates the people's understanding as faulty, preferring "Son of God" (contra Kingsbury, *Matthew*, pp. 22, 88–89).

Notes

---

3 Zerwick (par. 280) rightly points out that the verb ἐρεῖτε (*ereite*, lit., "you will say"; NIV, "tell") is one of the rare instances when a future indicative in the NT has imperatival force (apart from passages where the NT cites the LXX).

11 Note this use of ἀπό (*apo*, "from," "away from") to denote place of origin instead of ἐκ (*ek*, "from," "out from"; cf. BDF, par. 209[3]).

---

b. *Jesus at the temple*

21:12–17

12Jesus entered the temple area and drove out all who were buying and selling there. He overturned the tables of the money changers and the benches of those selling doves. 13"It is written," he said to them, " 'My house will be called a house of prayer,' but you are making it a 'den of robbers.' "

14The blind and the lame came to him at the temple, and he healed them. 15But when the chief priests and the teachers of the law saw the wonderful things he did and the children shouting in the temple area, "Hosanna to the Son of David," they were indignant.

16"Do you hear what these children are saying?" they asked him.

"Yes," replied Jesus, "have you never read,

" 'From the lips of children and infants
you have ordained praise'?"

17And he left them and went out of the city to Bethany, where he spent the night.

Matthew is considerably more condensed than Mark (11:11–19; cf. Luke 19:45–48; John 2:13–22). Matthew omits, among other things, Mark's more precise chronology, all mention of the habit of carrying merchandise through the temple courts, and reference to the Gentiles in the quotation from Isaiah 56:7. It is doubtful whether

Matthew's silence in any of these things reflects major theological motivation, but see on v.13. Matthew focuses on the cleansing of the temple as the work of the Son of David (vv.9, 15) and as of as much messianic significance as any of Jesus' miracles.

The great majority of contemporary scholars believe there was only one cleansing of the temple and debate about whether the synoptists or John put it at the right time in Jesus' ministry. Although some argue that the event occurred early in Jesus' ministry (John), more side with the Synoptics in placing it late. Certainly we have ample evidence that the evangelists arranged some materials topically; yet there are, in this instance, numerous reasons for the possibility, indeed the likelihood, of two separate cleansings—something most commentators never seriously consider.

1. Leon Morris (*John,* pp. 288ff.) has shown the striking differences between the details John provides and those the Synoptics provide. If there was but one cleansing, some of these differences became surprising; if two cleansings, they became quite reasonable.

2. Those who hold that John's placing of the cleansing is topical usually assume that he does so to lead up to the saying, "Destroy this temple, and I will raise it again in three days" (John 2:19), part of his "replacement" theme—viz., that Jesus himself replaces much of the Jewish cultic milieu. But this view fails to provide any reason for shifting the temple's cleansing so as to make it an *early* theme in Jesus' ministry. Moreover in this particular case the temple-replacement theme is reflected in the trial of Jesus in two of the Synoptics (Matt 26:61; Mark 14:58).

3. If the Synoptics fail to mention the earlier cleansing, this may go back to their omission of Jesus' entire early Judean ministry.

4. Some hold that if Jesus had inaugurated his ministry by cleansing the temple, the authorities would not have let him do it a second time. But two or three years have elapsed. The money changers and merchants, protected by the temple police, doubtless returned the day after the first cleansing. But it is doubtful that tight security would have been kept up for months and years. This second cleansing took a few dramatic minutes and could not have been prevented, and its prophetic symbolism quickly spread throughout Jerusalem.

5. It is difficult to tell from the Gospels how much the cleansing(s) of the temple contributed to official action against Jesus, and to overstate the evidence is easy (cf. E. Trocmé, "L'expulsion des marchands du Temple," NTS 15 [1968–69]: 1–22). But a second cleansing as Passover drew near was far more likely to have led to the authorities' violent reaction than the first one.

12 Jesus entered the *hieron* ("temple area"). Temple service required provision to be made for getting what was needed for the sacrifices—animals, wood, oil, etc.—especially for pilgrims from afar. The money changers converted the standard Greek and Roman currency into temple currency, in which the half-shekel temple tax had to be paid (cf. 17:24–27). (For some of the customs and regulations, cf. M *Shekalim;* LTJM, 1:367–74.) But letting these things go on at the temple site transformed a place of solemn worship into a market where the hum of trade mingled with the bleating and cooing of animals and birds. Moreover, especially on the great feasts, opportunities for extortion abounded. Jesus drove the lot out.

13 Jesus here refers to Scripture, much as he did when confronted by the devil (4:1–10). His first words are from Isaiah 56:7. Isaiah looked forward to a time when the temple would be called a house of prayer. But now, at the dawn of the Messianic Age, Jesus finds a "den of robbers." The words come from Jeremiah 7:11, which warns against the futility of superstitious reverence for the temple compounded with wickedness that dishonors it. This suggests that the Greek *lēstai* ("robbers") should be given its normal meaning of "nationalist rebel" (see on 27:16). The temple was meant to be a house of prayer, but they had made it "a nationalist stronghold" (cf. C.K. Barrett, "The House of Prayer and the Den of Thieves," in Ellis and Grässer, p. 16).

The point is even clearer in Mark, who retains "house of prayer for all nations" (Isa 56:7 uses the longer form once and the shorter one once). The temple was not fulfilling its God-ordained role as witness to the nations but had become, like the first temple, the premier symbol of a superstitious belief that God would protect and rally his people irrespective of their conformity to his will. The temple would therefore be destroyed (vv.18–22; 24:2). Matthew does not omit "for all nations" because he writes after the temple has been destroyed and therefore recognizes the promise in Isaiah no longer capable of fulfillment. Even Mark knows the temple cannot stand and that this temple could never become a rallying place "for all nations." The omission may simply be for conciseness; but it shifts the contrast from "temple mission—nationalist stronghold" (Mark) to "house of prayer—nationalist stronghold" (Matthew)—a shift that focuses attention more on spiritual neglect and mistaken political priorities than on neglect of what the temple was really for. These are the things Jesus denounces.

The Lord whom the people see now comes to his temple (Mal 3:1). Purification of Jerusalem and the temple was part of Jewish expectation (cf. Pss Sol 17:30). So for those with eyes to see, Jesus' action was one of self-disclosure and an implicit claim to eschatological authority over the Holy Place. That the purification would entail destruction and building a new temple (John 2:19–22) none but Jesus could yet foresee.

14 Verses 14–15 are found only in Matthew. Not only is v.14 the last mention of Jesus' healing ministry, but it takes place *en tō hierō* ("at the temple [site]") and probably within the temple precincts in the Court of the Gentiles. It was not uncommon for the chronically ill to beg at the approaches to the temple (Acts 3:2); but where the lame, blind, deaf, or otherwise handicapped could go in the temple area was restricted. The Court of the Gentiles was open to them all, and there were even crippled priests. But restrictions were imposed when the handicap required certain kinds of cushions, pads, or supports that might introduce "uncleanness" (cf. Jeremias, *Jerusalem*, pp. 117f.).

Most Jewish authorities forbade any person lame, blind, deaf, or mute from offering a sacrifice, from "appearing before Yahweh in his temple." The Qumran covenanters wanted to go further and exclude all cripples from the congregation, the messianic battle, and the messianic banquet (1QSa 2:5–22; 1QM 7:4–5). But Jesus heals them, thus showing that "one greater than the temple is here" (12:6). He himself cannot be contaminated, and he heals and makes clean those who come into contact with him. These two actions—cleansing the temple and the healing miracles—jointly declare his superiority over the temple (Heil, "Healing Miracles," pp. 283f.) and raise the question of the source of his authority (v.23).

15–16 The "chief priests and teachers of the law" (v.15; see on 2:4; 26:59) express indignation, not so much at what he has done, as at the acclamation he is receiving for it. The children cry out, "Hosanna to the Son of David" (see on v.9); and if Jesus is prepared to accept such praise, then "the wonderful things" he is doing must have messianic significance. When challenged, Jesus supports the children by quoting Psalm 8:2, introducing it with his "have you never read" (v.16), which exposes the theological ignorance of the Scripture experts (cf. 12:3; 19:4; 21:42; 22:31). God *has* ordained praise for himself from "children and infants" (lit., "infants and sucklings" —nursing sometimes continued among the Jews to the age of three: cf. 2 Macc 7:27). Jesus' answer is a masterstroke and simultaneously accomplishes three things.

1. It provides some kind of biblical basis for letting the children go on with their exuberant praise and thus stifles, for the moment, the objections of the temple leaders.

2. At the same time thoughtful persons, reflecting on the incident later (especially after the Resurrection), perceive that Jesus was saying much more. The children's "Hosannas" are not being directed to God but to the Son of David, the Messiah. Jesus is therefore not only acknowledging his messiahship but justifying the praise of the children by applying to himself a passage of Scripture applicable only to God (cf. Notes).

3. The quotation confirms that the humble perceive spiritual truths more readily than the sophisticated (cf. 19:13–15). The children have picked up the cry of the earlier procession and, lacking inhibitions and skepticism, enthusiastically repeat the chant, arriving at the truth more quickly than those who think themselves wise and knowledgeable.

17 During the festivals Jerusalem was crowded. So Jesus spent his last nights at Bethany, on a spur of the eastern slopes of the Mount of Olives (cf. Mark 11:19; Luke 21:37). The home where he stayed was probably that of Mary, Martha, and Lazarus.

Notes

---

16 Part of the interpretation of this verse given above depends on the view that Ps 8 is not messianic. This is almost certainly the case; and even application of Ps 8:5–7 to Jesus in 1 Cor 15:27; Heb 2:6 is due, not to the Psalm's messianic character, but to Jesus' role in introducing humanity to the heights God designed for it, as most expositors now acknowledge. The treatment of Ps 8 as messianic by ancient Jewish authorities in the Targum on Ps 8 (cf. F.J. Maloney, "The Targum on Ps. 8 and the New Testament," *Salesianum* 37 [1975]: 326–36) almost certainly postdates the NT.

---

c. *The fig tree*

21:18–22

[18]Early in the morning, as he was on his way back to the city, he was hungry. [19]Seeing a fig tree by the road, he went up to it but found nothing on it except leaves. Then he said to it, "May you never bear fruit again!" Immediately the tree withered.

[20]When the disciples saw this, they were amazed. "How did the fig tree wither so quickly?" they asked.

> 21 Jesus replied, "I tell you the truth, if you have faith and do not doubt, not only can you do what was done to the fig tree, but also you can say to this mountain, 'Go, throw yourself into the sea,' and it will be done. 22 If you believe, you will receive whatever you ask for in prayer."

This story is found only here and in Mark, where it is split into two parts (11:12–14, 20–26), with the temple's cleansing in between. Chronologically Mark is more detailed. If the Triumphal Entry was on Sunday, then, according to Mark, the cursing of the fig tree was on Monday; and the disciples' surprise at the tree's quick withering, along with Jesus' words about faith, were on Tuesday. Matthew has simply put the two parts together in a typical topical arrangement. He leaves indistinct (v.20) the time when the disciples see the withered fig tree, though he implies it was the same day. Compare the condensation in 9:18–25.

The most recent major study on this passage is by William R. Telford (*The Barren Temple and the Withered Tree* [Sheffield: JSOT, 1980]). Though he admirably surveys earlier studies, his own is less convincing (cf. review by D. Wenham, EQ 72 [1980]: 245–48). The idea that "this mountain" (v.21) refers to the temple, thus making the cursing of the fig tree a sign of the temple's doom, is unlikely. More probably it refers to the Mount of Olives as a sample of any mountain. Telford's exhaustive examination of the uses of "fig tree" as a metaphor does no more than show that "fig tree" could be applied metaphorically to many different things; but only the context of the metaphor is determinative. Still less convincing is the view that this story is a mere dramatization of the parable in Luke 13:6–9 (so van der Loos, pp. 692–96); for, apart from the question of whether such "historicization" of parabolic material ever occurs, the latter treats *delay* in judgment, whereas the present passage is concerned with *imminent* judgment.

It is commonly held that 21:20–22 and the corresponding Markan material is a separate tradition unrelated to the original. Preferable is the view that the awkward transition reflects the historical chronology, which Mark preserved. Cursing the fig tree is, then, an acted parable related to cleansing the temple and conveying a message about Israel. But when the next day the disciples see how quickly the fig tree has withered, their initial—and shallow—response is to wonder how it was done; and this leads to Jesus' remarks on faith. So this single historical event teaches two theological lessons.

18–19 Somewhere on the road between Bethany and Jerusalem, Jesus approached a fig tree in the hope of staunching his hunger (v.18). Mark tells us that though it was not the season for figs, the tree was in leaf. Fig leaves appear about the same time as the fruit or a little after. The green figs are edible, though sufficiently disagreeable as not usually to be eaten till June. Thus the leaves normally point to every prospect of fruit, even if not fully ripe. Sometimes, however, the green figs fall off and leave nothing but leaves. All this Matthew's succinct remark—"He . . . found nothing on it except leaves" (v.19)—implies; his Jewish readers would infer the rest. This understanding of the text confirms the chronology established at 21:1–11. If these events took place at Dedication, when figs were plentiful, not only would Mark's explicit statement be incorrect (11:13), but in both Matthew and Mark Jesus' cursing of the tree would be harder to understand, for if he was hungry, he could simply go to the next tree.

Many commentators think otherwise and suppose that by omitting Mark's statement "it was not the season for figs," Matthew has eliminated a moral difficulty. Why should Jesus curse a tree for not bearing fruit when it was not the season for fruit? But this theory misses the point. That it was not the season for figs explains why Jesus went to this particular tree, which stood out because it was in leaf. Its leaves advertised that it was bearing, but the advertisement was false. Jesus, unable to satisfy his hunger, saw the opportunity of teaching a memorable object lesson and cursed the tree, not because it was not bearing fruit, whether in season or out, but because it made a show of life that promised fruit yet was bearing none.

Most scholars interpret the cursing of the fig tree as a symbolic cursing of the people of Israel for failing to produce faith and righteousness, as evidenced primarily in their attitude to Jesus. The fig tree then becomes akin to the imagery of the vine in Isaiah 5:1–7 or the figs in Jeremiah 8:13; 24:1–8: sterility, the absence of fruit, or bad fruit—all lead to judgment. Walvoord objects, insisting that there is no place in the Bible where a fig tree serves as a type of Israel (Jer 24:1–8 is dismissed because the good and bad figs refer to captives versus those who remain in the land). The Gospel pericope is a lesson on faith and the miraculous, no more. But if the common interpretation will not stand, Walvoord's reductionism will not withstand close scrutiny either.

1. Mark's arrangement of the material, with the temple's cleansing sandwiched between the two parts, must be taken into account. Even Matthew, who condenses Mark's arrangement and eliminates the division of the pericope into two, places this immediately after the cleansing of the temple and right before the questioning of Jesus' authority. We have learned to respect Matthew's arrangement of pericopes enough to see them linked; and therefore to read vv. 18–22 as nothing more than a lesson on faith forfeits the obvious links.

2. Jeremiah 24:1–8 may provide a closer parallel than Walvoord thinks, for even in the Gospels Jesus is not saying that all Jews fall under whatever curse this may be; after all, his disciples at this point in history were all Jews. In the Synoptics, as in Jeremiah, there is a division between Jew and Jew.

3. Yet even if Jeremiah 24:1–8 is not too close a parallel, one cannot make too much of the fig tree's not being a type of Israel; for one could similarly argue that there is no other example in the Bible of Jesus' performing a miracle *simply* to teach faith, without there being some organic connection with the narrative.

This does not mean the common interpretation—that the fig tree represents Israel, cursed for not bearing fruit—is correct. In light of the discussion on the relation between leaves and fruit, Jesus is cursing those who make a show of bearing much fruit but are spiritually barren. This has four advantages.

1. It deftly handles both Mark and Matthew on the fig tree and its leaves.

2. It directs the attack against the hypocrites among the Jewish people, a constant target in all four Gospels, but especially in Matthew (e.g., 6:2, 5, 16; 7:5; 15:7; 22:18; and we now approach 23:1–39!).

3. It is compatible with the cleansing of the temple, which criticizes, not the Jewish children and their praise, or the Jewish blind and lame who came to be healed (vv. 14–15), but those who used the temple to make a large profit, and those who stifled the children's praises of Messiah. These, like this leafy fig tree, Jesus finds full of advertised piety without any fruit; and them he curses.

4. Unlike other passages (3:9; 8:11–12), there is no mention of something being taken from the Jews and given to Gentiles. The cursing of the fig tree is an acted parable cursing hypocrites, not Jews or Judaism.

The cursing of the fig tree is not so far out of character for Jesus as some would have us believe. The same Jesus exorcised demons so that two thousand pigs were drowned (8:28–34), drove the animals and money changers out of the temple precincts with a whip, and says not a little about the torments of hell. Perhaps the fact that the two punitive miracles—the swine and the fig tree—are not directed against men should teach us something of Jesus' compassion. He who is to save his people from their sin and its consequences resorts to prophetic actions not directed against his people, in order to warn them of the binding power of the devil (the destruction of the swine) and of God's enmity against all hypocritical piety (the cursing of the fig tree).

20–22 Though it is uncertain whether v.20 is a question or an exclamation (cf. Moule, *Idiom Book*, p. 207), the effect is the same. The substance of Jesus' response has already been given in 17:20, which implies that the figure of a mountain cast into the sea was common in Jesus' teaching. Here, however, attention shifts "from the smallest effective amount of faith to the opposition of faith to doubt" (Hill, *Matthew*). The miracle Jesus selects to teach the power of faith—throwing a mountain into the sea (v.21)—is no more than a hyperbolic example of a miracle. But because the Dead Sea can be seen from the Mount of Olives, some have suggested an allusion to Zechariah 14:4 (Lane, *Mark*, p. 410)—viz., what the disciples must pray for is the coming eschatological reign. This seems unlikely, for Zechariah speaks of the splitting of the Mount of Olives rather than its removal into the sea.

Jesus used the fig tree to teach the power of *believing* prayer, an extrapolation on the theme of faith, the lesson just taught by the immediate withering of the fig tree. But belief in the NT is never reduced to forcing oneself to "believe" what he does not really believe. Instead, it is related to genuine trust in God and obedience to and discernment of his will (see on 19:20; cf. Carson, *Farewell Discourse*, pp. 43, 108–11). Though exercised by the believer, such faith reposes on the will of God who acts.

Notes

19 Μίαν (*mian*, lit., "one") here has the force of enclitic τις (*tis*, "a certain," "a"): see on 8:19; 9:18; cf. 19:16; 21:24; BDF, par. 247(2).

d. *Controversies in the temple court* (21:23–22:46)

1) *The question of authority*

21:23–27

23Jesus entered the temple courts, and, while he was teaching, the chief priests and the elders of the people came to him. "By what authority are you doing these things?" they asked. "And who gave you this authority?"
24Jesus replied, "I will also ask you one question. If you answer me, I will tell you by what authority I am doing these things. 25John's baptism—where did it come from? Was it from heaven, or from men?"
They discussed it among themselves and said, "If we say, 'From heaven,' he

will ask, 'Then why didn't you believe him?' [26]But if we say, 'From men'—we are afraid of the people, for they all hold that John was a prophet."
[27]So they answered Jesus, "We don't know."
Then he said, "Neither will I tell you by what authority I am doing these things.

This long section (21:23–22:46) is characterized by a number of controversies with various Jewish leaders, along with several parables that must be interpreted in the light of such controversies. In Mark's chronology these controversies apparently took place on Tuesday, the third day of Passion Week. It was customary to stop well-known teachers and ask them questions (cf. 22:16, 23, 35), and the crowds delighted in these exchanges. Eventually Jesus turned primarily to the crowds and addressed them without excluding the Pharisees and teachers of the law (ch. 23); and then, as evening fell, he retired to the Mount of Olives and gave his last "discourse" to his disciples (chs. 24–25).

In the first exchange (vv.23–27), Matthew follows Mark (11:27–33) fairly closely (cf. Luke 20:1–8).

23 Jesus' teaching takes place in the "temple courts," probably in one of the porticos surrounding the Court of the Gentiles. The chief priests were high temple functionaries, elevated members of the priestly aristocracy who were part of the Sanhedrin (see on 2:4); the elders were in this case probably nonpriestly members of the Sanhedrin, heads of the most influential lay families (cf. Jeremias, *Jerusalem*, pp. 222ff.). In other words, representative members of the Sanhedrin, described in terms of their clerical status rather than their theological positions (e.g., Sadducees and Pharisees), approached Jesus and challenged his authority to do "these things" —viz., the cleansing of the temple, the miraculous healings, and perhaps also his teaching (v.23). Their first question was therefore not narrowly theological but concerned Jesus' authority; yet their concern in asking who gave him this authority (cf. Acts 4:7) sprang less from a desire to identify him than from a desire to stifle and perhaps ensnare him.

24–26 Jesus' reply is masterful. He responds to their question with a question of his own (v.24), a common enough procedure in rabbinic debate. "John's baptism" (v.25) is a way of referring to the Baptist's entire ministry (cf. v.25b and the reference to *believing* John, not simply being *baptized* by him). Jesus asks whether that ministry was from heaven or from men. He does not raise this question as a simple rebuke—as if to say that if the authorities cannot make up their minds about John, neither will they be able to do so about him. His question is far more profound. If the religious authorities rightly answer it, they will already have the correct answer to their own question. If they respond, "From heaven," then they are morally bound to believe John—and John pointed to Jesus (see on 11:7–10; cf. John 1:19, 26–27; 3:25–30). They would therefore have their answer about Jesus and his authority. If they respond, "From men" (v.26), they offer the wrong answer; but they will not dare utter it for fear of the people. The religious authorities share Herod's timidity (14:5).

Far from avoiding the religious leaders' question, Jesus answers it so that the honest seeker of truth, unswayed by public opinion, will not fail to see who he is, while those interested only in snaring him with a captious question are blocked by a hurdle their own shallow pragmatism forbids them to cross. At the same time

Jesus' question rather strongly hints to the rulers that their false step goes back to broader issues than Jesus' identity. It they cannot discern Jesus' authority, it is because their previous unbelief has blinded their minds to God's revelation.

27 "We don't know," they said—which is not so much a lie as a misrepresentation of the categories that bound them in public indecision. Their equivocation gave Jesus a reason for refusing to answer their question. Rejection of revelation already given is indeed a slender basis on which to ask for more. In one sense the Sanhedrin enjoyed not only the right but the duty to check the credentials of those who claimed to be spokesmen for God. But because they misunderstood the revelation already given in the Scriptures and rejected the witness of the Baptist, the leaders proved unequal to their responsibility. They raised the question of Jesus' authority; he raised the question of their competence to judge such an issue.

2) *The parable of the two sons*

21:28–32

28"What do you think? There was a man who had two sons. He went to the first and said, 'Son, go and work today in the vineyard.'

29" 'I will not,' he answered, but later he changed his mind and went.

30"Then the father went to the other son and said the same thing. He answered, 'I will, sir,' but he did not go.

31"Which of the two did what his father wanted?"

"The first," they answered.

Jesus said to them, "I tell you the truth, the tax collectors and the prostitutes are entering the kingdom of God ahead of you. 32For John came to you to show you the way of righteousness, and you did not believe him, but the tax collectors and the prostitutes did. And even after you saw this, you did not repent and believe him.

This is the first of three parables by which Jesus rebukes the Jewish leaders (vv.28–32, 33–46; 22:1–14). The first and third of these are peculiar to Matthew. There is no convincing evidence that this first parable is only a variation of Luke 15:11–32. Helmut Merkel ("Das Gleichnis von den 'ungleichen Söhnen' [Matth. xxi.28–32]," NTS 20 [1974]: 254–61) argues that the entire parable is inauthentic; but his approach—isolating, sometimes on doubtful grounds, Matthew's redaction and wondering if enough of the parable is left for us to posit an authentic core—is so one-sided that few follow it. It is much more common to deny the authenticity of v.32 (e.g., Strecker, *Weg*, p. 153; Ogawa, pp. 121ff.), or of the last clause of v.32 (van Tilborg, pp. 52–54). Jeremias (*Parables*, pp. 80f.) argues for the authenticity of the whole.

That the verb *metamelomai* ("I change my mind") occurs in the Synoptics only in Matthew (21:29, 32; 27:3) is scarcely evidence against authenticity (so Strecker) because (1) the figures are so low (three occurrences) as to be statistically useless—one might as cogently argue that the verse is Pauline since Paul uses the verb once; (2) its use in this parable (v.29) might as easily suggest the entire parable is traditional; and (3) even if the language is Matthean—and the evidence is not conclusive either way—such considerations are not themselves conclusive concerning content (cf. Introduction, section 2). As we shall see, the entire parable makes excellent sense in context; indeed, van Tilborg (pp. 47–52) has convincingly argued that all three parables belong together as a block, even if Matthew has tightened the connections. This supports the view that 21:23–22:46 constitutes a block of confrontations and warnings that took place on the one occasion (see on 21:23).

28 The particular wording "What do you think?" is distinctively Matthean (17:25; 18:12; 22:17). The parable is introduced without any preamble other than the question. The normal way to take *prōteros* ("first") and *deuteros* ("second") in this context is "older" and "younger" son respectively (Derrett, *NT Studies*, 1:78).

29–31 The last point has a useful bearing on the complex textual problem in these verses. The evidence is neatly set out by Metzger (*Textual Commentary*, pp. 55–56) along with some useful bibliography (cf. also Derrett, *NT Studies*, 1:76ff.). When the textual evidence is sifted, three choices remain.

1. The older son says no, but repents and goes; the second son says yes, but does nothing. Who performs the Father's will? The first.
2. The older son says yes, but does nothing; the second son says no, but repents and goes. Who performs the Father's will? The younger, or the last, or the second.
3. The older son says no, but repents and goes; the second son says yes, but does nothing. Who performs the Father's will? The last.

Clearly 3 is the hardest reading; and from the time of Jerome, some have defended it for precisely that reason (Merx, Wellhausen). But not only is this reading weakly attested (Jerome knew of some Greek MSS supporting it, but only versional evidence remains today), it is either nonsensical, or else we must say the Jews are represented as perversely giving a farcical answer to avoid the application to themselves. This is not very convincing. If we do not adopt the position of WH, who suggest that a primitive textual error lies behind all extant copies, we must choose between 1 and 2. Many choose 1—as NIV—largely on the grounds that it has somewhat better external attestation than 2 and that the change from 1 to 2 can easily be envisaged. For one thing, if the first son actually went, the second might not be necessary. Also, it was natural to identify the older son with the disobedient one and the younger son with the obedient one, once the interpretation of the Fathers was widely adopted—viz., that the disobedient son stands for the Jew (who chronologically came first) and the obedient son stands for Gentile sinners. The first of these two arguments is irrelevant: there is nothing whatsoever to suggest that only one son was needed in the vineyard. The second argument is, by itself, more convincing; but it needs to face another possibility.

Derrett (*NT Studies*, 1:76ff.) has shown that in the world of Jesus' day option 2 is psychologically far more natural. The older son is somewhat pampered and favored because he is the heir, whereas the younger son is sullen and resentful but has to go out of his way to prove himself to his father. The change from 2 to 1 may have occurred if copyists supposed that in this context the father stands for John the Baptist (so, for instance, Jülicher, Jeremias), whom tax-gatherers and prostitutes, open sinners, first denied and then believed. The evidence does not admit of certain resolution, but perhaps the balance of probabilities slightly favors NASB (option 2) rather than NIV.

Either way the story is fairly straightforward. *Metamelomai* ("he changed his mind," v.29) may or may not be followed by change of purpose in the NT, unlike *metanoeō* ("I repent"). For the first time Jesus openly makes a personal application of one of his parables to the Jewish leaders. "I tell you the truth" (v.31; see on 5:16) he solemnly begins, "the tax collectors and the prostitutes enter the kingdom of God—and you do not"—for so the verb *proagō* must be translated here, rather than "are entering . . . ahead of you" (NIV; cf. Bonnard; Jeremias, *Parables*, p. 101, n. 54; TDNT, 8:105, n. 158; BDF, par. 245a[3]).

The shock value of Jesus' statement can only be appreciated when the low esteem in which tax collectors (see on 5:46) were held, not to mention prostitutes, is taken into account. In our day of soft pornography on TV, we are not shocked by "prostitutes." But Jesus is saying that the scum of society, though it says no to God, repents, performs the Father's will, and enters the kingdom, whereas the religious authorities loudly say yes to God but never do what he says, and therefore they fail to enter. Their righteousness is not enough (cf. 5:20). Thus the parable makes no distinction between Jew and Gentile but between religious leader and public sinner.

32 This verse links the parable to the preceding pericope, where the importance of believing John has already been established (vv.23–27). John pointed the way to the kingdom (11:12), which sinners are now entering (21:31). NIV interprets 21:32 in much the same way; but strictly speaking the Greek text says, "John came to you in the way of righteousness," not "John came to show you the way of righteousness." This probably means that John came preaching God's will about what was right (cf. "the way of God" in 22:16; cf. Przybylski, pp. 94–96). But in Matthew's thought John's preaching includes the demand for ethical reformation in light of the imminent coming of the kingdom (cf. 3:2–3). In this way John pointed to Jesus and the kingdom's superior righteousness (5:20). But the religious leaders did not believe John's witness, even after seeing society's vilest sinners repenting and believing him and his message.

Notes

32 Hill (*Greek Words*, pp. 124f.), Przybylski (pp. 94–96), and others rightly insist that δικαιοσύνη (*dikaiosynē*, "righteousness") in Matthew means "righteousness that is practiced," "performing the will of God." But this does not necessarily mean that practicing righteousness *in itself* gains entrance into the kingdom; for if Matthew says that John taught men to repent, he equally makes clear that John's ministry pointed to Jesus and the kingdom. If John is believed, men are led to Jesus. "Righteousness," or, better, "doing what is right, in accordance with the Father's will," includes not merely ethics, narrowly conceived, but believing Jesus and welcoming him as Messiah: the Father's will focuses on Jesus (11:25–27), who comes not only to set an example but to give his life as a ransom for many (20:28) and to inaugurate the new covenant in his blood (26:27–28). Word studies on "righteousness" by Hill and Przybylski, sound as they are, must not blind us to the larger themes in Matthew with which "righteousness" is inextricably connected.

3) *The parable of the tenants*

21:33–46

33"Listen to another parable: There was a landowner who planted a vineyard.
He put a wall around it, dug a winepress in it and built a watchtower. Then he

rented the vineyard to some farmers and went away on a journey. [34]When the harvest time approached, he sent his servants to the tenants to collect his fruit.
[35]"The tenants seized his servants; they beat one, killed another, and stoned a third. [36]Then he sent other servants to them, more than the first time, and the tenants treated them the same way. [37]Last of all, he sent his son to them. 'They will respect my son,' he said.
[38]"But when the tenants saw the son, they said to each other, 'This is the heir. Come, let's kill him and take his inheritance.' [39]So they took him and threw him out of the vineyard and killed him.
[40]"Therefore, when the owner of the vineyard comes, what will he do to those tenants?"
[41]"He will bring those wretches to a wretched end," they replied, "and he will rent the vineyard to other tenants, who will give him his share of the crop at harvest time."
[42]Jesus said to them, "Have you never read in the Scriptures:

" 'The stone the builders rejected
has become the capstone;
the Lord has done this,
and it is marvelous in our eyes'?

[43]"Therefore I tell you that the kingdom of God will be taken away from you and given to a people who will produce its fruit. [44]He who falls on this stone will be broken to pieces, but he on whom it falls will be crushed."
[45]When the chief priests and the Pharisees heard Jesus' parables, they knew he was talking about them. [46]They looked for a way to arrest him, but they were afraid of the crowd because the people held that he was a prophet.

This parable has long been a battleground for complex debate. It is marginally easier to account for synoptic differences (cf. Mark 12:1–12; Luke 20:9–19) postulating both a Markan and a Q recension; but this is by no means certain (cf. chart and discussion at 19:1–2).

On the face of it, the parable continues to make a statement against the Jewish religious authorities. The metaphorical equivalences are obvious: the landowner is God, the vineyard Israel, the tenants the leaders of the nation, the servants the prophets, and the son is Jesus Messiah. Such obvious metaphors have troubled many scholars, who detect late "allegorizing," which, they judge, could not have been part of the original parable but belongs only to the church's interpretation of it.

The reconstructed parable is therefore given other interpretations (cf. Jeremias, *Parables*, p. 76; Dodd, *Parables*, pp. 124–32) so far removed from the texts as we have them that others have despaired of reconstructing the original. W.G. Kümmel ("Das Gleichnis von den bösen Weingärtnern [Mark.12.1–9]," *Aux Sources de la Tradition Chrétienne*, edd. O. Cullmann and P. Menoud [Neuchâtel: Delachaux et Niestlé, 1950], pp. 120–38) argues that the creative milieu from which this parable springs is neither Galilee, nor the ministry of Jesus, but the first-century church influenced by its own interpretation of Isaiah 5. The following observations, however, point in a different direction.

1. We have already noted (see on 13:3a) that to draw a rigid line between "parable" and "allegory" or "parable" and "interpretation" has no methodological base.

2. Certainly Jesus himself faced opposition from the religious leaders of his people and day. There is no historical reason to think he could not himself have referred to Isaiah 5 in this connection and substantial formal literary reason for thinking that the parable, as the Synoptics preserve it, fits in with some of Jesus'

established patterns of teaching (cf. E.E. Ellis, "New Directions," in Strecker, *Jesus Christus*, pp. 299–315, esp. pp. 312–14).

3. Recognizing these things, some scholars have argued that the "son" motif in the parable itself depends on the logic of the story and therefore must not be judged inauthentic (Hill, *Matthew;* cf. J. Blank, "Die Sendung des Sohnes," in Gnilka, *Neues Testament*, pp. 11–41). This is surely right. But to assign the identification of this "son" as Jesus only to the church seems a rather artificial expedient. Even the most skeptical approach to the Gospels acknowledges that Jesus enjoyed a sense of special sonship to the Father. It is almost inconceivable, therefore, that Jesus could use this "son" language in defending his mission and not be thinking of himself. It is far more natural to read the "son" language of the parable as yet another veiled messianic self-reference, especially in light of the use of "Son of God" as a messianic title in 4QFlor (see on 2:15; 3:17; 11:27).

4. As far as source criticism is concerned, it will no longer do to postulate that the Gospel of Thomas 65–66 preserves the original form of the parable. K.R. Snodgrass ("The Parable of the Wicked Husbandmen: Is the Gospel of Thomas Version the Original?" NTS 21 [1975]: 142–44), along with reviewing the evidence that argues that the omissions in Thomas owe something to Gnostic influence, shows the dependence of this version on the Syriac Gospels.

33–34 This parable is probably addressed not only to Jewish rulers (v.23) but to the crowds in the temple courts, not excluding the rulers (cf. Luke 20:9). "Another" (v.33) links this parable with the last one (cf. pl. "parables" in v.45). Verses 33–34 clearly allude to Isaiah 5:1–7 and Psalm 80:6–16: Jesus' parable is an old theme with new variations. The pains the landowner takes show his care for the vineyard. He builds a wall to keep out animals, a watchtower to guard against thieves and fire, and digs a winepress to squeeze the grapes right there. All this shows his confidence that his vineyard will bear fruit. The tenant farmers take care of the vineyard during the owner's absence and pay rent in kind.

The "servants" are the owner's agents sent "to collect his fruit." Mark stipulates merely "some of the fruit of the vineyard"; and some over-zealous critics think *tous karpous autou* ("his fruit," NIV; but possibly "its fruit" [i.e., the vineyard's] as in v.43, where the "its" refers to the kingdom) in Matthew represents the *whole* crop. That any first-century reader would take words referring to rent this way is very doubtful (v.33). Mark mentions one servant at a time but says that many others were sent (cf. v.36); again, it is very doubtful that any profound theological issue hangs on the differences.

35–37 The verb *derō* ("beat," v.35) can also mean "flay" or "flog" and stands for general bodily ill-treatment (cf. Jer 20:1–2; 37:15; for Micaiah, cf. 1 Kings 22:24). Killing the prophets is attested in the OT (1 Kings 18:4, 13; Jer 26:20–23), as is stoning (2 Chron 24:21–22; cf. Matt 23:37; Heb 11:37). The landowner sends more servants (some commentators detect an allusion to the Jewish distinction between "former" and "latter" prophets) who are treated in the same brutal way (v.36). "Last of all" (v.37) he sends his son—there is a note of pathos here—hoping the tenants will respect him. This is not as implausible as it might seem to a Western reader (cf. Derrett, *NT Studies*, 2:97–98); here it shows the landowner's forbearance with his wicked tenant farmers (cf. Rom 2:4) and motivates the ultimate implacability of his wrath.

38–41 The action of the tenants is consistently callous. Precisely how it applies to Jesus is not entirely clear. Many object that the Jewish leaders did not recognize Jesus and did not desire to kill Messiah and usurp his place (v.38). But these objections miss the mark; they run into the danger of making the details of the parable run on all fours. Matthew does not take so tolerant a view as some modern scholars do of the way the Jewish leaders discharged their responsibility. Elsewhere he shows (23:37) their fundamental unwillingness to come to terms with Jesus' identity and claims (see also on 21:23–27) because they did not want to bow to his authority. True, their attitude was not, according to the synoptic record, "This is the Messiah: come, let us kill him"; yet, in the light of the Scriptures, their rejection of him was no less culpable than if it had been that. Therefore, though all the parable's details may not be pressed, rejection of the son (v.39) by the leaders *is* the final straw that brings divine wrath on them.

For six months Jesus has been telling his disciples that the rulers at Jerusalem would kill him (16:21; 17:23; 20:18). Now he tells the rulers themselves, albeit in a parable form, which, at some level, the leaders understand (vv.45–46). Undoubtedly some who heard Peter a few weeks later (Acts 2:23–37; 3:14–15) were the more convicted when they remembered these words of Jesus.

Many take the order of events—"threw him out of the vineyard and killed him" (Matthew and Luke in the best texts), the reverse of Mark (12:8)—as the result of an attempt to align the parable a little more closely with Jesus' passion: he was taken outside the city wall and then crucified (a point made by all four Gospels). This is possible. But if Matthew and Luke here depend on Q, it is at least equally possible that they preserve the original order; and Mark has a climactic arrangement: the tenants kill the son and throw him out of the vineyard. Nothing in the parable suggests that the vineyard stands for Jerusalem.

In Matthew alone Jesus elicits the self-condemning response (vv.40–41) of the hearers of the parable, thus concluding his teaching in this parable, instead of simply presenting it. Of course the conclusion remains his, regardless of how he gets it across. NIV nicely preserves the verbal assonance in the Greek ("wretches . . . wretched end").

42 In the NT, only Jesus asks, "Have you never read?" (12:3; 19:4; 21:16; Mark 12:10); and in each case he is saying, in effect, that the Scriptures point to him (John 5:39–40). The quotation is from Psalm 118:22–23 (LXX, which faithfully renders MT; cf. Notes). Luke adds a free translation of Isaiah 8:14 (cf. Isa 28:16), which appears in Matthew 21:44. "Stone" symbolism was important in the early church (Acts 4:11; Rom 9:33; 1 Peter 2:6) to help Christians understand why Jesus was rejected by so many of his own people; and doubtless its effectiveness was enhanced by Jesus' use of it.

Jesus now turns to the image of a building. The "capstone" (lit., "head of the corner") is most probably the top stone of roof parapets, exterior staircases, and city walls (cf. Derrett, *NT Studies*, 1:61). Psalm 118 may have been written about David, the type of his greater Son. All the "builders"—Goliath, David's own family, even Samuel—overlooked or rejected David, but God chose him. So in Jesus' day the builders (leaders of the people) rejected David's antitype, Jesus. But God makes him the Capstone. Alternatively, and more probably, the psalm concerns Israel. The nation was despised and threatened on all sides, but God made it the capstone. Jesus, who recapitulates Israel (see on 2:15) and is the true center of Israel, receives similar treatment from his opponents, but God vindicates him (cf. 23:39).

The building metaphor makes no explicit allusion to the church: the point is christological, not ecclesiastical. The reversal of what man holds dear, the elevation of what he rejects, can only be the Lord's doing; "and it is marvelous in our eyes."

43 This verse, found only in Matthew (cf. van Tilborg, pp. 54–58), further explains the parable. Up to this time the Jewish religious leaders were the principal means by which God exercised his reign over his people. But the leaders failed so badly in handling God's "vineyard" and rejecting God's Son that God gave the responsibility to another people who would produce the kingdom's fruit (cf. 7:16–20). For a somewhat similar explanation, see Stonehouse (*Witness of Matthew*, p. 230). Strictly speaking, then, v.43 does not speak of transferring the locus of the people of God from Jews to Gentiles, though it may hint at this insofar as that locus now extends far beyond the authority of the Jewish rulers (cf. Acts 13:46; 18:5–6; 1 Peter 2:9); instead, it speaks of the ending of the role the Jewish religious leaders played in mediating God's authority (see further on 23:2–3; so also Ogawa, pp. 127–39, though he unsuccessfully questions the authenticity of v.43).

44–46 Jesus' words are confirmed by what "the chief priests [mostly Sadducees] and the Pharisees" (v.45)—the two principal voices of authority in the Judaism of Jesus' day—understood this parable to mean: "they knew he was talking about them." Verse 44 is inserted in many MSS. It is certainly dominical but may be an assimilation to Luke 20:18. A "capstone," if too low, could be tripped over by an unwary person, sending him over the parapet; if too light or insecurely fastened, leaning against it could dislodge it and send it crashing onto the head of some passerby (v.44). There is probably an allusion to both Isaiah 8:14–15 and Daniel 2:35. This despised stone (v.42) is not only chosen by God and promoted to the premier place, it is also dangerous.

The pericope ends with magnificent yet tragic irony (v.46). The religious leaders are told they will reject Jesus and be crushed. But instead of taking the warning, they hunt for ways to arrest him, hindered only by fear of the people who accept Jesus as a prophet (see on v.11), and so trigger the very situation they have been warned about—a dramatic example of God's poetic justice. God in the Scriptures foretells this very event; and these men, prompted by hatred, rush to bring it to pass.

Notes

---

42 The words αὕτη (*hautē*, "this") and θαυμαστή (*thaumastē*, "marvelous") are feminine and could be construed with κεφαλή (*kephalē*, "head," as in "head of the corner" = "capstone"); but more likely this LXX feminine is a slavish rendering of the Hebrew, which has no neuter and often uses feminine for general ideas; i.e., זאת (*zō'ṯ*, "this") = *hautē*, and so forth (cf. BDF, par. 138[2]). The case of λίθον (*lithon*, "stone") has been determined by inverse relative attraction (cf. BDF, par. 295; Zerwick, par. 19).

On εἰς (*eis*, "for") plus an accusative as a substitute for the predicate nominative, see Zerwick, par. 32.

46 On εἰς (*eis*, "for") as substitute for the predicate accusative—an unmistakable trace of Semitic influence—see BDF, par. 157(5); Turner, *Syntax*, p. 266; Zerwick, par. 70.

---

4) *The parable of the wedding banquet*

22:1–14

[1]Jesus spoke to them again in parables, saying: [2]"The kingdom of heaven is like a king who prepared a wedding banquet for his son. [3]He sent his servants to those who had been invited to the banquet to tell them to come, but they refused to come.

[4]"Then he sent some more servants and said, 'Tell those who have been invited that I have prepared my dinner: My oxen and fattened cattle have been butchered, and everything is ready. Come to the wedding banquet.'

[5]"But they paid no attention and went off—one to his field, another to his business. [6]The rest seized his servants, mistreated them and killed them. [7]The king was enraged. He sent his army and destroyed those murderers and burned their city.

[8]"Then he said to his servants, 'The wedding banquet is ready, but those I invited did not deserve to come. [9]Go to the street corners and invite to the banquet anyone you find.' [10]So the servants went out into the streets and gathered all the people they could find, both good and bad, and the wedding hall was filled with guests.

[11]"But when the king came in to see the guests, he noticed a man there who was not wearing wedding clothes. [12]'Friend,' he asked, 'how did you get in here without wedding clothes?' The man was speechless.

[13]"Then the king told the attendants, 'Tie him hand and foot, and throw him outside, into the darkness, where there will be weeping and gnashing of teeth.'

[14]"For many are invited, but few are chosen."

The similarities between this parable and the one in Luke 14:16–24 lead most commentators to take them as separate developments of the same tradition, found also in the Gospel of Thomas (64). This almost inevitably leads to the view that Matthew is later on the grounds that it is more "allegorizing" (but cf. discussion on 13:3a) and that vv.6–7, 11–13 are secondary (e.g., Ogawa, p. 140), vv.11–13 perhaps representing another parable. Some go so far as to argue that the Thomas version is the most primitive of the three (but cf. Blomberg, "Tendencies of Tradition," esp. pp. 81ff.). Even when there is perfunctory recognition that Jesus may have repeated the same parable on many different occasions and applied it in quite different ways, the text is subjected to ingenious theories that "explain" all the differences without any attempt to explain the methodological grounds on which one may distinguish two historical accounts of the same or similar parables from one account considerably modified in the tradition and placed in an entirely different setting. (To cite one of many examples, cf. Robert W. Funk, *Language, Hermeneutic, and the Word of God* [New York: Harper and Row, 1966], pp. 163–87. For more recent literature, see van Tilborg, pp. 58–63; Ogawa, pp. 139–49; and for discussion on the general problem, see Introduction, section 6, and comments on 5:1–12.)

Until we have unambiguous criteria, it seems wiser to accept Matthew's setting and report and Luke's setting and report (for detailed discussion, cf. Stonehouse, *Origins*, pp. 35–42). This is especially so here because of the very small degree of verbal similarity between Matthew and Luke (see chart and discussion at 19:1–2).

In this instance the differences between Matthew and Luke are striking. In Luke the story concerns "a certain man," in Matthew "a king"; in Luke a great supper, in Matthew a wedding banquet for the king's son; in Luke one invitation, in Matthew two; in Luke the invited guests make excuses, in Matthew they refuse and turn violent; in Luke the invited guests are passed by, in Matthew they are destroyed. Each parable makes admirable sense in its own setting; and whereas the skeptical may judge such suitability to be due to editorial tampering, one might equally conclude from the evidence itself that the suitability of the two parables in their respective settings stems from two historical situations.

Moreover the alleged evidence for later "allegorizing" in Matthew, in addition to being of doubtful worth as an index of later editorial activity, since more and more scholars recognize that parables and allegorizing are not mutually exclusive, must be set against the view that Luke's very simplicity may argue for the lateness of his account. Both criteria—allegorizing and simplicity—are well-nigh useless for determining historical settings. And if Matthew's parable is much harsher than Luke's, may this not owe something to the historical situation—open confrontation with the Jewish leaders during Passion Week, which sets it considerably later than in Luke?

If the parable of the tenants exposes Israel's leaders' neglect of their covenanted duty, this one condemns the contempt with which Israel as a whole treats God's grace. The parable of the wedding banquet is therefore not redundant.

1 *Apokritheis* ("answered," NASB; untr. in NIV) may reflect Jesus' response to the Jewish leaders' desires (21:45–46), but it is probably merely formulaic (see on 11:25).

2–3 For "kingdom of heaven," see on 3:2. This kingdom has become like the following story (cf. Carson, "Word-Group"). The kingdom has already dawned; invitations to the banquet have gone out and are being refused. The son's wedding banquet doubtless hints at the messianic banquet; but this must not be pressed too hard, for when that banquet comes, there is no possibility of acceptance or refusal.

The king's son is clearly Messiah, not uncommonly represented as a bridegroom (9:15; 25:1; John 3:29; Eph 5:25–32; Rev 21:2, 9). Prospective guests to a major feast were invited in advance and then notified when the feast was ready, but these guests persistently refuse (imperfect tense).

4–5 The king not only graciously repeats his invitation but describes the feast's greatness in order to provide an incentive to attend it (v.4). *Ariston* ("dinner") properly means "breakfast." It refers to the first of two meals, usually taken about mid-morning (unlike Luke 14:16, where the word *deipnon* refers to the evening meal). But large wedding feasts went on for days in the ancient world. This *ariston* is therefore just the beginning of prolonged festivity. By v.13 the celebration is continuing at night. Those invited stay away for mundane and selfish reasons (v.5). They slight the king, whose invitation is both an honor and a command, and the marriage of whose son is a time for special joy.

6–7 The scene turns violent. Some of those invited treat the king's messengers outrageously (*hybrizō* is stronger than "mistreat," v.6). Enraged, the king sends his army (cf. Notes), destroys the murderers, and burns their city (v.7). Many object that vv.6–7 introduce an unexpectedly violent tone; but it is unexpected *only* if Luke 14:16–24 is presupposed to be the more primitive form of the story. Matthew's readers, who have just finished 21:38–41, would not find 22:6–7 out of place. Nor is there a veiled allusion to A.D. 70 (contra Hummel, pp. 85f., and many others); Reicke ("Synoptic Prophecies," p. 123) has shown how implausible this is because the language belongs to the general OT categories of judgment (cf. Introduction, section 6).

8–10 The situation having gone beyond that at normal wedding banquets, these shocking developments make their points that much more effectively. The king sends his servants to *tas diexodous tōn hodōn* ("street corners," v.9)—probably the forks of the roads, where they would find many people. They extend the king's invitation to all and succeed in drawing in all kinds of people, "both good and bad" (v.10). That Jesus is reported as saying this in Matthew clearly shows that the superior righteousness (5:20) believers must attain to enter the kingdom is not merely rigorous obedience to law. After all, this Gospel promises a Messiah who saves his people from their sins (1:21; 20:28).

11–13 Whether one is good or bad, there is an appropriate attire for this wedding feast (v.11). Evidence that the host in first-century Palestinian weddings furnished appropriate attire is inadequate and probably irrelevant to what Matthew is saying. The guest's speechlessness proves he knows he is guilty, even though the king gently calls him "friend" (v.12; cf. 20:13). In view of "good or bad" (v.10), it is difficult to believe that the wedding clothes symbolize righteousness, unless we construe it as a righteousness essential not to enter but to remain there. It is better to leave the symbolism a little vague and say no more than that the man, though invited, did not prepare acceptably for the feast. Thus, though the invitation is very broad, it does not follow that all who respond positively actually remain for the banquet. Some are tied (presumably so they can't get back in) and thrown outside into the darkness, where final judgment awaits (v.13).

14 The *gar* ("for") introduces a general, pithy conclusion explaining the parable (see on 18:7; Zerwick, pars. 474–75). Many are invited; but some refuse to come, and others who do come refuse to submit to the norms of the kingdom and are therefore rejected. Those who remain are called "chosen" (*eklektoi*), a word implicitly denying that the reversals in the parable in any way catch God unawares or remove sovereign grace from his control. At the same time it is clear from all three parables (21:28–22:14) that not the beginning but the end is crucial.

Notes

2 The plural γάμους (*gamous*, lit., "wedding feasts"), as in vv.3–4 (though sing. in vv.8, 11–12), may suggest a feast with successive stages (cf. English "nuptials"; TDNT, 1:648–57).

7 The words τὰ στρατεύματα αὐτοῦ (*ta strateumata autou*, lit., "his armies") might lead the English reader to think of vast numbers of soldiers but is probably no more specific than the English idiom "sending in the army" or "police."

5) *Paying taxes to Caesar*

22:15–22

[15]Then the Pharisees went out and laid plans to trap him in his words. [16]They
sent their disciples to him along with the Herodians. "Teacher," they said, "we
know you are a man of integrity and that you teach the way of God in accordance
with the truth. You aren't swayed by men, because you pay no attention to who
they are. [17]Tell us then, what is your opinion? Is it right to pay taxes to Caesar or
not?"
[18]But Jesus, knowing their evil intent, said, "You hypocrites, why are you trying
to trap me? [19]Show me the coin used for paying the tax." They brought him a
denarius, [20]and he asked them, "Whose portrait is this? And whose inscription?"
[21]"Caesar's," they replied.
Then he said to them, "Give to Caesar what is Caesar's, and to God what is
God's."
[22]When they heard this, they were amazed. So they left him and went away.

Matthew now rejoins Mark (12:13–17) and Luke (20:20–26) in a series of confrontations, the third of which Luke omits. In each one Jesus is confronted in an attempt to show he is no better than any other rabbi, or even to ensnare him in serious difficulties. Not only does Jesus respond with superlative wisdom, but he ends the exchanges by challenging his opponents with a question of his own they cannot answer (vv. 41–46)—another bit of veiled self-disclosure. All this probably takes place in the temple courts on Tuesday of Passion Week.

15–16a "Then" (*tote*, v.15) may have purely temporal force (Mark and Luke have "and"), but there is probably a logical connection as well: "then"—after Jesus' further self-disclosure and ample warning to the Jewish leaders—the Pharisees went out from the temple courts where Jesus was preaching (21:23) and "laid plans to trap him in his words." Mark (12:13) says that "they" (presumably "the chief priests, the teachers of the law and the elders," 11:27) sent "some of the Pharisees and Herodians" to ensnare Jesus. Matthew says the Pharisees laid the plan and sent their disciples along with Herodians (v.16). Many think this difference reflects Matthew's "anti-Pharisaic bias." But several cautions must be sounded.

1. If Mark's "they" includes "the chief priests, the teachers of the law and the elders," we must remember that most of the latter two groups were Pharisees. Both Gospels therefore recognize the Pharisees' part in this confrontation.

2. Matthew's motive for making the Pharisees instigators need not be "anti-Pharisaic bias," any more than mention of the Sadducees in v.23 and synoptic parallels reflects "anti-Sadducean bias." It may owe something to literary balance—an explicit party in v.23, an explicit party in v.15. Or it may even reflect historical awareness since the Sadducees, most of whom got along with the Roman overlord better than the Pharisees, would be less likely to think up this first confrontation.

3. Both Matthew and Mark specify that Pharisees and Herodians approached Jesus, and the reason for this is obvious. Unlike most of the Jews, the Herodians openly supported the reigning family of Herod and its pro-Roman sympathies. Clearly both Pharisees and Herodians are more than mere envoys: they are active participants, seeking to put Jesus between a rock and a hard place.

A common enemy makes strange bedfellows; and common animus against Jesus erupts in plans to trip him up by fair means or foul. The verb *pagideuō* ("ensnare," "entrap," used only here [v.15] in the NT) reveals the motive: this is no dispassionate inquiry into a proper attitude to the Roman overlord. Paying the poll tax was the most obvious sign of submission to Rome. In A.D. 6 Judas of Galilee led a revolt against the first procurator because he took a census for tax purposes (Jos. Antiq. XVIII, 3[i.1]). Zealots claimed the poll tax was a God-dishonoring badge of slavery to the pagans. The trap, then, put Jesus into the position where he would either alienate a major part of the population or else lay himself open to a charge of treason.

16–17 The title "Teacher" and the long preamble (v.16) reflect flattery and pressure for Jesus to speak. If he does not reply after such an introduction, then he is not a man of integrity and is swayed by men. The question "Is it right?" is theological, as all legal questions inevitably were to a first-century Jew. The question raised here, and others like it, exercised the rabbis (e.g., b *Pesahim* 112b; b *Baba Kamma* 113a).

By NT times "Caesar," the family name of Julius Caesar, had become a title (cf. Luke 2:1, of Augustus; 3:1, of Tiberius; Acts 17:7, of Claudius; 25:8–12; Phil 4:22, of Nero). The reference here is to Tiberius. The wording of the question, with its deft "or not," demands a yes or a no.

18–20 But Jesus will not be forced into a reductionistic reply. He recognizes the duplicity of his opponents. "Trap" (v.18) is not *pagideuō* (as in v.15) but *peirazō* ("test" or "tempt," as in 4:1; 16:1). Jesus chooses to answer them on his own terms and asks for the coin (*nomisma*, a NT *hapax legomenon*) used for paying this tax (v.19). That he has to ask may reflect his own poverty or the fact that he and his disciples had a common purse. It was customary, though not absolutely essential, to pay the tax in Roman currency; and that such coins bore an image of the emperor's head along wit' an offensive inscription ("Tiberius Caesar, son of the divine Augustus" on one side and "*pontifex maximus*"—which Jesus would understand as "high priest"—on the other) would offend most Palestinian Jews. They hand Jesus a denarius (v.19); and, as in 21:23–27, he asks his questioners a question—this time one they have to answer (v.20).

21–22 Superficially Jesus' answer accords with Jewish teaching that men ought to pay taxes to their foreign overlords, since the great, even the pagan great, owe their position to God (cf. Prov 8:15; Dan 2:21, 37–38). But Jesus' answer (v.21) is more profound than that and can be fully understood only in the light of religion-state relations in first-century Rome. The Jews, with their theocratic heritage, were ill-equipped to formulate a theological rationale for paying tribute to foreign and pagan overlords, unless, like the Jews of the Exile, they interpreted their situation as one of divine judgment. But it was not only Jewish monotheism that linked religion and state. Paganism customarily insisted even more strongly on the unity of what we distinguish as civil and religious obligations. Indeed, some decades later Christians faced the wrath of Rome because they refused to participate in emperor worship—a refusal the state judged to be treason.

Seen in this light, Jesus' response is not some witty way of getting out of a predicament; rather, it shows his full awareness of a major development in redemption history. Jesus does *not* side with the Zealots or with any who expect his messiahship to bring instant political independence from Rome. The messianic community he determines to build (16:18) must render to whatever Caesar who is in power whatever belongs to that Caesar, while never turning from its obligations to

God. The lesson was learned by both Paul and Peter (Rom 13:1–7; 1 Peter 2:13–17). Of course, Jesus' reply is not a legal statute resolving every issue. Where Caesar claims what is God's, the claims of God have priority (Acts 4:19; 5:29; much of Rev). Nevertheless Jesus' pithy words not only answer his enemies but also lay down the basis for the proper relationship of his people to government. The profundity of his reply is amazing (v.22); but some of his enemies, no doubt disappointed at their failure to ensnare him, later on lie to pretend that their snare had worked (Luke 23:2).

Notes

---

16 The clause οὐ γὰρ βλέπεις εἰς πρόσωπον ἀνθρώπων (*ou gar blepeis eis prosōpon anthrōpōn*, lit., "you do not look to the face of men") is idiomatically translated by NIV, "you pay no attention to who [men] are." The expression probably has the same force as לֹא תַכִּיר פָּנִים (*lō' ṭakîr pānîm*, "you shall not respect persons [NIV, 'show partiality'']," Deut 16:19; cf. Lev 19:15): cf. Sigal, "Halakah," pp. 74f.; contra Derrett, *Law*, pp. 313ff.

21 Some have interpreted ἀπόδοτε (*apodote*, "give") to mean "pay back": Give back to God what he has given you, and to Caesar what he has given you. Although the verb can have that force, it need only mean "give" or "pay"; but the former is more suitable in this context because in no real sense does Caesar "give back" his subjects' tax money. They pay what is his due, what properly belongs to him, not what he has given them.

---

6) *Marriage at the Resurrection*

22:23–33

[23]That same day the Sadducees, who say there is no resurrection, came to him
with a question. [24]"Teacher," they said, "Moses told us that if a man dies without
having children, his brother must marry the widow and have children for him.
[25]Now there were seven brothers among us. The first one married and died, and
since he had no children, he left his wife to his brother. [26]The same thing happened to the second and third brother, right on down to the seventh. [27]Finally, the
woman died. [28]Now then, at the resurrection, whose wife will she be of the seven,
since all of them were married to her?"
[29]Jesus replied, "You are in error because you do not know the Scriptures or
the power of God. [30]At the resurrection people will neither marry nor be given in
marriage; they will be like the angels in heaven. [31]But about the resurrection of
the dead—have you not read what God said to you, [32]'I am the God of Abraham,
the God of Isaac, and the God of Jacob'? He is not the God of the dead but of the
living."
[33]When the crowds heard this, they were astonished at his teaching.

The questioners' intent is as malicious as in the last pericope. They hope to embroil Jesus in a theological debate where he must choose sides; but instead the exchange again demonstrates his wisdom and authority (cf. Mark 12:18–27; Luke 20:27–40).

23 "That same day" (lit., "in that hour") places this confrontation in the same situation as the former one. Pharisees believed in a resurrection from the dead, basing their belief in part on Isaiah 26:19 and Daniel 12:2. But Sadducees did not believe in a resurrection: both body and soul, they held, perish at death (cf. Acts 23:8; Jos. Antiq. XVIII, 12–17 [i.3–4]; Wars II, 162–66 [viii.14]). At Jesus' time Judaism as a whole held surprisingly diverse views of death and what lies beyond it (cf. G.W.E. Nickelsburg, *Resurrection, Immortality, and Eternal Life in Intertestamental Judaism* [Cambridge: Harvard University Press, 1972]). In support of his view that Matthew was written so late that it retains only vague and inaccurate impressions of Sadducees (who largely died out after A.D. 70), Hummel (pp. 18–20), followed by Bonnard, argues that this verse says that only *some* of the Sadducees say there is no resurrection; but the Greek text knows no such restriction, whatever variant is chosen (cf. Notes).

24–28 Like the Pharisees and Herodians, the Sadducees approach Jesus with insincere respect ("Teacher," v.24; cf. v.16). They begin by citing the Mosaic levirate law (Deut 25:5–6). The text form in Matthew is either a little closer to the Hebrew than in Mark and Luke, or else it assimilates more closely to Genesis 38:8 (LXX). According to biblical law, if a man dies without children (the pl. is generalizing: Zerwick, par. 7; and see on 2:20), his younger brother is to marry the widow and "have children for him," i.e., sire children who would legally be heirs of the deceased brother. Levirate marriage antedates Moses in the canon (Gen 38:8); i.e., Moses regulated the practice but did not initiate it. The OT gives us no case of it, though levirate law stands behind Ruth 1:11–13; 4:1–22. Probably in Jesus' day the law was little observed, the younger brother's right to decline taking precedence over his obligation.

Though the case brought by the Sadducees (vv.25–27) *could* have happened, it is probably hypothetical, fabricated to confound Pharisees and others who believed in resurrection. Their question presupposes that resurrection life is an exact counterpart to earthly life; and if so, the resurrected woman (v.28) must be guilty of incestuous marriages (see on 19:9) or arbitrarily designated the wife of one of the brothers. And if so, which one? Or—and this is the answer the Sadducees pressed for—the whole notion of resurrection is absurd.

29–30 In Jesus' mind the Sadducees were denying Scripture (v.29) because they approached its clear teaching on the subject (Isa 26:19; Dan 12:2; cf. Job 19:25–27), assuming that if God raises the dead he must bring them back to an existence just like this one. Jesus' response was acute. The Sadducees, Jesus insists, betray their ignorance of the Scriptures, which *do* teach resurrection, and of the power of God, who is capable of raising the dead to an existence quite unlike this present one. "For" (*gar*, untr. in NIV)—introducing an explanation as to how the power of God will manifest itself—"in" (*en*, not "at" [NIV]) viewing the Resurrection, not as a single event, but as a state inaugurated by the event) "the resurrection" there will be a change in sexual relationships (v.30). In this way we shall be "like the angels in heaven," and marriage as we know it will be no more. In fact Jesus' use of angels contains a double thrust since the Sadducees denied their existence (cf. Acts 23:8).

Some have concluded from Jesus' answer that in heaven there will be no memory of earlier existence and its relationships, but this is a gratuitous assumption. The greatness of the changes at the Resurrection (cf. 1 Cor 15:44; Phil 3:21; 1 John 3:1–2) will doubtless make the wife of even seven brothers (vv.24–27) capable of loving all and the object of the love of all—as a good mother today loves all her children and is loved by them.

31–32 Jesus now turns from the power of God to the word of Scripture (cf. v.29). He may have drawn the passage to which he appeals (Exod 3:6) from the Pentateuch, because the Sadducees prized the Pentateuch more highly than the rest of Scripture. "Have you not read?" (v.31) is a rebuke (see on 21:42).

If God is the God of Abraham, Isaac, and Jacob even when addressing Moses, hundreds of years after the first three patriarchs died, then they must be alive to him (v.32), "for to him all are alive" (Luke 20:38). God is the eternal God of the covenant, a fact especially stressed wherever reference is made to the patriarchs (e.g., Gen 24:12, 27, 48; 26:24; 28:13; 32:9; 46:1, 3–4; 48:15–16; 49:25). He always loves and blesses his people; therefore it is inconceivable that his blessings cease when his people die (cf. Pss 16:10–11; 17:15; 49:14–15; 73:23–26). Yet at first glance the text Jesus cites is sufficient, along the lines of this argument, to prove immortality but not resurrection. Two observations largely alleviate the problem.

1. The Sadducees denied the existence of spirits as thoroughly as they denied the existence of angels (Acts 23:8). Their concern was therefore not to choose between immortality and resurrection but between death as finality and life beyond death, whatever its mode.

2. The mode that was the principal (though certainly not exclusive) option in Palestinian piety was a rather shadowy existence in Sheol followed by final resurrection.

Our problem is that we force on the text a neoplatonic dualism and demand a choice between immortality and resurrection (cf. Warfield, *Shorter Writings*, 1:339–47). The point is simply "that God will raise the dead because he cannot fail to keep his promises to them that he will be their God" (Marshall, *Luke*, p. 743), read against the background of biblical anthropology and eschatology (cf. also F. Dreyfus, "L'argument scripturaire de Jésus in faveur de la résurrection des morts [Mark, XII, 26–27]," RB 66 [1959]: 213–24—though he handles Luke 20:37–38 rather disappointingly).

33 Matthew does not tell us that the Sadducees are convinced but that the crowds are astonished at Jesus' teaching. The cause of the astonishment is probably Jesus' authority and incisive insight into biblical truth (cf. 7:28–29; 13:54; 22:22). Luke (20:39) remarks that some teachers of the law, almost certainly of Pharisaic persuasion, responded, "Well said, teacher!"

Notes

---

23 The two principal readings are "Sadducees saying" and "Sadducees, those who say" (for textual details, cf. Metzger, *Textual Criticism*, p. 58). The former is likely original, both on external evidence and because it almost suggests the Sadducees began the conversation with a denial, an unprecedented approach (though it is possible their "saying" is understood to be an aside, under their breath as it were). The second reading is then a partial assimilation to Mark 12:18; Luke 20:27. But even if the second reading is original, it is quite unnecessary to suppose "those who say" refers to some *part* of the Sadducees. The words most plausibly belong in apposition: "Sadducees, i.e., those who say." Matthew treats the verb ἔρχονται (*erchontai,* "come") in Mark 12:18 as a historical present; and if "saying" is a dependent participle, it takes on the same temporal force as Matthew's προσῆλθον (*prosēlthon,* "came").

31 This is the only place in the NT that speaks of resurrection τῶν νεκρῶν (*tōn nekrōn,* "of the dead"), though Rom 1:4 uses the anarthrous expression. More common is the insertion of the preposition ἐκ (*ek,* "from"). Despite various theories to explain these differences, the diverse forms are probably synonymous.

---

7) *The greatest commandments*

22:34–40

[34]Hearing that Jesus had silenced the Sadducees, the Pharisees got together. [35]One of them, an expert in the law, tested him with this question: [36]"Teacher, which is the greatest commandment in the Law?"

[37]Jesus replied: " 'Love the Lord your God with all your heart and with all your soul and with all your mind.' [38]This is the first and greatest commandment. [39]And the second is like it: 'Love your neighbor as yourself.' [40]All the Law and the Prophets hang on these two commandments."

The account as we have it is not in Luke (cf. Mark 12:28–34), though Luke 10:25–28 has something similar introducing the parable of the Good Samaritan. Because there are several verbal agreements between Matthew and Luke against Mark, it is usually held that the "double commandment" came down separately in Mark and Q (for recent discussion, cf. R.H. Fuller in Schottroff et al., pp. 41–56). This is quite possible; and the Lukan pericope (10:25–37) is so loosely connected to its setting that it could have come from almost any period in Jesus' ministry.

On the other hand, the rabbis of Jesus' day were much exercised to find summary statements of OT laws and establish their relative importance; and in all probability the question arose enough times in Jesus' ministry that he developed a fairly standard response to the question. In Luke, Jesus elicits the correct answer from the expert in the law, rather than providing it himself; but we have already seen this kind of diversity when the synoptists recount the same event (e.g., Mark 12:9 and Matt 21:40–41; cf. Mark 12:35–36 and Matt 22:42–44), so the distinction may not be significant. More telling is the fact that the pericope in Luke focuses primarily, not on the question of the greatest commandment, but on the question of how to inherit eternal life. While this is scarcely conclusive, it may suggest quite separate occasions (cf. E.E. Ellis, "New Directions," in Strecker, *Jesus Christus,* pp. 310–12).

34 Mark says that a teacher of the law—most of whom were Pharisees—posed the question (12:28) and gives a rather positive picture of the man. But Matthew maintains the polemical tone and portrays this confrontation as owing something to the machinations of the Pharisees, who saw how Jesus had silenced the Sadducees. Historically the Pharisees' leaders sent one of their "disciples" (cf. v.16)—himself a Pharisee—who turned out to be more sympathetic than his seniors. Mark focuses on the confrontation; Matthew looks at its core from the perspective of the Pharisees who plotted it. (For similar dissension among high Jewish authorities when assessing Jesus, see John 7:45–52; Acts 5:33–39.)

35–36 The *nomikos* ("expert in the law," assuming this is the correct reading and not an interpolation from Luke) is here a Pharisee, a "scribe" or "teacher of the law" considered particularly learned (v.35). The "law," of course, is Scripture, perhaps especially the Pentateuch. But because Scripture was applied to every area of life—including all civil matters—by means of certain interpretive rules and a vast complex of tradition, such an expert was, by modern standards, both a learned theologian and a legal expert. He "tested" Jesus, asking which is the greatest commandment (v.36; the positive is used for the superlative, a not uncommon way to speak of a group or class: Moulton, *Accidence*, p. 442; BDF, par. 245[2]; Zerwick, par. 146).

The Jews quite commonly drew distinctions among the laws of Scripture—great and small, light and heavy. Jesus does something similar in 23:23. Testament of Issachar 6 gives certain Scriptures as the epitome of the law; and Akiba's "negative golden rule" (see on 7:12) is proclaimed as "the whole law. The rest is commentary" (cf. b *Shabbath* 31a). Yet the Jewish evidence is not univocal. *Mekilta* Exodus 6 and *Sifre* Deuteronomy 12:8; 19:11 speak of the equal importance of all commandments (cf. futher SBK, 1:902ff.). We must allow not only for diversity of opinion among Jewish authorities but also for various opinions with different aims. Moreover, equality of various laws can refer to equality of reward for keeping them; Akiba's dictum was a response to a Gentile challenge to explain the whole law during the time he could stand on one leg.

Verse 36 shows that the question of the expert was probably a hotly debated one (cf. Urbach, 1:345–65). The scene is like an ordination council where the candidate is doing so well that some of the most learned ministers ask him questions they themselves have been unable to answer—in the hope of tripping him up or of finding answers.

37–39 Jesus first quotes Deuteronomy 6:5 (part of the Shema [Deut 6:4–9; 11:13–21; Num 15:38–41]) and then Leviticus 19:18. The first is from the MT; the second from the LXX (cf. Gundry, *Use of OT*, pp. 22–25). From the viewpoint of biblical anthropology, "heart," "soul," and "mind" (v.37) are not mutually exclusive but overlapping categories, together demanding our love for God to come from our whole person, our every faculty and capacity. "First and greatest" (v.38) refers to one, not two, qualities: the "and" is explicative, i.e., this command is primary because it is the greatest. The second (v.39) also concerns love, this time toward one's "neighbor," which in Leviticus 19:18 applies to a fellow Israelite or resident alien, but which Luke 10:29–37 expands to anyone who needs our help.

Bringing these two texts together does not originate with Jesus, as Luke's parallel suggests (confirmed also by T Issachar 5:2, 7:6; T Dan 5:3, if these texts are pre-Christian).

40 This verse is distinctive though enigmatic. "All the Law and the Prophets hang on [lit., 'are suspended from'] these two commandments." The following observations bring out the principal points of this summary.

1. The two commandments, Jesus says, stand together. The first without the second is intrinsically impossible (cf. 1 John 4:20), and the second cannot stand without the first—even theoretically—because disciplined altruism is not love. Love in the truest sense demands abandonment of self to God, and God alone is the adequate incentive for such abandonment.

2. But in what sense do the Law and the Prophets "hang" on these two commandments? It is unlikely that the verb implies "derivation"—that the Law and the Prophets can be deduced from these two commandments (so Berger, *Gesetzesauslegung*, pp. 227–32). Jesus has expanded the initial category ("the greatest commandment in the Law," v.36) to include all Scripture ("all the Law and the Prophets"). So even if "all the Law" could be derived from these two commandments, how could the same be said of "all the Prophets"?

3. It is equally unlikely that Jesus is appealing to these two commandments to abolish the necessity of formal adherence to all other law, thus entirely abandoning the rabbinical approach to the law and perhaps even making the love commandments a kind of hermeneutical canon for interpreting all OT law. This view, in one form or another, is very popular (Bornkamm, *Tradition*, pp. 76–78; id., "Das Doppelgebot der Liebe," *Geschichte*, pp. 37–45; Hummel, pp. 51ff.; and esp. B. Gerhardsson, "The Hermeneutic Program in Matthew 22:37–40," *Jesus, Greeks, and Christians*, edd. R. Hamerton-Kelly and R. Scroggs [Leiden: Brill, 1976], pp. 129–50). This radical interpretation of Jesus' answer is said to be necessary to make sense of the fact this confrontation is a test (Bornkamm, *Tradition*, p. 78). But the test can be understood in other ways (see on v.36); and the fact that Jesus' opponents are testing him does not require his answer to be radical, any more than in vv.23–33. There is no positive evidence in the text to support this view, if a better one can be found; and Moo ("Jesus") has rightly pointed out that in no case in the Gospels does love serve as grounds for abrogating any commandment (the Sabbath controversies are no exception, since there concern for fellow human beings is recognized as one important factor within the Sabbath law itself; see on 12:1–13). Indeed, G. Barth (Bornkamm, *Tradition*, p. 78) is reduced to pitting the love commands *against* the "jot and tittle" of 5:18, though both are taught by Jesus.

4. Kaiser rightly points out that this passage is in keeping with the prophetic tradition of the OT, which equally demands a heart relationship with God (Deut 10:12; 1 Sam 15:22; Isa 1:11–18; 43:22–24; Hos 6:6; Amos 5:21–24; Mic 6:6–8; cf. Prov. 15:8; 21:27; 28:9). Sterile religion, no matter how disciplined, was never regarded as adequate. Unfortunately Kaiser then arbitrarily links this pericope too closely with passages like 23:23–24 and argues that Jesus is saying that "the meticulous Scribes and punctilious Pharisees . . . must penetrate to the *more significant and abiding aspects of the law*" (p. 185; emphasis mine). But that is just what Jesus does *not* say at this point. The relative "greatness" of this command or some other one has no connection whatever in synoptic pericopes to continuity or discontinuity between the Testaments.

5. Nevertheless Kaiser's initial linking of 22:34–40 with the OT tradition demanding heart religion is valid. This matter is well treated by Moo ("Jesus"). There is no question here of the priority of love over law—i.e., one system over another—but of the priority of love within the law. These two commandments are the greatest because all Scripture "hangs" on them; i.e., nothing in Scripture can cohere or be truly obeyed unless these two are observed. The entire biblical revelation demands heart religion marked by total allegiance to God, loving him and loving one's neighbor. Without these two commandments the Bible is sterile. This pericope prepares the way for the denunciations of 23:1–36 and conforms fully to Jesus' teaching elsewhere. "Love is the greatest commandment, but it is not the *only* one; and the validity and applicability of other commandments cannot be decided by appeal to its paramount demand" (Moo, "Jesus," p. 12). The question of the continuity or discon-

tinuity of OT law within the teaching of Jesus is determined not with reference to the love commands but by a salvation-historical perspective focusing on prophecy and fulfillment (see on 5:17–48).

Notes

40 It is doubtful whether Paul (Rom 13:8–10) goes beyond the interpretation given above: see C.E.B. Cranfield, *The Epistle to the Romans*, 2 vols. (Edinburgh: T. & T. Clark, 1975, 1979), 2:673–79. This does not mean that Cranfield's entire view on the law in Paul is to be endorsed but that he rightly perceives the relation between love and law. For fairly detailed discussion of the place of law in the history of redemption, cf. Carson, *Sabbath*.

8) *The son of David*

22:41–46

41While the Pharisees were gathered together, Jesus asked them, 42"What do
you think about the Christ? Whose son is he?"
"The son of David," they replied
43He said to them, "How is it then that David, speaking by the Spirit, calls him
'Lord'? For he says,

> 44" 'The Lord said to my Lord:
> "Sit at my right hand
> until I put your enemies
> under your feet." '

45If then David calls him 'Lord,' how can he be his son?" 46No one could say a
word in reply, and from that day on no one dared to ask him any more questions.

After silencing the Jewish leaders, Jesus in turn asks them a question. His purpose is not to win a debate but to elicit from them what the Scriptures themselves teach about the Messiah, thus helping people to recognize who he really is. The passage speaks to crucial christological and hermeneutical issues (see esp. on vv.43–44).

The synoptic parallels (Mark 12:35–37; Luke 20:41–44) do not show that Jesus' questions were addressed to the Pharisees, or that they replied (see on 22:34–40). The historical setting is the temple courts, where crowds and leaders mingled together and alternately listened to the teacher from Nazareth and fired questions at him (21:23–23:36). Matthew's details probably stem from his memory of the events. That he mentions the Pharisees may reveal his desire to show his readers where the Pharisees were wrong. But one cannot be dogmatic about this, since Matthew omits Mark's gentle snub: "The large crowd listened to him with delight" (12:37), which shows that Mark, too, knows that Jesus aimed his exegesis of Psalm 110 against the biblical experts of his day.

41–42 Jesus' question (v.41) focuses on the real issue—christology, not resurrection or taxes—that turned the authorities into his enemies. The Messiah's identity according to the Scriptures must be determined. One way to do that is to ask whose son he is (v.42). The Pharisees gave the accepted reply: "The son of David"—based on passages like 2 Samuel 7:13–14; Isaiah 11:1, 10; Jeremiah 23:5 (see on 1:1; 9:27–28; cf. Moore, *Judaism*, 2:328–29; Guthrie, *NT Theology*, pp. 253–56; Fitzmyer, *Semitic Background*, pp. 113–26; Longenecker, *Christology*, pp. 109–10).

43–45 But this view, though not wrong, is too simple because, as Jesus points out, David called the Messiah his Lord (v.43). How then could Messiah be David's son? The force of Jesus' argument depends on his use of Psalm 110, the most frequently quoted OT chapter in the NT. The Davidic authorship of the psalm, affirmed by the psalm's superscription, is not only assumed by Jesus but is essential to his argument. If the psalm was written by anyone else, then *David* did not call Messiah his Lord. The phrase "speaking by the Spirit" not only assumes that all Scripture is Spirit-inspired (cf. Acts 4:25; Heb 3:7; 9:8; 10:15; 2 Peter 1:21) but here reinforces the truth of what David said so it may be integrated into the beliefs of the hearers (cf. "and the Scripture cannot be broken," John 10:35). The text of Psalm 110:1 quoted by all three Synoptics is essentially Septuagintal (cf. Gundry, *Use of OT*, p. 25; on the variants, cf. Fee, pp. 163–64). The "right hand" (v.44) is the position of highest honor and authority (cf. Ps 45:9; Matt 19:28).

Many but not all Jews in Jesus' day regarded Psalm 110 as messianic (cf. SBK, 4:452–65; LTJM, app. 9; David M. Hay, *Glory at the Right Hand: Psalm 110 in Early Christianity* [Nashville: Abingdon, 1973], pp. 11–33). Most modern scholars say that Psalm 110 was not Davidic but was written *about* David or some other king, making "my Lord" a monarchical reference by an unknown psalmist. Because Psalm 110 is so frequently quoted in the NT, some scholars try to establish the "entry" of the psalm into Christian tradition, associating it with, say, "the pre-Pauline formula in Rom 1:3f." (D.C. Duling, "The Promises to David and Their Entrance into Christianity," NTS 20 [1974]: 55–77) or Pentecost (M. Gourgues, "Lecture christologique du Psaume cx et Fête de la Pentecôte," RB 83 [1976]: 1–24). A pattern is then plotted for the score of NT uses of Psalm 110, on which Matthew 22:41–46 plus parallels appear too late to be authentic words of Jesus.

Nevertheless there are many arguments for an interpretation more in conformity with the texts as we have them.

1. That Psalm 110 is about the king makes sense only if the superscription is ignored. If David is indeed the author, as both the psalm's superscription and Jesus insist, then either the psalm deals with some figure other than David or else David, caught up in high prophetic vision, is writing about himself in the third person.

2. The latter is by no means implausible. But we have already seen that much prophecy and fulfillment is in OT paradigms pointing forward, sometimes with the understanding of the OT writers, sometimes not (see on 2:15, 5:17; 8:16–17). David is regularly portrayed, even in the OT, as the model for the coming Anointed One; and David himself understood at least something of the messianic promise (2 Sam 7:13–14).

3. Psalm 110 uses language so reckless and extravagant ("forever," v.4; the mysterious Melchizedek reference, v.4; the scope of the king's victory, v.6) that one must either say the psalm is using hyperbole or that it points beyond David. That is exactly the sort of argument Peter uses in Acts 2:25–31 concerning another Davidic psalm (Ps 16).

4. Psalm 110 contains no allusion to the much later Maccabeans, who were priest-

kings, for they were priests who became "kings," whereas the figure in Psalm 110 is a king who becomes a priest.

5. As the text stands, this pericope has important christological implications. The widely held, if not dominant, view was that the coming Messiah would be the son of David (cf. Pss Sol 17). Jesus not only declares that view inadequate, but he insists that the OT itself tells us it is inadequate. If Messiah is not David's son, *whose son is he?* The solution is given by the prologue to Matthew (chs. 1–2) and by the voice of God himself (3:17; 17:5): Jesus is the Son of God. Even the title "Son of Man" (see on 8:20) offers a transcendent conception of messiahship.

6. However, in spite of Bultmann (*Synoptic Tradition*, pp. 136–37) and many others, this does not mean that Jesus or Matthew is *denying* that the Messiah is David's son, replacing this notion with a more transcendent perspective. This Gospel repeatedly recognizes that Jesus the Messiah is Son of David, not only by title (1:1; 9:27; 15:22; 20:30–31; 21:9, 15; cf. 12:23) and by the genealogy (1:2–16) but also by its portrayal of Jesus as King of the Jews (2:2; 21:5; 27:11, 29, 37, 42: cf. Hay, *Glory*, pp. 116–17). What Jesus does is synthesize the concept of a human Messiah in David's line with the concept of a divine Messiah who transcends human limitations (e.g., Ps 45:6–7; Isa 9:6; Jer 23:5–6; 33:15–16; Zech 12:10 [MT]; 13:7 [NASB]), even as Matthew elsewhere synthesizes kingship and the Suffering Servant. The OT itself looked forward to one who would be both the offshoot and the root of David (Isa 11:1, 10; cf. Rev 22:16).

7. Even the fact that Jesus' use of Psalm 110:1 was susceptible to an interpretation denying that the Messiah must be of Davidic descent argues strongly for the authenticity of this exegesis of the psalm, for it is unlikely that Christians would have placed this psalm on Jesus' lips when his Davidic sonship is taught throughout the NT (in addition to Matthew, cf. Mark 10:47–48; 11:10; Luke 1:32; 18:38–39; Rom 1:3; 2 Tim 2:8; Rev 3:7; 5:5; 22:16). Jesus' question (v.45) is not a denial of Messiah's Davidic sonship but a demand for recognizing how Scripture itself teaches that Messiah is more than David's son.

8. Against those who hold that this transcendent sonship could only have arisen as an issue after the Passion (e.g., Lindars, *Apologetic*, pp. 46f.), we must ask why Jesus himself could not have expressed the paradox of Messiah's dual paternity, since he certainly knew God as uniquely his "Father" (see esp. 11:27) and applies the transcendent title "Son of Man" to himself as well.

9. If this approach is substantially correct, then the entrance of Psalm 110 into Christian theology is traceable to Jesus himself. Moreover it can be credibly argued that *his* approach to the OT is adopted by the NT writers, even when they do not focus on the same OT texts to which he gave his primary attention.

10. Finally, the text has some eschatological implications, even though they are not of primary interest. Messiah is pictured at God's right hand of authority during a period of hostility from God's enemies, a hostility to be crushed at the end (cf. 28:18–20).

46 In Mark the opponents' silence (12:34) concludes the pericope of the greatest commandment. Matthew uses this comment to finish the entire section of confrontations (21:23–22:46). Many who were silenced were not saved; so Jesus' enemies went underground for a short time before the Crucifixion. Yet even their silence was a tribute. The teacher who never attended the right schools (John 7:15–18) confounds the greatest theologians in the land. And if his question (v.45) was unanswerable at this time, a young Pharisee, who may have been in Jerusalem at the time, was to answer it in due course (Rom 1:1–4; 9:5).

Notes

44 The variants "under your feet" or "your footstool" (cf. Nestle) were easily exchangeable in Greek because of (1) similarity in the Greek terms ὑποκάτω (*hypokatō*, "under") and ὑποπόδιον (*hypopodion*, "footstool"); (2) the demonstrable influence of Ps 8:6; and (3) the obvious relation between the two expressions (a footstool by definition is under one's feet). On the significance of the idea, cf. Josh 10:24; Ps 47:3.

e. *Seven woes on the teachers of the law and the Pharisees* (23:1–36)

1) *Warning the crowds and the disciples*

23:1–12

[1]Then Jesus said to the crowds and to his disciples: [2]"The teachers of the law and the Pharisees sit in Moses' seat. [3]So you must obey them and do everything they tell you. But do not do what they do, for they do not practice what they preach. [4]They tie up heavy loads and put them on men's shoulders, but they themselves are not willing to lift a finger to move them.

[5]"Everything they do is done for men to see: They make their phylacteries wide and the tassels on their garments long; [6]they love the place of honor at banquets and the most important seats in the synagogues; [7]they love to be greeted in the marketplaces and to have men call them 'Rabbi.'

[8]"But you are not to be called 'Rabbi,' for you have only one Master and you are all brothers. [9]And do not call anyone on earth 'father,' for you have one Father, and he is in heaven. [10]Nor are you to be called 'teacher,' for you have one Teacher, the Christ. [11]The greatest among you will be your servant. [12]For whoever exalts himself will be humbled, and whoever humbles himself will be exalted.

Structurally, it is difficult to decide just where Matthew 23 belongs. Because it is essentially discourse, some have held that it either belongs to Matthew 24–25 or else is a separate discourse and must be treated as such. But the different audiences (23:1; 24:3) separate chapter 23 from chapters 24–25, as do their distinct, though related, themes. Nor is Matthew 23 a discourse on a par with the five major discourses of Matthew: it lacks the characteristic discourse ending (see on 7:28–29). Moreover, from a thematic viewpoint Matthew 23 is best perceived as the climax of the preceding confrontations.

Solutions to many of the important questions raised by Matthew 23 gradually emerge from exegesis of the whole; but several preliminary considerations will point the way ahead.

1. The literary origins of this chapter are disputed. Some see vv.1–12 as free expansion—by Matthew—of Mark 12:38–39, and vv.13–36 of Mark 12:40. Others hold that Mark has reduced material in Matthew because he is not interested in this debate; and still others that the two Gospels spring at this juncture from separate traditions. There is no way of proving the rightness of one of these options. Yet it must be said that Matthew's material is remarkably coherent and, when viewed dispassionately (see below), believably dominical. Even the changes of addressees

(23:1, 13, 37) admirably suit the larger context (21:23–22:46), with crowds and authorities milling around and coming and going, and the preacher addressing first this part of his audience, then that. The chapter *may* be a montage of sayings: there is ample evidence that Luke often compiled sayings in that way, without pretense of doing otherwise. On the other hand, there is no good reason for thinking 23:2–36 cannot be a report of what Jesus said on this occasion.

2. Attempts to define the situation in Matthew's church on the basis of this chapter are precarious. These turn on attitude toward the law (cf. vv.2–3 and v.23) or toward the Jewish religious leaders and lead to extended debate as to whether Matthew's church has broken from the synagogue and is therefore appealing to it, denouncing it from without, or still trying to win it over from within. Objections to the contrary, there is no real anachronism to warrant such discussion, which is scarcely more than fanciful though learned speculation. Obviously Matthew is telling us what Jesus says, not what the church says. Even if we assume that Matthew's choice of what he includes largely reflects the situation at the time he wrote, it is naive to think twentieth-century scholars can reconstruct the situation in detail (cf. Introduction, section 2). A certain amount of personal interest or a need to show his readers "how we got from there to here" may have led Matthew to many of his choices. The space he allots to it implies that he is interested in the continuity between the OT people of God and the church, the people of the Messiah, and how it happened that so many Jews, including the religious authorities, rejected Jesus. But Paul had similar aims in writing Romans, and no one thinks the church at Rome is theologically akin to Matthew's church in this respect.

3. The literary context of the chapter is extremely important. Not only does Matthew 23 climax a series of controversies with the Jewish religious authorities (21:23–22:46), but it immediately follows the christologically crucial confrontation of 22:41–46. The question "What do you think about Christ?" raised by Jesus (v.42) "was not simply a theological curiosity which could be thrashed out in the seminar room," as Garland (p. 24) puts it; it stands at the heart of the gospel. The failure of the Pharisees to recognize Jesus as the Messiah prophesied in Scripture is itself already an indictment, the more so since they "sit in Moses' seat" (see on v.2); and the woes that follow are therefore judicial and go some way toward explaining the prophesied destruction of Jerusalem in the Olivet Discourse (24:4–25:46).

4. Thus Jesus' strong language in this chapter ("fools," "hypocrites," "blind guides," "son of hell") is not the language of personal irritation at religious competition, nor the language of a suffering church tired of the restrictions and unbelief of the synagogue in the ninth decade A.D., but the language of divine warning (cf. vv.37–39) and condemnation. Those who see Matthew 23 as inconsistent with the Sermon on the Mount (esp. 5:43–48) neglect two things. First, they overlook the limitations inherent to the sermon itself: the love Jesus demands of his followers is more radical and more discriminating than modern liberal sentimentality usually allows. Second, the Sermon on the Mount, not less than Matthew 23, also presents Jesus as eschatological Judge who pronounces solemn malediction on those he does not recognize and who fail to do his word (7:21–23). To read Matthew 23 as little more than Matthew's pique about A.D. 85 is not only without adequate historical and literary justification but fails dismally to understand the historical Jesus, who not only taught his followers to love their enemies and gave his own life in supreme self-sacrifice, but proclaimed that he came not to bring peace but a sword (10:34) and presented himself as eschatological Judge (e.g., 7:21–23; 25:31–46).

1 Perhaps a year earlier Jesus had begun to denounce the Pharisees (15:7). Subsequently he warned his disciples of the teaching of the Pharisees and Sadducees (16:5–12). Now his warnings and denunciations are public. Current scholarship tends to see "crowds" and "his disciples" either as unhistorical, perhaps an invented transition (Walker, pp. 68–70), or else as an ambiguous pastiche of historical reminiscence and contemporizing, the "crowds" referring to Jews in Matthew's day and "disciples" to Christians in his day. All this is groundless. In the setting—the temple courts a few days before Passover (21:23)—"crowds" along with "disciples" and some religious authorities are to be expected. Matthew mentions both groups because he sees that the essential thrust of Jesus' warnings is to compel men to follow him, the Messiah as defined in 22:41–46, or the religious leaders. And those who do the latter will share their leaders' condemnation. The scene is therefore set for Jesus' lament over Jerusalem (vv.37–39) and the judgment that follows (chs. 24–25; cf. Garland, pp. 34–41).

2 Only here in Matthew do the Greek words behind "teachers of the law" and "Pharisees" take separate articles, implying two separate groups (cf. RHG, pp. 758f.). Therein lies a problem, for whereas "scribes" (NIV, "teachers of the law") had teaching authority, the Pharisees as such did not. Many were laymen without authority or responsibility to teach. Grundmann suggests that *kai* ("and") is epexegetical ("scribes, that is, the Pharisees"); Gaechter, that the phrase is a hendiadys ("scribes of the Pharisees"). But both views are unnatural and do not account for the use of "Pharisees" in ch. 23.

On the other hand, some hold that the "Pharisees" represent Matthew's opponents in A.D. 85 and are therefore anachronistically inserted into the Gospel (Kilpatrick, *Origins*, p. 113; Hummel, p. 31; Bonnard; and many others). Garland (p. 44, n. 32, and pp. 218–21), however, has pointed out that Luke attacks the Pharisees as vigorously as Matthew; yet no one holds that Pharisaic Judaism was a major concern for Luke's church. Walker (p. 20), van Tilborg (p. 106), and Garland (pp. 43–46) conclude that all categories of Jewish leaders (Pharisee, scribe, Sadducee, chief priest, etc.) in Matthew lose all historical distinction and become synonymous, ciphers for Jewish leadership in general that failed to recognize Jesus as Messiah. But some passages preserve fine historical distinctions (e.g., 21:23); and it is intrinsically unlikely that a writer as sensitive to Jewish background as Matthew would use words so clumsily. The problem is one of demanding too narrow definition of certain categories and, when they don't fit, charging the writer with anachronism.

A better approach is possible (cf. Carson, "Jewish Leaders"). The "teachers of the law," most of them Pharisees in Matthew's time, were primarily responsible for teaching. "Pharisee" defines a loose theological position, not a profession like "teacher." The two terms are distinct, even if there is much overlap on the personal level. An analogy might be the Puritan John Owen's denouncing "the prelates and Roman Catholics" and then continuing his discourse with epithets like "you prelates, you Catholics," "you prelates, Catholics." "Prelates" defines roles but does not mean that the only prelates are Catholics (some were Anglicans); the other—"Catholics"—defines theological position but does not require all Catholics to be prelates. This is how Jesus was attacking a theological position and those who promulgated it.

These leaders "sit in Moses' seat." E.L. Sukenik (*Ancient Synagogues in Palestine and Greece* [London: OUP, 1934], pp. 57–61) has shown that synagogues had a stone seat at the front where the authoritative teacher, usually a *grammateus* ("teacher of the law"), sat. Moreover, "to sit on X's seat" often means "to succeed X" (Exod 11:5; 12:29; 1 Kings 1:35, 46; 2:12; 16:11; 2 Kings 15:12; Ps 132:12; cf. Jos. Antiq. VII, 353[xiv.5]; XVIII, 2[i.1]). This would imply that the "teachers of the law" are Moses' legal successors, possessing all his authority—a view the scribes themselves held (M *Sanhedrin* 11:3; cf. Ecclus 45:15–17; M *Aboth* 1:1; M *Yebamoth* 2:4; 9:3).

3 The astounding authority conceded "the teachers of the law and the Pharisees" in v.2 becomes explicit in v.3. Even if the emphasis in v.3 falls at the end, where Jesus denounces the Jewish leaders' hypocrisy, the beginning of the verse gives them full authority in all they teach, even if they do not live up to it. *Panta hosa* ("everything") is a strong expression and cannot be limited to "that teaching of the law that is in Jesus' view a faithful interpretation of it"; they cover *everything* the leaders teach, including the oral tradition as well (Garland, pp. 48f.; contra Allen; Plummer; Schlatter; Stonehouse, *Witness of Matthew,* pp. 196f.; and others). Nor does the text say their authority rests in their roles but not in their doctrine: on the contrary, v.3 affirms their doctrine but condemns their practice. Meier (*Law,* pp. 106, 119, 156) argues that this pertains only to Jesus' earlier ministry but not to the church from the Resurrection on. But this settles nothing, because Jesus has during his ministry repeatedly criticized the scribes and Pharisees for their teaching, not least their oral tradition (5:21–48; 15:3–14; 16:12), will do so again (23:16–36), and has just finished exposing their ignorance of the Scriptures (22:41–46).

Many scholars hold that vv.2–3 reflect an earlier tradition, reflecting a time when Matthew's church was still part of and under the authority of the Jewish leaders and that somehow that early tradition was awkwardly preserved in a book that, on the whole, reflects later theological developments. But it is doubtful whether there ever was such a time (cf. Acts 3–4); and in any case the theory makes Matthew an extraordinarily incompetent editor.

The way around this thorny point, according to Hummel, van Tilborg, and Schweizer, is to recognize that Matthew preserves vv.2–3 because the rupture between synagogue and church has not yet taken place. So Matthew incorporates vv.2–3 to mollify and if possible win Jewish opponents, while at the same time giving a qualified interpretation of the statement in line with 5:17–20 (Schweizer). The remarkable thing, however, is that vv.2–3 are not in themselves qualified but are about as strong as can be imagined. If Matthew was interested in preventing a threatening rupture in the alleged union between synagogue and church, why does he not elsewhere mitigate his strong denunciation of the Jewish leaders' teaching and include the praise of the scribe (Mark 12:34)? First-century readers were no less alert than we. Could they not see that the Gospel repeatedly criticizes the Pharisees' doctrine, making the assurance of vv.2–3 empty and mocking?

Before proposing a solution, we must consider the force of v.4.

4 The Qumran covenanters called the Pharisees "the expounders of smooth things," because their casuistry made life easier than the covenanters themselves approved. To reconcile this DSS evidence with v.4, some have held that though the Pharisees made things easier for themselves, proving the covenanters right, they made it harder for everyone else; so v.4 is correct (cf. Hill, *Matthew*). The distinction is doubtful. Most Pharisees, including rabbis, worked in some full-time trade: they were not secluded scholars but active members of society. It is hard therefore to see how their rulings could benefit only themselves. We must not forget that the DSS came out of a monastic community, which would negatively judge all rules less rigorous than their own. The real question about v.4 is whether (1) it contrasts in some way with vv.2–3 or (2) it merely illustrates v.3b. The latter will not stand close scrutiny (cf. Garland, pp. 50ff.).

Verse 4 speaks of the leaders' putting "heavy loads on men's shoulders—laying down irksome rules—and then refusing "to lift a finger" to help. This does not mean they were unwilling to obey burdensome rules themselves (contra Josef Schmid, in loc.; Bornkamm, *Tradition*, p. 24; Schweizer, *Matthew;* Sand, p. 89) but that they refused to help those who collapsed under their rules (Manson, *Sayings*, p. 101; McNeile; Filson; Garland, p. 51). This is the natural interpretation of *kinēsai* ("to move"; cf. BAGD, s.v.) and fits the allusion to 11:28–30. Thus the Pharisees are unlike Jesus, whose burden is light and who promises rest. But this means that v.4 does more than illustrate v.3b: it shows how the Pharisees are by their teaching doing more harm than good.

Thus vv.2–3 stand alone in their emphasis: their contexts flatly contradict them. It will not do to treat vv.2–3 as a concession to the leaders that Matthew then modifies, a "rhetorical preparation" drawn from conservative tradition that the evangelist proceeds to modify (Banks, *Jesus*, p. 176; Garland, pp. 54f.), for the tension is too sharp. The only way to make sense of the text is to follow Jeremias (*Theology*, p. 210) and see in vv.2–3 an instance of biting irony, bordering on sarcasm. This position is self-consistent and does not weaken the strong statements in vv.2–3. Moreover it is strengthened by the verb *ekathisan* ("sit") in v.2. The aorist is not normally translated as a present. In response many point out that the same aorist verb is used in Mark 16:19; Hebrews 1:3; 8:1; 10:12; Revelation 3:21—all of which refer to Jesus as still sitting. But that misses the point. The emphasis in each of these instances is not that Jesus is still sitting, though that is doubtless presupposed, but on the fact that as a result of his triumph he *sat down*. The aorist does not *require* that the action be at one point in time; it is the context that in each of these instances presupposes it. Moreover the gnomic aorist in the indicative mood (which is how NIV's "sit" takes the Greek in v.2) is so rare in the NT that it should not be our first option. But if vv.2–3a are ironic, then the aorist can have its natural force: the teachers of the law and the Pharisees *sat down* in Moses' seat (cf. NASB's "have seated themselves," which may be overtranslated but has the right idea). The Jewish religious leaders have "presumed" to sit in Moses' seat (so Adalbert Merx, *Das Evangelium Matthaeus* [Berlin: Georg Reimer, 1902]; Moulton, *Prolegomena*, p. 458; Zahn). It is, of course, of no help to say that such a translation must be followed in v.3a by "therefore, pay no attention to what they say" (contra Plummer; Banks, *Jesus*, p. 175; Garland, p. 48), for v.3a continues the irony. This generates a neat chiasm:

A: v.2—the leaders have taken on Moses' teaching authority } irony
    B: v.3a—do what they say
    B¹: v.3b—do not what they do } nonironical advice
A¹: v.4—their teaching merely binds men

Thus the first two elements are ironic, and the last two reveal in reverse order the painful futility of following the teachers of the law. Jesus warns the crowds and his disciples in the sharpest way possible. The reluctance of many scholars to admit that vv.2–3 are biting irony overlooks the tone of much of this chapter (e.g., vv.23–28) and superb parallels elsewhere in the NT (e.g., 1 Cor 4:8a, 10).

5–7 These verses illustrate some of the leaders' practices not to be copied (v.3b; cf. Mark 12:38–39; Luke 20:46). Jesus accuses them of being time-servers and applause-seekers (6:1–18). "Phylacteries" (v.5) were small leather or parchment boxes containing a piece of vellum inscribed with four texts from the law (Exod 13:2–10, 11–16; Deut 6:4–9; 11:13–21). They were worn on the arm or tied to the forehead according to Exodus 13:9, 16; Deuteronomy 6:8; 11:18 (though originally these passages were probably metaphorical). The peculiar term used here only in the NT has pagan associations ("amulet") and may insinuate that the *ṭôṭāpōt* ("frontlets," as they were called, though they are now referred to by Jews as *tᵉpillîn* [lit., "prayers"]) had become like pagan charms (cf. ZPEB, 4:786–87; SBK, 4:250–76; Urbach, 1:130, 366f.).

To show their piety to the world, these leaders made large, showy phylacteries. The same ostentation affected the length of tassels, worn by all Jews (including Jesus, 9:20; 14:36) on the corners of the outer garment, in obedience to Numbers 15:37–41; Deuteronomy 22:12. (The view that *ta kraspeda* ["tassels"] means "borders" [KJV] of garments is unlikely in this context: cf. BAGD, s.v.; on the details of Jewish ritualism, HJP, 2:479ff.)

Seeking a reputation for piety goes with seeking places of honor at great dinners or the most important seats—as close as possible to the law scrolls—in the synagogues (v.6). "Rabbi" (v.7), the transliteration of the Hebrew word meaning "my master" or "my teacher," was used in Hillel's time, a generation before Jesus; but it probably did not signify official ordination till after the Fall of Jerusalem. The title, originally merely a mark of respect, was applied to Jesus (26:25, 49; John 1:38; 3:26). But like other common terms, it became inflated. By Talmudic times a rabbi's status was immense: his disciple had to obey him without question, never walk beside or in front of him, never greet him first, and so forth (cf. Moses Aberbach, "The Relations Between Master and Disciple in the Talmudic Age," *Essays Presented to Chief Rabbi Brodie*, 2 vols., ed. H.J. Zimmels [London: Soncino, 1966–67]. 1:1–24; cf. Albright and Mann). The situation had not developed so far in Jesus' day; but if the process had begun, one can well imagine Jesus' exposing it (esp. in light of 18:1–5; 20:25–28; cf. also Introduction, section 11.f).

8–10 The "you" (v.8) is emphatic, but this does not mean that vv.8–10 are out of place in an address before a mixed audience. It is not implausible that out of the crowd Jesus is here speaking primarily to his disciples, just as he later addresses the Pharisees directly (vv.13–36). A good preacher knows that forthright words about what is required of believers can be at the same time a powerful incentive to decision on the part of the sympathetic but uncommitted. These verses could therefore serve as warning not to follow the "teachers of the law and the Pharisees" while laying down normative patterns for relationships among Jesus' disciples.

Unlike the religious authorities, Jesus says, his disciples are not to be called "Rabbi" (v.8), for they have but one *didaskalos* (better rendered "Teacher" than "Master"). The "one Teacher" is not God but Jesus himself (cf. v.10); but either way, in view of 22:41–46; 23:4, 13–36, this verse not only proscribes self-exaltation in teaching divine things but rejects the authority of the religious teachers of Jesus' day. Such authority has been taken from them (see on 21:43). Among those who follow Jesus, a brotherly relationship (see on 5:22–24, 47; 18:15, 21, 35; 25:40; 28:10) is required.

Verse 9 moves from "Rabbi" or "Teacher" to "Father." To the best of our knowledge, rabbis were not directly addressed as "Fathers." Some have therefore argued that the text is referring to the patriarchs ("fathers") and is saying, "Do not rely on your racial tie to Abraham, Isaac, and Jacob" (cf. 3:9; so J.T. Townsend, "Matthew xxiii.9," JTS 12 [1961]: 56–59; Schweizer *Matthew*; and others). Nothing in the context supports this, still less the suggestion that Greek Stoicism stands in the background (van Tilborg, p. 138). But K. Kohler ("Abba, Father. Title of Spiritual Leader and Saint," JQR 13 [1900–1901]: 567–80) showed long ago that "the fathers" became a very common way of referring to earlier teachers of the law, especially the great masters (cf. also Urbach, 1:186; 2:906, n. 38). The practice may have stretched back to the days of the prophets (cf. 2 Kings 2:12).

"On earth" does not mean the "fathers" were alive in Jesus' time but simply contrasts them with the Father in heaven: their domain is not exalted enough to warrant the latter title. This explains the change from the passive ("do not be called," vv.8, 10) to the active ("do not call [i.e., someone else," v.9): "do not be called" would be inappropriate since the title was not bestowed till after the teachers of law died and were memorialized. There may be an allusion to Malachi 2:7–10: like the priests of Malachi's day whose teaching caused many to stumble, so the revered Jewish fathers have so misinterpreted Scripture that they must not be called "fathers." There is but one Father, God.

But where, then, *is* the voice of authoritative teaching? Jesus returns to that theme in v.10, completing an A-B-A chiasm. Thus v.10 largely repeats v.8, using a different word for "Teacher" (cf. Notes); but it is not repetitious, still less anticlimactic, because it ends by identifying the sole Teacher as the Christ, the Messiah (Kingsbury, *Matthew*, p. 93). This not only picks up the theme of 1:1 and 16:16 but echoes the confrontation in 22:41–46 regarding Messiah. Jesus' enemies, the certified teachers of Israel, could not answer basic biblical questions about the Messiah. Now he, Jesus the Messiah, declares in the wake of that travesty that he himself is the only one qualified to sit in Moses' seat—to succeed him as authoritative Teacher of God's will and mind.

Two further observations need to be made. First, it is untrue to Jesus' teaching to deduce from this passage that no Jewish leader was sympathetic to his cause, nor that there is no place for distinctions in roles or respect for leaders in his church, any more than his prohibition of oaths (5:33–37) means it is unchristian to swear on oath in court. Certainly Jesus was not justifying that particularly perverse pride that cloaks itself in discourtesy. Yet once this has been noted, we must say that the risen Christ is as displeased with those in his church who demand unquestioning submission to themselves and their opinions and confuse a reputation for showy piety with godly surrender to his teaching as he ever was with any Pharisee.

Second, the continuing modern discussion as to what these verses show about the structure of Matthew's church finds no valid source here. For instance, Hummel (pp. 27f.) holds that vv.8–10 show that there must have been a sort of Christian rabbinate in Matthew's day, which Matthew was combatting or attempting to guide. That may be so, but the text does not say so. In any case other reasons for Matthew's including this material spring readily to mind. If Matthew *is* concerned to show Christian-Jewish readers of his own day "how we got from there to here," and if this material is basically authentic, no further reason is needed. The truth is that we know about Matthew's situation only from what he chose to write about Jesus, not a late first-century church.

11–12 The substance of v.11 is in 20:26: Matthew repeatedly emphasizes humility. For instances of exalting oneself, see on 20:20–28; of humbling oneself, on 18:4 (cf. Prov 15:33; 22:4; James 4:6; 1 Peter 5:5–6). "Will be your servant," "will be humbled," and "will be exalted" are pure futures without imperatival force (contra Zerwick, par. 280). The latter two could not be otherwise; so v.11 should be read the same way. The principle enunciated in these verses reflects not natural law but kingdom law: the eschatological reward will humble the self-exalted and exalt the self-humbled, after the pattern in Ezekiel 21:26. What is commended is humility, not humbug; service, not servility. The supreme example—the Messiah himself—makes this clear (20:26–28); for his astonishing humility and service to others was untainted by servility and was perfectly compatible with exercising the highest authority. Having done the greatest service, he has been most highly exalted.

Notes

---

4 For the variant "and hard to carry" (as in Luke 11:46), see Metzger, *Textual Commentary*, pp. 59–60.

8 For literature on the question of whether this use of "Rabbi" is anachronistic, see Garland, p. 58; Sigal, "Halakah."

9 The Greek word order suggests the rendering "for, for you there is only *one* Father—the heavenly Father" (Moule, *Idiom Book*, p. 166).

10 Καθηγητής (*kathēgētēs*, "teacher") is used only here in the NT. Many suggestions have been made as to why it should replace "rabbi" and διδάσκαλος (*didaskalos*, "teacher") in v.8. Some have assumed it to be Matthew's translation for Gentile readers (Grundmann; Strecker, *Weg*, p. 217) or an addition to dissociate Jesus from Hellenistic teachers as much as from "teachers of the law" (Frankemölle, pp. 99–100). C. Spicq ("Une Allusion au Docteur de Justice dans Matthieu, XXIII, 10?" RB 66 [1959]: esp. 393–96) suggests the word is the Greek equivalent of the Hebrew מוֹרֶה (*môreh*, "teacher"), used in the DSS for the "Teacher of Righteousness" at Qumran. Jesus is then seen as denouncing the sectarian religious authorities as well as the scribes. But the linguistic evidence is unconvincing, and it seems wiser to take *kathēgētēs* as a synonym for *didaskalos*, possibly prompted by homophony with ἐκάθισαν (*ekathisan*, "*they sat down*") *and* καθέδρα (*kathedra*, "seat") in v.2. "This would be further evidence that the authority of the scribes and Pharisees is null and void for Matthew" (Garlad, p. 60, n. 100).

---

2) *The seven woes* (23:13–36)

Compare the six woes of Luke 11:37–54. The overlaps are considerable but the differences in order and wording no less remarkable. The three chief options are (1) Luke preserves the correct setting, and Matthew adds the woes to the end of vv.1–12; (2) Matthew preserves the correct setting, and Luke inserts some of the woes into his narrative; and (3) Jesus pronounced such woes on the Pharisees fairly frequently, perhaps following the pattern of the six woes of Isaiah 5:8–23 or the five woes of Habakkuk 2:6–20. (For discussion, cf. Marshall, *Luke*, pp. 491–93.)

The seven woes Matthew records fit into a neat chiastic pattern:

- A: First woe (v.13)—failing to recognize Jesus as the Messiah
  - B: Second woe (v.15)—superficially zealous, yet doing more harm than good
    - C: Third woe (vv.16–22)—misguided use of the Scripture
      - D: Fourth woe (vv.23–24)—fundamental failure to discern the thrust of Scripture
    - C′: Fifth woe (vv.25–26)—misguided use of the Scripture
  - B′: Sixth woe (vv.27–28)—superficially zealous, yet doing more harm than good
- A′: Seventh woe (vv.29–32)—heirs of those who failed to recognize the prophets.

What stands out is the centrality of rightly understanding the Scriptures—a theme that is reflected in all the preceding controversies and is no less related to Jesus' rejection of the claims of the teachers of the law.

a) *First woe*

23:13[14]

> [13]"Woe to you, teachers of the law and Pharisees, you hypocrites! You shut the kingdom of heaven in men's faces. You yourselves do not enter, nor will you let those enter who are trying to.

13[14] Verse 14 must be taken as an interpolation, derived from Mark 12:40; Luke 20:47. This is made clear, not only by its absence from the best and earliest Matthew MSS, but from the fact that the MSS that do include it divide on where to place it—before or after v.13. (For the meaning of v.14, cf. Derrett, *NT Studies*, 1:118–27.)

Verse 13 begins the first of seven "woes." A "woe" can be a compassionate "alas!" (24:19), a strong condemnation (11:21), or a combination of the two (18:17; 26:24). In Matthew 23 condemnation predominates; but it is neither vindictive nor spiteful so much as judicial. Jesus the Messiah pronounces judgment.

"Teachers of the Law" and "Pharisees" are anarthrous from here on throughout the chapter (see on 2:4; 3:7; 23:2; Introduction, section 11.f). (For "hypocrites," see on 1:2; for "kingdom of heaven," on 3:2.) The syntax of v.13 (cf. Notes) assumes that the messianic reign has begun. The teachers of the law and the Pharisees are "hypocrites" since they claim to teach God's way but refuse to enter the messianic kingdom and hinder those who try to do so. This does not refer to their casuistry that obscured fundamental questions of conduct and made it difficult for people to obey God's law fully, though this is the dominant interpretation (e.g., Hill, *Matthew*). Conduct is not mentioned here, only entrance into the kingdom. Though proper conduct is essential, it admits no one into the kingdom.

The last controversy (22:41–46) reveals the real failure—the teachers of the law and the Pharisees do not enter the kingdom because they refuse to recognize who

Jesus is. When the crowds begin to marvel at Jesus and suggest he may be the Messiah, the authorities do all they can to dissuade them (cf. 9:33–34; 11:19; 12:23–24; 21:15). The sheep of Israel are "lost" (10:6; 15:24) because the shepherds have led them astray. The "woe" pronounced on the authorities is therefore of a piece with 18:6–7.

Notes

13 The present substantival participle τοὺς εἰσερχομένους (*tous eiserchomenous,* "those entering") need not in itself have present force but can refer to sustained effort in the past (as in 2:20; for discussion, cf. BDF, par. 339[3]; RHG, pp. 858–64, 891–92; Zerwick, par. 274). However, in the context of the present finite verb οὐδὲ . . . ἀφίετε (*oude . . . aphiete,* "nor . . . do you permit"), there can be no doubt that the action envisaged by both participle and finite verb is portrayed as simultaneous with the speaker's words.

b) *Second woe*

23:15

15 "Woe to you, teachers of the law and Pharisees, you hypocrites! You travel over land and sea to win a single convert, and when he becomes one, you make him twice as much a son of hell as you are.

15 External sources for assessing the Pharisees' zeal to win converts are not easy to interpret, though a sizable body of scholarship convincingly argues that the first century A.D. till the Fall of Jerusalem marks the most remarkable period of Jewish missionary zeal and corresponding success (see esp. B.J. Bamberger, *Proselytism in the Talmudic Period* [Cincinnati: Hebrew Union, 1939]; W.G. Braude, *Jewish Proselytizing in the First Five Centuries of the Common Era* [Providence, R.I.: Brown University Press, 1940]; F.M. Derwacter, *Preparing the Way for Paul: The Proselyte Movement in Later Judaism* [New York: Macmillan, 1930]; D. Georgi, *Die Gegner des Paulus im 2. Korintherbrief* [Neukirchen-Vluyn: Neukirchener Verlag, 1964], pp. 83–187; Jeremias, *Promise,* pp. 11ff.; cf. Rom 2:24). Not the least important fact, as W. Paul Bowers observed ("Studies in Paul's Understanding of His Missicn," Ph.D. dissertation, Cambridge, 1976), is that there is no evidence that Jews in any way opposed Paul's or anyone else's Christian Gentile mission: rather, what they disputed was the basis of admission to the people of God.

How much of the Pharisees' activity was aimed at converting to their views those who had already become loose adherents of Judaism (cf. Jos. Antiq. XX, 34–48[ii.3–4]), we cannot know for certain. But whether the scribes and Pharisees were winning raw pagans or sympathizers of Judaism, they were winning them to their own position. The converts in view, therefore, are not converts to Judaism but to Pharisaism. Pharisees and teachers of the law would travel extensively to make one "proselyte"—a word used in the NT only here and in Acts 2:11; 6.5; 13:43 and one that at this time probably refers to those who have been circumcised and have pledged to submit to the full rigors of Jewish law, including the oral tradition for which the Pharisees were so zealous.

Jesus did not criticize the *fact* of the Pharisees' extensive missionary effort but its *results:* the "converts" became twice as much a "son of hell" (gehenna; see on 5:32) as the scribes and Pharisees who won them. This means that the Pharisees' interpretations and the rules deduced from Scripture became so fully those of their converts that they "out-Phariseed" the Pharisees. Psychologically this is entirely possible, as every teacher of converts knows. As for the converts of whom Jesus was speaking, the Pharisees' teaching locked them into a theological frame that left no room for Jesus the Messiah and therefore no possibility of entering the messianic kingdom.

c) *Third woe*

23:16–22

16"Woe to you, blind guides! You say, 'If anyone swears by the temple, it means nothing; but if anyone swears by the gold of the temple, he is bound by his oath.' 17You blind fools! Which is greater: the gold, or the temple that makes the gold sacred? 18You also say, 'If anyone swears by the altar, it means nothing; but if anyone swears by the gift on it, he is bound by his oath.' 19You blind men! Which is greater: the gift, or the altar that makes the gift sacred? 20Therefore, he who swears by the altar swears by it and by everything on it. 21And he who swears by the temple swears by it and by the one who dwells in it. 22And he who swears by heaven swears by God's throne and by the one who sits on it.

16–22 See on 5:33–37 for the background and thrust of these verses. The striking designation "blind guides" (v.16) was introduced at 15:14. The "temple" here is *naos* (see on 4:5).

Because of the references to the temple—its gold, altar, and offerings—a surprising number of scholars focus on Matthew's attitude toward the cultic aspects of the temple (Hummel, pp. 78–82; van Tilborg, p. 105). This quite misses the point (Gaston, *No Stone*, p. 94). The pericope simply uses the language of the cultus in discussing the kinds of distinctions in oaths often favored in Jewish circles. Saul Lieberman (*Greek in Jewish Palestine* [New York: Jewish Theological Seminary, 1942], pp. 115–43), after studying the difficult and conflicting Jewish evidence, argues that the rabbis fought the abuses of oaths and vows among the unlearned masses. This is doubtless so. But the way they fought them was by differentiating between what was binding and what was not. In that sense, wittingly or unwittingly they encouraged evasive oaths and therefore lying. Jesus cut through these complexities by insisting that men must tell the truth.

Some writers have supposed that 5:33–37—which, formally at least, abolishes oaths—contradicts 23:20–22, which maintains that all oaths are binding but does not abolish them. In fact, however, vv.20–22 provide the rationale for 5:33–37. All oaths are in some way related to God. All are therefore binding, and thus evasive oaths are disallowed. On the other hand, the heart of the issue is telling the truth; and it is probably a new kind of casuistry that, failing to see this, insists that Jesus in 5:33–37 abolishes all oaths of every kind.

In the context of Matthew 23, Jesus charges the teachers of the law and the Pharisees with mishandling the Scriptures they claimed to defend and promulgate.

Notes

16–22 References to the temple and the cultus, which no longer existed after A.D. 70, do not prove that this Gospel was composed before that date, since Matthew, writing later, may be incorporating older material and describing what Jesus said at the time of his ministry. But the pericope is consistent with an early date; and, more importantly, if we think instead that Matthew writes about A.D. 85 but carefully preserves the right tense and distinctions appropriate to Jesus' ministry, why should we not expect him to be equally careful elsewhere?

d) *Fourth woe*

23:23–24

[23]"Woe to you, teachers of the law and Pharisees, you hypocrites! You give a tenth of your spices—mint, dill and cummin. But you have neglected the more important matters of the law—justice, mercy and faithfulness. You should have practiced the latter, without neglecting the former. [24]You blind guides! You strain out a gnat but swallow a camel.

23–24 The OT law on tithing (Deut 14:22–29) specifies grain, wine, and oil, though Leviticus 27:30 is more comprehensive. Certainly in the first century there was debate about how far the law of tithing should extend. The consensus was to include greens and garden herbs (v.23; SBK, 1:932). Jesus does not condemn scrupulous observance in these things ("without neglecting the former"), but insists that to fuss over them while neglecting the "more important matters of the law" (cf. 22:34–40)—justice, mercy, and *pistis* (here rightly translated "faithfulness")—is to strain out a gnat but swallow a camel (v.24), both unclean creatures.

Several points deserve notice.

1. The "weightier" matters do not refer to the "more difficult" or "harder" but to the "more central," "most decisive" (Ridderbos, p. 302) or (as in NIV) "more important" versus "peripheral" or "trifling" ones (cf. TDNT, 1:554, 558; Kaiser, p. 184).

2. Yet it goes much too far to interpret vv.23–24 as expanding the love command into the central feature of the law (see on 22:34–40 and literature cited there; also Garland, p. 139).

3. In essence what Jesus accuses the teachers of the law and the Pharisees of is a massive distortion of God's will as revealed in Scripture. At a fundamental level, they fail to focus on the thrust of Scripture, a point made with equal force in the two references to Hosea 6:6 in this Gospel (see on 9:9–13; 12:1–14).

4. The chiastic structure of the "woes" centers on this fourth one, where the basic failure of the Pharisaic teachers is laid bare. Moving out from this center, it becomes clear that where Scripture is interpreted by the Pharisees, there is danger of misappropriation of truth (woes 3 and 5) and of corrupting other people (woes 2 and 6), coupled with blindness to true revelation when it comes supremely in the person of Jesus the Messiah (woes 1 and 7).

5. All this presupposes that Jesus holds readers of the OT responsible for discerning its purpose and recognizing its most important emphases (see on 22:40). Only

those who do this please God and recognize the Messiah (cf. Luke 24:44–46; John 5:39–40).

6. The current debate over the words "without neglecting the former"—viz., whether they show Jesus or Matthew as a very conservative interpreter of the law, or whether they can possibly come from the historical Jesus (cf. Garland, p. 140, n. 66; Westerholm, pp. 58f.)—badly misses the point. For neither Jesus nor Matthew do these verses focus on the problem of continuity–discontinuity between the OT and the reign of Jesus Messiah but on the relative importance of material within the OT. Jesus describes what the Pharisees should have done; he is not here questioning how the "former" will relate to the reign he now inaugurates (12:28) or the church he will build (16:19), any more than in vv.16–22 he discusses what role the temple altar plays under the new covenant.

Notes

24 Black (*Aramaic Approach*, pp. 175f.) points out that in Aramaic this saying would be something of a pun, since "gnat" and "camel" sound much alike: קַמְלָא (*qamlā'*) and גַּמְלָא (*gamlā'*) respectively.

e) *Fifth woe*

23:25–26

[25]"Woe to you, teachers of the law and Pharisees, you hypocrites! You clean the outside of the cup and dish, but inside they are full of greed and self-indulgence. [26]Blind Pharisee! First clean the inside of the cup and dish, and then the outside also will be clean.

25–26 The most common interpretation of these verses is that Jesus begins with the metaphor of the cup and dish (v.25a), reveals his nonmetaphorical concerns in the last words of v.25, then returns to his metaphor in v.26 now that its real purpose has been exposed. The Pharisees have been occupied with external religion instead of that of the inner person. Within themselves they remain "full of greed and self-indulgence [*akrasia*, found in the NT only here and in 1 Cor 7:5]." In the metaphor, cleaning the inside is basic and guarantees cleanliness of the outside.

Jacob Neusner (" 'First Cleanse the Inside,' " NTS 22 [1976]: 486–95) holds, largely on form-critical grounds, that pre–A.D. 70 Judaism was divided on the issue of clean vessels. The Hillelites thought that cleaning the inside of a vessel declared it "clean." The Shammaites, predominant before A.D. 70, held it was necessary to cleanse both inside and outside; the one did not affect the status of the other (cf. esp. M *Kelim* 2:1; 25:1, 7–9; j *Berakoth* 8:2). Consequently Jesus could not be refuting the Hillelites (who did not become predominant until after A.D. 70), telling them *first* to cleanse the inside, since they would have cleaned *only* the inside. Rather, the admonition was for the Shammaites.

From this debate about cleansing, it is argued, the saying was variously interpreted and applied (cf. Luke 11:41) in metaphorical ways. Garland (pp. 148–50) thinks the first part of v.25 is literal but was taken over by Matthew to make his point. In his view the *ex* clause should not be rendered "full *of* greed and self-indulgence" but "full *because of* greed and self-indulgence" (Turner, *Syntax*, p. 260; Schweizer, McNeile, and others think this is possible). In other words Matthew turns the original saying into one that says the inside is most important but then draws "attention to the fact that the vessels were filled with food and drink which was [sic] obtained unjustly and consumed intemperately—a circumstance which cultic washing could not cleanse—and ultimately made the entire issue moot" (Garland, p. 149).

This interpretation will not do. The Pharisees were not as a class intemperate in food and drink but abstemious (cf. Luke 18:11–12). Moreover, if they were full *because* of greed and self-indulgence, the preceding "but" is nonsensical: the first clause should read "you empty the cup and dish," not "you clean the outside." Rather, the kind of historical background envisaged by Neusner is being used by Jesus to point away from the ceremonial question altogether. The Pharisees (here Shammaites) debate about what must be cleansed for a cup to be clean, without seeing that they themselves need to become inwardly clean. This approach is very close to the traditional interpretation of these verses (above; cf. Westerholm, pp. 85–90). Yet it also hints that Jesus holds that OT ceremonial distinctions have moral implications the avoiding of which betrays deep misunderstanding.

"Blind Pharisee!" (v.26, the singular has generic force), says the one who came to save his people from their sin (1:21), "first clean the inside . . . and then the outside also will be clean." "Inside" does not here encourage privatized pietism but total, moral renewal in terms of "justice, mercy, and faithfulness." The "outside," the bits of religious observance easily seen by men, will then take care of itself.

f) *Sixth woe*

23:27–28

[27]"Woe to you, teachers of the law and Pharisees, you hypocrites! You are like whitewashed tombs, which look beautiful on the outside but on the inside are full of dead men's bones and everything unclean. [28]In the same way, on the outside you appear to people as righteous but on the inside you are full of hypocrisy and wickedness.

27–28 During the month of Adar, just before Passover, it was customary to whitewash with lime graves or grave-sites that might not be instantly identified as such (v.27), in order to warn pilgrims to steer clear of the area and avoid ritual uncleanness from contact with corpses (cf. M *Shekalim* 1:1; M *Kelim* 1:4; M *Moed Katan* 1:2; M *Masser Sheni* 5:1). Such uncleanness would prevent participation in the Passover (M *Kelim* 1:4; for similar concerns, cf. John 11:55; 18:28). But in that case whitewashed tombs would not have been objects of beauty ("which look beautiful on the outside") but of disgust: they were places to be shunned (cf. Luke 11:44, which mentions neither whitewash nor beauty).

Various solutions have been put forward (for a list, cf. S.T. Lachs, "On Matthew 23: 27–28," HTR 68 [1975]: 385–88). Perhaps the best proposal is Garland's (pp. 150–57), who suggests that the graves were beautiful because of their structure (cf. v.29), not their whitewash. Monuments were normally considered pure unless marked with whitewash; so if the memorial was built right over a grave, it would probably be whitewashed. Thus Jesus' mention of whitewashing has nothing to do with the beauty of sepulchers but is a further thrust at the Pharisees based on their distinctive preoccupation with avoiding defilement from corpses (cf. b *Baba Kamma* 57a; b *Baba Metzia* 85b). Jesus is saying that the scribes and Pharisees are sources of uncleanness just as much as the whitewashed graves are. There may also be an allusion to the white linen clothes that some men, impressed with their own eminence, used to wear (cf. b *Kiddushin* 72a; b *Shabbath* 25b; b *Nedarim* 20b; Jos. War II, 123 [viii.3]).

In the context of Matthew 23, the point Jesus is making is not that the scribes and Pharisees were deliberate and self-conscious hypocrites, but that in their scrupulous regulations they appeared magnificently virtuous but were actually contaminating the people. This woe parallels the second (v.15). The supreme irony is that their preoccupation with their law (*nomos*) left them steeped in *anomia*—a general term for "wickedness" (v.28; cf. 13:41; TDNT, 4:1085–86) but which may here suggest that their fundamental approach to the law was in fact, from the perspective of Jesus' hermeneutic, plain "lawlessness."

g) *Seventh woe*

23:29–32

> [29]"Woe to you, teachers of the law and Pharisees, you hypocrites! You build tombs for the prophets and decorate the graves of the righteous. [30]And you say, 'If we had lived in the days of our forefathers, we would not have taken part with them in shedding the blood of the prophets.' [31]So you testify against yourselves that you are the descendants of those who murdered the prophets. [32]Fill up, then, the measure of the sin of your forefathers!

29–30 Derrett (*NT Studies*, 2:68ff.) denies that Pharisees in Jesus' day would have been involved in building memorial tombs, but his evidence is late and may well represent reaction against earlier excesses (cf. Garland, p. 164). Herod led the way in tomb building (cf. Jos. Antiq. XVI, 179–82 [vii.1]; XVIII, 108 [iv.6]; XX, 95 [iv.3])—to atone for his attempts to plunder them! Jewish building was more likely to be commemorative; by erecting monuments the religious leaders thought themselves morally and spiritually above their forebears who had persecuted the prophets whose monuments they were building (v.29). They believed that they would not have joined their forebears in murdering the prophets (v.30)—just as many Christians today naively think they would have responded better to Jesus than the disciples or the crowds that cried, "Crucify him!"

31 But the distinction the Jews draw in v.30 Jesus now denies. Their own saying (not the tomb-building) testifies against them. They speak of their forefathers and so acknowledge themselves to be the sons (NIV, "descendants") of those who shed the blood of the prophets. But Jesus sees further irony here, based on the ambiguity of "fathers" and "sons" (see on 5:9). The Jews think in terms of their physical descent. Jesus responds by saying in effect that they are sons all right—more than they realize. They show their paternity by resembling their fathers. While piously claiming to be different, they are already plotting ways to put an end to Jesus (21:38–39, 46).

32 The conclusion is defiant and ironical. The idea behind "the measure of the sin" is that God can only tolerate so much sin; and then, when the measure is "full," he must respond in wrath (cf. Gen 15:16; 1 Thess 2:14–16). The idea is common in the intertestamental literature (e.g., Jub 14:16; 1 Enoch 50:2; 2 Esd 4:36–37; 4Q185 2: 9–10), but never before was the concept applied to Israel.

3) *Conclusion*

23:33–36

[33]"You snakes! You brood of vipers! How will you escape being condemned to hell? [34]Therefore I am sending you prophets and wise men and teachers. Some of them you will kill and crucify; others you will flog in your synagogues and pursue from town to town. [35]And so upon you will come all the righteous blood that has been shed on earth, from the blood of righteous Abel to the blood of Zechariah son of Berekiah, whom you murdered between the temple and the altar. [36]I tell you the truth, all this will come upon this generation.

33 See on 3:7 and 12:34 for the epithets. The transition from the preceding verse is clear: if the teachers of the law and Pharisees are filling up the measure of the sin of their forefathers, how can they possibly escape the condemnation of hell (see on 5:22; 23:15)?

34 If this verse shares a common source (Q?) with Luke 11:49 (see above on 23:1–12), the differences between Matthew and Luke are noteworthy, though perhaps not quite so problematic as many think. The most noteworthy feature is the change from "the wisdom of God" (NIV, "God in his wisdom") as the sender of the emissaries to an emphatic "I." Not only is there little doubt that Christians identified Jesus with God's wisdom, but he who assigned to himself messianic titles and even OT texts referring exclusively to Yahweh would not have hesitated to make the same identification. Matthew's interpretation is therefore not necessarily wrong, even if a single saying stands behind both Luke and Matthew.

Hare (pp. 87–88) thinks the introductory *dia touto* ("Because of this," Luke 11:49; "Therefore," Matt 23:34) is drastically altered. In Luke it refers to 11:47–48—a tacit admission of blood-guiltiness for the prophets' death and for which reason "the wisdom of God" sends more prophets so that "this generation" (Luke 11:50) will be accountable. In Matthew, however, vv.32–33 separate the tacit admission from *dia touto* ("Therefore," v.34) so that the connective no longer explains God's wisdom in the past but an act Jesus performed in the present. But Hare's contrast is exaggerated. It is formally correct that *dia touto* in Luke 11:49 explains a statement made in the past by the wisdom of God. But that explains only that a statement was made, not the statement's content—which refers to an act done in the present, viz., Jesus' sending emissaries. Thus the two renderings of *dia touto* are very close and share the same function: they point out that because of the Jewish leaders' wicked reception of God's messengers, more messengers will "therefore" be sent; and they will be treated the same way. This will fill up the full measure of iniquity, and judgment will fall.

Luke (11:49) has "prophets and apostles," Matthew "prophets and wise men and teachers." The "wise man" and the "teacher" were "materially identical" (Garland, p. 175; TDNT, 8:505–7) at this time. Both Matthew and Luke here look forward to the sending out of Christian missionaries—disciples of Jesus (cf. 5:10–12; 9:37–38;

28:18–20). The terms used do not reflect post-A.D. 70 terminology (cf. van Tilborg, pp. 140f.).

Matthew adds "crucify." There is no evidence Jews used crucifixion as a mode of capital punishment after 63 B.C. "Crucify" may mean "cause to be crucified" (as in Acts 2:36; 4:10), surely a better possibility than Hare's suggestion (pp. 89–92) that the words "and crucify" are a gloss on what Matthew wrote. Garland (p. 177) holds that "and crucify" refers to Jesus' death. But this, too, requires a causative sense and seems strange when it is Jesus who is sending the emissaries to their deaths and Jesus who is (in this view) among those sent and killed. Perhaps v.34 echoes 10:24–25: the servant is not above his master. If Jesus is to be crucified, his servants may expect the same.

35 The very messengers who were beaten and killed for calling the people to repentance in the mystery of providence fill up the measure of the peoples' sin (v.32)—viz., shedding righteous blood of God's emissaries from Abel to Zechariah (cf. Notes). Verse 35 anticipates 27:24–25: Pilate tries to evade responsibility for crucifying Jesus, and the Jews clamor for that same dreadful responsibility because of their skepticism about who Jesus is. On the question of alleged anti-Semitism, see on 26:57–68.

36 All along in this chapter, the teachers of the law and the Pharisees have been Jesus' primary target. Now the reference is to "this generation," because the leaders represent the people (see on 21:43) and the people, despite Jesus' warnings, do not abandon their leaders for Jesus, Messiah. This sets the stage for the concluding lament over Jerusalem (vv.37–39).

Notes

34 On flogging, see on 10:17; on persecution from city to city, cf. 10:23; Acts 9:2; 13:50–51; 14:4–7; 17:10–15. On indifference toward and harsh treatment of OT prophets, cf. 1 Kings 18:4, 13; 19:10, 14; 2 Kings 17:13–17; 1 Chron 16:22; 2 Chron 24:19; 36:14–16; Ps 105:15; Jer 7:25–26; 25:4; 26:5, 20–23; 29:19; 35:15; 44:4; Lam 2:20; 4:16.

35 Abel is the first victim of murder in the Scriptures (Gen 4:8); but the identity of this "Zechariah son of Berekiah" is problematic. Principal possibilities include:

1. It could refer to Zechariah the father of John the Baptist, but there is no evidence he was martyred.

2. It could be Zechariah son of Baris or Baruch or Bariscaeus (MSS vary), who was murdered by two Zealots in the temple (Jos. War IV, 334–44 [v.4]). But there is no evidence he was a prophet or a martyr; and, though he was killed ἐν μέσῳ (*en mesō*, "in the midst") of the temple precincts, it is unlikely he was killed between the actual sanctuary and the altar unless he was a priest; and there is no evidence for this.

3. It could be a reference to the OT prophet Zechariah son of Berekiah (Zech 1:1). But there is no account of his being killed.

4. It may be a Zechariah of whom we have no knowledge (Albright and Mann). This is possible but without proof.

5. Another possibility is Zechariah the son of Jehoiada (2 Chron 24:20–22). His murder took place in the courtyard of the temple and is related toward the end of what was probably the last book in the Hebrew canon. The sweep runs (to use Christian terms)

"from Genesis to Revelation." The problem is the patronymic. There is a possible solution. Just as Zechariah the prophet is alternately given his father's patronymic (Zech 1:1) or his grandfather's (Ezra 6:14), so it is possible Jehoiada was the grandfather (not father) of the Zechariah of 2 Chron 24—a suggestion that Jehoiada's living to be 130 years old (2 Chron 24:15) makes more plausible, since Zechariah's ministry immediately followed Jehoiada's death. An otherwise unknown Berekiah would therefore have had time to sire Zechariah, live to a good age, and die before the death of his own father gave him opportunity to serve as chief priest. That would allow time for a father named Berekiah. But we do not know. Substantive text-critical uncertainties in the relevant traditions (esp. LXX) complicate the problem. For literature and discussion, cf. Gundry, *Use of OT*, pp. 86–88; Garland, pp. 182–83.

---

f. *Lament over Jerusalem*

23:37–39

[37]"O Jerusalem, Jerusalem, you who kill the prophets and stone those sent to you, how often I have longed to gather your children together, as a hen gathers her chicks under her wings, but you were not willing. [38]Look, your house is left to you desolate. [39]For I tell you, you will not see me again until you say, 'Blessed is he who comes in the name of the Lord.' "

Almost exact verbal equivalence between these verses and Luke 13:34–35 makes it nearly certain that both Matthew and Luke are following the same written source (Q?) and therefore that at least one of the two evangelists displaced this prayer from its setting in the life of Jesus. Certainly the lament is more integral to the setting in Matthew than in Luke (cf. Suggs, pp. 64–66; Garland, pp. 187–97). Jesus undoubtedly lamented over the city on other occasions (Luke 19:41–44), and the broad compassion of his words is characteristic (Matt 9:35–38).

The effect of the lament is twofold. First, it tinges all the preceding woes with compassion (note the doubling of "Jerusalem" [cf. 2 Sam 18:33; 1 Kings 13:2; Jer 22:29; Luke 10:41; 22:31]). There is also a change of number from Jerusalem to people of Jerusalem: "you [sing.] who kill . . . sent to you [sing.] . . . your [sing.] children . . . your [pl.] house . . . you [pl.] will not see." The effect is to move from the abstraction of the city to the concrete reality of people. Jesus' woes in Matthew 23 therefore go far beyond personal frustrations: they are divine judgments that, though wrathful, never call in question the reality of divine love (see discussion on 5:44–45).

Second, the christological implications are unavoidable, for Jesus, whether identifying himself with God or with wisdom, claims to be the one who has longed to gather and protect this rebellious nation. Phrased in such terms, Jesus' longing can only belong to Israel's Savior, not to one of her prophets. The authenticity of the lament is frequently denied on the ground that the historical Jesus could not possibly have said it (e.g., Suggs, p. 66). But it is a strange criticism that a priori obliterates any possibility of listening to the text in such a way as to hear a historical Jesus who was not only conscious of his transcendent origins but who in many ways laid claims to his origins as part of his compassionate and redemptive self-disclosure.

37 Verses 37–39 preserve Jesus' last recorded public words to Israel. Jerusalem, the city of David, the city where God revealed himself in his temple, had become known as the city that killed the prophets and stoned those sent to her. Stoning to death, prescribed in the law of Moses for idolatry (Deut 17:5, 7), sorcery (Lev 20:27), and several other crimes, is also laid down in the Mishnah (M *Sanhedrin* 7:4) for false prophets. It could also be the outcome of mob violence (21:35; Acts 7:57–58) or conspiracy, which apparently is how Zechariah died (2 Chron 24:21). "How often" may look back over Israel's history—viz., Jesus' identifying himself with God's transcendent, historical perspective (John 8:58); but more probably "how often" refers to the duration of Jesus' ministry. During it he "often" longed to gather and shelter Jerusalem (by metonymy including all Jews) as a hen her chicks (cf. Deut 32:11; Pss 17:8; 36:7; 91:4; Jer 48:40); for despite the woes, Jesus, like the "Sovereign LORD" in Ezekiel 18:32, took "no pleasure in the death of anyone."

38 This verse may allude to both Jeremiah 12:7 and 22:5 (cf. Notes). "Your house" in this context could refer to Jerusalem, since the lament is first addressed to her (Klostermann; McNeile; Trilling [p. 86]), to Israel (Schniewind; Green; cf. Gal 4:25–26 for a similar use of "Jerusalem"), or to the temple in whose precincts Jesus was preaching (21:23; 24:1) and whose destruction was about to be predicted (24:2; cf. Manson [*Sayings*, p. 127]; Davies [*Setting*, p. 298]). There seems to be no need to choose only one of these options; all three are closely allied and rise and fall together. If "desolate" (*erēmos*) is not part of the text (cf. Notes), the verse means "your house is abandoned to the consequences of your misdeeds" (Plummer). More probably *erēmos* is original and makes the implied destruction explicit. Your "house" is left to you (i.e., abandoned), whether by God (as in Jer 12:7) or Jesus (cf. 24:1), who is "Immanuel," "God with us" (1:23; cf. Garland, pp. 202–3). The verb "left" (*aphietai*) can mean "abandoned to enemies," not just "abandoned." But since the ideas are related, a choice is unnecessary.

39 E. Haenchen ("Matthäus 23," *Zeitschrift für Katholische Theologie* 48 [1951]: 56) holds that in vv.33–36 "Wisdom" (cf. Luke 11:49) looks *forward* prophetically to sending the prophets but in vv.37–39 looks *back* on the sending of prophets. The latter passage must therefore be anachronistic. But the temporal relation between the two passages is not so sharp. If vv.33–36 look forward to the sending of the prophets, they also speak of judgment on "this generation." If vv.37–39 look backward on prophets already killed, the reference is to the way Jerusalem has acted in the *past* (v.37), a past that is even now bringing judgment (v.38), and that looks *forward* to future consummation (v.39).

The quotation is from Psalm 118:26 (also in 21:9; cf. 21:42 for another quotation from this psalm). The words may have been used by the priests in greeting the worshipers at the temple. Jesus, too, the true locus of Israel, must come, victorious and exalted, and receive greetings and homage from the religious authorities (cf. France, *Jesus*, pp. 58f.). Because of its location in Luke, "until" could refer to Palm Sunday, when people cried such words (Luke 19:38; cf. Matt 21:9); but as Marshall (*Luke*, pp. 576–77) points out, if Palm Sunday is in view in Luke, the cries of the people are but an ironic fulfillment that still looks forward to the consummation.

What Matthew refers to is perfectly clear. The Greek literally translated reads, "You will not see me from now (*ap' arti*) until you say"; and *ap' arti* is tied to the consummation (cf. 26:29, 64). Thus v.39 looks, not to Jesus' resurrection appearances, but to his parousia. When he returns, all will acknowledge him. The context strongly implies that the Parousia spells judgment (cf. 24:30–31; Phil 2:9–11; Rev 1:7); but the quotation of Psalm 118 keeps open the way Jesus will be received—as consuming Judge or welcomed King (cf. Benoit; Schlatter; Goulder, pp. 429–30; Bonnard; contra Garland, pp. 207–9 and the literature there cited). But whatever the outcome, the immediate prospect is disaster: "for I tell you, you will not see me, etc."; i.e., the proof that judgment is imminent is that Jesus turns away and will not be seen again till the End.

So Jesus leaves the temple and goes away (24:1); and his words, which have dealt with judgment on Israel and with the consummation, evoke his disciples' two-pronged question (24:3) and lead to the Olivet Discourse (chs. 24–25).

Notes

---

38 If ἔρημος (*erēmos,* "desolate") be omitted, as in B L [1 184] it[ff2] et al., the allusion is to Jer 12:7 alone; if included, there may also be an allusion to Jer 22:5 (cf. Gundry, *Use of OT*, p. 88). WH, relying too heavily on B, omit it; but the external evidence is strong for inclusion in Matthew, even if omission in Luke—where the evidence is much weaker and principally Western—is more likely (cf. Garland, pp. 200–201, n. 120). The presence of the word makes the judgment theme slightly more emphatic.

B. *Fifth Discourse: The Olivet Discourse*

24:1–25:46

Few chapters of the Bible have called forth more disagreement among interpreters than Matthew 24 and its parallels in Mark 13 and Luke 21. The history of the interpretation of this chapter is immensely complex. G.R. Beasley-Murray's *Jesus and the Future* (London: Macmillan, 1954) is an admirable guide for works up to 1954; and David Wenham's "Recent Study of Mark 13" (*TSF Bulletin* 71 [Spring, 1975]: 6–15; 72 [Summer, 1975]: 1–9) succinctly summarizes and critiques several more recent works up to 1975, including A.L. Moore, *The Parousia in the New Testament* (Leiden: Brill, 1966); Lars Hartman, *Prophecy Interpreted: The Function of Some Jewish Apocalyptic Texts and of the Eschatological Discourse, Mark 13 Par.* (Lund: CWK Gleerup, 1966); J. Lambrecht, *Die Redaktion der Markus-Apokalypse: Literarische Analyse und Strukturuntersuchung* (Rome: PBI, 1967); R. Pesch, *Naherwartungen: Tradition und Redaktion in Markus 13* (Dusseldorf: Patmos, 1968); Gaston; and France (*Jesus*). In addition, there are major commentaries on each of the synoptic Gospels, as well as several important articles on these chapters, and some popular works on eschatology, not a few of them by conservatives (cf. the bibliography in Hoekema). Some of the difficulties and exegetical turning points must be cursorily introduced:

1. The literary nature of chapters 24–25 and of the parallels in Mark and Luke has occupied much scholarly attention. For a century or two before and after Jesus, writings now described as "apocalyptic literature" flourished in Jewish and Christian circles. At best the label is not precise, and the genre's various forms tend to fray around the edges. G.E. Ladd ("Why Not Prophetic-Apocalyptic?" JBL 76 [1957]:

192–200) has wisely suggested that the NT apocalypses, especially this chapter and most of Revelation, read like a merging of apocalyptic and prophetic literature. The symbolism is not so sharp as in works indisputably apocalyptic, and the "above–below" dualism typical of apocalyptic is here rather muted. Other features of this discourse are often noted, especially the frequent imperatives, whether in the second person ("Watch out that no one deceives you," v.4; "See to it that you are not alarmed," v.6) or the third person ("Let no one in the field go back," v.18).

2. As for the sources, first there is the question of whether the synoptists have simply put together a pastiche of Jesus' sayings (some of which may represent an "Olivet Discourse"), mingled with other traditions, or have selected and shaped material deriving from a single historical utterance. They undoubtedly give the latter impression. Matthew, with his framing formulas (see on 5:1–2; 7:28–29), is especially clear about this. Though this view is a minority one, nevertheless it can be strenuously argued that each evangelist felt his report of the discourse to be coherent. And if this is so, it seems too much to postulate, on the basis of disputable conceptual and grammatical discrepancies, unambiguous sources stemming from various traditions.

Second, the relation among the three synoptic accounts is still disputed. Some have argued that Luke 21 is sufficiently distinctive to spring from a separate tradition. Touching on both these questions, David Wenham, in some unpublished papers soon to appear in book form, argues for a source-critical solution, not only tying together all the synoptic Gospel records of this discourse, but also uniting them into a single comprehensive record. While Wenham's reconstruction is far from certain, the fact that he is able to develop his view so rigorously shows the dangers of the facile historical and literary disjunctions of which many critics are so fond.

Third, the Olivet Discourse is studded with OT quotations and allusions that add to the complexity.

Fourth, the discourse itself is undoubtedly a source for the Thessalonian Epistles (cf. G. Henry Waterman, "The Sources of Paul's Teaching on the 2nd Coming of Christ in 1 and 2 Thessalonians," JETS 18 [1975]: 105–13; David Wenham, "Paul and the Synoptic Apocalypse," France and Wenham, 2:345–75) and Revelation (cf. Gregory Kimball Beale, "The Use of Daniel in Jewish Apocalyptic Literature and in the Revelation of St. John [Ph.D. diss., Cambridge University, 1980], pp. 260–64, and the literature cited there). If so, then we may say that Jesus himself sets the pattern for the church's eschatology.

3. This last statement presupposes, of course, the authenticity of the discourse material in the Gospels. However, this is frequently denied on the grounds that the "prophecy" of the Fall of Jerusalem must in reality be *ex eventu*, based on the event itself. This will not do because, apart from antisupernatural presuppositions, Reicke ("Synoptic Prophecies") has shown the language in the Olivet Discourse prophesying the Fall of Jerusalem to be largely in OT categories. Not only is it general, it does not describe any detail peculiar to the known history of the Jewish War (A.D. 66–73). Reicke goes so far as to conclude that the Olivet Discourse as found in any of the Synoptics *could not* have been composed after A.D. 70, and that therefore the Synoptics themselves have earlier dates (cf. Introduction, section 6).

4. Numerous details in the text are much disputed and hard to understand: the meaning of "the abomination that causes desolation" (24:15), the significance of "let the reader understand" (v.15), whether the "coming of the Son of Man" (vv.27, 30) refers to his return at the consummation or to something else (the Resurrection,

Pentecost, the Fall of Jerusalem, and the growth of the church have all been suggested), the extent of "this generation" (v.34). The ideal solution is the one that treats all of these in the most natural way possible.

5. A disputed term, not in the text but in the forefront of interpretive theory, is "imminent," which has two related but distinct problems. One concerns the expectations of the historical Jesus and is linked to the way the various parts of the discourse relate to one another and to v.34: "I tell you the truth, this generation will certainly not pass away until all these things have happened." How "imminent" did Jesus think the coming of the Son of Man was? (See below, under 6.)

The other problem concerns the meaning of the word "imminent" itself as used in theological—especially evangelical—discussion. A dictionary defines it as "impending": as applied to Christ's return, an "imminent return of Christ" would then mean Christ's return was near, impending. Hardly anyone uses "imminent" that way but understands it in a specialized, theological sense to mean "at any time": "the imminent return of Christ" then means Christ may return at any time. But the evangelical writers who use the word divide on whether "imminent" in the sense of "at any time" should be pressed to mean "at any second" or something looser such as "at any period" or "in any generation."

Resolution turns on two issues. First, how are the various "signs" presaging Christ's return to be related to an "imminent" return? The classic dispensational response is to postulate two returns (or, as they hold, one return in two stages): one before any of the "signs" appear, a "Rapture" that removes the church alone and which could take place at any second; the other after the signs appear, a return that consummates history as we know it. Most will agree that no passage in the Bible unambiguously teaches a two-stage return. The theory is in the best sense a theological harmonization—certainly not a wrong approach in itself—of disparate texts.

Other theories clamor for attention, including that of J. Barton Payne (*The Imminent Appearing of Christ* [Grand Rapids: Eerdmans, 1962]), who proposes that, with the events of A.D. 70 now behind us, all the remaining "signs" are so general that they may be "fulfilled" in any generation. Distinctions regarding "imminency" therefore become moot. Other theories are not lacking. Unfortunately the meaning of "imminent" is so comprehensive a question that each theory is in fact an entire eschatological scheme, complete with detailed exegesis and sweeping synthesis. While the approach of this commentary is inductive and limited primarily to the text of Matthew, some implications for the debate will be spelled out in due course.

Second, on what is the "any second" view of imminency based and how well does it withstand close scrutiny? The truth is that the biblical evidence nowhere unambiguously endorses the "any second" view and frequently militates against it, as R.H. Gundry (*The Church and the Tribulation* [Grand Rapids: Zondervan, 1973], esp. pp. 29ff.) has demonstrated. Not only do all the relevant NT verbs for "looking forward to" or "expecting" or "waiting for" have a semantic range including necessary delay, but many NT passages also implicitly rule out an "any second" imminency (24:45–51 [see below]; 25:5, 19; Luke 19:11–27; John 21:18–19 [cf. 2 Peter 1:14]; Acts 9:15; 22:21; 23:11; 27:24). Yet the terms "imminent" and "imminency" retain theological usefulness if they focus attention on the eager expectancy of the Lord's return characteristic of many NT passages, a return that could take place soon, i.e., within a fairly brief period of time, without specifying that the period must be one second or less! This is not so rigid as the "any second" view, and it more fairly represents the exegetical evidence.

6. But the most difficult interpretive questions concern the structure of the discourse—how the parts relate to each other, to the initial questions of the disciples, and to the whole. On the face of it, the disciples' questions and the tenor of the discourse argue that Jesus is dealing with at least two issues—the Fall of Jerusalem and the return of the Son of Man. But these two issues appear to be so tightly intertwined that it is impossible to separate them, and therefore Jesus or Matthew wrongly (as it turned out) tied them together.

Many modern scholars adopt this view, and it has recently been given a new twist by Desmond Ford (*The Abomination of Desolation in Biblical Eschatology* [Washington, D.C.: University Press of America, 1979], p. 76). He argues that Jesus meant to say that the Parousia would immediately succeed the Fall of Jerusalem, all within the generation of his hearers, but that this was in reality a contingent promise, like Jonah's "Forty more days and Nineveh will be destroyed" (Jonah 3:4). Hence "it is possible that he [Jesus] believed that if the early church proved faithful to its missionary commission, and if the chastened Jewish nation repented, the end would transpire in the same Age."

But the parallel with Jonah is not very close, if only because the Parousia is invariably treated in the NT as qualitatively unlike all other divine visitations. It alone marks the end of history, the final outpouring of judgment and blessing, and thus is not an event that can be postponed. More important, v.22 seems to say that God will hasten the consummation, not postpone it; for the days of tribulation are shortened. And nowhere in the NT is there any clear suggestion that the delay of the Parousia was the result of the church's sin (2 Peter 3:12 is not a genuine exception). Yet Ford's view highlights the problem of the relation between the Fall of Jerusalem and the Parousia.

At the risk of oversimplification, we may lump together some other major interpretations of the Olivet Discourse according to their treatment of this problem.

a. In 1864, T. Colani published his "little apocalypse" theory. According to him the historical Jesus exhibited no interest in any future kingdom: as far as Jesus was concerned, the kingdom was exclusively present. The genesis of Mark 13 and parallels therefore must be accounted for as a tract by first-century Jewish Christians facing persecution just before A.D. 70. The answer of the historical Jesus to the disciples' questions was simply Mark 13:32 (Matt 24:36). Few follow Colani now, though some have tried to find in the Olivet Discourse not one "little apocalypse" but a number of different sources. Taken together, such theories follow a unifying method: the material in the discourse is assumed to be so disparate that it can only be accounted for by appealing to distinct sources not very well integrated by the evangelist-redactor. But too many details in the various theories seem unconvincing and fail to deal adequately with how each synoptist thought of the material he was editing. If he detected some unity, it must be found; and if found, then what methodological principle distinguishes between the unity imposed by a synoptist-redactor and a unity latent in a discourse delivered by Jesus? Indeed, one could make an a priori case for the apparent textual discrepancies based, not on the synoptist's failure to integrate separate sources, but on its condensed and selective reporting of much longer unified material in terms understandable to the first readers but more susceptible to misunderstanding today.

b. Among commentators who find comprehensive theological cohesion in the Olivet Discourse, the most common approach—and that of most evangelicals today—is exemplified by Broadus and Lane (*Mark*). Broadus holds that vv.15–21, 34 foretell the destruction of Jerusalem, and at least vv.29–31 foretell the Lord's return; but "every attempt to assign a definite point of division between the two topics has proved a failure." If Christ's return is placed between v.28 and v.29, then v.34 is difficult; if after v.34, v.36, or v.42, how are we to interpret vv.30–31, 36? The solution is that the two are purposely intertwined, perhaps under some kind of "prophetic foreshortening." The near event, the destruction of Jerusalem, serves as a symbol for the far event. (In addition to the commentaries, cf. also Hoekema; Ridderbos, *Kingdom,* pp. 477–510.) This approach is possible but has two weaknesses. It has to skate gingerly around the *time* references in the discourse (e.g., "immediately after those days," v.29; "this generation," v.34), and it leads some of its adherents to the view that on the *timing* of the Parousia Jesus was in error (e.g., Beasley-Murray). Verse 36 is scarcely sufficient to support all this, since it is one thing to admit ignorance and another to be quite mistaken.

c. A number of scholars have denied that any part of the Olivet Discourse deals with the Fall of Jerusalem: all of it concerns the Parousia. One form or another of this theory is held by Lagrange, Schlatter, Schniewind, and Zahn. Lagrange thinks the "abomination of desolation" deals with Jerusalem but not the "great distress" (v.21). Almost all who hold this view are forced to say that Luke 21:20–24, which is unavoidably historical, stems from another discourse or has been consciously modified by Luke. The latter suggestion seems a desperate expedient in support of a weak theory. It is very difficult to imagine that a Christian reader of any of the Synoptics at any period during the first one hundred years of the existence of these documents would fail to see a reference to the destruction of Jerusalem. Methodologically this approach belongs with those who flatten the discourse in other ways —e.g., by claiming that it represents a continuous account of Christian history.

d. An older view (e.g., Alexander), now again popular (Tasker; J.M. Kik, *Matthew Twenty-Four* [Swengel: Bible Truth Depot, 1948]) and newly given exegetical support (France, *Jesus,* pp. 231ff.), holds that the Fall of Jerusalem is in view in the discourse till the end of v.35. Only with the opening of v.36 does the second advent come into view. This interpretation has the advantage of being neat: there is a clear division between the two parts of the discourse and eliminates flipping back and forth or appealing to "prophetic foreshortening" or the like. Its proponents point out that this interpretation answers both questions put by the disciples. The first, concerning the destruction of Jerusalem and its temple, elicits the anticipation of an answer in v.15 ("When you see . . .") but finds an explicit answer only in vv.29–31. The verses before v.29 tell of great anguish *preceding* the events of A.D. 70. But unless vv.29–35 deal with the Fall of Jerusalem itself, it is held, the disciples' first question is never satisfactorily answered.

If someone objects that vv.29–35 more naturally read as a prophecy foretelling the Second Advent than the destruction of Jerusalem, this, we are told, would not be so obvious to the first readers. The celestial disturbances (v.29) are figurative, symbolic of political and national disasters (as in Isa 13:10; 34:4). The coming of the Son of Man in glory and power (v.30) is not Jesus' return to earth but, as in Daniel 7, a heavenly coming for vindication, a reference either to Jesus' vindication after the Resurrection or to the Fall of Jerusalem itself (26:64 is then commonly interpreted the same way). The sending of the "angels" is the commissioning of "messengers" or "missionaries" to gather the elect in the church (v.31); for despite the Lord's judgment on the Jews, the gathering in of the elect continues through the preaching of the gospel.

Casey (pp. 172ff.) has raised some criticisms, a few of them cogent. Detailed rebuttal is impossible, but the following difficulties in this interpretation must be faced.

1) Even if v.15 speaks only of the beginning of the Jerusalem distress (and this is debated), if France's view is right, it is hard to explain how vv.21–22 could describe the mere preliminaries to Jerusalem's fall. Verse 22 speaks of those days being cut short: surely this does not mean the preliminaries to the Fall of Jerusalem were cut short for the elect's sake, for that would entail the conclusion that the fall itself was a mercy on the elect.

2) Although vv.14–22 do not explicitly mention the Fall of Jerusalem, the same can be said with even greater vigor of vv.29–35. Similarly, if vv.29–35 do not mention the coming of the Son of Man *to the earth*, the same can be said of 1 Thessalonians 4:16, where in my opinion that is implied. In any case there may be other reasons for Jesus' not mentioning the Fall of Jerusalem explicitly in vv.15–22. The cryptic "let the reader understand" (v.15) may be thought hint enough of the true import of Jesus' reference to Daniel's "abomination that causes desolation"; or it may even be that the synoptists thought the Jerusalem reference obvious. Apparently Luke thought so (cf. Luke 21:20–24; and comments on v.15, below).

3) Although there can be no objection to coming-of-the-Son-of-Man language occasionally referring to something other than the Parousia (see on 10:23; 16:28), yet when that occurs the interpretive problems are invariably notoriously complex. This is because the *regular* way of taking this expression and related language is as a reference to the Parousia. Compare closely 13:40–41; 16:27; 25:31; 1 Corinthians 11:26; 15:52; 16:22; 1 Thessalonians 4:14–17; 2 Thessalonians 1:7; 2:1–8; 2 Peter 3:10–12; Revelation 1:7 (cf. *Didache* 16). Here are references to the Son of Man's coming, angels gathering the elect, trumpet call, clouds, glory, tribes of the earth mourning, celestial disturbances—all unambiguously related to the Second Advent. It seems very doubtful, to say the least, that the natural way to understand vv.29–35 is as a reference to the Fall of Jerusalem.

4) This approach to vv.29–35 is psychologically unconvincing for two reasons. First, it demands a close connection between the Fall of Jerusalem and the Gentile mission (v.31), when in fact the Gentile mission had been prospering, first informally and then formally, for several decades. The fall of the temple doubtless helped support Christian theology about Jesus as the true sacrifice, priest, and temple; but it did not clearly motivate Gentile mission per se. Why, then, should the link be tendered here, almost as the climax of the pericope? Second, even on the basis of the interpretation under review, Christians saw the destruction of Jerusalem as a terrible thing and the onslaught by the pagan Romans as an abomination. If they also saw it as Jesus' vindication and as judgment on the Jewish nation, that is comprehensible enough; but could they see it as fulfillment of Daniel 7? Daniel 7 portrays something glorious and wonderful, the end of the pagan emperor's reign; but A.D. 70 marks success by the pagan emperor. Even if one supposes that the Synoptics are operating under a reverse typology—the OT pagans being now equated with the Jews—is it psychologically convincing to hold that antipathy between Jews and Christians was running so high that the latter could be told the sack of Jerusalem was their "redemption" (Luke 21:28)?

5) The interpretation France (*Jesus*, pp. 236–38) offers of v.30, though plausible, is not convincing. He says that all the (Jewish) *tribes* of the land (*gē;* NIV, "earth"; see on 5:5) shall mourn. The word "tribe" (*phylē;* NIV, "nation"), used with cer-

tainty of Gentiles elsewhere in the NT only in Revelation, is not determinative (Rev 1:7; 5:9; 7:9; 11:9; 13:7; 14:6), though it must be admitted that all the other NT references either refer to a specific Jewish tribe or make a specifically Jewish connection unambiguous. More importantly, however, v.30 contains an allusion to Zechariah 12:10–12; and other similar NT use of this passage supports the view that the verse refers to the Parousia. This appears to be sufficient evidence to set against the ambiguous meaning of *phylē* proposed by France.

6) There are already hints, early in the discourse (esp. in Matt), that the reader is to bear in mind that there are at least two topics under discussion, not one: the Fall of Jerusalem and the Second Advent (cf. vv.3, 5, 14, 23–27). Thus, since the reader is already primed to expect mention of the Second Advent, it would be difficult for him to take vv.29–31 in any other way.

e. A strong minority of evangelicals adopts one form or another of the dispensationalist interpretation of the discourse (S.E. English; A.C. Gaebelein; Walvoord; cf. John F. Walvoord, "Christ's Olivet Discourse on the End of the Age," BS 128 [1971]: 109–16; 129 [1972]: 20–32, 99–105, 206–10, 307–15). Perhaps the most common view along these lines takes vv.36–40 to refer to a secret "Rapture" of the church, which could take place at any second, and vv.4–28 (or 15–28) to refer to the Great Tribulation, lasting seven years and culminating in the Second Advent (vv. 29–35). Walvoord adds refinements. He holds that v.2 refers to the destruction at A.D. 70. The disciples' question of v.3 is in *three* parts, the first of which, dealing with the Fall of Jerusalem, Jesus does not answer.

At this point there is a curious intersection of views with writers like Hare (pp. 177–79), who argues that Matthew, writing after the events of A.D. 70, eliminates all reference to the destruction of Jerusalem and "eschatologizes" even vv.15–28, and so does not answer the disciples' first question. Under Hare's view of Matthew's editorial activity, the strange thing is that Matthew retains that first question. The entire discourse, in Walvoord's view, deals with the general characteristics of the age (vv.4–14), the Great Tribulation (vv.15–25), and the Second Advent (vv.26–31), because the "Rapture" is not revealed till Paul. Thus "taken" in vv.40–41 means "taken in judgment." "This generation" (v.34) Walvoord takes to mean either "this race" or something like "the generation that is alive when the great tribulation starts."

This interpretation is difficult to discuss adequately without delving into dispensationalism, including its "parenthesis" view of the church, something beyond the range of this commentary. If dispensationalism were unambiguously defined elsewhere in Scripture, then the least to be said for its interpretation of chapter 24 is that it is self-consistent and makes sense of the time indicators (e.g., "Immediately after the distress of those days," v.29, etc.). Even then, however, this interpretation faces several difficulties, one or two of them well-nigh insuperable.

1) It is forced to adopt a possible but extraordinarily unlikely meaning for "this generation" (v.34; see below).

2) It rests heavily on Matthew's report of the Olivet Discourse and makes less sense of the parallels in Mark and Luke. One of many examples of problems it involves is Matthew's recording the disciples' question differently from Mark and Luke; and Walvoord's interpretation of the discourse depends almost entirely on Matthew. Even if through harmonizing Walvoord can show that v.3 best preserves the tripartite nature of the disciples' historical question, one must still ask why Mark and Luke have it as they do. If the discourse as they present it can only be ade-

quately explained by reference to the disciples' question as Matthew preserves it, then Mark and Luke cannot be intelligently read without referring to Matthew.

3) Much dispensationalism, especially the older kind, holds that the "Rapture" is not mentioned in this chapter and justifies this view on the ground that Jesus is not talking to the church but to Jews. Dispensationalists use this disjunction to justify a number of theological points, but they are insensitive to historical realities. Even after Pentecost the earliest church was entirely Jewish. Here, before the Passion, Jesus is not addressing the church, in its post-Pentecost sense; but he *is* addressing, not his Jewish opponents, but his Jewish disciples who will constitute the church. Rigid application of this doubtful disjunction between Jews and church likewise banishes the church from the Sermon on the Mount; but it fails to observe that 18:15–20, dealing with the church, is also addressed, before the Passion, to Jewish disciples.

4) Granted the dispensational interpretation, Jesus' answer must have not only been opaque to his auditors but almost deceptive. Their first question concerns Jerusalem's judgment. But since a substantial part of Jesus' answer is couched in terms dealing with Jerusalem's destruction, how could the disciples think Jesus was *not* answering their question but describing a *second* destruction of the city, unless Jesus explicitly disavowed their understanding? But he does nothing of the kind. So perhaps it is not surprising that the dispensational identification of vv.15–28 *exclusively* with the Great Tribulation after the Rapture of the church, whether revealed or unrevealed, finds no exponent till the nineteenth century. The dispensational approach to the Olivet Discourse must be judged historically implausible in reference to both the history of Jesus and the history of interpretation.

f. The view of Matthew 24 this commentary advocates finds clear breaks in the Olivet Discourse, thus differing from the second option, but deals with the location and significance of these breaks in a novel way. David Wenham and the writer, to our mutual surprise, came to independent but similar conclusions about the Olivet Discourse. Sustained discussion has benefited us both and enabled us to develop the original ideas with the result that I cannot say exactly what each of us contributed to the thinking of the other. Wenham will doubtless publish his own view of the discourse. But here I acknowledge indebtedness to him.

In my understanding of the Olivet Discourse, the *disciples* think of Jerusalem's destruction and the eschatological end as a single complex web of events. This accounts for the form of their questions. Jesus warns that there will be delay *before* the End—a delay characterized by persecution and tribulation for his followers (vv.4–28), but with one particularly violent display of judgment in the Fall of Jerusalem (vv.15–21; Mark 13:14–20; Luke 21:20–24). Immediately after the days of that sustained persecution characterizing the interadvent period comes the Second Advent (vv.29–31; cf. Guthrie, *NT Theology*, pp. 795–96). The warning in vv.32–35 describes the whole tribulation period, from the Ascension to the Second Advent. The tribulation period will certainly come, and the generation to which Jesus is speaking will experience all its features that point to the Lord's return. But the exact time of that return no one but the Father knows (vv.36–44). This structure works out in all three Synoptics (though with significant differences in emphasis), and the main themes developed have important ties with other NT books. The disciples' questions are answered, and the reader is exhorted to look forward to the Lord's return and meanwhile to live responsibly, faithfully, compassionately, and courageously while the Master is away (24:45–25:46).

1. *Setting*

24:1–3

> [1]Jesus left the temple and was walking away when his disciples came up to him to call his attention to its buildings. [2]"Do you see all these things?" he asked. "I tell you the truth, not one stone here will be left on another; every one will be thrown down."
>
> [3]As Jesus was sitting on the Mount of Olives, the disciples came to him privately. "Tell us," they said, "when will this happen, and what will be the sign of your coming and of the end of the age?"

Unlike Mark (12:41–44) and Luke (21:1–4), Matthew omits the story of the widow's offering, thus linking the Olivet Discourse more closely to the "woes" in chapter 23. This does not mean that chapters 24–25 continue a single discourse—the setting, audience, and principal themes all change. But Matthew does tie the prediction of desolation (23:37–39) to the destruction of the temple (24:1–2; for discussion, cf. Hummel, pp. 85–86; J. Lambrecht, "The Parousia Discourse," in Didier, pp. 314–18).

1 Jesus' departure from the *hieron* ("temple complex") may be symbolic (see on 23:39). It also gives the disciples a chance to call Jesus' attention to its various structures. In Mark and Luke the disciples call Jesus' attention to the beauty of the temple buildings and the great stones on which it rests (cf. Jos. Antiq. XV, 391–402 [xi.3]; Wars V, 184–226 [v.1–6]; Tacitus *Histories* 5.8.12). Whether or not the disciples thought they were speaking piously, they show that they have underestimated or even misunderstood the force of Jesus' denunciations in chapter 23 and Luke 11. They still focus on the temple, on which Jesus has pronounced doom, since the true center of the relation between God and man has shifted to himself. In chapter 23 Jesus has already insisted that what Israel does with him, not the temple, determines the fate of the temple and of Israel nationally.

2 Because *tauta panta* ("all these things") is neuter and "buildings" (v.1) feminine, some have suggested that Jesus' question refers, not to the buildings, but to the discourse in chapter 23, especially v.36, and should be rendered "You do understand [metaphorically 'see'] these things, don't you?"—the positive answer being suggested by the presence of the particle *ou* ("not," untr. in NIV). This may be oversubtle: the Greek demonstrative pronoun may have an irregular antecedent for various reasons (RHG, p. 704). Moreover, the particle *ou*, anticipating a positive response, detracts from this novel interpretation; for if Jesus thinks his disciples have understood, why then does he go on immediately to answer their question unequivocally? But if the sentence is taken in the usual way (NIV), then the expectation of a positive response is most natural: of course the disciples see the buildings! (Moule is nevertheless right in saying that English idiom prefers an open question here; cf. *Idiom Book*, p. 159.)

Jesus' forecast of the destruction of the temple complex is unambiguous, cast in OT language (cf. Jer 26:6, 18; Mic 3:12) and repeated variously elsewhere (23:38; 26:61; Luke 23:28–31).

3 The Mount of Olives (see on 21:1, 17) is an appropriate site for a discourse dealing with the Parousia (cf. Zech 14:4). Mark specifies that Peter, James, John, and Andrew (the first four in Matt 10:2) asked the question privately. Whether this means that they were the only disciples present or that they were the ones who raised the question is uncertain, since "privately" in both Matthew and Mark sets the disciples apart from the crowds, not some disciples from others. The form of the question varies from Gospel to Gospel, with Matthew showing the greatest independence. Yet if we make the reasonable assumption that in the disciples' mind their question as to the temple's destruction and the signs that will presage it are linked to the end of the age and Jesus' return (cf. 16:27–28; 23:39; Luke 19:11–27) there is little problem. Matthew makes explicit what was implicit and what Jesus recognized as implicit in their question.

"The end of the age" is used six times in the NT (13:39, 40, 49; 24:3; 28:20; Heb 9:26), five of which are in Matthew and look to final judgment and the consummation of all things. (Hebrews 9:26 sees the Cross as introducing the coming age and thereby marking out "the end of the ages" [NIV].) *Parousia* ("coming") is found twenty-four times in the NT, four of which are in Matthew 24 (3, 27, 37, 39). The term can refer to "presence," "arrival," or "coming"—the first stage of "presence"—and need not have eschatological overtones (2 Cor 7:6; 10:10). Yet *parousia* is closely tied with Jesus' glorious "appearing" or "coming" at the end of human history. (For views of its relation to NT eschatology, cf. Turner, *Christian Words*, pp. 404–8; DNTT, 2:898–935.)

2. *The birth pains* (24:4–28)

a. *General description of the birth pains*

24:4–14

4Jesus answered: "Watch out that no one deceives you. 5For many will come in
my name, claiming, 'I am the Christ,' and will deceive many. 6You will hear of
wars and rumors of wars, but see to it that you are not alarmed. Such things must
happen, but the end is still to come. 7Nation will rise against nation, and kingdom
against kingdom. There will be famines and earthquakes in various places. 8All
these are the beginning of birth pains.

9"Then you will be handed over to be persecuted and put to death, and you will
be hated by all nations because of me. 10At that time many will turn away from the
faith and will betray and hate each other, 11and many false prophets will appear
and deceive many people. 12Because of the increase of wickedness, the love of
most will grow cold, 13but he who stands firm to the end will be saved. 14And this
gospel of the kingdom will be preached in the whole world as a testimony to all
nations, and then the end will come.

Alexander goes too far in saying that Jesus' purpose in these verses "is not to tell what are but what are not the premonitions of the great catastrophe to which he refers." Instead, all things (vv.5–7) are signs that Jesus is coming back, and they all will be manifest before the generation Jesus was addressing had died. But though these things show that the End is near, none of them stipulates how near; and the tenor of the warning is that the delay will be substantial and that during this period Jesus' disciples must not be deceived by false messiahs.

4–5 One of the greatest temptations in times of difficulty is to follow blindly any self-proclaimed savior who promises help. It is the temptation to repose confidence (v.4) in false Christs. Those who "come in my name" (v.5) may refer to those who come as Jesus' representatives; but because of the words that follow, we must assume that their claim goes farther. They claim to be Messiah, Christ himself. They come "in his name," as if they were he. Would-be deliverers have appeared in every age, not least the first century (Acts 5:36; Jos. Antiq. XX, 97–99 [v.1], 160–72 [viii.5–6], 188 [viii.10]; Wars II, 259 [xiii.5], 433–56 [xvii.8–10]; VI, 285–87 [v.2]). That this governs vv.4–28 is made clear by the second half of the literary inclusion (vv.26–28) that brackets the section. (On Mark's parallel "I am he," see Lane, *Mark*, p. 457, n. 43.)

6–8 "Birth pains" (v.8) in this context (elsewhere in the NT in Acts 2:24 ["agony"]; 1 Thess 5:3) stems from such OT passages as Isaiah (13:8; 26:17), Jeremiah (4:31; 6:24), Micah (4:9–10). By this time it was almost a special term for "the birthpangs of the Messiah," the period of distress preceding the Messianic Age (cf. SBK, 1:905; 4:977–78; TDNT, 9:667–74; cf. 2 Baruch 27:1–30:1; b *Shabbath* 118a; b *Sanhedrin* 98b). But the "wars and rumors of war, . . . famines and earthquakes" (vv.6–7, of which there were not a few in the first century, cf. Alford) do not so point to the End as to validate the false Christs' claims. Jesus' followers are not to be alarmed by these events. "Such things must happen"; yet the End is still to come (v.6). These are only "the beginning of [the] birth pains" that stretch over the period between the advents. Why "must [they] happen"? The reason may be hidden in God's providence, which can provide a haven for faith (cf. 26:54). But it may also be that during this time of inaugurated reign before the Messianic Age attains its splendor, conflict is inevitable, precisely because the kingdom is only inaugurated. The conflict extends not only to families (10:34–37), but to nations and even nature (cf. Rom 8:20–21; Col 1:16, 20).

The effect of these verses, then, is not to curb enthusiasm for the Lord's return but to warn against false claimants and an expectation of a premature return based on misconstrued signs.

9–13 *Tote* ("then," v.9) is an elusive word (see on 2:7). In this chapter alone it occurs in vv.9, 10, 14, 16, 21, 23, 30, 40. Translated "then" in v.9, it occurs as "At that time" in v.10. Certainly there is no suggestion of *sequence* between v.8 and v.9; it is *during* the "birth pains" that Jesus' disciples will be persecuted and killed. "You" quite clearly extends beyond the immediate disciples and includes all the followers Jesus will have. Persecution would break out early (cf. Acts 4:1–30; 7:59–8:3; 12:1–5; Rev 2:10, 12) and keep on during the "birth pains," against a background of hatred by the whole world (cf. Acts 28:22).

Thlipsis ("persecution," "tribulation," "distress") occurs four times in Matthew, three in this chapter (13:21; 24:9, 21, 29) and relates significantly to the chapter's structure (see on vv.21, 29). Jesus establishes *thlipsis* as characteristic of this age (cf. 10:16–39)—a time when many will "turn away" (*skandalisthēsontas*) from the faith (for the verb, see on 5:29; 13:21, 57) and hate each other (v.10).

In this chapter there are several allusions to Daniel (cf. Dan 11:35; linguistically some LXX MSS of Dan 11:41; cf. D. Wenham, "A Note on Matthew 24:10–12," *Tyndale Bulletin* 31 [1980]: 155–62, and esp. Trotter) and a certain parallelism between v.10 and vv.11–12. Those who turn away from the faith are deceived by false prophets, and those who hate each other do so because wickedness abounds and the love of most grows cold (cf. Trotter). Professing believers are either included in this description or are the focus of interest; but only those who endure—in love (v.12) and despite persecution (vv.9–11; cf. Rev 2:10)—will be saved (v.13). They must "stand firm" [endure] to the *end*": individual responsibility persists to the end of life, but corporate responsibility to the final consummation. Part of the effect of this "tribulation," therefore, is to purify the body of professed disciples: those who endure are saved, as in Daniel (11:32, 34–35) and elsewhere in Matthew (see on 12:32; 13:21, 41; cf. 2 Tim 2:3, 10–13; 3:11; Heb 10:32; 11:27; 12:2–3; James 1:12; 5:11).

The reasons for falling away may differ. In 13:21 the cause is *thlipsis* ("persecution" or "tribulation"), and in 24:10–12 it is false prophets (see on 7:15–23). But even here the false prophecy finds some of its appeal in the matrix of trouble and persecution (vv.4–9) from which it emerges; and Matthew cares little whether faith is lost owing to fear of physical violence or to deception effected by false prophets. The result is the same and is to be expected throughout this age (cf. 7:15–23; 24:24; Acts 20:29–30; 2 Peter 2:1; 1 John 4:1).

14 But none of this means that the gospel of the kingdom (see on 4:23) is not preached or that its saving message does not spread throughout the world. Despite persecution—and often because of it (Acts 8:1, 4)—the Good News is "preached" (*kērychthēsetai*, see on 4:17) "as a testimony to all nations." The expression is itself neutral (see on 8:4) and the gospel will bring either salvation or a curse, depending on how it is received. Thus the theme of Gentile mission is again made explicit (see on 1:1; 2:1–12; 3:9; 4:15–16; 8:11–12; 21:43; 28:18–20).

Notes

10 The reciprocal pronoun ἀλλήλους (*allēlous*, "one another"), used twice in this verse, can scarcely be strictly reciprocal in either case.

b. *The sharp pain: the Fall of Jerusalem*

24:15–21

[15]"So when you see standing in the holy place 'the abomination that causes desolation,' spoken of through the prophet Daniel—let the reader understand—[16]then let those who are in Judea flee to the mountains. [17]Let no one on the roof of his house go down to take anything out of the house. [18]Let no one in the field go back to get his cloak. [19]How dreadful it will be in those days for pregnant women and nursing mothers! [20]Pray that your flight will not take place in winter or on the Sabbath. [21]For then there will be great distress, unequaled from the beginning of the world until now—and never to be equaled again.

Although many commentators hold that Matthew (but probably not Mark and certainly not Luke) here portrays not just the Fall of Jerusalem but also the Great tribulation before Antichrist comes (e.g., Hill, *Matthew*), the details in vv.16–21 are too limited geographically and culturally to justify that view. For other interpretations, see comments at the beginning of this chapter. For justification of a pericope termination at v.21 instead of the more common v.22, see below (on vv.21–22).

15 *Oun* ("so") can serve as either an inferential or merely a transitional conjunction (cf. BAGD, pp. 592–93; BDF, par. 451.1 plus app.; RHG, pp. 1191–92; Turner, *Syntax*, pp. 337–38), which can sometimes be left untranslated; it does not introduce something *temporally* new. If it retains any inferential force in this passage, it is very light—"accordingly, when you see . . . then flee." Having characterized the entire age during which the gospel of the kingdom is preached as a time of *thlipsis* ("distress"), Jesus goes on to talk about one part of it when there will be particularly "great distress."

To bdelygma tēs erēmōseōs means "the abomination characterized by desolation," leaving it unclear whether the abomination "causes" desolation (NIV; cf. McNeile, "the abominable thing that layeth waste"; RSV, "the desolating sacrilege") or is simply a token of it. The former is more likely. The expression occurs four times in Daniel (8:13; 9:27; 11:31; 12:11). Daniel 11:31 clearly refers to the desecration under Antiochus Epiphanes (168 B.C.; cf. 1 Macc 1:54–61), who erected an altar to Zeus over the altar of burned offering, sacrificed a swine on it, and made the practice of Judaism a capital offense. The other references in Daniel are more disputed. Matthew and Mark agree with the LXX of Daniel 12:11 only; and, "[despite] the primary importance of Dan 9:27 for the meaning of the expression, 12:11 is contextually the more suitable reference so far as the gospels are concerned, because allusions to Dan 11:40–12:13 surround this reference to the abomination of desolation" (Gundry, *Use of OT*, p. 48).

Jesus, then, is identifying Daniel 9:27 and 12:11 with certain events about to take place; and the parenthetical "let the reader understand" is designed to draw the attention of the *reader of Daniel* to the passages' true meaning. This parenthetical aside is not a Matthean addition (unless one holds to Matthew's priority), for it is already in Mark. Matthew clearly understood it, not as an aside by Mark to draw the attention of his readers to the importance of this Gospel text, but as an aside by Jesus to draw the attention of his hearers who read Daniel to the importance of Daniel's words; hence Jesus' mention of "the prophet Daniel." Whether the identification Jesus makes is a prediction fulfillment or a typological fulfillment largely depends on how one understands the various "abomination of desolation" passages in Daniel.

But to what event does Jesus make this text from Daniel refer? Some have suggested Caligula's plan to set up a pagan altar and standards in the temple precincts (A.D. 40), a plan never carried out; but the description in the following verses cannot apply to that. The obvious occasion, in general terms, is A.D. 70, though certain difficulties must be faced. Although *topos* ("place") can refer to the city of Jerusalem (cf. BAGD, p. 822), the normal meaning of *hagios topos* ("holy place") is the temple complex (cf. BAGD; Isa 60:13; 2 Macc 1:29; 2:18; Acts 6:13; 21:28). But by the time the Romans had actually desecrated the temple in A.D. 70, it was too late for anyone in the city to flee.

Mark's language is less explicit: "standing where it does not belong" (Mark 13:14) instead of "standing in the holy place." Luke resolves the matter: "When you see Jerusalem surrounded by armies, you will know that its desolation is near" (Luke 21:20)—but now there is no explicit mention of "the abomination of desolation." Possibly Jesus said something ambiguous, such as Mark reports. Luke, writing for a Gentile audience less concerned with Daniel, emphasizes the aspect of warning. Matthew, believing the allusions to Daniel important for his Jewish audience because Jesus drew attention to them, makes explicit reference to "the abomination of desolation" and to "the holy place," since the setting up of the abomination in the holy place is the inevitable result of the pagan attack.

By the time the Roman military standards (an eagle in silver or bronze over the imperial bust, to which soldiers paid homage not far removed from worship) surrounded Jerusalem, the city was defiled. Some have held that though Luke refers to the approaching armies, Matthew and Mark refer to the Zealot excesses that polluted the temple before A.D. 70 (including murder and the installation of a false high priest; cf. Jos. War IV, 147–57 [iii.6–8], 162–92 [iii.10], 334–44 [v.4]) when there was still time to flee (e.g., Lane, *Mark*, p. 469; Gaston, *No Stone*, pp. 458ff.). In any case, there is reasonably good tradition that Christians abandoned the city, perhaps in A.D. 68, about halfway through the siege.

16–19 The instructions Jesus gives his disciples about what to do in view of v.15 are so specific that they must be related to the Jewish War. The devastation would stretch far beyond the city; people throughout Judea should flee to the mountains, where the Maccabeans had hidden in caves. Most roofs were flat (cf. Deut 22:8; Mark 2:4; Acts 10:9)—pleasant places in the cool of the day. Verse 17 implies such haste that fugitives will not take time to run downstairs for anything to take with them but will run from roof to roof to evacuate the city as quickly as possible (cf. Jos. Antiq. XIII, 140 [v.3]). People in the fields will not have time to go home for their cloaks (see on 5:40). It will be especially dreadful (lit., "woe," here like a compassionate "alas!") for pregnant women and nursing mothers.

20 Flight is obviously harder in winter. As for fleeing on the Sabbath, travel would become more difficult because few would help, and many would try to prevent traveling farther than a Sabbath day's journey. Jesus clearly expects these events to take place while the strict Sabbath law is in effect.

21 "For" introduces the reason for flight (in vv.17–20: *thlipsis* ("distress," "tribulation") and unprecedented suffering (cf. Dan 12:1; 1 Macc 9:27; Rev 7:14; Gundry, *Use of OT*, pp. 49f.). The savagery, slaughter, disease, and famine (mothers eating their own children) were monstrous (cf. Jos. War V, 424–38 [x.2–3]) "unequaled from the beginning of the world until now," and, according to Jesus, "never to be equaled again." There have been greater numbers of deaths—six million in the Nazi death camps, mostly Jews, and an estimated twenty million under Stalin—but never so high a percentage of a great city's population so thoroughly and painfully exterminated and enslaved as during the Fall of Jerusalem.

From this "great distress" Jesus' followers were to flee. Eusebius (*Ecclesiastical History* 3.5.2–3) says that during the siege under Titus (who did not replace his father Vespasian as commanding officer till A.D. 69, after the death of Galba) many were permitted to leave (cf. Jos. War V, 420–23 [x.1]). Others hold that the Christians left in 66 or 68.

That Jesus in v.21 promises that such "great distress" is never to be equaled implies that it cannot refer to the Tribulation at the end of the age; for if what happens next is the Millennium or the new heaven and the new earth, it seems inane to say that such "great distress" will not take place again. At the same time, by these remarks Jesus finishes his description of Jerusalem in Matthew and Mark (Luke goes to 21:24). (For the way Luke's version of the discourse fits this framework, see the forthcoming monograph by Wenham.)

Notes

18 Only here and in Luke 7:38 is ὀπίσω (*opisō*, "back") used as an adverb (cf. Moule, *Idiom Book*, p. 86).

c. *Warnings against false messiahs during the birth pains*

24:22–28

22If those days had not been cut short, no one would survive, but for the sake
of the elect those days will be shortened. 23At that time if anyone says to you,
'Look, here is the Christ!' or, 'There he is!' do not believe it. 24For false Christs
and false prophets will appear and perform great signs and miracles to deceive
even the elect—if that were possible. 25See, I have told you ahead of time.
26"So if anyone tells you, 'There he is, out in the desert,' do not go out; or, 'Here
he is, in the inner rooms,' do not believe it. 27For as the lightning that comes from
the east is visible even in the west, so will be the coming of the Son of Man.
28Wherever there is a carcass, there the vultures will gather.

22 Many problems in interpreting the Olivet Discourse relate to the assumption that "those days" refers to the period described in vv.15–21 and also to v.29. But there are excellent reasons for concluding that vv.22–28 refer to the general period of distress introduced by vv.4–14 and that therefore "those days" refers to the entire period of which vv.15–21 are only one part—the "great distress" (v.21).

1. The term "elect" (in Matthew only at 22:14; 24:22, 24, 31; plus the variant at 20:16) most naturally refers to all true believers, chosen by God; so it is reasonable to assume that it does so here.

2. Similarly, *pasa sarx* (lit., "all flesh"; NIV, "no one"; cf. Notes) normally refers to all mankind and is more sweeping than "no one in Jerusalem."

3. The themes of the ensuing verses have already been taken up as characteristics of the entire age (vv.4–14), especially the warning against false Christs (cf. vv.4–5).

4. It has already been shown that v.21 makes a suitable ending to vv.15–21.

5. Wenham, in his forthcoming work (see at v.21), posits a neat presynoptic tradition that embraces the content of all three Gospels and suggests reasons for individual selection of materials. That tradition (slightly modified from Wenham) runs approximately as follows: Matthew 24:15–20 = Mark 13:14–18 = Luke 21:20–23a; Luke 21:23b–24; Matthew 24:20 = Mark 13:19; Matthew 24:22–28 = Mark 13:20–23; Matthew 24:29–42 = Mark 13:24–37 = Luke 21:25–36. Right or wrong as to source-critical details, this reconstruction at least makes sense of the relationship among the Synoptics at this point and supports a logical break between v.21 and v.22 of Matthew 24.

6. Further literary and structural arguments suggest that vv.4–28 must be taken as one time period, with vv.15–21 a critical part of it (see on v.29).

While none of these arguments is decisive, all are reasonable and help us understand the whole discourse. If they are correct, then v.22 tells us that this age of evangelism and distress—wars, famines, persecution, hatred, false prophets—will become so bad that, if not checked, no one would survive. In a century that has seen two world wars, now lives under the threat of extinction by nuclear holocaust, and has had more Christian martyrs than in all the previous nineteen centuries put together, Jesus' prediction does not seem farfetched. But the age will not run its course; it will be cut short. (For a somewhat similar idea, see the Jewish apocalypse 2 Baruch 20:1–2; 83:1.) This promise enables believers to look for God's sovereign, climactic intervention without predicting dates.

23–25 Empty-headed credulity is as great an enemy of true faith as chronic skepticism. Christian faith involves the sober responsibility of neither believing lies nor trusting imposters. As false Christs and false prophets proliferate (v.24), so will their heralds (v.23). Jesus' disciples are not to be deceived, even by spectacular signs and miracles (see on 7:21–23; 16:1; for the terms, 12:38; 18:12–13; cf. 24:4–5, 11). The imposter is perennial (Deut 13:1–4; Rev 13:13).

Ei dynaton ("if that were possible") no more calls in question the security of the elect (contra I.H. Marshall, *Kept by the Power of God*, rev. ed. [Minneapolis: Bethany, 1975], pp. 72–73) than it calls in question the inevitability of Jesus' cup (26:39). If "deceive" is telic (i.e., "in order to deceive" (cf. Notes)) the "if possible" refers to the intent of the deceivers: they intend to deceive, if possible, even the elect—without any comment on how ultimately successful such attacks will be. "If that were possible" clearly suggests that "deceive" is not ecbatic (i.e., "with the result that"). That Jesus tells these things in advance (v.25) not only warns and strengthens his followers (cf. John 16:4) but also authenticates him (cf. Deut 13:1–4; John 14:29).

26–27 It is pointless to look for Messiah's return in the desert (v.26; cf. 4:1) or in inner rooms (cf. 6:6)—whether in some desert monastic community or in some hidden, unrecognized enclave for insiders (cf. Stendahl, Peake). Far from it! The coming of the Son of Man (see on 8:20; here his coming is clearly identified as "your [Jesus'] coming," v.3, and Messiah's coming, vv.23–24) will be public, unquestionable, and not confined to some little group of initiates. As the lightning (cf. Ps 97:4; Zech 9:14) comes out of the east but is everywhere visible, as far away as the west (Weiss, Broadus), so also the coming of the Son of Man will be visible to all people everywhere (TDNT, 8:433–34).

28 Here Jesus quotes a proverb (cf. Job 39:30; Luke 17:37). "Eagle" (KJV) is wrong: "vulture" (NIV) is correct. *Aetos* can mean "eagle," "kite," or "vulture"; but eagles are not normally carrion eaters. The proverb itself is a difficult one.

1. Calvin, following some of the Fathers, sees it portraying God's children, gathering to feed on Christ. But identifying carrion with Christ is strange indeed!
2. Others see an allusion to Roman military eagles, with the Roman forces swarming over corrupt Jerusalem. But eagles are not vultures; and the preceding verse relates to the Parousia, not the Fall of Jerusalem.
3. Hill and others think that the vultures' gathering indicates that the Parousia is near. But there must be carrion before the vultures gather; so the symbolism breaks down, because the "signs" attest the reality only after the fact.
4. Manson (*Sayings*, p. 147) emphasizes the swiftness of the coming of the Son of Man: the carrion is no sooner there than the vultures swoop down (Ezek 17:3, 7; Rev 4:7; 8:13; 12:4). But in passages where the *aetos* ("eagle" or "vulture") symbolizes speed, it is understood to mean an "eagle." Why then assign it to a setting where it must be taken as a vulture?

5. The proverb may be a colorful way of saying that things come to pass at just the right time (Broadus); so the proverb applies here and in Luke 17:37 to the Parousia of the Son of Man. Concluding this broader section (vv.4–28) is this thought: Do not be too eager for Christ's coming, or you will be deceived by false claimants (vv.23–26). When he comes, his coming will be unmistakable (v.27), in God's own time (v.28)—a time when the world will be ripe for judgment (Zahn; see on v.6).

6. Or this enigmatic proverb may simply mean that it will be as impossible for humanity not to see the coming of the Son of Man (cf. v.27) as it is for vultures to miss seeing carrion (Klostermann).

Notes

---

22 On the aorist verbs in this verse, see Zerwick, par. 317. The οὐ . . . πᾶς (*ou . . . pas*, lit., "not . . . all") construction is often said to represent the Hebrew כֹּל . . . לֹא (*lō' . . . kōl*), equivalent to Greek οὐδείς (*oudeis*, "no one"; e.g., Zerwick, par. 446; but the Semitizing stretches even farther to οὐ . . . πᾶσα σάρξ (*ou . . . pasa sarx*, lit., "not . . . all flesh," i.e., no person).

24 The construction ὥστε πλανῆσαι (*hōste planēsai*, "to deceive") would most naturally be expected to be consecutive, and so it may be (Moule, *Idiom Book*, p. 143); but the same construction can have final force (Zerwick, par. 352), as does the parallel expression in Mark 13:22.

---

3. *The coming of the Son of Man*

24:29–31

29"Immediately after the distress of those days

"'the sun will be darkened,
and the moon will not give its light;
the stars will fall from the sky,
and the heavenly bodies will be shaken.'

30"At that time the sign of the Son of Man will appear in the sky, and all the nations of the earth will mourn. They will see the Son of Man coming on the clouds of the sky, with power and great glory. 31And he will send his angels with a loud trumpet call, and they will gather his elect from the four winds, from one end of the heavens to the other."

Matthew essentially follows Mark (13:24–27; cf. Luke 21:25–28) but adds the allusion to Zechariah about mourning (v.30) and the trumpet call (v.31).

29 For general arguments that vv.29–31 refer to the Parousia, not the coming of the Son of Man in the events of A.D. 70, see on vv.1–3. Mark brackets the last section (Mark 13:5–23 parallels Matt 24:4–28) with *blepete* ("watch out") in Mark 13:5, 23. Matthew has nothing similar, but the effect is the same because v.29 begins the new stage with "Immediately after the distress [*thlipsis*] of those days," a clear reference back to the *thlipsis* of vv.9, 22, not to the "great distress" of vv.15–21. Thus the celestial signs and the coming of the Son of Man do not immediately follow "the abomination that causes desolation" but "the distress of those days"—i.e., of the entire interadvent period of *thlipsis*.

The cosmic portents (cf. esp. Isa 13:9–10; 34:4; but also Ezek 32:7; Joel 2:31; 3:15; Amos 8:9; Rev 6:12) are probably meant to be taken literally, because of the climactic nature of the Son of Man's final self-disclosure. Yet this is not certain, since in some political contexts similar expressions are used metaphorically (see on 24:1–13).

30 "The sign of the Son of Man" has been interpreted in three principal ways.

1. Some of the Fathers after the Constantinian settlement thought it referred to Constantine's vision of a cross in the sky, with the words "In this sign, conquer"—an interpretation both anachronistic and fanciful.

2. More commonly "the sign" is assumed to be Jesus' coming, with "of the Son of Man . . . in the sky" being taken as standing in epexegetical relation to "the sign." The Jews had repeatedly asked for a sign (12:38; 16:1; cf. John 2:18), and the disciples had just asked for the sign of his coming (v.3). The supreme "sign" is his parousia at the end of the age. This interpretation is possible, though perhaps a bit forced. When the Jews asked for a sign, Jesus referred them to "the sign of Jonah" (12:39–41), not to his parousia. His disciples' more specific question (v.3) was partially answered by vv.4–28, with a fuller answer in vv.32–35.

3. T.F. Glasson ("The Ensign of the Son of Man (Matt. xxiv, 30)," JTS [1964]: 299f.) offers the best explanation. He points out that careful comparison of vv.30–31 with the synoptic parallels shows Matthew has added mention of both "sign" and "trumpet." But *sēmeion* ("sign") commonly meant "ensign" or "standard," both in pagan Greek literature and in the LXX; and "standard" and "trumpet" are both regularly associated with the eschatological gathering of the people of God (cf. v.31; Isa 11:12; 18:3; 27:13; 49:22; Jer 4:21; 6:1; 51:27; 1QM 3:1–4:2). Therefore *sēmeion* has two different meanings in this chapter (vv.3, 30)—a phenomenon common enough in the NT. Theologically this means that the kingdom is being consummated. The standard, the banner of the Son of Man, unfurls in the heavens, as he himself returns in splendor and power.

The event will prompt "all the nations of the earth" to mourn, an allusion to Zechariah 12:10–12, probably directly from the MT (cf. Gundry, *Use of OT*, p. 53; cf. John 19:37; Rev 1:7). In Zechariah the reference is to the tribes of Israel in the land, and the mourning is that of repentance. Those who follow Kik and France want to keep the first link with the OT (the tribes of Israel) but not the second (the mourning; see on 24:1–3). Most scholars see the mourning (v.30) as that of despair, not repentance (Rev 1:7; 6:15–17); and we have already argued for the translation "all the nations of the earth" (NIV) over "all the tribes of the land." So it seems that neither link with the OT is simple, and we must probe for a deeper link.

What we discover is an implicit a fortiori argument. In Zechariah 12, Yahweh enables the house of David and Judah to crush its enemies; and as a result the Jews weep, apparently in contrition for their past sins in light of Yahweh's merciful deliverance and salvation (cf. also Zech 13:1–2). But it is the Gentile enemies who are crushed. If, then, the Jews face judgment and mourning (vv.15–21), even though not only Jerusalem but also *all nations* (v.9) have hated Jesus' disciples, *how much more* will all the nations of the earth, to whom the gospel has been preached (v.14), also mourn at the Parousia, when the lost opportunities and the persecution of Jesus through persecuting his disciples are seen as they truly are?

The next allusion in v.30 is to Daniel 7:13–14. Some have objected that since in

Daniel's vision "one like a son of man" approaches the throne of "the Ancient of Days" and does not descend to earth, v.30 and parallels cannot be speaking about the Parousia, which requires the descent to earth. The objection misses the point. In Daniel "one like a son of man" approaches God to receive all authority, glory, sovereign power—"an everlasting dominion that will not pass away." In the framework of NT eschatology, we may imagine Jesus the Son of Man receiving the kingdom through his resurrection and ascension, his divine vindication, so that now all authority is his (28:18). Yet it is equally possible to think of him receiving the kingdom at the consummation, when his reign or kingdom becomes direct and immediate, uncontested and universal. Unless one thinks of the location of the Ancient of Days in some physical and spatial sense, it is hard to imagine why Christ's approaching God the Father to receive the kingdom might not be combined with his returning to earth to set up the consummated kingdom. This interpretation goes well with its vivid context.

The Son of Man, whose standard has been unfurled, comes "on [*epi*] the clouds of heaven" (cf. 26:64; Rev 14:14–16); it is doubtful whether sharp distinctions are to be drawn between this expression and "in [*en*] the clouds of heaven" (Mark 13:26; Luke 21:27) or "with [*meta*] the clouds of heaven" (Mark 14:62 [NIV, "on"]; Rev 1:7). The clouds symbolize God's presence (see on 17:5): Immanuel ("God with us") comes "with power and great glory." The latter phrase not only ensures that the coming is universally witnessed and unmistakably plain (cf. vv.26–28, 30) but may allude to Isaiah 11:10: the nations will rally to "the Root of Jesse," and his place of rest will be (lit.) "the Glory" (cf. M.G. Kline, "Primal Parousia," WTJ 40 [1977-78]: 274).

31 The sound of a loud trumpet (cf. Isa 27:13; 1 Cor 15:52; 1 Thess 4:16) is an eschatological figure (see on v.30). Only with considerable difficulty can v.31 be interpreted as referring to Christian missions: its natural linguistic relations are in 13:41. For comments on "his elect," see on 22:14; 24:22. The "four winds" represent the four points of the compass (Ezek 37:9; Dan 8:8; 11:4): the elect are gathered from all over (cf. 8:11), "from one end of the heavens to the other" (from every place under the sky), since that is how far the gospel of the kingdom will have been preached (v.14). Although all nations of the earth will mourn, nevertheless the elect are drawn from them.

4. *The significance of the birth pains*

24:32–35

> [32]"Now learn this lesson from the fig tree: As soon as its twigs get tender and its leaves come out, you know that summer is near. [33]Even so, when you see all these things, you know that it is near, right at the door. [34]I tell you the truth, this generation will certainly not pass away until all these things have happened. [35]Heaven and earth will pass away, but my words will never pass away.

32–33 This "lesson" (*parabolē*, lit., "parable"; see on 13:3a; 15:15) of the fig tree (cf. 21:18–22) is based on the common observation that the twigs get tender before summer and arouse expectations of summer (v.32). Although the Greek is ambiguous, NIV's "you know" is preferable to KJV's imperative ("know"). The "parable" points to the relation between "all these things" and "it is near" (v.33). It is uncertain whether the antecedent of "it" is the Parousia or Jesus, the Son of Man. Jesus sometimes spoke of himself in the third person (v.31) and may be doing so here. But whatever "it" refers to, it is certainly the nearness of the Second Advent that is in view.

"All these things" is more problematic. If the words include the celestial signs *and the Parousia itself* (vv.29–31), then vv.32–33 are illogical, because any distinction between "all these things" and "it is near" would be destroyed. Thus many have suggested that vv.32–33 constitute a displaced parable—once again making the synoptists out to be less intelligent than their critics two millennia later. The more natural way to take "all these things" is to see them as referring to the distress of vv.4–28, the tribulation that comes on believers throughout the period between Jesus' ascension and the Parousia.

Having warned his disciples of the course of this age (vv.4–28) and told them of its climax in the Parousia (vv.29–31), Jesus in these verses answers the part of his disciples' questions (v.3) dealing with timing. He makes two points. First, "all these things" (vv.4–28) must happen; and then the Parousia is "near, right at the door"—"imminent." In other words the Parousia is the next major step in God's redemptive purposes. Second, this does not mean that the period of distress pinpoints the Parousia, for "no one knows about that day or hour" (vv.36–42).

34 "I tell you the truth" emphasizes the importance of what it introduces. "This generation" (see on 11:16; 12:41–42; 23:36; cf. 10:23; 16:28) can only with the greatest difficulty be made to mean anything other than the generation living when Jesus spoke. Even if "generation" by itself can have a slightly larger semantic range, to make "*this* generation" refer to all believers in every age, or the generation of believers alive when eschatological events start to happen, is highly artificial. Yet it does not follow that Jesus mistakenly thought the Parousia would occur within his hearers' lifetime. If our interpretation of this chapter is right, all that v.34 demands is that the distress of vv.4–28, including Jerusalem's fall, happen within the lifetime of the generation then living. This does *not* mean that the distress must end within that time but only that "all these things" must happen within it. Therefore v.34 sets a *terminus a quo* for the Parousia: it cannot happen till the events in vv.4–28 take place, all within a generation of A.D. 30. But there is no *terminus ad quem* to this distress other than the Parousia itself, and "only the Father" knows when it will happen (v.36).

35 The authority and eternal validity of Jesus' words are nothing less than the authority and eternal validity of God's words (Ps 119: 89–90; Isa 40:6–8).

5. *The day and hour unknown: the need to be prepared* (24:36–42)

a. *The principle*

24:36

36"No one knows about that day or hour, not even the angels in heaven, nor the Son, but only the Father.

36 Many commentators read v.36 with the preceding paragraph; but it goes much better with the following verses, which constitute an exhortation to vigilance precisely because, the day and the hour being unknown to humanity, life goes on as it always has. The *gar* ("for") at the beginning of v.37 must not be overlooked, as in NIV.

The gist of v.36 is clear enough. Jesus' disciples are morally bound to repress all desires to know what no one knows but the Father—not even angels (cf. 18:10; 4 Ezra 4:52) or the Son (cf. Notes). If the Son himself does not know the time of the Parousia, "how cheerfully should we his followers rest in ignorance that cannot be removed, trusting in all things to our Heavenly Father's wisdom and goodness, striving to obey his clearly revealed will, and leaning on his goodness for support" (Broadus). Moreover it is ridiculous quibbling divorced from the context to say that though the day and hour remain unknown, we ascertain the year or month.

Jesus' self-confessed ignorance on this point has generated not a little debate. In fact, it is part of the NT pattern of his humiliation and incarnation (e.g., 20:23; Luke 2:52; Acts 1:7; Phil 2:7). John's Gospel, the one of the four Gospels most clearly insisting on Jesus' deity, also insists with equal vigor on Jesus' dependence on and obedience to his Father—a dependence reaching even to his knowledge of the divine. How NT insistence on Jesus' deity is to be combined with NT insistence on his ignorance and dependence is a matter of profound importance to the church; and attempts to jettison one truth for the sake of preserving the other must be avoided. (For an attempt to work some of these things out, cf. Carson, *Divine Sovereignty*, pp. 146–60.)

Notes

36 The words "nor the Son," while textually secure in Mark 13:32, are disputed here. The omission is supported by most late MSS and by ℵ[a]. Such omission may have been prompted by the doctrinal difficulty presented by the words; but it is mildly surprising that Mark 13:32 has not suffered similar distortion. One might in fact argue that the omission in Matthew is original and that the words were added by assimilation to Mark. The most convincing argument in favor of retaining the words in Matthew is grammatical (cf. Metzger, *Textual Commentary*, p. 62). The curious suggestion of Jeremias (*Prayers*, p. 37), that "nor the Son" is a late addition in both Matthew and Mark that makes explicit the implications of "but only the Father," is not only without textual warrant but also an intrinsically unlikely christological development.

b. *Analogy of the days of Noah*

24:37–39

37 As it was in the days of Noah, so it will be at the coming of the Son of Man.
38 For in the days before the flood, people were eating and drinking, marrying and
giving in marriage, up to the day Noah entered the ark; 39 and they knew nothing
about what would happen until the flood came and took them all away. That is
how it will be at the coming of the Son of Man.

37–39 (See also Mark 13:33 and Luke 17:28–32, though the latter is in a different context and has quite different structure and wording.) The *gar* ("for") in the best

MSS further elucidates v.36: that the coming of the Son of Man takes place at an unknown time can only be true if in fact life seems to be going on pretty much as usual—just as in the days before the Flood (v.37). People follow their ordinary pursuits (v.38). Despite the distress, persecutions, and upheavals (vv.4–28), life goes on: people eat, drink, and marry. There is no overt typological usage of the Flood as judgment here, nor any mention of the sin of that generation. Yet Jesus' warning may well have given rise to 1 Peter 3:20–21. Jesus expects ceaseless vigilance of his followers, for the final climax of human history will suddenly come on ordinary life. In the human condition massive distress and normal life patterns coexist. For the believer the former point to the end; the latter warn of its unexpectedness.

c. *Two in the field; two with a mill*

24:40–41

> 40Two men will be in the field; one will be taken and the other left. 41Two women will be grinding with a hand mill; one will be taken and the other left.

40–41 These two vignettes do not "stress the sharp cleavage caused by the coming of the Son of Man, *rather than* the unexpectedness of the event" (Hill, *Matthew*, emphasis mine) but the unexpectedness of the event *by means of* the sudden cleavage. Two men are working in a field; one is taken, the other left (v.40). Two women work their hand mill (v.41)—one normally operated by two women squatting opposite each other with the mill between them, each woman in turn pulling the stone around 180 degrees. The two are apt to be sisters, mother and daughter, or two household slaves. Yet no matter how close their relationship, one is taken, the other left (cf. 10:35–36). It is neither clear nor particularly important whether "taken" means "taken in judgment" (cf. v.39, though the verb "took . . . away" differs from "taken" in vv.40–41) or "taken to be gathered with the elect" (v.31).

6. *Parabolic teaching: variations on watchfulness* (24:42–25:46)

a. *The homeowner and the thief*

24:42–44

> 42"Therefore keep watch, because you do not know on what day your Lord will come. 43But understand this: If the owner of the house had known at what time of night the thief was coming, he would have kept watch and would not have let his house be broken into. 44So you also must be ready, because the Son of Man will come at an hour when you do not expect him.

The exact relation between vv.42–51 and Mark 13:33–37 is obscure and has not been satisfactorily explained. On the nature of parables, see on 13:3a; on comparison with Luke 12:39–40, see discussion and chart at 19:1–2. Each of the five parables in 24:42–25:46 deal with some aspect of watchfulness. But watchfulness is not always passive: duties and responsibilities must be discharged (24:45–51), and foresight and wisdom are important (25:1–13). Responsible living under Jesus' directives is rewarded in the end (vv.14–46).

42–44 The first parable teaches both the unexpectedness of the return of "your Lord" (*kyrios*, v.42)—an expression that is not only identical to "the master" in the next parable (v.45), but lays the foundation for the church's cry, "Come, O Lord!" (1 Cor 16:22)—and her willingness to call Jesus *ho kyrios* ("the Lord"), a title hitherto reserved in its religious use by the Jews for God himself (1 Cor 12:3; Phil 4:5; 2 Thess 2:2; James 5:7; see on 8:2; 17:4, 14–16; 21:3; 22:41–46). It might be better to take *ginōskete* not as an imperative ("understand," NIV, v.43) but as an indicative ("you know"): the disciples know the owner of a house would watch if he knew when the thief was coming (on the tenses of the verb, cf. Zerwick, par. 317), so the thief could not break in (on the verb, see on 6:19). Since no one knows at what time, or during what "watch," the thief might strike, constant vigilance is required. "So you also must be ready" (v.44), because in this one respect—the unexpectedness of his coming—the Son of Man (see on vv.37, 39; 8:20) resembles a thief.

b. *The two servants*

24:45–51

> 45"Who then is the faithful and wise servant, whom the master has put in charge of the servants in his household to give them their food at the proper time? 46It will be good for that servant whose master finds him doing so when he returns. 47I tell you the truth, he will put him in charge of all his possessions. 48But suppose that servant is wicked and says to himself, 'My master is staying away a long time,' 49and he then begins to beat his fellow servants and to eat and drink with drunkards. 50The master of that servant will come on a day when he does not expect him and at an hour he is not aware of. 51He will cut him to pieces and assign him a place with the hypocrites, where there will be weeping and gnashing of teeth.

The good servant is prepared for his Lord at any time, is faithful throughout his delay, and in the end is highly rewarded. The wicked servant is faithless in his responsibilities, abusive to fellow servants, lax in waiting for his master's return, and ultimately earns the punishment that is his due (see chart and discussion at 19:1–2; cf. 21:34–36; cf. also Mark 13:34–37; Luke 12:35–38, 42–46).

45–47 The *doulos* ("servant") in this parable is the head over all the domestics (v.45). This, however, does not so much limit the application of the parable to leaders as establish that their responsibilities entail good personal relationships (v.49), requiring exemplary conduct and precluding harshness and lording it over others. The good servant is faithful and "wise" (i.e., prudent, judicious—cf. 7:24; 10:16) doing what is assigned him. When his master returns (v.46), he is *makarios* ("blessed"; NIV, "will be good"; see on 5:3) and promoted (v.47; cf. 25:21). In Mark 13:37 Jesus applies the necessity of watching to "everyone."

48–51 If the servant is wicked (v.48) and lacking faithfulness and wisdom (v.45), he may convince himself that the master "is staying away a long time"—perhaps a subtle hint that the Parousia could be considerably delayed (cf. 25:19). The wicked servant uses the delay to abuse his fellow servants and carouse (v.49). (For "begins to beat," cf. 11:7, 20.) But the wicked servant, surprised and unprepared for his master's return (v.50), is put with the "hypocrites" (v.51): his lot is with the punishment given those most constantly held up as vile in this Gospel (6:2, 5, 16; 16:3;

23:13–29). The master "will cut him to pieces" (cf. 1 Sam 15:33; Heb 11:37; Sus 55; on the punishments accorded Jewish slaves, cf. SBK, 4:698–744). *Dichotomeō* literally is "I cut in two" (found in the NT only here and Luke 12:46). Alleged parallels (in 1QS 1:10–11; 2:16–17; 6:24–25; 7:1, 2, 16; 8:21–23) are unconvincing: the Hebrew "cut off from the midst of the sons of light" refers to excommunication. Here, however, the wicked servant is not cut off from anything; he is cut in pieces—a most severe and awful punishment—and joins the hypocrites in weeping and grinding of teeth (cf. 8:12).

Notes

---

50 This is one of only three places in Matthew where the relative pronoun is attracted to the case of its antecedent (see on 18:19; cf. 25:24).

---

c. *The ten virgins*

25:1–13

1"At that time the kingdom of heaven will be like ten virgins who took their lamps and went out to meet the bridegroom. 2Five of them were foolish and five were wise. 3The foolish ones took their lamps but did not take any oil with them. 4The wise, however, took oil in jars along with their lamps. 5The bridegroom was a long time in coming, and they all became drowsy and fell asleep.

6"At midnight the cry rang out: 'Here's the bridegroom! Come out to meet him!'

7"Then all the virgins woke up and trimmed their lamps. 8The foolish ones said to the wise, 'Give us some of your oil; our lamps are going out.'

9" 'No,' they replied, 'there may not be enough for both us and you. Instead, go to those who sell oil and buy some for yourselves.'

10"But while they were on their way to buy the oil, the bridegroom arrived. The virgins who were ready went in with him to the wedding banquet. And the door was shut.

11"Later the others also came. 'Sir! Sir!' they said. 'Open the door for us!'

12"But he replied, 'I tell you the truth, I don't know you.'

13"Therefore keep watch, because you do not know the day or the hour.

This parable has been widely discussed. Hill (*Matthew*), largely following Jeremias (*Parables*, pp. 51–53) notes the "allegorical" elements (bridegroom's coming = coming of the Son of Man; ten virgins = expectant Christian community; tarrying = delay of the Parousia; rejection of the foolish virgins = final judgment) and claims there is evidence for thinking these to be later additions by the church. This view is strengthened, it is claimed, by the fact that the equation Messiah = bridegroom is virtually unknown in late Judaism (cf. ibid., p. 52) and first appears in 2 Corinthians 11:2. The story Jesus actually told, stripped of its "allegorical accretions," involved wedding preparations and warned his hearers of the impending eschatological crisis. But this will not do. We have already seen that source criticism of Gospel parables based on theoretical distinctions between "parable" and "allegory" is ill-founded (see on 13:3a). The idea of Messiah as bridegroom springs from such OT passages as Isaiah 54:4–6; 62:4–5; Ezekiel 16:7–34; Hosea 2:19. There Yahweh is portrayed as the "husband" of his people. We have noted how readily Jesus in his parables places himself in Yahweh's place (see on 13:37–39). Moreover both John the Baptist (John 3:27–30) and Jesus himself (Matt 9:15; Mark 2:19–20) have already made the equation Jesus = Messiah = bridegroom, unless we deny the historicity of these passages. But the parable makes sense in its own setting and as it stands.

While dispensationalists divide on whether this parable relates to the "Rapture" of the church (A.C. Gaebelein) or the Second Advent, following the Tribulation (Walvoord), both views introduce eschatological structures that do not emerge naturally from the text (see above on 24:1–3). W. Schenk ("Auferweckung der Toten oder Gericht nach den Werken: Tradition und Redaktion in Matthäus xxv 1–3," NovTest 20 [1978]: 278–99) reconstructs a very simple "original" parable in which all the virgins have enough oil but only five of them sleep. When the bridegroom comes, they all enter and enjoy the feast. The point is that when the bridegroom comes, some are asleep and some are awake; but all enjoy the festivities (as in 1 Thess 4:15–17). But Matthew has allegorized this parable and required a store of good works (oil) as qualification for entry. It is hard to decide which of Schenk's options is more wrong—his reconstruction of the alleged original or his interpretation of the parable as it stands in Matthew.

Scarcely less idiosyncratic is J.M. Ford ("The Parable of the Foolish Scholars," NovTest 9 [1967]: 107–23), who, arguing largely from late rabbinic sources, claims the virgins represent Jewish scholars, the lamps Torah, and the oil good deeds. The foolish virgins are Jewish scholars who study Torah but who fail to practice good deeds. They are therefore excluded from the Chamber of Instruction.

Such ingenuity ignores both the narrative and the context, as J.M. Sherriff ("Matthew 25:1–13. A Summary of Matthean Eschatology?" in Livingstone, 2:301–5) has pointed out. The plot turns on the bridegroom's delay. The foolish virgins do not *forget* to bring oil; rather the delay of the bridegroom shows they did not bring enough. The oil cannot easily apply to "good works" or "Holy Spirit." It is merely an element in the narrative showing that the foolish virgins were unprepared for the delay and so shut out in the end. In a real sense it is the bridegroom's delay that distinguishes the wise from the foolish virgins. Any interpretation that ignores this central element in the story is bound to go astray (cf. also G. Bornkamm, "Die Verzögerung der Parusie," *Geschichte*, pp. 49f.). The context similarly shows that the overriding theme is preparedness for the coming of the Son of Man. Even when this involves certain forms of behavior (24:45–51; 25:14–30), that behavior is called forth by the unexpectedness of the master's return.

From this perspective vv.1–13 fit well into this sequence of parables and agree with what we know Jesus taught. There is no good reason for doubting its authenticity or retreating to one of several reconstructed cores. The first parable (24:42–44) warns of the unexpectedness of Messiah's coming. The second (24:45–51) shows that more than passive watchfulness is required: there must be behavior acceptable to the master, the discharge of allotted responsibilities. This third parable (25:1–13) stresses the need for preparedness in the face of an unexpectedly long delay.

1 *Tote* ("At that time") is sufficiently vague in Matthew's usage (see on 2:7; 24:9) that not much can be built on it. The most natural way to take it here is as a reference to the coming of the Son of Man (cf. 24:29–31, 36–44). "At that time" the kingdom of heaven will become like the story of the ten virgins (so the Gr.; cf. Carson, "Word-Group")—i.e., the parable deals with the onset of the consummated kingdom.

The setting is fairly clear from what we know of the marriage customs of the day (cf. Broadus; Jeremias, *Parables*, pp. 173–74; TDNT, 4:1100; and esp. H. Granquist, *Marriage Conditions in a Palestinian Village*, 2 vols [Helsingfors: Centraltryckeriet, 1931, 1935]). Normally the bridegroom with some close friends left his home to go to the bride's home, where there were various ceremonies, followed by a procession through the streets—after nightfall—to his home. The ten virgins may be bridesmaids who have been assisting the bride; and they expect to meet the groom as he comes from the bride's house (cf. Kistemaker, p. 130), though this is uncertain. Everyone in the procession was expected to carry his or her own torch. Those without a torch would be assumed to be party crashers or even brigands. The festivities, which might last several days, would formally get under way at the groom's house.

That the bride is not mentioned in the best MSS (cf. Notes) has been variously interpreted. Some have thought this is the trip to the bride's house or that this is one of those rare occasions when all the festivities took place at her home, because the groom lived at a considerable distance. But then the bride's father, not the groom, would have refused entrance to the foolish virgins. To demand the presence of the bride is to demand that the parable walk on all fours: mention of her is not essential to the story.

For the meaning of *parthenos* ("virgin"), see on 1:23. The point is not these girls' virginity, which is assumed, but simply that they are ten (a favorite round number; e.g., Ruth 4:2; Luke 19:13; Jos. War VI, 423–24 [ix.3]) maidens invited to the wedding. The "lamps" (not the same word as in 5:15) are here either small oil-fed lamps or, more plausibly, torches whose rags would need periodic dowsing with oil to keep them burning. In either case the prudent would bring along a flask with an additional oil supply.

2–5 The "wise" (v.2) are called such because they are prepared (v.4) for the bridegroom's delayed coming. Both wise and foolish wait and doze (v.5); no praise or blame attaches to either group for this. There is no point in seeing hidden meanings in the oil or sleep. The sole distinction between the two groups is this: the wise bring not only oil in their lamps but an extra supply in separate jars, while the foolish bring no oil (either no extra oil or no oil at all [cf. Robertson, 1:196; Hendriksen; Lenski]: if the latter, then the lamps going out [v.8] is the sputtering of wicks or rags that burn brightly but don't last). The wise are prepared for delay; the foolish expect to meet the groom, but are either utterly unprepared or unprepared if he is delayed. And the bridegroom is a long time coming (24:48; 25:19).

6–9 At midnight (v.6), symbol of eschatological climax, "the cry rang out"—an admirable paraphrase of *kraugē gegonen* (lit., "a cry has arisen": the perfect is unusual and probably dramatic; cf. Moule, *Idiom Book*, pp. 14, 202; BDF, par. 343[3]). All the virgins wake up and trim their lamps (v.7); but the lamps of the foolish virgins quickly go out (present tense, "are going out," contra KJV's "are gone out"). Apart from the identification of "oil" with "grace," Matthew Henry's observation is pertinent: "They will see their need of grace hereafter, when it should save them, who will not see their need of grace now, when it should sanctify and rule them." The wise virgins cannot help them. Whether the text reads "there may not be enough" or "there will certainly not be enough" (cf. Notes), the effect is the same: the foresight and preparedness of the wise virgins cannot benefit the foolish virgins when the eschatological crisis dawns (vv.8–9). Preparedness can neither be transferred nor shared.

10–12 The bridegroom comes, the wise virgins enter, and the door is shut (v.10; cf. 7:22–23; Luke 13:25). The intense cries of the ill-prepared and foolish latecomers—"Sir! Sir!" (on the doubling, cf. BDF, par. 493[1]; 7:21–23; 23:37)—are of no avail (v.11). Because this parable concerns the consummation, the refusal to recognize or admit the foolish virgins (v.12) must not be construed as calloused rejection of their lifelong desire to enter the kingdom. Far from it: it is the rejection of those who, despite appearances, never made preparation for the coming of the kingdom.

13 The theme is reiterated once more (cf. 24:36, 42, 44, 50). Jeremias (*Parables*, p. 52) and others suggest this verse is a late addition to the parable, since it is at variance with the fact that both the wise and the foolish virgins fell asleep. But this misses the purpose of v.13. "Keep watch" does not mean "keep awake," as if an ability to fight off sleep were relevant to the story. Rather, in the light of the entire parable, the dominant exhortation of this discourse is repeated: Be prepared! Keep watching!

Notes

1 The words "and the bride," attested by D X* Θ f[1] et al., may have been added out of a sense of propriety, a desire for a well-rounded story in which the bride should be present. Alternatively one might argue that the words were original but omitted out of the widely held view that Christ would come and fetch his bride, the church. These and other internal considerations (how much did copyists know about marriage customs in Jesus' day?) are indecisive. On external evidence alone, omission is more likely original.

9 The two readings are (1) μήποτε οὐκ ἀρκέσῃ (*mēpote ouk arkesē*, "no, there may not be enough"), supported by ℵ A L Z (Θ) f[13] et al.; and (2) μήποτε οὐ μὴ ἀρκέσῃ (*mēpote ou mē arkesē*, perhaps "no, there will certainly not be enough"), attested by B C D K W Δ et al. The second option might be taken to introduce into the parable the notion of the absolute untransferability of the oil. But three things must be borne in mind: (1) though the grammatical points are much discussed, there is some ground for thinking that by NT times the second construction (*ou mē* plus the subjunctive) could itself be softened to the first meaning (cf. Zerwick, par. 444); (2) on internal grounds the first reading is considerably more likely, since copyists might well wish to change an *ouk* to an *ou mē* before the subjunctive; and (3) the effect on the story is the same—whether the wise virgins are certain they will not have enough oil to share or doubt that they will, the outcome is the same; and the reasons differ but little.

d. *The talents*

25:14–30

[14]"Again, it will be like a man going on a journey, who called his servants and entrusted his property to them. [15]To one he gave five talents of money, to another two talents, and to another one talent, each according to his ability. Then he went on his journey. [16]The man who had received the five talents went at once and put his money to work and gained five more. [17]So also, the one with the two talents

gained two more. [18]But the man who had received the one talent went off, dug a hole in the ground and hid his master's money.

[19]"After a long time the master of those servants returned and settled accounts with them. [20]The man who had received the five talents brought the other five. 'Master,' he said, 'you entrusted me with five talents. See, I have gained five more.'

[21]"His master replied, 'Well done, good and faithful servant! You have been faithful with a few things; I will put you in charge of many things. Come and share your master's happiness!'

[22]"The man with the two talents also came. 'Master,' he said, 'you entrusted me with two talents; see, I have gained two more.'

[23]"His master replied, 'Well done, good and faithful servant! You have been faithful with a few things; I will put you in charge of many things. Come and share your master's happiness!'

[24]"Then the man who had received the one talent came. 'Master,' he said, 'I knew that you are a hard man, harvesting where you have not sown and gathering where you have not scattered seed. [25]So I was afraid and went out and hid your talent in the ground. See, here is what belongs to you.'

[26]"His master replied, 'You wicked, lazy servant! So you knew that I harvest where I have not sown and gather where I have not scattered seed? [27]Well then, you should have put my money on deposit with the bankers, so that when I returned I would have received it back with interest.

[28]" 'Take the talent from him and give it to the one who has the ten talents. [29]For everyone who has will be given more, and he will have an abundance. Whoever does not have, even what he has will be taken from him. [30]And throw that worthless servant outside, into the darkness, where there will be weeping and gnashing of teeth.'

This parable goes beyond the first three (24:42–25:13) in that it expects the watchfulness of the servants to manifest itself during the master's absence, not only in preparedness and performance of duty, even if there is a long delay, but in an improvement of the allotted "talents" till the day of reckoning.

The parable is frequently compared with Luke 19:11–27, the parable of the ten minas. The majority opinion today is that there is only one original and that most likely Luke has borrowed from Matthew's version or from a precursor of it (cf. Marshall, *Luke*, pp. 700–703; chart and discussion at 19:1–2). Borrowing the other way is scarcely conceivable. Would Matthew, for instance, be likely to eliminate the "king" theme found in Luke? The language of the two pericopes is rather different, and most of the differing details cannot be reconciled on normal grounds. The few parallels are well within the bounds of the speech variation of any itinerant preacher. Moreover the emphasis in each of the two parables is somewhat different, and Luke's is tightly tied to the Zacchaeus episode. The somewhat similar parable in the later noncanonical Gospel of the Nazaraeans (Hennecke, 1:149) is undoubtedly secondary and dependent on Matthew. On the whole it seems best to side with certain older commentators (Plummer, Zahn) who discern two separate parables.

14 The introduction to this parable in the Greek is somewhat abrupt (lit., "for as," without mention of the kingdom, "it" [NIV]; or a verb [NIV, "will be"]: the closest parallel is Mark 13:34). Probably this parable is so tightly associated with the last one as to share its introduction (see on v.1).

Slaves in the ancient world could enjoy considerable responsibility and authority. The man going on a journey entrusts his cash assets to three of his slaves who are understood to be almost partners in his affairs and who may share some of his profits (cf. Derrett, *Laws*, p. 18). The departure and the property are integral parts of the story and should not be allegorized (to refer to the Ascension and the gifts of the Spirit), though doubtless some early readers after Pentecost read these into the text.

15 Modern English uses the word "talent" for skills and mental powers God has entrusted to men; but in NT times the *talanton* ("talent") was a unit of exchange. Estimates of its value vary enormously for four reasons.

1. A talent could be of gold, silver, or copper, each with its own value. *Argyrion* in v.18, a word that can mean either "money" or "silver," may hint at the second option.

2. The talent was first a measure according to weight, between fifty-eight and eighty pounds (twenty-six to thirty-six kg), and then a unit of coinage, one common value assigned it being six thousand denarii.

3. Although it is possible to calculate by weight or metallic value, another problem remains. For instance, eighty pounds of silver at fifteen dollars an ounce would mean that a talent was worth about nineteen thousand dollars. But modern inflation changes silver values so quickly that prices are soon obsolete. Yet such equivalences are passed on from generation to generation of reference texts (e.g., BAG [1957] and BAGD [1979] have the same figures!).

4. It may be more sensible to compare the talent with modern currency in terms of earning power. If a talent was worth six thousand denarii, then it would take a day laborer twenty years to earn so much—perhaps three hundred-thousand dollars. On any reckoning NIV's footnote ("more than a thousand dollars") is much too low.

So the sums are vast—much larger than in Luke 19:11–27, where a "mina" (one hundred drachmas) is very close to one hundred denarii, or one-third of a year's wages (perhaps five thousand dollars). Moreover in Matthew's parable the talents are distributed according to the master's evaluation of his servants' capacities, whereas in Luke each servant is given the same amount. In Matthew, therefore, the parable lays intrinsic emphasis on the principle "to whom much is given, from him also shall much be required."

Attempts to identify the talents with spiritual gifts, the law, natural endowments, the gospel, or whatever else, lead to a narrowing of the parable with which Jesus would have been uncomfortable. Perhaps he chose the talent or mina symbolism because of its capacity for varied application.

16–18 "At once" (v.16) relates to the servant's promptness to put the money to work (NIV), not with the owner's departure (KJV; cf. Metzger, *Textual Commentary*, p. 63). The point is that the good servants felt the responsibility of their assignment and went to work without delay. NIV's "put his money to work" does not mean the servant invested the money in some lending agency. Rather he set up some business and *worked* with the capital to make it grow. But one servant, unwilling to work or take risks, merely dug a hole and buried the money (v.18). This was safer than the deposit systems of the time. (In Luke's parable the money of the last servant is hidden in a piece of cloth.)

19–23 The accounting begins "after a long time" (v.19), the implication being that the consummation of the kingdom will be long delayed (24:48; 25:5). "Settled accounts" (*synairei logon*) is a standard commercial term (Deiss LAE, pp. 118–19). The first servant, who doubled his five talents (v.20), is praised, especially for his faithfulness, and given two things (vv.21, 23): increased responsibility and a share in his master's *chara* ("joy," as in John 15:11). But we should not conclude that the sole reward of fulfilled responsibility is increased responsibility. The eschatological setting, coupled with the promise of joy that bursts the natural limits of the story, guarantees that the consummated kingdom provides glorious new responsibilities and holy delight (cf. Rom 8:17).

The parallelism of vv.22–23 with vv.20–21 is not exact but close (cf. 7:26–27 with 7:24–25) and reflects a Semitic cast. The second servant has been faithful with what has been given him (v.22) and hears the same words as his more able fellow servant (v.23). Probably the "many things" assigned the two men are not exactly the same. The point is not egalitarianism, whether here (cf. 13:23) or in the consummated kingdom, but increased responsibility and a share in the master's joy to the limits of each faithful servant's capacity.

24–25 The third servant accuses his master of being a "hard" (*sklēros*) man (v.24). The word, both in Greek and English, can mean various things (elsewhere in the NT it is found only in John 6:60; Acts 26:14; James 3:4; Jude 15). The servant is saying that the master is grasping, exploiting the labor of others ("harvesting where you have not sown"), and putting the servant in an invidious position. Should he take the risk of trying to increase the one talent entrusted to him, he would see little of the profit. If he failed and lost everything, he would incur the master's wrath. Perhaps, too, he is piqued at having been given much less than the other two (cf. Derrett, *Law*, p. 26); so, in a rather spiteful act, he returns to his master what belongs to him, no more and no less (v.25).

What this servant overlooks is his responsibility to his master and his obligation to discharge his assigned duties. His failure betrays his lack of love for his master, which he masks by blaming his master and excusing himself. Only the wicked servant blames his master. "The foolish virgins failed from thinking their part too easy; the wicked servant fails from thinking his too hard" (Alf). Grace never condones irresponsibility; even those given less are obligated to use and develop what they have.

26–27 The master condemns the servant on the basis of the servant's own words, which prove his guilt (v.26). If the master was so hard and grasping, should not the servant have put the money where it would have been relatively safe, earn interest, and require no work (v.27)?

The OT forbade Israelites from charging interest against one another (Exod 22:25; Lev 25:35–37; Deut 23:19; cf. Ps 15:5; "usury" is from Lat. *usura*, "use," and came to refer to the interest charged for the use of money); but interest on money loaned to Gentiles was permitted (Deut 23:20). Doubtless the law was frequently broken (e.g., Neh 5:10–12). By NT times Jewish scholars already distinguished between "lending at interest" and "usury" (in the modern sense). According to Roman law the maximum rate of interest was 12 percent (cf. W.W. Buckland, *A Textbook of Roman Law*, 3d ed. [Cambridge: University Press, 1963], p. 465). It is wrong to assume that Jesus is here either supporting or setting aside the OT law. The question does not arise, for Jesus' parables are so flexible that he sometimes uses examples of evil to make a point about good (e.g., Luke 16:1–9; 18:1–8).

28–30 The talent entrusted to this wicked servant is taken from him (v.28); the relationship between master and servant is severed (cf. Derrett, *Law*, p. 28). It is given to the man who now has ten talents, following the kingdom rule (v.29) Jesus had already taught in 13:12. Moreover, there is OT warrant for this pattern: on this basis the kingdom of Israel was stripped from Saul and given to David (cf. also 21:43). The wicked servant is "worthless" (*achreios*, used only here [v.30] and in Luke 17:10), for to fail to do good and use what God has entrusted to us to use is grievous sin, which issues not only in the loss of neglected resources but in rejection by the master, banishment from his presence, and tears and gnashing of teeth.

The parable insists that the watchfulness that must mark all Jesus' disciples does not lead to passivity but to doing one's duty, to growing, to husbanding and developing the resources God entrusts to us, till "after a long time" (v.19) the master returns and settles accounts. The parable applies widely and cannot be restricted to Christian leaders or Jews who fail to recognize their Messiah.

e. *The sheep and the goats*

25:31–46

31"When the Son of Man comes in his glory, and all the angels with him, he will
sit on his throne in heavenly glory. 32All the nations will be gathered before him,
and he will separate the people one from another as a shepherd separates the
sheep from the goats. 33He will put the sheep on his right and the goats on his
left.

34"Then the King will say to those on his right, 'Come, you who are blessed by
my Father; take your inheritance, the kingdom prepared for you since the creation
of the world. 35For I was hungry and you gave me something to eat, I was thirsty
and you gave me something to drink, I was a stranger and you invited me in, 36I
needed clothes and you clothed me, I was sick and you looked after me, I was in
prison and you came to visit me.'

37"Then the righteous will answer him, 'Lord, when did we see you hungry and
feed you, or thirsty and give you something to drink? 38When did we see you a
stranger and invite you in, or needing clothes and clothe you? 39When did we see
you sick or in prison and go to visit you?'

40"The King will reply, 'I tell you the truth, whatever you did for one of the least
of these brothers of mine, you did for me.'

41"Then he will say to those on his left, 'Depart from me, you who are cursed,
into the eternal fire prepared for the devil and his angels. 42For I was hungry and
you gave me nothing to eat, I was thirsty and you gave me nothing to drink, 43I
was a stranger and you did not invite me in, I needed clothes and you did not
clothe me, I was sick and in prison and you did not look after me.'

44"They also will answer, 'Lord, when did we see you hungry or thirsty or a
stranger or needing clothes or sick or in prison, and did not help you?'

45"He will reply, 'I tell you the truth, whatever you did not do for one of the least
of these, you did not do for me.'

46"Then they will go away to eternal punishment, but the righteous to eternal
life."

Strictly speaking, this passage is not a parable. Its only parabolic elements are the shepherd, the sheep, the goats, and the actual separation. Moreover, because the pericope is unique to Matthew, criticism based on close parallels is impossible. It clearly functions in this discourse somewhat as 10:40–42 (with which it has some connections) does in the second discourse. Almost everyone praises the simplicity and power of the passage. Alford remarks, "It will heighten our estimation of the wonderful sublimity of this description, when we recollect that it was spoken by the Lord *only three days before His sufferings*" (emphasis his). But there is disagreement over the meaning and literary history of these eloquent words.

1. The great majority of scholars understand "the least of these brothers of mine" (vv.40, 45) to refer to all who are hungry, distressed, needy. The basis of acceptance into the kingdom is thus established by deeds of mercy and compassion. This interpretation is often allied with a misunderstanding of 22:34–40 (see comments there). The overall interpretation can take on varying forms as it relies on source-critical conclusions or particular views of the "Son of Man" (U. Wilckens, "Gottes geringste Brüder—zu Mt 25, 31–46," in Ellis and Grässer, pp. 363–83; David R. Catchpole, "The Poor on Earth and the Son of Man in Heaven: A Re-appraisal of Matthew xxv. 31–46," BJRL 61 [1978–79]: 355–97).

Most authors stress the Jewish parallels relating to compassion and almsgiving. Bornkamm (*Tradition*, pp. 23–24) holds that the parable (as we shall call it) not only eliminates distinction between Jews and Gentiles but also between Jesus' disciples and unbelievers. All will ultimately be judged by their response to human need, and on this basis some from each group will be numbered among the sheep (cf. P. Christian, *Jesus und seine geringsten Brüder* [Leipzig: St. Benno, 1975], who holds this is a sermon for the Christian church concerning the eschatological significance of human solidarity). J. Friedrich's tome (*Gott im Brüder?* [Stuttgart: Calwer, 1977]) includes much useful information about how this pericope has been interpreted, but its basic point—that Matthew narrowed down to Christians Jesus' teaching that the eschatological judgment would decide the fate of all men according to their response to all human need—is unconvincing because it rests on a redaction-critical methodology of dubious worth.

The weakness of this general position is the identification of the least of Jesus' brothers with the poor and needy without distinction. There is no parallel for this, but there are one or two excellent alternative interpretations with strong NT parallels.

2. If the first interpretation extends "one of the least of these brothers of mine" too far, the second does not go far enough. Several scholars (e.g., J.R. Michaels, "Apostolic Hardships and Righteous Gentiles," JBL 84 [1965]: 27–37; J. Mánek, "Mit wem identifiziert sich Jesus (Matt. 25:31–46)?" *Christ and Spirit in the New Testament*, edd. B. Lindars and S.S. Smalley [Cambridge: University Press, 1973], pp. 15–25) argue that Jesus' "least brothers" are apostles and other Christian missionaries, the treatment of whom determines the fate of all men. Those who receive them receive Christ; those who reject them reject Christ (cf. 10:40–42). This interpretation is much closer to the text than the first one. The only hesitation concerns the restriction to apostles and missionaries in any technical sense. Appeal to Matthew 10 cuts two ways: though that mission was first restricted to the Twelve, it is clear that Jesus was looking beyond the Twelve to all true disciples, who without exception must confess him before men (10:32–33). Proclaiming the gospel of the kingdom to all nations (24:14) takes place in obedience to a universal mandate (28:18–20); and the suffering that Jesus envisages for his disciples (24:9–13) is not restricted to missionaries, even if sometimes theirs is a special share of it. Without detracting from the Twelve, Matthew's report of Jesus' words makes it clear that all true disciples are his emissaries.

3. Another restrictive interpretation is that of George Gay ("The Judgment of the Gentiles in Matthew's Theology," *Scripture, Tradition, and Interpretation*, edd.

W.W. Gasque and W.S. LaSor [Grand Rapids: Eerdmans, 1978], pp. 199–215). Relying on Matthew 18, Gay holds that three mutually exclusive groups are involved: those outside the Christian community who think they are part of it, those inside the community but not the "little ones," and the "little ones" within the community. The basis for judgment is the attitude of professing believers to the "little ones," Jesus' favorites. The judgment is therefore not the judgment of the nations ("It would be unfair and illogical to judge the unrepentant who have never made any commitment to Jesus and know nothing of the demands of the Kingdom on the same basis" [ibid., p. 210]).

But Matthew 18 does not support Gay's tripartite distinction, and 12:46–50 makes it clear that Jesus' brothers are his disciples. Moreover the language of vv.31–32, 46, including a reference to "all the nations" gathered before the Son of Man "on his throne in heavenly glory," cannot easily be made to apply to anything as restricted as Gay suggests.

4. Dispensational writers see a reference to the Second Coming, after the church has been removed at the Rapture. Jesus' "brothers" are Jews who have been converted during the Tribulation; and the "nations" are converted Gentiles (the "sheep") because they side with the converted Jews during this period. But unconverted Gentiles (the "goats") continue to oppose Jesus' brothers (Jews converted during the Tribulation). The sheep enter the millennial kingdom with Jesus' "brothers." "All the nations" (v.32) therefore excludes Jews—though it is doubtful whether the same interpretation would be pressed in 28:18–20. Some older writers argue that the judgment determines what nations as opposed to individuals are admitted to the millennial kingdom, but see on 28:18–20. One or two nondispensationalist writers (e.g., Allen) think the "brothers" are Christian Jews.

This interpretation fails unless the dispensational interpretation of chapters 24–25 is sustained, something we have rejected on other grounds (see on 24:1–3). Moreover there is no such pinpointing in the passage itself. Jesus never speaks of Jews as his brothers, though he does speak of his disciples in that way (12:46–50).

5. By far the best interpretation is that Jesus' "brothers" are his disciples (12:48–49; 28:10; cf. 23:8). The fate of the nations will be determined by how they respond to Jesus' followers, who, "missionaries" or not, are charged with spreading the gospel and do so in the face of hunger, thirst, illness, and imprisonment. Good deeds done to Jesus' followers, even the least of them, are not only works of compassion and morality but reflect where people stand in relation to the kingdom and to Jesus himself. Jesus identifies himself with the fate of his followers and makes compassion for them equivalent to compassion for himself (cf. Kistemaker, pp. 146ff.; Manson, *Sayings*, p. 251; J.-C. Ingelaere, "La 'Parabole' du jugement dernier [Matthew 25/31–46]," *Revue de l'histoire et de philosophie religieuses* 50 [1970]: 23–60; G.E. Ladd, "The Parable of the Sheep and the Goats in Recent Interpretation," in Longenecker and Tenney, pp. 191–99; cf. Matt 10:40–42; Mark 13:13; John 15:5, 18, 20; 17:10, 23, 26; Acts 9:4; 22:7; 26:14; 1 Cor 12:27; Heb 2:17).

To the objection that this interpretation does not preserve an adequate distinction between the "sheep" and "the least of these brothers of mine," the answer is that (1) a similar ambiguity occurs in Matthew 18; (2) this interpretation emphasizes the kind of loving relationships that must exist within the Christian community, a constant theme in the NT; and (3) it prepares the way for the surprise shown by both sheep and goats (vv.37–39, 44) and for some important theological implications (see below).

31 Nowhere in this discourse does Jesus explicitly identify the "Son of Man" (see on 8:20) with himself (24:27, 30, 37, 39, 44). But since this epithet is used in answer to the question "What will be the sign of your coming?" (24:3), the inference is inescapable. There are clear allusions to Zechariah 14:5 (cf. also Dan 7; Joel 3:1–12); but the role of eschatological Judge is, like many other things (see on 13:37–39), transferred without hesitation from Yahweh to Jesus. The Son of Man will come "in his heavenly glory" (cf. 16:27; 24:30; 1 Thess 4:16; 2 Thess 1:8) for "nothing earthly could furnish the images for an adequate description" (Broadus). He sits on his throne, not only as Judge, but as King (see v.34); for all of divine authority is mediated through him (28:18; cf. 1 Cor 15:25; Heb 12:2). (On the role of the angels, see 13:41–42; 24:31; 2 Thess 1:7–8; Rev 14:17–20.)

32–33 Presupposed is the fulfillment of 24:14. "All the nations" (*panta ta ethnē*, v.32) means "all peoples" and clearly implies that "all the nations" includes more than Gentiles only (see on 28:18–20). As the gospel of the kingdom is preached to Gentiles as well as Jews (see on 1:1; 2:1–12; 3:15–16; 8:11), so also must all stand before the King.

In the countryside sheep and goats mingled during the day. At night they were often separated: sheep tolerate the cool air, but goats have to be herded together for warmth. In sparse grazing areas the animals might be separated during the day as well. But now these well-known, simple, pastoral details are freighted with symbolism. The right hand is the place of power and honor.

34–40 The change from "Son of Man" (see excursus on 8:20) to "King" (vv.31, 34) is not at all unnatural; for the Son of Man in Daniel 7:13–14 approaches the Ancient of Days to receive "a kingdom," and here that kingdom is consummated (see on 24:30). The kingship motif has long since been hinted at or, on occasion, made fairly explicit to certain persons (see on 3:2; 4:17; 5:35; 16:28; 19:28; 27:42). Yet Jesus still associates his work with his Father, something he loves to do (10:32–33; 11:25–27; 15:13; 16:17, 27; 18:10, 19; 20:23; 26:29, 53; and many references in John). He addresses the sheep, "Come, you who are blessed *by my Father*" (v.34). "Blessed" is not *makarioi* (as in 5:3) but *eulogēmenoi* (as in 21:9; 23:39). They are "blessed" inasmuch as they now take their inheritance (Rom 8:17; Rev 21:7), which presupposes a relationship with the Father. That inheritance is the kingdom (see on 3:2) prepared for them "since the creation of the world" (John 17:24; Eph 1:4; 1 Peter 1:20). This glorious inheritance, the consummated kingdom, was the Father's plan for them from the beginning.

The reason they are welcomed and invited to take their inheritance is that they have served the King's brothers (cf. Isa 58:7). The thought is antithetical to Paul only if we think this is all Matthew says and that all Paul says touches immediately on grace. Both assumptions are false: 2 Corinthians 5:10 is related to the thought of this parable, and Matthew has other things to say about the salvation of men and women (1:21; 11:25–30; 20:28). The reason for admission to the kingdom in this parable is more evidential than causative. This is suggested by the surprise of the righteous (vv.37–39; see further below). When he is questioned, the King replies that doing the deeds mentioned to the least of his brothers is equivalent to doing it to him (v.40), and by implication to refuse help to the King's brothers is sacrilege (Calvin).

There is no awkwardness in the scene that requires a disjunction between the sheep (the righteous) and "the least of these brothers of mine"; for in pronouncing sentence on each one, the King could point out surrounding brothers who had been compassionately treated.

41–45 The condemnation is even more awful than in 7:23. The "goats" are cursed: they are banished from the King's presence and sent to the eternal fire (v.41). Hell is here described in categories familiar to Jews (see on 3:12; 5:22; 18:8; cf. Jude 7; Rev 20:10–15). The kingdom was prepared for the righteous (v.34). Hell was prepared for the Devil (see on 4:1) and his angels (demons; see on 8:31; cf. Jude 6; Rev 12:7) but now also serves as the doom of those guilty of the sins of omission of which Jesus here speaks: they have refused to show compassion to King Messiah through helping the least of his brothers. There is no significance in the fact that the "goats" address Jesus as "Lord" (v.44); for at this point there is no exception whatever to confessing Jesus as Lord (cf. Phil 2:11).

More important is the surprise of the sheep (vv.37–39) and the goats (v.44), a major part of the parable, though rarely discussed. Three things can be said with confidence.

1. Contrary to what some have suggested (e.g., Gay, "Judgment of Gentiles") neither the sheep nor the goats are surprised at the place the King assigns them but at the reason he gives for this—viz., that they are admitted or excluded on the basis of how they treated Jesus. Thus there is no need to say the goats expected to be welcomed or the sheep expected to be rejected.

2. Zumstein (p. 348) is right to point out that the surprise of the righteous makes it impossible to think that works of righteousness win salvation. How the sheep and the goats treated Jesus' brothers was not for the purpose of being accepted or rejected by the King. The sheep did not show love to gain an eschatological reward, nor did the goats fail to show it to flout eschatological retribution.

3. The parable therefore presents a test eliminating the possibility of hypocrisy. If the goats had thought that their treatment of Jesus' "brothers" would gain them eschatological felicity, they would doubtless have treated them compassionately. But Jesus is interested in a righteousness of the whole person, a righteousness from the heart (see on 5:20; 13:52). As people respond to his disciples, or "brothers," and align themselves with their distress and afflictions, they align themselves with the Messiah who identifies himself with them (v.45). True disciples will love one another and serve the least brother with compassion; in so doing they unconsciously serve Christ. Those who have little sympathy for the gospel of the kingdom will remain indifferent and, in so doing, reject King Messiah. So Paul learned at his conversion! Determined to persecute Christians, he heard the Voice from the heavenly glory declaring, "I am Jesus, whom you are persecuting" (Acts 9:5).

We must not think that the Bible is unconcerned for the poor and the oppressed (Deut 15:11; Matt 22:37–40; 26:11; Gal 2:10). But that is not the center of interest here.

46 The same word "eternal" (*aiōnion*) modifies "punishment" as modifies "life." *Aiōnion* can refer to life or punishment in the age to come, or it can be limited to the duration of the thing to which it refers (as in 21:19). But in apocalyptic and eschatological contexts, the word not only connotes "pertaining to the [messianic] age" but, because that age is always lived in God's presence, also "everlasting" (cf. BAGD, s.v.; and esp. DNTT, 3:826–33). (On penal notions in NT theology, cf. J.I.

Packer, "What Did the Cross Achieve? The Logic of Penal Substitution," *Tyndale Bulletin* 25 [1974]: 3–45.)

The final separation of "sheep" and "goats" is a recurring theme in the NT, including Matthew (e.g., 7:21–23; 13:40–43). Some have argued that this doctrine has turned many people into infidels; but so have other Christian doctrines. The question is not how men respond to a doctrine but what Jesus and the NT writers actually teach about it. Human response is a secondary consideration and may reveal as much about us as about the doctrine being rejected. Nevertheless two things should be kept in mind: (1) as there are degrees of felicity and responsibility in the consummated kingdom (e.g., 25:14–30; cf. 1 Cor 3:10–15), so also are there degrees of punishment (e.g., Matt 11:22; Luke 12:47–48); and (2) there is no shred of evidence in the NT that hell ever brings about genuine repentance. Sin continues as part of the punishment and the ground for it.

7. *Transitional conclusion: fourth major passion prediction and the plot against Jesus*

26:1–5

[1]When Jesus had finished saying all these things, he said to his disciples, [2]"As you know, the Passover is two days away—and the Son of Man will be handed over to be crucified."

[3]Then the chief priests and the elders of the people assembled in the palace of the high priest, whose name was Caiaphas, [4]and they plotted to arrest Jesus in some way and kill him. [5]"But not during the Feast," they said, "or there may be a riot among the people."

1–2 For the other major passion predictions, see on 16:21; 17:22–23; 20:18–19. One last time Matthew uses the formula by which he brings all his discourses to a close (v.1; see on 7:28–29). In the narrative line of Matthew, this pericope is a masterpiece of irony. The Judge of the universe, King Messiah, the glorious Son of Man, is about to be judged. After Jesus' warnings against hypocrisy (23:12–31) and his demand for righteousness that involves the whole person (25:31–46), the plot moves on by stealth and by a morally bankrupt expediency (26:4–5). The Passion begins.

The Passover began Thursday afternoon with the slaughter of the lamb. "Two days" (v.2) must be somewhat under forty-eight hours, or the "two days" would be "three days" (see on 12:40). According to the tentative chronology (see on 21:23–22:46; 23:1–36; 24:1–3), Jesus speaks these words on the Mount of Olives late Tuesday evening, which, by Jewish reckoning, would be the beginning of Wednesday.

The "Son of Man" (see on 8:20) is here both glorious and suffering: as often, the themes merge. The Passover is two days away; and it is during that festival, Jesus now reveals for the first time, that the Son of Man will be handed over (for reasons to take the Greek present as a future, cf. Moule, *Idiom Book*, p. 7) to be crucified. Thus Jesus provides a framework for his disciples to interpret his death correctly after it happens—a framework alluded to a little more clearly in the institution of the Lord's Supper (vv.17–29).

3–5 *Tote* ("then," v.3) is such a loose connective (see on 2:7) that it does not mean that the Jewish leaders only began to plot after Jesus had delivered his final passion prediction (vv.1–2). Certainly the opposition had been rising for some time (cf. 12:14; 21:45–46). On the other hand, by placing vv.3–5 immediately after vv.1–2,

Matthew gives the narrative the flavor of God's sovereign control. The leaders may plot; but if Jesus dies, he dies as a voluntary Passover sacrifice (vv.53–54; John 10:18).

Matthew mentions the chief priests and elders, probably meaning the clerical and lay members of the Sanhedrin (see on 21:23). The word *aulē* can mean "courtyard," "farm" or "farmyard," "temple court," or the "prince's court," hence, "palace" (NIV). Caiaphas is called the high priest in Matthew and John (11:49); Luke (3:2; Acts 4:6) specifies Annas. There is no real conflict. Annas was deposed by the secular authorities in A.D. 15 and replaced by Caiaphas, who lived and ruled till his death in A.D. 36. But since according to the OT the high priest was not to be replaced till after his death, the transfer of power was illegal. Doubtless some continued to call either man "high priest." Certainly Annas, Caiaphas's father-in-law (John 18:13), continued to exercise great authority behind the scenes. This joint high priesthood is presupposed by Luke 3:2 and probably by John 18, where the most natural reading of the passage names Caiaphas as high priest in v.13 but Annas as high priest in v.19 (cf. v.24).

The combination of *synagō* ("assembled") and *bouleuomai* ("plotted") in vv.3–4 strongly suggests an allusion to Psalm 31:13. Psalm 31 is the lament of a righteous sufferer and the source of Jesus' word from the cross in Luke 23:46 (cf. Moo, "Use of OT," pp. 234–35). Earlier that day the leaders had wanted to arrest Jesus but dared not do so for fear of the people (21:46; apparently earlier attempts had also failed, John 7:32, 45–52). Now they decide to do away with Jesus (v.4), recognizing that they must do this by *dolos* ("stealth," "cunning," "guile") so as not to excite the crowds and start a riot (v.5).

The leaders were right in fearing the people. Jerusalem's population swelled perhaps fivefold during the feast; and with religious fervor and national messianism at a high pitch, a spark might set off an explosion. They decided to suspend action; but Judas's offer to hand Jesus over at a time and place when the crowds were not present was too good an opportunity to pass up (vv.14–16). Thus in God's providence the connection between Passover and Jesus' death that he had just predicted (vv.1–2) came about.

VII. The Passion and Resurrection of Jesus (26:6–28:20)

A. *The Passion* (26:6–27:66)

1. *Anointed at Bethany*

26:6–13

6While Jesus was in Bethany in the home of a man known as Simon the Leper,
7a woman came to him with an alabaster jar of very expensive perfume, which
she poured on his head as he was reclining at the table.
8When the disciples saw this, they were indignant. "Why this waste?" they
asked. 9"This perfume could have been sold at a high price and the money given
to the poor."
10Aware of this, Jesus said to them, "Why are you bothering this woman? She
has done a beautiful thing to me. 11The poor you will always have with you, but
you will not always have me. 12When she poured this perfume on my body, she
did it to prepare me for burial. 13I tell you the truth, wherever this gospel is
preached throughout the world, what she has done will also be told, in memory of
her."

Because of the structure the five discourses impose on Matthew, some scholars (Bacon, *Studies in Matthew;* Stendahl, *School,* pp. 20ff.) have thought that the passion and resurrection narratives (26:6–28:20) stand outside the main framework, perhaps as a kind of epilogue to balance the "prologue" (Matt 1–2). But I have argued (see Introduction, section 14; and on 28:18–20) that the familiar pattern of narrative elements followed by discourse teaching continues here in a *sixth* section. In this case, however, the "teaching" part of the narrative-and-teaching structure is continued by the church after Jesus' ascension (28:18–20). From another viewpoint the Passion and Resurrection must, as in all the Gospels, be seen as the climax toward which a great deal of the earlier narrative has been moving.

As often noted, Matthew from now on follows Mark quite closely, though he omits Mark 14:51–52; 15:21b, adds certain bits (e.g., 27:3–10, 51–53), provides a completely independent ending, and offers a number of minor changes (e.g., some third-person reports in Mark are now given in direct speech). Many attempts have been made to identify what is exclusively Matthean in the passion narrative; but not a few such attempts suffer from reductionism. For instance, Dahl (*Jesus in Memory,* pp. 37–51) holds that Matthew's account is designed to highlight differences between church and synagogue. The former has accepted Jesus as Messiah; the latter has rejected and condemned him (cf. also Trilling, pp. 66–74). Others think Jesus' passion in Matthew has an ethical cast, designed to help young disciples learn obedience (e.g., Strecker, *Weg,* pp. 183–84). Many others see various christological elements in Matthew's account. Barth (Bornkamm, *Tradition*) claims that by his suffering and death, Jesus fulfills God's redemptive plan and establishes the kingdom; and Kingsbury (*Matthew*) stresses the confession of Jesus as "Son of God." (For an excellent survey, cf. D. Senior, "The Passion Narrative in the Gospel of Matthew," in Didier, pp. 343–57; A. Descamps, in Didier, pp. 359–415.)

Virtually every theme thought to be particularly strong in Matthew can be shown to be present in one or more of the other Gospels. For instance, that the events are all under God's control or that Jesus dies voluntarily is even more strongly attested in John than in Matthew. This is not to deny that Matthew has his own contribution to make. Instead it is to say that what Matthew offers is a great deal of commonly held theology, presented with a rich allusiveness and a complex intertwining of themes, subtly blended to lay stress on one part or another of the narrative, and capped with a few additions unknown in any other source. Thus it is best to examine Matthew's material inductively and trace its unfolding.

The first pericope (vv.6–13) is problematic because of its disputed relation to other Gospel accounts (Mark 14:3–9; John 12:2–8; cf. Luke 7:36–50). Some ancient commentators (e.g., Origen) thought there were three anointings: first, Luke 7:36–50, in Galilee; second, John 12:2–8, a few days earlier than the third, Mark 14:3–9 and Matthew 26:6–13. Most modern scholars believe that there was only one anointing and that variations in details arose during oral transmission and because of the hortatory use by each evangelist (see esp. R. Holst, "The One Anointing of Jesus: Another Application of the Form-Critical Method," JBL 95 [1976]: 435–46); but there is no consensus among these scholars as to the original setting or purpose of the story.

On the whole a third alternative seems preferable: there were two anointings, one in Galilee (recorded by Luke) and the other in Bethany (recorded by Matthew, Mark, and John; so Broadus; McNeile; A. Legault, "An Application of the Form-Critique Method to the Anointings in Galilee and Bethany," CBQ 16 [1954]: 131–

45). The only real similarities between the two incidents are the anointing by a woman and the name Simon. But "Simon," like "Judas," was a very common name; and the two incidents differ in many details. In Luke the woman is a "sinner"; in the other account there is no mention of this, and John says she is Mary of Bethany. In Luke the host is a Pharisee, in a Galilean home; here the host is "Simon the leper," at a home in Bethany. In Luke the host is critical of the woman's actions; here the disciples criticize her.

Small differences among Matthew, Mark, and John are fairly easily reconciled. John may place the incident where he does because he has just spoken of Bethany and will mention that town no more; but his links with the historical setting seem fairly strong and the most natural interpretation of his account is that the anointing took place before the Triumphal Entry (John 12:2, 12). Mark and Matthew, on the other hand, provide no chronological connection, only a thematic one. Out of Jesus' rebuke to the disciples, Judas Iscariot sets his course of betrayal (cf. John 12:4–6). To object to this two-incident theory on the grounds that the methodology and many of the presuppositions "are out of date due to the scholarly advances in the disciplines of form and redaction criticism. . . .[so that there is] no trajectory or *tendency* to explain the complexities of the final editions of the stories" (Holst, "The One Anointing," p. 435, emphasis his) is to make these tools intrinsically incapable of recognizing two superficially similar incidents.

6–7 For Bethany (v.6), see on 21:17. Contrary to common opinion, John does not say this took place at the home of Lazarus, Mary, and Martha; he may only mean that the well-known family was present. That Martha served is quite in keeping with village life at the time. Mark and Matthew set the scene in the home of "Simon the Leper," who was presumably cured—or else all there were violating Mosaic law. The action of the woman was not unprecedented: a distinguished rabbi might have been so honored. The evangelists stress the cost of the "perfume" (v.7, most likely a fairly viscous fluid, possibly from the nard plant native to India), which was extracted from the thin-necked alabaster flask by snapping off the neck. According to John 12:3, the nard was worth about three hundred denarii—approximately a year's salary for a working man.

8–9 Matthew mentions "the disciples" (v.8), Mark "some of those present," and John "Judas Iscariot." If the three accounts represent the same incident, it could be that, just as Peter voiced the sentiments of the group (v.35) and was answered directly by Jesus, so with Judas. Matthew shows the disciples' failure to understand what is taking place, not only in the anointing, but also in who Jesus truly is and in the rush of events toward the Cross (see on 16:21–28; 17:22–23; 20:18–19). Doubtless there were thousands of really poor people within a few miles of this anointing. Whatever Judas's motives (John 12:6), some people at least were motivated by righteous indignation (v.9); and thus in Jesus' view they revealed their distorted values and blindness as to the unique redemptive event about to take place.

10–11 The Greek *gnous de* ("aware of this") is also behind 16:8 ("Aware of their discussion"). It is possible that Jesus' knowledge is here supernatural; but perhaps the complaints were whispered and came to Jesus' attention because they troubled the woman. Jesus begins his rebuke by accusing the disciples of "bothering" her (v.10; the Greek idiom, found in the NT only here and in Luke 11:7; Gal 6:17, is a strong one). What they call waste, Jesus calls "a beautiful thing."

Hill's claim (*Matthew*) that Jesus' further statement (v.11) "distinguishes between a good work (i.e., almsgiving) and one done with reference to himself while he is present (with his disciples, and also as the 'living Christ' in the Matthean church)" entirely misses the point. Jesus distinguishes between giving to the poor and the extravagance lavished on himself *on the grounds that he will not always be there to receive it*. Far from referring to Jesus' spiritual presence in the church, Matthew *distinguishes* between Jesus' earthly presence and his postascension spiritual presence (28:20). His followers will always find poor people to help (cf. Deut 15:11); they will not always have the incarnate Jesus with them. Implicitly, the distinction Jesus makes is a high christological claim, for it not only shows that he foresees his impending departure but also that he himself, who is truly "gentle and humble in heart" (11:29), *deserves* this lavish outpouring of love and expense.

Lane (*Mark* pp. 493–94) follows F.W. Danker, ("The Literary Unity of Mark 14, 1–25," JBL 85 [1966]: 467–72) in suggesting that Psalm 41 may also be alluded to here—a psalm that speaks of the poor yet righteous sufferer who is betrayed by his closest friend, yet vindicated by God in the end. Jesus is the poor, righteous Sufferer par excellence; and the opportunity to help him in any way will soon be gone forever.

12 The anointing does not designate Jesus as Messiah but "prepares" him for his burial after dying the death of a criminal, for only in that circumstance would the customary anointing of the body be omitted (cf. D. Daube, "The Anointing at Bethany and Jesus' Burial," *AThR* 32 [1950]: 187–88). Jesus' defense of the woman does not necessarily mean that the woman understood what she was doing, though it allows this. Jesus may well be using the anointing to intimate again his impending crucifixion (cf. v.2).

13 Interpretations of this verse, with its solemn promise, differ. Jeremias (*Prayers*, pp. 112–24; *Promise*, p. 22) takes the saying as authentic but says that *hopou* here means not "wherever" (NIV) but "when"—i.e., when the triumphal news of this gospel is proclaimed by God's angel (cf. Rev 14:6–11) at the Parousia, before all the world, then her act will be remembered. Jeremias thus avoids any prediction by Jesus of a worldwide mission. But this uses "gospel" strangely and is too tightly linked with assumptions about what Jesus could or could not have said. Jesus did foresee Gentiles entering the kingdom (8:11), in response to his disciples' preaching, and that the word of God would be preached in the world (13:37; 24:14). Thus the groundwork has already been laid for this saying and also for the Great Commission (28:18–20).

The most natural interpretation of v.13 is that the woman and her deed would be remembered "wherever" the "gospel of the kingdom" would be preached (cf. Moore, pp. 203f.). Broadus remarks: "This very remarkable promise . . . was already in process of fulfillment when John wrote his Gospel, probably sixty years afterwards; for he distinguishes this Bethany from the one beyond Jordan (John 1:28) by calling it (John 11:1f.) the village of Mary (placed first) and Martha; and then makes all definite and clear by adding, 'It was that Mary who anointed the Lord with ointment', etc. He has not yet in his Gospel told the story of the anointing, but he assumes that it is familiar to all Christian readers."

2. *Judas's betrayal agreement*

26:14–16

[14]Then one of the Twelve—the one called Judas Iscariot—went to the chief priests [15]and asked, "What are you willing to give me if I hand him over to you?" So they counted out for him thirty silver coins. [16]From then on Judas watched for an opportunity to hand him over.

All the Gospels speak of Judas's important role in Jesus' death (cf. Mark 14:10–11; Luke 22:3–6); but none explains what motives prompted his treachery. Like most human motives, his were mixed and doubtless included avarice and jealousy combined with profound disappointment that Jesus was not acting like the Messiah he had expected.

14–16 While *tote* ("then") is generally difficult to translate (see on 2:7), here (v.14) there is probably a logical connection with the preceding pericope. In Judas's view Jesus was acting less and less regal and more and more like a defeatist on his way to death. If Matthew's anointing (vv.6–13) is the same as the one in John 12:1–8, Judas may also have been smarting from Jesus' rebuke. Moreover, *if* his name ties him in with the Zealot movement (see on 10:4), then his disappointment is the more understandable, though not more excusable. He approaches the "chief priests" (see on 21:23). (One may ask in passing why Matthew makes no mention of the Pharisees if his antipathy toward them is as strong as some say.)

The chief priests "counted out for him thirty silver coins" (v.15); but Matthew's language (lit., "they weighed out to him"), unlike Mark's, is the distinctive language of the LXX and calls to mind Zechariah 11:12, to which Matthew will return in 27:3–10 (Moo, "Use of OT," pp. 187–89). In Zechariah 11, thirty pieces of silver is a paltry amount ("the handsome price at which they priced me" [v.13] is ironic)—the value of a slave accidentally gored to death by an ox (Exod 21:32). That Jesus is lightly esteemed is reflected not only in his betrayal but in the low sum agreed on by Judas and the chief priests.

Excursus

The traditional date of Jesus' death has been A.D. 30. But Hoehner (*Chronological Aspects*, pp. 65–93) has made a plausible case for A.D. 33, though the exact year has little effect on the exegesis. More important is the problem of the relationship between the synoptic Gospels and John. The Synoptics seem to indicate that Jesus and his disciples ate the Passover meal the evening before the Crucifixion (see esp. Mark 14:12–16; 15:1–25, and parallels), whereas John seems to suggest that the Passover lamb was slaughtered at the moment Jesus was being put to death, which would of course mean that he and his disciples did not eat the Passover at the Last Supper (cf. esp. John 18:28; 19:14).

The question is of more than chronological interest; for quite apart from harmonization of disparate historical records, the meaning of the Lord's Supper is affected by its connection with Passover. The literature about this question is immense. The aim of this excursus is to list some of the principal options and defend briefly the interpretation adopted here. Essential bibliography includes Hoehner, *Chronological Aspects*, pp. 81–90; Jeremias, *Eucharistic Words*, pp. 41ff.; SBK, 2:847–52; A. Jaubert, *The Date of the Last Supper* (Staten Island,

N.J.: Alba, 1965); E. Ruckstuhl, *Chronology of the Last Days of Jesus* (New York: Desclée, 1965); G. Ogg, "The Chronology of the Last Supper," *Historicity and Chronology in the New Testament*, ed. D.E. Nineham (London: SPCK, 1965), pp. 75–96; J.B. Segal, *The Hebrew Passover from the Earliest Times to A.D. 70* (London: OUP, 1963); S. Dockx, *Chronologies néotestamentaires et Vie de l'Eglise primitive* (Paris/Gembloux: Duculot, 1976), *passim;* Marshall, *Last Supper*, esp. pp. 57ff., and Table 4 (pp. 184–85); Moo, "Use of OT," pp. 318–23; and the major commentaries on the Gospels.

1. Many scholars maintain that the discrepancies are not historically reconcilable—that either the Synoptics are right or John is. There are many indications that the synoptists understand the Last Supper to be a Passover meal (see esp. Jeremias, *Eucharistic Words*, pp. 41–62; Marshall, *Last Supper*, pp. 59–62). Therefore attempts to turn the meal into something else—a *Kiddush* (prayer meal), though this was unknown till several centuries later, or an *Habburah* (fellowship meal) eaten just before Passover—are not convincing. That the meal was not Passover supper but that such elements were read back into it is a counsel of despair, especially in light of the Passover associations as early as 1 Corinthians 11.

Any theory of this kind depends on its explanation of why the discrepancy was introduced. If the Synoptics are historically correct (Jeremias), perhaps John changed the date to correspond with his Jesus–Passover-lamb typology; if John is historically correct (Ogg), perhaps the synoptists changed the date to make the Last Supper fit the Passover symbolism. Either way it is necessary to trace a theological development; but to date no such work has proved convincing. To argue that John has identified Jesus with the Passover lamb by so flimsy a device as changing two or three chronological references is not very credible in a book abounding with explanatory statements (1:42; 2:21–22; 12:38; 13:18 et al.). In fact, only the Synoptics mention the day the lambs were sacrificed (Mark 14:12; Luke 22:7). Finding theological motivation for a putative change in the Synoptics is even more problematic, because of the highly disputed question of which evangelist preserves the oldest form of the institution of the Lord's Supper (cf. Marshall, *Last Supper*, pp. 30ff.).

2. The second group of options brings together various theories of calendrical disputes in the first century. Jaubert argues that Jesus, as reported by the synoptists, was using a solar calendar known to us from Jubilees and apparently adopted at Qumran. Passover always occurred on *Tuesday* evening (14–15 Nisan); so Jesus and his men ate their Passover that night. But the "official" Pharisaic lunar calendar, followed by the fourth Gospel, places the Cross and the Sacrifice on the *lunar* 14–15 Nisan (Thursday–Friday, from nightfall to nightfall). In a somewhat different scheme some have argued that the Pharisees and Sadducees adopted different calendars (SBK), or that Jesus followed a Galilean (i.e., the Pharisees') calendar (Synoptics) and John reports on the basis of the Judean (Sadducees') equivalent (so Hoehner).

At least all these theories based on diverse calendars join in affirming that Jesus and his disciples ate a Passover meal, whatever the date. But beyond that all these calendrical solutions have severe drawbacks. Part of Jaubert's view, for instance, turns on a third-century document (the *Didascalia*) concerned with justifying current fasting practices by appeal to Passion Week, rather than giving any useful historical information about that week. There is no evidence that Jesus followed a sectarian calendar; and quite certainly sacrifices were not offered in the temple on any day other than the "official" (lunar calendar) day. Moreover all four evangelists seem to agree that Jesus was arrested the evening before his crucifixion; and, despite objections, there was enough time between his arrest

Thursday night and his crucifixion Friday to allow for the various events discussed below. Some of the other theories are highly suspect because of poor attestation in primary sources and are little more than last resorts.

3. The third approach is to attempt historical harmonization between John and the Synoptics as they stand. Of these attempts, one, pursued at various times in church history, is reasonably successful.

Matthew 26:17 speaks of "the first day of the Feast of Unleavened Bread." According to Leviticus 23:6 and Numbers 28:17, Jews were forbidden to use yeast in their bread for seven days from 15 Nisan. However, Exodus 12:18 says that yeast should be removed from the house on 14 Nisan; and there is some evidence that Jews customarily removed it at noon on 14 Nisan so as to have everything ready in good time. Thus Josephus can in one place speak of the beginning of the feast as occurring on 15 Nisan (Antiq. III, 248–50 [x.5]) and in another as occurring on 14 Nisan (War V, 99 [iii.1]; cf. also Antiq. II, 315–16 [xv.1]). Matthew seems to presuppose Thursday, 14 Nisan. According to Exodus 12:6 and Numbers 9:3, the Jews were directed to kill the paschal lamb "at twilight" (NIV), i.e., "between the two evenings," which in Jesus' day meant middle to late afternoon till sundown (Deut 16:6). Hence Josephus (War VI, 423 [ix.3]) says the lambs were killed from the ninth to the eleventh hour (3:00 P.M. to 5:00 P.M.) and that on one occasion the number killed was 256,500—almost certainly an inflated figure.

It seems, then, that Jesus' disciples entered the city shortly after noon on Thursday, 14 Nisan, procured the room, took a lamb to the temple court and killed it, roasted it with bitter herbs (Exod 12:8–9), and made other arrangements for the meal, including the purchase of wine and unleavened bread. Matthew 26:19 explicitly says that they "prepared the Passover." After nightfall on Thursday evening, when it was 15 Nisan, Jesus joined his disciples and they ate the Passover. On these points the Synoptics agree; and this places Jesus' death on Friday, 15 Nisan, probably about 3:00 P.M.

The following passages in John are the most difficult to harmonize with this scheme.

John 13:1 "It was just before the Passover Feast" need not set the stage for the meal, which was about to be eaten, but for the footwashing. The footwashing took place before the "Passover Feast." John 13:2 in the best texts does not contradict this: we should not read "supper being ended" (KJV) but the "meal was being served" (NIV).

John 13:27 "What you are about to do, do quickly." John adds (13:29) that some of those present thought Jesus was telling Judas to buy what was necessary for the feast, or else give something to the poor. How could they think this, if they were just then *finishing* the feast? But one may also ask why, if the feast was still twenty-four hours away, anyone would think that there would be any rush to buy things. It is more reasonable to think that the disciples thought Judas needed to make some purchases for the *continuing* "Feast of Unleavened Bread"—e.g., some more unleavened bread. Since the next day, still Friday, 15 Nisan, was a high feast day and the day after a Sabbath, it was best to do things immediately. By Jewish reckoning the high feast day (15 Nisan) had begun that Thursday evening; but purchases were more than likely still possible, though inconvenient. After all one could buy necessities even on a Sabbath if it fell before a Passover, provided it was done by leaving something in trust rather than paying cash (M *Sanhedrin* 23:1). Moreover it was customary to give alms to the poor on Passover night. The temple gates were left open from midnight on, and beggars congregated there (cf. Jeremias, *Eucharistic Words*, p. 54; Ruckstuhl, *Last Days*, p. 132). On any other night it is difficult to imagine why the disciples would think Judas was being sent out for this purpose; the next day would have done as well.

John 18:28 Jesus stands before Pilate. "By now it was early morning, and to avoid ceremonial uncleanness the Jews did not enter the palace; they wanted to be able to eat the Passover." The precise nature of this "ceremonial uncleanness" is highly disputed. Certainly Jews had to purify themselves for Passover (cf. 2 Chron 30:18; Ezra 6:19–21; cf. John 11:55; 12:1), and Pilate respected the Jews' scruples (John 18:28–29). Contamination might come from the road dust brought in by foreign visitors (cf. M *Berakoth* 9:5), or from contact with Gentiles who had eaten or touched something unclean (e.g., a corpse or a menstruous woman). While there are numerous other possibilities, uncleanness from any of these sources could have been eliminated at the end of one day by a purifying wash at sundown (cf. Lev 15:5–11, 16–18; 22:5–7; cf. j *Peshahim* 36b, 92b); and then the Passover could be eaten. Thus close attention to John's text and the historical background makes it unlikely that John 18:28 can be used to defend the view that Jesus ate a meal the evening before Passover night. Instead, John 18:28 is more plausibly interpreted in one of two other ways.

1. It is possible that the priests had intended to eat the Passover that night; but, pressed by their temple duties and the thousands of sacrifices they had to perform, interrupted by Judas's unexpected offer of instant betrayal and delayed by the headlong pace of the ensuing judicial examinations, they still had not yet eaten their own Passover. This view is unlikely if Exodus 12:8–10, forbidding delay of the Passover dinner beyond midnight (M *Peshahim* 10:9; M *Zebahim* 5:8), was strictly interpreted. But these traditions may be late; and *Mekilta* on Exodus says that some rabbis interpreted Exodus 12:8–10 as being satisfied if the Passover were eaten by dawn. Even so, these Jewish leaders were being caught out by at least two or three hours.

2. More plausibly, "to eat the Passover" in John 18:28 may refer, not to the Passover meal itself, but to the continuing feast, and in particular to the *chagigah,* the feast-offering offered on the morning of the first full paschal day (cf. Num 28:18–19). This could explain the Jews' concern: ritual purification could be regained by nightfall, but not by the morning *chagigah*. Of course the *chagigah* could be eaten later in the week; but it is unlikely that the leaders, conscious of their public status, would be eager to delay it unless absolutely unavoidable. Deuteronomy 16:3 speaks of eating the Passover food of unleavened bread seven days. It may be, then, that the leaders wanted to avoid ritual uncleanness in order to continue full participation in the entire feast. Moreover this becomes the more plausible if our treatment of John 19:31 is correct. Morris's objection (*John,* pp. 778–79) that one may concede that "the Passover" can refer to Passover plus the Feast of Unleavened Bread but certainly not to the Feast of Unleavened Bread without the Passover meal may be setting up a straw man; for the interpretation being defended here does not claim that "the Passover" here refers to the Feast of Unleavened Bread *apart from* the Passover meal itself but to *the entire Passover festival*. Ritual uncleanness at this point in the festival would force temporary withdrawal from the festivities, from "eating the Passover."

John 19:14 Referring to the day of Jesus' crucifixion, the verse reads, "It was *paraskeuē tou pascha*" (lit., "the Preparation of the Passover"). There is strong evidence to suggest that *paraskeuē* ("Preparation [Day]") had already become a technical name for Friday, since Friday was normally the day on which one prepared for the Sabbath (Saturday); and we have no evidence that the term was used in the evangelist's time to refer to the eve of any festal day other than the Sabbath (cf. C.C. Torrey, "The Date of the Crucifixion according to the Fourth Gospel," JBL 50 [1931]: 241). In this context, then, *tou pascha* means "of Passover Week" or "of the Passover festival." Several diverse strands of evidence support this meaning of *pascha*. Josephus (Antiq. XIV, 21 [ii.1]; cf. XVII, 213

[ix.3]; War II, 10 [i.3]) uses "Passover" to refer to the entire Feast of Unleavened Bread, unless he is directly dependent on an OT passage, when he tends to keep the two distinct (Antiq. III, 248–51 [x.5]; cf. BAGD, s.v.). The same extended usage is found not only in M *Peshahim* 9:5 but in the NT (cf. Luke 22:1: "the Feast of Unleavened Bread, called the Passover," and probably also such passages as John 2:23; 6:4; 13:1; 19:31, 42). Thus John 19:14 most probably means "Friday in Passover Week" (hence NIV, "the day of Preparation of Passover Week"); and this understanding of *pascha* reinforces the comments on 18:28.
John 19:31 "And the next day was to be a special Sabbath." The most plausible view is that this does not refer to the day of the Passover meal but to Saturday, which would be considered a "high" or "special" Sabbath, not only because it fell during the Passover Feast, but because on the second paschal day, in this case a Sabbath (Saturday), the very important sheaf offering fell (cf. SBK, 2:582; Philo *De Specialibus Legibus* 2).
John 19:36 This verse refers to Exodus 12:46 to explain that Jesus, the Passover Lamb, did not have any of his bones broken; and some have thought this suggests that Jesus must have died while the lambs were being slaughtered. But this does not follow. John makes no such temporal connection; and the theological connection could spring either from the tradition regarding the witness of John the Baptist (John 1:29, 36) or from Jesus' words at the institution of the Lord's Supper, reported by the synoptists and Paul.

It seems, then, that the fourth Gospel can be fairly harmonized with the Synoptics as far as the chronology of the Last Supper and Jesus' death are concerned.

One final question remains. How could conscientious Jews be party to a trial and execution on a feast day, which, in terms of prohibitions and legal procedure, was to be regarded as a Sabbath (cf. Exod 12:16; Lev 23:7; Num 28:18; M *Betzah* 5:2)? But Mishnah (*Sanhedrin* 11:4) insists that the execution of a rebellious teacher *should* take place on one of the three principal feasts so that all the people would hear and fear (cf. also Deut 17:13; SBK, 2:826). Jeremias (*Eucharistic Words*, p. 79) examines other events reported in the Gospels (e.g., Jesus' burial) and alleged to be inconsistent with the sabbatical nature of Passover feast day and concludes that "the passion narratives portray no incident which could not have taken place on Nisan 15." There are numerous irregularities connected with the Sanhedrin trial; these, however, bear only marginally on the chronological problems and are treated in situ (see on 26:57–68).

Therefore we seem to be on safe ground in arguing that the Last Supper was a Passover meal and that some of its associations must be seen in that light.

3. *The Lord's Supper* (26:17–30)

a. *Preparations for the Passover*

26:17–19

[17]On the first day of the Feast of Unleavened Bread, the disciples came to Jesus and asked, "Where do you want us to make preparations for you to eat the Passover?"

[18]He replied, "Go into the city to a certain man and tell him, 'The Teacher says: My appointed time is near. I am going to celebrate the Passover with my disciples at your house.' " [19]So the disciples did as Jesus had directed them and prepared the Passover.

17 Problems of chronology and some of the steps needed to prepare for the Passover are discussed in the preceding excursus. A few more details shed light on the situation. Toward midafternoon of Thursday, 14 Nisan, the lambs (one per "household"—a convenient group of perhaps ten or twelve people) would be brought to the temple court where the priests sacrificed them. The priests took the blood and passed it in basins along a line till it was poured out at the foot of the altar. They also burned the lambs' fat on the altar of burnt offerings. The singing of the *Hallel* (Pss 113–18) accompanied these steps.

After sunset (i.e., now 15 Nisan), the "household" would gather in a home to eat the Passover lamb, which by this time would have been roasted with bitter herbs. The head of the household began the meal with the thanksgiving for that feast day (the Passover *Kiddush*) and for the wine, praying over the first of four cups. A preliminary course of greens and bitter herbs was, apparently, followed by the Passover *haggadah*—in which a boy would ask the meaning of all this, and the head of the household would explain the symbols in terms of the Exodus (cf. M *Pesahim* 10:4–5)—and the singing of the first part of the *Hallel* (Ps 113 or Pss 113–14). Though the precise order is disputed, apparently a second cup of wine introduced the main course, which was followed by a third cup, known as the "cup of blessing," accompanied by another prayer of thanksgiving. The participants then sang the rest of the *Hallel* (Pss 114–18 or 115–18) and probably drank a fourth cup of wine. Thus the preparations about which the disciples were asking were extensive.

18–19 Matthew's account is much simpler than Mark's. *Pros ton deina* ("to a certain man") refers to somebody one cannot or does not wish to name (v.18). A case can be made that the home belonged to the father of John Mark (Zahn), but this is far from certain. It is not clear whether Jesus had made previous arrangements or called on supernatural knowledge (cf. 21:1–3). Either way Jesus was carefully taking charge of this final Passover meal. Jesus' words "My appointed time is near" were probably purposely ambiguous. To the disciples and the owner of the house, they might have implied Jesus' timing for the Passover meal and prior arrangements for it. In the light of Easter, the words must refer to the now impending Crucifixion, the fulfillment of Jesus' mission.

The disciples do as Jesus has "directed" (v.19) or "instructed" them (*syntassō* is used in the NT only here and in 21:6; 27:10). *Syntassō* does not relate to discipleship, as many maintain, and still less to Jesus' authority in any abstract sense. Instead, it prepares the way for the Last Supper and Jesus' death and demonstrates that he is quietly and consciously taking the steps to complete his mission of tragedy and glory.

b. *Prediction of the betrayal*

26:20–25

[20]When evening came, Jesus was reclining at the table with the Twelve. [21]And while they were eating, he said, "I tell you the truth, one of you will betray me."

[22]They were very sad and began to say to him one after the other, "Surely not I, Lord?"

[23]Jesus replied, "The one who has dipped his hand into the bowl with me will betray me. [24]The Son of Man will go just as it is written about him. But woe to that man who betrays the Son of Man! It would be better for him if he had not been born."

[25]Then Judas, the one who would betray him, said, "Surely not I, Rabbi?"

Jesus answered, "Yes, it is you."

Matthew agrees with Mark in placing this scene before the words of institution, whereas Luke's briefer account gives the impression that Judas did not leave till after those words. We cannot be certain which Gospel has preserved the chronological sequence; perhaps the Lukan account betrays greater marks of condensation and topical arrangement. Matthew omits the allusion to Psalm 41:9 preserved in Mark 14:18 but adds the brief exchange between Jesus and Judas in v.25 (cf. Mark 14:18–21; Luke 22:21–23; John 13:21–30).

20–22 The Passover meal could not be eaten till after sundown; and for those living within Palestine, it had to be eaten inside Jerusalem or not at all. That is why we find Jesus reclining at a table in a room in the city "when evening came" (v.20). Once the meal began—we do not know at what stage—Jesus solemnly says, "I tell you the truth, one of you will betray me" (v.21). The disciples respond uniformly: one after another, as the enormity of the charge sinks in, each man asks, "Surely not I, Lord?" (v.22).

23 NIV's "The one who has dipped his hand into the bowl" attempts to render an aorist participle (*ho embapsas*): contrast the present tense "one who dips" in Mark 14:20 (*ho embaptomenos*). Nevertheless NIV is misleading: it gives the impression that a particular "one" is in view, when in fact most if not all those present would have dipped into the same bowl as Jesus, given the eating styles of the day. Jesus' point is that the betrayer is a friend, someone close, someone sharing the common dish, thus heightening the enormity of the betrayal. The identification in John 13:22–30 probably took place just after this. If the main course, the roast lamb, was being eaten, the "bowl" would contain herbs and a fruit puree, which would be scooped out with bread.

24 For "woe," see on 23:13; for "Son of Man," see the excursus on 8:20. Here the Son of Man is simultaneously the glorious messianic figure who receives a kingdom and the Suffering Servant; indeed, the former highlights the evil of the person who hands him over to the latter role. No OT quotation explains "as it is written of him"; but one may think of OT passages such as Isaiah 53:7–9; Daniel 9:26, or else suppose that an entire prophetic typology (see on 2:15; 5:17–20) is in view, such as the Passover lamb, or some combination of the two.

The divine necessity for the sacrifice of the Son of Man, grounded in the Word of God, does not excuse or mitigate the crime of betrayal (cf. Acts 1:16–18; 4:27–28). Nor is this an instance of divine "overruling" after the fact. Instead divine sovereignty and human responsibility are both involved in Judas's treason, the one effecting salvation and bringing redemption history to its fulfillment, the other answering the promptings of an evil heart. The one results in salvation from sin for Messiah's people (1:21), the other in personal and eternal ruin (cf. Carson, *Divine Sovereignty*, pp. 130–32).

25 This exchange, preserved only in Matthew, magnifies Judas's effrontery and brackets the words of institution (vv.26–30) with the deceit of the betrayer (v.25) and the empty boast of the one who would disown Jesus with oaths (vv.31–35). Doubtless Judas felt he had to speak up; silence at this stage might have given him away to the others. Both here and in v.49, Judas uses "Rabbi" (see on 8:19; 23:7) which, in the pre-Easter setting, was probably more unambiguously honorific than the versatile *kyrios* ("Lord," v.22). As in v.22, the form of the question (using *mēti*) anticipates a negative answer; but the expected answer bears no necessary relation to the real answer (BDF, par. 427[2]). Jesus' response is identical in Greek to that in 26:64. It is affirmative but depends somewhat on spoken intonation for its full force. It could be taken to mean "You have said it, not I"; yet in fact it is enough of an affirmative to give Judas a jolt without removing all ambiguity from the ears of the other disciples. See further on v.64.

c. *The words of institution*

26:26–30

> [26]While they were eating, Jesus took bread, gave thanks and broke it, and gave it to his disciples, saying, "Take and eat; this is my body."
> [27]Then he took the cup, gave thanks and offered it to them, saying, "Drink from it, all of you. [28]This is my blood of the covenant, which is poured out for many for the forgiveness of sins. [29]I tell you, I will not drink of this fruit of the vine from now on until that day when I drink it anew with you in my Father's kingdom."
> [30]When they had sung a hymn, they went out to the Mount of Olives.

John records nothing of the words of institution. Matthew and Mark are fairly close in their formulations, as are Luke and Paul; but Luke and Paul are sufficiently distinct to make it better to speak of three accounts instead of two (cf. Mark 14:23–26; Luke 22:19–20; 1 Cor 11:23–25). The numerous text-critical variations confirm the tendency toward assimilation, especially in material at the heart of Christian liturgy. The literature attempting to trace Jesus' exact words and to determine which of the synoptic forms is most primitive is immense (cf. Jeremias, *Eucharistic Words*, pp. 96–105; Marshall, *Last Supper*, pp. 30–56). Marshall's caution is sensible: "It must be emphasized that there is no good reason for supposing that any one of the three versions must necessarily be closer to the original form of the account than any of the others" (p. 38).

We may go farther and ask why we must limit ourselves to just one "original account." There were eleven or twelve witnesses. We have repeatedly referred to the evangelists' interest in reporting Jesus' *ipsissima vox*, not his *ipsissima verba* (see note on 3:17). The various criteria for getting behind this (number of Semitisms, redaction-critical distinctions) are inadequate. A good translation may reduce Semitisms but preserve authentic content; redaction criticism may determine that some statement is traditional but cannot prove authenticity or, conversely, that some formulation is redactional without disproving authenticity. We must be satisfied with the sources we have. (On the question of discerning by critical means Jesus' understanding of his own death, see esp. H. Schürmann, "Wie hat Jesus seinen Tod bestanden und verstanden? Eine methodenkritische Besinnung," in Hoffmann et al., *Orientierung*, pp. 325–63; and cf. Guthrie, *NT Theology*, pp. 436–48.)

Close comparison of Mark and Matthew reveals few distinctive elements in Matthew. The first evangelist, unlike Mark, has "eat" in v.26 and replaces "they all drank from it" (Mark 14:23) with "Drink from it, all of you" (26:27). Matthew is usually judged more "liturgical" (Lohmeyer, Stendahl, Hill). This, though possible, is no more than a guess; we know almost nothing about first-century liturgy, and the variations are no more revealing in this regard than variations between Mark and Matthew in "nonliturgical" sections.

Appeal to liturgical influence is commonplace in current NT scholarship, and therefore the frequent assumption of such influence lends credibility to the claim; but it is in urgent need of reexamination. There may have been considerable diversity in the formulations used in church worship even *within each congregation*, as today in many nonliturgical denominations. Once again we must confess that our sources are inadequate for a confident conclusion. What is certain is that Jesus bids us commemorate, not his birth, nor his life, nor his miracles, but his death (cf. 20:28; 26:26–29).

26 This is the second thing Matthew records that takes place "while they were eating" (cf. v.21). Jesus takes *artos*, which can refer to "bread" generally (4:4; 6:11; 15:2, 26) but more commonly refers to a loaf or cake (4:3; 12:4; 14:17, 19; 15:33–34; 16:5–12). This loaf was unleavened (cf. Exod 12:15; 13:3, 7; Deut 16:3). He then gives thanks, probably with some such traditional formula as "Blessed art thou, O Lord our God, King of the universe, who bringest forth bread from the earth." He breaks it, distributes it (if the imperfect indicative variant is original, it may imply that he personally gave the bread to each of them), and says, "Take and eat; this is my body."

Few clauses of four words have evoked more debate than the last one. But three things must be said.

1. The words "this is my body" had no place in the Passover ritual; and as an innovation, they must have had stunning effect, an effect that would grow with the increased understanding gained after Easter.

2. Both the breaking and the distributing are probably significant: the bread (body) is broken, and all must partake of it. The sacrificial overtones are clearer in vv.27–28, but the unambiguous sacrificial language connected with Jesus' blood requires that v.26 be interpreted in a similar way.

3. Much of the debate on the force of "is" (In what sense *is* the bread Jesus' body?) is anachronistic. The verb itself has a wide semantic range and proves very little. "Take this, it means my body" (Mof) has its attractions, though it is scarcely less ambiguous. But what must be remembered is that this is a Passover meal. The new rite Jesus institutes has links with redemption history. As the bread has just been broken, so will Jesus' body be broken; and just as the people of Israel associated their deliverance from Egypt with eating the paschal meal prescribed as a divine ordinance, so also Messiah's people are to associate Jesus' redemptive death with eating this bread by Jesus' authority.

27 Assuming this is a Passover meal, this "cup" (with or without the article, by assimilation to Mark 14:23 or Luke 22:17 respectively) is probably the third, the "cup of blessing." Jesus again gives thanks, probably with some such prayer as "Blessed art thou, O Lord our God, King of the universe, Creator of the fruit of the vine." The wine was not grape juice, though it was customary to cut the wine with a double or triple quantity of water. Unlike Mark, Matthew records, not the performance, but the command: "Drink from it, all of you." As in Luke and Paul, this has the effect of describing exclusively what Jesus did, not what the disciples did. It should be noted that the participle *eucharistēsas* ("gave thanks"), cognate with *eucharistē* ("thanksgiving"), has given us the word "Eucharist." Some Protestants have avoided the term because of its associations with the traditional Roman Catholic mass, but the term itself is surely not objectionable.

28 This verse is rich in allusions; so attempts to narrow down its OT background to but one passage are reductionistic. "Blood" and "covenant" are found together in only two OT passages (Exod 24:8; Zech 9:11). Lindars (*Apologetic*, pp. 132–33) represents those who think the allusion must be to the latter, because allusion to the former would presuppose a typological exegesis not used so early in the tradition. But this fails to reckon with the extensive use of typology at Qumran; and the textual affinities are clearly in favor of Exodus 24:8 (see Gundry, *Use of OT*, pp. 57–58; Moo, "Use of OT," pp. 301ff.). The conclusion seems to be that, once again, we can penetrate near the heart of Jesus' own understanding of his relation to the OT (see on 5:17–20; 9:16–17; 11:9–13; 12:28; 13:52). And it is *his* understanding that sets a paradigm, not only for Matthew (see on 1:23; 2:15, 23; 8:16–17; 12:15–21; 13:35), but for other NT writers also (e.g., Heb 9:20). Equally without support are those theories that hold the covenant language to be original but not the blood–sacrifice language, making the primary allusion to Jeremiah 31:31–34; or that the sacrifice language is original but not the concept of covenant, making the primary allusion to the OT sacrificial system or to Isaiah 52:13–53:12. The primary reference is to Exodus 24:8, though other allusions are certainly present.

This means that Jesus understands the violent and sacrificial death he is about to undergo (i.e., his "blood"; cf. Morris, *Apostolic Preaching*, pp. 112–28; A.M. Stibbs, *The Meaning of the Word 'Blood' in Scripture* [London: Tyndale, 1954]) as the ratification of the covenant he is inaugurating with his people, even as Moses in Exodus 24:8 ratified the covenant of Sinai by the shedding of blood. "Covenant" is thus a crucial category (cf. DNTT, 1:365–72; Ridderbos, *Kingdom*, pp. 200–201; Morris, *Apostolic Preaching*, pp. 65–111; John J. Hughes, "Hebrews ix 15ff. and Galatians iii 15ff.; a Study in Covenant Practice and Procedure," NovTest 21 [1979]: 27–96; cf. Heb 8:1–13; 9:11–10:18, 29; 13:20). The event through which Messiah saves his people from their sins (1:21) is his sacrificial death; and the resulting relation between God and the messianic community is definable in terms of covenant, an agreement with stipulations—promises of blessing and sustenance and with threats of cursing all brought here into legal force by the shedding of blood.

Luke and Paul use the adjective "new" before covenant and thus allude to Jeremiah 31:31–34. Mark almost certainly omits the adjective; and the textual evidence for the word in Matthew is finely divided. But the passage from Jeremiah was almost certainly in Jesus' mind, as Matthew reports him, because "for the forgiveness of sins" reflects Jeremiah 31:34. Matthew has already shown his grasp of the significance of Jesus' allusion to covenant terminology in general and to the "new covenant" in particular; in 2:18 (see comments there) he cites Jeremiah 31 so as to show that he interprets the coming of Jesus as the real end of the Exile and the inauguration of the new covenant.

The words *to peri pollōn ekchynnomenon* ("which is poured out for many") could not fail to be understood as a reference to the Passover sacrifice in which so much blood had just been "poured out" (see on v.17). They also connote other sacrificial implications (e.g., Lev 1–7, 16), especially significant since at least *Jesus'* crucifixion did entail much bloodshed. The Mishnah (*Pesahim* 10:6), which in this instance may well preserve traditions alive in Jesus' day, uses Exodus 24:8 to interpret the Passover wine as a metaphor for blood that seals a covenant between God and his people. Jeremias (*Eucharistic Words*, pp. 222ff.) theorizes that the reason no mention is made of the Passover *lamb* in our accounts is that Jesus had already identified himself as the Lamb. This is possible because the failure to mention the lamb in any of the Synoptics is startling. But like most arguments from silence, it falls short of proof. Yet the allusions to the Passover—not least being the timing of the Last Supper—are cumulatively compelling.

It appears, then, that Jesus understands the covenant he is introducing to be the fulfillment of Jeremiah's prophecies and the antitype of the Sinai covenant. His sacrifice is thus foretold both in redemption history and in the prophetic word. The Exodus becomes a "type" of a new and greater deliverance; and as the people of God in the OT prospectively celebrated in the first Passover their escape from Egypt, anticipating their arrival in the Promised Land, so the people of God here prospectively celebrate their deliverance from sin and bondage, anticipating the coming kingdom (see on v.29).

Some take the preposition *peri* ("for [many]") to mean "on account of many" or "because of many" (BDF, par. 229[1]). But it is more likely equivalent in meaning to the *hyper* (NIV, "for [many]") of the parallel in Mark (Moule, *Idiom Book*, p. 63; Zerwick, par. 96) and possibly has the force of *anti* in 20:28 (cf. Morris, *Apostolic Preaching*, pp. 63, 172, 204, 206). As Karl Barth noted, the three prepositions point to Christ's "activity as our Representative and Substitute. . . . They cannot be understood if—quite apart from the particular view of the atonement made in Him which dominates these passages—we do not see that in general these prepositions speak of a place which ought to be ours, that we ought to have taken this place, that we have been taken from it, that it is occupied by another, that this other acts in this place as only He can, in our cause and interest" (cited in Morris, *Apostolic Preaching*, p. 63). For comments on "many," see on 20:28.

"For the forgiveness of sins" (cf. Heb 9:22) occurs in the words of institution only in Matthew and alludes to Jeremiah 31:31–34. Because the identical phrase is found in Mark 1:4 to describe the purpose of John's baptism but is omitted from the parallel in Matthew (3:1–2, 11), many suggest that Matthew purposely suppressed the phrase there because he wanted to attach it here and connect it exclusively to the work of Jesus Messiah. This is possible: NT writers understand that repentance and forgiveness of sin are tied together as tightly in the OT as in the period following Jesus' death, even though Jesus' death provides the real basis for forgiveness, a basis long promised by revelatory word, cultic act, and redemptive event. In one sense Mark might be willing to speak of John's baptism as a "baptism of repentance for the forgiveness of sins," while in another Matthew might be more interested in the ultimate ground of that "forgiveness of sin" and so reserve the phrase for Jesus. But several cautions should be kept in mind.

1. Matthew so regularly condenses Mark that it is usually risky to base too much on an omission.

2. Even in Matthew, John's baptism requires repentance (3:11) that demands confession of sin (3:6). It is hard to believe that Matthew thought that those who thus repented and confessed their sins were *not* forgiven!

3. Matthew may have slightly abbreviated the report of the Baptist's preaching (3:2) to maintain formal similarity to Jesus' early preaching (4:17).

4. In any case, a more important connection with v.28 is to be found in 1:21. It is by Jesus' death, by the pouring out of his blood, that he will save his people from their sins.

One more OT allusion is worth emphasizing. As in 20:28, it is very probable that Jesus is also portraying himself as Isaiah's Suffering Servant (cf. Moo, "Use of OT," pp. 127–32; France, "Servant of the Lord," pp. 37–39). This is based on three things: (1) "my blood of the covenant" calls to mind that the servant is twice presented as "a covenant for the people" (Isa 42:6; 49:8)—i.e., he will reestablish the covenant; (2) *ekchynnomenon* ("poured out") may well reflect Isaiah 53:12; and (3) "for many" again recalls the work of the Servant in Isaiah 52:13–53:12 (see on 20:28).

29 The "fruit of the vine" is a common Jewish way of referring in prayers to wine (cf. M *Berakoth* 6:1). Contrary to Jeremias (*Eucharistic Words*, pp. 207–18), Jesus' promise does not mean that he is abstaining from the cup of wine in this first "Lord's Supper" (cf. Hill, *Matthew*). Rather, just as the first Passover looks forward not only to deliverance but to settlement in the land, so also the Lord's Supper looks forward to deliverance and life in the consummated kingdom. The disciples will keep this celebration till Jesus comes (cf. 1 Cor 11:26); but Jesus will not participate in it with them till the consummation, when he will sit down with them at the messianic banquet (Isa 25:6; 1 Enoch 72:14; see on Matt 8:11; cf. Luke 22:29–30) in his Father's kingdom, which is equally Jesus' kingdom (cf. Luke 22:16, 18, 29–30; see on Matt 16:28; 25:31, 34). This point is greatly strengthened if we assume that Jesus speaks after drinking the *fourth* cup (see on v.17).

The four cups were meant to correspond to the fourfold promise of Exodus 6:6–7. The third cup, the "cup of blessing" used by Jesus in the words of institution, is thus associated with redemption (Exod 6:6); but the fourth cup corresponds to the promise "I will take you as my own people, and I will be your God" (Exod 6:7; cf. Daube, *New Testament*, pp. 330–31; Lane, *Mark*, pp. 508–9). Thus Jesus is simultaneously pledging that he will drink the "bitter cup" immediately ahead of him and vowing not to drink the cup of consummation, the cup that promises the divine presence, till the kingdom in all its fullness has been ushered in. Then he will drink the cup with his people. This is a veiled farewell and implies a sustained absence (see on 24:14; 25:5, 19). The Lord's Supper therefore points both to the past and to the future, both to Jesus' sacrifice at Calvary and to the messianic banquet.

30 The "hymn" normally sung was the last part of the *Hallel* (Pss 114–18 or 115–18). It was sung antiphonally: Jesus as the leader would sing the lines, and his followers would respond with "Hallelujah!" Parts of it must have been deeply moving to the disciples when after the Resurrection they remembered that Jesus sang words pledging that he would keep his vows (Ps 116:12–13), ultimately triumph despite rejection (Ps 118), and call all nations to praise Yahweh and his covenant love (Ps 117). It may be that Jewish exegesis had already interpreted Psalm 118:25–26 as a reference to Messiah's parousia (Jeremias, *Eucharistic Words*, pp. 255–62).

Notes

29 BDF, par. 12(3) points out that *απαρτι* (*aparti*) is ambiguous: it should most likely be taken as *ἀπ᾽ ἄρτι* (*ap' arti*, "from now on," NIV); but it could be construed as Ionic and Attic *ἀπαρτί* (*aparti*, "exactly," "certainly"), as, possibly, in Rev 14:13. But the customary rendering fits the context well and should be given the benefit of the doubt.

4. *Prediction of abandonment and denial*

26:31–35

[31]Then Jesus told them, "This very night you will all fall away on account of me, for it is written:

"'I will strike the shepherd,
and the sheep of the flock will be scattered.'

[32]But after I have risen, I will go ahead of you into Galilee."
[33]Peter replied, "Even if all fall away on account of you, I never will."
[34]"I tell you the truth," Jesus answered, "this very night, before the rooster crows, you will disown me three times."
[35]But Peter declared, "Even if I have to die with you, I will never disown you." And all the other disciples said the same.

Mark (14:27–31) and Matthew place this pericope after Jesus and his disciples have left the Upper Room. Luke (21:31–38) implies that its contents occur before the departure for the Mount of Olives; John (13:36–38) clearly places it during the supper and before the farewell discourse. The abruptness with which Mark begins this pericope suggests that he displaced it, perhaps to keep intact the theological coherence of the preceding pericope. Matthew does the same thing and for the same reason: this use of *tote* ("then") is inconsequential (see on 2:7). It seems likely, therefore, that John gives us the historical sequence at this point, while Matthew and Mark place this pericope where it will emphasize the gravity of the disciples' defection and Peter's denial. Matthew adds some touches, such as the personal pronouns in v.31 (emphasis mine): "*You* will all fall away *on account of me*"—*you*, of all people, on account of *me*, your Messiah, by your own confession. Moreover, in laying out in advance much of the tragedy of the coming hours, the pericope shows that Jesus is not a blind victim of fate but a voluntary sacrifice; and simultaneously he is preparing his disciples for their dark night of doubt.

31 "This very night" makes clear how very soon the disciples' defection and Peter's denial will happen. The intimacy of the Last Supper is shortly to be replaced by disloyalty and cowardice. The disciples will all "fall away" on account of Jesus: they will find him an obstacle to devotion and will forsake him (for the verb, see on 5:29). As the quotation from Zechariah makes clear, their falling away is related to the "striking" of the Shepherd. Jesus has repeatedly predicted his death and resurrection, but his disciples are still unable to grasp how such things could happen to the Messiah to whom they have been looking (16:21–23; 17:22–23; see on v.33).

Yet Jesus' words "for it is written" show that the disciples' defection, though tragic and irresponsible, does not fall outside God's sovereign plan. The textual questions relating to Zechariah 13:7 are complex (Gundry, *Use of OT*, pp. 25–28; Moo, "Use of OT," pp. 182ff.; cf. John 16:32); apparently the quotation rests on a pre-Christian recension of the LXX or on the MT or on some combination of both. There is no reason to think that Zechariah's words have been altered to fit the events of Jesus' passion and thereby accord with Christian tradition to make the "prophecy" after the event seem to be scriptural (Jeremias, *NT Theology*, pp. 297f.). The change to the future *pataxō* ("I will strike") from the imperative *pataxon* ("Strike") is the only word that provides nominal support for this theory. However, the grammatical change was probably necessitated by the omission of a definite subject when the

Zechariah passage was condensed (France, *Jesus*, pp. 107–8) rather than by the pressure of an *ex eventu* "prophecy" or by a stress on the divine initiative for theological reasons—something already accomplished by "it is written." Even if it is the "sword" that does the striking in MT, it does so at Yahweh's command.

Matthew alone (cf. Mark) includes "of the flock" in the second line of the quotation (following LXX) but to what does "the flock" refer? In light of the context of Zechariah 13:1–6, many have suggested that a wicked prophet is in view there. But this is incompatible with "the man who is close to me [i.e., to Yahweh]" (13:7b). Instead, Yahweh pictures a day when, owing to the prevailing apostasy, the Shepherd who is close to him (as opposed to the false shepherd in Zech 11) is cut down and the sheep scattered. In 13:8–9 most of the sheep perish; but one-third are left, after being refined, to become "my people"—those who will say, "Yahweh is our God." If Jesus' quotation of Zechariah in the Gospels presupposes the full context of Zechariah 13:7, then the disciples themselves join Israel, the sheep of God, in being scattered as the result of the "striking" of the Shepherd. Their falling away "this very night" continues to the Cross and beyond and is emblematic of the coming dispersion of the whole nation. But a purified remnant, a "third," will survive the refining and make up the people of God, "my people." Thus at the very instant Jesus' disciples show by their scattering that they temporarily side with the unbelieving and apostate nation, God is taking action to make them his true people.

32 Lohmeyer (*Matthäus*) originated the notion that this verse refers to Jesus' future parousia, not his resurrection appearances. The Parousia is to take place, Lohmeyer thinks, in Galilee. But R.H. Stein ("A Short Note on Mark xiv.28 and xvi.7," NTS 20 [1974]: 445–52) has conclusively shown that v.32 must refer to a resurrection appearance. Others see in the verb *proagō* (which may mean either "will go ahead" [NIV] or "will lead" [as does a shepherd]) a continuation of the shepherd imagery. But the most natural way to take the verse, and one that vitiates the frequent insistence that it ill suits its context, is that of Stonehouse (*Witness*, pp. 170–73). The prediction that the shepherd will be stricken and the sheep scattered might suggest, apart from any further word, that the disciples would return disconsolate to their homes in Galilee, leaving Jesus behind in a grave in Judea. But this new word (v.32) promises that after Jesus has risen, he will arrive in Galilee before they get there: he will "go ahead of [them]."

33 Some have objected that Jesus' prediction of the scattering of *all* the disciples (v.31) conflicts with Peter's following Jesus into the high priest's courtyard (e.g., G. Klein, "Die Verleugnung des Petrus: Eine traditionsgeschichtliche Untersuchung," *Zeitschrift für Theologie und Kirche* 58 [1961]: 297; M. Wilcox, "The Denial-Sequence in Mark xiv.26–31, 66–72," NTS 17 [1970–71]: 426–36). But this overlooks the fact that all the disciples actually fled (v.56) and that Peter followed only "at a distance" (v.58) and then denied Jesus. At the end of the day, all the sheep were scattered; all had fallen away.

Peter does not respond directly to Jesus' quotation, nor to his promise to meet him in Galilee. But this does not mean that vv.31b–32 are misplaced redactional additions, for Peter's reply is psychologically convincing. On the one hand, he has learned more about Jesus than he knew at Caesarea Philippi (16:21–28); and as a result he is able to accept the idea of suffering for both Jesus and himself. On the other hand, his notion of suffering is bound up with the heroism of men like the

Maccabean martyrs, not with voluntary sacrifice—hence v.51 (cf. John 8:10). He is prepared for suffering but is not yet ready for what he thinks of as defeat. More important, he reacts on a primal level to Jesus' prediction in v.31a: "It would be natural for him to be too taken up with the implied slur on his loyalty to pay much attention to anything else" (Cranfield, *Mark*, p. 429).

34 Jesus' "I tell you the truth" (see on 5:18) introduces another warning about how near Peter's own defection is: "this very night," indeed, "before the rooster crows." If the idea of *two* cock crowings, preserved only in certain MSS of Mark 14:30, 68, 72, is original (and it may not be: cf. John W. Wenham, "How Many Cock-Crowings? The Problem of Harmonistic Text-Variants," NTS 25 [1978–79]: 523–25), then the "difference is the same as that between saying 'before the bell rings' and 'before the second bell rings' (for church or dinner)" (Alexander). Apparently it was usual for roosters in Palestine to crow about 12:30, 1:30, and 2:30 A.M. (Hans Kosmala, "The Time of the Cock-Crow," *Annual of Swedish Theological Institute* 2 [1963]: 118–20; 6 [1967–68]: 132–34); so the Romans gave the term "cock-crow" to the watch from 12:00 to 3:00 A.M. Despite Peter's claims of undeviating loyalty (v.33), Jesus says that Peter is within hours of disowning (same verb as in 16:24) him three times.

35 The language of Peter's protest (the rare subjunctive of *dei*) shows that he does not really think that Jesus' death was likely; he still has his visions of heroism. Nor is he alone in his brash protestations of loyalty—only quicker and more vehement than his peers.

5. *Gethsemane*

26:36–46

36Then Jesus went with his disciples to a place called Gethsemane, and he
said to them, "Sit here while I go over there and pray." 37He took Peter and the
two sons of Zebedee along with him, and he began to be sorrowful and troubled.
38Then he said to them, "My soul is overwhelmed with sorrow to the point of
death. Stay here and keep watch with me."
39Going a little farther, he fell with his face to the ground and prayed, "My
Father, if it is possible, may this cup be taken from me. Yet not as I will, but as you
will."
40Then he returned to his disciples and found them sleeping. "Could you men
not keep watch with me for one hour?" he asked Peter. 41"Watch and pray so that
you will not fall into temptation. The spirit is willing, but the body is weak."
42He went away a second time and prayed, "My Father, if it is not possible for
this cup to be taken away unless I drink it, may your will be done."
43When he came back, he again found them sleeping, because their eyes were
heavy. 44So he left them and went away once more and prayed the third time,
saying the same thing.
45Then he returned to the disciples and said to them, "Are you still sleeping and
resting? Look, the hour is near, and the Son of Man is betrayed into the hands of
sinners. 46Rise, let us go! Here comes my betrayer!"

Scholars usually see in this pericope an exhortation to foster vigilance and prayerfulness in the face of temptation (cf. Mark 14:32–42; Luke 22:40–46; also, John 12:28–33; 13:21; 16:32). Though this is doubtless present, far more central is the light the pericope sheds on Jesus' perception of what he is about to do. If the exegesis of v.39 is correct, we must ask why this Jesus who has for so long calmly faced the prospect of death (16:21; 17:22–23; 20:17–19; 26:1–2) should now seem to be less courageous than the Maccabean martyrs or the many thousands of his disciples who have faced martyrdom with great courage. The anguish in Gethsemane is not lightly to be passed over: three times Jesus prayed in deep emotional distress. The answer is found even in this first Gospel. The pericope must be interpreted in light of 1:21 and 20:28, on the one hand, and, on the other, in light of the reader's recognition that Jesus is the Messiah, the Son of God, "God with us," whose *sacrificial* death inaugurates the new covenant (vv.26–30) and redeems his people from their sins. Small wonder that NT writers make much of Jesus' unique and redemptive death (Rom 3:21–26; 4:25; 5:6, 9; 1 Cor 1:23; 2 Cor 5:21; Heb 2:18; 4:15; 5:7–9; 1 Peter 2:24).

Jesus did not suffer martyrdom. Can anyone imagine the words of 26:53 on the lips of a Maccabean martyr? Many of Jesus' followers throughout the centuries willingly suffer martyrdom because of the strength Jesus' death and resurrection give them. But Jesus went to his death knowing that it was his Father's will that he face death completely alone (27:46) as the sacrificial, wrath-averting Passover Lamb. As his death was unique, so also his anguish; and our best response to it is hushed worship (see K. Schilder, *Christ in His Suffering*, tr. H. Zylstra [Grand Rapids: Eerdmans, 1938], pp. 289–309).

36–38 "Gethsemane" (v.36) means "oil press," and here probably gave the name to the *chōrion* ("place"), usually a field or an *enclosed* piece of ground (cf. John 18:4, "went out") to which it was attached. Jesus and his disciples often frequented this spot (John 18:1–2) on the western slopes of Mount Olivet, separated from Jerusalem by the Kidron. Eight disciples remain at some distance, perhaps outside the enclosure, and the inner three join him (v.37). Jesus with stern self-control has so far masked his anguish; now he begins "to be sorrowful [*lypeisthai*, which connotes deep grief] and troubled" (*adēmonein*, found in the NT only here, in the parallel in Mark 14:33, and in Phil 2:26, and connoting deep distress).

Jesus' next words—"My soul is overwhelmed with sorrow" (v.38)—are almost a quotation from the refrain of Psalms 42–43 (LXX). The phrase *heōs thanatou* ("to the point of death") is so common in the LXX (e.g., Isa 38:1) that it should not be thought an allusion to Jonah 4:9 (contra Gundry, *Use of OT*, p. 59) but "merely a reflection of the OT-tinged language which Jesus used" (Moo, "Use of OT," p. 241). It suggests a sorrow so deep it almost kills (Taylor, *Mark*, p. 553; Hill, *Matthew;* and many others), not that Jesus is so sorrowful he would rather be dead (contra Bultmann, TDNT, 4:323, n. 2). Having revealed his deepest emotions and thus given his disciples the most compelling of reasons to do what he asks, he tells them to stay and "keep watch with me" while he goes a little farther on to pray alone. His words could be taken as no more than a request to protect him from intrusion in his deep anguish (so many older commentaries). But his words "with me" (only in Matthew) imply that he wanted them to keep awake and go on praying.

39 Jesus prays, prostrate in his intense anguish. He addresses God as "My Father" (see on 6:9); and Mark preserves the Aramaic *Abba*. The "cup" (*potērion*) refers not only to suffering and death but, as often in the OT (Pss 11:6 ["lot," NIV]; 75:7–8; Isa 51:19, 22; Jer 25:15–16, 27–29; 49:12; 51:57; Lam 4:21; Ezek 23:31–34; Hab 2:16; Zech 12:2; cf. Job 21:20; Ps 60:3; Isa 63:6; Obad 16), also to God's wrath (cf. C.E.B.

Cranfield, "The Cup Metaphor in Mark xiv.36 and Parallels," ExpT 59 [1947–48]: 137f.; Goppelt, TDNT, 6:153; Blaising, pp. 339–40). The frequent OT allusions in the passion narrative demand an OT meaning for *potērion* instead of "cup of death" in other Jewish literature. Thus the meaning here is fuller than in 20:22–23 and anticipates 27:46.

In one sense all things are possible with God (see on 19:26; Mark 14:36); in another some things are impossible. The two passages (Mark 14:36 and Matt 26:39) complement each other: all things are possible with God; and so, if it be morally consistent with the Father's redeeming purpose that this "cup" (Matthew) or "hour" (Mark) be taken from Jesus, that is what he deeply desires. But more deeply still, Jesus desires to do his Father's will. Though the precise wording of the synoptic accounts varies somewhat, if the prayer was of some duration ("one hour," v.40), and if Jesus after his resurrection told his disciples its contents, or if the disciples were within earshot, some variation in the tradition is not surprising. Jesus' deep commitment to his Father's will cannot be doubted. But in this crisis, the worst since 4:1–11, Jesus is tempted to seek an alternative to sin-bearing suffering as the route by which to fulfill his Father's redemptive purposes. As with his self-confessed ignorance in 24:36, Jesus may simply not have known whether any other way was possible. He prays in agony; and though he is supernaturally strengthened (Luke 22:43), he learns only that the Cross is unavoidable if he is to obey his Father's will.

Blaising has recently proposed an alternative exegesis. He observes that, whatever the wording in the Synoptics, the conditional clause is grammatically "first class," a so-called real condition, which he interprets as follows: "This class of condition assumes the condition to be a reality and the conclusion follows logically and naturally from that assumption" (p. 337; cf. RHG, p. 1007). From this Blaising concludes that what Jesus is asking for *is* possible with the Father and that Jesus knows it; so he cannot be asking that the cup (i.e., his passion) not come to him, an impossibility, for Jesus has repeatedly spoken of it, but that the cup not *remain* with him. In other words Jesus is tempted to fear that the "cup" of God's wrath will not pass away from him after he has drunk it but that it will consume him forever, and there would be no resurrection. He prays with faith, because he knows it is the Father's will: "Father, as you have promised in your Word, take the cup from me after I drink it; yet this is not my will alone, it is your will that this be done" (Blaising, p. 343).

This interpretation has certain attractions; yet along with several questionable details, it has two insuperable difficulties.

1. Despite Blaising's appeal to A.T. Robertson (i.e., RHG, p. 1007), a first-class condition in Greek does not necessarily assume the reality of the protasis but only that the protasis is as real as the apodosis. The speaker assumes the reality of the protasis for the sake of argument but does not thereby indicate that the condition described in the protasis is in fact real. Were Blaising to apply his understanding of first-class conditional clauses to Matthew 12:26–27; Mark 3:24–26, the result would be theologically incoherent, as Robertson himself recognizes (RHG, p. 1008; cf. Zerwick, pars. 303ff.).

2. Blaising introduces a novel interpretation, but only the traditional view continues the line of temptation Jesus has earlier found most difficult to confront—viz., the temptation to avoid the Cross (see on 4:1–11; 16:21–23).

40–41 Jesus returns to his disciples—i.e., the inner three—and finds them sleeping (v.40; Luke 22:45 adds "exhausted from sorrow"). Jesus' question is addressed to

Peter but is in the plural and therefore includes them all (see on 16:16; 26:33–35). Though "one hour" need not be exact, it certainly indicates that Jesus has been praying for some time. "Watch and pray" could be a hendiadys (cf. Notes); alternatively it may suggest two components: spiritual alertness and intercession.

It is doubtful that "so that you will not fall into temptation" (v.41) means only "so that you will stay awake and not fall into the temptation to sleep." Indeed, Jesus' prediction of their spiritual defection that "very night" (v.31) should have served as an urgent call to prayer. So now he tells them that only urgent prayer will save them from falling into the coming "temptation" (see on 4:1; 6:13). Even in his own extremity, when he needs and seeks his Father's face, Jesus thinks of the impending but much lesser trial his followers will face. He speaks compassionately: "The spirit is willing, but the body [*sarx,* 'flesh'] is weak." This is not a reference to the Holy Spirit but makes a "distinction between man's physical weakness and the noble desires of his will" (Hill, *Matthew;* id., *Greek Words,* p. 242; Bonnard). But though compassionate, these words, which doubtless hark back to v.35, are not an excuse but a warning and incentive (Broadus). Spiritual eagerness is often accompanied by carnal weakness—a danger amply experienced by successive generations of Christians.

42–44 Some interpreters have seen a certain progression in Jesus' three prayers, but Matthew says that Jesus said "the same thing" (v.44). The variations between v.39 and v.42 must therefore be incidental. "May your will be done" mirrors one of the petitions of the prayer Jesus taught his disciples (6:10). As Jesus learned obedience (Heb 5:7–9), so he became the supreme model for his own teaching. In the first garden "Not your will but mine" changed Paradise to desert and brought man from Eden to Gethsemane. Now "Not my will but yours" brings anguish to the man who prays it but transforms the desert into the kingdom and brings man from Gethsemane to the gates of glory.

45–46 The word *loipon* as an adverb does not naturally mean "still" (NIV, v.45) or "meanwhile" but points to the future ("henceforth") or is inferential ("it follows that"). Therefore Jesus' words should not be taken as a question (NIV) but as a gently ironic command (cf. KJV, "Sleep on now, and take your rest"; cf. the irony in 23:2–3; cf. Moule, *Idiom Book,* p. 161). The hour of the Passion is near: it is too late to pray and gain strength for the temptations ahead. His disciples may as well sleep. The Son of Man (see on 8:20) is betrayed into the hands of sinners: he who is the resplendent, messianic King takes the path of suffering. Doubtless Jesus could see and hear the party approaching as it crossed the Kidron with torches and climbed up the path to Gethsemane. The sleepers for whom he would die have lost their opportunity to gain strength through prayer. By contrast Jesus has prayed in agony but now rises with poise and advances to meet his betrayer.

Notes

---

39 The distinctions Thrall (pp. 67–70) draws between Mark's (14:36) ἀλλά (*alla,* "but") and Matthew's πλήν (*plēn,* "but") are dubious, because the former adversative particle has so broad a semantic range.

41 If the ἵνα (*hina*, "that") clause is dependent only on the verb "pray," then it is probably nonfinal (as in 5:29) and gives the content of the prayer. If it depends on "watch and pray" together, it may have telic force.

43 The periphrastic pluperfect ἦσαν . . . βεβαρημένοι (*ēsan . . . bebarēmenoi*, lit., "were having been weighed down"; NIV, "were heavy") provides a good instance in which the perfect passive participle probably has no more than adjectival force (cf. Moule, *Idiom Book*, p. 19).

---

6. *The arrest*

26:47–56

47While he was still speaking, Judas, one of the Twelve, arrived. With him was a large crowd armed with swords and clubs, sent from the chief priests and the elders of the people. 48Now the betrayer had arranged a signal with them: "The one I kiss is the man; arrest him." 49Going at once to Jesus, Judas said, "Greetings, Rabbi!" and kissed him.

50Jesus replied, "Friend, do what you came for."

Then the men stepped forward, seized Jesus and arrested him. 51With that, one of Jesus' companions reached for his sword, drew it out and struck the servant of the high priest, cutting off his ear.

52"Put your sword back in its place," Jesus said to him, "for all who draw the sword will die by the sword. 53Do you think I cannot call on my Father, and he will at once put at my disposal more than twelve legions of angels? 54But how then would the Scriptures be fulfilled that say it must happen in this way?"

55At that time Jesus said to the crowd, "Am I leading a rebellion, that you have come out with swords and clubs to capture me? Every day I sat in the temple courts teaching, and you did not arrest me. 56But this has all taken place that the writings of the prophets might be fulfilled." Then all the disciples deserted him and fled.

47 Judas Iscariot (see on 10:4; 26:14–16, 25; 27:3–10) arrived with armed men. What he received payment for was probably information as to where Jesus could be arrested in a quiet setting with little danger of mob violence. He may have first led the "large crowd" to the Upper Room and, finding it empty, surmised where Jesus and his disciples had gone (cf. John 18:1–3). The "large crowd" accompanying Judas had been sent "from the chief priests and the elders of the people"—the clergy and lay members of the Sanhedrin (see on 21:23). Luke 22:52 says some chief priests and elders accompanied the crowd. The military terms in John 18:3, 12 suggest that some Roman soldiers were among the number along with temple police and some others. Although many scholars have argued that no Romans were involved at this time, it is not unlikely that some were present. Especially during the feasts the Romans took extra pains to ensure public order; so a request for a small detachment from the cohort would not likely be turned down. Thus Pilate might have had some inkling of the plot from the beginning, and if he shared it with his wife, it might help explain her dream (27:19).

48–50 The need for pointing out the right man was especially acute, not only because it was dark, but because, in a time long before photography, the faces of even great celebrities would not be nearly so widely known as today. To identify Jesus, Judas chose the kiss (thereby turning it into a symbol of betrayal. "Greetings,

Rabbi!" (v.49; see on 8;19; 23:8), a tragic mockery, was for the crowd's ears, not Jesus'.

"Friend" (v.50) is an open-hearted but not intimate greeting. The next words, *eph ho parei* ("what you came for"), are notoriously ambiguous. If the relative pronoun *ho* functions as a direct interrogative pronoun, the expression means "Why [lit., 'for what'] have you come?" (NIV mg.; cf. Zerwick, par. 223; Turner, *Insights*, pp. 69–71; id., *Syntax*, pp. 49–50; BDF, pars. 495–96), and some verb like "do" must be supplied (NIV text; cf. BDF, par. 300[2]). If the clause is an imperatival statement, its force is like John 13:27 and reflects Jesus' newly regained poise and his sovereignty in these events. If it is a question, it elicits no information but administers a rebuke steeped in the irony of professed ignorance that knows very well why Judas has come.

51–54 "With that" (v.51) is NIV's acceptable effort to render *idou* in this context (cf. "Look," v.45; "Here," v.46; untr., v.47; see on 1:20). Many are skeptical of the authenticity of this passage, finding it out of keeping with the restrained spirit of the pericope as a whole and wondering why the offending disciple was not arrested. Moreover it is the latest Gospel that names Jesus' sword-wielding disciple (Peter) and his target (Malchus [John 18:10]). This might suggest that the story was growing and gaining accretions. Noteworthy are the following points.

1. The restraint belongs to Jesus, not the pericope. Moreover, we have already seen that earlier protestations of loyalty (vv.33–35) were probably grounded in some form of nationalistic messianism; so Peter's response is scarcely unexpected.

2. His response is psychologically convincing. After repeated warnings of defection, Peter may have felt that the crucial test of loyalty had arrived. He is magnificent and pathetic—magnificent because he rushes in to defend Jesus with characteristic courage and impetuousness, pathetic because his courage evaporates when Jesus undoes Peter's damage, forbids violence, and faces the Passion without resisting.

3. However one interprets the difficult verses in Luke 22:36–38, they show that the disciples had two swords with them; and if Peter actually wielded the sword, other disciples had the same idea (Luke 22:49).

4. There were probably many reasons why Peter was not arrested. Jesus not only quickly cooled the situation but healed the wound (omitted by Matthew). It was one thing to escort a nonresisting prisoner quietly back to the city; it was another to escort twelve men, eleven of them frightened and ready to fight. In any case before decisive action could be taken, the disciples fled in the darkness (v.56).

5. Over the centuries pious Christian imaginations have provided names for those not named in the NT (cf. B.M. Metzger, "Names for the Nameless in the New Testament: A Study in the Growth of Christian Tradition," *NT Studies*, pp. 23–43). Within the NT the evidence is mixed. Whatever order the Synoptics were written in, we must note that Matthew may preserve a name omitted by Mark (Matt 26:57; Mark 14:53) or drop a name preserved by Mark (Matt 9:18; Mark 5:22). Matthew and Luke both drop Mark's Bartimaeus (Mark 10:46) and Alexander and Rufus (Mark 15:21). Add to this the fact that many scholars now insist that John does not represent late tradition, and there remains little reason for skepticism concerning this sorry scene.

Some take Jesus' response—"for all who draw the sword will die by the sword" (v.52)—as a call to pacifism, whereas others observe that Jesus told Peter to put his sword "back in its place," not to throw it away. Both views ask the text to answer questions of no immediate relevance. The least we can say is that violence *in defense of Christ* is completely unjustified: certainly verse 52 separates Jesus from the Zealots. Moreover a simple request to his Father (the aorist infinitive is significant; cf. BDF, par. 471[2]) would bring twelve legions of angels (a full Roman legion was six thousand; cf. ZPEB, 3:907–8) to his assistance—perhaps one legion for Jesus and one for each of the Eleven (v.53). This is more than the eyes of faith seeing help as in 2 Kings 6:17 but the knowledge that help is available, while refusing to use it (cf. John 10:18). In addition, Jesus' stance regarding his own death is grounded on the fact the "Scriptures" (plural, v.54) must be fulfilled (see on vv.24, 31; cf. Luke 24:25–26). This divine "must" (*dei*) is not for Jesus sheer inevitability, since he still believes it possible to gain instant aid from his Father. Instead, it is the commingling of divine sovereignty and Jesus' unflagging determination to obey his Father's will.

Many commentators note that in 1QM 7:6 the angels are represented as joining forces with the righteous at the End. Jesus himself elsewhere pictures angelic participation at the consummation (e.g., 13:41; 24:30–31). But at this point in redemptive history, the angels are not called on. Jesus faces this battle alone, and the consummation of all things is not yet.

55–56 Every day for the preceding week, and presumably on earlier visits to the Holy City, Jesus had been teaching in the temple courts (v.55); yet the authorities had not arrested him. Why then do they seize him now as if he were a rebel (*lēstēs*, see on 27:16)? The implication is that there is no need to arrest him secretly and violently, except for reasons in their own minds that reveal more about them than about him. "At that time" (lit., "In that hour") seems a rather heavy-handed transition, but perhaps what follows it was a well-known saying of Jesus among Christians to whom Matthew was writing; and he is pointing out that this was the time when he spoke it.

After questioning the display of force by those who arrested him, Jesus said, "This has all taken place [see on 1:22; 21:4] that the writings [or 'Scriptures'] of the prophets might be fulfilled." Mark (14:49) simply has "But the Scriptures must be fulfilled." Matthew gives us more, doubtless because he is more interested in the prophetic nature of the Scriptures (see Introduction, section 11.b). "The writings of the prophets" therefore probably does not exclude the Law and the Writings, for elsewhere Moses and David are also considered "prophets." The reference is to the Scriptures (as in v.54), their human authors being considered primarily as prophets, not lawgivers, wise men, or psalmists.

All the disciples then fulfill one specific prophecy (see on v.31) and flee. Mark 14:51–52 adds the account of the young man who flees naked. Probably at this time Jesus is bound (John 18:12).

7. *Jesus before the Sanhedrin*

26:57–68

[57]Those who had arrested Jesus took him to Caiaphas, the high priest, where the teachers of the law and the elders had assembled. [58]But Peter followed him at a distance, right up to the courtyard of the high priest. He entered and sat down with the guards to see the outcome.

[59]The chief priests and the whole Sanhedrin were looking for false evidence

against Jesus so that they could put him to death. [60]But they did not find any, though many false witnesses came forward.

Finally two came forward [61]and declared, "This fellow said, 'I am able to destroy the temple of God and rebuild it in three days.' "

[62]Then the high priest stood up and said to Jesus, "Are you not going to answer? What is this testimony that these men are bringing against you?" [63]But Jesus remained silent.

The high priest said to him, "I charge you under oath by the living God: Tell us if you are the Christ, the Son of God."

[64]"Yes, it is as you say," Jesus replied. "But I say to all of you: In the future you will see the Son of Man sitting at the right hand of the Mighty One and coming on the clouds of heaven."

[65]Then the high priest tore his clothes and said, "He has spoken blasphemy! Why do we need any more witnesses? Look, now you have heard the blasphemy. [66]What do you think?"

"He is worthy of death," they answered.

[67]Then they spit in his face and struck him with their fists. Others slapped him [68]and said, "Prophesy to us, Christ. Who hit you?"

Few topics have caused more tension between Jews and Christians than the trial of Jesus. Those who have committed abominable atrocities against the Jews have often based their actions on the ground that Jews are the murderers of their Messiah, or God-killers, and have all too frequently turned to Matthew 27:25 for backing. As a reaction to this reprehensible attitude, more recent study (both Jewish and Christian) has argued that the Jews were very little involved and that most of the blame should be placed on the Romans. An excellent survey of Jewish and Christian exegesis of the trial narratives, from 1770 to the late 1960s, is given by Catchpole (*Trial of Jesus*); and representative modern treatments, in addition to commentaries and articles, are included in our bibliography under Bammel, Blinzler, Brandon, Cohn, Winter, Sherwin-White (ch. 2), and Benoit (*Jesus*, pp. 123–66).

Though there is no consensus, the dominant view in current scholarship runs something like this: The four Gospel accounts of the trial before the Sanhedrin cannot readily be reconciled. But the fourth Gospel, though making clear that both Jewish and Roman authorities were involved from the beginning (John 18:3, 12), stresses that the Sanhedrin did not have the power to inflict the death penalty (John 18:31) and places much more emphasis on the Roman trial. By contrast the Synoptics lay more blame on the Jews; and Matthew goes so far as to tell us that Pilate washed his hands of the whole affair, while the Jews called down curses on themselves (27:24–25). On the face of it, John's account is the more historically reliable, whereas the Synoptics are more seriously tainted by later church-synagogue tensions. In short, anti-Semitism has colored their narratives.

This is confirmed, it is alleged, when all the illegalities of the Jewish proceedings are noted. The Mishnah (*Sanhedrin*) makes it clear that legal procedure in capital cases forbade night trials, required at least two consecutive days, and provided for private interrogation of witnesses. The breaches in law are so numerous as to be unbelievable; and one Jewish writer (Cohn) has gone so far in reconstructing the evidence that he concludes the Sanhedrin actually tried to *save* Jesus from the Roman courts. Any trace of evidence that counters this thesis he ascribes to the polemic of later deteriorating church-synagogue relationships, compounded with the natural desire in Christian writers to avoid blaming the powerful Roman authorities.

Yet some things must not be overlooked.

1. The problem of illegalities in Jesus' trial is more complex than is customarily recognized. We have already shown (see excursus at v. 17) that executions under certain circumstances could take place on a major feast day. Other irregularities include (1) the proceedings that apparently took place in Caiaphas's home, not the temple precincts; (2) Jesus' not being offered a defense attorney; (3) his being charged with blasphemy without actually blaspheming in the legally defined sense, which required that the accused actually pronounce the name of God; (4) the verdict's being rushed through at night without the minimum two days required in capital cases, which had the effect of banning the new opening of capital trials from the day before Sabbaths or festival days (M *Sanhedrin* 4:1). But quite apart from the difficult problem of dating Mishnaic traditions—for the sake of argument we may agree that they all date back to the beginning of the first century or earlier—five factors challenge the idea that legal considerations invalidate the authenticity of the Gospels on these points.

a. Some Mishnaic stipulations, not least in the tractate Sanhedrin, are almost certainly theoretical formulations only, which never had the force of obeyed law. Is there any independent historical evidence, for instance, that "burnings" of the sort described in *Sanhedrin* 7:2 ever took place?

b. Dalman (pp. 98–100) provides references to other occasions of flagrant breach of judicial regulations on the ground that "the hour demands it."

c. Similarly there is evidence that expediency partially motivated the religious authorities (cf. John 11:49–50). This could account for numerous irregularities. If the leaders feared mob violence, haste was required. Moreover it was legitimate to execute certain criminals on feast days, but not on the Sabbath. If Jesus was arrested Thursday night (Friday by Jewish reckoning), things had to move swiftly if he was to be buried by dusk on Friday, the onset of Sabbath. An all-night session of the Jewish authorities was demanded by the fact that Roman officials like Pilate worked very early in the morning and then refused to take on new cases for the rest of the day. If Jesus could not be presented to Pilate early Friday morning, the case would drag on till after Sabbath—along with mounting risks of mob violence.

d. The sources are sufficiently difficult that we do not know the precise relationship between the Pharisees of Jesus' day and the rabbis who compiled Mishnah. Even if Sigal (cf. Introduction, section 11.f) has exaggerated the distinctions, we may not always be wise in reading rabbinic regulations back into Jesus' day. For instance, the narrow and technical definitions of blasphemy in Mishnah may not have been popular with all Pharisees. After all, large parts of the population held to extraordinarily broad notions of blasphemy: Josephus (Antiq. XX, 108[v.2]) records that an angry crowd accused a Roman soldier of blasphemy because he had exposed his genitals to them. And we have *no* evidence for the way the Sadducees understood blasphemy.

e. We may go farther. A strong, if not entirely convincing, case can be made for distinguishing between *Sanhedrin* and *Beth Din*. The NT speaks of the former; the relevant Mishnaic tractate, though traditionally called *Sanhedrin*, in fact speaks almost thirty times of the latter and only three times of the former. From this some have deduced that what the Gospels describe is *not* the "Sanhedrin" in the religious, scholarly sense but the "Sanhedrin" that was essentially political and, to some extent, corrupt (most recently, cf. E. Rivkin, "Beth Din, Boule, Sanhedrin: A

Tragedy of Errors," HUCA 46 [1975]: 181–99). Even if this distinction does not prove valid, it must be admitted that "a way of removing an undesirable enemy is usually found when the will is there" (S. Rosenblatt, "The Crucifixion of Jesus from the Standpoint of Pharisaic Law," JBL 75 [1956]: 319 [though Rosenblatt does not accept the accounts as we have them in the Gospels]). Catchpole (*Trial of Jesus*, pp. 268f.) has convincingly shown that "the debate about illegalities should be regarded as a dead end, and at most able to make only a minor contribution."

2. More distinction is found between John and the Synoptics and between Matthew and Mark–Luke than is actually there. Although John places more emphasis on the Roman trial, only in John 19:12, and never in the Synoptics, do we find *the Jews* manipulating Pilate in order to secure a guilty verdict and a capital sentence. It is surely false to attribute the lesser prominence of Pilate in the Synoptics to Christian concern to get on with Rome; for long before the evangelists wrote, Pilate was deposed and banished by Rome. Moreover it is not at all clear that Matthew sees 27:24 as an effective absolution for Pilate; Matthew frequently records denunciations of hypocrisy and expects persecution from Gentile "governors and kings" (10:18–19). Equally it is not at all clear that 27:25 should be interpreted to mean that all Jews remain under a continuing curse. The first disciples were Jews to a man; and the fact that Matthew clearly insists the authorities were afraid of mob action (vv.3–4) shows he understands that many Jews were enthusiastically if superficially *for* Jesus, even if few of them were committed disciples.

3. But if such sharp distinctions between John's treatment of the trial and that of the Synoptics are scarcely supported by the text, even less defensible are sharp disjunctions. The attempt to blame the Romans and exonerate the Jews finds little support in the fourth Gospel; but even if it were an unquestionable theme there, responsible historiography attempts a synthesis of the sources, not a priori historical disjunctions—one of the classic "historians' fallacies" (cf. Fischer). And a believable synthesis is indeed possible (see below).

4. John 18:31, frequently cited to absolve the Sanhedrin, is not only historically credible (cf. Sherwin-White, pp. 35–43; Catchpole, *Trial of Jesus*, pp. 247–48) but also provides an important clue to the roles played by Jews and Romans. All the Gospels attest, repeatedly and in highly diverse ways, that many Jewish leaders wanted Jesus' removal because of his claims of messianic authority, coupled with his popularity among the populace at large and the unexpected kind of "messiah" he was proving to be—and especially his failure to show more respect to the religious authorities. When he finally came into their hands, political circumstances forced them to seek the death sentence from Pilate. For this purpose it was necessary for the Jewish leaders to tinge the charges against Jesus with political color. Thus he was made to seem less a Messiah than a competitor of Caesar. Only by a very selective handling of the evidence (e.g., S.G.F. Brandon, *The Trial of Jesus of Nazareth* [London: Batsford, 1968] can one conclude that the political charge came first, making Jesus some kind of Zealot rebel.

5. The Holocaust and other atrocities have blinded the eyes of both Jewish and Christian historians. Not a few modern Jews insist that the Holocaust is the result of centuries of bigoted Christian tradition, and that Christian solidarity entails corporate Christian guilt. Yet they would be loathe to assume that Jewish solidarity entails for the Jewish race a corporate Jewish guilt because of the contribution of a few Jews to the death of Jesus. Meanwhile Christian historians, alive to the legacy of

Western Christendom's persecution of the Jews, are embarrassed into making irresponsible judgments against the historical evidence, as a sort of atonement for past injustices. It is easier to blame the Romans, who are not present to defend themselves, than to face the survivors of the Holocaust with unpleasant historical realities. The wisest scholars of both sides have seen this. The Jewish scholar Samuel Sandmel writes: "Perhaps we might be willing to say to ourselves that it is not at all impossible that some Jews, even leading Jews, recommended the death of Jesus to Pilate. We are averse to saying this to ourselves, for so total has been the charge against us that we have been constrained to make a total denial" (*We Jews and Jesus* [London and New York: OUP, 1965], p. 141).

It is helpful to remember that, whatever Christendom has done, the NT writers, most if not all of whom were Jews, can scarcely or reasonably be labeled "anti-Semitic." Matthew and the other evangelists certainly blame some Jews for Jesus' death. They also blame some Romans. But the reasons for the blame are historical, theological, spiritual—not racial. The Twelve are Jews; and after the Crucifixion a Jew from Arimathea (27:57–60) shows great concern for Jesus' burial. The NT writers assess people by their response to Jesus, whom they have come to know as King Messiah and Son of God, not by their race.

6. From the viewpoint of NT theology, Christians must repeatedly remind themselves of two things. First, from a theological perspective every Christian is as guilty of putting Jesus on the cross as Caiaphas. Thoughtful believers will surely admit that their own guilt is the more basic of the two; for if we believe Matthew's witness, and Jesus could have escaped the clutches of Caiaphas (v.53), then what drove Jesus to the cross was his commitment to the Father's redemptive purposes. While this does not excuse Caiaphas and his peers, it keeps Christians from supercilious judgment of the Jews. Second, even if first-century Christians, whether Jews or Gentiles, rightly saw God's judgment in the destruction of Jerusalem and Judea (A.D. 66–73), that could not give them the right to put themselves in God's place and execute his judgment for him. Judgment belongs only to God. Any other view, including that which has often dominated Christendom, fails to recognize essential NT distinctions between the kingdom and the church (see on 13:37–39).

At this point we should consider one of several ways in which the complementary accounts of Jesus' passion in our Gospels can be reasonably harmonized so as to show how the proceedings against Jesus could have been completed within the few hours the chronology permits. There were two trials, one Jewish and the other Roman. The Jewish trial began with an informal examination by Annas (John 18:12–14, 19–23), perhaps while members of the Sanhedrin were being hurriedly gathered. A decision by a session of the Sanhedrin (vv.57–68; Mark 14:53–65) was followed by a formal decision at dawn and a dispatch to Pilate (27:1–2; Luke 22:66–71). The Roman trial began with a first examination before Pilate (vv.11–14; John 18:28–38a) and was quickly followed by Herod's interrogation (Luke 23:6–12) and the final appearance before Pilate (27:15–31; John 18:38b–19:16). This reconstruction is merely tentative; but it usefully coordinates the biblical data.

57 For the relationship between Annas and Caiaphas, see on v.3. If both men concurred in finding Jesus guilty and recommending the death penalty, the action would more likely win the acceptance of both the populace and the Romans than if only one agreed. Well-to-do homes were often built in a square shape with an open, central courtyard. If Annas lived in rooms on one wing of the court, then it is possible that he interviewed Jesus (John 18:14–16) in one wing while the Sanhedrin was assembling in another (NIV's "had assembled" is too strong: the Greek verb means no more than "assembled"). Not much time would be required.

Matthew mentions the teachers of the law and the elders; Mark 14:53 adds the chief priests, to whom Matthew refers in v.59. There is probably little significance to such variations, but they warn us against reading too much into particular details. No Pharisees are mentioned, though doubtless many teachers and lay elders belonged to that party. Their absence from Matthew's passion account is important for two reasons. First, it calls in question theories that pit the Matthean church against "Pharisees" of A.D. 85; for if Matthew sees the Pharisees as prime enemies of Jesus, why are they not mentioned in this final confrontation? Second, it accurately reflects the little we know of Jerusalem politics at the time. The Pharisees doubtless exercised throughout the land strong theological and social influence and through the synagogues in the towns and villages a great deal of moral persuasion and some political power. But for the Sanhedrin, where the final act of confrontation with Jewish leaders was played out, the shape of power was different. The high priest, almost certainly a Sadducee, presided; the priests, primarily if not exclusively Sadducees, enjoyed large and perhaps dominant influence; and the Pharisees exercised power only through the decision of the entire assembly.

58 Peter followed Jesus "at a distance," midway between courage (v.51) and cowardice (v.70) (Bengel). John 18:15–16 provides additional information on how Peter secured entrance to the high priest's courtyard. Peter joined the "servants" (the term is general but probably includes both household servants and temple police—hence NIV's "guards") around the courtyard fire, waiting to see the outcome.

59–63a If there was but one central Sanhedrin (see above), it was composed of three groups: leading priests (see on 21:23), teachers of the law, and elders. It had seventy members plus the high priest, but a mere twenty-three made a quorum. The "whole Sanhedrin" need not mean that everyone was present (cf. Luke 23:50–51) but only that the Sanhedrin as a body was involved. We do not know what proportion of the seventy came from constituent groups or whether the proportion had to be preserved in the quorum.

Many equate this meeting of the Sanhedrin with the one at daybreak described by Luke (22:66–71). But Matthew seems to make a distinction between the two (cf. 27:1–2). Perhaps the later meeting was in the temple precincts (the usual place) and was more fully attended; and if so, Luke may well be conflating the proceedings.

Matthew says the Sanhedrin was looking "for false evidence" (*pseudomartyria*, v.59) and obtained it from "false witnesses" (*pseudomartyres*, v.60). It is unlikely this means that the Sanhedrin sought liars only; if so, why not simply fabricate the evidence? Rather, the Sanhedrin, already convinced of Jesus' guilt, went through the motions of securing evidence against him. When people hate, they readily accept false witness; and the Sanhedrin eventually heard and believed just about what it wanted. Matthew knew that Jesus was not guilty and could not be; so he describes the evidence as "false."

The two men who came forward (v.60) may or may not have been suborned (cf. Acts 6:11). At least two witnesses were required in a capital case. In Greek *houtos* does not necessarily carry a sneering tone (NIV, "This fellow," v.61; similarly v.71) but may serve as an emphatic pronoun or equivalent to the British "this chap."

Their witness had some element of truth but was evilly motivated and disregarded what Jesus meant in John 2:19–21 (the reference is not to Matthew 24:2, where only disciples were present; see on 21:12–17). John did not interpret Jesus' saying allegorically (Hill, *Matthew*) but typologically. Though some will insist that even typological exegesis must be traced to the later church, we have already noted enough typological exegesis in Jesus' own teaching (see on v.28) to acknowledge that Jesus himself led the way in this regard. Interpreted with crass literalism, Jesus' words might be taken as a threat to desecrate the temple, one of the pillars of Judaism. Desecration of sacred places was almost universally regarded as a capital offense in the ancient world, and in this Jews were not different from the pagans (e.g., Jer 26:1–19; *Tosephta Sanhedrin* 13:5; b *Rosh ha-Shanah* 17a).

But what do Jesus' words in John 2:19–21 mean? If Jesus sees himself as the antitype of the Passover lamb, the true Suffering Servant, the revelation of the Father, and the fulfillment of OT Scriptures (e.g., vv.27–30; cf. 5:17–20; 11:25–30), it is not at all unlikely he would also see himself as the true temple, the ultimate point of meeting between God and man. In that case John's words accurately reflect Jesus' thought.

We have penetrated very close to the heart of the dispute between early Christianity and Judaism as attested elsewhere in the NT—a dispute that may be summarized by a series of questions: What is the nature of the continuity between the old covenant and the new? Must Gentiles become Jews before they can become Christians? In what sense and to what degree does the Mosaic law have binding force on Jesus' followers? The place of the temple is one element in that debate, raised in earliest Christianity (Acts 6:13–14), but traceable back to Jesus himself and a contributing factor to his own condemnation.

NIV and NASB are probably correct in translating v.62 as two questions from the high priest (cf. BDF, pars. 298[4]; 299[1]). He probably hoped Jesus would incriminate himself. But, true to Isaiah 53:7, Jesus kept silent (v.63a; cf. Moo, "Use of OT," pp. 148–51).

63b The high priest, frustrated by Jesus' silence, tried a bold stroke that cut to the central issue: Was Jesus the Messiah or was he not? The question has been raised before in one form or another (see on 12:38–42; 16:1–4; 21:1–11, 14–16, 23) and may have been prompted in the high priest's mind by Jesus' mention of the temple, since some branches of Judaism anticipated a renewal of the temple's glory when Messiah came (cf. Lane, *Mark*, p. 535). But whether or not this explains his motive, the high priest boldly charges Jesus to answer "under oath by the living God" (cf. McNeile; Benoit, *Jesus*, for justification of this rendering).

The form of the question in Mark 14:61 is slightly different: "Are you the Christ [see on 1:1; 2:4], the Son of the Blessed One?" Instead of the latter, Matthew uses his preferred title, "the Son of God." The two titles are formally equivalent and both may have been used at various points in the trial (cf. John 19:7). "Son of God" in Judaism can be equivalent to Messiah (see on 2:15; 3:17; 11:27; 16:13–20).

The outcome is now inevitable. If Jesus refuses to answer, he breaks a legally imposed oath. If he denies he is the Messiah, the crisis is over—but so is his influence. If he affirms it, then, given the commitments of the court, Jesus must be false. After all, how could the true Messiah allow himself to be imprisoned and put in jeopardy? The Gospels' evidence suggests that the Sanhedrin was prepared to see Jesus' unequivocal claim to messiahship as meriting the death penalty, and their unbelief precluded them from allowing any other possibility.

64 Perhaps this is what is meant by Jesus' "good confession" (1 Tim 6:13). There are four points of interest.

1. Unlike the unambiguous "I am" in Mark 14:62, Matthew uses an expression, found also in 26:25, that many have taken to be purposely ambiguous (e.g., Turner, *Insights*, pp. 72–75). But Catchpole has convincingly shown that the expression is "affirmative in content, and reluctant or circumlocutory in formulation" (David R. Catchpole, "The Answer of Jesus to Caiaphas (Matt.xxvi.64)," NTS 17 [1970–71]: 213–26). Certainly Caiaphas understood it as positive (v.65). The next clause, beginning with *plēn legō hymin* ("But I say to all of you"), found also in 11:22, 24, means something like "Indeed I tell you": there is likely no adversative force (Thrall, pp. 72–78). Instead it expresses "an expansion or a qualification" (Catchpole, "Answer of Jesus," p. 223) of the preceding statement. Jesus speaks in this way, not because Caiaphas has spoken the truth of himself without any revelation (Kingsbury, *Matthew*, p. 64) but because Caiaphas's understanding of "Messiah" and "Son of God" is fundamentally inadequate. Jesus is indeed the Messiah and so must answer affirmatively. But he is not quite the Messiah Caiaphas has in mind; so he must answer cautiously and with some explanation.

2. That explanation comes in allusions to two passages—Psalm 110:1 (see on 22:41–46) and Daniel 7:13 (see on 8:20; 24:1–3, 30–31). Jesus is not to be primarily considered a political Messiah but as the one who, in receiving a kingdom, is exalted high above David and at the Mighty One's right hand, the hand of honor and power (cf. 16:27; 23:39; 24:30–31; 26:29). This is Jesus' climactic self-disclosure to the authorities and it combines revelation with threat.

3. Jesus uses "Son of Man" (see on 8:20) instead of "Christ" or "Son of God" (cf. v.63). Efforts to interpret "Son of Man" in terms of "Son of God" (Kingsbury, *Matthew*, pp. 113ff.) badly miss the point (cf. Hill, "Son and Servant"). The titles are parallel, and each is messianic. Certainly Caiaphas understands "Son of Man" that way. The most ambiguous title now reveals most about Jesus: it is his self-designation, associated with the glory of the Parousia, but uttered at the culmination of Jesus' ministry and in the face of suffering and death.

4. The Greek phrase *ap' arti* (lit., "from now; NIV, "in the future"; see on v.29) is difficult. Some have found it so difficult that they say v.64 must refer, not to the Parousia, but to the Resurrection (e.g., L. Hartman, "Scriptural Exegesis," in Didier, p. 145). But if "from now" or "from now on" ill suits the delay till the Parousia, it is equally unsuited to the delay till the Resurrection and the Ascension (see on 28:18–20). Moreover the records show that the high priest and other august leaders were not witnesses of the Resurrection; for according to the NT, no human being saw the actual event happen.

The best explanation of v.64 is that Jesus is telling the members of the Sanhedrin ("you" is pl.) that from then on they would not see him as he now stands before them but only in his capacity as undisputed King Messiah and sovereign Judge. "From now on" (i.e., "in the future," NIV) that is the way they will see him. Matthew does not include the word "only" or the like (e.g., "From now on you will only see the Son of Man sitting on the right hand. . . .") because it would imply a possibility they might not see him at all, which is not true. The phrase "from now on" makes this a forceful warning that at least some Sanhedrin members doubtless remembered after the Resurrection.

65–66 Rending garments (v.65) was prescribed for blasphemy (M *Sanhedrin* 7:5) but can also express indignation or grief (cf. 2 Kings 18:37; Jud 14:19; 1 Macc 11:71;

Acts 14:14). It appears that the definition of "blasphemy" varied over the years (see above, on vv.57–68; cf. John 5:18; 10:33). Whether the Sanhedrin thought Jesus was blaspheming because he claimed to be Messiah, because he put himself on the Mighty One's right hand, or because God had not especially attested who Jesus was (a requirement in certain rabbinic traditions) is uncertain. The decision of the assembled members of the Sanhedrin appears to have been by acclamation. "Worthy" (*enochos,* v.66) is the same word used in 5:21: Jesus is "liable" to the death penalty, mandated for blasphemy (Lev 24:16).

67–68 Although Luke portrays the examination and condemnation only at the trial that takes place after dawn (parallel to Matt 27:1–2), even he has this outrage first (Luke 22:63–65), which, in agreement with Matthew and Mark, suggests that some decisions had already been made. Though "they" (v.67) might well mean the members of the Sanhedrin, it might also refer to those under their control, their immediate servants (cf. Luke 22:63–65). In any case the messianic claims of the accused do not impress the Sanhedrin; and the indignities to which he is now subjected are probably meant to deride his false pretensions. The true Messiah would vanquish all foes and, according to some Jewish traditions, would be able to judge by smell without the need of sight (see Lane, *Mark*, pp. 539–40 and references there; cf. also Pss Sol 17:37ff.). But here is Jesus, spit on, punched, slapped (cf. Isa 50:6; the verb for "slapped" is also used in 5:39 and may mean "clubbed"), blindfolded (Mark 14:65; Matthew does not mention this detail), and taunted, without displaying any power.

"Prophesy" (v.68) does not here imply foretelling the future but revealing hidden knowledge (cf. 11:13): Messiah should be able to tell who hit him, even when blindfolded. The easiest way to explain Matthew's not mentioning blindfolding while including "Who hit you?" (not in Mark) is that Matthew and Mark have each kept one part of what Luke has kept intact (Notes). In any case Jesus remains silent, confirming their suspicions while fulfilling Isaiah 53:7.

Notes

---

61 The peculiar expression διὰ τριῶν ἡμερῶν (*dia triōn hēmerōn,* "in three days") uses the preposition in its primary sense of "between," which then extends to the notion of interval (contra B.F. Meyer; cf. Zerwick, par. 115; Moule, *Idiom Book*, p. 56).

63 Some MSS preserve only καί (*kai,* "and"), others καὶ ἀποκριθεὶς (*kai apokritheis,* "and he answered"), and a few ἀποκριθεὶς οὖν (*apokritheis oun,* "therefore he answered"). Although some have argued that the shortest reading came about because copyists felt "answered" was inappropriate immediately after a statement about Jesus' silence, Metzger (*Textual Commentary*, p. 65) says the majority of the UBS Committee preferred the shortest reading on the external evidence. But it is difficult to imagine why "answered" would have been introduced into the shortest reading, and easy to understand how the second reading could have generated the other two. If original, "answered" must be understood as in 11:25.

68 Although this is a remarkably clear "minor agreement" of Matthew and Luke (22:64) against Mark (14:65), it is scarcely adequate to overturn Mark's priority (cf. Introduction, section 3); but at very least it suggests that more independent accounts of the synoptic passion narratives were circulating (cf. Luke 1:1–4) than is commonly recognized. Some detect Luke's dependence on Matthew here. The literary relationships are too complex to sort out with certainty; but in view of the apparent independence of Luke's trial narrative as a whole, it seems wise to think that on this one point—the *combination* of the blindfolding and the question "Who hit you?"—Luke has preserved the *historical* connection, of which Matthew and Mark have each given one part (Tasker; for discussion and literature, cf. Moo, "Use of OT," p. 142, n. 2).

---

8. *Peter's denial of Jesus*

26:69–75

69Now Peter was sitting out in the courtyard, and a servant girl came to him. "You also were with Jesus of Galilee," she said.
70But he denied it before them all. "I don't know what you're talking about," he said.
71Then he went out to the gateway, where another girl saw him and said to the people there, "This fellow was with Jesus of Nazareth."
72He denied it again, with an oath: "I don't know the man!"
73After a little while, those standing there went up to Peter and said, "Surely you are one of them, for your accent gives you away."
74Then he began to call down curses on himself and he swore to them, "I don't know the man!"
Immediately a rooster crowed. 75Then Peter remembered the word Jesus had spoken: "Before the rooster crows, you will disown me three times." And he went outside and wept bitterly.

The four Gospel accounts, though brief (cf. Mark 14:66–72; Luke 22:54–62; John 18:15–18, 25–27 and see above on v.34 for comments regarding two cock crowings [Mark]), contain substantial differences, and a variety of solutions have been proposed. Matthew and Mark are in close agreement and list three denials: (1) before a servant girl, in the courtyard; (2) before another girl, but out by the gateway; (3) before bystanders, apparently in the court. Luke also lists three: (1) before a servant girl, apparently near the fire; (2) before another person, place not specified; (3) before yet another person, still in the courtyard (22:60–61). The three denials recorded by John are (1) before a servant girl at the door; then, after a break in the narrative, (2) before some people—the verb is plural but may be a generalizing one—(3) before one of the high priest's servants, a relative of Malchus.

Several things may be said.

1. Some attempts to harmonize the texts have resulted in Jesus' predicting *three* denials at each of *two* different times, making *six* denials (most recently, cf. H. Lindsell, *The Battle for the Bible* [Grand Rapids: Zondervan, 1976], pp. 174–76). This is not only intrinsically unlikely but introduces major source-critical problems never addressed and handled.

2. It may help us to look at the location of the relevant pericopes in the four Gospels. If our treatment of the trial sequence is correct (see on vv.57–68), Matthew and Mark do not record the examination before Annas but simply say that Peter followed Jesus into the courtyard. Then they place Peter's three denials after the preliminary trial before the Sanhedrin. Luke records neither the examination before Annas nor the preliminary trial before the Sanhedrin and therefore places Peter's

three denials before recording the Sanhedrin trial at dawn. John has nothing about the Jewish trial (though it may be hinted at in 19:24) except Jesus' examination before Annas. If Peter's first denial took place about the time of that examination, it is understandable that John separates it from the other two, which he describes after Jesus has been led before Caiaphas.

3. The order of the first two denials may be reversed between John and the Synoptics (cf. the order of the temptations; see on 4:1–11), but which Gospel has the historical order cannot easily be determined. John has "the girl at the gate" asking the first question and implies, but does not state, that this occurs on Peter's way in. Matthew and Mark have Jesus move back out to the gate as the setting for their second denial. Several possibilities come to mind, but no adequate way of testing them.

4. Remaining differences are minor and are capable of many solutions. Problems arise from the brevity of the accounts. In a setting around a fire, two or three may speak up at once (see below on vv.69–70); or, more probably, the plural in the second denial (in John's order) is generalizing (as in Matt 2:20). The differences in the reports of the denial cannot adequately be accounted for on redactional grounds.

69–70 The article "a" in "a servant girl" masks an idiomatic use of "one" (*mia*, v.69; see on 8:19; 21:19; cf. Moule, *Idiom Book*, p. 125). Her remark to Peter reflects both an accusation and her curiosity; and "Jesus of Galilee" (Mark 14:67: "that Nazarene, Jesus") is the kind of derogatory remark one might expect from a Jerusalemite convinced of her geographical and cultural superiority. Peter denies her words "before them all" (v.70), implying that several people were listening and that some may have joined in the questioning. The form of Peter's denial is akin to a formal, legal oath (cf. M *Shebuoth* 8:3).

71–72 Peter "went out" (v.71) to the gateway, apparently retiring from the brighter light of the fire into the darkness of the forecourt. Again he denies the accusation, this time with an oath. "Oath" here (v.72) does not refer to "swearing" as we know it in profanity; rather, Peter invokes a solemn curse on himself if he is lying and professes his "truthfulness" by appealing to something sacred (see on 5:33–34; 23:16–22).

73–75 A little more time elapses (v.73). Luke says "about an hour later" (22:59). In any age accent in speaking varies with geography (e.g., Judg 12:5–6), and Peter's speech shows him to be a Galilean (cf. Hoehner, *Herod Antipas*, pp. 61–64). That one of those present at Peter's denial said that his accent proved him to be a disciple of Jesus shows how much Jesus' ministry had been in Galilee and how relatively few of his disciples were from Judea. Having lied twice Peter finds himself forced to lie again, this time with more oaths (v.74). Immediately the rooster crows, a bitter reminder (v.75) of Jesus' words (v.34). He who thought he could stand has fallen terribly (cf. 1 Cor 10:12). Luke tells us that Jesus looked at Peter—perhaps through a window or as he was being led across the courtyard. If we cannot credit the legend that after this Peter never heard a cock crow without weeping, we may justifiably assume that Peter's bitter tears led to his being "poorer in spirit" (5:3) the remainder of his days than he had ever been before.

Matthew does not mention Peter again.

9. *Formal decision of the Sanhedrin*

27:1–2

[1]Early in the morning, all the chief priests and the elders of the people came to the decision to put Jesus to death. [2]They bound him, led him away and handed him over to Pilate, the governor.

Whether this formal decision was reached as a final stage of the first meeting or at a separate meeting held either in Caiaphas's house or the temple precincts, we cannot say with certainty (see on vv.57–68). But Luke 22:66 implies a meeting in the council chamber (Catchpole, *Trial of Jesus*, pp. 191f.).

1 *Symboulion elabon* ("came to the decision") is a Latinism for *consilium capere* (cf. RHG, p. 109; BDF, par. 5[3b]) and does not mean "hold a council" (Hill, *Matthew*). On the other hand, Catchpole (*Trial of Jesus*, p. 191) seems to go too far in denying that it refers to the same event as Luke 22:66–71. The term can refer to a plot (as in 12:14; 22:15) and also to an agreed decision (28:12) as here. *Hōste* plus the infinitive here clearly refers to intention (cf. Zerwick, par. 352; Moule, *Idiom Book*, p. 140). Probably, too, the religious authorities decided just how to present their case to Pilate. If their own concern was Jesus' "blasphemy" (26:65), they were nevertheless more likely to get Pilate to sentence him to death by stressing the royal side of messiahship rather than blasphemy, as to Pilate that would suggest treason (cf. Acts 17:5–9 for a similar reference to treason).

2 Jesus is led to Pontius Pilate, the "governor" (for the variant, cf. Metzger, *Textual Commentary*, p. 65). "Governor" is here a general title (cf. 10:18; 1 Peter 2:14). Pilate was in fact appointed prefect or procurator by Tiberius Caesar in A.D. 26 (cf. IBD, 3:1229–31; ZPEB, 4:790–93). Prefects governed small, troubled areas; and in judicial matters they possessed powers like those of the far more powerful proconsuls and imperial legates; in short, they held the power of life and death, apart from appeal to Caesar. Following the banishment of Archelaus in A.D. 6, Judea and Samaria were made into one Roman province governed by a prefect or procurator who normally lived at Caesarea but often came to Jerusalem during the feasts to be close to the potential trouble spot.

Extrabiblical sources portray Pilate as a cruel, imperious, and insensitive ruler who hated his Jewish subjects and took few pains to understand them (e.g., Jos. Antiq. XVIII, 35 [ii.2], 55–62 [iii.1–2], 177–78 [vi.5]; War II, 169–77 [ix.2–4]; Philo, *ad Gaium* 38; cf. Hoehner, *Herod Antipas*, pp. 172–83). He stole korban (see on 15:5) money to build an aqueduct; and when the population of Jerusalem rioted in protest, he sent in soldiers who killed many. He defiled Jerusalem more than once (cf. Luke 13:1). These known facts about Pilate are often thought to render the Gospel accounts incredible, for here Pilate is portrayed as weak, ineffectual, and cowardly, judicially fair enough to want to release Jesus but too cowardly to stand up to the Sanhedrin's brow-beating tactics. This transformation of Pilate's character, it is claimed, results from the evangelists' desire to exculpate the Romans and condemn the Jews.

Hoehner (*Chronological Aspects*, pp. 105–14) responds to these problems with his crucifixion date of A.D. 33, *after* Pilate had set up the embossed shields in Jerusalem that Tiberius Caesar directly ordered removed, and *after* the execution of Pilate's patron, the anti-Semite Sejanus (d. 19 Oct. A.D. 31), whose death endangered Pilate. At this time the Sanhedrin would have found it easier to make direct and telling application to the emperor. In Hoehner's view Pilate appears weak in the Gospels because he has just been severely rebuked by Caesar and fears that the Jews' threat (John 19:12) could lead to another rebuke. By A.D. 33 Pilate's administration had become so bad that in A.D. 36 he was recalled and finally banished.

Even without this chronology, far too wide a historical gap between the Pilate of the Gospels and the Pilate of extrabiblical sources is being assumed.

1. Modern psychology helps us understand that the weak, insecure, selfish man elevated to a position of authority may become despotic and insensitive. Thus the evidence about Pilate may be complementary rather than disjunctive.

2. Pilate hated the Jews and especially the Jewish leaders. In the crisis forced on him by the Sanhedrin, though he may have seemed to be *for* Jesus, in reality he was probably *against* the Sanhedrin. His final decision betrayed no trace of sympathy for the Sanhedrin; rather, the Jews' threat (John 19:12) could well have intimidated so corrupt a man at any point in his career.

3. Jesus was not the criminal or guerrilla fighter with which Pilate was familiar. Jesus' silence and poise, the wisdom of his brief answers, and the dreams of Pilate's wife (v.19) may have prompted less drastic action than Pilate usually took.

4. Arguably, v.24 does not exculpate Pilate or reserve exclusive blame for the Jews (see on vv.24–25). Instead, as in vv.3–5, Matthew uses irony to say that no one connected with this crisis could escape personal responsibility.

5. Both the Sanhedrin trial and the trial before Pilate were necessary for capital punishment. Without the Sanhedrin, Pilate would never have taken action against Jesus unless he had become convinced Jesus was a dangerous Zealot leader; without Pilate the Sanhedrin might whip up mob violence against Jesus, but not a legally binding death sentence (cf. John 18:31).

10. *The death of Judas*

27:3–10

[3]When Judas, who had betrayed him, saw that Jesus was condemned, he was seized with remorse and returned the thirty silver coins to the chief priests and the elders. [4]"I have sinned," he said, "for I have betrayed innocent blood."

"What is that to us?" they replied. "That's your responsibility."

[5]So Judas threw the money into the temple and left. Then he went away and hanged himself.

[6]The chief priests picked up the coins and said, "It is against the law to put this into the treasury, since it is blood money." [7]So they decided to use the money to buy the potter's field as a burial place for foreigners. [8]That is why it has been called the Field of Blood to this day. [9]Then what was spoken by Jeremiah the prophet was fulfilled: "They took the thirty silver coins, the price set on him by the people of Israel, [10]and they used them to buy the potter's field, as the Lord commanded me."

This account is peculiar to Matthew, though Acts 1:16–19 also records Judas's death. The differences between the two are considerable; and many scholars hold that Acts 1:16–19 or something like it circulated as a bit of independent tradition Matthew adapted to develop his "fulfillment" theme further. But Benoit (*Jesus*, pp. 189–207) finds greater historical accuracy in Matthew than in Acts. Many believe the only historically fixed points are Judas's sudden death and the purchase of a piece of land called "the Field of Blood" (cf. Stendahl, *School of Matthew*, pp. 120–27; Lindars, *Apologetic*, pp. 116–22). But if Matthew developed a fulfillment theme by adding to or changing an earlier tradition, numerous difficulties, including even misnaming the prophet (v.9), show that he botched the job.

Hill's suggestion that Matthew placed the story of Judas's suicide here to show that Judas's remorse depends on the Sanhedrin's decision, not Pilate's, is only a possibility. No matter where Matthew located the pericope, it would interrupt the narrative at this point; and other reasons may have led him to place it here. Matthew's prime interest in this pericope is to continue the fulfillment theme—that not only Jesus' death but the major events surrounding it were prophesied in Scripture. Verse 4 again stresses Jesus' innocence and sees the fulfillment of another of Jesus' predictions (26:24), which sets up an apologetic tool (cf. "to this day," v.8). In any case, neither Peter's tears nor Judas's remorse can remove their guilt.

3 On "the chief priests and elders," here governed by a single article suggesting a single entity (the Sanhedrin), see on 21:23. Verse 3 looks back to 10:4; 26:14–16, 20–25. Judas's "remorse" is not necessarily repentance, though the two Greek verbs *metamelomai* (here and in 21:29) and *metanoeō* can overlap.

4 Judas recognizes that he is not only guilty of betrayal but that Jesus whom he has betrayed is "innocent" (cf. Metzger, *Textual Commentary*, p. 66). The Jewish leaders' callous response "What is that to us?" is both a Semitic and classical idiom (cf. BDF, pars. 127[3], 299[3]). But their own words condemn them, for it *should* have been something to them. Judas has betrayed innocent blood; they have condemned innocent blood. "That's your responsibility" (lit., "you will see [to it]," as in v.24), they say—a remark correct in content but wrong in implying that they are absolved.

5–8 Exactly where Judas threw the money (v.5) is uncertain (cf. Notes). He then went out and hanged himself. *Apēnxato* ("hanged himself") occurs in 2 Samuel 17:23 LXX. On this basis some have made lengthy comparisons between Judas and Ahithophel—the one a treacherous friend of David, the other a treacherous friend of David's greater Son (e.g., B.F. Meyer, McNeile); but that Matthew intended such a comparison is doubtful (cf. Moo, "Use of OT," pp. 189–91).

The chief priests, in accord with Deuteronomy 23:18, refuse to allow the blood money to supplement the funds of the *korbanas* ("treasury," v.6; used only here in the NT—the place where a consecrated article is deposited and cognate with *korban;* see on 15:5; Jos. War II, 175 [ix.4]). Many scholars suggest that elements of the OT quotation (vv.9–10) have generated these "historical" details. They hold that the Hebrew *yôṣēr* ("potter") in Zechariah 11–13 was either confused with *'ôṣār* ("treasury") or that the latter was found in Matthew's copy of Zechariah (as in Peshitta). Alternatively *yôṣēr* can mean "smith," i.e., a worker in metals, and is so rendered by LXX. Does Zechariah therefore throw his money "to the potter" (NIV), to the treasury, or to the temple foundry, which made temple vessels and coins? The problem with this alternative to the MT is that if Matthew (or the tradition he used) understood the OT to refer to the treasury, then where did he find his reference to "potter" (vv.7, 10)? The OT text is indeed difficult, though a better analysis is possible (see below). What is clear is that Matthew is again pointing out the propensity of the Jewish leaders for ceremonial probity even in the face of gross injustice (cf. 12:9–14; 15:1–9; 23:23; 28:12–13; cf. John 18:28).

With this probity in view, the chief priests decide (same construction as in v.1) to buy the potter's field to meet a public need (v.7)—an accepted use of ill-gotten gains (cf. SBK, 1:37; Jeremias, *Jerusalem*, p. 140). The potter's field, used for the burial of foreigners, probably did not belong to "the potter" (surely there was more than one potter in Jerusalem) but was a well-known place, perhaps the place where potters had long obtained their clay. If depleted, it might have been offered for sale. There are no reliable early traditions of its location, though Matthew's "to this day" shows it was well known when he wrote. The best assumption is that it lay in the valley of Hinnom near the juncture with the Kidron.

There are three significant differences between these verses and Acts 1:18–19.

1. Matthew says that the chief priests bought the field; Acts, that Judas did. But if the priests bought it with Judas's money, it may well have been regarded as his. More important, the language in Acts is fine spun: "With the reward of unrighteousness, he acquired [*ktaomai*, not necessarily 'bought'] a field" (lit. tr.). "The money bought him a burial-place; that was to him the sole financial outcome of the iniquitous transaction" (Broadus).

2. Matthew says Judas hanged himself; Acts, that "he fell headlong, his body burst open and all his intestines spilled out." This does not imply a disease, or that Judas tripped, as some have held. If Judas hanged himself, no Jew would want to defile himself during the Feast of Unleavened Bread by burying the corpse; and a hot sun might have brought on rapid decomposition till the body fell to the ground and burst open. Alternatively, one long tradition in the church claims Judas hanged himself from a tree branch that leaned over a ravine (of which there are many in the area); and when the branch broke, whether before or after he died, Judas fell to a messy end. We are not so much beset by contradictory accounts as by paucity of information, making it difficult to decide which of several alternatives we should choose in working out the complementarity of the two accounts.

3. Matthew seems to ascribe the name "Field of Blood" to its being purchased with blood money; Acts, to the fact that Judas's blood was shed there. But again the paucity of information faces us with several possibilities. All the circumstances must have become public knowledge; and one reason, far from ruling out the other, actually complements it—provided that Judas died in the field purchased by the priests. Perhaps the priests bought the field (not necessarily the same day—Sunday would have been adequate); and Judas, informed as to what had been done with the blood money and driven to despair by futile remorse, decided to commit suicide in a field for the burial of aliens to Israel's covenants.

Moreover we must at least raise the question whether Acts 1:18–19 associates "Field of Blood" with Judas's blood. "Everyone in Jerusalem heard about this" (Acts 1:19); but does "this" refer to Judas's body splitting open, without mention of blood, or to securing the field with blood money, also without explicit mention of blood? This is not an attempt at forced harmonization. But if it is bad historiography to squeeze two diverse accounts of one incident into a contrived union, it is equally bad historiography to mistake an instance of too little information for contradiction.

9–10 Four aspects of this complex quotation need discussion.

1. *The ascription to Jeremiah*. On the face of it, the quotation is a rough rendering of Zechariah 11:12–13, with "I took" changed to "they took" and the price interpreted as referring to the sum paid for Jesus. The only obvious allusions to Jeremiah are 18:2–6; 32:6–15—Jeremiah did visit a potter and buy a field. But

though some of the language of those passages may have influenced Matthew 27:9–10, it is difficult to imagine why Matthew mentioned Jeremiah instead of Zechariah, even though Jeremiah is important in this Gospel (cf. 2:17; 16:14). Highly improbable "solutions" abound. Some have followed the minor textual variant "Zechariah" instead of "Jeremiah"; others have argued for an original text with no mention of the prophet's name, attributing "Jeremiah" to a copyist's error; many have assumed that Matthew made a minor error; others have appealed to a hypothetical writing of Jeremiah now lost; others have held that Jeremiah wrote Zechariah 9–11—though it is surely "a critical anachronism" (Morison) to see Matthew as anticipating modern source theories; and still others assume that Matthew is referring to the entire collection of prophetic books grouped under the name of the first book (though it is not at all certain that Jeremiah was first in Matthew's day).

The most believable solution comes from Hengstenberg (pp. 1095ff.) and is developed by Gundry (*Use of OT*, pp. 122–27), Senior (*Passion Narrative*, pp. 359ff.), and especially by Moo ("Use of OT," pp. 191–210). They note that no extant version of Zechariah 11 refers to a field; and Matthew's attributing the quotation to Jeremiah suggests we ought to look to that book. Jeremiah 19:1–13 (not Jer 18 or 32) is the obvious candidate. There Jeremiah is told to purchase a potter's jar and take some elders and priests to the Valley of Ben Hinnom, where he is to warn of the destruction of Jerusalem for her sin, illustrated by smashing the jar. A further linguistic link is "innocent blood" (Jer 19:4); and thematic links include renaming a locality associated with potters (19:1) with a name ("Valley of Slaughter") denoting violence (19:6). The place will henceforth be used as a burial ground (19:11), as a token of God's judgment. In the last clause in Matthew's quotation, "as the Lord commanded me" (v. 19), Lindars (*Apologetic*, p. 121) sees an allusion to Exodus 9:12; but Moo ("Use of OT," pp. 196f.) has shown this is at best tenuous.

We have not yet tried to explain what Matthew understands by these OT texts, or what he means by "fulfillment." But it is fair to say that the quotation appears to refer to Jeremiah 19:1–13 along with phraseology drawn mostly from Zechariah 11:12–13 (MT in both cases), with the concluding clause a traditional "obedience formula" (cf. R. Pesch, "Eine alttestamentliche Ausführungsformel im Matthäus-Evangelium," *Biblische Zeitschrift* 10 [1966]: 220–45) used to paraphrase the opening words of Zechariah 11:13: "And the LORD said to me." Such fusing of sources under one "quotation" is not unknown elsewhere in Scripture (e.g., Mark 1:2–3; cf. 2 Chron 36:21, verbally drawn from Lev 26:34–35, yet ascribed to Jeremiah [25:12; 29:10; cf. Gundry, *Use of OT*, p. 125]; and see on Matt 3:17). Jeremiah alone is mentioned, perhaps because he is the more important of the two prophets, and perhaps also because, though Jeremiah 19 is the less obvious reference, it is the more important as to prophecy and fulfillment.

2. *Prophecy and history*. Many scholars hold that Matthew presents as history a number of "fulfillments" that did not happen. Rather he deduces that they must have happened because his chosen OT texts predict, as he understands them, that such events would take place. To this there are two objections. First, the more complex and composite a quotation (as here), the less likely is it that the "fulfillment" was invented. It is far easier to believe that certain historical events led Matthew to look for Scriptures relating to them. We may then ask how he has treated these Scriptures, but that is a separate problem. Second, when we examine Matthew's quotation clause by clause, we can see impressive reasons for holding that the narrative does not grow out of the prophecy (see esp. Moo, "Use of OT,"

pp. 198ff.) To give but one instance, the "thirty silver coins" (v.3) are mentioned in Zechariah 11:13; but Mark speaks of betrayal money without mentioning Zechariah. Even if Mark does not specify the amount, the *fact* that Judas had been paid became well known, independent of any Christian interpretation of Zechariah 11:12–13; and it is not unreasonable to suppose that the *amount* of money *also* became common knowledge.

3. *Meaning*. How did Matthew understand the OT texts he was quoting? The question is not easy, because the two OT passages themselves can be variously explained. It appears that in Zechariah 11 the "buyers" (v.5) and the three shepherds (vv.5, 8, 17) apparently represent Israel's leaders, who are slaughtering the sheep. God commands Zechariah to shepherd the "flock marked for slaughter" (v.7), and he tries to clean up the leadership by sacking the false shepherds. But he discovers that not only is the leadership corrupt, but the flock detests him (v.8). Thus Zechariah comes to understand the Lord's decision to have no more pity on the people of the land (v.6).

Zechariah decides to resign (11:9–10), exposing the flock to ravages. Because he has broken the contract, Zechariah cannot claim his pay (presumably from the "buyers"); but they pay him off with thirty pieces of silver (v.12). But now Yahweh tells Zechariah to throw this "handsome price at which they priced me" (probably ironical; cf. Notes) to the potter in the "house of the LORD," i.e., the temple (v.13). Temple ritual required a constant supply of new vessels (cf. Lev 6:28) so a guild of potters worked somewhere in the temple precincts. Certainly Jeremiah could point to a potter as he preached and could purchase pottery somewhere near the temple (Jer 18:6; 19:1).

The purpose of Zechariah's action is uncertain. Because a *yôṣēr* (lit., "shaper") was both a potter and a metal worker, it may be that the money in Zechariah 11:12–13 was thrown to the *yôṣēr* so that it would be melted down and turned into a figurine, a little "god." The people did not want the Lord's shepherd, and so they will be saddled with a silver figurine (cf. Ezek 16:17; Hos 2:8)—betrayal money, in effect, since it pays off the good shepherd who would have kept the people true to the Lord's covenant and who has been rejected by the people. The result can only be catastrophic judgment (11:14–17).

The parallel between Zechariah 11 and Matthew 26–27 is not exact. In Zechariah the money is paid to the good shepherd; in Matthew it is paid to Judas and returned to the Jewish leaders. In Zechariah the money goes directly to the "potter" in the temple; in Matthew, after being thrown into the temple, it purchases "the potter's field"—though at this point the influence of Jeremiah 19 has been introduced (see below). Nevertheless the central parallel is stunning: in both instances Yahweh's shepherd is rejected by the people of Israel and valued at the price of a slave. And in both instances the money is flung into the temple and ends up purchasing something that pollutes.

The reference to Jeremiah 19 (cf. above, under 1) provides equally telling parallels. The rulers have forsaken Yahweh and made Jerusalem a place of foreign gods (19:4); so the day is coming when this valley, where the prophecy is given and the potter's jar smashed, will be called the Valley of Slaughter, symbolic of the ruin of Judah and Jerusalem (19:6–7). Similarly in Matthew the rejection of Jesus (Yahweh; see on 2:6; 3:3; 13:37–39) leads to a polluted field, a symbol of death and the destruction of the nation about to be buried as "foreigners."

4. *Fulfillment*. In the light of these relationships between the events surrounding

Jesus' death and the two key OT passages that make up Matthew's quotation, what does the evangelist mean by saying that the prophecy "was fulfilled"? As in 2:17, the form of this introductory formula shrinks from making Judas's horrible crime the immediate result of the Lord's word, while nevertheless insisting that all has taken place in fulfillment of Scripture (cf. 1:22 with 2:17). Beyond that there is a tendency to apply standard Jewish categories to this use of the OT by Matthew. For instance, Doeve (pp. 185f.) characterizes Matthew 27:3–10 as "haggadah," a creative story the starting point of which was the link between "innocent blood" in v.4 and in Jeremiah 26:15, which led on by associations of word and theme to Jeremiah 19, 32 and Zechariah 11:13. But "innocent blood" is not an uncommon expression and is therefore an inadequate link between Matthew and Jeremiah. Lindars (*Apologetic*, pp. 116–22) detects an elaborate Midrashic development along somewhat different lines, and Stendahl (*School of Matthew*, pp. 120–26; 196–98) finds a parallel in Midrash Pesher at Qumran. Though these are invaluable studies, several cautions are needed.

France (*Jesus*, pp. 206–7) draws attention to two differences between Matthew's use of the OT in this passage and the Pesharim at Qumran, which claimed that various OT texts were in reality referring to certain recent historical events. First, Matthew changes the wording far more than was done at Qumran; second, he respects the central intentions of the OT authors far more than at Qumran. These two points are linked: Matthew does not need to devise farfetched explanations for each word and phrase, because in each case he has truly represented the central theme. The verbal differences he introduces in citing the OT are not an embarrassment to him, because he is not claiming that the OT text is a prophecy to be fulfilled by a simple one-on-one pattern. Pesher claims that what the OT text refers to *is* the specified historical event; and there are close parallels to this claim elsewhere in the NT (e.g., Acts 2:16). But what we find in Matthew, including vv.9–10, is not *identification* of the text *with* an event but *fulfillment* of the text *in* an event, based on a broad typology governing how both Jesus and Matthew read the OT (see on 2:15; 8:17; 13:35; 26:28, 54).

Because of this typological model, Matthew introduces the commonly noticed changes: the one on whom a price is set is no longer the prophet ("me," Zech 11:13) but Jesus ("him," Matt 27:9). Even Matthew's use of the concluding obedience formula—"as the Lord commanded me"—is best accounted for as a hint of the prophecy-fulfillment pattern. Here "me" can only refer to the prophet; yet Matthew keeps it even though he changes other parts of the quotation to "him," because he believes that in obeying the Lord, the prophet—whether Jeremiah or Zechariah—was setting forth typological paradigms that truly did point to Jesus and the greatest rejection of all.

"Midrash" and "haggadah" are deceptive categories. We have maintained that Matthew did not make up the events he relates to illustrate Scripture but that they stand as independent historical realities he now relates to Scripture. Normally, late Midrash (the only kind that is well defined: cf. Introduction, section 12.b) begins with the text as the point of departure, but in Matthew the narrative is the point of departure. The element of "fulfillment" is not present in Midrash in the way it is everywhere presupposed in the NT.

This is not a surreptitious plea to divorce Matthew from his Jewish roots. Doubtless it is correct to say that Matthew uses "midrashic techniques," at least on the level of what Moo calls "appropriation techniques"—i.e., devices by which an OT text is applied to or appropriated by events contemporary with the evangelist. But such procedures are so universally used that the expression "midrashic technique" conceals more than it reveals: it is a little like saying "interpretative techniques." What must not be overlooked is that, unlike any other broad, hermeneutical category used by the Jews, NT approaches to the OT are steeped in a salvation-historical perspective that finds in the sacred text entire patterns of prophetic anticipation (see esp. on 2:15; 5:17–20; 8:17; 11:11–13; 13:34–35). In this sense Matthew sees in Jeremiah 19 and Zechariah 11 not merely a number of verbal and thematic parallels to Jesus' betrayal but a pattern of apostasy and rejection that must find its ultimate fulfillment in the rejection of Jesus, who was cheaply valued, rejected by the Jews, and whose betrayal money was put to a purpose that pointed to the destruction of the nation (see on 15:7–9; 21:42).

Notes

5 The question of where Judas threw the money is beset by two problems.

1. O. Michel (TDNT, 4:882–85) and G. Schrenk (TDNT, 3:235) argue that there is no necessary difference between ναός (*naos*, "temple [sanctuary]") and ἱερόν (*hieron*, "temple [and its precincts]"). If so, then the use of the former in this verse means no more than that Judas threw the money somewhere in the temple area. But a fairly strong case can be made for maintaining a distinction between the words in Matthew's usage: *naos* is used only of the temple proper, the sanctuary, in 23:16–17, 21; 27:51, and, metaphorically, in 26:61; 27:40; whereas *hieron* is used of the temple and its precincts in 4:5; 21:12, 14–15, 23; 24:1; 26:55 (cf. Garland, p. 199, n. 117). It is possible that *hieron* is a trifle forced in 12:5; but since it is the encompassing term and not all the priests' functions took place in the temple proper, the use still admits the traditional distinction between the terms. That leaves only 27:5; but in the narrow sense of *naos*, Judas would normally not have been allowed to enter. That may be just the point: feeling damned already, he has nothing more to lose; and in desperation he runs into the temple proper and flings down his money before he can be stopped. Thus he deeply incriminates the priests, a further example of 23:35.

2. It is very difficult to decide between the variant εἰς τὸν ναόν (*eis ton naon*, "into the temple") and ἐν τῷ ναῷ (*en tō naō*, "in the temple") (cf. Metzger, *Textual Commentary*, p. 66).

8 The aorist passive ἐκλήθη (*eklēthē*, lit., "it was called") here takes on perfective force ("it has been called") because of the ἕως (*heōs*, "until") clause that follows (cf. Burton, *Syntax*, par. 18; Moule, *Idiom Book*, p. 14; somewhat similar, 28:15).

9 Although thirty shekels is the price of a slave (Exod 21:32), some argue (e.g., Joyce Baldwin, *Haggai, Zechariah, Malachi*, TOTC [London: Tyndale, 1972], pp. 183–86) that the amount is not paltry. The Code of Hammurabi distinguishes an ordinary citizen from a slave by saying that when either is gored to death by an ox, the payment in the former case is one-half mina, in the latter one-third mina, when a mina was probably worth about fifty shekels. Doubtless the biblical law puts more value on a human life, slave or not; but the fact remains that thirty shekels is a slave's price. If Baldwin is correct, then "the handsome price" of Zech 11:13 is not ironic but must be an indication of how willing the buyers were to get rid of this shepherd. This seems unlikely since Zechariah is going to leave anyway. If, however, "the handsome price" is meant sardonically, this makes good sense; for even if the amount represents a substantial sum, it is still the price of a slave and representative of how God's prophet is valued by an apostate people. The same kind of irony probably stands behind the paronomasia of Matt 27:9: τὴν τιμὴν τοῦ τετιμημένου ὃν ἐτιμήσαντο (*tēn timēn tou tetimēmenou hon etimēsanto*, lit., "the price of the one whose price had been priced [by the sons of Israel]").

10 The third person plural ἔδωκαν (*edōkan*, "they gave"; NIV, "they used") is to be preferred above the first person singular ἔδωκα (*edōka*, "I gave,") because the OT text and the "me" of the next clause would be strong inducement to change to the first person (cf. Senior, *Passion Narrative*, p. 356).

---

11. *Jesus before Pilate*

27:11–26

[11]Meanwhile Jesus stood before the governor, and the governor asked him, "Are you the king of the Jews?"

"Yes, it is as you say," Jesus replied.

[12]When he was accused by the chief priests and the elders, he gave no answer. [13]Then Pilate asked him, "Don't you hear the testimony they are bringing against you?" [14]But Jesus made no reply, not even to a single charge—to the great amazement of the governor.

[15]Now it was the governor's custom at the Feast to release a prisoner chosen by the crowd. [16]At that time they had a notorious prisoner, called Barabbas. [17]So when the crowd had gathered, Pilate asked them, "Which one do you want me to release to you: Barabbas, or Jesus who is called Christ?" [18]For he knew it was out of envy that they had handed Jesus over to him.

[19]While Pilate was sitting on the judge's seat, his wife sent him this message: "Don't have anything to do with that innocent man, for I have suffered a great deal today in a dream because of him."

[20]But the chief priests and the elders persuaded the crowd to ask for Barabbas and to have Jesus executed.

[21]"Which of the two do you want me to release to you?" asked the governor.

"Barabbas," they answered.

[22]"What shall I do, then, with Jesus who is called Christ?" Pilate asked.

They all answered, "Crucify him!"

[23]"Why? What crime has he committed?" asked Pilate.

But they shouted all the louder, "Crucify him!"

[24]When Pilate saw that he was getting nowhere, but that instead an uproar was starting, he took water and washed his hands in front of the crowd. "I am innocent of this man's blood," he said. "It is your responsibility!"

[25]All the people answered, "Let his blood be on us and on our children!"

[26]Then he released Barabbas to them. But he had Jesus flogged, and handed him over to be crucified.

John gives most details of the trial before Pilate; Luke adds the account of the intervening trial before Herod; and Matthew follows Mark rather closely, but vv.19, 24–25 have no parallel (cf. Mark 15:2–15; Luke 23:2–25; John 18:28–19:26).

The setting is uncertain. It might be the Tower of Antonia, on the northwest corner of the temple area; but more probably it is Herod's old palace on the west side of the city near the Jaffa gate (cf. Jos. Antiq. XX, 110; [v.3]; War II, 328 [xv.5]; Philo *ad Gaium* 38). The word "Praetorium" (v.27) can refer to a princely palace as readily as to a judicial or military seat. Probably Herod Antipas, tetrarch of Galilee, would also stay in his father's palace whenever he came to Jerusalem, which could explain the ease with which Jesus' brief interview with Herod (Luke 23:8–12) was arranged.

11 For comments regarding Pilate, see on vv.1–2. Matthew's report, in which Pilate asks, "Are you the king of the Jews?" presupposes the background of Luke 23:2 and John 18:28–33. The Sanhedrin's concern with Jesus' "blasphemy" becomes his claim to kingship, a charge of treason with overtones of Zealot sedition, capped with a claim that Jesus refuses to pay taxes (see on 22:15–22). In Roman trials the magistrate normally heard the charges first, questioned the defendant and listened to his defense, sometimes permitted several such exchanges, and then retired with his advisors to decide on a verdict, which was then promptly carried out. The first step, the charge by the Jewish leaders, led to this particular formulation of Pilate's question to Jesus. Jesus answers, as in 26:25, 64, in an affirmative but qualified way. He is indeed the king of the Jews, but not exactly in the sense Pilate might think. The nature of Jesus' kingship is defined in the more detailed exchange John reports (18:34–37).

Verse 11 is important theologically as well as historically. It stands behind the inscription on the cross (v.37) and prepares the way for Christianity, which rests on the conviction that Jesus of Nazareth, who rose from the dead, is indeed the promised Messiah, the King of the Jews—basic themes in Matthew even in the prologue. In other words, the vindicated Lord is the crucified Messiah (cf. N.A. Dahl, *The Crucified Messiah* [Minneapolis: Augsburg, 1974], pp. 10–36).

12–14 Persistent charges by "the chief priests and the elders" (v.12) evoke only silence from Jesus. If Jesus had said nothing at all, Pilate would be bound to condemn him (Sherwin-White, pp. 25–26) since in the Roman system the defense depended heavily on the defendant's response. But Jesus *has* spoken (v.11). Now, surrounded by unbelief and conscious that the hour has come, he makes no reply (v.13). Thus he continues to fulfill Isaiah 53:7 (see on 26:63). Pilate's "great amazement" (v.14) appears to be mingled with respect for Jesus and antipathy for the Jewish leaders, and so he takes tentative steps to release the prisoner. Meanwhile Jesus' silence testifies mutely to his willingness (cf. 26:53) to suffer as "a ransom for many" (20:28).

15 In Roman law an imperial magistrate could acquit a prisoner not yet condemned or pardon one already condemned; but the Gospel accounts makes this a regular custom, apparently associated with Judea alone (on the grammar, cf. Moule, *Idiom Book*, p. 59). Blinzler (pp. 218–21), followed by Lane (*Mark*, pp. 552f.) has shown that M *Pesahim* 8:6 ("they may slaughter [viz., a Passover lamb] for one . . . whom they have promised to bring out of prison") presupposes some kind of regular paschal amnesty; and the tractate in question is universally recognized as recording very old traditions.

16 "Barabbas" seems a strange name: "bar Abba" means "son of Abba," i.e., "son of the father." But there is evidence that the name or nickname was not unknown in rabbinic families (SBK, 1:1031). Perhaps Barabbas was the son of a famous rabbi (on such a use of "father," see on 23:9). Some MSS preserve his name as "Jesus Barabbas" (cf. Notes), but with what authority we cannot now be certain. Matthew says he was an *episēmos* ("notorious," NIV) prisoner. NIV's translation of the word implies Barabbas was universally reprobated, but the Greek is neutral ("notable," "conspicuous"); and in the only other NT occurrence of the word, NIV renders it "outstanding" (Rom 16:7). The point is not academic, for Barabbas was no ordinary villain but a *lēstēs* (cf. Mark 15:7; Luke 23:19; John 18:40). Although *lēstēs* can refer to a robber (as perhaps in John 10:1), it more probably refers to insurrectionists (cf. 26:55; John 18:40), and Josephus constantly uses it of the Zealots. Neither theft nor violent robbery was a capital offense, but insurrection was. Revolts and bloodshed fostered by guerrilla action were common (cf. Jos. Antiq. XVIII, 3–10 [i.1], 60–62 [iii.2]; Luke 13:1), and Barabbas had been caught. In the eyes of many of the people he would not be a "notorious" villain but a hero.

It may be that the two who were crucified with Jesus were co-rebels with Barabbas, for Matthew 27:38 calls them *lēstai* (better "rebels," "guerrillas," or "insurrectionists" than NIV's "robbers"), and their crucifixion indicates they were judged guilty of more than robbery. The fact that three crosses were prepared strongly suggests that Pilate had already ordered that preparations be made for the execution of the three rebels. If so, Jesus the Messiah actually took the place of the rebel [Jesus] Barabbas because the people preferred the political rebel and nationalist hero to the Son of God.

17–18 The "crowd" (v.17) was not a crowd of Jesus' accusers but of those trying to influence the selection of the prisoner who would receive the paschal amnesty (cf. Mark 15:8). It is possible, though far from certain, that the crowd, knowing little as yet of the arrest and trial of Jesus Christ, was voicing its support for "Jesus" (i.e., Jesus Barabbas—if the variant is supported); and Pilate mistook their pleas as support for Jesus Christ (cf. Lane, *Mark*, p. 554, n. 29).

What is certain is that Pilate sized up the real motivation of the Jewish leaders (v.18). They had no special loyalty to Rome; so if they were accusing Jesus of being a traitor to Rome, he must have been disturbing them for other reasons; and they were simply using Pilate to eliminate Jesus' challenge to them. Pilate, with his network of spies and informers, would be aware of how much popularity Jesus Christ enjoyed among the people at large. He could hardly have been unaware of the upsurge of acclaim the previous Sunday (21:1–16). He thought to administer a reversal to Sanhedrin policy by using the paschal amnesty to encourage the crowd to free Jesus; and therefore he offered them a choice: Barabbas or Jesus "who is called Christ." The last clause may be contemptuous.

19 In A.D. 21 it had been proposed in the Roman Senate that no provincial magistrate could be accompanied by his wife (cf. Tacitus *Annales* 3.33–35). The proposal was defeated; so Pilate's wife was on hand to speak of her dream. If Roman troops were involved in Jesus' arrest (see on 26:47–56), Pilate and perhaps his wife would have been informed. Her dream calls to mind the five dreams of Matthew 1–2; but it is quite unlike them and may not have been supernatural. God gave the earlier dreams for guidance to be obeyed, but this dream combines suffering with intimations of gloom. In any event the interruption of Pilate's wife while he was sitting "on the judge's seat" (cf. Jos. War II, 301[xiv.8]) further stresses Jesus' innocence (NIV rightly renders *dikaios* by "innocent") and gives the chief priests and elders a few moments to influence the crowd. On the idiom "Don't have anything to do with," see Turner (*Insights*, pp. 43–47).

20–23 Matthew and Mark both insist that the leaders ("chief priests," Mark; "chief priests and elders," Matthew) helped persuade the crowd (v.20). But it is wrong to infer that either Matthew or Mark is whitewashing the crowd (contra Hill et al.), for then "all the people" (v.25) would make no sense. Historically the description of the crowd's response is comprehensible enough. They have come to demand Barabbas's release (see on v.17). When they are confronted with the choice of Barabbas or Jesus (v.21), both of whom were widely popular, their momentary faltering is resolved by their leaders. If the crowd must choose between Pilate's choice and the Sanhedrin's choice, especially if the Sanhedrin members are circulating stories of Jesus' "blasphemy," then there can be little doubt on which side of the issue they will come down. In Judea it was common to confront the Roman authorities with as noisy and large a delegation as possible (cf. Jos. Antiq. XVIII, 269–72[viii.3]). And now mob mentality begins to take over.

Tactically Pilate has blundered. Trying to save face he asks more questions. The first (v.22) offers the hope of milder sentence (high treason could be punished by crucifixion, facing wild animals in the arena, or banishment); and the second (v.23) attests Jesus' innocence (on NIV's sensitive rendering of *gar* [lit., "for"], cf. BDF, par. 423[1]). But mob psychology prevails (cf. Acts 19:34). The demand for crucifixion also assured that the executed person would be declared accursed (see on vv.32–44).

The people indicate their preference for a murderous, nationalistic guerrilla leader over their Messiah, who exhorted the people to love their enemies and said he would die as a ransom for many. As Luke points out, it would not be long before Peter would remind the people of Israel at large (not just the leaders): "You handed [Jesus] over to be killed, and you disowned him before Pilate, though he had decided to let him go. You disowned the Holy and Righteous One and asked that a murderer be released to you" (Acts 3:13b–14).

24 It is customary to interpret this verse as Matthew's fictitious attempt to show Pilate's positive response to his wife's advice (v.19) and place guilt on the Jews (cf. v.25). But this is not the most natural interpretation.

1. To the best of our knowledge, this hand washing was not a Roman custom. After living several years among the Jews he detested, Pilate picked up one of their own customs (Deut 21:6; cf. Ps 26:6) and contemptuously used it against them.

2. There is little reason to think the hand washing incompatible with the proceedings, because, whatever his motives, Pilate tried repeatedly to release Jesus. He sent him to Herod (Luke), suggested that the paschal amnesty be applied to him, proposed a compromise with a scourging (Luke), tried to turn the case back to Jewish authorities (John), remonstrated before pronouncing sentence (John), and here washes his hands. Matthew gives us only two of these steps; so it is difficult to see why he should be charged with exculpating the Romans simply because one of his two is the only one not mentioned by the other evangelists.

3. If Matthew were interested in exculpating Pilate, would he have included the soldiers' savage mockery of Jesus (vv.27–31)?

4. Pilate's claim to be "innocent of this man's blood" is no stronger than Luke 23:14. Why then should this verse in Matthew be thought to color the first gospel's passion narrative so uniquely?

5. We cannot be certain that Pilate actually thought his action would excuse him; it may have reflected his contempt for the Jews or have been a taunt. And even if he thought he had exculpated himself, he should have known better. Plumptre quotes Ovid's lines: "Too easy souls, who dream the crystal flood/Can wash away the fearful guilt of blood."

6. But regardless of what Pilate thought, Matthew does not think the hand washing exonerated Pilate. We have already seen how Matthew shows that all connected with Jesus' death are guilty (see on vv.2, 4–5). Now Matthew insists that Pilate's action was not prompted by desire for justice but by political and moral cowardice and fear of a mob. The Romans expected their magistrates to maintain peace. An uproar, especially one tinged with complaint to Caesar (John), would be enough to intimidate a corrupt governor whose past has caught up with him (see on 26:57–68). So when Pilate says, "It is your responsibility" (27:24), Matthew intends his readers to remember the same words spoken by the chief priests and elders to Judas (v.4).

7. Too much of the debate about v.24 implies that the text merely reflects church-synagogue relations at the end of the first century, with little connection with the trial of Jesus. This has led to so many historical disjunctions as to be no longer credible. Is it not remarkable that the fourth Gospel, which in recent literature is also regularly interpreted as a clash between church and synagogue, should contain much more about the Roman trial than the Synoptics?

25 To Pilate's words, "all the people" answer, "Let his blood be on us and on our children!" The idiom is familiar (2 Sam 1:16; 3:28; Acts 18:6; 20:26). In the narrative this is a swift retort to Pilate's taunt and mob pressure for him to pronounce the verdict. But it clearly is more than that. How much more? Many say that by "all the people" Matthew is saying that *the Jews as a whole* reject Jesus (Frankmölle, pp. 204–11) and therefore have incurred collective guilt. Thus v.25 becomes a prophecy of the destruction of Jerusalem and the nation; and a new people of God, the church, take over. There is some truth in this view, but it needs qualification.

1. Matthew probably means "all the people" to refer to the entire crowd that cries, "Let his blood be upon us," rather than limiting these words to the chief priests and elders (see on v.20).

2. Even if there is symbolism (as there appears to be) whereby the crowd's response reflects the response of the nation as a whole (cf. 23:37–39), Matthew certainly knows that *all* the first disciples were Jews. Thus the Gospel's denunciations of the Jews are not more severe than those of many OT prophets, and in both instances it is understood that a faithful remnant remains. So what Matthew actually says cannot be judged as anti-Semitic. It is only when Matthew's account is read as a description, not of Jesus' trial, but of later church-synagogue relations, that it begins to bear anti-Semitic nuances fostered, not by the trial itself, but by the expansion of the remnant to include Gentile believers. Thus the anachronism of the church-synagogue conflict, consciously adopted by more liberal critics and unconsciously presupposed by more conservative ones, injects into the passion narratives more "anti-Semitic" bias than was actually present in the events they describe. If v.25 joins Matthew 25 in anticipating the judgment of A.D. 70, it does so in a way akin to Jeremiah's prophecies of the Exile and not with the often cynical detachment of Gentile believers from the Fathers on.

26 Among the Jews scourging was limited to forty lashes (Deut 25:3; cf. 2 Cor 11:24), but the Romans were restricted by nothing but their strength and whim. The whip was the dreaded *flagellum*, made by plaiting pieces of bone or lead into leather thongs. The victim was stripped and tied to a post. Severe flogging not only reduced the flesh to bloody pulp but could open up the body until the bones were visible and the entrails exposed (cf. TDNT, 4:510–12; Jos. War II, 612[xxi.5]; VI,

304[v.3]) Flogging as an independent punishment not infrequently ended in death. It was also used to weaken the prisoner before crucifixion. Jesus' flogging took place before the verdict (cf. Luke 23:16, 22; John 19:1–5; cf. Blinzler, pp. 222ff.) and so was not repeated after the verdict. Repetition would doubtless have killed him. Pilate, after further entreaty (John 19:1–16) then "handed him over to be crucified" (v.16); the words recall the Suffering Servant (Isa 53:6, 12 LXX).

Notes

16–17 Only witnesses of the Caesarean text (e.g., Θ f^1 700* syr[s]) preserve the name "Jesus" before "Barabbas"; but Origen knows the reading, as do several marginal glosses (in one uncial, S, and in about twenty miniscules); and it is probably presupposed in the ancestors of B 1010. The external evidence is not strong enough to be at all certain; but on the whole it is more likely that scribes deleted the name out of reverence for Jesus than added it in order to set a startling if grotesque choice before the Jews. The problem is compounded in v.17, where, in an uncial script, the abbreviated form of the accusative of "Jesus" could be easily lost by haplography (YMINI̅N̅). See Metzger, *Textual Commentary*, pp. 67–68. UBS 3d edition and Nestle 26th edition include "Jesus" in brackets.

---

12. *The soldiers' treatment of Jesus*

27:27–31

27Then the governor's soldiers took Jesus into the Praetorium and gathered the whole company of soldiers around him. 28They stripped him and put a scarlet robe on him, 29and then twisted together a crown of thorns and set it on his head. They put a staff in his right hand and knelt in front of him and mocked him. "Hail, king of the Jews!" they said. 30They spit on him, and took the staff and struck him on the head again and again. 31After they had mocked him, they took off the robe and put his own clothes on him. Then they led him away to crucify him.

Many think it unlikely that troops (auxiliary soldiers recruited from the non-Jewish population of Palestine and under Pilate's direct control) would mock a prisoner just scourged; but close parallels are not hard to find (Philo *In Flaccum* 6.36–39; Dio Cassius *History* 15.20–21; cf. Luther R. Delbrueck, "Antiquarisches zu den Verspottungen Jesu," ZNW 41 [1942]: 124–45). This pericope is meant to fulfill 17:22–23; 20:17–19 (cf. Mark 15:16–20; John 19:2–3).

27 That the governor's troops are the ones involved in these shameful actions belies any suggestion that Matthew exculpates Pilate (see on v.24). The "Praetorium" is probably the old palace of Herod (see on vv.11–26; cf. Benoit, *Jesus*, pp. 167–88); the soldiers take Jesus into the palace courtyard. The "whole company" would number six hundred if the cohort were at full strength and all were on duty, but more likely the expression simply refers to all the soldiers present.

28–31 Here we have humanity at its worst—a scene of vicious mockery. The Jews have mocked Jesus as Messiah (26:67–68); here the Roman soldiers ridicule him as king. Matthew's readers recognize that the soldiers speak more truly than they know, for Jesus is both King and Suffering Servant. The "robe" (*chlamys*, in the NT only here and in v.31) is probably the short red cloak worn by Roman military and civilian officials (v.28). Mark and John describe it as "purple," Matthew as "scarlet." Commentators have speculated that this redactional change serves to symbolize blood and its concomitant suffering. Such efforts are strained. The ancients did not discriminate among colors as closely as we do, and BAGD (p. 694) adduces a reference in which a Roman soldier's cloak is said to be "purple." The "purple" (Mark; John) calls to mind the robes worn by vassal kings (cf. 1 Macc 10:20, 62; 11:58; 14:43–44), and the "scarlet" (Matthew) shows what the garment probably was—a trooper's cloak.

For a crown (v.29) the soldiers plaited a wreath of thorns from palm spines or acanthus and crushed it down on Jesus' head in imitation of the circlet on the coins of Tiberius Caesar (cf. TDNT, 7:615–24, 632f.). The staff they put in his hand stood for a royal scepter; and the mocking "Hail, King of the Jews!" corresponded to the Roman acclamation "Ave, Caesar!" and capped the flamboyant kneeling. Not content with the ridicule and the torture of the thorns, they spat on him (v.30) and used the staff, the symbol of his kingly authority, to hit him on the head "again and again" (cf. the imperfect tense of the verb).

"After they had mocked him" (v.31, an aorist with pluperfect force; see on v.8; Moule, *Idiom Book*, p. 16), they dressed him again in his own clothes and led him off to be crucified. Normally a prisoner went naked to his place of execution and was scourged along the route. That this custom was not followed with Jesus may be because he had already been flogged and more flogging might have killed him. Or it may reflect an attempt not to offend too many Jewish sensibilities during a feast time. Jesus was led away by the execution squad of four soldiers, dragging the crosspiece to which his hands would be nailed (John 19:17, 23).

13. *The Crucifixion and mocking*

27:32–44

32As they were going out, they met a man from Cyrene, named Simon, and
they forced him to carry the cross. 33They came to a place called Golgotha (which
means The Place of the Skull). 34There they offered Jesus wine to drink, mixed
with gall; but after tasting it, he refused to drink it. 35When they had crucified him,
they divided up his clothes by casting lots. 36And sitting down, they kept watch
over him there. 37Above his head they placed the written charge against him: THIS
IS JESUS, THE KING OF THE JEWS. 38Two robbers were crucified with him, one on his
right and one on his left. 39Those who passed by hurled insults at him, shaking
their heads 40and saying, "You who are going to destroy the temple and build it in
three days, save yourself! Come down from the cross, if you are the Son of God!"

41In the same way the chief priests, the teachers of the law and the elders
mocked him. 42"He saved others," they said, "but he can't save himself! He's the
King of Israel! Let him come down now from the cross, and we will believe in him.
43He trusts in God. Let God rescue him now if he wants him, for he said, 'I am the
Son of God.' " 44In the same way the robbers who were crucified with him also
heaped insults on him.

Two thousand years of pious Christian tradition have largely domesticated the cross, making it hard for us to realize how it was viewed in Jesus' time. Two excellent recent studies discuss the relevant evidence (M. Hengel, *Crucifixion* [London:

SCM, 1977]; J.A. Fitzmyer, "Crucifixion in Ancient Palestine, Qumran Literature, and the New Testament," CBQ 40 [1978]: 493–513). Crucifixion was unspeakably painful and degrading. Whether tied or nailed to the cross, the victim endured countless paroxysms as he pulled with his arms and pushed with his legs to keep his chest cavity open for breathing and then collapsed in exhaustion until the demand for oxygen demanded renewed paroxysms. The scourging, the loss of blood, the shock from the pain, all produced agony that could go on for days, ending at last by suffocation, cardiac arrest, or loss of blood. When there was reason to hasten death, the execution squad would smash the victim's legs. Death followed almost immediately, either from shock or from collapse that cut off breathing.

Beyond the pain was the shame. The later rabbis excluded crucifixion as a form of capital punishment for just this reason, though there is some evidence that the Pharisees, their probable predecessors, did not oppose it in principle (cf. David T. Halperin, "Crucifixion, the Nahum Pesher, and the Rabbinic Penalty of Strangulation," *Journal of Jewish Studies* 32 [1981]: 32–46). In ancient sources crucifixion was universally viewed with horror. In Roman law it was reserved only for the worst criminals and lowest classes. No Roman citizen could be crucified without a direct edict from Caesar.

Among Jews the horror of the cross was greater still because of Deuteronomy 21:23: "Anyone who is hanged on a tree is under God's curse." In Israelite law this meant the corpse of a judicially executed criminal was hung up for public exposure that branded him as cursed by God. The words were also applied in Jesus' day to anyone crucified; and therefore the Jews' demand that Jesus be crucified rather than banished was aimed at arousing maximum public revulsion toward him. But in Christian perspective the curse on Jesus at the cross fulfills all OT sacrifices: it is a curse that removes the curse from believers—the fusion of divine, royal prerogative and Suffering Servant, the heart of the gospel, the inauguration of a new humanity, the supreme model for Christian ethics, the ratification of the new covenant, and the power of God (1 Cor 1:23–24; Gal 3:13; Rom 5:12–21; Col 2:14; Hebrews; 1 Peter 2:18–25, cf. Matt 3:17; 8:17; 16:21; 24–25; 20:25–28; 21:38–42; 26:26–29).

All four Gospels record the Crucifixion. No Gospel says much about the Crucifixion itself; the details were all too well known, and theological interest does not lie so much in crucifixion per se as in the attendant circumstances and their significance. Each evangelist gives his narrative an independent cast by what he includes or omits, though these differences are often exaggerated. Matthew largely follows Mark; but whereas Mark alludes to the OT, Matthew tends to be somewhat more explicit (v.34, Ps 69:21; v.35, Ps 22:18; v.39, Ps 22:7; v.43, Ps 22:8). The dominant note of the pericope is the continuing mockery (Bonnard); but the mockery by an awful irony reveals more than the mocker thinks, for Jesus is indeed King of the Jews (v.37), the new meeting place with God (v.40), the Savior of men (v.42), the King of Israel (v.42), and the Son of God (v.43).

The date is 15 Nisan A.D. 30 or 33, and the time fairly early in the morning, as the interchanges with Pilate and Herod and the scourging and the mocking need not have consumed more than two to three hours.

32 "As they were going out" presupposes "of the city," not "from the Praetorium," as Mark says that Simon was coming in "from the country." Executions normally took place outside the city walls (Lev 24:14; Num 15:35–36; 1 Kings 21:13; Acts 7:58), symbolizing still further rejection (cf. Heb 13:13). This suggests that Jesus, weak as he was, managed to carry the crossbeam as far as the city gates (cf. John 19:17). There the soldiers forced Simon to assume the load. His name suggests, but does not prove, that he was a Jew. He came from Cyrene, an old Greek settlement on the coast of North Africa (Acts 2:10; 6:9; 11:20; 13:1). Mark says that he was the father of Alexander and Rufus, who may be referred to in Acts 19:33 and Romans 16:13 and were obviously well-known to Mark's readers; but because the names were common, these passages may refer to other persons.

In 1941, N. Avigad ("A Depository of Inscribed Ossuaries in the Kidron Valley," IEJ 12 [1962]: 1–12) published an account of the discovery of a burial cave belonging to Cyrenian Jews, located on the southwest slope of the Kidron and dating from pre-A.D. 70. An ossuary from this find is twice inscribed in Greek: "Alexander son of Simon." But we cannot be certain the same family is in view.

The efforts of Christian piety to make Simon's act a deed of sympathetic magnanimity are invalid. Simon had no choice, and the text says nothing about his sympathy for Jesus.

33 The site of Golgotha (transliteration of Aram. *gālgāltā'*["skull"]) is uncertain. Gordon's Calvary is not an option (cf. Parrot, pp. 59–65). The most likely place is one near the Church of the Holy Sepulchre, in an area outside the northern wall, on a hill near the city wall (John 19:20), and not far from the road (Matt 27:39). Our English "Calvary" comes from the Latin *calva* ("a skull").

34 Mark says they offered Jesus wine mingled with myrrh, and he refused it; Matthew, that they offered him wine mingled with gall, and he tasted it and then refused it. A common explanation is that Mark describes a custom in which women of Jerusalem, responding to Proverbs 31:6–7 (the alleged custom is Jewish, not Roman), prepared a drink of wine and [frank]incense—Mark's mention of myrrh instead of frankincense is variously explained (e.g., Lane, *Mark*, p. 124)—as a narcotic to ease the pain of the sufferers (b *Sanhedrin* 43a). This Jesus refused so as to drink the full draught of suffering with all his senses intact. Matthew then changed "myrrh" (Mark) to "gall" in order to link the event to Psalm 69:21.

Though this interpretation remains popular, another one is more convincing (cf. Moo, "Use of OT," pp. 249–52). Neither Mark nor Matthew mentions women, and both imply that the soldiers administered the drink. Moreover that Matthew says Jesus tasted it before refusing it argues against the view that it was a customary narcotic to dull pain; for if customary, he would know what it contained: why should he have tasted it if he would in the end refuse it? It is much better to assume that the gesture in both Matthew and Mark was not one of compassion but of torment.

Myrrh may have been used with wine to strengthen the drink (TDNT, 7:458), but it has no effect on pain (cf. John Wilkinson, "The Seven Words from the Cross," SJT 17 [1964]: 77, n. 1). But myrrh tastes bitter; so a large dose of it mingled with wine would make the latter undrinkable. Whether customary or not, the drink was offered to Jesus; but it was so bitter he refused it, and, according to this view, the soldiers were amused. Mark keeps the word "myrrh" to describe the content, and Matthew uses "gall" to describe the taste and to provide a link with Psalm 69:21. In both Hebrew and Greek, the words for "gall" in Psalm 69:21 (*rō'š* and *cholē* respectively) refer to various bitter or poisonous substances. Like David his father, Jesus looked for sympathy but found none (Ps 69:20–21).

35 The victim was either tied or nailed to the crossbeam (in Jesus' case, the latter), which was then hoisted to its place on the upright. The feet were sometimes tied or, as in this instance, nailed to the upright. Crosses were made in various shapes—an X, a T, or the traditional † . The latter is in view here (v.37). How high the victim was from the ground varied from a few inches to several feet, in Jesus' case the latter (v.48; John 19:29). The Romans crucified their victims naked. Whether they permitted a loin cloth to avoid transgressing Jewish stipulations (M *Sanhedrin* 6:3) is unknown. The victim's clothes customarily became the perquisite of the executioners; here they divided them—probably an inner and outer garment, a belt, and a pair of sandals—among themselves by casting lots, oblivious to the OT lament in Psalm 22:18 that John 19:23–24 says was now fulfilled. (The variant reading in Matthew, preserved in NIV margin, is an assimilation to John.) Mark says this took place at the third hour, about 9.00 A.M.

36 This verse is peculiar to Matthew. The soldiers kept watch to prevent rescue (men were known to have lived after being taken down from a cross). Perhaps Matthew gives us this detail to eliminate any suggestion that Jesus was removed from the cross without dying.

37 The statement of the crime was often written on a white tablet in red or black letters and displayed on the cross. The charge against Jesus, written in Hebrew, Greek, and Latin (John 19:20), is highly ironic: Pilate, though desiring to offend the Jews (John 19:19–22), wrote more of the truth than he knew. Pilate rubs the noses of the Jews' in their vassal status. To a Jew, "king of the Jews" meant "Messiah"; so the charge on which Jesus was executed was, according to Pilate, that he was a messianic pretender. Matthew's Christian reader will remember the intertwining strands of royal Son and Suffering Servant and see their climax here.

38 On the two *lēstai* ("rebel guerrillas"; NIV, "robbers") see on v.16. The King of the Jews is crucified along with rebels. Matthew may be thinking of Isaiah 53:12, but this is uncertain (cf. Moo, "Use of OT," pp. 154–55).

39–40 Crucifixion was always carried out publicly as a warning to others. With the day of the paschal meal behind them (see excursus at 26:17) and the restrictions of Sabbath not to begin till sundown, there was time and opportunity for people to walk by on the nearby road and "hurl insults" (*blasphēmeō*, v.39, as in 9:3; 12:31; 26:65) at Jesus. Shaking their heads, and so calling to mind the derision in Psalms (22:7; 109:25; Lamentations 2:15, the passers-by threw up the charge in Matthew (26:60–61). The Greek should probably be rendered "You who were trying to destroy the temple and rebuild it in three days" (v.40; cf. 2:20; cf. BDF, par. 339[3]; Turner, *Syntax*, pp. 80–81). The derision was palpable and identifies the mockers as those who had witnessed the proceedings of the Sanhedrin or had some report of them.

The second taunt, "If you are the Son of God," not only harks back to the trial (26:63), but for Matthew's readers recalls a dramatic parallel (4:3, 6). Through the passers-by Satan was still trying to get Jesus to evade the Father's will and avoid further suffering (Lohmeyer; cf. also 16:21–23).

41–43 The "chief priests, teachers of the law and the elders" (v.41) represent all the principal groups of the Sanhedrin (see on 21:23; 26:59). They do not address Jesus directly but speak of him in the third person, in a stage whisper meant for his ears. "He saved others" (v.42) is probably an oblique reference to Jesus' supernatural healing ministry. "But he can't save himself" is cutting because it questions that same supernatural power. But there is level on level of meaning. For the Christian reader "save" has full eschatological overtones. And though Jesus *could* have saved himself (26:53), he could *not* have saved himself if he was to save others.

The second of the three taunts, "He's the king of Israel," substitutes the covenant term Israel for "the Jews" in Pilate's words (v.11) and is in fact the normal Palestinian form of Jesus' claim (cf. TDNT, 3:359–62, 375f.). The words "Let him come down from the cross, and we will believe in him" have several levels of meaning. They constitute a malicious barb directed at Jesus' helplessness, while having the effrontery to suggest that the leaders' failure to believe was his fault. The taunt piously promises faith if Jesus will but step down from the cross; but the reader knows that, in the mystery of providence, if Jesus did step down, there would be no "blood of the covenant for the forgiveness of sins" (26:26–29), no ransom (20:28), no salvation from sin (1:21), no theological basis for healing (8:16–17), no gospel of the kingdom to be proclaimed to nations everywhere (28:18–20), no fulfillment of Scripture.

In an unconscious allusion to Psalm 22:8 (as Caiaphas uttered an unconscious prophecy in John 11:51–52), the religious leaders launch their third taunt: "He trusts in God" (v.43). They recognize that Jesus' claim to be the "Son of God" was at least a claim to messiahship and perhaps more. So assuming that God must crown every effort of Messiah with success, they conclude that Jesus' hopeless condition is proof enough of the vanity of his pretensions. Again their malice masks the ironic redemptive purposes of God. On the one hand, as Christian readers know, God will indeed vindicate his Son at the Resurrection: Matthew ends his Gospel, not at 27:56, but at 28:20 (cf. Acts 2:23–24; Rom 1:3–4). On the other hand, the leaders are right: Jesus is now facing his most severe test, the loss of his Father's presence, leading to the heart-rending cry of the following verses (esp. v.46).

44 The *lēstai* ("robbers"; see on v.16) crucified with him join in the abuse (cf. Luke 23:39–43; Zerwick, par. 7).

14. *The death of Jesus*

27:45–50

> 45From the sixth hour until the ninth hour darkness came over all the land.
> 46About the ninth hour Jesus cried out in a loud voice, "*Eloi, Eloi, lama sabachthani?*"—which means, "My God, my God, why have you forsaken me?"
> 47When some of those standing there heard this, they said, "He's calling Elijah."
> 48Immediately one of them ran and got a sponge. He filled it with wine vinegar, put it on a stick, and offered it to Jesus to drink. 49The rest said, "Now leave him alone. Let's see if Elijah comes to save him."
> 50And when Jesus had cried out again in a loud voice, he gave up his spirit.

45 The darkness that "came over all the land" from noon till 3:00 P.M. (that is what "sixth hour" and "ninth hour" refer to) was a sign of judgment and/or tragedy. The

Greek *gē* means "land" rather than "earth," since the darkness was meant to be a sign relating both to Jesus' death and to the Jewish people; and beyond the borders of Israel the darkness would lose this significance. SBK (1:1040–42) gives numerous rabbinic parallels, and Wettstein an array of Greek and Latin authors. But the most-telling background is Amos 8:9–10, and to a lesser extent Exodus 10:21–22. Both passages portray darkness as a sign of judgment; but Amos mentions noon, the turning of religious feasts into mourning, and says, "I will make that time like mourning for an only son" (Amos 8:10; see also on Matt 2:15). The judgment is therefore a judgment on the land and its people (cf. Best, pp. 98f.). But it is also a judgment on Jesus; for out of this darkness comes his cry of desolation (v.46). The cosmic blackness hints at the deep judgment that was taking place (20:28; 26:26–29; Gal 3:13).

It is futile to argue whether the darkness was caused by an eclipse of three hours(!) or by atmospheric conditions caused by a sirocco or something else, not because it did not happen, but because we do not know how it happened, anymore than we know how Jesus walked on the water or multiplied the loaves. The evangelists are chiefly interested in the theological implications that rise out of the historical phenomena.

46 The "cry of desolation" raises two important questions.

1. In what language did Jesus utter it? Almost all recognize that the words echo Psalm 22:1 (for a list of exceptions, cf. Moo, "Use of OT," pp. 264f.). But among the variant readings of a confused textual history (cf. Notes), Matthew keeps *"Eli, Eli"* (NIV, *"Eloi, Eloi")*, representing a Hebrew original, and Mark *"Eloi, Eloi,"* representing an Aramaic original. The remaining words, *"lama sabachthani,"* are Aramaic. Many suggest that Jesus quoted Psalm 22:1 in Hebrew, reverting to the ancient language of Scripture in his hour of utmost agony. Only this, it is argued, accounts for the confusion with "Elijah" in v.47 and provides a plausible explanation for the rendering "my power" (*hē dynamis mou,* presupposing Semitic *ḥêlî*) in the apocryphal Gospel of Peter. In this view Mark, or an early copyist of Mark, has turned Jesus' words into Aramaic, recognizing that Jesus more commonly spoke Aramaic than Hebrew.

However, though Jesus was probably at least trilingual (Hebrew, Aramaic, Greek—with perhaps some Latin), the overwhelming textual evidence for the rest of the cry supports an Aramaic original. Even Matthew's Hebraic-sounding "Eli" may in fact support an Aramaic original, because the Targum (written in Aramaic) to Psalm 22:1 has *'ēlî*. Apparently some Aramaic speakers preserved the Hebrew name for God in the same way some English speakers sometimes refer to him as Yahweh. The evidence of the Gospel of Peter is not decisive because "my power" may not rest on a Semitic original but may be an independent periphrasis for God, akin to 26:64. Moreover on the lips of a dying man crying out in agony, *"Eloi"* could as easily be mistaken for Elijah as *"Eli"* (cf. discussion by Broadus; Lagrange; Gundry, *Use of OT*, pp. 63–66; Moo, "Use of OT," pp. 264–75). Jesus' cry was most probably in Aramaic; and at least some of the variants stem from the difficulty of transliterating a Semitic language into Greek and others from the influence of the OT.

2. What does this psalm quotation signify? A large number of recent interpreters have interpreted the cry against the background of the *whole* of Psalm 22, which begins with this sense of desolation but ends with the triumphant vindication of the righteous sufferer. The chief difficulty with this is that though OT texts are frequent-

ly cited with their full contexts in mind, they are never cited in such a way that the OT context effectively annuls what the text itself affirms (Bonnard; Moo, "Use of OT," p. 272). If the context of Psalm 22 is carried along with the actual reference to Psalm 22:1, the reader of the Gospel is to understand that the vindication comes with the Resurrection in Matthew 28, not that Jesus' cry reflects full confidence instead of black despair.

Equally futile is the suggestion of Schweizer and others that these words constitute a more or less standard cry of a pious man dying with the words of a psalm on his lips. But why *this* psalm when others would be more suitable? Evidence for such a use of Psalm 22 is sparse and late. It is better to take the words at face value: Jesus is conscious of being abandoned by his Father. For one who knew the intimacy of Matthew 11:27, such abandonment must have been agony; and for the same reason it is inadequate to hypothesize that Jesus felt abandoned but was not truly abandoned (contra Bonnard; Green; McNeile; Senior, *Passion Narrative*, p. 298), because "it seems difficult to understand how Jesus, who had lived in the closest possible fellowship with the Father, could have been unaware whether he had, in fact, been abandoned" (Moo, "Use of OT," p. 274).

If we ask in what ontological sense the Father and the Son are here divided, the answer must be that we do not know because we are not told. If we ask for what purpose they are divided, the ultimate answer must be tied in with Gethsemane, the Last Supper, passion passages such as 1:21; 20:28 (see also 26:26–29, 39–44), and the theological interpretation articulated by Paul (e.g., Rom 3:21–26). In this cry of dereliction, the horror of the world's sin and the cost of our salvation are revealed. In the words of Elizabeth Browning:

Yea, once Immanuel's orphaned cry his universe hath shaken.
It went up single, echoless, "My God, I am forsaken!"
It went up from the Holy's lips amid his lost creation,
That, of the lost, no son should use those words of desolation.

47 According to 2 Kings 2:1–12, Elijah did not die but was taken alive to heaven in a whirlwind. Some Jewish tradition, perhaps as old as the first century, held that he would come and rescue the righteous in their distress (cf. Jeremias, TDNT, 2:930–31; SBK, 4:769–771).

48–49 See on v.34. The allusion is again to Psalm 69:21. What is not clear is whether the offer of a drink is meant as a gesture of mercy or as mockery (v.48). The Gospel parallels are somewhat ambiguous. The best explanation is that of mockery. *Oxos* (lit., "vinegar") probably refers to "wine vinegar" (NIV), sour wine diluted with vinegar drunk by foot soldiers; but this does not make the offer a compassionate act, since its purpose may have been to prolong life and agony, while with false piety the onlookers say they will wait for Elijah to rescue him (v.49). But if the Father has abandoned Jesus, will Elijah save him? The offer of a drink not only fulfills Scripture but makes the cry of dereliction (v.46) all the bleaker.

In this interpretation NIV's "But" (v.49) is too adversative a rendering of *de*, and "Leave him alone" should be taken to suggest (as in NIV on Mark 15:36) "Leave him alone now"—i.e., the proffered drink provides the context for more mocking. It is not clear whether Luke 23:36, where mockery is clearly intended, properly parallels Matthew 27:34 or 27:48–49. John's Gospel (19:28–29) is interested only in the fact of Scripture fulfillment, not the question of whether mockery is intended.

50 This loud cry reminds us once more of Jesus' hideous agony. Matthew's "he gave up his spirit" ("spirit" here is equivalent to "life") suggests Jesus' sovereignty over the exact time of his own death. It was at this moment, when he was experiencing the abyss of his alienation from the Father and was being cruelly mocked by those he came to serve, that he chose to yield up his life a "ransom for many" (see on 20:28).

Notes

46 Instead of ηλι or ηλει (*ēli* or *ēlei,*) from the Hebrew אֵלִי (*'ēlî,* "my God"), some MSS agree with Mark 15:34: ελωι (*elōi*), from the Aramaic אֱלָהִי (*'ᵉlāhî,* "my God"), the long *ō* in Greek representing the Semitic *ā* by influence of Hebrew *'ᵉlōhay*. It is perhaps more probable that some MSS of Matthew have been assimilated to Mark than to MT. For other variants, see Metzger, *Textual Criticism,* pp. 70, 119.

49 The future participle σώσων (*sōsōn,* "to save") here functions as a supplement to the main verb. The construction is rare in the NT (cf. BDF, pars. 351 [1], 418 [4]; Zerwick, par. 282).

15. *Immediate impact of the death*

27:51–56

51At that moment the curtain of the temple was torn in two from top to bottom. The earth shook and the rocks split. 52The tombs broke open and the bodies of many holy people who had died were raised to life. 53They came out of the tombs, and after Jesus' resurrection they went into the holy city and appeared to many people.

54When the centurion and those with him who were guarding Jesus saw the earthquake and all that had happened, they were terrified, and exclaimed, "Surely he was the Son of God!"

55Many women were there, watching from a distance. They had followed Jesus from Galilee to care for his needs. 56Among them were Mary Magdalene, Mary the mother of James and Joses, and the mother of Zebedee's sons.

51a There were two temple curtains, one dividing the Most Holy Place from the Holy Place and the other separating the Holy Place from the court. Tearing the latter would be more public, but tearing the inner veil could hardly be hushed up. Jewish parallels are interesting (b *Yoma* 39b reports the doors of the temple opened of their own accord during the forty years before the destruction of the temple) but difficult to interpret. The inner veil is presupposed in Hebrews 4:16; 6:19–20; 9:11–28; 10:19–22. Destruction of the outer veil would primarily symbolize the forthcoming destruction of the temple, while destruction of the inner veil would primarily symbolize open access to God (Best, *Temptation,* p. 99); but destruction of either veil could point in both directions.

There is more. If the death of Jesus opened up a fresh access to God that made the OT sacrificial system and the Levitical high priesthood obsolete, then an entire change in the Mosaic covenant must follow. It is impossible to grapple with Matthew's fulfillment themes (cf. esp. on 5:17–20; 11:11–13) and see how even the law points prophetically to Messiah and hear Jesus' promise of a new covenant grounded in his death (26:26–29) without seeing that the tearing of the veil signifies the obsolescence of the temple ritual and the law governing it. Jesus himself is the New Temple, the meeting place of God and man (see on 26:61); the old is obsolete. The rent veil does indeed serve as a sign of the temple's impending destruction—a destruction conceived not as a brute fact but as a theological necessity.

51b–53 On problems concerning the historicity of this narrative, see D. Wenham, "Resurrection" (esp. pp. 42–46). Only Matthew reports it, but it is of a piece with the tearing of the temple veil. Both are part of the initial impact of Jesus' death, along with the centurion's exclamation (v.54). Moreover, the earthquake apparently links them: it is possible that Matthew sees the earthquake (v.51b), itself a symbol of judgment and theophanic glory (cf. 1 Kings 19:11; Isa 29:6; Jer 10:10; Ezek 26:18; and esp. see the background materials gathered by R.J. Bauckham, "The Eschatological Earthquake in the Apocalypse of John," NovTest 19 [1977]: 224–33), as the means of tearing the veil as well as opening the tombs. The temple area lies on a geological fault; and the Muslim shrines on the site today have been damaged by tremors from time to time (cf. D. Baly, *The Geography of the Bible* [New York: Harper and Row, 1974], p. 25).

But the resurrection of the *hagioi* ("saints," i.e., "holy people," v.52) remains extraordinarily difficult for two reasons. First, its extreme brevity and lack of parallels raise many unanswered questions: What kind of bodies do these "holy people" have? Do they die again? How many people saw them? How public were these appearances? Second, a quick reading of the text gives the impression that though the holy people were raised when Jesus died, they did not leave the tombs and appear to the citizens of the "holy city" till after Jesus' resurrection (v.53). What were they doing in between?

The passage has elicited various explanations. Hutton thinks it a displaced resurrection account, originally connected with the earthquake of 28:2. Others have thought it a primitive Christian hymn. D. Senior ("The Death of Jesus and the Resurrection of the Holy Ones [Matthew 27:51–53]," CBQ 38 [1976]: 312–29), in addition to criticizing some other views, represents the approach currently most popular: these verses are a midrash, a symbolic representation of certain theological ideas about the triumph of Jesus and the dawning of the new age. But apart from questions of literary genre (cf. Introduction, section 12.b), one wonders why the evangelist, if he had nothing historical to go on, did not invent a midrash with fewer problems.

J.W. Wenham ("When Were the Saints Raised?" JTS 32 [1981]: 150–52) offers an alternative view. He has convincingly argued that a full stop should be placed, not after "split" (v.51), but after "broke open" (v.52). The tearing of the veil and the opening of the tombs together symbolize the first of twin foci in Jesus' death and resurrection. On the one hand, Jesus' sacrificial death blots out sin, defeats the powers of evil and death, and opens up access to God. On the other, Jesus' victorious resurrection and vindication promise the final resurrection of those who die in him.

The resurrection of "the holy people" begins a new sentence and is tied up only with Jesus' resurrection. So Matthew does not intend his readers to think that these "holy people" were resurrected when Jesus died and then waited in their tombs till

Easter Sunday before showing themselves. The idea is a trifle absurd anyway: there is no more reason to think they were impeded by material substance than was the resurrected Lord, the covering rock of whose grave was removed to let the witnesses in, not to let him out. The "holy people" were raised, came out of the tombs, and were seen by many after Jesus rose from the dead. There is no need to connect the earthquake and the breaking open of the tombs with the rising of "the holy people": the two foci must be differentiated.

On several details we are told little. For instance, it is unclear whether the resurrection of the "holy people" was to natural bodies (cf. Lazarus, John 11) or to supernatural bodies. The latter is perhaps more likely; and in that case they did not return to the tombs, and their rising testifies that the Last Day had dawned. Where they ultimately went Matthew does not say. Were they "translated"? Nor does he tell us who they were; but the language implies, though it does not prove, that they were certain well-known OT and intertestamental Jewish "saints," spiritual heroes and martyrs in Israel's history (cf. the terminology in Isa 4:3; Dan 7:18; Tobit 8:15; 1 Enoch 38:4–5; T Levi 18:10–11). If so, then Matthew is telling us, among other things, that the resurrection of people who lived before Jesus Messiah is as dependent on Jesus' triumph as the resurrection of those who come after him. The idea is not fanciful, given Matthew's grasp of prophecy and fulfillment (see on 5:17; Introduction, section 11.a).

One must still reflect on why the evangelist placed the account here instead of in chapter 28. He probably had at least three reasons.

1. The pericope would disrupt the narrative in Matthew 28.

2. The account is held together by two foci—Jesus' death and resurrection. Therefore Matthew's putting it with the resurrection pericopes would have possibly been even more awkward than putting it with the passion pericopes. Linking the Cross and the empty tomb in a unified theological application is not without its difficulties, regardless of whether the pericope in question is placed with the story of the Cross or with the account of the Resurrection.

3. More positively the placement of this pericope with other verses dealing with the immediate impact of Jesus' death may be peculiarly appropriate since they too point to the future. No Christian reader who saw in the torn veil a reference to judgment on the temple would fail to see the new means opening up for the meeting of God and man, a means dependent on Jesus' resurrection and continued ministry. Similarly the confession that Jesus was the Son of God (v.54) would appear to thoughtful readers as a deeper truth than the centurion and his men could have known, for Matthew 28 lies just ahead. Furthermore, if the text had ended at "broke open" (v.52) and resumed with v.54, the reader would have been given a wholly wrong impression. Jesus' work on the cross is tied to his impending resurrection; together they open up the new age and promise eschatological life.

54 Despite the fact that "Son of God" is one of several major christological titles in Matthew, it also appears in Mark as the climax of the Passion (Mark 15:38–39). What is not certain is exactly what the soldiers meant by "Son of God" (cf. Blair, pp. 60–68). They may have used the term in a Hellenistic sense, "a son of God" referring to a divine being in a pagan sense. But the governor's soldiers were probably non-Jewish natives of the land (see on 27:27). If so, or even if they were Romans who had been assigned to Palestine for some time, they may well have understood "Son of God" in a messianic sense (see on 26:63). Certainly the anarthrous noun

"Son" can mean "*the* Son" instead of "*a* Son" in this construction (cf. Moule, *Idiom Book*, p. 116).

The darkness, the earthquake, and the cry of dereliction convinced the soldiers that this was no ordinary execution. The portents terrified them and probably led them to believe that these things testified to heaven's wrath at the perpetration of such a crime, in which the soldiers had participated. But this confession tells us something more: Jesus as the promised Messiah and unique Son of God is seen most clearly in his passion and death; but again the Jewish religious establishment, mistaking the nature of his messiahship, mocked him with the very title (vv.41–44) by which the pagans now confessed him (see also on 8:5–13; 15:21–28).

55–56 Along with the soldiers, certain women, generally not highly regarded in Jewish society, watched to the bitter end. They kept their distance (v.55), whether through timidity or modesty; and last at the cross, they were first at the tomb (28:1). Not only do they provide continuity to the narrative, but they prove that God has chosen the lowly and despised things of the world to shame the wise and strong (cf. 1 Cor 1:27–31). These women were Galileans who often traveled with the disciples to care for Jesus' needs out of their own resources (cf. Luke 8:2–3).

Comparison of the lists of names in Matthew, Mark, and John (19:25) produces these results:

Matthew	*Mark*	*John*
Mary Magdalene	Mary Magdalene	Jesus' mother
Mary the mother of James and Joses	Mary the mother of James the younger and Joses	Jesus' mother's sister
Mother of Zebedee's sons	Salome	Mary wife of Clopas
		Mary of Magdala

If we make two assumptions—(1) that John's second entry is distinguished from his third (i.e., they are not in apposition) and (2) that John's list of four includes the list of three in Matthew and Mark—then certain things become probable. First, the mother of Zebedee's sons was called Salome, unless a different woman is here introduced. Second, if Mary the mother of James and Joseph (or Joses) is Jesus' mother (cf. 13:55), then Jesus' mother and Mary Magdalene (of Magdala) appear on all three lists. That would make Salome Jesus' mother's sister—his aunt on his mother's side. Others suppose that Mary the wife of Clopas is the mother of James and Joses, who are not Jesus' half-brothers. Yet the result still equates Salome and Jesus' aunt on his mother's side. Although none of this is certain, it would help explain 20:20.

16. *The burial of Jesus*

27:57–61

57 As evening approached, there came a rich man from Arimathea, named Joseph, who had himself become a disciple of Jesus. 58 Going to Pilate, he asked for
Jesus' body, and Pilate ordered that it be given to him. 59 Joseph took the body,
wrapped it in a clean linen cloth, 60 and placed it in his own new tomb that he had
cut out of the rock. He rolled a big stone in front of the entrance to the tomb and
went away. 61 Mary Magdalene and the other Mary were sitting there opposite the
tomb.

Because of Deuteronomy 21:22–23, Jesus' body, according to Jewish custom, could not remain on the cross overnight. The Roman custom was to let bodies of crucified criminals hang in full view till they rotted away. If they were buried at all, it was only by express permission of the imperial magistrate. Such permission was usually granted to friends and relatives of the deceased who made application, but never in the case of high treason.

57 The approaching evening—about 6:00 P.M. at that time of year—would mark the end of Friday and the beginning of Sabbath. Mark and Luke portray Joseph of Arimathea (the place is uncertain, but the best guess is Ramathaim, northwest of Lydda) as a prominent member of the Sanhedrin, and Luke says Joseph had not consented to the Sanhedrin's action. Only Matthew mentions he was rich. This may direct attention to Isaiah 53:9–12: though Jesus was numbered with the transgressors, yet in his death he was with the rich. To own a new tomb and use the quantity of spices reported by John, Joseph must have been well-to-do. Matthew tells us Joseph had become a disciple (on the verbal form, cf. BDF, par. 148[3]; Zerwick, par. 66; see on 13:52; 28:19); he learned from Jesus and to some extent was committed to following him, even if his discipleship was secret (John).

58–60 Matthew's account is more condensed than Mark's, who mentions Pilate's checking that Jesus was actually dead and describes Joseph's purchases. Joseph's initiative is remarkably courageous; and Pilate granted his request only because he was convinced that Jesus was not really guilty of high treason (v.58). Joseph could not have acted alone: removal of the body, washing, the weight of spices, and other preparations would be too much for one man with limited time. John mentions the assistance of Nicodemus; probably their servants also helped. Matthew does not mention the seventy-five pounds of spices (John) wrapped up with Jesus in the linen cloth.

The Church of the Holy Sepulchre is most probably the correct site of the tomb (cf. Parrot). Some centuries earlier the place had been a stone quarry, and the resulting rugged face became a place where tombs were cut from the rock. Joseph had prepared this tomb for his own use (v.60), but now he laid Jesus' body in it. Tombs were of various kinds. Many were sealed with some sort of boulder wedged into place to discourage wild animals and grave robbers. But an expensive tomb consisted of an antechamber hewn out of the rock face, with a low passage (cf. "bent over," John 20:5, 11) leading into the burial chamber that was sealed with a cut, disk-shaped stone that rolled in a slot cut into the rock. The slot was on an incline, making the grave easy to seal but difficult to open: several men might be needed to roll the stone back up the incline. This sort of tomb is presupposed in the Gospel records (cf. Parrot, pp. 43ff.).

61 No mourning was permitted for those executed under Roman law. The women followed with broken but silent grief and watched the burial. In addition to Joseph of Arimathea and Nicodemus, the women saw Jesus buried. This can only be factual, since the Jews placed little value on the testimony borne by women (M *Rosh ha-Shanah* 1:8). The witness of the women also prepares the way for 28:1. That Jesus was actually buried became an integral part of gospel proclamation (cf. 1 Cor 15:4).

17. *The guard at the tomb*

27:62–66

> [62]The next day, the one after Preparation Day, the chief priests and the Pharisees went to Pilate. [63]"Sir," they said, "we remember that while he was still alive that deceiver said, 'After three days I will rise again.' [64]So give the order for the tomb to be made secure until the third day. Otherwise, his disciples may come and steal the body and tell the people that he has been raised from the dead. This last deception will be worse than the first."
>
> [65]"Take a guard," Pilate answered. "Go, make the tomb as secure as you know how." [66]So they went and made the tomb secure by putting a seal on the stone and posting the guard.

This pericope is peculiar to Matthew; and it is often viewed as a piece of "creative writing" designed to provide "witnesses" to the Resurrection (Schniewind) or to provide "evidence" that Jesus' body had not been stolen. But there are several things in favor of the pericope's historicity.

1. It must be taken with 28:11–15. Thus the account of the guards at the tomb does less to assure us that the body was not stolen than to provide background for the report that it was.
2. This may be the reason why the other evangelists omit it. In the circles they were writing for, the report circulated by the Jews may not have been current; so no explanation was necessary. In Matthew's Jewish environment, he could not avoid dealing with the subject.
3. Matthew has regularly given information in the passion narrative that the other evangelists omit (e.g., 27:19, 34–35, 62–63); and it is methodologically wrong to doubt the historicity of all details that lack multiple attestation—not least because such "multiple attestation" may sometimes go back to one literary source.
4. If Matthew were trying to prove Jesus' body was not stolen, why does he not have the guards posted immediately, instead of waiting till the next day (v.62)?
5. On the other hand, the chief priests and the Pharisees would not necessarily be defiling themselves by approaching Pilate on the Sabbath, provided they did not travel more than a Sabbath day's journey to get there and did not enter his residence (cf. John 18:28). Their action is not implausible if they still saw some potential threat in the remains of the Jesus movement. A few more details are mentioned below. (See further D. Wenham, "Resurrection," esp. pp. 47–51.)

62 This strange way of referring to the Sabbath (for "Preparation Day," see excursus at 26:17) cannot reasonably be taken to spring from Matthew's desire to use the word he omitted at 27:57 (Mark 15:42; so Bonnard, Hill): Matthew is nowhere committed to using all of Mark's words. Rather, this may be a way to avoid using the word "Sabbath," which can be ambiguous during a feast, since it could refer to the last day of the week or to a feast-Sabbath.

63–64 "Sir" (*kyrie*, v.63) is merely a polite form of address. For comments on the phrase "after three days," see on 12:40. The objection that this scene is implausible because it shows the Jewish leaders believing something the disciples themselves cannot yet believe is insubstantial. They may have heard something of the content of 16:21; 17:9; 20:19 from Judas. Whatever the source of their information, they certainly do not *believe* Jesus' prediction, they are merely afraid of fraud—a fear fostered perhaps by the report that Jesus' body, against all judicial custom (see on vv.57–61), had been taken down from the cross and returned to Jesus' disciples by Joseph and Nicodemus. This could also account for the delay in the request to post a guard (v.64). The disciples disbelieved Jesus' words about rising again, not because they could not understand the plain words, but because they had no frame of reference capable of integrating a dying and rising Messiah into their own messianic expectations. Shattered by the demoralizing turn of events, they cowered in fear (John 20:19), unable and even unwilling to trust their judgment and understanding on anything, except for the terrible fact that their Messiah had been crucified.

The Jews could take no military action without Roman sanction; so they asked Pilate that a guard be posted against the possibility of the body being stolen (v.64). Jesus' "first deception" was his claim to messiahship; his "last deception" was his claim that he would rise from the dead. From their viewpoint, the Jewish leaders are protecting themselves and the people from deception; from Matthew's perspective they are deceiving themselves.

65–66 Greek *echete koustōdia* (v.65) could be imperative ("Take a guard," NIV), but it is more likely indicative ("You have a guard of soldiers," RSV; cf. KJV). Pilate refuses to use his troops but tells the Jewish authorities that they have the temple police at their disposal; and he grants the leaders permission to use them. This explains why, after the Resurrection, the guards reported to the chief priests, not to Pilate (28:11). Pilate's answer in v.65 must therefore be construed as cynical. He is saying, "You were afraid of this man when he was alive; now he is dead, and you are still afraid! By all means secure the tomb as tightly as possible, if you think that will help; but use your own police." So guards are posted and the stone sealed with cord and an official wax seal (v.66). But "death cannot keep his prey." With the dawn all the efforts to eliminate Jesus Messiah from the stage of redemptive history are held up for heavenly derision (Ps 2:4) in the irresistible triumph of the Resurrection.

B. *The Resurrection* (28:1–15)

1. *The empty tomb*

28:1–7

[1]After the Sabbath, at dawn on the first day of the week, Mary Magdalene and the other Mary went to look at the tomb.

[2]There was a violent earthquake, for an angel of the Lord came down from heaven and, going to the tomb, rolled back the stone and sat on it. [3]His appearance was like lightning, and his clothes were white as snow. [4]The guards were so afraid of him that they shook and became like dead men.

[5]The angel said to the women, "Do not be afraid, for I know that you are looking for Jesus, who was crucified. [6]He is not here; he has risen, just as he said. Come and see the place where he lay. [7]Then go quickly and tell his disciples: 'He has risen from the dead and is going ahead of you into Galilee. There you will see him.' Now I have told you."

Because the Resurrection is central to Christian theology, few subjects have received more attention. Paul goes so far as to say that if Christ was not raised from the dead, Christian faith is vain; and we are still dead in our sins. Useful examples of modern redaction-critical approaches to the resurrection narratives are provided by N. Perrin, *The Resurrection Narratives* (London: SCM, 1977), and especially John E. Alsup, *The Post-Resurrection Appearance Stories of the Gospel-Tradition* (Stuttgart: Calwer, 1975). Older works like B.F. Westcott's *The Gospel of the Resurrection: Thoughts on Its Relation to Reason and History* (London and New York: Macmillan, 1906) are too readily passed over in the modern debate. Yet more recent treatments are also necessary to answer questions raised from new literary and philosophical angles. A useful place to begin is with G.E. Ladd, *I Believe in the Resurrection of Jesus* (London: Hodder and Stoughton; Grand Rapids; Eerdmans, 1975); Daniel P. Fuller, *Easter Faith and History* (Grand Rapids: Eerdmans, 1965); and two essays by W.L. Craig, "The Bodily Resurrection of Jesus" (in France and Wenham, 1:47–74) and "The Empty Tomb of Jesus" (France and Wenham, 2:173–200).

The textual problems at the end of Mark compound the difficulties in sorting out literary relationships. Most now hold that Mark intended to end his Gospel with 16:8, though some still cling to the authenticity of the "long ending" (Mark 16:9–20); others suggest some such ending as Matthew 28:9–10. What is certain is that, for those who wish to attempt it, the various resurrection appearances can be harmonized in at least three different ways (cf. Broadus; Ladd). But it is more important to come to grips with the distinctive emphasis of each NT writer.

The considerable number of "minor agreements" between Matthew and Luke over against Mark strongly suggests that Matthew and Luke, if they did not simply follow one account independent of Mark, either shared as one source a written account of some resurrection appearances, or one evangelist borrowed from the other. The theological implications of the Resurrection are not treated at length by the evangelists; but the theme constantly recurs in Paul (e.g., Rom 4:24–25; 6:4; 8:34; 10:9; 1 Cor 15; 2 Cor 5:1–10, 15; Phil 3:10–11; Col 2:12–13; 3:1–4; 1 Thess 4:14). Thought-provoking works in this area include W. Künneth, *The Theology of the Resurrection* (tr. J.W. Leitch [London: SCM, 1965]); T.F. Torrance, *Space, Time and Resurrection* (Edinburgh: Handsel, 1976).

1 The Greek *opse de sabbatōn* can be understood as meaning "late on the Sabbath"; then the next phrase would mean "as it began to dawn toward the first day of the week." Taken together these two temporal phrases must then mean one of two things: (1) unlike Mark 16:1, not to mention the consistent witness of the NT, the events described take place on *Saturday* evening, the end of the Sabbath; or (2) this is evidence for a scheme of counting days from sunrise to sunrise and takes place early Sunday morning.

Instead, it is far better to take *opse* as an irregular preposition, meaning "after" (as in NIV; cf. BDF, par. 164[4]; RHG, pp. 645f.; Moule, *Idiom Book*, p. 86). "After the Sabbath" is then a general time indicator; i.e., the women would not walk far *during* the Sabbath; so they waited till *after* the Sabbath. But by then Saturday night was drawing on; so early on the first day of the week (i.e., at dawn: cf. BAGD, p. 304), Mary Magdalene and "the other Mary"—the other one mentioned in 27:56 (still others are mentioned in Mark 16:1; Luke 24:10)—"went to look at the tomb." Mark says they "bought spices so that they might go to anoint Jesus' body." It has been argued that Matthew must make the change to "late on the Sabbath" because he alone introduces the account of the posting of the guard (26:62–66), which would make admittance by the women impossible. The women would not have come once the guards were posted; so they must be presented as slipping in earlier. But if the women stayed home on the Sabbath and the guard was not posted till the Sabbath, would the women be likely to learn of it till they arrived on Sunday morning?

Matthew's brief "to look at the tomb" preserves the theme of witness (27:56, 61); but in addition it may reflect an ancient Jewish tradition that says Jews visited the tombs of the deceased till the third day to ensure that the party was truly dead (cf. Thomas R.W. Longstaff, "The Women at the Tomb: Matthew 28:1 Re-examined," NTS 27 [1981] 277–82).

2–4 The clause introduced by "for" (v.2) either suggests that the violent earthquake (see 27:51) came with the "angel of the Lord" (on angels, cf. 1:20–23; 18:10) or was the means the angel used to open the tomb. In Matthew and Luke the angel is more clearly portrayed as an angel than in Mark ("a young man dressed in a white robe"). But the distinction should not be pressed, as angelic beings often appear in human form in the OT; and Mark's "young man" is clearly an angel (cf. Lane, *Mark*, pp. 586–87; compare Jos. Antiq. V, 277 [viii.2]). The guards witnessed the earthquake, saw the angel, and "became like dead men" (v.4—i.e., "fainted in terror" or the like). There is no implication that the earthquake had anything to do with releasing Jesus: the stone was rolled back, the seal broken, and the soldiers made helpless, not to let the risen Messiah escape, but to let the first witnesses in.

Too much speculative "theologizing" has accompanied some modern treatments of these verses. In particular there is nothing to suggest that the soldiers were in any sense pagan witnesses of the Resurrection. They neither heard the angel's words nor saw the risen Jesus; and they would shortly lie about what really had happened (vv.11–15). Furthermore it is doubtful whether Matthew intended to contrast the soldiers' terror, based on failure to understand, with the women's joy, who received the word of revelation. There is no evidence that the women witnessed the earthquake and the first descent of the angel; moreover their joy was mingled with fear (v.8), for the angel's "Do not be afraid" (v.5) is meaningless unless they were afraid. What is stunningly clear is the restrained sobriety of these accounts as compared with the later apocryphal Gospels (e.g., *Gospel of Peter*, 9:35–11:44).

5–7 The angel speaks (lit., "answered"; see on 11:25) words that allay the women's fears (cf. Mark 16:5–7; Luke 24:4–8). The empty tomb by itself is capable of several explanations (cf. John 20:10–15). This explanatory word of revelation narrows the potential interpretations down to one: Jesus has risen from the dead (v.6), a truth to be confirmed by personal appearances. In Matthew and Luke, but not in Mark, the fact of Jesus' resurrection, announced by the angel, is also tied into Jesus' promises —"as he said" (cf. 16:21; 17:23; 20:18–19). This is one of several significant "minor agreements" of Matthew and Luke against Mark in the resurrection narratives. The women are invited to see the place where Jesus lay and commanded to go "quickly" (v.7, a happy touch) to give his disciples the joyous message. Unlike Mark, Matthew does not explicitly mention Peter.

Jesus had promised to go ahead of his disciples into Galilee (see on 26:32); and the angel now reminds them of this (v.7). The present tense *proagei* ("is going ahead") cannot mean that Jesus is already on his way, because (1) v.10 places him still in Jerusalem; and (2) a verb like "go ahead," if pressed to mean Jesus was actually traveling, "would also seem to presuppose that the disciples also were on the way to Galilee" (Stonehouse, *Witness of Matthew*, p. 173). The verb is not a progressive present but a vivid future. As he promised, Jesus will arrive in Galilee before they do and meet them there, contrary to their expectation (see on 26:32; 28:10).

2. *First encounter with the risen Christ*

28:8–10

> [8]So the women hurried away from the tomb, afraid yet filled with joy, and ran to tell his disciples. [9]Suddenly Jesus met them. "Greetings," he said. They came to him, clasped his feet and worshiped him. [10]Then Jesus said to them, "Do not be afraid. Go and tell my brothers to go to Galilee; there they will see me."

8–9 With mingled fear and joy, the women run to tell their news to the disciples (v.8), when "suddenly" (the probable force of *idou*, "behold," in this context) Jesus meets them (v.9). "Greetings" *(chairete)* is a normal Greek salutation (cf. 26:49). The women clasp his feet (possibly a generalizing plural: cf. Turner, *Insights*, p. 76; cf. John 20:11–14) and worship him. *Prosekynēsan* ("worshiped") can mean simply "knelt before" (see on 8:2). The same verb occurs in the only other resurrection appearance in Matthew (v.17) and encourages the view that the "kneeling" has instinctively become worship.

10 Like the angel (v.5), Jesus stills the women's fears and gives them a similar commission. Some have held that "my brothers" raises the status of Jesus' eleven surviving disciples. This ignores the use of the term in Matthew; for apart from the places where "brothers" denotes a natural relationship, the term is employed of spiritual relationships—even before the Passion—explicitly referring to the fellowship of those who acknowledge Jesus as Messiah (18:15; 23:8; cf. 5:22–24; 7:3–5; 18:21, 35). In the two other places where Jesus uses the full expression "my brothers" (12:49–50; 25:40), it refers to all Jesus' disciples and cannot possibly be limited to the apostles (cf. Stonehouse, *Witness of Matthew*, pp. 176–77).

Therefore the natural way to interpret "my brothers" in v.10 is not as a reference to the Eleven but to all those attached to his cause who were then in Jerusalem, most of whom had followed him from Galilee to Jerusalem as his "disciples" (see on 5:1–2, and esp. 26:32; 28:7). There were many others in addition to the Twelve who had followed Jesus (e.g., 20:17; 21:8–9, 15; 27:55; cf. 20:29; 21:46; 23:1). Apart from the Galileans, Joseph of Arimathea was certainly not Jesus' sole disciple from the Jerusalem region (19:13–15; 27:57–61).

If this interpretation of Jesus' words is reasonable, several interesting conclusions or possibilities are evident.

1. The view that interprets the "some" of v.17 as a reference to others than the apostles is supported, and the resurrection appearance of vv.16–20 may well be equivalent to the appearance before five hundred reported by Paul (1 Cor 15:6).

2. Obviously Matthew does not tell all he knows or recount every resurrection appearance of which he has information. Therefore it is tendentious to argue that 28:10, 16–20 means that Matthew thinks Jesus appeared to his disciples only in Galilee and denies any Jerusalem appearances.

3. The interpretation of v.10 offered here looks back to 26:32; 28:7: Jesus now confirms his earlier promise that, far from being left behind as a rotting corpse when his disciples return to Galilee, he will precede them there and meet them there. But now, after the resurrection, he makes the promise a command and includes all

his "brothers." Taken this way v.10 is far from eliminating other appearances to the believers (cf. John 20:3–10; Luke 24:13–49; John 20:11–29) before they return to Galilee. It is simply that Matthew, for his immediate purposes, is not interested in them.

4. But why not? Or why does Matthew record only the resurrection appearance to the women and the appearance in Galilee to his followers? Some have suggested that Galilee is introduced because it is the place of revelation and ministry, whereas Jerusalem is the place of rejection and judgment (see esp. E. Lohmeyer, *Galiläa und Jerusalem* [Göttingen: Vandenhoeck und Ruprecht, 1936], pp. 36ff.; R.H. Lightfoot, *Locality and Doctrine* [London: Hodder and Stoughton, 1938], pp. 66ff., 128ff.). But one must wonder whether enough weight has been assigned to various facts: viz., Jesus' ministry was not only to Galilee but to the whole of Israel (10:6, 23; 15:24); opposition was directed against Jesus in Galilee as well as in Jerusalem, where the plots to kill him were hatched; at Jerusalem Jesus revealed himself as King in fulfillment of Zechariah's prophecy (21:1–7); and Jerusalem, called the "holy city" (4:5; 27:53), peculiarly drew out Jesus' compassion (23:37–39), whereas cities in Galilee were excoriated (11:20–24).

Why, then, Matthew's record of a resurrection appearance in Galilee? The answer surely lies in the combination of two themes that have permeated the entire Gospel. First, the Messiah emerges from a despised area (see on 2:23) and first sheds his light on a despised people (see on 4:15–16); for the kingdom of heaven belongs to the poor in spirit (5:3). For this reason, too, the risen Jesus first appears to women whose value as witnesses among Jews is worthless (see on 27:55–56, 61; 28:1, 5–7). Second, "Galilee of the Gentiles" (4:15) is compatible with the growing theme of Gentile mission in this Gospel (see on 1:1; 2:1–12; 4:15–16; 8:5–13; 10:18; 12:21; 13:37; 15:21–28; 24:14 et al.) and prepares for the Great Commission (28:18–20).

3. *First fraudulent denials of Jesus' resurrection*

28:11–15

11While the women were on their way, some of the guards went into the city
and reported to the chief priests everything that had happened. 12When the chief
priests had met with the elders and devised a plan, they gave the soldiers a large
sum of money, 13telling them, "You are to say, 'His disciples came during the
night and stole him away while we were asleep.' 14If this report gets to the governor, we will satisfy him and keep you out of trouble." 15So the soldiers took the
money and did as they were instructed. And this story has been widely circulated
among the Jews to this very day.

There is no sure way of dating the writing of this pericope by the closing words, "to this very day" (v.15). To conclude from *this* pericope that Matthew had in mind a period ten or fifteen years after the Fall of Jerusalem (so Bonnard) stretches the evidence too far. Matthew simply intends this paragraph to be an explanation of the stolen-corpse theory and an apologetic against it. He may also be drawing out a startling contrast: the chief priests use bribe money to commission the soldiers to spread lies, while the resurrected Jesus uses the promise of his presence to commission his followers to spread the gospel (vv.16–20).

11 Some of the guards (presumably the rest waited to be officially relieved) reported, not to Pilate, but to the chief priests; probably they were temple police (see on 27:65–66). When Matthew says the guards reported "everything that had happened," he is not suggesting that they actually witnessed the Resurrection but the earthquake, angel, and empty tomb (Bonnard).

12–14 It is very difficult to believe that the soldiers of Pilate would admit falling asleep (v.13): that would be tantamount to suicide. But the temple police could more easily be bribed, even though it took "a large sum of money" (v.12), and could more easily be protected from Pilate's anger. The plan devised (see on 12:14; 27:1) by the chief priests and elders (v.12; see on 21:23) proves to Matthew that their pious promises to believe if Jesus would only come down from the cross (27:42) were empty. Once again the instinctive concern of the Jewish leaders relates to expedience and the people's reaction, not to the truth. The story they concoct shows how desperate they are for an explanation, for if the guards were asleep, they could not know of the alleged theft; and if one of them awoke, why was not an alarm sounded and the disciples arrested? Molesting graves was a serious offense in the ancient world, subject at times to the death penalty. The famous "Nazareth Inscription," recording an ordinance of Caesar to this effect, confirms this, though the relation of this inscription to Jesus' death and burial is uncertain (cf. B.M. Metzger, "The Nazareth Inscription Once Again," in Ellis and Grässer, pp. 221–38).

It is equally improbable that the timid and fearful disciples could have mustered up the courage to open Jesus' tomb and run the risk of a capital indictment, or that the Jewish authorities would have failed to prosecute the disciples if they had possessed a scrap of evidence pointing to the disciples' guilt. Nor was the "large sum of money" an adequate measure of how far the Jewish leaders would go, for to "satisfy" the governor may well have involved further bribery (cf. parallels in Wettstein).

15 And this, Matthew explains, was the origin of the "widely circulated" Jewish explanation for the empty tomb, still common in the days of Justin Martyr (*Dialogue* 108).

C. *The Risen Messiah and His Disciples* (28:16–20)

1. *Jesus in Galilee*

28:16–17

[16]Then the eleven disciples went to Galilee, to the mountain where Jesus had told them to go. [17]When they saw him, they worshiped him; but some doubted.

Partly because there is no close Gospel parallel to these verses, and partly because as the conclusion to Matthew's Gospel they have great significance, an enormous amount of study has centered on these verses. Much of it has gone into trying to distinguish between tradition and redaction or in establishing the *Gattung* or literary genre (e.g., B.J. Malina, "The Literary Structure and Form of Matthew 28:16–20," NTS 17 [1970–71]: 87–103; J. Lange, *Das Erscheinen des Auferstandenen im Evangelium nach Matthäus* [Würzburg: Echter, 1973]; B.J. Hubbard, *The Matthean Redaction of a Primitive Apostolic Commissioning: An Exegesis of Matthew 28:16–20* [SBLDS 19; Missoula: Scholars, 1974]). The most believable opinion is that of Hubbard, who avoids the classifications of his predecessors (enthronement hymn, official decree, covenant renewal manifesto) and opts for a commissioning narrative patterned after similar OT commissionings (e.g., Gen 12:1–4; Exod 3:1–10;

Josh 1:1–11; Isa 6; 49:1–6). After examining twenty-seven such narratives and finding a basic form consisting of seven elements, Hubbard finds five of them in Matthew 28:16–20: introduction (v.16), confrontation (vv.17–18a), reaction (v.17b), the commission (vv.19–20a), reassurance (v.20b). Missing are the protest before the reassurance and a conclusion stating the work is being carried out.

But several questions persist. Hubbard himself concedes that the form is not monolithic even in the OT; and absence of two of the seven common elements is disconcerting, the more so since Matthew's final clause is a perfectly suitable conclusion to his Gospel. More important, all the OT commissions Hubbard refers to are to individuals, whereas this one is to the disciples as a group. Some of the OT commissions are in reality the establishment of covenants; and if Frankmölle (pp. 42ff.) has somewhat exaggerated this theme in Matthew, it cannot be entirely ignored in a book that promises a new covenant (26:26–29) and seeks to demonstrate the continuity with and fulfillment of the OT covenant people in the messianic community being gathered around Jesus.

It seems best to conclude with John P. Meier ("Two Disputed Questions in Matt 28:16–20," JBL 96 [1977]: 407–24; cf. P.T. O'Brien, pp. 254–67) that this pericope does not easily fit any known literary form and must not be squeezed into a poorly fitting mold. Yet Meier's principal reason for this conclusion could be strengthened. He argues that these verses constitute a tradition so heavily redacted by the evangelist that conformity to a *Gattung* (or form) shaped primarily by oral transmission is in principal unlikely. That may be so, but this conclusion by no means makes impregnable judgments about the way the material came into Matthew's hands (cf. Introduction, section 2). Above all, the temptation to ascribe authenticity to "tradition" but not to "redaction" must be resisted (cf. Carson, "Redaction Criticism"; cf. G.R. Beasley-Murray, *Baptism in the New Testament* [London: Macmillan, 1962], pp. 77ff.).

Some have distinguished between "Christepiphanies" (appearances of the resurrected Christ on earth, as in 28:9) and "Christophanies" (appearances of the resurrected Christ from heaven, as at Paul's conversion, Acts 9; cf. Dunn, *Jesus*, pp. 116, 123). Those who make this helpful distinction are uncertain how to classify the resurrection appearance of vv.16–20. The dilemma is a false one. There has been no mention of the Ascension; and Paul seems to put his own experience of the risen Christ into a class of one (1 Cor 15:8), the sole "Christophany," which must also be distinguished from John's visionary experiences (e.g., Rev 1:12–16).

It is often pointed out that vv.16–20 recapitulate many of Matthew's themes. The point can be overstressed (e.g., Peter F. Ellis, *Matthew: His Mind and His Message* [Collegeville, Minn.: Liturgical, 1974]) but is an important insight that ties up several loose ends.

16 "Then" translates the mildly adversative *de* ("but"), not *tote* (see on 2:7). The fraudulent explanation of the empty tomb was purchased with a bribe and was widely circulated (vv.11–15), *but* the Eleven (designated as such in the NT only here and four times in Luke and Acts) do what Jesus says and go to Galilee. They go "to the mountain where Jesus had told them to go": the subordinate clause makes the expression *eis to oros* ("to the mountain") specific, though by itself it customarily means "into the hills." We do not know what mountain is meant, but the verse presupposes the arrangements implicit in 26:32; 28:7, 10. Associating the Great Commission (vv.18–20) with Galilee not only has nuances with Jesus' humble background and the theme of Gentile mission (see on v.10) but "ensures that the risen Christ and his teaching are not thought of as a substitute for, but as continuous with, Jesus' ministry and teaching in Galilee" (Hill, *Matthew*).

17 Doubt about Jesus' resurrection is expressed elsewhere (Luke 24:10–11; John 20:24–29), but only by those who have heard reports of Jesus' resurrection without actually seeing him. This verse is therefore unique. Two difficulties must be considered.

1. Does "some" refer to "some of the Eleven" or to "some others" in addition to the Eleven? The question is partly decided by one's interpretation of v.10, though more can be said. If *proskyneō* here means not merely "kneel" or "make obeisance to" but "worship" (see on v.9), then the "eleven disciples" and the "some" probably constitute two groups; for doubt about who Jesus is or about the reality of his resurrection does not seem appropriate for true worship. Especially if Matthew was an eyewitness, it is easy to believe that he describes a scene vivid in his own memory without taking all the precautions that would remove questions from the minds of readers who were not there. As a result, both here and in v.10 Matthew in an incidental fashion alludes to the larger crowd without providing useful specifics. Moreover *hoi de*, here as in 26:67, means "but some," in contrast with those already mentioned, rather than "but they" (cf. Gundry, *Matthew*). While this solution is not certain, the problem is not helped by suggesting that "some" refers to those in Matthew's community who have doubts (Hill, *Matthew*).

2. But why was there doubt at all? The verb used (*edistasan*, "[some] doubted") occurs in the NT only here and in 14:31 and does not denote disbelief but hesitation (cf. "though some hesitated," JB; cf. I.P. Ellis, "'But some doubted,'" NTS 14 [1967–68]: 574–80). Even so, why did they hesitate, and why does Matthew include this information here? Even if others than the Eleven are the ones who hesitate, this does not solve the problem; it merely shifts it from the Eleven to other followers of Jesus.

Several solutions have been proposed, none of them convincing. There is no evidence of scribal emendation. It is barely possible that some doubted not the fact of the Resurrection but just who this person was (Hendriksen, Grosheide, Filson, Walvoord et al.). The pattern would then be somewhat akin to Luke 24:16; John 21:4–14, where the resurrected Jesus is not instantly recognized. But it must be admitted that this introduces a very subtle distinction into Matthew 28; and the parallels in Luke and John are not all that close, since Luke says the two on the Emmaus road "were kept from recognizing him," and John's narrative has other uncertainties—distance from shore and the aside in 21:12b. The most that can be said for this interpretation is that other passages show that Jesus in his postresurrection appearances was not always instantly recognized. Far less likely is the view of L.G. Parkhurst ("Matthew 28:16–20 Reconsidered," ExpT 90 [1978–79]: 179f.), who says that some doubted, not who Jesus was, nor the facticity of the Resurrection, but the propriety of worshiping the resurrected Jesus; and this hesitation Jesus dispels by the words of v.18: "All authority . . . has been given to me." Somewhat similar is the position of Gundry, who argues that vv.17–20 are Matthew's way of saying that only Jesus' *word* quiets doubt, and even the resurrection appearances will not do this. According to Gundry *(Matthew)*, we "could hardly ask for better evidence of the authority of Jesus' teaching in Matthew's theology." But thematically v.18 is tightly related to v.19, not v.17. It is not at all clear that v.18 alleviates the doubt of v.17 (cf. Dunn, *Jesus*, p. 124; and to the contrary, Bornkamm, *Tradition*, p. 132). At very least we must admit that the text does not say that all doubts were removed, as is the case in Luke 24 and John 21. More important, Matthew's use of *proskyneō* ("worship") has been sufficiently ambiguous (see on 8:2; 28:9) that he would have needed to use a stronger verb such as *latreuō* ("worship," "serve [God]") if he were trying to make the various points Parkhurst and Gundry suggest.

We are left with some uncertainty about what Matthew means, owing primarily to the conciseness of his account. Perhaps it is best to conclude that, especially if the "some" refers not to the Eleven but to other followers, the move from unbelief and fear to faith and joy was for them a "hesitant" one. The Eleven, who according to the other Gospels had already seen the risen Jesus at least twice (Peter at least three times, Thomas at least once), respond instantly with worship on the occasion of this new epiphany, but some (others) hesitated—without further specification as to their subsequent belief or doubt. If this is what Matthew means, he may be using this historical reminiscence to stress the fact that Jesus' resurrection was not an anticipated episode that required only enthusiasm and gullibility to win adherents among Jesus' followers. Far from it, they still were hesitant; and their failure to understand his repeated predictions of his resurrection, compounded with their despair after his crucifixion, worked to maintain their hesitancy for some time before they came to full faith. Jesus' resurrection did not instantly transform men of little faith and faltering understanding into spiritual giants.

Another thing (not dealt with by Matthew) was necessary, viz., the enduement of the Spirit at Pentecost. Matthew's concise account presupposes this—for it is impossible that any evangelist could have been ignorant of that transforming event—but omits it in favor of pressing on to the Great Commission, which ties together some of his own thematic interests.

2. *The Great Commission*

28:18–20

> 18Then Jesus came to them and said, "All authority in heaven and on earth has been given to me. 19Therefore go and make disciples of all nations, baptizing them in the name of the Father and of the Son and of the Holy Spirit, 20and teaching them to obey everything I have commanded you. And surely I am with you always, to the very end of the age."

18 "All" dominates vv.18–20 and ties these verses together: *all* authority, *all* nations, *all* things ("everything," NIV), *all* the days ("always," NIV). The authority of Jesus Messiah has already been heavily stressed in this Gospel (e.g., 7:29; 10:1, 7–8; 11:27; 22:43–44; 24:35; cf. John 17:2). Therefore it is incautious, if not altogether wrong, to claim that the Resurrection conferred on Jesus an authority incomparably greater than what he enjoyed before his crucifixion. The truth is more subtle. It is not that anything he teaches or does during the days of his flesh is *less* authoritative than what he now says and does: even during his ministry his words, like God's, cannot pass away (24:35); and he, like God, forgives sin (9:6). It is not Jesus' authority per se that becomes more absolute. Rather, the spheres in which he now exercises absolute authority are enlarged to include all heaven and earth, i.e., the universe. This authority has been "given" him by the Father; and so, of course, the Father is exempt from the Son's authority (cf. 1 Cor 15:27–28). The Son becomes the one through whom *all* God's authority is mediated. He is, as it were, the mediatorial King. This well-defined exercise of authority is given Jesus as the climactic vindication of his humiliation (cf. Phil 2:5–11); and it marks a turning point in redemptive history, for Messiah's "kingdom" (i.e., his "king-dominion," the exercise of his divine and saving authority; see on 3:2; 13:37–39) has dawned in new power. This is still clearer if we accept the view that there is a conscious allusion here to Daniel 7:13–14 (see esp. France, *Jesus,* pp. 142–43): the Son of Man, once humiliated and suffering, is given universal authority (same word in LXX).

Contrary to France, it does not follow from this that Matthew 26:64 and Mark 14:62 refer to this exaltation and not the Parousia. In the first place, the chief priests in no way witnessed this coming of the Son of Man; and, in the second place, we have repeatedly observed how the coming of the Son of Man to kingly authority cannot be reduced to a single moment in redemptive history.

19 "Therefore" is probably the correct reading; but even if the word is absent, the logical connection is presupposed by the flow of the commission. Two features tie the command to Jesus' universal authority.

1. Because he *now* has this authority, *therefore* his disciples are to go and make disciples—i.e., the dawning of the new age of messianic authority changes the circumstances and impels his disciples forward to a universal ministry he himself never engaged in during the days of his flesh, "except in reluctant anticipation" (Stendahl, Peake, 695k; Hill, *Matthew*). His promotion to universal authority serves as an eschatological marker inaugurating the beginning of his universal mission.

2. Because of that authority, his followers may go in confidence that their Lord is in sovereign control of "everything in heaven and on earth" (cf. Rom 8:28).

In the Greek, "go"—like "baptizing" and "teaching"—is a participle. Only the verb "make disciples" (see below) is imperative. Some have deduced from this that Jesus' commission is simply to make disciples "as we go" (i.e., wherever we are) and constitutes no basis for *going* somewhere special in order to serve as missionaries (e.g., Gaechter, *Matthäus;* R.D. Culver, "What Is the Church's Commission?" BS 125 [1968]: 243–53). There is something to this view, but it needs three careful qualifications.

1. When a participle functions as a circumstantial participle dependent on an imperative, it normally gains some imperatival force (cf. 2:8, 13; 9:13; 11:4; 17:27; cf. C. Rogers, "The Great Commission," BS 130 [1973]: 258–67).

2. While it remains true to say that the main imperatival force rests with "make disciples," not with "go," in a context that demands that this ministry extend to "all nations," it is difficult to believe that "go" has lost all imperatival force.

3. From the perspective of mission strategy, it is important to remember that the Great Commission is preserved in several complementary forms that, taken together, can only be circumvented by considerable exegetical ingenuity (e.g., Luke 24:45–49; John 20:21; Acts 1:8; cf. Matt 4:19; 10:16–20; 13:38; 24:14; see further below).

The main emphasis, then, is on the command to "make disciples," which in Greek is one word, *mathēteusate,* normally an intransitive verb, here used transitively (a not uncommon Hellenization; cf. BDF, par. 148[3]; Zerwick, par. 66; see on 13:52; 27:57). "To disciple a person to Christ is to bring him into the relation of pupil to teacher, 'taking his yoke' of authoritative instruction (11:29), accepting what he says as true because he says it, and submitting to his requirements as right because he makes them" (Broadus). Disciples are those who hear, understand, and obey Jesus' teaching (12:46–50). The injunction is given at least to the Eleven, but to the Eleven in their own role as disciples (v.16). Therefore they are paradigms for all disciples. Plausibly the command is given to a larger gathering of disciples (see on vv.10, 16–17). Either way it is binding on *all* Jesus' disciples to make others what they themselves are—disciples of Jesus Christ.

The words *panta ta ethnē* ("all nations") have been understood primarily in two ways.

1. They refer to all Gentiles—i.e., all nations except Israel. Israel has forfeited her place, and now the preaching of the Gospel must be kept from her (so Hare, *Jewish Persecutions*, pp. 147–48; Walker, pp. 111–13; D.R.A. Hare and D.J. Harrington, " 'Make Disciples of All the Gentiles' (Mt 28–19)," CBQ 37 [1975]: 359–69).

2. They refer to all people, including Israel (so Trilling, pp. 26–28; Hill, *Matthew;* Hubbard, *Matthean Reaction*, pp. 84–87; John P. Meier, "Nations or Gentiles in Matthew 28:19?" CBQ 39 [1977]: 94–102; O'Brien, pp. 262–63).

Now *ta ethnē* in its eight occurrences in Matthew (4:15; 6:32; 10:5, 18; 12:18, 21; 20:19, 25) normally denotes Gentiles, often pagans; but 21:43, where *ethnos* is used anarthrously, is an instance where "people" does not exclude Jews. Moreover, contrary to Hare and Harrington, a good case can be made for saying that the full expression, *panta ta ethnē*, used four times in Matthew (24:9, 14; 25:32; here), uses *ethnē* in its basic sense of "tribes," "nations," or "peoples" and means "all peoples [without distinction]" or "all nations [without distinction]," thereby including Jews. Could Matthew really be excluding Israel as one source of the hate his followers will have to endure (24:9)? Would he say that any Jewish Christians in any church known to him should not be baptized and taught?

More telling yet, Matthew's Gospel is now, in its final verses, returning to the theme introduced in the very first verse (see on 1:1)—that the blessings promised to Abraham and through him to all peoples on earth (Gen 12:3) are now to be fulfilled in Jesus the Messiah. And when that covenant promise is reiterated in Genesis 18:18; 22:18, the LXX uses the same words found here: *panta ta ethnē*. The expression is comprehensive; and, in line with all the anticipatory hints of Gentile witness in Matthew's Gospel (1:1; 2:1–12; 4:15–16; 8:5–13; 10:18; 13:38; 24:14 et al.), it would be as wrong to conclude that only Gentiles are in view as it would be to set up another restriction and see this commission as a command to evangelize only *Jewish* tribes.

Adherents of the "church growth movement" have attempted to justify their entire "people movement" principle on the basis of this phrase, used here and elsewhere, arguing that *ethnos* properly means "tribe" or "people" (most comprehensively, perhaps, by H.C. Goerner, *All Nations in God's Purpose* [Nashville: Broadman, 1979]). The latter point is readily conceded, but the conclusion is linguistically illegitimate. Plural collectives may have all-embracing force, whether in Greek or English. Doubtless God may convert people by using a "people movement"; but to deduce such a principle from this text requires a "city movement" principle based on Acts 8:40, where the same construction occurs with the noun "cities." In neither case may missiologists legitimately establish the normativeness of their theories.

The aim of Jesus' disciples, therefore, is to make disciples of all men everywhere, without distinction. Hill *(Matthew)* insists that such a command cannot possibly be authentic: "Had Christ given the command to 'make disciples of all nations,' the opposition in Paul's time to the admission of Gentiles to the Church would be inexplicable. It must be assumed that the Church, having learned and experienced the universality of the Christian message, assigned that knowledge to a direct command of the living Lord." But we have already seen how slow the disciples were to grasp what Jesus taught. More important, Acts and the Epistles betray no trace of opposition whatsoever to the *fact* of a Gentile mission. The debate between Paul and his Judaizing opponents was over *the conditions of entrance* into the Christian community (see on 23:15). The many hints throughout Jesus' ministry that show he anticipated a Gentile ministry after some delay (e.g., see on 10:16–20; 13:37–39; 24:14) would make it incongruous for him to have not given some commission about this.

The syntax of the Greek participles for "baptizing" and "teaching" forbids the conclusion that baptizing and teaching are to be construed solely as the *means* of making disciples (cf. also Allen, Klostermann, Lagrange, Schlatter); but their precise relationship to the main verb is not easy to delineate. Neither participle is bound to the other or to the main verb with the conjunction *kai* or a particle; and therefore "they must be viewed as dependent on one another or depending in differing ways on the chief verb" (Beasley-Murray, *Baptism*, p. 89; cf. BDF, par. 421). Most likely some imperative force is present, since the disciples are certainly to baptize and teach; but computer studies of the Greek NT have shown that although a participle dependent on an imperative normally gains imperatival force when it *precedes* the imperative, its chief force is not normally imperatival when it *follows* the imperative. Luke 6:35 has a close syntactic parallel: "And lend [*daneizete*] to them without expecting to get anything back [*apelpizontes*]." Not expecting anything in return is certainly not the *means* of the lending, but it is modal in that it characterizes the lending; and at the same time at least some imperatival force tinges the participle, even if the participle is primarily modal.

Similarly baptizing and teaching are not the *means* of making disciples, but they characterize it. Envisaged is that proclamation of the gospel that will result in repentance and faith, for *mathēteuō* ("I disciple") entails both preaching and response. The response of discipleship is baptism and instruction. Therefore baptism and teaching are not coordinate—either grammatically or conceptually—with the action of making disciples. The masculine pronouns *autous* ("them," vv.19–20) hint at the same thing, since *ethnē* ("nations") is neuter: the "them" who are baptized and taught are those who have been made disciples. But this is uncertain, because the case of "them" may be *ad sensum* (i.e., merely according to the general sense). In any case it would certainly misconstrue the text to absolutize the division between discipleship and baptism-instruction. The NT can scarcely conceive of a disciple who is not baptized or is not instructed. Indeed, the force of this command is to make Jesus' disciples responsible for making disciples of others, a task characterized by baptism and instruction.

Those who become disciples are to be baptized *eis* ("into," NIV mg.) the name of the Trinity. Matthew, unlike some NT writers, apparently avoids the confusion of *eis* (strictly "into") and *en* (strictly "in"; cf. Zerwick, par. 106) common in Hellenistic Greek; and if so, the preposition "into" strongly suggests a coming-into-relationship-with or a coming-under-the-Lordship-of (cf. Allen; Albright and Mann). For comments about baptism, see on 3:6, 11, 13–17. It is a sign both of entrance into Messiah's covenant community and of pledged submission to his lordship (cf. Beasley-Murray, *Baptism*, pp. 90–92).

The triple formula containing Father (or God), Son (or Christ), and Spirit occurs frequently in the NT (cf. 1 Cor 12:4–6; 2 Cor 13:14; Eph 4:4–6; 2 Thess 2:13–14; 1 Peter 1:2; Rev 1:4–6). Individually these texts do not prove there is any Trinitarian consciousness in the NT, since other threefold phrases occur (e.g., "God and Christ Jesus and the elect angels," 1 Tim 5:21). But contributing evidence makes it difficult to deny the presence of Trinitarian thought in the NT documents: (1) the frequency of the God–Christ–Spirit formulas; (2) their context and use: it is impossible, for instance, to imagine baptism into the name of God, Christ, and the elect angels; (3) the recognition by NT writers that the attributes of Yahweh may be comprehensively applied to Jesus and, so far as we have evidence, to the Spirit (cf. C.F.D. Moule, *The Holy Spirit* [London: Mowbrays, 1978], pp. 24–26; Carson, *Farewell Discourse*, esp. pp. 65–66).

Many deny the authenticity of this Trinitarian formula, however, not on the basis of doubtful reconstructions of the development of doctrine, but on the basis of the fact that the only evidence we have of actual Christian baptisms indicates a consistent monadic formula—baptism in Jesus' name (Acts 2:38; 8:16; 10:48; 19:5; similarly, passages such as Rom 6:3). If Jesus gave the Trinitarian formula, why was it shortened? Is it not easier to believe that the Trinitarian formula was a relatively late development? But certain reflections give us pause.

1. It is possible, though historically improbable, that the full Trinitarian formula was used for pagan converts, and "in the name of Jesus" for Jews and proselytes. But this is doubtful, not least because Paul, the Apostle to the Gentiles, never uses a Trinitarian formula for baptism.

2. Trinitarian ideas are found in the resurrection accounts of both Luke and John, even if these evangelists do not report the Trinitarian baptismal formula. The faith to be proclaimed was in some sense Trinitarian from the beginning. "This conclusion should not come as a great surprise: the Trinitarian tendencies of the early church are most easily explained if they go back to Jesus Himself; but the importance of the point for our study is that it means that Matthew's reference to the Trinity in chapter 28 is not a white elephant thoroughly out of context" (D. Wenham, "Resurrection," p. 53).

3. The term "formula" is tripping us up. There is no evidence we have Jesus' *ipsissima verba* here and still less that the church regarded Jesus' command as a baptismal *formula*, a liturgical form the ignoring of which was a breach of canon law. The problem has too often been cast in anachronistic terms. E. Riggenbach (*Der Trinitarische Taufbefehl Matt. 28:19* [Gütersloh: C. Bertelsmann, 1901]) points out that as late as the Didache, baptism in the name of Jesus and baptism in the name of the Trinity coexist side by side: the church was not bound by precise "formulas" and felt no embarrassment at a multiplicity of them, precisely because Jesus' instruction, which may not have been in these precise words, was not regarded as a binding formula.

20 Those who are discipled must not only be baptized but also taught. The content of this instruction (see on 3:1 for comments concerning *kerygma* ["preaching"] and *didache* ["teaching"]) is everything Jesus commanded the first disciples. Five things stand out.

1. The focus is on *Jesus'* commands, not OT law. Jesus' words, like the words of Scripture, are more enduring than heaven and earth (24:35); and the peculiar expression "everything I have commanded you" is, as Trilling (p. 37) has pointed

out, reminiscent of the authority of Yahweh (Exod 29:35; Deut 1:3, 41; 7:11; 12:11, 14). This confirms our exegesis of 5:17–20. The revelation of Jesus Messiah at this late stage in salvation history brings the fulfillment of everything to which the OT Scriptures pointed and constitutes their valid continuity; but this means that the focus is necessarily on Jesus.

2. Remarkably, Jesus does not foresee a time when any part of his teaching will be rightly judged needless, outmoded, superseded, or untrue: *everything* he has commanded must be passed on "to the very end of the age."

3. What the disciples teach is not mere dogma steeped in abstract theorizing but content to be *obeyed*.

4. It then follows that by carefully passing on everything Jesus taught, the first disciples—themselves eyewitnesses—call into being new generations of "earwitnesses" (O'Brien, pp. 264f.). These in turn pass on the truth they received. So a means is provided for successive generations to remain in contact with Jesus' teachings (cf. 2 Tim 2:2).

5. Christianity must spread by an internal necessity or it has already decayed; for one of Jesus' commands is to teach all he commands. Failure to disciple, baptize, and teach the peoples of the world is already itself one of the failures of our own discipleship.

But the Gospel ends, not with command, but with the promise of Jesus' comforting presence, which, if not made explicitly conditional on the disciples' obedience to the Great Commission, is at least closely tied to it. "Surely" captures the force of *idou* here (see on 1:20): he who is introduced to us in the prologue as Immanuel, "God with us" (1:23; cf. also 18:20), is still God with us, "to the very end of the age." The English adverb "always" renders an expression found in the NT only here—viz., *pasas tēs hēmeras,* strictly "the whole of every day" (Moule, *Idiom Book*, p. 34). Not just the horizon is in view, but each day as we live it. This continues to the end of the age (for this expression, see on 13:39–40, 49; 24:3; cf. Heb 9:26)—the end of history as we know it, when the kingdom will be consummated. Perhaps there is a small hint of judgment: the church dare not drift, because it, too, rushes to the consummation. The period between the commission and the consummation is of indefinite length; but whatever its duration, it is the time of the church's mission and of preliminary enjoyment of her Lord's presence.

Matthew's Gospel ends with the expectation of continued mission and teaching. The five preceding sections always conclude with a block of *Jesus'* teaching (3:1–26:5); but the passion and resurrection of Jesus end with a commission *to his disciples* to carry on that same ministry (see Introduction, section 14), in the light of the Cross, the empty tomb, and the triumphant vindication and exaltation of the risen Lord. In this sense the Gospel of Matthew is not a closed book till the consummation. The final chapter is being written in the mission and teaching of Jesus' disciples.

9 780310 499718